The Psychology of Women and Gender

Ninth Edition

To Raeka and Isador, for the insight and perspective. (NEQ)

*To Margaret and Luke, the two best kids a
professor/author/mom could ever have. (JSH)*

The Psychology of Women and Gender

Half the Human Experience +

Ninth Edition

Nicole M. Else-Quest

University of Maryland, Baltimore County

Janet Shibley Hyde

University of Wisconsin–Madison

Los Angeles | London | New Delhi
Singapore | Washington DC | Melbourne

FOR INFORMATION:

SAGE Publications, Inc.
2455 Teller Road
Thousand Oaks, California 91320
E-mail: order@sagepub.com

SAGE Publications Ltd.
1 Oliver's Yard
55 City Road
London EC1Y 1SP
United Kingdom

SAGE Publications India Pvt. Ltd.
B 1/I 1 Mohan Cooperative Industrial Area
Mathura Road, New Delhi 110 044
India

SAGE Publications Asia-Pacific Pte. Ltd.
3 Church Street
#10-04 Samsung Hub
Singapore 049483

Printed in the United States of America

ISBN 978-1-5063-8282-1

This book is printed on acid-free paper.

Acquisitions Editor: Lara Parra
Editorial Assistant: Zachary Valladon
Production Editor: Laureen Gleason
Copy Editor: Sarah J. Duffy
Typesetter: C&M Digitals (P) Ltd.
Proofreader: Scott Oney
Indexer: Jeanne Busemeyer
Cover Designer: Janet Kiesel
Marketing Manager: Katherine Hepburn

18 19 20 21 10 9 8 7 6 5 4 3 2

Contents

3   Gender Stereotypes and Gender Differences   61

4   The Intersection of Gender and Ethnicity   83

8. Abilities, Motivation, and Achievement — 181

9. Gender and Work — 201

10 Biology and Gender 223

11 Psychology, Gender, and Health 241

15 Gender and Mental Health Issues 339

16 The Psychology of Men and Masculinity 367

17 Retrospect and Prospect 395

Preface

Our textbook *Half the Human Experience: The Psychology of Women* had a good run, through eight editions. But then, in the short time between finishing the 8th edition in 2012 and the present, many things changed, foremost among them the transgender activist movement, blossoming new research on transgender individuals, and fundamental challenges to the gender binary. At the same time, scholars and activists increasingly called for a more intersectional approach to the psychology of women and gender. In light of these major shifts, we decided that the field needed not a new edition, but a very new book. We sought a new publisher and were impressed with Sage's resonance with our ideas. We set out to write a new, cutting-edge textbook that thoroughly integrated intersectionality and transgender research. We developed a new title that pays homage to the textbook from which it was derived and simultaneously recognizes the new thinking about gender: *The Psychology of Women and Gender: Half the Human Experience +*.

Within the field of gender and women's studies today, we face a tension between the traditional emphasis on cisgender women and the new emphasis on transgender people. Transgender activists and the new research on trans people make us rethink what we mean by the term *gender*. We have tried hard to include that new thinking in this textbook. Yet women remain oppressed in our society and most societies in the world, and women's issues continue to deserve a focus in our courses and textbooks. Therefore, we have tried to strike a balance between an emphasis on women and an emphasis on trans folks and the new thinking about gender. Strikingly, there are many commonalities among women and trans people, the persistent challenges they face, and the profound resilience they display.

Language is extremely important. Our goal was to create a trans-inclusive textbook written in trans-inclusive language. Yet that turns out to be more difficult than it might sound. Within the trans community, there are often disagreements about preferred terminology, and terminology often changes over time. We have done our best to use respectful language based on 2017 norms, but it is possible, indeed likely, that preferred terms will change over the years. All of us need to keep up with these trends. A good basic rule is that people should be called what they prefer to be called.

Intersectionality has become a more and more prominent force in gender and women's studies, and it is increasingly making its way into psychology. We began to introduce intersectionality into the textbook in its previous incarnation. This time we integrated it thoroughly, examining its place in each chapter. This time, we had much more to work with, because intersectionality research is blossoming in psychology.

Overall, our goal has been to create a text on the psychology of women and gender written in such a way that it will be accessible to undergraduates who may have little background in psychology—perhaps only an introductory course—yet also challenging and thought-provoking for senior psychology majors or gender and women's studies majors. We want students to feel excited to learn about the psychology of women and gender, and we hope that our excitement about the field shows through for them in the book. This is truly one of the most meaningful courses that a student can take. It can be life changing. Those of us who teach it can feel a deep pride in the body of research from which we can draw.

Three characteristics of this book—its readability, comprehensiveness, and scholarship—have been well received in previous versions, and we have worked to retain and improve those features. We believe that the readability of textbooks is a feminist principle. One of the goals of feminists has been to demystify science, and as part of that effort we must demystify psychology, including the psychology of women and gender. Our goal therefore has been to provide a text with solid, cutting-edge scholarship, clearly explained so that students can grasp it—indeed, be captivated by it.

Each of us has taught psychology of women and gender numerous times using earlier versions of this textbook. We have used those experiences to polish and improve the book. For example, if students have problems with a question on an exam, is it because that passage in the book is not clearly written? If so, we fix it. Both of us have a deep understanding of what is fascinating and what is difficult for students, and we put that knowledge into our crafting of the book.

What's new in this edition? We have kept the chapter numbering the same, although the titles of many chapters changed with the new emphasis on both transgender and intersectionality. The following are some of the highlights, although we can't begin to list all of the additions and updates.

Chapter 1: Introduction

- Updated and expanded material on important language and terminology regarding gender

- New sections on the intersectionality of gender and critiquing the gender binary

- New material on transnational feminism and gender equality around the world, mixed methods, and critical theory

Chapter 2: Theoretical Perspectives on Gender

- Added material on queer theory and intersectionality

- New Focus box: Feminist Theory in Psychology: Objectification Theory

- Expanded material on the cognitive-developmental theory of gender and the feminist critique and reformulation of evolutionary psychology

Chapter 3: Gender Stereotypes and Gender Differences

- New sections: The Gender Similarities Hypothesis and Stereotypes About Trans Individuals, including an intervention to reduce cisgenderism

- New material on gender differences in impulsivity and in narcissism

Chapter 4: The Intersection of Gender and Ethnicity

- New sections: Immigration and Feminisms of Color
- New material on historical trauma and intergenerational transmission of trauma
- Integrated content on trans people of color, intersectionality, and gendered racism

Chapter 5: Gender and Communication

- New sections on gendered language, expansive/contractive posture, misgendering language, and clinical applications of research on gender and language for transgender people
- New data on interruptions, gender-linked language, and effects of sexist language

Chapter 6: Gender and Emotion

- Expanded coverage of the politics of gender and emotion
- New sections on gender differences in temperament, self-conscious emotional experience, emotional expression in childhood, and intersectional approaches to emotion
- New section: Emotions Beyond the Binary, on gender and emotion in transgender individuals

Chapter 7: Lifespan Development

- Added exciting new research on gender-differentiated maternal touch, infants' abilities to discern gender congruent and incongruent faces and bodies, and learning of the gender binary
- New sections on transgender gender identity development in early childhood and pubertal development in cisgender and transgender adolescents
- New section: Gender and Cognitive Aging

Chapter 8: Abilities, Motivation, and Achievement

- New data on gender, ethnicity, and academic achievement
- New section: The Gender Gap in STEM
- New section on motivation, framed around expectancy-value theory

Chapter 9: Gender and Work

- New section: The Motherhood Penalty
- New data on the gender wage gap and occupational segregation by gender
- New Focus box: Psychology and Public Policy: Employment Discrimination in the United States

Chapter 10: Biology and Gender

- New Focus box: Feminist Biology
- New sections: Are There Genes for Being Transgender? and Transgender and the Brain
- New research on the brain gender mosaic

Chapter 11: Psychology, Gender, and Health

- New sections: Transgender Persons and the Health Care System, Trans Health Issues, and Miscarriage
- New Focus box: Gender and Infectious Disease, which incorporates a transnational feminist perspective
- New and expanded material on pregnancy, abortion, and childbirth

Chapter 12: Gender and Sexuality

- New section, The Sexuality of Transgender Persons
- New section on the search for a female Viagra
- Data table on intersectionality updated
- Disorders updated to DSM-5, with critique of DSM-5

Chapter 13: Gender and Sexual Orientation

- New section: Queer Theory
- Old section on civil unions deleted, replaced with new section on gay marriage
- Queer of color critique added

Chapter 14: Gender and Victimization

- New data and research on gender-based violence, with integrated coverage of violence against trans individuals

- New section: Human Trafficking
- New Focus box: The Violence Against Women Act and Vulnerable Populations

Chapter 15: Gender and Mental Health Issues

- New section: Psychological Practice With Trans People
- Mental health issues updated to DSM-5, with critique of DSM-5
- New Focus box: The Politics of Psychiatric Diagnosis: Gender Dysphoria

Chapter 16: The Psychology of Men and Masculinity

- New material on masculinities and the male role among men of color
- Expanded discussion of precarious manhood, the gender role strain paradigm
- New material on father involvement

Chapter 17: Retrospect and Prospect

- New research on gender, affiliative behavior, and stress
- New section: The Continuing Feminist Revolution and Backlash

Learning Aids

Strong resources for students' learning are included in the text.

- *Chapter outlines.* Each chapter begins with an outline, providing students with the structure of the chapter, which will help their cognitive processing of it.

- *Margin glossary.* Each chapter has a margin glossary, with terms defined clearly when they are first mentioned. A comprehensive glossary can be found at the end of the book. These features help students learn the meaning of important terms in the field.

- *Experience the Research boxes.* Each chapter has a boxed insert toward the end that is designed to give students active experience with research in the psychology of women and gender. Each one includes an exercise such as collecting a small amount of data from friends to replicate a study in the text or analyzing the gendered content of computer games in a local store. Although each individual student may collect only a small amount of data, if data are pooled across all students in the class, a data set large enough for statistical analysis can be produced. We hope that students will benefit from these experiences and that faculty will find them useful for assignments.

- *Focus boxes.* This feature draws from research, theory, and case studies to examine key issues in depth. Topics include "Health at the Intersection of Gender and Disability," "Gender Diversity and Athletics," and "The Politics of Psychiatric Diagnosis: Premenstrual Dysphoric Disorder."

Ancillaries

SAGE Publishing offers an array of instructor resources to instructors on the cutting edge of teaching and learning. Go to **study.sagepub.com/else-quest9e** to access the companion site.

SAGE for Instructors

The SAGE Instructor Companion Site, a password-protected resource, supports teaching by making the classroom a learning-rich environment for students. The following assets are available on the teaching site:

- Sample syllabi—for semester, quarter, and online courses—provide suggested models for instructors to use when creating the syllabi for their courses.

- A Microsoft Word test bank is available containing multiple-choice, true/false, short-answer and essay questions for each chapter. The test bank provides a diverse range of prewritten options as well as the opportunity to edit any question and insert personalized questions to effectively assess students' progress and understanding.

- Editable, chapter-specific Microsoft PowerPoint slides offer complete flexibility in easily creating a multimedia presentation for your course.

- Carefully crafted lecture notes follow the structure of each chapter and can be used alongside the PowerPoint slides, providing an essential reference and teaching tool for course lectures.

- Lively and stimulating chapter-specific activity ideas reinforce active learning and critical thinking, and can be used in individual or group settings in the classroom or assigned as homework.

Acknowledgments With Gratitude

We have many people for whose help we are very grateful. We thank our university colleagues. NEQ thanks her Psychology and Gender and Women's Studies faculty colleagues at the University of Maryland, Baltimore County, for their support and intellectual inspiration. I am especially grateful to Julie Murphy for helping me think more deeply and critically about trans psychology, disability, and the diagnosis of mental health issues. I thank Chris Murphy for his guidance in understanding the complexities of intimate partner violence perpetration, prevention, and treatment. I thank Rachel Salk at the University of Pittsburgh School of Medicine for her guidance on research on gender and mental health issues. I am also grateful for the guidance and encouragement of Kim Acquaviva, at the George Washington University School of Nursing, for expanding my thinking about LGBTQ issues. And I remain deeply grateful to my graduate and undergraduate students at UMBC for challenging me and teaching me about their daily experience of the intersectionality of gender.

JSH thanks her University of Wisconsin faculty colleagues in both Psychology and Gender and Women's Studies (GWS). My Psychology colleagues have made me a better scientist. Among them, I especially thank Judy Harackiewicz for getting me involved in interventions designed to close social class and race gaps in academic achievement. And I am grateful to grad student Sarah Gavac for persistently yet kindly enhancing my understanding of transgender issues. My GWS colleagues have taught me immense amounts about both intersectionality and transgender. I am particularly grateful for the transgender pedagogy workshop.

We thank expert reviewers who reviewed our chapters for their coverage of intersectionality and transgender: Stephanie Budge, Sabra Katz-Wise, and Charlotte Tate. In addition, these reviewers contributed other useful comments: Jennifer Bradley, Northampton Community College; Marianna E. Carlucci, Loyola University Maryland; Jeannie DiClementi, Purdue University; Leanne M. Epling, University of Pikeville; Andrea Hinds, University of Rochester; Chivi Kapungu, Massachusetts Institute of Technology; Iva Katzarska-Miller, Transylvania University; Sabra L. Katz-Wise, Boston Children's Hospital and Harvard Medical School; Linda Scacco, University of Hartford; and Suzan Tessier, Rochester Institute of Technology.

Finally, we thank the many people at Sage for their commitment to producing a top-quality book and for their commitment to this book in particular: Lara Parra (editor) and Zach Valladon (editorial assistant). It has been a joy to work with all of you!

We hope that *The Psychology of Women and Gender: Half the Human Experience +* will help students and faculty alike gain a deeper, richer, more growth-enhancing understanding of the psychology of women and gender.

Nicole M. Else-Quest
Janet Shibley Hyde
December 2017

Sara Miller McCune founded SAGE Publishing in 1965 to support the dissemination of usable knowledge and educate a global community. SAGE publishes more than 1000 journals and over 800 new books each year, spanning a wide range of subject areas. Our growing selection of library products includes archives, data, case studies and video. SAGE remains majority owned by our founder and after her lifetime will become owned by a charitable trust that secures the company's continued independence.

Los Angeles | London | New Delhi | Singapore | Washington DC | Melbourne

Introduction

Pregnant people are commonly asked, "What are you having?" Unless the person is ordering food at a restaurant, the question has to do with whether they are expecting a girl or a boy. About two-thirds of pregnant women in the United States want to find out in advance whether they'll give birth to a daughter or son (Kearin et al., 2014). Today, advances in medical technology mean that many expectant parents may obtain relatively detailed ultrasound images of the developing fetus; that technology can be used to identify the fetus's genitals. Most expectant parents assume that if the ultrasound shows that the fetus has a penis, they'll have a son, and if it doesn't, they'll have a daughter. Seems simple, right? Parents soon imagine gendered names, clothing, colors, toys, activities, and so on for the child, all on the basis of whether or not they saw a penis on that ultrasound.

The question "What are you having?" is ubiquitous because most people understand gender as an essential and central characteristic of humans. We tend to have a hard time perceiving or thinking about a person without knowing their gender. To some extent,

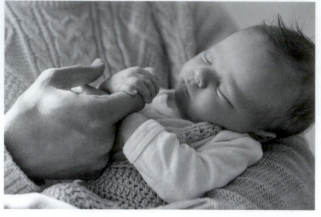

istock.com/Mikolette.

PHOTO 1.1
What is this baby's gender? How does it matter?

Cisgender: A person whose gender identity matches the gender they were assigned at birth.

that's not surprising; our social world is organized on the basis of gender. Public restrooms are often segregated by gender, as are sports teams, social clubs and organizations, items in clothing stores and toy stores, and sometimes even classrooms and schools. In addition, power and status are conferred by gender; around the world, men have more power and higher status relative to women (United Nations Development Programme, 2015; see Focus 1.1 for more on this). In short, gender matters.

Gender is also complex. Our goal in this textbook is to help you understand the complexity of gender, that is, when, why, and how gender matters in psychology. Historically, **cisgender** men have dominated in society and in psychological science. To redress this balance, we focus on women and, when possible, trans and nonbinary people. Each of these groups has been marginalized, "othered," or oppressed because of their gender. We examine gender broadly: its impact on people's lives and alternatives to a two-category gender system.

Why Study the Psychology of Women and Gender?

In thinking about why students might take a course on the psychology of women and gender, we (as professors and researchers) immediately reflect on why we would write a book or teach a course on the psychology of women and gender. One of the main reasons is simple: It is a fascinating topic. The questions we ask in our psychology of women and gender courses are unique and provocative. What does it mean to be a woman? How is that identity shaped by things like race or ethnicity, class, or sexual orientation? What roles do our hormones or brains play in our gender? How does our gender influence how others treat us? In some cases, these questions have complex answers that lead to more questions. In others, we have only begun to gather the evidence needed to answer the questions. And, often, the answers surprise us.

The psychology of women and gender is personally meaningful. Students take this course for a variety of reasons. For example, many women take the course to understand themselves better, a goal they may feel was not met by their other psychology courses. Some students may take this course because they have questions about their own gender and how they fit into the world.

The psychology of women and gender is essential to psychology. That is, there are many academic reasons to study the psychology of women and gender. For example, many traditional psychological theories have literally been theories about men (as you'll learn in Chapter 2). Sexism or gender bias exists not only in our everyday experiences, but also in the science of psychology. As a result, the experiences of cisgender men have been considered the norm and the experiences of women and anyone who doesn't fit into the traditional masculine role have been marginalized, ignored, or devalued. One way to address these biases in psychology is to study the psychology of women as well as trans and nonbinary people and to think critically about gender.

The psychology of women and gender is relevant to understanding our society and improving people's lives. That is, just as our social world is organized on the basis of gender, that social organization shapes the opportunities and experiences available to all of society's members. One of the central themes of the feminist movement has been that "the personal is political." What this means is that social roles, norms, policies, and laws play an important role in determining many aspects of our lives. In some circumstances, our gender may offer unearned privileges or disadvantages. Understanding how our personal experiences are connected to the context of our community and culture is important not only for our own knowledge, but also for improving the conditions in which we all live.

Sex, Gender, Transgender, and Cisgender

Language is constantly evolving and changing, especially within the psychology of women and gender. The fact that the meanings and connotations of words are in flux can lead to misunderstandings and different interpretations. In the interest of establishing a common vocabulary for readers, we clarify our language here (see also Table 1.1).

In the English language the term *sex* is often used ambiguously. That is, sometimes it is used to refer to sexual behaviors such as sexual intercourse, sometimes it is used to refer to physical or physiological characteristics of maleness and femaleness, and sometimes it is used as way of categorizing a species based on reproductive function. Often, the meaning is clear from the context. For example, if a job application says, "Sex: ____," you don't write, "As often as possible." Yet what is the topic of a book titled *Sex and*

TABLE 1.1   **Language and terminology about gender are constantly evolving. Below is a list of some of the terms we use throughout this book.**

Term	Definition
Gender	The state of being male, female, both male and female, or neither male nor female
Sex	Physical or physiological characteristics of maleness and femaleness; sexual behaviors
Gender binary	A system of conceptualizing gender as having two distinct and opposing groups or kinds (i.e., male and female)
Genderqueer	A gender category that is not exclusively male or female and therefore is not captured by the gender binary
Gender identity	A person's internal sense of their own gender
Cisgender	Describes a person whose gender identity matches the gender they were assigned at birth
Transgender	Describes a person whose gender identity differs from the gender they were assigned at birth
Intersex	A variety of conditions in which a person is born with genitals or reproductive anatomy that is not typical of female or male people. Also termed *disorders of sex development* in the DSM-5 and *differences of sex development* or *genital diversity*.
Trans	An umbrella term for the transgender spectrum; may include people who identify as transgender, genderqueer, cross-dressing, gender nonconforming, gender fluid, or other nonbinary identity

Source: Created by the authors.

Temperament in Three Primitive Societies? Is it about female roles and male roles in those societies, or is it about the sexual behavior of people in those societies? To reduce this ambiguity, in this book we generally use the term *sex* to refer to sexual behaviors.

Gender: The state of being male, female, both male and female, or neither male nor female.

Sometimes people use *sex* interchangeably with **gender**, which we define as the state of being male, female, both male and female, or neither male nor female. Gender has, at least in Western cultures, long been understood as a binary, such that individuals are *either* male or female, but never both or neither (a theme we revisit later in this chapter). The **gender binary** is a system of thinking about gender as having two distinct and opposing groups or kinds (that is, male and female). It is evident in phrases such as "the opposite sex" and in assuming that all people must fit squarely into one of these two groups. When you apply for a driver's license, for example, you typically must choose *either* male or female for gender; in nearly all states, you may choose only one of these options, and there are no others. Today, we know that people may identify themselves as being either within or outside the gender binary, such as belonging to a third gender category like **genderqueer** or as being *nonbinary*.

Gender binary: A system of conceptualizing gender as having two distinct and opposing groups or kinds (i.e., male and female).

Genderqueer: A gender category that is not exclusively male or female and therefore is not captured by the gender binary.

Similarly, in recent years we have seen increased visibility and awareness of transgender men and women. A person who is **transgender** is a person whose self-identified gender differs from the gender they were assigned at birth, typically based on the appearance of external genitalia (sometimes called *natal gender*). A transgender woman, then, is a person who identifies as female but was assigned a male gender at birth, and a transgender man is a person who identifies as male but was assigned a female gender at birth. Still, it is important to note that not all people whose self-identified gender differs from their assigned gender will label themselves transgender. By contrast, a person who is cisgender is a person whose self-identified gender matches the gender they were assigned at birth. The prefixes *cis-* ("on the same side of") and *trans-* ("across or on the other side of") come from Latin and appear in chemistry, which uses *cis* and *trans* for different pairs of molecules.

Transgender: Describes a person whose gender identity differs from the gender they were assigned at birth.

Some people use *trans* as an umbrella term to refer to anyone who is not a cisgender man or cisgender woman, such as transgender men and women and genderqueer people. You will notice that our definition of gender allows for some flexibility and avoids adhering to the gender binary.

Cisgenderism: Prejudice against people who are outside the gender binary; also refers to bias that recognizes a person's birth-assigned gender but not their gender identity. Also termed anti-trans prejudice.

Nonetheless, psychology has, until recently, neglected the study of transgender men and women or considered them as abnormal (dickey, Hendricks, & Bockting, 2016), operating from **cisgenderism**. Cisgenderism refers to prejudice against people who are outside the gender binary or bias that recognizes a person's birth-assigned gender but not their gender identity (Ansara & Hegarty, 2012). While we believe awareness of cisgenderism is improving and research on the experiences of transgender persons is blossoming, the field still has a long way to go.

The fact that most empirical research in psychology has not accommodated the experiences of transgender persons raises questions about the psychology of women and gender. In psychology, *gender differences* has generally been used to refer to differences between men and women. Thus, gender differences research is rooted in the gender binary. In this book, because we review the existing science, we follow this convention and use the term *gender differences* to refer to male-female differences because the vast majority of empirical research in psychology has assumed the gender binary. We believe it is possible to be sophisticated consumers of that research without adopting the gender binary (a point we'll return to later in this chapter).

With regard to describing psychological differences between men and women, we recognize that other scholars have adopted other conventions. For example, some scholars prefer to use the term *sex differences* to refer to innate or biologically produced differences between men and women and *gender differences* to refer to male-female differences that result from learning and the social roles of men and women (e.g., Unger, 1979). The problem with this terminology is that studies often document a difference between men and women without providing any evidence as to what causes it—biology, society, or both. Furthermore, the sharp distinction between biological causes and cultural causes fails to recognize that biology and culture often interact. Sometimes, the distinction between sex and gender isn't obvious or even possible to make. Therefore, we simply use the term *gender differences* for differences between men and women, and leave their causation as a separate question.

Sexism and Feminism

Sexism

Another term that will you will find throughout this book is *sexism*. **Sexism** or gender bias can be defined as discrimination or bias against people based on their gender. Some people feel uncomfortable using the term *sexism* because they think of it as a nasty or inflammatory label to hurl at someone or something. In fact, it is a good, legitimate term that describes a particular phenomenon—namely, discrimination on the basis of gender. It will be used in that spirit in this book, not as a form of name-calling. It is also important to recognize that anyone, regardless of their gender, can engage in sexist behavior or hold sexist attitudes.

Social psychologists have studied sexism extensively, and their research has yielded several findings that are relevant here. First, sexism isn't what it used to be. **Old-fashioned sexism**, the kind that was prevalent in the 1950s and earlier, was characterized by open or overt prejudice against women. An example would be the belief—common in the 1950s and 1960s in the United States—that women could not be anchors on TV news programs because they wouldn't be good at it and because viewers wouldn't accept the news as authoritative if it were delivered by a woman. Today, of course, news programs often have coanchors, one male and one female, and the old view seems ridiculous. Old-fashioned sexism has been replaced by **modern sexism** or neosexism, which refers to covert or subtle prejudiced beliefs about women (Swim et al., 1995). Psychologists measure old-fashioned sexism with items like "Women are generally not as smart as men"; 50 or more years ago, many people would have agreed with such a statement. Modern sexism, in contrast, is more subtle and consists of three components: denial that there is continuing discrimination against women, antagonistic feelings about women's "demands," and resentment about perceived special favors granted to women (Swim et al., 1995). Although anyone can be sexist, modern sexist beliefs are most strongly endorsed by White men (Hayes & Swim, 2013).

Even in the 21st century, experiences with sexism are common. In one study of a large sample of girls between the ages of 12 and 18, 23% reported that they had been discouraged in math, science, or computers by teachers because they were girls, and 32% reported that boys had discouraged them in these areas (Leaper & Brown, 2008). Many had also been discouraged in athletics because of being a girl: 28% had been discouraged by teachers or coaches, and 54% had been discouraged by boys.

Social psychologists Peter Glick and Susan Fiske (2001) have documented two other types of sexism today: hostile and benevolent. **Hostile sexism** refers to negative, hostile attitudes toward women and adversarial beliefs about gender relations in which women

Sexism: Discrimination or bias against other people based on their gender; also termed gender bias or sex bias.

Old-fashioned sexism: Open or overt prejudice against women.

Modern sexism: Subtle prejudiced beliefs about women; also termed neosexism.

Hostile sexism: Negative, hostile attitudes toward women and adversarial beliefs about gender relations.

Paul Thompson/Hulton Archive/Getty Images.

Benevolent sexism:
Beliefs about women that seem to be kind or benevolent; women are seen as pure and morally superior beings who should be protected and adored.

are thought to spend most of their time trying to control men, whether through sexuality or feminism. **Benevolent sexism**, in contrast, consists of beliefs about women that seem to the perpetrator to be kind or benevolent—in which women are honored and put on the proverbial pedestal. In the benevolent view, women are seen as pure beings who should be protected and adored. Although this view may seem harmless, it is still a form of sexism because it stereotypes women as weak and dependent on men, and being put on a pedestal is extremely confining, both literally and figuratively.

Feminism

Feminist: A person who favors political, economic, and social equality of all people, regardless of gender, and therefore favors the legal and social changes necessary to achieve gender equality.

Another important term that needs to be defined in this context is *feminist*. A **feminist** is a person who favors political, economic, and social equality of all people, regardless of gender, and therefore favors the legal and social changes necessary to achieve gender equality. While most Americans support the feminist principle and goal of gender equality, a much smaller percentage identify themselves as feminists (Gallup, 2002). A well-sampled national survey conducted in 2009 by ABC News/*Washington Post* asked the question "Do you consider yourself to be a feminist or not?"; 29% of the women and 17% of the men said yes (Roper Center, 2011). Clearly feminism is more than a tiny splinter group.

A 2006 national survey of women and men by CBS News asked, "Has the women's movement achieved anything that has made your life better?" (Roper Center, 2011). A majority (55%) of the respondents said yes. Those who responded yes were then asked what the main thing was that had made their lives better. The top choice was equality/more rights (17% of respondents), followed by better jobs (15%), more choices (14%), the right to vote (10%—good not to forget that one), and better/equal pay (9%). As we discuss in Focus 1.1, the feminist goal of gender equality has not yet been met.

Just as sexism has changed over time, so has feminism. Historically, there have been four periods of heightened feminist activism, termed *first-wave* feminism, *second-wave* feminism, *third-wave* feminism, and *fourth-wave* feminism. First-wave feminism occurred in the late 1800s and early 1900s in Britain, Canada, and the United States. These feminists fought for women's voting rights, and they succeeded! In the United States, women's right to vote was won when the Nineteenth Amendment to the U.S. Constitution was ratified in 1920.

Second-wave feminism began in the 1960s and extended into the 1990s. Second-wave feminists could build on the successes of their predecessors and take on a much wider range of issues: sexual freedom; reproductive rights, especially contraception and abortion; pay equity; equal opportunity in education; and gender-based violence. The movement proposed the Equal Rights Amendment to the U.S. Constitution, which declared, "Equality of rights under the law shall not be denied or abridged by the United States or by any State on account of sex." The amendment passed in the House and Senate in 1972 but ultimately failed at the stage of ratification by the states.

PHOTO 1.2
First-wave feminists, often called suffragettes, fought for women's voting rights.

By the 1990s, many goals of the second wave had been accomplished, and some declared that feminism was dead and that the nation had passed into the "postfeminist" era. There was actually no good scientific evidence of a decline in feminism (E. J. Hall & Rodriguez, 2003), but a new kind of feminism began to emerge sometime in the 1990s, known as third-wave feminism (Snyder, 2008). In part, it represents a rebellion against second-wave foremothers and attempts to rectify some of the perceived weaknesses of the second wave. One of the key criticisms of second-wave feminism is that it tended to essentialize and oversimplify the category of "women" by focusing on "universal" female experiences such as motherhood. In so doing, it ignored the great diversity among women along lines of race and social class. Second-wave feminists were also accused of being rigid in their ideology, saying that certain approaches were feminist and others definitely were not. Responding to these issues, third-wave feminism emphasized intersectionality—an approach originating in Black feminism—and diversity among women rather than universality of female experience. In addition, it favors the individual's right to define feminism, instead of everyone accepting a uniform ideology.

We are currently in the early years of the fourth wave of feminism, which has been fueled by recent advances in online technology, including user-generated content, such as blogs, and social media, such as Twitter, Facebook, and Instagram (Naly & Smith, 2015). Building on the third wave, it also includes greater emphasis on intersectionality and critique and rejection of the gender binary. Thus, transgender issues are more prominent than in previous waves.

Feminism is a political movement and ideology as well as a theoretical perspective. There is a rich literature within feminist psychology, and a wide spectrum of feminist theoretical perspectives exists, which we describe in Chapter 2.

Themes in the Psychology of Women and Gender

A number of themes will recur in this book. Some of these themes are rooted in history, taking somewhat different forms across cultures but remaining essentially the same. Some themes are rooted in feminism. Other themes are derived from current scientific psychological research on women and gender. We focus here on five themes that are central to understanding the psychology of women and gender.

Feminine Evil

One theme rooted in history is **feminine evil**. One of the clearest images of women in mythology is their portrayal as the source of evil (Hays, 1964). In the Judeo-Christian tradition, Eve disobeyed God's orders and ate from the fruit of the tree of knowledge. As a result, Adam and Eve were forced to leave the Garden of Eden, and Eve, the woman, became the source of original sin, responsible for the fall of humanity. In a more ancient myth, the Greek god Zeus ordered Vulcan to create the lovely maiden Pandora to bring misery to earth in revenge for the theft of fire by Prometheus. Pandora was given a box containing all the evils of the world, which she was told not to open. But Pandora opened the box, and thus all the evils it contained spread over the world. In addition, in Chinese mythology the two forces, yin and yang, correspond to feminine and masculine, and yin, the feminine, is seen as the dark, or evil, side of nature.

Historically, perhaps the most frightening manifestation of the belief in feminine evil was the persecution of witches beginning in the Middle Ages and persisting into Puritan America. Guided by the Catholic Church in a papal bull of 1484, the Malleus Maleficarum, the Inquisition tortured or put to death unknown numbers of witches. The vast majority

Feminine evil: The belief that women are the source of evil or immorality in the world, as in the Adam and Eve story.

FOCUS 1.1

GENDER EQUALITY AROUND THE WORLD AND TRANSNATIONAL FEMINISM

In 1995, at the Fourth World Conference on Women in Beijing, China, 17,000 participants and 30,000 activists met and created the Beijing Declaration and Platform for Action. The Platform for Action affirmed a commitment to gender equality and described specific steps that needed to be taken in order to improve the lives of girls and women and achieve gender equity. It stated, "The status of women has advanced in some important respects in the past decade but that progress has been uneven, inequalities between women and men have persisted and major obstacles remain, with serious consequences for the well-being of all people" (*Beijing Declaration and Platform for Action,* 1995, p. 2). As a result, the United Nations now regularly publishes data on how women are doing in all nations of the world, and these data are used to monitor progress toward gender equality.

What does gender equality look like? Gender equality has several aspects, such as education, politics, economics, health, and gender-based violence (Else-Quest & Hamilton, 2018). For example, educational gender equality would entail equal numbers of men and women attending high school or university, or equal numbers of men and women being able to read and write. Political gender equality could include equal political representation or having equal numbers of men and women elected to congress or parliament. Economic gender equality would entail equal pay for equal work and adequate family leave policies, regardless of gender. Gender equality in health would include improving women's access to prenatal care and reducing maternal mortality and adolescent pregnancy rates. With regard to gender-based violence, gender equality would mean freedom from forms of violence in which men are the predominant perpetrators and women are the predominant victims (such as rape and intimate partner violence, discussed further in Chapter 14). All of these aspects of gender equality are important and were described in the Beijing Declaration and Platform for Action.

Data from 20 countries are shown in Table 1.2. The United Nations Development Programme computes a Gender Inequality Index (GII), which is one of many measures of country-level gender equality. The GII indexes inequality of women relative to men in three areas: reproductive health (measured by adolescent pregnancy and maternal mortality), empowerment (measured by

educational attainment and representation of women in parliament), and labor force participation. Low scores indicate less inequality (i.e., greater equality). A country's overall rank, shown in the left column of Table 1.2, results from an average of these indicators. As the data show, no country in the world can claim to be truly gender equal.

American readers may be surprised that the United States does not rank first; some believe that we have a great deal of gender equality in this country, but it's clear we still have areas of inequality. We rank only 55th and are beaten by some European nations, Canada, and Japan. The United States does not fare so well because of our high teen pregnancy rate (31.0, compared with 1.9 in Switzerland) and our persistent underrepresentation of women in Congress. What would we have to do to get the United States in first place?

Psychological research has shown data such as these are linked to individual endorsement of sexism and hostile sexism against women (Brandt, 2011; Glick et al., 2000; Napier et al., 2010). That is, countries that have more gender inequality also have more people who hold sexist beliefs. So, achieving gender equality means more than just changing laws and improving our scores on the GII. It also means changing people's beliefs about gender and the roles of women so that women can be free to make their own choices.

Transnational feminism advocates for gender equality across countries and points out that we need to carefully consider women's and girls' experiences not only across countries, but also within them (Grabe & Else-Quest, 2012). That is, within each culture and country, behaviors and roles have different meanings. Consider gender-based violence, where we see differences across cultures and countries in the types of gender-based violence and the meaning of specific violent acts. A man in Sri Lanka might throw a shoe at his wife to punish her for cooking a meal he did not like. Even if the woman was not physically injured, such an act is considered humiliating and degrading (Marecek, 2012). In most Western countries, however, such a behavior might seem simply strange or rude and probably wouldn't be identified in a screening or survey of gender-based violence. Thus, transnational feminists point out that we need to carefully consider women's and girls' experiences not only across countries, but also within them.

TABLE 1.2 Gender Inequality Index (GII) scores and ranks of 20 countries.

GII Rank	Country	GII Value
1	Slovenia	0.016
2	Switzerland	0.028
3	Germany	0.041
4	Denmark	0.048
5	Austria	0.053
11	Finland	0.075
19	Australia	0.110
25	Canada	0.129
26	Japan	0.133
40	China	0.191
54	Russian Federation	0.276
55	United States	0.280
68	Cuba	0.356
74	Mexico	0.373
83	South Africa	0.407
110	Indonesia	0.494
130	India	0.563
131	Egypt	0.573
135	Sudan	0.591
152	Afghanistan	0.693

Source: Created by Nicole Else-Quest based on data from United Nations Development Programme (2015).

Transnational feminists such as Chandra Mohanty (2003, p. 503) advocate for "noncolonizing feminist solidarity across borders," cautioning that we should avoid viewing girls' and women's experiences through a Western lens and imposing Western standards on other cultures. What can we do to empower girls and women around the world without dictating that they should adopt Western ways? Can gender equality be universalized to every country? If so, what do you think it would look like?

of those accused and tried were women (Hays, 1964). Thus, it is woman who is seen as being in collaboration with the devil, visiting evil upon humans.

Today, people who hold hostile sexist attitudes, as discussed earlier in this chapter, believe that women use their sexuality to ensnare helpless men (Glick & Fiske, 2001). Again, women are believed to exert an evil influence on men.

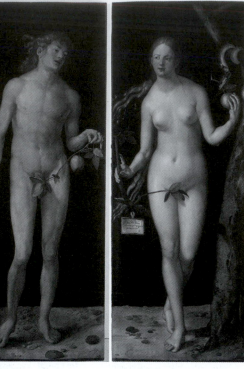

PHOTO 1.3

The male as normative is a theme throughout history. An example is the Adam and Eve story, in which Adam is created first and Eve is later made from his rib.

Male as normative: A model in which the male is seen as the norm for all humans and the female is seen as a deviation from the norm.

Androcentrism: Male centered; the belief that the male is the norm.

Gender differences: Differences between genders.

Gender similarities: Similarities among genders.

Male as Normative

Another enduring historical theme is the **male as normative**. Throughout mythology the male is seen as normative, the female as a variant or deviation. That is, the male is the important one, the major representative of the species, the "normal" one, and the female is a variation on him. As Simone de Beauvoir (1952) expressed it, woman is the Other.

In the biblical creation story (Genesis 2), Adam, the man, is created first; Eve, the woman, is later fashioned out of his rib, almost as an afterthought. In this and many other creation myths, man is created first; he is the major, important part of the species. Woman comes second and is only a variant on the man, the normative. There are even myths in which a woman is created by castrating a man.

Perhaps the clearest example of the male-as-normative theme is in our language. The word *man* is used to refer not only to a male person, but to people in general. When the gender of a person is unknown, the pronoun *he* is used to refer to "him." (Would we dare have said "to refer to her"?) The species as a whole is man; woman is merely a subset. This topic will be discussed in detail in Chapter 5.

A closely related concept is **androcentrism** (Bem, 1993). It means, literally, male-centeredness, or the belief that males are the standard or norm. This concept crops up in a number of places in modern psychology, including some of the theories discussed in Chapter 2.

To be the deviation from the norm is, often, to be marginalized, ignored, or devalued. Thus, embedded within the theme of male as normative and androcentrism is the lower social status of women relative to men. Throughout the world, women do not enjoy the same rights, freedoms, and opportunities as men (United Nations Development Programme, 2015). Focus 1.1 describes gender equity around the world, demonstrating that we still have a way to go before men and women are treated as equals. For this reason, our book is about the psychology of gender and focuses especially on the experiences of women.

Gender Differences and Similarities

There is a paradox in trying to understand the psychology of women and gender: Women and men are at once different and similar. Although **gender differences** are important in the psychology of gender, **gender similarities** are equally important. Both scientific and nonscientific views of women have concentrated on how they differ from men; this lopsided emphasis on gender differences has led to a distorted understanding of the psychology of women and gender. The study of psychological gender similarities is essential to a comprehensive and unbiased psychology of women and gender (Hyde, 2005a). This paradoxical tension between gender differences and gender similarities will be a continuing theme throughout this book.

Historically, the overemphasis on gender differences combined with male-as-normative thinking have fostered the pervasiveness of female deficit models. That is, we spend so much time and energy demonstrating that men and women are different and that men are the norm or the standard, we end up concluding that women are abnormal or deficient. In the 19th century, scientists found that women had slightly smaller brains than men and interpreted this as a sure reason why women were not as intelligent as men (Shields, 1975). Today some researchers continue to argue that girls are not as good at math as boys are. No matter the century, researchers always seem to try to find female deficits. In Chapter 3, we will delve into the study of psychological gender differences and similarities in detail.

Critiquing the Gender Binary

The overemphasis on gender differences and neglect of gender similarities is deeply rooted in the gender binary. There are many problems with the gender binary, which, with only the categories of male and female, is very narrow and restrictive in its range. According to the gender binary, gender is defined based on physical characteristics (such as sex chromosomes, hormones, and external genitalia), which are assumed to be consistent with one another. Thus, the binary assumes that our gender identities stem from these physical characteristics. In turn, the gender binary also assumes that everyone is cisgender.

Because of these faulty assumptions, the most glaring problems with the binary are that it excludes anyone who is transgender, **intersex**, or genderqueer. Many people do not fit within the gender binary; there is *gender diversity* beyond two rigid gender categories. Critiquing the gender binary requires thinking differently about gender and asking difficult questions. For example, should we think of gender as having distinct categories or groups? Or should we think of it as being a continuum? If there are distinct genders, how many are there? Can gender change, or is it stable and permanent? Critiquing the gender binary—and exploring the implications of that critique for research—is an important theme in the psychology of women and gender.

Intersex: A variety of conditions in which a person is born with genitals or reproductive anatomy that is not typical of females or males. Also termed disorders of sex development in the DSM-5 and differences of sex development or genital diversity.

Intersectionality of Gender

A recurring theme in the psychology of women, rooted in Black feminism, is intersectionality. **Intersectionality** can be defined as an approach or perspective that simultaneously considers the meaning and consequences of multiple categories of identity, difference, and disadvantage (E. R. Cole, 2009; Else-Quest & Hyde, 2016). That is, according to this approach, we should not consider the effects of gender in isolation. Instead, we should consider the experience and effects of gender, race, social class, and sexual orientation simultaneously. When we talk about the category "women," we are talking about a complex group that differs along many dimensions and categories, including ethnicity, social class, and sexual orientation.

Intersectionality: A feminist approach that simultaneously considers the meaning and consequences of multiple categories of identity, difference, and disadvantage.

The Black abolitionist and women's rights activist Sojourner Truth described the essence of intersectionality in a speech at the Ohio Women's Rights Convention in 1851. One of 12 children born to James and Elizabeth Baumfree, Truth (a self-given name) was born into slavery sometime around 1797 and sold to four different slave owners before walking to freedom in 1826. While she never learned to read or write, she traveled and preached on abolition, women's suffrage, and prison reform.

At the Ohio Women's Rights Convention, Truth spoke extemporaneously about the importance of women's rights for all women, not just White women. Though her exact words were not recorded, an excerpt of the speech attributed to her at the Convention reflects a need for intersectionality in the feminist movement:

> That man over there says that women need to be helped into carriages, and lifted over ditches, and to have the best place everywhere. Nobody ever helps me into carriages, or over mud-puddles, or gives me any best place! And ain't I a woman? Look at me! Look at my arm! I have ploughed and planted, and gathered into barns, and no man could head me! And ain't I a woman? I could work as much and eat as much as a man—when I could get it—and bear the lash as well! And ain't I a woman? I have borne 13 children, and seen most all sold off to slavery, and when I cried out with my mother's grief, none but Jesus heard me! And ain't I a woman?

Several themes are evident in her speech and continue to be described within intersectionality writing. One theme is that femininity and womanhood have often been defined with White, middle- and upper-class women in mind, and thus the experiences of poor women and women of color have often been marginalized or made invisible. Intersectional approaches recognize that gender may be constructed differently by other racial, ethnic, and socioeconomic groups. The issues that are important to White women may not be as relevant to women of color, and vice versa.

Critical theory: A theoretical perspective that seeks to redress power inequalities and achieve equity and equality.

Recognizing that diversity and giving voice to everyone—but especially to those who lack power—is essential within intersectionality. Therefore, another theme in her speech is that, despite the different needs and issues that matter to diverse groups of women, there are also commonalities. Truth was speaking about the importance of all women's voices being heard. All women in the United States, regardless of race, were disenfranchised at this time. In sum, intersectionality holds both the diversity and commonality of experiences of people who are oppressed. As a **critical theory**, intersectionality is focused on power and inequality, how they are maintained, and how to achieve equity and equality.

Within this perspective, it becomes clear that some groups experience multiple disadvantages, such as poor Black women or lesbian women of color. Others may be part of a disadvantaged group but also part of a privileged group, such as White women with disabilities. The experience of gender differs for the women at each of these intersections, but there are also similarities. Transgender women and cisgender women may experience their gender in some ways that are different and some ways that are similar.

We will consider intersectionality throughout this book, when research is available. The overreliance on middle-class White college students as research participants makes it difficult to find an intersectional approach in much of psychology. Thus, we will return to intersectionality especially in Chapter 2, "Theoretical Perspectives on Gender"; Chapter 4, "The Intersection of Gender and Ethnicity"; and Chapter 13, "Gender and Sexual Orientation." As a brief example here, women's attitudes about gender roles vary as a function of their race or ethnicity

By Randall Studio - National Portrait Gallery, Smithsonian Institution, Public Domain.

PHOTO 1.4

Black abolitionist and women's rights activist Sojourner Truth.

(E. R. Cole & Zucker, 2007). Feminists of any race or ethnicity, for instance, have readily recognized that White men oppress White women. Black feminists, on the other hand, have emphasized that the oppression of Black women by Black men can be understood only in the context of the fact that Black men themselves are oppressed by White persons. Gender intersects with a number of other social categories, and understanding the psychology of women and gender requires examining and understanding those many intersections.

The Social Construction of Gender

Many of these themes in the psychology of women and gender reflect the social construction of gender. Feminist theorists view gender not as a biologically created reality, but as a socially constructed phenomenon (Crawford & Kaufman, 2005; Hare-Mustin & Marecek, 1988; Marecek et al., 2004). The basic position of **social constructionism** is that people—including scientists—do not discover reality; rather, they construct or invent it (Watzlawick, 1984). According to social constructionism, we do not experience reality directly. Instead, we actively construct meanings for events in the environment based on our own prior experiences, social interactions, and predispositions. Thus, concepts like the gender binary are a product of social interactions and culture.

The extent to which we socially construct gender becomes clearer if we view how gender is constructed within other cultures. In European American cultures, the gender binary is assumed by most people. To them, it is perfectly obvious—a clear reality—that there are two genders, male and female. However, among many American Indian tribes, including the Cherokee, Shoshone, Navajo, Lakota, and Zuni, there is another category of gender, known generally as **Two Spirit** (however, each tribe has a unique name for this category). Two Spirits are people who feel they possess both male and female spirits, so they may dress as and adopt roles traditional for both men and women or for a gender that contrasts with the gender they were assigned at birth. Some indigenous tribes consider the Two Spirit to be a third or fourth gender, and it is perfectly clear in their culture that there are more than two genders (M. T. Garrett & Barret, 2003; S.-E. Jacobs et al., 1997; S. J. Kessler & McKenna, 1985). What seems like an obvious reality to European Americans, that there are only two genders, turns out to be a social construction, which becomes clear when we see that other cultures have constructed the categories differently.

Processes closely related to gender are also socially constructed. For example, Americans are quite sure of the reality that women typically feel tired after giving birth, because they have gone through a physically exhausting process. Other societies, though, have the couvade, which is practiced among the Ainu of Japan and the Timbira of Brazil (Gregersen, 1996). The couvade consists of elaborate rituals that are based on the assumption that the father, not the mother, is the main contributor of effort in childbirth. After the mother gives birth, the baby is given to the father, and he rests for several days to overcome his fatigue, whereas the mother returns to work immediately because she is believed not to need rest. The contribution of the father to childbirth, and his fatigue following it, is a clear reality to people in these cultures. Again, European American notions of women's contributions to childbirth are challenged, and we see the extent to which such events are socially constructed.

Social constructionism: A theoretical viewpoint that humans do not discover reality directly; rather, they construct meanings for events in the environment based on their own prior experiences and beliefs.

Two Spirit: Among some American Indian tribes, a gender category for individuals who feel they possess both male and female spirits.

By Unknown—The Library at The College of Staten Island of the City University of New York, PD-US.

PHOTO 1.5

We'wha was a Two Spirit person from the Zuni tribe. She was born with a male body but adopted traditionally feminine traits. We'wha was often misgendered by White Americans, who understood gender only as a binary system and assumed she was a cisgender woman.

Feminist psychologists have noted that gender is not only a person variable (as traditional psychology has maintained) but also a stimulus variable (e.g., Grady, 1979). By saying that gender is a *person variable*, we mean that it is a characteristic of the individual; this point of view leads to the study of gender differences, a pursuit that has occupied some traditional psychologists and some feminist psychologists (see Chapter 3). By saying that gender is also a *stimulus variable*, we mean that a person's gender has a profound impact on the way others react to that person. Our understanding of an individual—that is, our social construction of that individual—is in part determined by our knowledge of that individual's gender. This point of view stimulated an area of research in which participants are led to believe that a particular piece of work was done by a man or a woman, or that a particular infant is male or female; their responses to the work or the infant can then be studied as a function of the gender they believe it to be (see Chapters 7 and 9 for examples). Therefore, gender is both a personal characteristic and a stimulus variable.

Social constructionism, then, argues that these processes occur in at least three areas: (1) The individual engages in social constructions, for example, reacting to another person differently depending on whether that person is male or female; (2) the society or culture provides a set of social constructions of gender, for example, whether there are two genders or more; and (3) scientists socially construct gender by the way they construct their research.

Among other things, this view that notions of gender are socially constructed challenges the belief that science is fundamentally objective (Hare-Mustin & Marecek, 1988). Scientific knowledge, like all other knowledge, is shaped by the values and presuppositions of the perceiver—in this case, the scientist.

Continuing Topics in Psychology

You will also notice other topics or issues that return throughout this book, which are present throughout psychology. For example, you will learn about theories of women's behavior, some of which have solid data (empirical evidence) backing them, some of which do not. Not every theory is true, nor is every one a good description or explanation of behavior. Just because Freud said something does not make it true (or false). Readers need to become critical thinkers about the difference between statements based on theory and statements based on empirical evidence.

Another important topic in psychology is the distinction between internal and external determinants of behavior. Is human behavior determined more by internal factors, such as a person's enduring personality traits, or more by external factors, such as the particular situation the person is in. Advocates of the latter position point out how inconsistent people's behavior can be from one situation to another—for example, a man may be aggressive toward a business competitor, but passive or nurturant toward his spouse. This suggests that his behavior is not determined by an enduring personality trait (aggressiveness), but rather by the particular situation he is in. This distinction also has practical implications for improving people's lives, which is the primary goal of psychology.

Sources of Bias in Psychological Research

Research in the psychology of women and gender is progressing at a rapid pace. Certainly we will be able to provide you with much important information about the psychology of women and gender in this book, but there are still more questions yet to be answered. With research on the psychology of women and gender expanding so rapidly, many important discoveries will be made in the next 10 to 20 years. Therefore, someone who takes a course on the psychology of women and gender should do more than just learn what is currently known about women and gender. It is even more valuable to gain the skills to become a "sophisticated consumer" of psychological research. That is, it is very important that you be able to evaluate future studies about gender that you may find in newspapers, magazines, blogs, websites, or scholarly journals. To do this, you need to develop at least three skills: (1) Know how psychologists go about doing research, (2) be aware of ways in which gender bias may affect research, and (3) be aware of problems that may exist in research on gender roles or the psychology of women. In general, one of the most valuable things you can get from a college education is the development of *critical thinking skills*. The feminist perspective encourages thinking about psychological research and theory. The following discussion is designed to help you develop these skills.

How Psychologists Do Research

Figure 1.1 is a diagram of the process that psychologists go through in doing research, shown in rectangles. The diagram also indicates points at which gender bias may enter, shown in ovals.

The process, in brief, is generally this: The scientist starts with some theoretical model, whether a formal model, such as gender schema theory (see Chapter 2), or merely a set of personal assumptions. Based on the model or assumptions, the scientist then formulates a question. The purpose of the research is to answer that question. Next, they design the research, which involves several substeps: A behavior must be selected, a way to measure the behavior must be devised, a group of appropriate participants must be chosen, and a research design must be developed. One of these substeps—finding a way to measure the behavior—is probably the most fundamental aspect of quantitative psychological research. The next step is for the scientist to collect the data. The data are then analyzed (often, but not always, using statistics) and the results are interpreted. Next, the scientist publishes the results, which are read by other scientists and incorporated into the body of scientific knowledge (and also put into textbooks). Finally, the system comes full circle, because the results are fed into the theoretical models that other scientists will use in formulating new research.

Now let us consider some of the ways in which gender bias—bias that may affect our understanding of the psychology of women or gender—may enter into each stage of this process (Caplan & Caplan, 2009).

Bias in Theory

The theoretical model or set of assumptions the scientist begins with has a profound effect on the outcome of the research. Gender bias may enter if the scientist begins with a biased theoretical model. Perhaps the best example of a biased theoretical model is psychoanalytic theory as formulated by Freud (see Chapter 2). A person with a psychoanalytic orientation might design research to document the presence of penis envy or immature superego in women; someone with a different theoretical orientation wouldn't even think to ask such questions. It is important to be sensitive to the theoretical orientation of a scientist reporting a piece of research—and sometimes the theoretical orientation isn't stated; it needs to be ferreted out—because that orientation affects the rest of the research and the conclusions that are drawn.

FIGURE 1.1   **Ways that gender bias may enter each of the stages of the research process.**

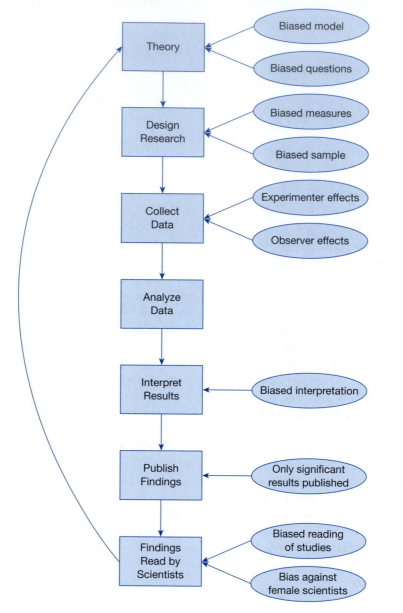

Source: Created by the authors.

Feminist scholars advocate an important method for overcoming the problems of biased theoretical models and stereotyped research questions: Go to the community of people to be studied and ask them about their lives and what the significant questions are. For example, research on transgender women may be limited if it is conducted by cisgender women working from theories developed by cisgender men. It is better scientific practice to begin by asking transgender women for input on the research design. Theories can be built at a later stage, once a firm foundation has been laid beginning from the women's own experiences and perspectives.

Bias in Research Design

As shown in Figure 1.1, the next step in psychological research is designing the research. Research methods in psychology can be roughly classified into two categories: laboratory experiments and naturalistic observations. In the experiment, the research participant is brought into the psychologist's laboratory, and their behavior is manipulated in some way in order to study the phenomenon in question. In contrast, with naturalistic observations, researchers observe people's behavior as it occurs in naturalistic settings, and they do not attempt to manipulate the behavior. In practice, the distinction between these categories is not so clear-cut. For example, it is possible to conduct an experiment in a naturalistic setting. However, regardless of where an experiment takes place, true experiments must always include (a) the researcher randomly assigning participants to conditions, (b) some kind of experimental control to rule out confounds, and (c) the manipulation of an independent variable.

It is also possible to talk about **quasi-experimental designs** (*quasi* meaning "not quite"). This term refers to designs that don't meet these three criteria. For example, a quasi-experiment might compare two or more groups of participants on their response to a treatment without randomly assigning the participants to the treatment conditions. Thus, studies of gender differences are not true experiments, but rather quasi-experiments, because the researcher cannot randomly assign participants to be male or female.

Some scholars argue that laboratory experiments are inherently gender biased, although this point is controversial (Peplau & Conrad, 1989). This question will be considered in greater detail later in this chapter.

When psychologists study a trait or behavior, they must clearly define it for the purposes of their study, or create an *operational definition*. **Quantitative research methods** use operational definitions that involve **psychological measurement**, or the assignment of numbers to psychological characteristics. Psychological measurement may take many forms. If the researcher wants to measure aggressive behavior in preschool children, the measurement technique may involve having trained observers sit unobtrusively in a preschool classroom and make check marks on a research form every time a child engages in an aggressive act. Here, however, we will concentrate on psychological tests, some of which have been the objects of sharp criticism for problems of gender bias (Baker & Mason, 2010).

Let's consider as an example the mathematics portion of the SAT, which is taken widely by high school seniors who are planning to attend college. The SAT Math has been criticized a great deal on the grounds that it is biased against women. In 2015, for example, women taking it scored an average of 496, compared with an average of 527 for men (College Board, 2015). How could such a test be biased against women? One major issue is the content and wording of questions. If the content of an item involves situations that men experience more frequently, or requires knowledge to which men have more access, then the item is gender biased. As an example, consider the following item, which actually appeared on the SAT in 1986:

Quasi-experimental design: A research design that compares two or more groups but is not a true experiment because participants are not randomly assigned to groups; an example is a study comparing men and women.

Quantitative research methods: Research methods that involve psychological measurement and the use of statistics to analyze data, often with the goal of generalizing from a sample to a population.

Psychological measurement: The processes of assigning numbers to people's characteristics, such as aggressiveness or intelligence; essential to quantitative methods.

A high school basketball team has won 40% of its first 15 games. Beginning with the sixteenth game, how many games in a row does the team now have to win in order to have a 55% winning record?

(a) 3

(b) 5

(c) 6

(d) 11

(e) 15

Men, who tend to have more experience with team sports and computing win-loss records, have an advantage. There is a direct algebraic solution, which a woman could do if she had mastered algebra, but it is time-consuming, and the test is timed. A man might say, "I know that 11 out of 20 is a 55% record. Will that work? Yes. The answer is 5."

If women score lower than men on a particular psychological test, there often are two possible interpretations: (1) Women are not as skilled at the ability being measured, or (2) the gender difference simply indicates that the test itself contained biased items.

Another area of gender bias in research design has to do with sampling. There is a long history of gender bias in choosing participants for psychological research. Men have been used more frequently as participants than women have been, though the tide is changing. For example, in 1970 in the *Journal of Abnormal Psychology*, 42% of the articles reported on male-only studies, and in 1990 the percentage was 20% (Gannon et al., 1992). By 2007, women were somewhat overrepresented as research participants in mainstream psychology journals, a pattern that may stem from the overreliance on undergraduate psychology students (who are disproportionately female) as research participants (Cundiff, 2012). The reliance on single-gender samples varies by discipline; while women are now somewhat overrepresented as participants in psychological research, they remain underrepresented as participants in biomedical and neuroscience research (Eagly & Riger, 2014).

Researchers can make a second error that compounds the effects of using an all-male sample: **overgeneralization**. That is, having used a single-gender sample, the researchers then discuss and interpret the results as if they were true of all people, regardless of their gender.

Overgeneralization:
A research error in which the results are said to apply to a broader group than the one sampled, for example, saying that results from an all-male sample are true for all people.

Although psychological research has become less prone to gender bias in sampling, problems remain. Psychologists have been guilty of an overreliance on college student samples, which are typically homogeneous in several ways, including age (most participants are between 18 and 22), race/ethnicity (mostly White), and social class (mostly middle class). Feminist psychologists argue for the importance of recognizing the diversity of human experience. Your family's ethnic group and social class influenced the environment in which you grew up and therefore influenced your development and behavior. Feminist psychologists urge researchers to use samples that will allow an exploration of ethnic and social class diversity.

Bias in Data Collection

In the step of research in which the data are collected, two important kinds of bias may enter: experimenter effects and observer effects.

Experimenter effects occur when some characteristic of the experimenter affects the way respondents behave and thus affects the outcome of the experiment. For example, in one experiment, a sex survey was administered by either a male or female researcher; men reported more sexual partners when they had a female researcher (Fisher, 2007). In another experiment, a test of rape myth acceptance was administered by a woman who was either provocatively or conservatively dressed (Bryant et al., 2001). Answers to the questionnaire differed significantly depending on the experimenter's clothing. It is rather disturbing to realize that an experiment might have different outcomes depending on whether the experimenter was a man or a woman, White or a person of color, or dressed in one set of clothes or another.

The problem of experimenter effects is not unsolvable. The situation can be handled by having several experimenters—for example, half of them female, half of them male—collect the data. This will minimize any experimenter effects due to the gender of the experimenter and demonstrate whether the gender of the experimenter did have an effect on the participants' behavior.

Another important bias that may enter at the stage of data collection is observer effects. **Observer effects** (sometimes also called *rater bias*) occur when the researcher's expectations for the outcome of the research influence their observations and recording of the data (Hoyt & Kerns, 1999; Lakes & Hoyt, 2009; R. Rosenthal, 1966). Scientists are no more immune than laypeople to having stereotyped expectations for the behavior of women and men. These stereotyped expectations might lead scientists to find stereotyped gender differences in behavior where there are none. As an example, consider research on gender differences in aggression among preschool children. If observers expect more aggression from boys, that may be just what they observe, even though the boys and the girls behaved identically.

The technical procedure that is generally used to guard against observer effects is the blind study. It simply means that observers are kept unaware of (blind to) which experimental group participants are in so that the observers' expectations cannot affect the outcome. Unfortunately, the blind method is virtually impossible in gender research, as the gender of a person is usually obvious from appearance, and therefore the observer cannot be blind to it or unaware of it.

One exception is infants and small children, whose gender is notoriously difficult to identify when they are clothed. This fact was used in a clever study that provides some information on whether observer effects do influence gender research. The study is discussed in detail in Chapter 6, but in brief, adults rated the behavior of an infant on a videotape (Condry & Condry, 1976). The infant was dressed in clothing that didn't signal their gender. Half the observers were told the infant was male and half were told the infant was female. When the infant showed a negative emotional response, those who thought the infant was male tended to rate the emotion as anger, whereas those who thought the infant was female rated "her" as showing fear. The observers rated behavior differently depending on whether they thought they were observing a male or female infant.

Experimenter effects:
When some characteristics of the experimenter affect the way participants behave and therefore affect the research outcome.

Observer effects:
When the researcher's expectations affect their observations and recording of the data; also called rater bias.

©iStockphoto.com/Wavebreakmedia.

PHOTO 1.6
If all researchers look like him, experimenter effects are likely.

Bias in Interpretation of Results

Once the scientist has collected the data and analyzed them statistically, the results must be interpreted. Sometimes the interpretation a scientist makes is at best a large leap of faith away from the results. Therefore, this is also a stage at which gender bias may enter (Hegarty & Pratto, 2010).

As an example, let us consider a fairly well-documented phenomenon of psychological gender differences. A class of students takes its first exam in Introductory Psychology. Immediately after taking the exam, but before getting the results back, the students are asked to estimate how many points (out of a possible 100) they got on the exam. On average, men will estimate that they got higher scores than women will estimate they got (see Chapter 3). At this point, the data have been collected and analyzed statistically. It can be stated (neutrally) that there are statistically significant gender differences, with men estimating more points than women. The next question is this: How do we interpret that result? The standard interpretation is that the result indicates that women lack self-confidence or have low confidence in their abilities. The interpretation that is not made, although it is just as logical, is that men have unrealistically high expectations for their own performance.

The point is that, given a statistically significant gender difference, such a result can often be interpreted in two opposite ways, one of which is favorable to men and one of which is favorable to women. A persistent tendency has existed in psychology to make interpretations that are favorable to men; these interpretations are essentially based on a **female deficit model**.

Female deficit model: A theory or interpretation of research in which women's behavior is seen as deficient.

Sometimes there is no way of verifying which interpretation is right. As it happens in the example above, there is a way, because we can find out how the students actually did on the exam. Those results indicate that women and girls underestimate their scores by about as much as men and boys overestimate theirs (D. Cole et al., 1999; Mednick & Thomas, 1993). Thus, the second interpretation is as accurate as the first.

Becoming sensitive to the point at which scientists go beyond their data to interpret them, and becoming aware of when those interpretations may be biased, is extremely important. Another example of bias in interpretations occurs in research on gender differences in language (Chapter 5).

Bias in Publishing Findings

Once the data have been analyzed and interpreted, the next step is to publish the findings. There is a strong tendency in psychological research to publish significant results only. This does not necessarily mean significant in the sense of important; it means significant in the sense of being the result of a statistical test that reaches the .05 level of significance. In other words, it means that if the study were repeated, there would be a less than 5% chance that the results would be different.

Why does it matter if we publish only significant findings in the psychology of gender? It means that there is a tendency to report statistically significant gender differences and to omit mention of gender similarities and nonsignificant gender differences. That is, we tend to hear about it when men and women differ, but we tend not to hear about it when men and women are the same. Thus there would be a bias toward emphasizing gender differences and ignoring gender similarities.

This bias may also enter into psychology of women and gender research when results are inconsistent with gender stereotypes or gender roles, for example, research on menstrual cycle mood fluctuations (a point to be discussed in detail in Chapter 11).

Bias Against Female Scientists

If there is a tendency for reports by female scientists to be considered less authoritative than reports by male scientists, this would introduce bias, particularly when combined with bias due to experimenter effects, as discussed previously. Evidence of such a gender bias might include the underrepresentation of women as lead authors of scientific journal articles and conference presentations. Research on the extent of this problem has produced mixed results (Hegarty & Buechel, 2006; Meredith, 2013; Swim et al., 1989), suggesting that bias against female scientists doesn't happen consistently. One analysis of over 8 million journal articles published across the natural sciences, social sciences, and humanities examined the representation of women as authors. The representation of women varied by fields, such that math and philosophy had the lowest percentage of women authors while demography, sociology, and education had the highest (J. D. West et al., 2013). In addition, the analysis found that the representation of women has been improving over time: From 1965 to 1989, only 15% of authors were women, but from 1990 to 2012, 27% of authors were women. A similar trend appears in psychology: From 1965 to 1974, only 12% of the articles in *Journal of Abnormal Psychology* had a woman as first author; by 1995–2004 that number had risen to 30% (Hegarty & Buechel, 2006). Thus, at least by the measure of women as authors of journal articles, it appears that bias against female scientists is on the decline.

Other Kinds of Gender Biases

Another kind of bias is introduced if scientists have a tendency to remember and use in their work only the studies that conform to their own biases or ideas and to ignore the studies that do not. This tendency would allow for dominant biases (such as bias against women and people of color) to be perpetuated in scientific research. Gender bias and cisgenderism in the language used in reports of psychological research are also a concern. We will address these forms of bias in language in depth in Chapter 5. In addition, research on women has long been considered a specialty or fringe topic, a perception that reflects the male as normative theme (which is discussed later in this chapter). Today, this bias has shifted such that mainstream research includes psychology of women (Eagly et al., 2012) but marginalizes research on people outside the gender binary.

Feminist Alternatives to Biased Research

We have discussed a number of problems with psychological research that may affect our understanding of women and men. Of course, these problems are not present in every study in the area, and certainly we don't mean to suggest that all psychological research is worthless. The point is to learn to think critically about biases that may or may not be present when you are reading reports of research. Thinking critically about the theoretical orientation of a scientist and about biased interpretations of results is important.

A more general point emerges from this whole discussion of gender bias in research methods in psychology. Traditional psychology has historically viewed itself as an objective and value-free science. Today, many psychologists, feminist psychologists among them, question whether psychological research can be objective and value-free (Peplau & Conrad, 1989). They point out that psychological research might more appropriately be viewed as an interaction between researcher and research participant that occurs in a particular context. The researcher brings to that interaction certain values that may influence the questions asked, the methods used, the results found, and the interpretations made. In short, psychological research cannot be totally objective. Acknowledging our values and reflecting on how they may shape the research process, then, is crucial.

Psychology, of course, is not the only science that has claimed to be objective and value-free when it isn't. Another example is physics and its groundbreaking discoveries of ways to generate nuclear power. These discoveries can be used to manufacture weapons capable of annihilating thousands, or they can be used to generate electricity for cities. Values are closely connected with science.

Feminist psychologists would say that, while the preceding criticisms are important and you should be aware of them, we need to go beyond those criticisms to offer some constructive alternatives. In doing so, we can think about gender-fair research and feminist research.

Gender-Fair and Feminist Research

Gender-fair research:
Research that is free of gender bias.

Gender-fair research is research that is not guilty of any of the gender biases discussed in the previous sections (Denmark et al., 1988; McHugh et al., 1986). Some characteristics of gender-fair research are as follows:

1. Single-gender research should rarely, if ever, be done. In some situations where a single-gender design might seem justified, the demands for gender fairness and inclusiveness might lead to better understandings. For example, a study exclusively examining women's mood fluctuations over the menstrual cycle would fail to identify systematic fluctuations in men's moods.

2. Theoretical models, underlying assumptions, and the kinds of questions asked should always be examined for gender fairness. For example, the minute someone proposes to do research on the effects of mothers' depression on their children, it also should be asked whether fathers' depression has an effect on their children. Otherwise, we assume that only mothers influence children and that fathers have no influence, which is unfair to both mothers and fathers.

3. Research teams should be diverse with regard to gender—as well as other social characteristics such as race or ethnicity—to limit experimenter effects.

4. Interpretations of data should always be examined carefully for gender fairness, and possibly several interpretations should be offered. For example, if there is a significant gender difference in the number of points students estimate they will get on an exam, two interpretations should be offered: that women underestimate and lack self-confidence and that men overestimate and have inflated expectations for their performance. In a sense, then, gender-fair research proposes that we continue to play the research game by the same set of rules it has always had—tight controls, careful interpretations, and so on—but that we improve procedures so that the rules are observed fairly.

Feminist research:
Research growing out of feminist theory, which seeks radical reform of traditional research methods.

Feminist researchers might argue that we need to go even further in reforming psychological research. There really is no single, comprehensive, definitive statement of the principles of **feminist research**, but many scholars have made contributions (e.g., Crawford & Kimmel, 1999; Else-Quest & Hyde, 2016; E. B. Kimmel & Crawford,

2001; Rabinowitz & Sechzer, 1993; Reinharz, 1992), and we present some of those ideas here.

Some feminist researchers have argued that the classic form of psychological research—the tightly controlled laboratory experiment—needs to be revised. They maintain that it is manipulative, intended to determine how manipulations of the independent variable cause changes in the dependent variable. It objectifies and dehumanizes the people it studies, calling them "subjects." It strips away the context of behavior, taking people out of their natural environments in order to control all those things the experimenter considers irrelevant. In all these senses—the manipulativeness, the objectification, the context stripping—traditional psychological experimentation might be accused of being masculine or patriarchal.

Feminist research includes several recommendations:

1. Do not manipulate people, but rather observe them in their natural environments and try to determine how they experience their natural lives and worlds.

2. Do not call the people who are studied "subjects," but rather "participants." This reaffirms their personhood and agency.

3. When determining the gender of research participants, it is best to follow this two-step method: First, ask participants what gender they were assigned at birth. Next, ask them to designate their gender identity using their own words. This two-step method is more inclusive and more accurate than asking participants to check a box indicating either "male" or "female" as their gender (dickey, Hendricks, & Bockting, 2016).

4. Devote specific research attention to the special concerns of women and members of marginalized groups.

5. Do not think in simple terms of variable A causing effects on variable B, but rather in terms of complex, interactive relationships in which A and B mutually influence each other. Complexity is emphasized.

6. Conduct critical research. That is, conduct research aimed at empowering members of marginalized or oppressed groups (such as women and transgender persons) and eliminating power inequities.

7. Consider diverse and innovative methods for studying human behavior (Crawford, 2013).

8. Keep in mind that scientific research and political activism are not necessarily contradictory activities (Wittig, 1985).

Values affect the scientific theories that are proposed and the way research is done (Rabinowitz & Sechzer, 1993). In particular, they affect the way research is interpreted, a point discussed earlier in the chapter. Readers need to become sensitive to the values expressed by a particular scientific position. At the same time, high-quality research that documents oppressive or harmful conditions and provides a prescription for eliminating inequities can facilitate social change. Psychologists who are engaged in political activism and have social justice as their goal can still do good research; such researchers are obligated to articulate their values, but clearly that is a good rule for all scientists!

Qualitative research methods: Research methods that do not use numbers or statistics, but may analyze text, in-depth interviews, participant observations, or focus groups for themes and meaning.

Mixed methods: Research methods that involve both quantitative and qualitative methods.

One example of innovative methods is the use of **qualitative research methods** or the combination of qualitative and quantitative methods, known as **mixed methods** (Denzin & Lincoln, 2005). Traditional psychological research has largely relied on quantitative methods (Eagly & Riger, 2014)—that is, behavior is studied by converting it to numbers, whether IQ scores or individuals' ratings of their attitudes toward legal abortion on a scale from 1 (strongly disapprove) to 7 (strongly approve). With qualitative methods, the data are often text, talk, or images. For example, an interviewer may pose open-ended questions in an interview or focus group, record and transcribe the respondent's answers, and then analyze the answers for themes. In one such study, Watson and her colleagues (2012) interviewed African American women about their experiences of sexual objectification, finding that their experiences were the result of bias based on gender, race, and class. The researchers argued that, since most of the research on sexual objectification had been with White women, African American women's experiences were marginalized and should be a focus of study. The possibilities of feminist research—using quantitative, qualitative, or mixed methods—are limitless and exciting, especially because they can address social inequality.

Both gender-fair research and feminist research can make valuable contributions. While the traditional psychological experiment needs reform, we shouldn't throw it out entirely. It is most effective when it is combined with naturalistic research examining complex mutual influences. Gender-fair research and feminist research may diverge on some issues, though. For example, feminist researchers would value the investigation of intimate partner violence against women as an issue of special importance. Gender-fair researchers may point out that intimate partner violence may be perpetrated by men and women alike, and that both should be studied. Feminist researchers might reply that intimate partner violence—which is most often perpetrated by men against women—is a gender-based crime and that feminist research should be especially concerned with this systematic form of gender-based oppression. We will revisit this issue in Chapter 14.

PHOTO 1.7

Today, scholarly journals such as *Psychology of Women Quarterly* publish empirical research on the psychology of women and gender.

Are We Making Progress?

Feminist psychologists began to publish their critiques of traditional research methods more than 45 years ago. Has there been any progress? Have psychologists changed their methods to respond to these criticisms?

Feminism has positively influenced psychology in a number of ways (Eagly & Riger, 2014; Hegarty & Buechel, 2006). Substantial shifts have been made toward nonsexist methods in psychological research. There are more women researchers and more equal representation of women among participants. However, other forms of bias—such as bias against transgender persons and those outside the gender binary—remain. It is critical that we continue monitoring our methods and commit to reducing all forms of bias in our discipline.

Chapter Previews

In the next chapter we will look at the contributions to the understanding of the psychology of women and gender that have been made by some of the major theoretical systems of psychology—psychoanalytic theory, social learning theory, and cognitive-developmental theory. A controversial theory, sociobiology, is examined, as are gender schema theory and feminist theories.

Following these theoretical views, later chapters will focus on research in content areas of the psychology of women and gender. Chapter 3 reviews evidence on gender stereotypes and gender differences to see the ways in which women and men differ and the ways in which they are similar. Chapter 4 examines the scholarship in psychology at the intersection of gender and ethnicity, focusing especially on women of color. Because feminist scholars have emphasized the importance of language, Chapter 5 is about gender and communication—whether there are gender differences in verbal and nonverbal communication and how women and trans or nonbinary people are treated in language. Chapter 6 presents the important new research on gender and emotion. In Chapter 7 we discuss gender development across the lifespan from birth to old age. We look at gender and achievement in Chapter 8 by considering research on gender differences in intellectual abilities and research on achievement in women. Chapter 9 is about gender and work, including discrimination and wage inequity as well as issues involved in balancing work and family roles.

Chapter 10 explores biological influences on gender and behavior, including research on persons who do not fit the gender binary. Chapter 11 discusses psychological research on several key women's health issues, including menstruation, abortion, and breast cancer, as well as transgender health issues. Chapter 12 explores gender and sexuality, including research on the physiology of sexual response and research on gender similarities and differences in sexuality.

Chapter 13 is about the intersection of gender and sexual orientation. Chapter 14 centers on gender-based violence as seen in rape, intimate partner violence, sexual harassment, child sexual abuse, and human trafficking, including the victimization of transgender persons. Chapter 15 considers mental health concerns that show gender disparities (such as depression and eating disorders) and feminist therapies.

In Chapter 16 we examine the psychology of men and masculinity from a feminist perspective. The final chapter discusses historical shifts and trends in the conceptualization of gender within psychology and social backlash against feminist progress.

Experience the Research

Understanding Gender Bias in Psychological Research

Design an experiment to determine whether adults are more likely to help a 4-year-old child who is crying and apparently lost, depending on whether the adult is alone and there are no other adults close by (no bystander condition) or there are other adults present (bystander condition). Design two versions of the experiment. First, create the experiment as a traditional, prefeminist psychologist might have done. Then, using Figure 1.1, make a list of all the examples of gender bias in the research. Finally, re-create the experiment to correct all the elements of gender bias so that it will meet the standards for gender-fair research.

CHAPTER SUMMARY

The psychology of women and gender is an exciting and constantly evolving field. Similarly, language on gender continues to evolve. Terms such as *sex, gender, transgender, cisgender, gender binary,* and *genderqueer* are important and used throughout this book. Table 1.1 clarifies many of these terms.

A chief concern in the psychology of women and gender is sexism. Sexism and its variations have changed over time, from old-fashioned sexism to modern sexism. Psychologists study sexism and its impact on psychological phenomena.

A feminist is a person who favors political, economic, and social equality of all people, regardless of gender, and therefore favors the legal and social changes necessary to achieve gender equality. We are currently in the fourth wave of feminism.

There are several pervasive themes in the psychology of women and gender. The male-as-normative theme results in women and nonbinary people being marginalized, ignored, or devalued. Androcentrism also fuels a lopsided emphasis on gender differences, despite evidence that women and men are both different and similar. In addition, critiquing the gender binary and analyzing gender with an intersectional approach are contemporary themes that challenge traditional approaches in psychology. We revisit these themes throughout this book.

Gender bias can shape the design of research, including the type of methods, measures, and sample used. Experimenter effects and observer effects can alter the outcome of research, and results may be interpreted with a female deficit model. There are many feminist alternatives to sexist research, and nonsexist research methods are now more commonly used.

SUGGESTIONS FOR FURTHER READING

Anderson, Kristin J. (2015). *Modern misogyny: Anti-feminism in a post-feminist era.* Oxford, UK: Oxford University Press. Anderson, a social psychologist, lays out the evidence for why feminism is as important today as ever.

Caplan, Paula J., & Caplan, Jeremy B. (2009). *Thinking critically about research on sex and gender* (3rd ed.). Boston, MA: Pearson/Allyn and Bacon. This brief book includes a feminist critique of several major areas of psychological research on women and provides helpful guides for critical thinking about research.

Theoretical Perspectives on Gender

Understanding gender differences has fascinated people probably since the dawn of the human species. In the past century, science has come to dominate intellectual thought. Thus, it is not surprising that scientific understandings of gender differences have developed. In this chapter we will examine some major psychological theories that have been formulated to explain the differences between women and men and how they develop.

At the outset, we think it is important to highlight the distinction between theory and empirical evidence. In the pages that follow, we will describe many of the theories about the psychology of women and gender that have been proposed. Some have solid data (empirical evidence) backing them, whereas others do not. Not every theory is true, nor is every one a good description or explanation of behavior. We all need to be critical thinkers about the difference between statements based on theory and statements based on empirical evidence.

Psychoanalytic Theory

One of the first scholarly explanations of differences between women and men was **psychoanalytic theory**, formulated by Sigmund Freud (1856–1939). Psychoanalytic theory has had an enormous impact on culture: It has permeated art, film, literature, and even the language and thinking of most laypeople. For these reasons alone, it is important to understand Freudian theory as a part of our history and culture.

Freud's Theory of Psychosexual Development

One of Freud's greatest contributions was to promote the view of human personality as being the result of development in the first 5 years of life. That is, he saw the personality of an adult as the product of previous experiences, and he believed that early childhood experiences were most critical. He proposed a stage theory of psychosexual development, each stage being characterized by a focus on one of the **erogenous zones,** parts of skin or mucous membranes highly endowed with nerve endings that are very sensitive to stimulation (e.g., the lips and mouth, the anal region, genitals). During stage 1, the oral stage, the infant derives pleasure from sucking and eating and experiences the world mainly through the mouth. Following this is the anal stage, in which pleasure is focused on defecating.

Freud proposed that boys and girls pass through the first two stages of psychosexual development, the oral and the anal, in a similar manner. However, during the **phallic stage,** around the ages of 3 to 6, the development of boys and girls diverges. As one might suspect from the name for this stage, girls will be at somewhat of a disadvantage in passing through it.

During the phallic stage, the boy becomes fascinated with his own penis, which is a rich source of pleasure and interest for him. At this stage boys experience the **Oedipal complex,** named for the Greek myth of Oedipus, who unknowingly killed his father and married his mother. In the Oedipal complex, the boy sexually desires his mother. His attachment to her is strong and intense. He also wishes to rid himself of the father, who is a rival for the mother's affection. But the father is too powerful an opponent, and the boy fears that the father will retaliate by castrating his son. This *castration anxiety* becomes so great that the boy seeks to resolve the problem, repressing his sexual desire for his mother and making the critical shift to *identify* with the father. In the process of identifying with the father, the boy introjects (takes into himself as his own) the values and ethics of society as represented by the father and thus develops a **superego**. But more important for our purposes is that, in identifying with the father, he comes to acquire his gender identity, taking on the qualities the father supposedly possesses—strength, power, and so on.

For girls, the phallic stage is quite different. According to Freud, the first critical event is the girl's stark realization that she has no penis. Presumably she recognizes that the penis is superior to her clitoris. She feels cheated and envious of boys, and thus comes to feel *penis envy*. She also feels mutilated, believing that at one time she possessed a penis, but that it had been cut off—indeed, Freud believed that the boy's castration anxiety stems from his observation of the girl's anatomy, which he sees as living proof

Psychoanalytic theory: A psychological theory originated by Sigmund Freud; its basic assumption is that part of the human psyche is unconscious.

Erogenous zones: Areas of the body that are particularly sensitive to sexual stimulation.

Phallic stage: The third stage of development in psychoanalytic theory, around 3 to 6 years of age, during which, for boys, the pleasure zone is the penis and sexual feelings arise toward the mother and, for girls, sexual feelings arise toward the father.

Oedipal complex: In psychoanalytic theory, a boy's sexual attraction to and intense love for his mother and his desire to do away with his father.

Superego: Freud's term for the part of the personality that contains the person's conscience.

of the reality of castration. Her penis envy can never be satisfied directly and instead is transformed into a desire to be impregnated by her father. Holding her mother responsible for her lack of a penis, she renounces her love for her mother and becomes intensely attracted to her father, thus forming her own version of the Oedipal complex, called the **Electra complex**. The desire to be impregnated by the father is a strong one and persists in the more general form of maternal urges, according to Freud.

According to Freud, the resolution of the Oedipal complex is critical for the boy's development, being necessary for the formation of his gender identity and superego. The prime motivation in his resolving his Oedipal complex was his overpowering castration anxiety. By contrast, for the girl, who believes she's already been castrated, the motivation to resolve her Electra complex is not so strong. She is motivated only by the comparatively abstract realization that her desires for her father cannot be gratified.

Freud theorized that the Electra complex is never as fully resolved for girls as the Oedipal complex is for boys. This leads the girl to lifelong feelings of inferiority, a predisposition to jealousy, and intense maternal desires. In addition, because she never fully resolves the Electra complex and introjects society's standards, her superego is immature. She is morally inferior and lacks a sense of justice, in large part because she lacks a penis. Thus, Freud postulated a theoretical model of early development with long-term consequences for male and female personality development.

Electra complex: In psychoanalytic theory, a girl's sexual attraction to and intense love for her father.

Phallocentric: Male centered or, specifically, penis centered.

Criticisms of Freud's Psychoanalytic Theory

Numerous general criticisms and feminist criticisms of Freudian theory have been made. From a scientific point of view, a major problem with psychoanalytic theory is that most of its concepts cannot be evaluated scientifically to see whether they are accurate. That is, because Freud placed so much value on unconscious desires—which cannot be directly observed, measured, or tested—it is impossible to evaluate the validity of his theory.

Another criticism that is often raised is that Freud derived his ideas almost exclusively from work with patients who sought therapy. In particular, his views on women may contain some truth about women who have problems of adjustment, but fail to describe typical or psychologically well women.

Many modern psychologists argue that Freud overemphasized biological determinants of human behavior and underemphasized social or cultural forces in shaping behavior. In particular, his views on the origin of differences between men and women, and on the nature of female personality, are heavily biological, relying mostly on anatomical differences—as the famous phrase has it, "Anatomy is destiny." In relying on anatomy as an explanation, Freud ignored the enormous forces of culture acting to create gender differences.

Feminists have raised numerous criticisms of Freudian theory, including those noted above (e.g., Lerman, 1986; J. A. Sherman, 1971; Weisstein, 1971). They are particularly critical of Freud's assumption that the clitoris and vagina are inferior to the penis. Thus, many have argued that Freudian theory is **phallocentric**.

By Max Halberstadt - Public Domain.

PHOTO 2.1
Sigmund Freud theorized that girls will inevitably realize that the penis is superior to the clitoris, thereby developing penis envy.

Feminists also note the similarities between psychoanalytic theory and some of the themes discussed in Chapter 1. In this context, Freud seems simply to be articulating age-old myths and images about women in "scientific" language. The image of women as sinful and the source of evil is translated into the scientific-sounding "immature superego." Certainly Freud's phallocentrism is a good example of a male-as-normative or andro-centric model. Basically, for Freud, a girl is a castrated boy. His model of development describes male development, female development being an inadequate variation on it.

Nonetheless, it is important to acknowledge Freud's contributions in his recognition of the importance of development in shaping human behavior and personality, and particularly in shaping gender identity.

Karen Horney

Several of the most prominent psychoanalytic theorists were women, and not surprisingly, they made some modifications to Freud's theory. Karen Horney's (1885–1952) theoretical papers show an evolution over time in her own thinking. Originally Horney (pronounced Horn-eye) accepted Freud's ideas wholeheartedly; in a 1924 paper she eagerly documented the origins of penis envy and of the castration complex in women. However, she soon became critical of these notions, and in a 1926 paper she pointed out that Freudian theory actually articulates the childish views boys have of girls and that Freud's psychological theory of women was phallocentric.

Her chief disagreement with Freud was over his notion that penis envy was the critical factor in female development. Horney used the master's tricks against him and postulated that the critical factor was male envy of women, particularly of female reproductive potential, which she called **womb envy**. She also suggested that male achievement represents an overcompensation for feelings of anatomical inferiority (i.e., a femininity complex).

Womb envy: In Horney's analytic theory, the man's envy of the woman's uterus and reproductive capacity.

Helene Deutsch

In 1944, Helene Deutsch (1884–1982) published a weighty two-volume work titled *The Psychology of Women*, the major attempt within the psychoanalytic school for a complete understanding of the psychological dynamics of women. Deutsch extended Freud's analysis of female development, which essentially ended with the phallic stage and Electra complex, to later stages of development. She began in the prepuberty period because she saw the critical processes in woman's psychological development revolving around the transition from being a girl to being a woman. She then continued to describe female development and personality in adolescence and adulthood.

Deutsch viewed motherhood as the most critical feature in women's psychological development. Indeed, the whole second volume of *The Psychology of Women* was devoted exclusively to this topic, and she saw prepuberty and adolescence as mainly an anticipation of motherhood. Retaining a Freudian orthodoxy in her thinking, she believed that to be a woman one must develop a "feminine core" in the personality, including the traits of *narcissism*, **masochism**, and *passivity*. The desire for motherhood is rooted in these traits, which are themselves rooted in her anatomy. Helene Deutsch (1944) wrote,

Masochism: The desire to experience pain.

> Thus woman acquires a tendency to passivity that intensifies the passive nature inherent in her biology and anatomy. She passively awaits fecundation: her life is fully active and rooted in reality only when she becomes a mother. Until then everything that is feminine in the woman, physiology and psychology, is passive, receptive. (p. 140)

Photo of Horney: Bettmann/Getty Images. Photo of Helene Deutsch: Public Domain.

PHOTO 2.2
Two women who made substantial contributions to psychoanalytic theory: Karen Horney (left) and Helene Deutsch (right).

Deutsch's view of the psychology of women is at once insightful and sexist. It is laden with the confusion of cultural and biological forces typical of psychoanalytic theory. For example, she believed that female passivity is a result of anatomy and biological functioning, failing to recognize that passivity is a culturally assigned part of the female role.

Nancy Chodorow

Nancy Chodorow's (1978) book *The Reproduction of Mothering* is a more recent addition to the psychoanalytic literature, representing second-wave feminism (L. C. Bell, 2004). Integrating psychoanalytic and feminist perspectives, Chodorow sought to answer this question: Why do women mother? That is, why is it that in all cultures women do almost all of the child care? She theorized that, when the child care is provided primarily by women, daughters and sons develop differently. That is, mothering produces daughters who want to mother—thereby reproducing mothering—and sons who dominate and devalue women.

Infants start life in a state of total dependency, and given the traditional division of labor (in which women care for children), those dependency needs are satisfied almost exclusively by the mother. In addition, infants are egocentric, or self-centered, and have trouble distinguishing between the primary caretaker—the mother—and themselves. Because mothers do such a good job of meeting their infants' every need, infants blissfully assume that mothers have no interests outside of mothering their children. As the children grow, the unpleasant reality eventually becomes clear as they come to understand that mothers do have other interests.

In her book, Chodorow theorized that the early, intensely intimate relationship with the mother affects the sense of self and attitudes toward women, for both daughters and sons. Boys and girls continue to expect women to be caring and sacrificing, and that forever shapes their attitudes toward women. The girl's sense of self is profoundly influenced because her intense relationship to her mother is never entirely broken. Therefore, girls never see themselves as separate in the way boys do, and girls and women continue to define themselves as caregivers of others.

By contrast, boys begin with the same intense attachment to the mother, but must repress that relationship in order to develop a masculine identity. Thus masculinity comes to be defined negatively, as the opposite or lack of femininity. Masculinity involves denying feminine maternal attachment. Therefore, the boy's need to separate himself from his mother (and all women) and define a masculine identity for himself fosters his devaluation of all women. Traditionally, fathers have been essentially absent or uninvolved in child care, thereby idealizing their masculine qualities and promoting the notion of masculine superiority. At the same time, men's capacity for providing child care is limited by their denial of relatedness.

According to Chodorow, women's relational needs are greater than men's relational needs, which are satisfied by a heterosexual relationship with a woman, in which they recapture the warmth of the infant's relationship with their mother. Yet women's greater relational needs cannot entirely be satisfied by a man. And so, women have babies, their relational needs are satisfied, and the cycle repeats itself.

Chodorow's question—Why do women mother?—is not so small as it might appear. Women's mothering perpetuates the whole division of labor by gender, because once women are committed to be the exclusive caregivers, men must do the other jobs necessary for society to continue. Moreover, women's mothering promotes the devaluation of women.

What makes Chodorow's psychoanalytic theory *feminist*? First, Chodorow offers a feminist revision of some of Freud's ideas. For example, she argues that penis envy results not from a girl's recognition of the inherent superiority of the penis (as Freud said), but rather from the fact that the penis symbolizes the power men have in our society. She argues that women's mothering was taken for granted and not given the attention it deserved (Chodorow, 2013). Second, Chodorow does not stop with her analysis of the family dynamics that perpetuate the devaluation of women; she gives a prescription for social change to eliminate inequities for women. She theorizes that the only way for the cycle to be broken is for men to begin participating equally in child care:

> Any strategy for change whose goal includes liberation from the constraints of an unequal social organization of gender must take account of the need for a fundamental reorganization of parenting, so that primary parenting is shared between men and women. (Chodorow, 1978, p. 215)

A few researchers have tested parts of Chodorow's theory. In one study, 4- and 5-year-olds were videotaped while playing with their mothers (Benenson et al., 1998). The results indicated that mother-daughter pairs were indeed closer to each other than mother-son pairs. This was true both physically—girls were physically closer to their mothers—and psychologically—mother-daughter pairs expressed more mutual enjoyment. These findings support Chodorow's assertion that girls are closer to their mothers and that boys separate themselves from their mothers.

Several key criticisms of Chodorow's theory should be noted (e.g., Lorber et al., 1981). First, the theory has a heterosexist and cisnormative bias. It explains in detail why children grow up heterosexual, consistent with the gender binary, assuming that all of them would, while making no attempt to understand the development of people with other sexual orientations (Rich, 1980). Second, as a feminist theory, Chodorow's theory has been criticized for lacking an intersectional approach, in that it focuses exclusively on gender and ignores race and social class (Spelman, 1988). Third, most of the evidence Chodorow cites in her book is clinical—that is, it comes from individual histories of people seeking psychotherapy. As such, Chodorow's theory is open to the same criticism that was made of Freud's theory—namely, that the theory is based on the experiences of people who are maladjusted, and thus their experiences are not generalizable.

Social Learning Theory

Psychoanalytic approaches, with their emphasis on unconscious desires, eventually gave way to a very different set of approaches in psychology—learning theories, which instead emphasize behaviors. *Social learning theory* is a major theoretical system in psychology, designed to describe the processes of human development (Bandura & Walters, 1963). It emphasizes several key mechanisms in development, including reinforcement, punishment, imitation, and observational learning. Thus, an explanation for psychological gender differences is that children *learn* how to behave differently based on their gender. That is, boys and girls act appropriately for their genders because they have been rewarded for doing some things and punished for doing others. The idea is that the operant conditioning mechanisms of reinforcement and punishment explain the acquisition of gender roles. Thus, children are rewarded or reinforced for displaying gender-appropriate behaviors and punished or not rewarded for displaying gender-inappropriate behaviors. For example, little girls are rewarded for being quiet and obedient, whereas little boys are rewarded for being athletic and tough. As a result, children are more likely to repeat the behaviors that have been reinforced, and gender differences in behavior develop.

Social learning theory also emphasizes the importance of two additional mechanisms: imitation and observational learning. **Imitation,** or **modeling**, means simply that children do what they see others (termed *models*) doing. **Observational learning** refers to situations in which children learn by observing the behavior of models, even though they may not actually perform the behavior at the time, perhaps not using the information until months or years later. These three mechanisms, then—reinforcement, imitation, and observational learning—are thought to underlie the process of **gender typing**—that is, the acquisition of gender-typed behaviors and learning of gender roles—according to social learning theory.

Children's imitation is motivated partly by the power of authority figures, so they are especially likely to imitate parents, other adults, or older peers. With regard to gender typing, the theory assumes that children tend to imitate models of a similar gender more than they imitate models of a different gender. Therefore, the little girl imitates her mother and other women more than she does men. This mechanism of imitation helps to explain the acquisition of the complex and subtle aspects of gender roles that probably have not been the object of reinforcements.

Children may learn behaviors but not perform them. A behavior may become part of the child's repertoire through observational learning. Such information may be stored up for use perhaps years later, when a situation in adolescence or adulthood calls for knowledge of gender-appropriate behaviors. For example, a young girl may observe her mother caring for an infant sibling. Although the little girl may not perform any

Imitation: People doing what they see others doing.

Modeling: Demonstrating gendered behavior for children; also refers to the child's imitation of the behavior.

Observational learning: Observing someone doing something and then doing it at a later time.

Gender typing: The acquisition of gender-typed behaviors and learning of gender roles.

©iStockphoto.com/martinedoucet.

PHOTO 2.3

Learning gendered behavior: After the birth of a new sibling, this preschooler uses a doll to imitate her mother's breastfeeding.

infant-care behaviors at the time, much less be rewarded for them, she nonetheless may store up the information for use when she herself is a mother. Children will also learn to anticipate the consequences of their actions. The little girl knows in advance that her attempts to join Little League will be not be reinforced, and perhaps will even be met with punishments.

According to social learning theory, then, gender typing results from differential rewards and punishments, as well as from imitation of same-gender models and observational learning.

Evidence for Social Learning Theory

Social learning theory has stimulated a great deal of research aimed at documenting the existence—or nonexistence—of the mechanisms it proposes. This research makes it possible to assess the adequacy of the social learning model for the development of gender differences.

Numerous studies have demonstrated the effectiveness of imitation and reinforcements in shaping children's behavior, particularly gender-typed behaviors such as aggression. A classic study by the social learning theorist Albert Bandura (1965) is a good example. In the first phase of this experiment, children were randomly assigned to view one of three films. In all of the films, an adult model was performing more than one aggressive behavior, but in one film the model was rewarded; in another, punished; and in the third, left alone without consequences. The children's aggressive behavior was then observed. As the social learning approach would predict, children who had viewed the model being punished performed the least aggressive behavior. Furthermore, and consistent with the findings of many other investigators (see Chapter 3), boys performed more aggressive behavior than girls. In the second phase of the experiment, the children were offered attractive reinforcements (pretty sticker pictures and juice treats) for performing as many of the model's aggressive responses as they could remember. Gender differences all but disappeared in this phase, and girls performed nearly as many aggressive behaviors as boys.

This experiment illustrates several important points. The first phase demonstrated that children do imitate and that they do so differentially depending on the perceived consequences of the behavior. Notice that in this phase the children themselves were not actually reinforced, but simply observed the model being reinforced. The second phase illustrated how gender differences in aggressive behavior can be influenced by reinforcements. When girls were given equal reinforcement for aggression, they were nearly as aggressive as boys. Certainly, the experiment is evidence of the power of imitation and reinforcement in shaping children's behavior.

There is evidence that parents treat boys and girls differently and that they differentially reward some—though certainly not all—behaviors in boys and girls. In one study, based on a review of 172 studies of parents' socialization practices, the authors concluded that there was a significant tendency for parents to encourage gender-typed activities in their children, especially in areas such as play and household chores (Lytton & Romney, 1991).

Of course, there is plenty of evidence of gender-stereotyped role models in the media. For example, in one study first and second graders were exposed to television commercials in which (a) all boys were playing with a gender-neutral toy (traditional condition), (b) all girls were playing with it (nontraditional condition), or (c) the commercial was not about toys (control; Pike & Jennings, 2005). After the viewing, children were asked to sort six toys into those that were for boys, those that were for girls, or those that were for both boys and girls. Among the six toys was the toy children had seen in the commercial. Children in the traditional condition were more likely to say that the toy was for boys, whereas children in the nontraditional condition were more likely to say that it was for both boys and girls. These results demonstrate that even television commercials can shape children's gender typing. We return to the role of media in gender role development in Chapter 7.

Cognitive Social Learning Theory

Social learning theorists have also incorporated cognitive approaches into their theories, which are now called cognitive social learning theory or social cognitive theory (Bandura, 1986; Bussey & Bandura, 1999). The emphasis on reinforcement, punishment, and imitation remains, and cognitive processes such as attention, self-regulation, and self-efficacy are added.

Every day, children observe thousands of behaviors in the complex environment surrounding them, yet they imitate or model only a few of them. Attention is the cognitive process that weeds out most of the behaviors that are irrelevant to the child and focuses on the few that are most relevant. Gender makes some behaviors relevant and others not. Once children can differentiate men and women, they pay more attention to same-gender than to other-gender models (Bussey & Bandura, 1992). As noted earlier, children tend to imitate same-gender models.

According to cognitive social learning theory, as children develop, regulation of their behavior shifts from externally imposed rewards and punishments to internalized standards and self-sanctions. As children learn to regulate themselves, they guide their own behavior (a process known as self-regulation), and as they learn the significance of gender, they monitor and regulate their own behavior according to

Self-efficacy: A person's belief in their ability to accomplish a particular task.

internalized gender norms. The data show that children are more likely to monitor their behavior for gender-appropriateness when they are in mixed-gender groups than when they are in single-gender groups (Bussey & Bandura, 1999).

Self-efficacy is an important concept in social cognitive theory. **Self-efficacy** refers to our beliefs about our ability to accomplish something, to produce a particular outcome. People can have a global sense of self-efficacy, but efficacy beliefs also tend to vary depending on the area or task. You may feel certain that you can earn an A in a psychology course but have no confidence that you can pass a

Jon Brenneis/The LIFE Images Collection/Getty Images.

PHOTO 2.4
Albert Bandura theorized that children pay more attention to same-gender models in order to learn gender-appropriate behaviors.

chemistry course. Efficacy beliefs are extremely important in individuals' lives. They affect the goals we set for ourselves, how much time and effort we put into attaining a goal, and whether we persist in the face of difficulties. People with strong efficacy beliefs redouble their efforts in the face of challenges, whereas those with a low sense of efficacy give up.

Efficacy beliefs, for example, play a large role in career choice and pursuing a career, perhaps over many years of necessary education (Bandura et al., 2001). Occupations are highly gendered (see Chapter 9). As girls observe teachers and see many women successfully doing the job, their sense of self-efficacy at being a teacher increases. By contrast, when they observe few women among airline pilots, their sense of efficacy at being a pilot declines and they don't even consider it an option.

Overall, though, cognitive social learning theory is an optimistic theory for those who want to see social change in gender roles. It says that children can and will learn a very different set of gender roles if powerful others—for example, parents and the media—change which behaviors they model and reinforce.

Cognitive-Developmental Theory

In terms of impact, perhaps the closest equivalent in the second half of the 20th century to Freud's work in the first half was the developmental theory proposed by Jean Piaget, together with his colleague Bärbel Inhelder. Lawrence Kohlberg (1966) then extended Piaget and Inhelder's cognitive principles to the realm of gender development.

Much of Piaget and Inhelder's thinking arose from their observations of the errors children made in answering questions such as those asked on intelligence tests. They concluded that these errors did not indicate that the children were stupid or ignorant, but rather that they had a different cognitive organization from that of adults. Piaget and Inhelder discovered that the cognitive organizations of children change systematically over time, and they constructed a stage theory of cognitive development to describe the progression of these changes. Interestingly, concepts of gender and gender identity undergo developmental changes parallel to the development of other concepts. Piagetian perspectives on cognitive development emphasize the importance of the child in constructing their own development, or being active and internally motivated to understand the meaning of concepts.

Gender constancy: The understanding that gender is a stable and consistent part of oneself.

Kohlberg theorized that **gender constancy**—the understanding that gender is a stable and consistent part of oneself—is critical to children's gender development. Put in Piagetian terms, when a child has gender constancy, they can *conserve* gender; conservation is the understanding that, even though something may change in appearance, its essence remains the same. Achieving gender constancy is a developmental process that begins with acquiring **gender identity**, or knowing their own gender. Children typically have gender identity around 2 years of age (Kohlberg, 1966; Zosuls et al., 2009). We provide a more detailed discussion of the stages of gender constancy development in Chapter 7.

Gender identity: The first stage of gender constancy development, in which children can identify and label their own gender and the gender of others.

Cognitive-developmental theory views gender role learning as one aspect of cognitive development. The child learns a set of rules regarding what men do and what women do, and behaves accordingly. In this theory, gender role learning is not entirely imposed by external forces, but rather is self-motivated and reflects children's engagement with their social environment. The child essentially engages in self-socialization and self-selects the behaviors to be learned and performed on the basis of rules regarding the gender appropriateness of the behavior. In Chapter 7, we revisit gender learning in childhood and discuss the self-socialization model of gender (Tobin et al., 2010).

FOCUS 2.1

FEMINIST REFORMULATION OF A THEORY OF MORAL DEVELOPMENT

Lawrence Kohlberg made another major contribution to psychology: a theory of moral development—that is, he developed a stage theory of how our understanding of morality and moral problem solving changes from early childhood through adolescence. First, you need to know how Kohlberg studied moral development and how he determined that there are stages in the development of moral reasoning.

Kohlberg studied moral thought by presenting children or adults with a moral dilemma, such as this one:

In Europe, a woman was near death from a special kind of cancer. There was one drug that the doctors thought might save her. It was a form of radium that a druggist in the same town had recently discovered. The drug was expensive to make, but the druggist was charging 10 times what the drug cost him to make. He paid $200 for the radium and charged $2,000 for a small dose of the drug. The sick woman's husband, Heinz, went to everyone he knew to borrow the money, but he could get together only about $1,000, which is half of what it cost. He told the druggist that his wife was dying and asked him to sell it cheaper or let him pay later. But the druggist said, "No, I discovered the drug and I'm going to make money from it." So Heinz gets desperate and considers breaking into the man's store to steal the drug for his wife.

Following presentation of the dilemma, the participant is asked a number of questions, such as whether Heinz should steal the drug and why. The important part is not whether the person says Heinz should or should not steal, but rather the person's answer to the question of why—which reflects the stage of development of moral reasoning.

Based on his research, Kohlberg concluded that people go through a series of three levels in their moral reasoning as they mature (in addition, each level is divided into two stages, for a total of six stages). His model is presented in Table 2.1. In Level I, *preconventional morality*, children (usually preschoolers) have little sense of rules and obey simply to avoid punishments or to obtain rewards. For example, Heinz should not steal because he

might get caught and put in jail. In Level II, *conventional morality*, children (usually beginning in elementary school) are well aware of society's rules and laws and conform to them rigidly; there is a law-and-order mentality and a desire to look good in front of others. For example, Heinz should not steal because stealing is against the law. Finally, in Level III, *postconventional morality*, a person transcends the rules and laws of society and instead behaves in accordance with an internal, self-defined set of ethical principles. For example, it is acceptable for Heinz to steal because human life is more important than property. In Level III, it might be judged acceptable to violate laws in some instances in which they are unjust.

Kohlberg reported evidence of gender differences in moral development, and here the interest for the psychology of women and gender begins. He found that, while most men make it to Stage 4, most women get to only Stage 3. From this it might be concluded that women have a less well-developed sense of morality.

One of the most influential critiques of Kohlberg's ideas is the feminist analysis by Carol Gilligan. In her influential book *In a Different Voice* (Gilligan, 1982), she offered a reformulation of moral development from a woman's point of view. Several of Gilligan's criticisms parallel our earlier discussion of sex bias in research. Some of the moral dilemmas Kohlberg used, like the Heinz dilemma, feature a male protagonist. Girls and women may find this a bit hard to relate to. Gilligan also pointed out that the people who formed the basis for Kohlberg's theorizing were a group of 84 men, whom he followed for 20 years, beginning in their childhood. When a theory is based on evidence from men, it is not surprising that it does not apply well to women; it's an error of overgeneralization. Finally, Gilligan identified a bias in Kohlberg's interpretation: The phenomenon that women reach only Stage 3 is interpreted as a deficiency in female development, whereas it might just as easily be interpreted as being a deficiency in Kohlberg's theory, which may not adequately describe female development.

Gilligan did not stop with a critique of Kohlberg's theory. She extended her analysis to provide a feminist reformulation of moral development. Her reformulation is based on the belief that women reason differently about the moral dilemmas—that is, they are speaking in a different voice—and that their voices had not been listened

(Continued)

(Continued)

TABLE 2.1   Kohlberg's and Gilligan's models of moral development.

Kohlberg's Levels and Stages	Kohlberg's Definitions	Gilligan's Levels
Level I. Preconventional morality		Concern for the self and survival
Stage 1. Punishment orientation	Obey rules to avoid punishment	
Stage 2. Naive reward orientation	Obey rules to get rewards, share to get returns	
Level II. Conventional morality		Concern for being responsible, caring for others
Stage 3. Good-boy/good-girl orientation	Conform to rules that are defined by others' approval/ disapproval	
Stage 4. Authority orientation	Rigid conformity to society's rules, law-and-order mentality, avoid censure for rule breaking	
Level III. Postconventional morality		Concern for self and others as interdependent
Stage 5. Social-contract orientation	More flexible understanding that we obey rules because they are necessary for social order, but the rules could be changed if there were better alternatives	
Stage 6. Morality of individual principles and conscience	Behavior conforms to internal principles (justice, equality) to avoid self-condemnation, and sometimes may violate society's rules	

to. She theorized that men reason about moral issues using a **justice perspective**, which views people as differentiated and standing alone and focuses on the rights of the individual, and that women reason using a **care perspective**, which emphasizes relatedness between people and communication. According to Gilligan, men focus on contracts between people, and women focus on attachments between people. Kohlberg devised his stages of moral reasoning with the male as norm; thus women's answers appear immature, when in fact they are simply based on different concerns.

What evidence is there for Gilligan's theorizing? Gilligan herself presented several studies in support of her views. Here we will consider one of these: the abortion decision study. She interviewed 29 women between the ages of 15 and 33, all of whom were in the first trimester of pregnancy and were considering abortion. They were interviewed a second time one year later. Notice how she shifted the moral dilemma from a male stranger named Heinz to an issue that is far more central to women. Just as Kohlberg saw three major levels of moral reasoning, so Gilligan found three levels among these women, but

the focus for the levels was different. Her model appears alongside Kohlberg's in Table 2.1. In Gilligan's Level I, preconventional morality, the woman making the abortion decision is concerned only for herself and her survival. An example is Susan, an 18-year-old, who was asked what she thought when she found out that she was pregnant:

> I really didn't think anything except that I didn't want it. . . . I didn't want it, I wasn't ready for it, and next year will be my last year and I want to go to school. (Gilligan, 1982, p. 75)

Women who have reached Level II have shifted their focus to being responsible and to caring for others, specifically for a potential child. Women in Level II see their previous, less mature Level I responses as selfish. These themes are articulated by Josie, a 17-year-old, in discussing her reaction to being pregnant:

> I started feeling really good about being pregnant instead of feeling really bad, because I wasn't looking at the situation realistically. I was looking at it

from my own sort of selfish needs, because I was lonely. Things weren't really going good for me, so I was looking at it that I could have a baby that I could take care of or something that was part of me, and that made me feel good. (Gilligan, 1982, p. 77)

Typical of Level II thinking, Josie sees Level I thinking as selfish, and shifts her concern to being responsible to the child. Notice that deciding to have an abortion or not to have an abortion is not what differentiates Level I from Level II. Either decision can be reached at either level.

Finally, in Level III moral reasoning, the self and others are seen as interdependent, and there is a focus on balancing caring for others (the fetus, the father, parents) with caring for oneself. A woman must have reasonably high self-esteem to reach this level, for without it the "caring for self" aspect looks like a return to the selfishness of earlier levels, rather than a complex balancing of care extended to all, including herself. A recapitulation of her earlier moral reasoning and her current balancing of caring is articulated by Sarah, who is faced with a second abortion:

Well, the pros for having the baby are all the admiration that you would get from being a single woman, alone, martyr, struggling, having the adoring love of this beautiful Gerber baby. . . . Cons against having the baby: it was going to hasten what is looking to be the inevitable end of the relationship with the man I am presently with. I was going to have to go on welfare. My parents were going to hate me for the rest of my life. I was going to lose a really good job that I have. I would lose a lot of independence. Solitude. . . . Con against having the abortion is having to face up to the guilt. And pros for having the abortion are I would be able to handle my deteriorating relation with [the father] with a lot more capability and a lot more responsibility for myself. . . . Having to face the guilt of a second abortion seemed like not exactly—well, exactly the lesser of two evils, but also the one that would pay off for me personally in the long run because, by looking at why I am pregnant again and subsequently have decided to have a second abortion, I have to face up to some things about myself. (Gilligan, 1982, p. 92)

Sarah's reasoning reflects the cognitive and moral sophistication of Level III, which entails wrestling with complicated and sometimes conflicting perspectives.

How good is Gilligan's theory? First, it is an example of many of the qualities of feminist scholarship. She detected the androcentric bias of Kohlberg's work, reconstructed the theory after listening to what women said, and shaped a developmental model from it. Still, much of Gilligan's writing sounds as though men display one kind of moral thinking and women display a totally different kind. Yet it seems likely that there are some men who show "female" moral reasoning of the kind quoted earlier and some women who display "male" moral reasoning. Here is the theme of the tension between gender similarities and gender differences.

What do the data say? A major meta-analysis (for an explanation of meta-analysis, see Chapter 3) of studies that had examined gender differences found that women score at the same moral level, on average, as men. That is, there is no evidence to support Gilligan's basic claim that Kohlberg's scales shortchange women and cause them to score as less morally mature. Another meta-analysis examined studies that had tested the use of the justice perspective versus the care perspective, to test Gilligan's assertion that men and women reason with different "moral voices." Averaged over all studies, the gender difference in care orientation did favor women, but was small: $d = -0.28$. (The d statistic is explained in Chapter 3.) The average gender difference in justice orientation favored men, but also was small: $d = 0.19$. In short, although women have a tendency to emphasize care reasoning and men have a tendency to emphasize justice reasoning, the differences are small, and most people use combinations of justice and care in their thinking about moral issues. It simply would not be accurate to say that girls and women speak in one moral voice and boys and men in another.

In sum, Gilligan's main contribution was to articulate a different side of moral reasoning, one based on relationships and caring. While gender differences in moral reasoning are small, it is important to recognize Gilligan's contribution in historical perspective: it offered a feminist reformulation of an androcentric theory based on gender-biased methods.

Sources: Colby et al. (1983); Gilligan (1982); Jaffee & Hyde (2000); Kohlberg (1969); Mednick (1989); L. J. Walker (1984).

Gender Schema Theory

A cognitive perspective on gender that is also feminist is psychologist Sandra Bem's (1981) gender schema theory. Schema is a concept from cognitive psychology, the branch of

Justice perspective:
According to Gilligan, an approach to moral reasoning that emphasizes fairness and the rights of the individual.

Care perspective:
According to Gilligan, an approach to moral reasoning that emphasizes relationships between people and caring for others and the self.

Schema: In cognitive psychology, a general knowledge framework that a person has about a particular topic; the schema then processes and organizes new information on that topic.

Gender schema: A person's general knowledge framework about gender; it processes and organizes information on the basis of gender-linked associations.

psychology that investigates how we think, perceive, process, and remember information. A **schema** is a general knowledge framework that a person has about a particular topic. A schema organizes and guides perception, and typically helps us process and remember information. Yet schemas also act to filter and interpret information, and they can therefore cause errors.

Bem (1981) applied schema theory to understanding the gender-typing process in her gender schema theory (see also C. L. Martin & Halverson, 1983; C. L. Martin et al., 2002). Her proposal was that each one of us has as part of our knowledge structure a **gender schema**, a set of gender-linked associations. Furthermore, the gender schema represents a basic predisposition to process information on the basis of gender. It represents our tendency to see many things as gender-related and to want to dichotomize things on the basis of gender. The gender schema processes new, incoming information, filtering and interpreting it.

Bem argued that the developmental process of gender typing or gender role acquisition in children is a result of the child's gradual learning of the content of their culture's gender schema. The gender-linked associations that form the schema are many: Girls wear dresses and boys don't; boys are strong and tough, girls are pretty (perhaps learned simply from the adjectives adults apply to children, rarely or never calling boys pretty, rarely or never calling girls tough); girls grow up to be mommies, boys don't.

In a further process, the gender schema becomes closely linked to the self-concept. Thus 5-year-old Maria knows she is a girl and also has a girl schema that she attaches to her own sense of girlhood. Maria's self-esteem then begins to be dependent on how well she measures up to her girl schema. At that point, she becomes internally motivated to conform to society's female gender role (a point much like Kohlberg's). Society does not have to force her into the role. She gladly does it herself and feels good about herself in the process. Finally, Bem postulated that different individuals have, to some extent, different gender schemas. The content of the schema varies from one person to the next, perhaps as a result of the kinds of gender information to which one is exposed in one's family throughout childhood. And the gender schema is more central to self-concept for some people than for others; gender schematic individuals are traditionally masculine men and feminine women, whereas gender aschematic individuals are less gender-typed.

Evidence for Gender Schema Theory

In one study, Bem (1981) gave a list of 61 words, in random order, to respondents who were college students. Some of the words were proper names, some referred to animals, some were verbs, and some were articles of clothing. Half the names were masculine and half were feminine. One-third of the animal words were masculine (gorilla), one-third were feminine (butterfly), and one-third were neutral (ant). Similarly, one-third of the verbs and the articles of clothing were each masculine, feminine, and neutral. The participants' task was to recall as many of the 61 words as they could, in any order. It is known from many previous studies that in memory tasks such as these, people tend to cluster words into categories based on similar meaning; this is indicated by the order in which they recall the words. For example, if the person organized the words according to gender, the recall order

Photo Courtesy of Emily Bem.

PHOTO 2.5
Gender schema theorist Sandra Bem proposed that our gender schema is closely linked to our self-concept.

might be gorilla, bull, trousers; but if the organization was according to animals, the recall order might be gorilla, butterfly, ant. If gender-typed people (masculine men and feminine women, as measured by the Bem Sex Role Inventory, a test discussed in Chapter 3) do possess a gender schema that they use to organize information, then they should cluster their recalled words into gender groupings. That is exactly what occurred. Gender-typed persons tended to cluster words according to gender, a result that supports gender schema theory.

In another experiment, 5- and 6-year-old children were shown pictures of boys and girls performing stereotype-consistent activities, such as girls baking, and stereotype-inconsistent activities, such as girls boxing (see Figure 2.1; C. L. Martin & Halverson, 1983). One week later the children were tested for their recall of the pictures. The results indicated that the children distorted information by changing the gender of the people in the stereotype-inconsistent pictures, while not making such changes for the stereotype-consistent pictures. That is, children tended to remember a picture of a girl sawing wood as having been a picture of a boy sawing wood. That result is just what would be predicted by gender schema theory: Incoming information that is inconsistent with the gender schema is filtered out and reinterpreted to be consistent with the gender schema. This study also indicates that the gender schema is present even in 5-year-olds. (For a review of the impact of Bem's theory, see Starr & Zurbriggen, 2017.)

FIGURE 2.1   **Gender schemas and children's memory.**

Pictures like these were used in the C. L. Martin and Halverson (1983) research on gender schemas and children's memory. (Left) A girl engaged in a stereotype-consistent activity. (Right) Girls engaged in a stereotype-inconsistent activity. In a test of recall a week later, children tended to distort the stereotype-inconsistent pictures to make them stereotype-consistent; for example, they remembered that they had seen boys boxing.

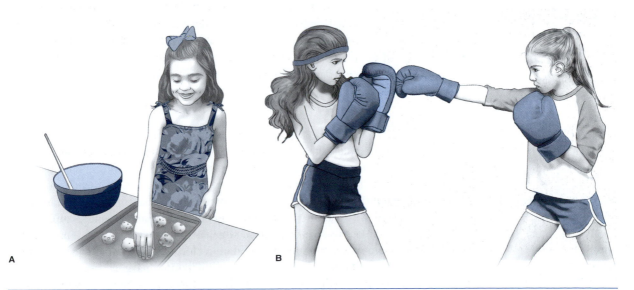

A   B

Source: Adapted from C. L. Martin and Halverson (1983).

Sociobiology and Evolutionary Psychology

Next we turn to two theories that argue that human gender differences are rooted in evolution. Sociobiology is a controversial theory initially proposed by Harvard biologist E. O. Wilson (1975b) in his book *Sociobiology: The New Synthesis*, a massive, 700-page work filled with countless examples from insect life.

Sociobiology can be defined as the application of Charles Darwin's theory of evolution by **natural selection** to understanding the social behavior of animals, including humans. That is, sociobiologists are specifically concerned with understanding how social behaviors—such as aggression or caring for the young—are the product of natural selection.

To understand what sociobiology has to say about women and gender roles, we must first discuss Darwin's theory. His basic observation was that living things over-reproduce—that is, they produce far more offspring than would be needed simply to replace themselves. Yet population sizes remain relatively constant because many individuals do not survive. There must be differential survival, with the "fittest" organisms surviving and reproducing viable offspring. **Evolutionary fitness** is defined in this theory as the relative number of genes an animal contributes to the next generation. The bottom line is producing lots of offspring—specifically, healthy and viable offspring. Thus, a man who jogs 10 miles a day, lifts weights, and has a 50-inch chest but whose sperm count is zero would be considered to have zero fitness according to sociobiologists. Over generations, there is differential reproduction, the fittest individuals producing the most offspring. Genes that produce fitness characteristics become more frequent, and fitness characteristics ("adaptive" characteristics) become more frequent; genes and associated characteristics that produce poor fitness become less frequent.

The basic idea of sociobiology is that the evolutionary theory of natural selection can be applied to social behaviors. That is, a particular form of social behavior—say, caring for one's young—would be adaptive, in the sense of increasing one's reproductive fitness. Other social behaviors—for example, female infanticide—would be maladaptive, decreasing one's reproductive fitness. Over the many generations of natural selection that have occurred, the maladaptive behaviors should have been weeded out, and we should be left with social behaviors that are adaptive because they are the product of evolutionary selection.

With this as background for the general principles of sociobiology, let us now consider some specific arguments of sociobiologists that are of special relevance to women.

Parental Investment

One of the things sociobiologists have attempted to explain is why it is typically the female of the species who does most of the care of offspring. Sociobiologists offer a very different explanation than Chodorow does for this phenomenon. The sociobiologist's explanation rests on the concept of **parental investment**, which refers to behaviors or other investments of the parent with respect to the offspring that increase the offspring's chance of survival but that also cost the parent something (Trivers, 1972). Females of a species generally have a much larger parental investment in their offspring than males do. At the moment of conception, the female has the greater parental investment—she has just contributed one of her precious eggs. The male has contributed merely a sperm. Eggs are precious because they are large cells and, at least in humans, only one egg is released each month. Sperm are "cheap" because they are small cells and are produced

Sociobiology: The application of evolutionary theory to explaining the social behavior of animals, including people.

Natural selection: According to Darwin, the process by which the fittest animals survive, reproduce, and pass on their genes to the next generation, whereas animals that are less fit do not reproduce and therefore do not pass on their genes.

Evolutionary fitness: In evolutionary theory, an animal's relative contribution of genes to the next generation.

Parental investment: In sociobiology, behaviors or other investments in the offspring by the parent that increase the offspring's chance of survival.

Rick Friedman/Corbis News/Getty Images.

PHOTO 2.6
Harvard biologist
E. O. Wilson (left)
developed the theory
of sociobiology, which
applies Charles Darwin's
(right) theory of evolution
by natural selection to
social behaviors.

in enormous numbers. For example, there are 200 million sperm in the average human male ejaculate, and a man can produce that number again in 48 hours (Malm et al., 2004). So at the moment of conception the female has invested much with her highly valuable egg, but the male has invested little with a single sperm. In mammals, the female then proceeds to gestate the young (for a period of 9 months in humans). Here again she makes an enormous investment of her body's resources, which otherwise could have been invested in doing something else. Then the offspring are born and, in the case of mammals, the female nurses them, once again investing time and energy.

It is most adaptive for whichever parent has the greater parental investment to continue caring for the offspring. For the female, who has invested her precious egg, gestation, and nursing, it would be evolutionary insanity to abandon the offspring when they still need more care in order to survive. By contrast, the male has invested relatively little and his best reproductive strategy is to impregnate as many females as possible, producing more offspring carrying his genes. This strategy is particularly effective if he can count on the female to take care of the offspring so that they survive.

Sociobiologists apply this logic to humans, arguing women are the ones doing the child care for two key reasons. The first reason is that the woman has a greater parental investment and therefore it is adaptive for her to continue caring for her children. The second reason arises from a basic fact: Maternity is always certain, whereas paternity is not. In other words, the woman is sure when a child is hers. The sociobiologist would say that she knows that the child carries her genes. The man cannot be sure that the child is his, carrying his genes. It is thus adaptive for the woman—that is, it increases her fitness—to care for the child to make sure that they, and her genes, survive. It does not increase the man's fitness to care for children that may not carry his genes. Therefore, women do the child care.

The basic pattern of females of a species having greater parental investment is found throughout the animal kingdom, with some exceptions that are worth considering. One is songbirds, who are notable because the male and female participate equally and cooperatively in the care of their young (Barash, 1982). But sociobiologists believe that their theory can explain the exception as well as the general rule. Songbirds have a monogamous mating system that makes paternity a near certainty. Thus it is adaptive for the male to care for the young because he can be sure that they carry his genes. In addition, young birds require an enormous amount of food per day. It is doubtful that they could survive on the amount of food brought to them by a single parent. Thus, it is highly adaptive for both parents to participate in care of the offspring, and it would be highly maladaptive for fathers or mothers to neglect them.

Sociobiologists have attempted to explain why female orgasm evolved in humans, given that it exists in few, if any, other species. They argue that human female orgasm has evolved because human babies are born particularly helpless, dependent, and in need of parental care (Barash, 1982). Essentially, human babies are more likely to survive if they have two parents. A monogamous mating system, with permanent pairing of mother and father, would be adaptive and favored in evolution. The female orgasm (and the female human's continuous interest in sex at all phases of the menstrual cycle) thus evolved to hold together that permanent pair.

Sociobiologists have also extended their theorizing to explain the sexual **double standard**—that is, that a man is allowed, even encouraged, to be promiscuous, whereas a woman is punished for engaging in promiscuous sex and instead is very careful and selective about whom she has sex with (Barash, 1982). The explanation has to do with that precious egg and those cheap sperm. It is adaptive for her to be careful of what happens to the egg, whereas it is adaptive for him to distribute sperm to as many women as possible. Anticipating her greater parental investment, the woman must also be careful about whose genes she mixes with her own. In essence, she chooses quality and he chooses quantity.

Sexual Selection

Sexual selection is an evolutionary mechanism originally proposed by Darwin to act in parallel to natural selection and to produce differences between males and females of a species. Essentially, sexual selection means that different selection pressures act on males and females, and thus males and females become different. Sexual selection consists of two processes: (1) Members of one gender (usually males) compete among themselves to gain mating privileges with members of the other gender (usually females), and (2) members of the other gender (usually females) have preferences for certain members of the first gender (usually males) and decide which of them they are willing to mate with. In short, males fight and females choose. Process (1) neatly explains why the males of most species are larger and more aggressive than the females—aggression is adaptive for males in competition, and they are the product of sexual selection. Sexual selection explains, for example, why among many species of birds it is the male that has the gorgeous plumage while the female is drab. Plumage is a way that males compete among themselves, and females are attracted to the most gorgeous males. Females, on the other hand, in their roles as choosers, need not be gorgeous and have not been selected to be so. Perhaps they have been selected for wisdom?

Sexual selection, then, is a mechanism that is used to explain differences between males and females of a species. It is particularly designed to explain the greater size, strength, and aggressiveness of males. Many more examples exist, but the thrust of the argument is clear: Sociobiologists argue that the social behaviors we see in animals and humans today evolved because these behaviors were adaptive, and they continue to be biologically programmed.

Evolutionary Psychology

Evolutionary psychology is an updated and more elaborate version of sociobiology proposed by psychologist David Buss and others (Buss, 1995; Buss & Schmitt, 1993; Geary,

Double standard:
The evaluation of male behavior and female behavior according to different standards, including tolerance of male promiscuity and disapproval of female promiscuity; used specifically to refer to holding more conservative, restrictive attitudes toward female sexuality.

Sexual selection:
According to Darwin, the processes by which members of one gender (usually males) compete with each other for mating privileges with members of another gender (usually females), who, in turn, choose to mate only with certain preferred members of the first gender (males).

Evolutionary psychology:
A theory that humans' complex psychological mechanisms are the result of evolutionary selection.

2010; Tooby & Cosmides, 1992). The basic idea is that humans' complex psychological mechanisms are the result of evolution based on natural selection. These evolved psychological mechanisms exist because, over thousands of years, they solved problems of survival or reproduction. For example, according to evolutionary psychology, fear of snakes is common precisely because it helped people avoid being bitten and poisoned by snakes.

Buss proposed *sexual strategies theory* as a way of articulating the evolved psychological mechanisms that are related to sexuality and, according to the theory, explain certain psychological gender differences (Buss & Schmitt, 1993). This theory distinguishes between short-term mating strategies (e.g., hooking up) and long-term mating strategies (e.g., marriage), and it proposes that women and men had different problems to solve in short-term as well as long-term mating. Because it is to men's evolutionary advantage to inseminate as many women as possible, men put more of their energy into short-term mating. Women, having the greater parental investment, are more interested in ensuring that their offspring survive and therefore put more of their energy into long-term mating strategies that will ensure the long-term commitment of a man who will provide resources for them and their children. Men's evolutionary problems centered on identifying fertile women and removing the uncertainty of paternity. Women, in contrast, had to identify men willing to make a long-term commitment who were also willing and able to provide resources. Thus men have evolved psychological mechanisms that lead them to prefer as sexual partners women who are in their 20s—even if the men are in their 60s—because women are at their peak fertility in their 20s. Women have evolved psychological mechanisms that lead them to prefer long-term mates who possess resources such as wealth, or qualities such as ambition or a law degree, that should indicate good capacity to provide resources in the future. Buss (1989) provided data supporting his theory from a study in which he collected data on mate preferences in 37 distinct cultures around the world and found results generally consistent with his predictions.

According to this perspective, men are also notoriously jealous about their mates' sexual infidelity because of the problem of paternity certainty. In short, if a man is going to provide resources to a female mate and her baby, he wants to be certain that the baby is his. By contrast, a woman will be more jealous if her male mate develops an emotional connection to another woman (termed emotional infidelity) because it represents a threat to the resources she needs for herself and her baby. Evolutionary psychology argues, then, that there are gender differences in responses to sexual versus emotional infidelity (Buss et al., 1992). However, the data don't support this argument: A meta-analysis of 54 studies on this topic found that both men and women report that sexual infidelity is more distressing than emotional infidelity (Carpenter, 2012).

Feminist Critique of Sociobiology and Evolutionary Psychology

Feminists have long been skeptical of sociobiology and evolutionary psychology (for feminist critiques, see J. Bianchi & Strang, 2013; Eagly & Wood, 2011; Fausto-Sterling, 1993; Janson-Smith, 1980; Weisstein, 1982), and some evolutionary psychologists have been dismissive of feminist approaches (e.g., A. Campbell, 2013). Many feminists are wary of biological explanations of anything, in large part because biology always seems to end up being a convenient justification for perpetuating the status quo.

For example, the sociobiologist's belief is that the greater aggression and dominance of men are a result of sexual selection and are controlled by genes. Therefore, men are genetically dominant and women are genetically subordinate, and the subordinate status of women will have to continue because it is genetic. That kind of logic is a red flag to a feminist, who believes the status quo can be changed. Sociobiologists do not ignore environmental influences completely, so this nature-nurture controversy has to do with relative emphasis, in that sociobiologists emphasize biology and feminists emphasize environment. Consider this passage from an article written by E. O. Wilson (1975a):

> In hunter-gatherer societies, men hunt and women stay at home. This strong bias persists in most agricultural and industrial societies and, on that ground alone, appears to have a genetic origin. No solid evidence exists as to when the division of labor appeared in man's ancestors or how resistant to change it might be during the continuing revolution for women's rights. My own guess is that the genetic bias is intense enough to cause a substantial division of labor even in the most free and most egalitarian of future societies. . . . Thus, even with identical education and equal access to all professions, men are likely to continue to play a disproportionate role in political life, business and science. (pp. 48–50)

If Wilson's claim were true, then we would not have witnessed the tremendous social changes that have occurred in the past century. As we will discuss in Chapters 8 and 9, women's achievements in some (though certainly not all) areas of education and work (including political life, business, and science) have matched or surpassed men's. In other words, sexual selection doesn't doom humanity to an eternity of gender inequity. Clearly, human behavior and culture are very complex.

Feminist scientists have pointed out the sexist bias in sociobiology and evolutionary psychology to ignore or minimize the significance of the active role of women in evolution (Gowaty, 1997; Hager, 1997; Sokol-Chang et al., 2013; Vandermassen, 2005). They argue that Darwin's portrayal of females as passive was inaccurate and androcentric (Hrdy, 2013). For example, evolutionary psychology has paid relatively little attention to mothering (a behavior which is pretty important for evolutionary fitness!) and women's role in the ancestral diet. By contrast, a considerable amount of attention has been given to rape as an adaptive reproductive strategy that evolved through natural selection (e.g., Thornhill & Palmer, 2000). Criticisms have also been raised about the representation of women among evolutionary psychologists (Meredith, 2013).

As another instance of androcentric bias, consider the case of a famous young female macaque (monkey) named Imo, living with her troop on an island off Japan. Scientists provisioned the troop there with sweet potatoes. Imo discovered that washing sweet potatoes got the sand off. Her discovery quickly spread among the other juniors in the troop, who then taught their mothers, who in turn taught their infants. Adult males never learned it. Next, scientists flung grains of wheat in the sand to see what the troop would do. Rather than laboriously picking the wheat out of the sand grain by grain, Imo discovered how to separate the wheat from the sand in one operation. Again, this spread from Imo's peers to mothers and infants, and, again, adult males never learned it. The fact that these Japanese macaques had a rudimentary culture has been widely heralded (Weisstein, 1982, p. 46).

Had the genders been reversed, with Imo being a male and the females being unable to learn, one can imagine the attention these facts would have been given by sociobiologists. They would have made much of the genius of the male and the lack of intelligence of females. As it is, Imo's gender is not discussed, and the learning failure of the males is similarly ignored. Sociobiologists, then, seem to ignore or minimize many animal examples that contradict human stereotypes.

Sociobiologists also rely heavily on data from nonindustrial societies, specifically hunter-gatherer societies that are supposed to be like those that existed at the dawn of the human species, millions of years ago. Once again, the emphasis is androcentrically selective. Sociobiologists emphasize "man the hunter" and how he evolved to be aggressive and have great physical prowess. In discussing this, E. O. Wilson (1978, p. 127) makes much of how natural selection for these traits is reflected in men's current superiority in Olympic track events. Later on the same page, he mentions that women are superior in precision archery and small-bore rifle shooting in the Olympics, but does not seem to see this as inconsistent with the evolution of only man as the hunter. "Woman the gatherer" is ignored, although she may have formed the foundation for early human social organization (Janson-Smith, 1980).

Sociobiology has been criticized for resting on an outmoded version of evolutionary theory that modern biologists consider naive (Gould, 1987). For example, sociobiology has focused mainly on the individual's struggle for survival, whereas modern biologists focus on more complex issues such as the survival of the group and the species, and the evolution of a successful adaptation between the species and its environment.

Many studies contradicting evolutionary psychology have emerged. As one example, evolutionary psychologist Devendra Singh (1993) presented evidence that women with a waist-to-hip ratio (WHR) of 0.70 are judged as most attractive by men, compared with women with greater WHRs. According to sexual strategies theory, men are constantly nonconsciously assessing the potential fertility of female partners and finding the most fertile ones to be the most attractive. WHR is an index of body fat distribution, and Singh argued that WHR is correlated with youth, sex hormone levels, and health. He found that Miss America contest winners and Playboy centerfolds have WHRs averaging 0.70 and vary little from that mark. This study has been much publicized, and the magical 0.70 ratio is well known, taking on the status of an academic urban legend. An independent team of investigators, however, reanalyzed the Playboy and the Miss America data and obtained three results that contradict Singh's claims (Freese & Meland, 2002). First, they found that there was actually considerable variation in the WHRs of Miss America winners, ranging from 0.61 (1963 winner) to 0.78 (1921). Second, the mean WHR for Miss America winners was 0.68, not the magical 0.70. Third, there was a systematic trend over time in the WHRs of the pageant winners and centerfolds, with the preferred WHR decreasing from the early to mid-20th century and then increasing after that. Claims that the preferred WHR is remarkably constant, supporting the contention that the preference was "hardwired" by evolution thousands of years ago, clearly are not accurate.

A second independent team noted that the other cultures in which evidence has been found for men's preference for a 0.70 WHR have all been exposed, often substantially, to Western media, and specifically to American beauty icons, thereby contaminating the results (Yu & Shepard, 1998). They studied the indigenous Matsigenka of Peru, who are isolated and thus have not been exposed to Western media. Men from that culture ranked as most attractive a female figure that was overweight with a 0.90 WHR, in contradiction to the claims of evolutionary psychologists. The more general point is that purported cross-cultural tests of evolutionary psychology are not truly cross-cultural because of globalization and the far reach of American media.

Space limitations don't permit us to catalog all of the studies that provide evidence contradicting some of the claims of evolutionary psychology. Suffice it to say that there are many more (e.g., Dantzker & Eisenman, 2003; Eastwick et al., 2014; Grice & Seely, 2000; C. R. Harris, 2002; W. C. Pedersen et al., 2002; Zentner & Eagly, 2015).

Heteronormativity: The belief that heterosexuality is the norm.

You may be noticing that, with all this focus on sexual selection and heterosexual mating preferences, evolutionary psychology seems deeply rooted in **heteronormativity** and the gender binary. That is, theories such as sexual strategies theory appear to assume that all people are innately heterosexual and either male or female. Such theories can thus contribute to the marginalization of individuals outside the gender binary. Sociobiology and evolutionary psychology have long struggled to explain the diversity of sexual orientations among humans (e.g., Confer et al., 2010). More recently, social psychologist Charlotte Tate, a lesbian and openly transgender woman, proposed an intersectional feminist approach to evolutionary psychology that avoids the assumptions of heteronormativity and the gender binary (e.g., Tate, 2013; Tate & Ledbetter, 2010).

The feminist criticisms, then, are that the evolutionary psychology theories of gender can justify or rationalize and perpetuate the subordination of women; that their evidence rests on a selective, androcentric citing of the data, ignoring many contradictions; that they rely on an androcentric and oversimplified view of evolution; and that they marginalize people outside the gender binary. In addition to these criticisms, evolutionary psychology has been criticized on the grounds that it is not an empirically *falsifiable* theory (e.g., Panksepp & Panksepp, 2000); that is, it is difficult (if not impossible) to imagine a pattern of results that would contradict evolutionary psychology. A good theory should be falsifiable.

Feminist Evolutionary Psychology and Feminist Sociobiology

Many of these feminist criticisms of evolutionary psychology have been raised by feminist evolutionary psychologists. Impossible, you say? Remember that feminists are focused on gender equity and equality, regardless of their field of study. This means there are feminist approaches throughout the sciences, including feminist evolutionary psychology, feminist sociobiology, and feminist biology (we'll return to feminist biology in Chapter 10).

Frustrated with the inattention to the active role of women in shaping human evolution, feminist evolutionary psychologists have responded with efforts to make their field higher quality and more equitable. In addition to providing these insightful critiques, they have conducted high-quality feminist research in sociobiology and evolutionary psychology. They have also formed the Feminist Evolutionary Psychology Society and contributed to a hefty volume on women's role in human evolution titled *Evolution's Empress: Darwinian Perspectives on the Nature of Women* (Fisher et al., 2013).

Feminist evolutionary psychologists argue that there are three core components of a feminist approach within evolutionary psychology. A direct response to the feminist criticisms discussed earlier, these components are (1) thinking critically about sex and gender, (2) explicitly recognizing women as active agents in evolutionary processes, and (3) explicitly recognizing women as active agents in human dynamics, including those related to sexual selection and competition for mates (Kruger et al., 2013).

An example of feminist sociobiology is the work of primatologist Sarah Blaffer Hrdy (1999, 2009), who has written several excellent books describing the crucial and complicated role of mothering (by mothers as well as aunts, grandmothers, sisters, and so on) in evolution. In *Mother Nature: Maternal Instincts and How They Shape the Human Species*, Hrdy (1999) assembled the evidence regarding evolutionary forces on mothering behaviors in humans and other species, while at the same time taking a decidedly feminist approach. Moreover, she has the biological sophistication and complex knowledge of primate behavior that many sociobiologists and evolutionary psychologists lack.

Hrdy's basic argument is that women have evolved to care for their children and ensure their survival, but in reality these evolved tendencies are miles away from romanticized Victorian notions of all-loving, self-sacrificing motherhood. Hrdy notes, for example, that female primates of all species combine work and family—that is, they must be ambitious, successful foragers or their babies will starve. Males are not the only ones who have status hierarchies; a female chimpanzee's status within her group has a powerful influence on whether her offspring survive and what the status of those offspring will be when they reach adulthood. In contrast to other sociobiologists' views of females as being highly selective about whom they mate with, Hrdy notes that female primates of many species will mate promiscuously with males invading their troop, even if they are already pregnant. Essentially, the females seem to be trying to create some confusion about paternity, because males happily commit infanticide against infants that are not theirs but generally work to protect infants they have sired. Under these circumstances the best thing a pregnant female can do for her unborn infant is to have sex with strangers! Hrdy's arguments subvert many ideas about traditional gender roles in humans and whether these roles have an evolutionary basis.

Handout/Getty Images News/Getty Images.

PHOTO 2.7
Feminist sociobiologist Sarah Blaffer Hrdy studies maternal behaviors among primates, such as these langurs.

Social Role Theory

Social psychologists Alice Eagly and Wendy Wood (1999) provided a probing critique of Buss's sexual strategies theory from evolutionary psychology and its explanations for psychological gender differences. They also articulated an alternative, social-structural explanation for Buss's findings that explains gender differences as resulting from women's and men's different positions in the social structure.

Eagly and Wood's alternative explanation, **social role theory** (also called *social structural theory*), emphasizes not cross-cultural universals, but rather the variability across cultures in patterns of gender differences. According to this view, a society's division of labor by gender (that is, gender roles) drives all other gender differences in behavior. Psychological gender differences result from individuals' accommodations or adaptations to the particular restrictions on or opportunities for their gender in their society. Social role theorists acknowledge biological differences between male and female bodies, such as differences in size and strength and the female body's capacity to bear and nurse children, but emphasize that these physical differences are important mainly because they are amplified by cultural beliefs. Men's greater size and strength have led them to pursue activities such as warfare that in turn gave them greater status, wealth, and power than women. Once men were in these roles of greater status and power, their behavior became more dominant and, similarly, women's behavior accommodated and became more subordinate. The gendered division of labor, in which women were responsible for home and family, led women to acquire such role-related skills as cooking and caring for children. In this way, women acquired nurturing behaviors and a facility for relationships. Men, specializing in paid employment in male-dominated occupations, adapted with assertive and independent behaviors.

Social role theory: A theory of the origin of psychological gender differences that focuses on the social structure, particularly the division of labor between men and women; also called social structural theory.

Eagly and Wood (1999) reanalyzed Buss's 37-cultures data to test the predictions of social role theory. Their basic hypothesis was that the greater the gender differences in status in a culture, the greater would be the psychological gender differences; societies characterized by gender equality would show far less psychological gender differentiation. Recall from Chapter 1 that the United Nations maintains a database that indexes gender inequality in countries around the world (described in Focus 1.1). Correlations were high between societies' gender inequality and the magnitude of the difference between women and men in a given society on psychological measures of mate preferences. In other words, in countries where opportunities for men and women were more equal, men and women were more similar. If mate preferences were determined by evolution thousands of years ago, they should not vary across cultures and they definitely should not correlate with a society's gender equality or lack thereof. These findings provide powerful evidence in support of social role theory.

Feminist Theories

Many people view the feminist movement as a political group with a particular set of goals, a lobbying group trying to serve its own ends, as the National Rifle Association does. What is less recognized is that feminism has a rich, articulated theoretical basis. This viewpoint spans many areas besides psychology and can be applied to any psychological approach or topic.

Feminist theories were created by no single person. Instead, numerous writers have contributed their ideas, consistent with the desire of feminists to avoid power hierarchies and not to have a single person become the sole authority. But it also means that the feminist perspective as we have crystallized it here has been drawn from many sources. For that reason, we have titled this section "Feminist Theories" rather than "Feminist Theory." Some of the central concepts and issues of feminist theories follow.

Gender as Status and Power

Feminists view gender as similar to a class variable in our society. That is, men and women are unequal just as the lower class, the working class, the middle class, and the upper class are unequal. Men and women are of unequal status, women having the lower status (Ridgeway & Bourg, 2004).

From the observation of the lesser status of women comes another basic feminist argument: Sexism is pervasive. Women are discriminated against in diverse ways, from the underrepresentation of women in Congress to the male-centeredness of psychological theories, from the different pay scales for women and men to the boss propositioning his secretary. Thus, sexism exists in many spheres: political, academic, economic, and interpersonal.

A closely related concept is the inequality of power between men and women, with men having greater power (Brace & Davidson, 2000; Pratto & Walker, 2004). Male dominance is therefore paired with female subordination. The areas of male power and dominance are diverse and occur at many levels, from institutions to marital interactions. Most political leaders are men, and men therefore have the power to pass laws that have a profound effect on women's lives. Feminist analysis has extended the power principle to many other areas, for example, to viewing rape not as a sexual act but as an expression of men's power over women (e.g., Brownmiller, 1975). The concept of power is key to feminist analysis (Enns, 2004).

One saying of the feminist movement has been "the personal is political" (MacKinnon, 1982). Once again, "political" refers to expressions of power. Feminists have reconceptualized many acts that were traditionally viewed as personal, as simple interactions between individuals, into acts that are seen as political, or expressions of power. As examples, Mr. Executive pats the ass of Miss Secretary, or Josh rapes Meghan. Traditionally, these were thought of as personal, individual acts. They were understood to be the product of an obnoxious individual such as Mr. Executive, or of a rare, disturbed individual such as Josh, or of the inappropriately seductive behavior of Miss Secretary or Meghan. The feminist recasts these not as personal acts, but as political expressions of men's power over women. The greater status of men gives them a sense of entitlement to engage in such acts. At the same time, men exert power and control over women when they engage in these acts.

Theorists believe that there are four basic sources of power when one person or group has power over another (Pratto & Walker, 2004): (1) the threat of violence or the potential to harm, (2) economic power or control of resources, (3) the ability of the powerful group to promote ideologies that tell others what they should desire (e.g., expensive cosmetics to make yourself look beautiful) or disdain (e.g., fat or even slightly overweight women), and (4) relational power, in which one person in a relationship needs the other more than the reverse. These sources of power can operate between any two unequal groups, such as Whites and African Americans in the United States, and you can see how directly they apply to relations between men and women. We will return to each of these sources of power in later chapters; for example, Chapter 14 is about violence against women by men.

Intersectionality

Feminists argue that attention to gender alone is not enough. Recall from Chapter 1 that intersectionality considers the meaning and consequences of multiple categories of identity, difference, and disadvantage simultaneously. Intersectionality is a concept that emerged and evolved largely within Black feminism and critical race theory (Else-Quest & Hyde, 2016; May, 2015). Kimberlé Crenshaw (1989, 1991), a legal scholar, first coined the term *intersectionality* and described how analyzing only gender or only race would exclude or ignore the unique experiences of women of color. Black feminists in the 1980s and 1990s described how they were marginalized by both the civil rights movement (which put Black men at the helm) and the second wave of the feminist movement (which focused on White women). Black women, they maintained, experienced "interlocking" systems of oppression (Combahee River Collective, 1982) in which racism and sexism (among other systems of oppression) worked hand in hand to marginalize and oppress them. While intersectionality was first used to talk about women of color, it is an important feminist approach throughout the psychology of women and gender.

Because intersectionality is a critical theory and not a scientific theory that should be held to the standard of falsifiability, it is best to evaluate intersectional research according to how well it adheres to the essential elements of intersectionality (Else-Quest & Hyde, 2016). The first element is that intersectional research

Tibrina Hobson/FilmMagic/Getty Images.

PHOTO 2.8
Legal scholar Kimberlé Crenshaw first coined the term *intersectionality*.

focuses on the experience and meaning of simultaneously belonging to multiple inter-twined social categories, such as gender, race/ethnicity, class, and sexual orientation. For example, how are cisgender women's experiences of gender identity similar to and different from transgender women's experiences? Such a question explores a dimension of diversity within the population of women.

The second element is that researchers must examine how power is connected to belonging in each of those intersecting categories. For example, what role does social inequality play in the different experiences of gender identity among cisgender and transgender women? Both groups are oppressed *as women*, but cisgender women have privilege relative to transgender women. An important point of intersectionality is that one intersecting category may confer disadvantage while another may grant privilege.

The third element of intersectional research is that social categories are examined as properties of a person as well as their social context, so those categories and their significance may change. For example, how does a transgender woman's gender identity develop within a particular culture and historical period? Are there times or situations when the importance of her being transgender is greater, such as when receiving medical care?

The new questions and perspectives that intersectionality inspires are limitless. The point is that social categories like gender, race/ethnicity, class, and sexual orientation (among others) are highly complex, and social justice and equality are always the goals of intersectional approaches.

Queer Theory

The word *queer* has a, well, queer history. Today, many use the word as an umbrella term for anyone who is not heterosexual. Yet, long used to mean "strange" or "odd," queer became a heterosexist slur in the middle of the 20th century. By the 1990s, however, the word had been reclaimed by feminist theorists within lesbian and gay studies, such as Michel Foucault (1978), Eve Sedgwick (1990), and Teresa de Lauretis (1991), who questioned the social construction of gender and sexuality (Halperin, 2003). **Queer theory** proposed that one's gender, gender identity, and sexual orientation are not stable, fixed, biologically based characteristics, but rather fluid and dynamic aspects of individuals shaped by culture. To be queer was not to be gay or lesbian, but to reject any boundaries or preconceived norms about gender and sexuality. Thus, queer theory is deeply rooted in social constructionism and the critique of the gender binary. Queer theorist Judith Butler explained,

Queer theory: A theoretical perspective that one's gender, gender identity, and sexual orientation are not stable, fixed, biologically based characteristics, but rather fluid and dynamic aspects of individuals shaped by culture.

> My understanding of queer is a term that desires that you don't have to present an identity card before entering a meeting. Heterosexuals can join the queer movement. Bisexuals can join the queer movement. Queer is not being lesbian. Queer is not being gay. It is an argument against lesbian specificity: that if I am a lesbian I have to desire in a certain way. Or if I am a gay I have to desire in a certain way. Queer is an argument against certain normativity, what a proper lesbian or gay identity is. (quoted in Michalik, 2001, para. 5)

Queer theory has made important contributions to the psychology of women and gender, particularly with regard to questioning the stability of gender and sexuality (B. B. Carr et al., 2017). We will revisit queer theory in greater depth in Chapter 13.

Gender Roles and Socialization

Feminists have highlighted the importance of gender roles and socialization in our culture. American society has well-defined roles for men and for women. From their earliest years, children are socialized to conform to these roles. In this regard, the feminist perspective is in close agreement with social learning theory. The feminist sees these roles as constricting to individuals. Essentially, gender roles tell children that there are certain things they may not do, whether telling a girl that she cannot be a physicist or a boy that he cannot be a nurse. Because gender roles limit individual potentials and aspirations, feminists believe that we would be better off without such roles, or at least that those roles need to be radically revised.

Anthropologists such as Margaret Mead (1935, 1949) have discovered that other cultures have gender roles considerably different from our own; for example, in some other cultures men are reputed to be the gossips, and women are thought to be the appropriate ones to carry heavy loads. But despite all the cross-cultural diversity in gender roles, one universal principle seems to hold: Every known society recognizes and elaborates gender differences (Rosaldo, 1974), a point that is consistent with feminists' emphasis on the power and pervasiveness of gender roles.

Beyond this recognition of the universality of gender roles, there is disagreement among feminist anthropologists. Some have argued that the male role, whatever it is, is always valued more (Mead, 1935; Rosaldo, 1974). For example, in some parts of New Guinea the women grow sweet potatoes and the men grow yams, but yams are the prestige food, the food used in important ceremonies. Even in this case where the labor of women and men is virtually identical, what the male does is valued more. This finding is consistent with the feminist concept of gender as a status variable. Other anthropologists argue that there are exceptions to the rule that the male role is always valued more. They point to societies in which there is gender equality or in which the female role is valued more (Lepowsky, 1993; Sanday, 1988). For example, the Minangkabau of West Sumatra are proud of being described as a matriarchate (a society in which many important activities are matri-centered, or female centered, and women are more important than men; Sanday, 1988). Members of that society say that men are dominant in matters related to traditions and customs, but that women are dominant in matters related to property. We cannot resolve this debate here, except to note that patriarchal societies are by far in the majority, and egalitarian or matriarchal societies, if they exist, constitute a small minority.

By University of California, Berkeley - CC0.

PHOTO 2.9
Queer theorist Judith Butler. Queer theory has made important contributions to the psychology of women and gender.

External Versus Internal Attributions of Problems

Latoya was raped; Sara is depressed. Traditional psychological analyses focus on the internal nature and causes of these women's problems. Latoya might be viewed as having brought on the rape by her seductive behavior. Sara might be viewed as having personal problems of adjustment. Feminists are critical of analyses that assume women's problems are caused by internal or personal factors. Feminists instead view the sources of women's problems as being external. Latoya's problem is recast as having its roots in a society that condones, indeed encourages, male aggression. Sara's problem is recast as having its roots in a society that attaches little value and recognition to being a housewife and mother. This theme of external factors will recur in Chapter 15 in the discussion of feminist therapy.

Consciousness Raising

In the late 1960s and early 1970s, as the second-wave feminist movement gained momentum, consciousness-raising (C-R) groups were popular. Ideally, such groups begin with a few women sharing their personal feelings and experiences; they then move to a feminist theoretical analysis of these feelings and experiences, and from this should flow action, whether it involves an individual woman restructuring her relationship with her partner or a group of women lobbying for a new law to be passed.

A great deal of consciousness raising now occurs on social media. The process of consciousness raising remains central to feminism and is a common feature of many gender and women's studies courses. It is a means for women to reflect on their experiences and understand themselves. It also involves a theoretical analysis or lens through which to view one's experiences. Women come to see that what they had perceived as individual problems are actually common and are rooted in external causes. For example, Lindsay has been beaten by her husband. In the C-R group, she discovers that three of the other women have also been beaten by husbands or lovers. In so doing, she comes to recognize two central points: that the personal is political (the individual beating by her husband is part of a larger pattern of power in society) and that the sources of her problems are external, rooted in the power structure of society, rather than a result of her own internal deficiencies. Finally, the C-R group becomes the power base for political action. Lindsay and the three other women might decide to establish a shelter for people victimized by intimate partner violence.

Diversity of Feminisms

One of the difficulties in writing this section on the feminist perspective is that there are actually several different kinds of feminism, differing in everything from their theoretical analysis to their model for social change to their vision of the ideal society. One method of categorization is to conceptualize the major types of feminism: (a) liberal feminism, (b) cultural feminism, (c) Marxist or socialist feminism, (d) radical feminism, (e) existentialist and postmodern feminism, (f) women of color feminism, and (g) ecofeminism (Enns & Sinacore, 2001; Tong, 2014). As discussed in Chapter 1, we can also distinguish between the first-wave, second-wave, third-wave, and fourth-wave feminist movements. While a diversity of feminist perspectives exists, all advocate for gender equality.

Liberal feminism holds that women should have opportunities and rights equal to those of men. Basically, liberal feminists believe in working within the system for reform. The liberal feminist position is exemplified by organizations such as NOW (National Organization for Women), which is the major group that lobbied for passage of the Equal Rights Amendment. The notion here is that American society is founded on basically good ideals, such as justice and freedom for all, but the justice and freedom need to be extended fully to women. Some would argue that liberal feminism can be credited with many of the educational and legal reforms that have improved women's lives in the United States over the last several decades (Tong, 2014).

Unlike the claims of liberal feminism, which sees men and women as basically alike but in need of equal rights, *cultural feminism* (sometimes called care-focused feminism) argues that women have special, unique qualities that differentiate them from men. The crucial task is to elevate and value those special qualities, which have been devalued in our patriarchal society. The special qualities include nurturing, connectedness, and intuition. Carol Gilligan's theorizing about moral development is a clear example of cultural or care-focused feminism.

Marxist or *socialist feminism* argues that the liberal feminist analysis of the problem is superficial and does not get to the deeper roots of the problem. Marxist feminism views the oppression of women as just one instance of oppression based on class, oppression that is rooted in capitalism. Marxist feminists, for example, point out the extent to which the capitalist system benefits from oppressing women in ways such as wage discrimination. What would happen to the average American corporation if it had to start paying all of its secretaries as much as plumbers earn? (Both jobs require a high school education and a certain amount of manual dexterity and specific skills.) The answer is that most corporations would find their economic structure ruined. Women's situation will not improve, according to this point of view, without a drastic reform of American society, including a complete overhaul of the capitalist economic system and the concept of private property. Marxist and socialist feminists also argue that unpaid domestic work should no longer be "women's work" and that men must perform an equal share of such work.

Radical feminists such as Shulamith Firestone (1970), Kate Millett (1969), and Andrea Dworkin (1987) view liberal feminism as entirely too optimistic about the sources of women's oppression and the changes needed to end it. Patriarchal values have saturated society to such an extent that radical change is necessary in everything from social institutions to patterns of thought. Radical feminists are split between *radical-libertarian feminists*—who argue that femininity limits women's development and instead advocate for androgyny among women—and *radical-cultural feminists*—who argue that femininity and feminine values (such as interdependence and community) are preferable to masculinity and masculine values (such as autonomy and domination) and that men should strive to be more feminine. Given the difficulty of changing social institutions, radical feminists sometimes advocate separatist communities in which women can come together to pursue their work free of men's oppression.

Existentialist and *postmodern feminists* have been influenced by the postmodern movement, which questions rationality and objectivity as methods for getting at truth, whether in the humanities or the sciences. Postmodern feminism has tended to be less focused on social action; rather, it is an academic movement that seeks to reform thought and research within colleges and universities. It is particularly concerned with the issue of epistemology, which is the question of how people—whether laypeople or scientists—know. How do we know about truth and reality? Traditional science has been based on positivism as its epistemology. Positivism claims that we can know reality directly through rational, objective scientific methods. Postmodernism questions that claim and instead advocates social constructionism as an epistemology, a concept discussed in Chapter 1.

Women of color feminism highlights the unique experiences of women of color as members of multiply marginalized groups and thus promotes a more inclusive and intersectional feminist perspective. Thus, this type of feminism is often critical of White feminists for focusing on "universal" female experiences such as reproductive freedom and neglecting the diversity of women's experiences (Bryant-Davis & Comas-Díaz, 2016; Enns & Sinacore, 2001). We discuss women of color feminism in depth in Chapter 4.

Ecofeminism links women's oppression to human beings' domination of nature. Women are often culturally tied to nature, and ecofeminists point out that patriarchy—which is hierarchical, dualistic, and oppressive—harms both women and nature (Tong, 2014; Warren, 1987). Ecofeminism has deep roots in the environmental movement and the work of environmentalists such as Rachel Carson and Aldo Leopold. Thus, issues such as climate change and sustainable development are understood as intertwined with gender equality and well-being. While there are multiple strains of ecofeminism, values such as interdependence and interconnection are central to all of them.

The point here is that not all feminists and not all feminist theories are alike. Instead, there is a wide spectrum of belief and practice. Most of the academic feminist psychologists who have contributed to the psychology of women would be classified as liberal feminists or postmodern feminists, but certainly there is a diversity of feminist approaches within the discipline.

Summary

Feminist theories generally highlight a number of points: (a) As discussed in Chapter 1, knowledge, in particular our understanding of gender, is socially constructed; (b) gender is a status and power variable, with men having power over women; (c) gender roles and gender role socialization are powerful forces in any culture; (d) many of women's problems are better conceptualized as being caused by external forces than by internal ones; (e) consciousness raising is an essential process for women to get in touch with themselves; and (f) according to intersectionality, race/ethnicity, sexual orientation, and class must be considered simultaneously with gender, as these social categories interact in influencing psychological phenomena.

Evaluation of Feminist Theories

Feminist theories span many disciplines and were not specifically proposed as scientific theories. This means that some of their propositions are difficult to evaluate scientifically. Yet many theories have been reformulated with a feminist approach or perspective. The notion of men as a class having power over women will recur in several studies mentioned later in this book; an example is gender-based violence such as rape (see Chapter 14). Also, the data on issues of sexuality for women are the focus in several later chapters (10, 11, 12, and 13). We don't mean to evade the question of the scientific evidence for feminist theories, but the issues raised by these theories are so broad that it is best to wait until you have read the rest of this book before attempting an evaluation.

In Conclusion

In this chapter we have presented seven major theoretical perspectives: psychoanalytic theory, social learning theory, cognitive-developmental theory, gender schema theory, sociobiology and evolutionary psychology, social role theory, and feminist theories. They operate from vastly different underlying assumptions and provide considerably different views of women and gender. Psychoanalytic theory and the evolutionary theories both see the nature of women and gender differences as rooted in biology: evolution, genes, and anatomy. Social learning theory falls at the other end of the nature-nurture continuum, seeing gender differences and gender roles as products of the social environment. Feminist theories, too, emphasize culture and society as the creator of gender roles. Cognitive-developmental theory is an interactionist theory, emphasizing the interaction between the state of the organism (stage of cognitive development) and the information available from the culture. Social role theory is also an interactionist theory. Gender schema theory emphasizes the cognitive aspects of gender typing and the interaction between the knowledge structures in the individual and the incoming information from the environment.

FOCUS 2.2

FEMINIST THEORY IN PSYCHOLOGY: OBJECTIFICATION THEORY

Feminist theory has made incredible contributions to modern psychology. As just one example, let's consider *objectification theory*. The feminine body is socially constructed as an object to be looked at, an object of the male gaze and male desire. That is, women are considered objects, not subjects. When women are objectified, their worth is reduced to the attractiveness of their body parts. This is plainly evident in the media, where a limited and unattainable standard of women's physical beauty is portrayed and linked to women's value.

Feminist psychologists Barbara Fredrickson and Tomi-Ann Roberts (1997) and Nita McKinley and Janet Hyde (1996) theorized that, as girls develop in a culture that objectifies women, they learn to view their own bodies as if they were outside observers. This experience of one's own body as an object to be viewed and evaluated is termed **objectified body consciousness** or **self-objectification.** Culturally constructed feminine beauty standards are internalized by girls and women so that they come to believe that these are their own personal standards. Women and girls constantly engage in body surveillance, monitoring their bodies to make sure that they conform to these standards. Of course, because standards are so unrealistic and unattainable, most girls and women will feel shame for not measuring up. Girls and women come to believe that they can control their appearance and, given enough effort, can achieve cultural standards of beauty and the perfect body. This can lead girls and women to diet excessively in order to force their unruly bodies to match a cultural ideal that is, in fact, unrealistic. Taken to the extreme, the results are eating disorders, anxiety, and depression.

Objectification theory has stimulated a great deal of research documenting its existence and effects. For example, objectified body consciousness and self-objectification impair cognitive performance. In one study, researchers randomly assigned women to wear either a bathing suit or a sweater and then gave the women a math test. Women in the bathing suit condition performed significantly worse on the math test! Links to negative affect, depression, eating disorders, and reduced sexual pleasure have also been established. In short, experiencing your own body as an object leads to some very negative psychological outcomes.

Objectification affects observers, too. More recent empirical evidence indicates that, when observers focus on women's physical appearance, they attribute less competence, warmth, and morality to those women. And when women's physical appearance is emphasized and scrutinized, women's faces and bodies are actually visually processed as objects. But the same is not true for men. That is, women are literally objectified by observers.

Objectification theory gives insight into the psychological dynamics that underlie girls' and women's internalization of cultural messages about their bodies. In doing so, it provides a sociocultural explanation for their internal experiences—in short, the personal is political.

Sources: American Psychological Association (2007b); Fredrickson & Roberts (1997); Heflick & Goldenberg (2014); McKinley & Hyde (1996); Szymanski et al. (2011).

With regard to scientific evidence for the various theories, certainly there are far more studies supporting social learning theory, gender schema theory, and cognitive-developmental theory than there are supporting psychoanalytic theory. The evidence concerning the tenets of evolutionary psychology is mixed.

Objectified body consciousness: The experience of one's own body as an object to be viewed and evaluated; includes components of surveillance, body shame, and control beliefs.

Self-objectification: Perceiving and valuing oneself as an object to be viewed and evaluated.

Experience the Research
Gender Schema Theory

Ask six friends to participate, individually, in a memory study that you are conducting. Collect the data in a quiet place that is free from distractions. Then give the following set of instructions to the person:

> I am going to read to you a list of 12 words. As soon as I finish, I would like you to recall the words for me, in any order. I want to see how many words you remember.

Then read the following words out loud, in exactly this order:

gorilla (M)	stepping (N)	ant (N)
Michael (M)	butterfly (F)	Mary (F)
blushing (F)	trousers (M)	bull (M)
hurling (M)	bikini (F)	dress (F)

Read the words slowly and clearly, with about one second between each. Write the words down as your friend recalls them, in exactly the order they are recalled. If the person responds quickly, you may need to abbreviate the words.

Does the pattern of results for your friends look like those that Sandra Bem obtained for her research on gender schemas? That is, did people cluster the words into groups on the basis of gender associations (*butterfly* and *dress* close together, *trousers* and *bull* close together) or on the basis of other categories (*trousers* and *dress* together, *butterfly* and *bull* together)?

CHAPTER SUMMARY

There are diverse theoretical perspectives from which we can study the psychology of women and gender. Each has strengths and weaknesses to consider. Psychoanalytic theory was first formulated by Freud, who theorized that gender differences in the development of the superego stem from girls' incomplete resolution of the Electra complex. Theorists such as Horney and Chodorow offered feminist approaches to psychoanalytic theory.

Bandura's social learning theory emphasizes the roles of reinforcement, punishment, observational learning, and imitation in the process of gender typing. Bandura's reformulation of this theory incorporated cognitive processes such as attention, self-regulation, and self-efficacy.

Cognitive-developmental theory emphasizes the development of gender constancy—the understanding that gender is a stable and consistent part of oneself—in gender typing. Bem's gender schema theory proposes that children develop gender schemas—a set of gender-linked associations that filter and interpret incoming information—which are essential to gender typing.

Sociobiology and evolutionary psychology apply Darwin's theory of evolution by natural selection to social behaviors. These theories emphasize parental investment and sexual selection in the development of gender differences.

Social role theory, proposed by Eagly and Wood, emphasizes not cross-cultural universals, but rather the variability across cultures in patterns of gender differences. This perspective proposes that a society's division of labor by gender fosters the development of psychological gender differences.

A diversity of feminist theories exists, but they share common themes and the goal of gender equality. Feminist theories emphasize men's power over women and the ways that other social categories, such as social class, race, and sexual orientation, intersect with gender. Gender and sexuality are understood as socially constructed, as in queer theory.

SUGGESTIONS FOR FURTHER READING

Fisher, Maryanne L., Garcia, Justin R., & Sokol Chang, Rosemarie. (2013). *Evolution's empress: Darwinian perspectives on the nature of women*. New York, NY: Oxford University Press. An excellent volume rich with feminist evolutionary psychology and sociobiology.

Tong, Rosemarie P. (2014). *Feminist thought: A more comprehensive introduction* (4th ed.). Boulder, CO: Westview Press. This book is a must-read for those interested in learning more about the diversity of feminist theories.

Gender Stereotypes and Gender Differences

> ❝ Man should be trained for war and woman for the recreation of the warrior. ❞

Nietzsche, *Thus Spoke Zarathustra* (1883)

Some people believe that this is the postfeminist era, that gender stereotypes have vanished, and that women (and men) can be anything they want to be. But then why are people so offended by a man who behaves in a feminine manner? Why are some people so upset by transgender and genderqueer folks, to the point that they pass legislation about which bathrooms they can use? Gender stereotypes and gender roles are still in force in contemporary culture, and violations of those roles and stereotypes seem very serious to some people.

Gender Stereotypes

Stereotypes About Men and Women

Gender stereotypes: A set of shared cultural beliefs about men's and women's behavior, appearance, interests, personality, and so on.

Gender stereotypes are simply a set of shared cultural beliefs about men's and women's behavior, appearance, interests, personality, and so on. Research shows that even in modern American society, and even among college students, there is a belief that men and women do differ psychologically in many ways. A list of these gender-stereotyped traits is given in Table 3.1.

How do researchers collect evidence of these stereotypes? In the study whose results are shown in Table 3.1, the researchers recruited a sample of undergraduates who were ethnically diverse (Ghavami & Peplau, 2013). Participants read instructions that said,

> We are all aware of *cultural stereotypes* of social groups. These may be ideas that you learned from movies, saw in magazines. . . . For example, people often perceive models as beautiful, tall, but dumb. Note that these characteristics may or may not reflect your own personal beliefs about these groups. In the space below, list at least 10 characteristics that are part of the current cultural stereotypes of [the target group] as a group rather than a specific individual you may know. Please note that we are *not* asking for your personal beliefs, but rather those held by people in general.

TABLE 3.1 **Gender role stereotypes. Americans believe the following are characteristics of men and women.**

Women	Men
Emotional	Tall
Caring	Physically strong
Soft	Respected
Care about appearance	Intelligent
Talkative	Have high status
Small build/petite	Leaders
Submissive	Sexist
Dependent	Like sports
Motherly	Providers
Feminine	Aggressive
Manipulative	Unfaithful
Attractive	Ambitious
Sexual objects	Arrogant
Materialistic	Messy
Jealous	Fixer-uppers

Source: Data from Ghavami & Peplau (2013).

Respondents received different groups for the target group, for example, women, Asian Americans, or Black women. It turns out that, if you ask the question this way, people will give you the stereotypes. Not every participant uses the same words to describe a quality, so the research team then groups synonyms together to come up with the lists. For example, one person might say *wealthy* and another might say *rich*. Those would be clustered together.

As shown in Table 3.1, women are believed to be emotional, caring, and talkative, stereotypes that have been around for decades. The same is true of the stereotypes of men as strong, intelligent, and leaders. Gender stereotypes have changed little from the early 1980s (Haines et al., 2016).

Although these gender *stereotypes* persist in modern American culture, the evidence indicates that *attitudes* about gender roles have changed considerably over the last 30 or more years. Some data on this point are shown in Table 3.2. For example, the attitude that the man should be the achiever outside the home and the woman should tend to the home and family went from 66% in 1977 to 32% in 2012 (Smith et al., 2012).

The data seem to present a paradox. Table 3.1 shows evidence of continuing old-fashioned gender stereotypes, whereas Table 3.2 shows that gender-related attitudes have changed considerably. How can that be? The answer is that both findings are actually compatible. Americans are deeply committed to the principles of equality and justice, and when feminists posed the issue of women's rights within that framework, many people were persuaded and changed their attitudes in the equal rights direction shown in Table 3.2. Yet gender stereotypes are powerful and seem harmless, and people privately believe that women are emotional and submissive and men are intelligent and leaders. Sarah is a woman, so she is emotional and submissive, and she has every right to run for president.

Why do people stereotype others? Social psychologists have uncovered two basic goals: comprehension and self-enhancement (Kunda & Spencer, 2003). As for the *comprehension* goal, when we meet a new person, we tend to fill in a lot of assumed information about that person so that we can understand them until we have more actual information. For example, breadwinner is a key aspect of the male role. When we meet a man, we are likely to invoke that stereotype and ask an opening question such as "What kind of work do you do?" Our first question is not "Are you a househusband?" When people stereotype for comprehension purposes, the stereotypes can be positive or negative. They are just trying to understand more about the person than they actually know. Of course, they may make errors in the process. We might actually be talking to a househusband, and he is offended by our assumption that he holds a job outside the home.

TABLE 3.2   **Changes over time in gender role attitudes.**

	Percentage Agreeing	
	1977	2012
1. It is much better for everyone involved if the man is the achiever outside the home and the woman takes care of the home and family.	66%	32%
2. Most men are better suited emotionally for politics than are most women.	49%	20%

Source: Data from Smith et al. (2012).

In contrast, when we stereotype for *self-enhancement* purposes, the stereotypes tend to be negative. We make ourselves feel better by denigrating another group. For example, if we say (or think), "Teenagers are so irresponsible," by implication we, as adults, are highly responsible.

In contrast to the conscious stereotypes shown in Table 3.1, **implicit stereotypes** are learned, automatic associations between social categories (e.g., women) and other attributes (e.g., nurse but not mathematician or scientist; Rudman & Glick, 2008). These stereotypes are not necessarily conscious. The method used to measure these implicit stereotypes is the Implicit Association Test (IAT), which measures an individual's relative strength of association between different pairs of concepts (Nosek et al., 2005). The key to measuring these associations is reaction time, which is measured on a computer in milliseconds. We react quickly to two concepts that we associate strongly and more slowly to two concepts that we do not associate strongly. One of the advantages of this measure is that people can't fake their reaction times. For example, they cannot hide their socially unacceptable stereotyped ideas. (If you want to try the IAT yourself, you can do it online at www.implicit.harvard.edu.)

In one important experiment, Mahzarin Banaji and her colleagues measured the association between gender and math (Nosek et al., 2002). In the practice phase, participants placed one finger on the left key of a keypad and another finger on the right key. They were instructed to press the left key if the word they saw on the screen in front of them was in the category *math* (e.g., algebra, equation) or if it was in the category *pleasant* (e.g., peace, love). They were to press the right key for topics in the *arts* (e.g., drama, poetry) or words that were *unpleasant* (e.g., hatred). After following this pattern for many trials, the instructions changed and they had to press the left key for math words and unpleasant words, and the right key for arts and pleasant words. All of this was practice for the real task. In the first phase of it, participants pressed the left key if the words were in the *math* category or the *male* category (e.g., male, boy) and the right key if the words were in the *arts* category or the *female* category (e.g., female, girls). Then in the second phase the pairings were reversed, so participants pressed the left key for the *math* category and the *female* category and the right key for the *arts* category and the *male* category. Implicit stereotyping is indicated if people respond faster to the male and math pairing than they do to the female and math pairing, and that is exactly what participants do! That is, people have an implicit association between math and male but not female.

In a similar study, researchers demonstrated an implicit association between *science* and *male* but not *female* (Carli et al., 2016). We will return to this finding in Chapter 8, when we consider why women are underrepresented in the STEM (science, technology, engineering, and mathematics) fields.

In an ambitious study, the researchers collected data on the implicit association between male and science for people from 34 nations around the world, using an online version of the IAT (Nosek et al., 2009). Implicit stereotyping is stronger in some nations than in others. The researchers also tapped international data on the gender gap in the science knowledge of eighth graders in these countries, using an approach similar to the one used by Eagly and Wood (1999; see the "Social Role Theory" section in Chapter 2). They found that the correlation, across nations, between implicit stereotyping of science as male and the gender gap in science performance was an amazing $r = 0.60$! That means that, to the extent that people in a country stereotype boys and men as better at science, boys in that country perform better than girls do on standardized science tests. The researchers believe that implicit stereotypes and the gender gap in science performance contribute to a vicious cycle. Implicit stereotypes

Implicit stereotypes: Learned, automatic associations between social categories (e.g., female) and other attributes (e.g., nurse but not mathematician).

held by adults and youth in a country discourage girls from studying science. And then, when girls do not do well in science (because they have studied it less), that strengthens the implicit stereotypes.

Intersectionality and Gender Stereotypes

As explained in earlier chapters, one of the essential principles of feminist theory is intersectionality. Here we will examine the intersection of gender and ethnicity when it comes to gender stereotypes. An intersectional approach tells us that gender stereotypes may not be the same in different ethnic groups.

Table 3.3 shows stereotypes about women and men from different ethnic groups in the United States (Ghavami & Peplau, 2013). Consistent with an intersectionality hypothesis, the gender-ethnic stereotypes contain distinct elements that do not represent adding gender stereotypes to ethnic stereotypes, or ethnic stereotypes to gender stereotypes. For example, Black women are stereotyped as athletic, but that stereotype is not found for Middle Eastern women, Latinx women, White women, or Asian American women. Latinx men are described as arrogant, as are White men and White women, but none of the other gender-ethnic groups. Essentially, then, within an ethnic group, men and women have some stereotyped traits in common, but also some that differ. For example, both Latinx men and Latinx women are described as hardworking, but Latinx men are described as arrogant whereas Latinx women are not. White women and Asian American women are stereotyped as intelligent, but women from the other ethnic groups are not. Given this intersectional analysis, it is difficult to talk simply about gender stereotypes in the United States, because those stereotypes are so specific to particular ethnic groups. Given the dominance of Whites in American society, what we have traditionally thought of as gender stereotypes are probably stereotypes about White men and women.

Stereotype Threat

Stereotypes are more than just abstract ideas. They can really hurt. Psychologist Claude Steele discovered a phenomenon he calls stereotype threat, and it documents the kind of subtle damage that stereotypes can inflict (Steele, 1997; Steele & Aronson, 1995). **Stereotype threat** can be defined as a situation in which there is a negative stereotype about a person's group, and the person is concerned about being judged or treated negatively on the basis of that stereotype (Spencer et al., 2016).

Steele's original work concerned ethnic stereotypes—specifically, the stereotype that African Americans are intellectually inferior. In one experiment, he administered a test of verbal intelligence to Black and White college students, all of whom were highly talented Stanford students. Half of each group were told that the test was diagnostic of intelligence and half were told it was not diagnostic of intelligence. The Black students who were told that the test measured intelligence performed worse than the Black students who were told it didn't, whereas White students' performance was unaffected by the instructions they received. The effect for the Black students demonstrates stereotype threat.

Other researchers then quickly moved to test whether stereotype threat applies to gender stereotypes—in particular, the stereotype that women are bad at math (Brown & Josephs, 1999; Quinn & Spencer, 2001; Schmader & Johns, 2003; Walsh et al., 1999). In one experiment, male and female college students with equivalent math backgrounds were tested (Spencer et al., 1999). Half were told that the math test had shown gender differences in the past and half were told that the test had been shown to be gender fair—that

Stereotype threat: A situation in which there is a negative stereotype about a person's group, and the person is concerned about being judged or treated negatively on the basis of that stereotype.

TABLE 3.3   **The intersection of gender and ethnicity: Stereotypes of men and women from different ethnic groups.**

Men	Women	Men	Women
Blacks		**Middle Easterners**	
Athletic	Have an attitude	Bearded	Quiet
Dark-skinned	Loud	Dark-skinned	Religious
Loud	Big butt	Terrorists	Covered
Quick to anger	Overweight	Sexist	Oppressed
Tall	Confident	Speak English with accent	Conservative
Violent	Dark-skinned	Dirty	Dark-skinned
Rapper	Hair weaves	Rich	Submissive
Dangerous	Assertive	Muslim	Attractive
Poor	Ghetto/unrefined	Wear turban	Dependent
Unintelligent	Athletic	Religious	Muslim
Latinx		**Whites**	
Macho	Feisty	Rich	Arrogant
Poor	Curvy	Tall	Blond
Dark-skinned	Loud	Intelligent	Rich
Day laborers	Attractive	Assertive	Attractive
Promiscuous	Good cooks	Arrogant	Small build/petite
Short	Dark-skinned	Successful	Ditsy
Hard workers	Uneducated	High status	Tall
Jealous	Have many children	Blond	Materialistic
Uneducated	Hard workers	Racist	Racist
Illegal immigrants	Promiscuous	All-American	Intelligent
Asian Americans			
Intelligent	Intelligent		
Short	Quiet		
Nerdy	Short		
Quiet	Bad drivers		
Good at math	Shy		
Bad drivers	Small build/petite		
Small build	Family-oriented		
Shy	Skinny		
Speak English with accent	Studious		
Skinny	Good at math		

Source: Data from Ghavami & Peplau (2013).

men and women had performed equally on it. Among those who believed that the test was gender fair, there were no gender differences in performance, but among those who believed it showed gender differences, women underperformed compared with men. Stereotypes about women and math hurt women's performance. In another experiment by the same researchers, women performed worse on the math test even when there was no mention of gender differences. The stereotype about women and mathematics is so much a part of the culture, it did not even have to be primed by the experimenters. The stereotype is simply there for women any time they encounter difficult mathematics problems.

Meta-analyses show that the size of the stereotype threat effect on women's math performance ranges between $d = 0.17$ and $d = 0.36$ (Spencer et al., 2016). The size of the stereotype threat effect for African Americans and Latinx on intellectual tests is somewhat larger, around $d = 0.50$ (Spencer et al., 2016).

What about the *intersection of gender and ethnicity* in stereotype threat? The case of Asian American women and mathematics is particularly interesting. As women, they are stereotyped as being bad at math, but as Asian Americans they are stereotyped as being good at math. Research shows that when Asian American women's ethnic identity is primed (highlighted), they perform better on math problems, and when their gender identity is primed, they perform worse, compared with a control group that has had neither identity primed (Shih et al., 1999).

Latinx women face a different set of challenges than Asian American women, because both their gender and their ethnic group are stereotyped as weak in math. In one experiment, Latinx men and women and White men and women were randomly assigned to either a stereotype threat condition (they were told that the math test they were about to take was diagnostic of their "actual abilities and limitations") or a no-threat condition (no reference to their ability was made; Gonzales et al., 2002). They then completed a difficult math test. The results are shown in Figure 3.1. Notice that

FIGURE 3.1   **Results of a study measuring the performance of Latinx and White women and men on a difficult math test under stereotype threat and no-threat conditions.**

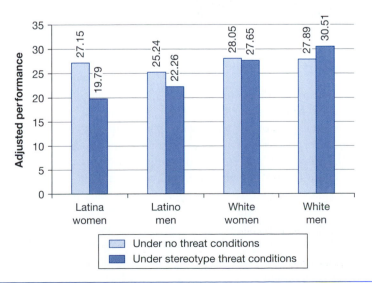

Source: Gonzales et al. (2002).

the performance of Latinx men is hurt somewhat under the stereotype threat (diagnostic) condition, but the performance of Latinx women is hurt more. Being the object of two negative stereotypes seems to hurt their performance twice as much. Notice also that stereotype threat actually helps the performance of White men, something that has been found in numerous studies and has been termed "stereotype lift" (Walton & Cohen, 2003).

What are the *psychological processes* that underlie stereotype threat effects? Two processes have been documented, and they may be in play for different individuals in different situations (Spencer et al., 2016).

1. *Underperformance due to extra pressure to succeed*: People in a stereotype threat situation are usually motivated to disconfirm the negative stereotype about their group. This leads to extra pressure to perform well, a pressure not experienced by others. This kind of pressure leads people to exert more effort, and sometimes that helps their performance (e.g., on easy tasks), but in other cases (e.g., difficult tasks) the pressure becomes highly stressful and hurts performance. The pressure can also deplete working memory capacity, which is needed for difficult intellectual tasks.

2. *Underperformance due to threats to self-integrity and belonging*: Stereotype threat can threaten people's sense of self-worth. To protect themselves, people may engage in various kinds of self-handicapping, such as setting lower goals for themselves so that they don't fail, which only makes them reach lesser goals. Stereotype threat can also reduce a person's sense of belonging, reducing their motivation and perhaps leading them to withdraw from the situation.

Can anything be done to counteract stereotype threat? Researchers have devised and tested a number of interventions designed to reduce stereotype-threat effects (Spencer et al., 2016). One intervention strategy involves guiding people to reconstrue (think differently about) a threatening situation as less threatening. For example, people may be taught to think differently about their anxiety. People can also be given coping strategies to deal with threatening situations and to maintain their self-integrity. For example, in one classroom study, a self-affirmation exercise with middle-schoolers closed the race gap in school performance by 40% (Cohen et al., 2006). These techniques need to be deployed widely in our schools.

Stereotypes About Trans Individuals

Gender stereotype research rests on the gender binary and tells us about stereotypes about women and stereotypes about men. There is little or no research on stereotypes about trans individuals, but we can glean some ideas from related research.

In one study, transgender individuals were asked whether they had had experiences of prejudice, discrimination, and stereotypes related to being transgender (Mizock & Hopwood, 2016). One stereotype is that trans individuals are gay or lesbian; that is, some people conflate sexual orientation and gender identity. Such people may not even be aware of gender diversity, and they react to a trans individual with anti-gay prejudice. In addition, gender-binary privilege and stereotypes can be highly salient for transgender individuals. For example, a trans woman has grown up enjoying male privilege but, after transitioning, loses that privilege in ways that may be quite disconcerting. As one participant in the study said,

The second they feminize their appearance, they've lost their true male privilege, but they haven't lost their voice. Women are so accustomed to being repressed, that these bold [trans] women who still retain their voice seem male to them. And that's not male [to be outspoken], it's them sticking up for themselves. (quoted in Mizock & Hopwood, 2016, p. 99)

Other research has shown that trans individuals are stereotyped as mentally ill (Reed et al., 2015), much as gays and lesbians were a few decades ago. Importantly, much of the prejudice against trans people seems to result from their violation of traditional gender role stereotypes. For example, on the Genderism and Transphobia Scale, one item is "I have behaved violently towards a woman because she was too masculine," and another is "I have teased a man because of his feminine appearance or behavior" (Hill & Willoughby, 2005). Thus cisgenderism—prejudice against people who are outside the gender binary—is deeply rooted in resentment toward those who violate gender role stereotypes.

Psychologists have begun to design interventions to reduce prejudice toward transgender people. In one case, researchers designed an intervention aimed at humanizing and perspective taking (Tompkins et al., 2015). Participants (college students) in the intervention condition viewed a video about Jazz, a transgender child, to humanize trans children for the participants. They then completed a writing assignment designed to promote perspective taking, in which they imagined that they were transgender and wrote a letter coming out to their parents as transgender. Participants in the control condition were presented with DSM criteria for gender dysphoria and heard a videotaped lecture by an expert. The intervention was successful at reducing trans prejudice. This study is a good first step along the way to developing successful interventions that could be used, for example, with all students entering college.

Meta-Analysis

At this point, studies of psychological gender differences number in the thousands. These studies are all based on the assumption of a *gender binary*—that is, that there are only two genders, female and male. Later in the chapter, we will consider how trans individuals might fit into this research in the future.

With these thousands of studies, we should have a thorough understanding of which behaviors show gender differences and which do not. Unfortunately, things are a bit more complicated than that. Often the results of different studies contradict each other. For example, some studies of gender differences in infants' activity levels find that boys are more active, whereas others find no gender difference. In such cases, what should we conclude?

Another problem is that sometimes a single study that finds a gender difference will be picked up by the media and included in textbooks, and the five other studies of the same behavior that found no gender difference will be ignored. It seems likely that this occurs particularly when a finding of gender differences confirms the stereotypes held by the scientists and the general public. Moreover, scientists and the general public are fascinated by findings of gender differences; they tend to find results indicating gender similarities to be, well, boring.

Meta-analysis is a technique that allows researchers to bring order out of this seeming chaos of sometimes contradictory studies (Lipsey & Wilson, 2001). **Meta-analysis** is a statistical method that allows the researcher to statistically combine the

Meta-analysis: A statistical technique that allows a researcher to combine the results of multiple research studies on a particular question.

results from all previous studies of the question of interest to determine what, taken together, the studies say. In conducting a meta-analysis, the researcher goes through three steps:

1. The researcher locates all previous studies on the question being investigated (e.g., gender differences in aggression). This step is typically done using computerized searches of databases such as PsycINFO or Web of Science.

2. For each study, the researcher computes a statistic that measures how big the difference between male participants and female participants was and what the direction of the difference was (male participants scoring higher or female participants scoring higher). This statistic is called d. The formula for it is

$$d = \frac{M_M - M_F}{s} ,$$

where M_M is the mean or average score for male participants, M_F is the mean score for female participants, and s is the average standard deviation of the male scores and the female scores. If you've studied statistics, you know what a standard deviation is. For those of you who haven't, the standard deviation is a measure of how much variability there is in a set of scores. For example, if the average score for people on test Q is 20 and all the scores fall between 19 and 21, then there is little variability and the standard deviation would be small. If, on the other hand, the average score for people is 20 and scores range from 0 to 40, then there is great variability and the standard deviation will be large. The d statistic, then, tells us, for a particular study, how big the difference between the male and female means was, relative to the variability in scores. If d is a positive value, then male participants scored higher; if d is negative, female participants scored higher; and if d is zero, there is no difference.

3. The researcher averages all the d values over all the studies that were located. When all studies are combined, this average d value tells what the direction of the gender difference is (whether male participants score higher or female participants score higher) and how large the difference is.

Although there is some disagreement among experts, a general guide is that a d of 0.20 is a small difference, a d of 0.50 is a moderate difference, and a d of 0.80 is a large difference (Cohen, 1969).

Numerous meta-analyses of gender differences are now available, most of them based on large numbers of studies. They are a much more reliable source than a single study. Meta-analyses, whenever available, will form the basis for the conclusions presented in this chapter and throughout this textbook.

It is also worth noting that meta-analysis can be used for synthesizing not just research on gender differences, but any research that uses a two-group design. For example, is cognitive-behavioral therapy effective, compared with a control group? How big is the effect?

Psychological Gender Differences

In this section, we will consider some of the scientific research on gender differences, focusing on aggressive behavior, impulsivity, activity, self-esteem, helping behavior, and anxiety. Discussions of other gender differences are found across the rest of the chapters in this book.

Aggressive Behavior

One of the most consistently documented psychological gender differences is in aggressive behavior, with boys and men being more aggressive than girls and women. Psychologists generally define **aggression** as behavior intended to harm another person. This gender difference holds up for many different kinds of aggression, especially physical aggression (Archer, 2004).

Aggression: Behavior intended to harm another person.

Developmentally, this gender difference appears about as early as children begin playing with each other, around the age of 2 (Alink et al., 2006; Baillargeon et al., 2007). The difference continues consistently throughout the school years. Of course, as people get older they become less aggressive, at least in the sense of physical aggression. It is rare to see adults rolling around on the floor as they punch each other, compared with the frequency with which that occurs on an elementary school playground. Less information is available on gender differences in adult aggression, but we do know that the great majority of crimes of violence are committed by men (although female crime is on the increase).

According to a meta-analysis, $d = 0.55$ for physical aggression, which is a moderate difference (Archer, 2004). For verbal aggression, $d = 0.09$, or close to no difference.

Recently there has been much publicity about "mean girls." The idea is that girls do not express their aggression physically the way boys do, but rather are mean to each other, spreading degrading rumors or excluding someone from a social group. Psychologists call this type of aggression *indirect aggression* or **relational aggression** (Crick & Grotpeter, 1995; Werner & Crick, 2004). Are girls really the mean ones, the relationally aggressive ones? Meta-analysis shows that the gender differences are not as large or as consistent as one would expect from the publicity. Girls scored higher, but the gender difference was small, whether assessed by peer ratings ($d = -0.19$, notice that the negative sign means that girls scored higher) or teacher reports ($d = -0.13$; Archer, 2004). Boys are nearly as mean as girls are.

Relational aggression: Behavior intended to hurt others by damaging their peer relationships. Also termed indirect aggression.

What causes the gender difference in aggression? Researchers debate between nature and nurture. The nature team attributes gender differences in physical aggressiveness to the greater size and muscle mass of male bodies and/or differences in the levels of the hormone testosterone. These factors will be discussed in detail in Chapter 10.

On the nurture side, a number of environmental forces might produce the observed gender difference. First, aggressiveness is a key part of the male role in our society, whereas aggressiveness is a violation of the female role. Following the logic of cognitive-developmental theory, as soon as children become aware of gender roles, girls realize that they are not supposed to be aggressive and boys know that they should be. As explained in Chapter 2, this reasoning does not work very well in explaining how gender differences develop so early, but it may be helpful in explaining gender differences among older children. Second, children imitate same-gender adults more than other-gender adults, and they see far more aggression in men than in women,

©iStockphoto.com/bowdenimages.

PHOTO 3.1
Gender differences in aggressiveness appear early.

particularly on TV and in the movies. In short, boys imitate men, who are aggressive, and girls imitate women, who are unaggressive. Third, boys receive more rewards for aggression and less punishment for it than girls do. These reinforcements and punishments might be in a physical form, such as spanking, or in a verbal form, such as comments from adults like "Boys will be boys" in response to a boy's aggression. Boys may also be rewarded in the form of status or respect from their peers for being aggressive, whereas girls receive no such reward from their peers and may even find that other girls don't want to play with them if they are aggressive. Research actually indicates that boys are punished more for aggression than girls are by both parents and teachers, thus posing a problem for this explanation. Yet psychologists believe that some kinds of punishments for aggression may actually increase a child's aggression rather than decrease it. Therefore, the punishments that boys receive may make them more aggressive.

One interesting experiment tested the first hypothesis stated above, that gender roles are a powerful force creating gender differences in aggression (Lightdale & Prentice, 1994). The researchers used the technique of deindividuation to produce a situation that removed the influences of gender roles. **Deindividuation** refers to a state in which the person has lost their individual identity; that is, the person has become anonymous. Under such conditions people feel no obligation to conform to social norms such as gender roles; deindividuation essentially places the individual in a situation free of gender roles. Half the participants were placed in an individuated condition (the opposite of deindividuation), by having them sit close to the experimenter, identify themselves by name, wear large name tags, and answer personal questions. Deindividuated participants sat far from the experimenter and were simply told to wait quietly. All participants were also told that the experiment required information from only half the participants, whose behavior would be monitored, and that the other half would remain anonymous. Next, the participants played a video game in which they first defended and then attacked by dropping bombs. The number of bombs dropped was the measure of aggressive behavior.

The results indicated that, in the individuated condition, men dropped significantly more bombs (31.1, on average) than women did (26.8, on average). In the deindividuated condition—that is, in the absence of gender roles—there were no significant gender differences. In short, the significant gender differences in aggression disappeared when the influences of gender roles were removed.

Deindividuation: A state in which a person has become anonymous and has therefore lost their individual identity—and therefore the pressure to conform to gender roles.

Impulsivity

Stereotypes hold that men are impulsive risk takers and that women are less so. Impulsivity refers to the tendency to act spontaneously and without careful thought (Cross et al., 2011). There are actually multiple aspects of impulsivity: reward sensitivity (being especially likely to do something because it will feel good right now), sensation seeking, risk taking, and impulse control (the opposite of impulsivity, i.e., being able to control one's actions).

A meta-analysis found that men did indeed score higher than women on risk taking ($d = 0.38$) and sensation seeking ($d = 0.22$). There were no gender differences in reward sensitivity or impulse control, though.

Men's greater tendency toward risk taking has negative implications for their health and life expectancy. (We will discuss this point in more detail in Chapter 16.) Yet there are also times in life when one has to take some calculated risks to achieve more—for example, taking the risk to start one's own business or taking the risk to apply to a high-status graduate program. Women may be disadvantaged in situations like this if they are less willing to take the leap.

Activity

Psychologists have debated whether gender differences in activity level exist. Certainly, if you ask the average parent or teacher, they will tell you that boys are more active, and most child psychology textbooks share this view.

A meta-analysis found that d was approximately 0.50—that is, that there is a moderate gender difference, with boys and men having the higher activity level (Eaton & Enns, 1986). Among infants, $d = 0.29$; it was 0.44 for preschoolers and 0.64 for older children and young adults. Thus a small difference is present from infancy, and the difference gets larger with age, at least among children. This meta-analysis was based on samples of children from the general population. In samples of hyperactive children, about 80% to 90% are boys (Biederman et al., 2002).

What causes this gender difference, and why does it get larger from infancy to childhood? One possibility is that the small difference in infancy is magnified by social interactions, especially when boys increasingly play actively with other boys and not with girls, something called the gender segregation effect (discussed in Chapter 7). Essentially, boys egg each other on to more and more active play. Another possibility has to do with the developmental precocity of girls. Girls are somewhat ahead of boys in development, including brain development. As children grow older, they learn to control their activity more. It might be, then, that the lower activity level of girls actually represents a greater ability to control activity because of their being somewhat more mature than boys.

Self-Esteem

Popular best sellers like Mary Pipher's (1994) *Reviving Ophelia* have spread the word that girls have major **self-esteem** problems beginning in early adolescence—and, by implication, that boys do not. Again, we have a meta-analysis available to speak to this issue (Kling et al., 1999; see also Major et al., 1999).

Averaged across all samples, the average effect size was $d = 0.21$. Male participants scored higher, on average, but the difference was small—certainly not the large gender gap that one would expect from the popular press.

Pipher and others have also argued that the pattern of gender differences changes developmentally with age. Elementary school girls may have self-esteem equal to that of boys, but the problems begin in early adolescence. To test this hypothesis, effect sizes were computed by age-group in the meta-analysis. The results showed that, for elementary school children (ages 7 to 10), $d = 0.16$; for middle school children (ages 11 to 14), $d = 0.23$; and for high schoolers, $d = 0.33$. That is, in early adolescence the gender difference is still small, and it grows larger in high school. Interestingly, for adults between the ages of 23 and 59, $d = 0.10$, and for those who are 60 and over, $d = 0.03$. In other words, the gender difference is close to zero in adulthood.

What about the intersection of gender and ethnicity? Is this gender difference found in all U.S. ethnic groups? For White samples the effect size was 0.20, whereas for Black samples it was –0.04. (For other ethnic groups, too few studies were available to compute effect sizes.) These results are a vivid illustration of the ways in which psychology has been a psychology of White people. The much-publicized gender difference in self-esteem is present for White Americans (and even then, it is small), but it is not found for Black Americans.

Self-esteem: The level of global positive regard that one has for oneself.

In sum, boys and men on average score higher on self-esteem measures, but the gender difference is small and may be true only for White Americans. The gender difference is tiny in the elementary school years and largest in the high school years, but even then it is not huge. On the other hand, it probably is large enough to be concerned about, in which case at least two of Mary Pipher's (1994) explanations ring true—that girls in the United States are subjected to a sex-saturated media environment that objectifies them and undermines their self-esteem and that they are victims of peer sexual harassment. Adolescent girls deserve a better environment.

Self-confidence: A person's belief that they can be successful at a particular task or in a particular domain such as athletics or academics.

To this point we have been talking about general self-esteem, one's global self-evaluation. We can also talk about domain-specific **self-confidence**—that is, confidence in specific areas such as athletics or academics. Another meta-analysis examined gender differences in domain-specific self-confidence (Gentile et al., 2009). The results indicate that male participants had more self-confidence in the domains of physical appearance ($d = 0.35$) and athletics ($d = 0.41$). Female participants had more self-confidence in the areas of behavioral conduct ($d = -0.17$) and morals or ethics ($d = -0.38$). At the same time, gender similarities were found in the areas of academics and social acceptance. If we consider an even more specific domain, math self-confidence, boys score higher than girls in the United States ($d = 0.26$) and in most other nations, with exceptions in a few places such as Eastern Europe (specifically, Estonia and Russia; Else-Quest et al., 2010).

These gender differences in self-confidence can be important in people's lives. People with low self-confidence avoid engaging in challenging tasks. Thus this gender difference in math self-confidence may have important effects on women's career choices, a point to be discussed further in Chapter 8.

Before leaving the topic of self-confidence, we need to consider one additional issue, namely, interpretation of the results. The objective, statistical result is that, for example, male students are more likely than female students to rate themselves at the top of their class in math ability. To use the terminology of Chapter 1, a typical interpretation of this result is that boys have more math self-confidence than girls or that girls are lacking in math self-confidence. This is a female-deficit interpretation. Would it be possible to make a different interpretation that would still be consistent with the data? An alternative interpretation is that boys' estimates are too high (rather than girls' being too low) and that boys are unrealistically overconfident. This alternative is just as reasonable an interpretation of the gender difference, but it implies a problem for boys. As it turns out, with tasks such as these it is possible to decide which interpretation is more accurate, because we can find out how students actually did on the math exam or in the course. In fact, boys and men do tend to overestimate their performance by about as much as girls and women underestimate theirs, although some studies find female participants' estimates to be accurate and male participants' to be inflated (Beyer, 1999; Cole et al., 1999). Therefore, there is some truth in each interpretation—men are probably somewhat overconfident and women somewhat underconfident.

Helping Behavior

Social psychologists have studied helping behavior extensively. Who do you think is more likely to help another person, women or men? A meta-analysis of studies of gender differences in helping behavior found that $d = 0.34$ (Eagly, 2009; Eagly & Crowley, 1986). The positive value indicates that men, on average, helped others more than women did and that the gender difference is somewhere in the small to moderate range. This finding may be somewhat surprising because helping or nurturing is an important part of the female role. In Table 3.1, caring is one of the stereotypes about women. To probe the findings more

FOCUS 3.1

WHO IS MORE NARCISSISTIC: MEN OR WOMEN?

Narcissism has been in the headlines a great deal recently, with the 2016 presidential election and with claims that millennials are a narcissistic bunch. Are there gender differences in narcissism?

Generally **narcissism** refers to a personality trait characterized by an excessive focus on oneself, along with a grandiose, exaggerated sense of one's own talents, an extreme need for admiration, and a lack of empathy for others. Who would we predict would be more narcissistic, men or women?

Using social theory (discussed in Chapter 2), we would consider which aspects of gender roles would be associated with narcissistic traits. Men are expected to be very self-confident, and arrogant is one of the male stereotypes shown in Table 3.1, so that would lead men to have an exaggerated sense of their own talents. Caring and being empathic are part of the female role, so men would be likelier to lack empathy. In general, then, the male role is more consistent with narcissistic traits than the female role is.

A meta-analysis found that men are more narcissistic, but only by a small amount, $d = 0.29$ (Grijalva et al., 2015). But it turns out that personality inventories include three facets of narcissism. For the Exploitative/Entitlement scale, $d = 0.29$, men scoring higher, and for Leadership/Authority, men also score higher, $d = 0.20$. However, for Grandiose/

Exhibitionism, $d = 0.04$, that is, there is no gender difference. There is also a newly discovered type of narcissism, vulnerable narcissism, which is characterized by low self-esteem, neuroticism, and introversion, all of which involve an excessive focus on the self. For this type of narcissism, there is also no gender difference, $d = -0.04$. Overall, then, we see gender similarities in some aspects of narcissism, but men scoring higher on the Exploitative/Entitlement facet.

The studies in the meta-analysis involved samples of the general population and a broad range of scores on personality scales. If we look at the extreme cases of diagnosable narcissistic personality disorder, men outnumber women, 7.7% to 4.8% (Stinson et al., 2008).

Why is narcissism important? A certain amount of narcissism probably helps propel people into leadership roles, which is advantageous. However, more extreme narcissism of the Exploitative/Entitlement type, where men score higher, can be disadvantageous or even disabling. The evidence indicates that people who are high on Exploitative/Entitlement are more likely to engage in antisocial behaviors at work, suffer poor adjustment to college, and experience poor relationship satisfaction (Grijalva et al., 2015). These are not outcomes that are desirable for the individual or for those who interact with them.

---

deeply, Alice Eagly and Maureen Crowley (1986) examined the kinds of situations that produced more helping by men and those that produced more helping by women. They noted that some kinds of helping are part of the male role and some are part of the female role. Helping that is heroic or chivalrous—rescuing your comrade injured in battle—falls within the male role, whereas nurturance and caretaking fall within the female role.

Consistent with these predictions from an analysis of social roles, Eagly and Crowley (1986) found that the tendency for men to help more was especially pronounced when the situation might involve danger (such as stopping to help a motorist with a flat tire). The tendency was also stronger when the helping was observed by others (rather than when the person needing help and the research participant were alone together). Helping that involves danger and that carries with it a crowd of onlookers has great potential for heroism, and that kind of helping is part of the male role.

The plot thickens, because social psychologists have spent most of their time studying precisely these kinds of helping behaviors—the ones that occur in relatively short-term encounters with strangers. They have devoted little research to the kind of caretaking and helping that is characteristic of the female role—the kind of behavior that more

Narcissism: A personality trait characterized by an excessive focus on oneself, along with a grandiose, exaggerated sense of one's own talents, an extreme need for admiration, and a lack of empathy for others.

©iStockphoto.com/bugphai &
©iStockphoto.com/Uberimages.

PHOTO 3.2
Research shows that
which gender helps more
depends on the situation
or context.

often occurs in the context of a long-term relationship, such as a mother helping her child. Therefore, the gender difference found in the meta-analysis, showing that men help more, is probably no more than an artifact of the kinds of helping that psychologists have studied and the kinds of helping that they have overlooked.

These results are consistent with a pattern: Gender differences are highly dependent on the situation or context in which they are observed (Zakriski et al., 2005).

Anxiety

Most studies show that girls and women are more fearful and anxious than boys and men, although the difference is not large. One large, cross-national study found $d = -0.38$ for self-reports of general anxiety (Löckenhoff et al., 2014). Because this study was based on self-reports, what we know is that girls and women are more willing to admit that they have anxieties and fears. It is possible that these self-reports reflect higher levels of anxiety in female respondents than in male respondents. But it is also possible that men experience the same levels of anxiety as women and that women are just more willing to admit them. Women are stereotyped as being more anxious than men (Löckenhoff et al., 2014). This stereotype would encourage women to admit their feelings and men to pretend not to have them. At this point, however, studies have not been able to resolve the issue.

The Gender Similarities Hypothesis

Our culture is dominated by the *differences model*, the belief that women and men are very different from each other. As one best-selling book title has it, *Men Are From Mars, Women Are From Venus* (Gray, 1992)—men and women are so different, it's like they are from different planets. Then there's *Boys and Girls Learn Differently! A Guide for Teachers and Parents* (Gurian, 2011), which has been read and taken seriously by thousands of parents and teachers.

Gender similarities hypothesis: The hypothesis that men and women are similar on most, but not all, psychological variables.

Yet the scientific evidence from meta-analyses leads to a very different conclusion: men and women are actually quite similar. The **gender similarities hypothesis** states that men and women are similar on most, but not all, psychological variables (Hyde, 2005a). That is, women and men are more similar than they are different.

Evidence for the gender similarities hypothesis comes from a review of 46 meta-analyses of psychological gender differences (Hyde, 2005a; for an update with the same conclusion, see Zell et al., 2015). Across those meta-analyses, 30% of the effect sizes were close to 0 ($d \leq 0.10$) and an additional 48% were small (d between 0.11 and 0.35). That is, 78% of the gender differences were small or smaller. We have seen some of these patterns of gender similarities already in this chapter. For example, self-esteem is viewed, in the culture, as showing a large gender difference, with girls and women having low self-esteem, yet a meta-analysis shows the gender difference to be small. We will continue to see other evidence of gender similarities in other chapters of this book.

The original statement of the gender similarities hypothesis did note that there are a few exceptions. One is aggressive behavior, where the gender difference is moderate in size, although not large. Another exception is some aspects of sexuality. We will consider these findings in Chapter 12.

Androgyny

Beginning in the 1970s, feminist psychologists sought to create new models of human behavior that would overcome gender stereotypes. One prominent alternative that emerged was **androgyny**, the combining of masculine and feminine characteristics in an individual (Bem, 1974). But before that, there was a history of several decades of psychologists measuring masculinity–femininity, so let's consider that first.

Androgyny: The combination of masculine and feminine psychological characteristics in an individual.

Psychologists' Traditional Views of Masculinity–Femininity

Psychologists' traditional view—beginning roughly in the 1930s—was that masculinity and femininity were at opposite ends of a single scale. We would call that a

---

FIGURE 3.2 **Progressive conceptualizations of masculinity–femininity.**

1. The unidimensional, bipolar continuum

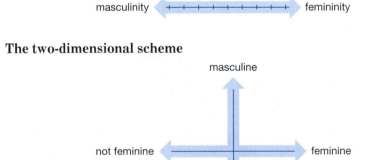

masculinity ⟷ femininity

2. The two-dimensional scheme

masculine

not feminine ⟷ feminine

not masculine

Source: Created by the authors.

unidimensional (one-dimensional) bipolar (two opposite ends) continuum. It is shown in Panel 1 of Figure 3.2.

One of these traditional scales was part of the California Psychological Inventory (Gough, 1957). It is simply a test on which you respond *true* or *false* about yourself to a series of items such as "I am somewhat afraid of the dark." Then a score is computed, over all the items, that places you at some point along the bipolar continuum.

Items were chosen for this scale in a simple way: They showed gender differences, with a much different percentage of men and women responding *true* to each one. Women are somewhat more likely to say *true* to "I am somewhat afraid of the dark," so that's why the item is on the scale. The implicit assumption, then, is that "femininity" is the quality of women that differentiates them from men.

In the 1970s, feminist psychologists raised a number of criticisms of masculinity–femininity scales (e.g., Constantinople, 1973). The basic issue is whether femininity and masculinity are really opposites of each other, so that the more feminine a person is, the less masculine they are. Is it possible to be both strongly feminine and strongly masculine? Of course it is. Enter androgyny.

The Concept of Androgyny

Most of us know people who have both masculine and feminine qualities. An example would be a woman who is both very nurturing to her children and a high-status leader on the job. The research on androgyny was designed to acknowledge and describe such people.

Androgyny means having both masculine and feminine psychological characteristics. It is derived from the Greek roots *andro*, meaning "man," and *gyn*, meaning "woman" (as in *gynecologist*). As shown in Figure 3.2, Panel 2, the concept of androgyny is based on a two-dimensional model of masculinity–femininity, in contrast to the traditional one-dimensional model. One of the dimensions is femininity, ranging from low to high, and the other is masculinity, ranging from low to high. With this conceptualization, a person could have a high score on both femininity and masculinity, and would therefore be androgynous. In Figure 3.2, those people would fall in the upper right quadrant.

Measuring Androgyny

Psychologist Sandra Bem (1974) constructed a test to measure androgyny (see also Spence & Helmreich, 1978). It consists of 60 adjectives or descriptive phrases. Respondents are asked to indicate, for each, how well it describes them on a scale from 1 (*never or almost never true*) to 7 (*always or almost always true*). Of the 60 adjectives, 20 are stereotypically feminine, 20 are stereotypically masculine, and 20 are neutral filler items—that is, not gender typed. In Table 3.4 we show only the stereotypically feminine and masculine items, because only they are relevant to computing scores. Items 1, 3, 5, and so on are masculine, and items 2, 4, 6, and so on are feminine.

How did Bem choose feminine items? She did so on the basis of characteristics that are considered socially desirable for women in our culture, and similarly for masculinity. She did this by asking a sample of people to list qualities that are socially desirable for women and qualities that are socially desirable for men.

A person who scores high (above the median) on both the masculinity and the femininity scales is classified as androgynous. A person who scores high on femininity but low on masculinity would be categorized as feminine. Someone who scores low on femininity

TABLE 3.4 Are you androgynous?

The following items make up the masculine and feminine scales of the Bem Sex Role Inventory. To find out whether you score as androgynous on it, first rate yourself on each item, on a scale from 1 (*never or almost never true*) to 7 (*always or almost always true*). Then see the instructions below the table to compute your score.

1. Self-reliant	15. Analytical	28. Warm
2. Yielding	16. Sympathetic	29. Willing to take a stand
3. Defends own beliefs	17. Has leadership abilities	30. Tender
4. Cheerful	18. Sensitive to the needs of others	31. Aggressive
5. Independent		32. Gullible
6. Shy	19. Willing to take risks	33. Acts as a leader
7. Athletic	20. Understanding	34. Childlike
8. Affectionate	21. Makes decisions easily	35. Individualistic
9. Assertive	22. Compassionate	36. Does not use harsh words
10. Flatterable	23. Self-sufficient	
11. Strong personality	24. Eager to soothe hurt feelings	37. Competitive
12. Loyal	25. Dominant	38. Loves children
13. Forceful	26. Soft-spoken	39. Ambitious
14. Feminine	27. Masculine	40. Gentle

SCORING:

(a) Add up your ratings for items 1, 3, 5, and so on (all the odd-numbered items). Divide the total by 20. That is your masculinity score.

(b) Add up your ratings for items 2, 4, 6, and so on (all the even-numbered items). Divide the total by 20. That is your femininity score.

(c) If your masculinity score is above 4.9 (the approximate median for the masculinity scale) and your femininity score is above 4.9 (the approximate femininity median), then you would be classified as androgynous according to the scale.

Source: Adapted from Bem (1974, 1977) and Hyde & Phillis (1979).

and high on masculinity would be categorized as masculine. And someone who scores low on both scales would be called undifferentiated.

Criticisms of Androgyny

Androgyny as a concept and a scale was an advance over previous masculinity–femininity scales because it acknowledged the possibility that people might be high on both masculinity and femininity. Nonetheless, criticisms can be raised. The major one is that the scale is now over 40 years old and cultural ideals of masculinity and femininity have changed a lot over those decades. We can't really know whether the same items would describe femininity and masculinity today.

Androgyny and Transgender

How does the concept of androgyny relate to the transgender spectrum and to the experience of trans or genderqueer individuals (Halberstam, 2012)? According to one view, the androgyny of the 1970s might be seen as a forerunner of the concept of genderqueer today. That is, the androgynous individual blends masculinity and femininity as the genderqueer individual does. To dig a bit deeper, though, androgyny is really about personality

Experience the Research

How Accurate Are People's Beliefs About Gender Differences?

Ask four people you know to provide you, individually, with some data. When you interview them, tell them that you want to determine how accurate people are in estimating the size of some psychological gender differences. Have them fill out the following form, explaining what they are to do. Be sure that they understand that they can give any number they want; for example, they do not have to answer just 0.20 or 0.50, but can give an answer like 0.35. Also be sure that they understand the importance of the difference between negative numbers and positive numbers. Negative numbers on this scale mean that women score higher than men, and positive numbers mean that men score higher than women.

1. Aggressive behavior among preschoolers

Girls > boys					Boys > girls	
−.80	−.50	−.20	0	.20	.50	.80
large	moderate	small	no difference	small	moderate	large

Your estimate: _____

2. Performance on math tests by elementary school children

Girls > boys					Boys > girls	
−.80	−.50	−.20	0	.20	.50	.80
large	moderate	small	no difference	small	moderate	large

Your estimate: _____

3. Approval of casual sex (i.e., two people engaging in sexual intercourse when they are only casually acquainted)

Women > men					Men > women	
−.80	−.50	−.20	0	.20	.50	.80
large	moderate	small	no difference	small	moderate	large

Your estimate: _____

How accurate were your respondents? Meta-analyses show that, among preschoolers, boys are more aggressive, $d = 0.58$. For math performance by elementary school children, $d = 0.0$; that is, there is no gender difference. For approval of two people engaging in sexual intercourse when they are only casually acquainted, $d = 0.45$; men are more approving (see Chapter 12).

traits and behaviors (independent, forceful, and so on), whereas genderqueer and transgender are about *identity* (I identify as a man, or I identify as a woman, or I identify as neither or both). Most people who score as androgynous on the Bem scale have definite cisgender identities. At that point, the link between androgyny and genderqueer breaks down.

CHAPTER SUMMARY

Gender stereotypes are a set of shared cultural beliefs about the characteristics of men and women. People stereotype for two reasons: comprehension and self-enhancement. Implicit gender stereotypes are learned automatic associations between a gender category (e.g., female) and other attributes (e.g., mathematics). An intersectional approach considering the intersection of gender and ethnicity finds that gender stereotypes vary across U.S. ethnic groups.

Stereotype threat occurs in a situation in which there is a negative stereotype about a person's group and the person is concerned about being judged or treated negatively because of the stereotype. Stereotype threat can hurt women's math performance and can doubly hurt Latinx women's math performance.

Little research is available on stereotypes about trans individuals, yet it is clear that there is prejudice against them. Psychologists have begun to design interventions to reduce anti-trans prejudice.

Meta-analysis is a statistical method for synthesizing the results of numerous studies on a particular question (e.g., gender differences in aggressive behavior). The effect size, d, measures how large a gender difference is. A d value of 0.20 is small, 0.50 is moderate, and 0.80 is large.

Gender differences are found in aggressive behavior, with boys and men being more aggressive; $d = 0.55$ for physical aggression. A deindividuation experiment showed that gender differences in aggression can be erased, though, if the force of gender roles is removed.

In regard to impulsivity, boys and men are higher in risk taking, $d = 0.38$. Boys and men also are higher in activity level, and the gender difference grows larger with age, from $d = 0.29$ in infancy to $d = 0.64$ in older children and young adults. Boys also account for 90% of hyperactive children.

Despite stereotypes that women are the ones with low self-esteem, $d = 0.21$, meaning that men have higher self-esteem but the difference is small. From an intersectional perspective, the gender difference is found for U.S. White samples, but not Black samples.

Research on gender differences in helping behavior provides evidence of the ways in which gender differences depend on the situation and context. Men help more in situations that involve danger, whereas women help more in situations that involve nurturing in the context of a long-term relationship.

Self-report studies find that women and girls are more anxious than men and boys are by a small to moderate amount.

The gender similarities hypothesis states that men and women are similar on most, but not all, psychological variables. Across 46 meta-analyses of gender differences, 78% of the effect sizes were small or very close to zero.

Androgyny refers to a combination of masculine and feminine characteristics in an individual. It is measured using a two-dimensional scale, with one dimension measuring femininity and the other measuring masculinity. In considering the relationship between being androgynous and being genderqueer, androgyny refers to personality characteristics and behaviors, whereas genderqueer refers to identity.

SUGGESTIONS FOR FURTHER READING

Hyde, Janet S. (2005). The gender similarities hypothesis. *American Psychologist, 60,* 581–592. This article represents the original statement of the gender similarities hypothesis and is accessible reading for college students.

Tompkins, Tanya L., Shields, Chloe N., Hillman, Kimberly M., & White, Kadi. (2015). Reducing stigma toward the transgender community: An evaluation of a humanizing and perspective-taking intervention. *Psychology of Sexual Orientation and Gender Diversity, 2,* 34–42. This article reports one of the first interventions designed to reduce anti-trans prejudice (cisgenderism). Because it is an early study, some aspects of it could be improved. How would you improve it?

The Intersection of Gender and Ethnicity

On January 21, 2017, 4.2 million people gathered for the Women's March on Washington and over 600 other "sister marches" throughout the United States. Hundreds of thousands more marched in countries across all seven continents. The Women's Marches were a response to the 2016 U.S. presidential election: The first female major party candidate for president, Hillary Rodham Clinton, won the popular vote, but a man widely criticized as sexist and racist, Donald J. Trump, won the required 270 electoral college delegates. The aims of the Women's Marches were explicitly feminist, yet not intially intersectional; at first, organizers did not fully consider the intersection of gender and ethnicity. When the perspectives of women of color and women from other intersectional locations (e.g., trans and queer persons) were incorporated into the platform, the marches became a powerful expression of their shared purpose and desire for gender equality.

At the intersection of gender and ethnicity, it is easy to see how people of diverse gender and ethnic groups may have very different experiences and yet have much in common. White women and women of color both encounter sexism. For White women, that sexism may be buffered by White privilege. For women of color, the combination of racism and sexism may result in double jeopardy. Meanwhile, for trans persons of color, sexism and cisgenderism may interact with racism. For example, trans people of color are disproportionately the target of hate violence (Waters et al., 2016).

When we study people of diverse racial and ethnic origins in the United States, it quickly becomes apparent that the different and complex social forces acting on them may result in diverse patterns of experiences. Among these forces are higher rates of poverty, discrimination, variations in family structures, identification with ethnic liberation movements, and evaluation of appearance by White standards of beauty.

Yet, before we dig into those diverse patterns of experiences, we must confront a serious problem in our field: Much of the scholarship on "the psychology of women" has been a psychology of White, middle-class, American cisgender women. Although many researchers have made great progress on this front, much work remains. Psychology has an important role to play in describing, explaining, and optimizing the experiences of all people, especially members of marginalized groups.

In this chapter we focus primarily on women and trans people in four major U.S. ethnic groups: African Americans, Latinx, Asian Americans, and American Indians. The purpose of the chapter is to provide important background information about the cultures and heritages of these ethnic groups as well as an overview of gender roles in these cultures. This background and overview will provide the context for more specific discussions of research on women and trans people of color that occur in other chapters throughout the book.

Recurring Themes

Two key themes recur throughout this chapter. The first theme, which stems from intersectionality, is of similarities and differences (Cole, 2009). That is, as the intersectional perspective suggests, women of diverse ethnic groups will be similar in some ways and different in others because both gender and ethnicity are influential. They share some common experiences (like objectification), despite having other unique experiences (such as different media representations and stereotypes). We will see that there are some profound differences, some resulting from differences in culture in the land of origin, others resulting from the greater poverty and discrimination experienced by members of some ethnic groups. Thus, the experience of their gender depends, in part, on their ethnicity.

The second recurring theme in this chapter is simultaneous oppression and strength. Women of color have a heritage of oppression, including slavery for African American women and internment in U.S. prison camps during World War II for Japanese American women. Current oppression, in the forms of racism, sexism, and **gendered racism**, persists. And it remains dangerous for many trans people of color to be open about their identities.

Gendered racism: A form of oppression and bias based simultaneously on both gender and race/ethnicity.

Yet, in the midst of this oppression, it would be a mistake to regard these individuals merely as victims. Instead, one sees enormous strength and resilience in them and in their lives. For example, research finds that trans people of color, despite experiencing oppression based on their race/ethnicity and gender identity and nonconformity, demonstrate tremendous resilience (Singh, 2013; Singh & McKleroy, 2011). Factors such as feeling pride in one's identity, recognizing oppression, and developing strong relationships within their families and communities promote resilience in the face of oppression. Thus, strength and resilience in the face of oppression is another continuing theme.

Ethnic Group Labels

Before we proceed, we need a brief discussion of terminology. The term **Hispanic** refers to all people with some Spanish heritage or a historical link to Spain (including those from countries once colonized by Spain), such as people from Puerto Rico, Cuba, Mexico, and other Caribbean, Central American, and South American countries or cultures. The label was introduced by the U.S. government in the 1970 census. **Latinos** refers to Latin Americans, including Brazilians (who would not be classified as Hispanic because they were colonized by Portugal, not Spain). Whereas **Latina** refers to female Latin Americans, the term Latino refers both to all Latinos *and* to male Latin Americans. Thus, the term Latino is an example of the familiar problem of masculine generics and the male as normative in language (discussed in Chapter 5).

PHOTO 4.1
Trans women of color, such as Janet Mock, demonstrate tremendous resilience in the face of multiple forms of discrimination.

In recent years, efforts to avoid the male-as-normative problem and be more inclusive of gender diversity have led to adoption of terms such as *Latin@*, which is visually inclusive of both the masculine and feminine forms. Similarly, **Latinx** (pronounced La-TEEN-ex), which is not marked by gender, has become increasingly popular (though not without controversy). More than half of Americans who would be classified as Hispanic on the U.S. Census prefer labels that reference their country of origin, such as *Dominican* or *Cuban* (Taylor et al., 2012). While *Latina/o* is an umbrella term that includes these diverse ethnic subgroups, it excludes individuals outside the gender binary. Therefore, we will use Latinx, an umbrella term that is more inclusive of gender diversity. We also use the term Hispanic when appropriate.

For Americans of African origin, language has steadily evolved. *Negro* was the respectful term prior to the 1960s. Then, with the emergence of the Black Power movement, activists urged the use of the term *Black* to connote pride in the very qualities that were the basis of discrimination, promoting slogans such as "Black Is Beautiful." In the late 1980s, as ties to Africa and pride in one's heritage were increasingly emphasized, we saw a shift to the term **African American**. The relative merit of the terms *Black* and *African American* has been debated (Swarns, 2004), so we will use both.

Similarly, there is controversy about the terms **American Indian** and **Native American**. Over half of U.S. Census respondents who identified as American Indian said they preferred *American Indian or Alaskan Native* to *Native American* (Tucker et al., 1995), so we will use American Indian here. While some argue that the term *Indian* reflects a geographical miscalculation, others contend that *Native American* excludes indigenous peoples (i.e., the original or native people of a region) from other countries in North and South America. In Canada, the indigenous peoples include the *First Nations, Métis,* and *Inuit* peoples.

For Americans of Asian origin, **Asian Americans** is the preferred term, replacing various slang or older terms that are now considered disrespectful (e.g., *Orientals*). People from the Indian subcontinent are usually considered Asian American as well. Often, people of Asian heritage are grouped with people of Pacific Islander heritage (e.g., Native Hawaiians and those from the Philippines, Guam, and Fiji) as *Asian and Pacific Islander* (or *API*). We'll generally use Asian American with the understanding that it includes Pacific Islanders.

Hispanic: People of Spanish descent, whether from Mexico, Puerto Rico, or elsewhere.

Latinos: Latin American people; also refers specifically to Latin American men.

Latina: A Latin American girl or woman.

Latinx: A Latin American person, unmarked by gender.

African Americans: Americans of African descent.

American Indians: The indigenous peoples of North America. Also called **Native Americans**.

Asian Americans: Americans of Asian descent.

The terms *White* and *Caucasian* are sometimes used interchangeably to refer to light-skinned people. These terms, however, are problematic. For example, *Caucasian* comes from the biological conceptualization of race (specifically the Caucasoid race), but also refers to people native to the Caucasus region between Europe and Asia. Also, many Hispanic Americans and people of Middle Eastern descent are light-skinned and might therefore be labeled as White, yet such people often do not experience life in the United States as White people. Moreover, many people exclude anyone who isn't of European origin when they speak of White people. An alternative that has been proposed for White is **European American** (or *Euro-American*). It has the advantage of being parallel to other terms, such as Asian American and African American, and places the emphasis on the group's cultural heritage rather than on skin color. Yet, in some situations, skin color is precisely the issue, as when people light in skin color are perceived more positively and may experience White privilege.

Adding another layer of complexity, many Americans are *biracial* or *multiracial*. About 3% of Americans identify as being from two or more racial groups (U.S. Census Bureau, 2015). For example, singer Alicia Keys's father is Black and her mother is White. Actress, producer, and author Rashida Jones's father (the producer Quincy Jones) is Black and her mother (the actress Peggy Lipton) is of Ashkenazi Jewish heritage. These women's appearances may not be good guides to their ethnic heritage. The experiences of multiracial people have become a focus of psychological research in recent years (Charmaraman et al., 2014; Landor & Halpern, 2016).

An Ethnic/Cultural Critique of Psychological Research

In Chapter 1 we discussed possible sources of gender bias in psychological research. Here we provide a parallel ethnic/cultural critique and discuss possible sources of race bias in psychological research (Jones, 2010; Landrine et al., 1995; Yoder & Kahn, 1993). There are several that warrant discussion.

The first issue has to do with the concept of **race**. Race—as it has been used in psychology over the last 100 years—is problematic (Betancourt & Lopez, 1993; Helms et al., 2005; Smedley & Smedley, 2005). Originally devised by White colonists, race was long

European American: White Americans of European descent; an alternative to the term Whites. Also, Euro-Americans.

Race: A socially constructed system of human classification, once considered a biological concept referring to discrete and exclusive groups of people with common physical features.

PHOTO 4.2
The experiences of multiracial people have become a focus of psychological research in recent years. Here, two multiracial women, actress and author Rashida Jones and singer Alicia Keys.

considered a biological concept that referred to distinct and exclusive groups of people, each with a common set of physical features, such as skin color, hair texture and color, and so on (Smedley & Smedley, 2005). One of the problems with the concept of race is the assumption that racial groups are distinct and exclusive; in other words, that races are "pure" and that people have mated exclusively with other members of their race and not with members of other races. Yet people have long mated outside of their racial groups, which means the groups cannot possibly be distinct or exclusive. For example, in the case of a woman in the United States with very dark skin, 50% of her ancestors may be of African heritage and 50% of European heritage. The existence of people like her renders race as a biological concept useless.

Nonetheless, this woman may have grown up identifying as Black, may have been socialized within the culture of a Black community, and may be perceived and treated by others as Black. Today, we understand that race is socially constructed and not rooted in biology. Thus, terms like *ethnicity* and *culture*, which emphasize shared traits, are generally preferable to race. Shared traits are learned and transmitted socially, not rooted in biology. The term **ethnic group** refers to a group that shares a common culture, language, geographical origin, and so on. Ethnic groups are flexible and often self-defined.

Ethnic group: A group of people who share a common culture and language.

Another problem with race as a biological concept is that it promotes essentialism and denies the contextual factors that oppress people of color. That is, racial group differences in, say, educational achievement are considered an outcome of innate, biologically based differences in intelligence between racial groups, rather than an outcome of systemic racism. In turn, racism is perpetuated. If this pattern sounds familiar, it's because a similar form of essentialism has long been used to perpetuate the oppression of women.

Second, just as men have been the norm in psychological research, so have European Americans been the norm (Jones, 2010). As one critic put it, "Even the rat was White" (Guthrie, 1976). Basing studies exclusively on samples of White college students or other samples of European Americans has been considered perfectly acceptable methodology. In part, this is just bad science. It involves making an unjustified inference from an all-White sample to all people. This is the error of overgeneralization (see Chapter 1). Moreover, the experiences of people of color are then marginalized and made invisible. The consequence is that Whites represent "people," and everyone else becomes "subcultures" (Landrine et al., 1995). Similar criticisms have been made about researchers' overreliance on samples from Western, industrialized, educated, and democratic countries, thereby ignoring a huge proportion of the world's people (Henrich et al., 2010). The point is, if psychology is to be a science of all people, then the field needs to study people of diverse origins.

Third, psychological research has ignored the different meanings that may be attached to different words, gestures, and so on by people from different ethnic groups (Corral & Landrine, 2010). We learn the meanings of various words from the culture in which we grow up. Therefore, two different ethnic groups (for example, African Americans and European Americans) may have different understandings of the meanings of words even though both groups speak the same language (English). This language issue quickly becomes a radical critique of methods in psychological research, because it means that standardized tests, many of which were normed on White samples, may include words that are defined differently by people from other ethnic groups. As a result, the tests might be measuring different things across different ethnic groups.

To demonstrate this problem, a group of researchers administered the Bem Sex Role Inventory (BSRI), which measures androgyny (see Chapter 3), to 71 White women and 67 women of color (Landrine et al., 1995). The women first rated themselves on each adjective and then chose, from among several choices, the phrase that best defined that term for them. Overall, there were no differences between the European American women and the women of color in their average scores on the BSRI—that is, there were ethnic group similarities. Yet there were major differences between the groups in how White women and women of color defined the adjectives on the BSRI. For example, for the term *passive*, White women most frequently chose the definition "am laid-back/easy-going," whereas women of color most frequently chose "don't say what I really think." That is, these adjectives meant significantly different things to these two groups of women. Such findings imply that we need to go back to the very beginning with many psychological tests to determine how people from various ethnic groups understand the terms used in the tests.

A fourth criticism has to do with the possibility of observer effects (discussed in Chapter 1) and, namely, race bias in observations. In thinking about biased observations, it seems likely that there would be in-group favoritism, that is, that observers would give higher or more positive ratings to members of their own group. In one study, Black, White, and Latinx undergraduates rated videos of mother-child interactions (Harvey et al., 2009). The mother-child pairs were themselves either Black, White, or Latinx. For the most part, observers of different ethnicities rated the mother-child interactions similarly. However, Black and White raters differed in their ratings of Black and White children's defiance. Members of each group rated children of their own group more positively. Overall, then, there were effects depending on the ethnicity of both the observer and the children, and they showed in-group favoritism. If psychological researchers are predominantly White, what are the implications for research on people of color?

A fifth criticism has to do with possible bias in interpretation of results. If European Americans are the norm, then the behaviors and experiences of people of color are interpreted as being deficient—much as we have seen in examples of female deficit models (Bryant-Davis & Comas-Díaz, 2016). Just as the latter bias is often called androcentrism, so the former bias can be called **ethnocentrism** or, more specifically, **Eurocentrism**. As an example of such bias, viewed through the eyes of White researchers, the African American family has generally been described as deficient.

As we review some of the psychological research on the intersection of gender and ethnicity, then, we must be conscious of how both androcentrism and Eurocentrism have permeated much of the traditional research. While progress has been made on this front, we continue to need more research that is both gender fair and race/ethnicity fair.

Ethnocentrism: The tendency to regard one's own ethnic group as superior to others and to believe that its customs and way of life are the standards by which other cultures should be judged.

Eurocentrism: The tendency to view the world from a European American point of view and to evaluate other ethnic groups in reference to European Americans.

Guidelines for Research With People of Color

In response to the issues raised by the ethnic/cultural critique of psychological research, psychological researchers (who are also people of color) have now proposed guidelines for research with people of color (American Psychological Association, 2003; Corral & Landrine, 2010; McDonald, 2000; Myers et al., 2000; Santos de Barona & Barona, 2000; Sue & Sue, 2000). Fundamental to each of these guidelines is the assumption that conducting research with people of a specific ethnic group is valuable:

1. *Collaboration*: Are researchers from the ethnic group under study included as collaborators? As outsiders, all-White teams of researchers may get it wrong.

2. *Theory*: Is the theory that is the basis for the research appropriate for this ethnic group? If it is inappropriate, it should be revised or a new theory should be formulated.

©iStockphoto.com/Yue_

PHOTO 4.3

When conducting research with people of color, it is important to include researchers from the ethnic group under study as collaborators.

3. *Measurement*: Are the psychological measures being used reliable and valid in this ethnic group? If a measure does not meet standards, it should be revised or a new measure should be devised.

The measurement issue is quite complex. Scales and the constructs they are designed to measure should demonstrate equivalence. Experts distinguish between conceptual equivalence and translational equivalence (Sue & Sue, 2000). **Conceptual equivalence** refers to the consistency of psychological constructs across different cultures. It is important that a concept developed by, say, a European American psychologist actually exists and has the same meaning in whatever other cultures are being studied. For example, some cultures have no concept of "homosexuality" (Herdt, 1998, 2006). And in other cultures, behaviors considered to be homosexual differ considerably from what most European Americans would assume. Among Mexicans, for instance, if two men engage in anal intercourse, the inserting partner is not considered gay because his behavior is like the man's in heterosexual intercourse. The man who takes the receptive role is the only one who is considered gay (Magaña & Carrier, 1991). Asking about sexual orientation in these cultures either may not compute or may lead the respondent to answer with a very different idea in mind than the researcher intended.

Conceptual equivalence: In multicultural research, the construct measured by a scale has the same meaning in all cultures being studied.

Translational equivalence refers to consistency of meaning between languages. For example, a scale originally written in English but then translated into Spanish needs to have the same meaning in both languages. The technique used to check for translational equivalence involves both translation and back-translation. That is, the scale would be translated from English to Spanish by a fluently bilingual person, and then translated from Spanish back to English by a second fluently bilingual person. If the back-translated version matched the original, that would be evidence for translational equivalence.

Translational equivalence: In multicultural research, whether a scale written in one language and translated into another has the same meaning in both languages.

FOCUS 4.1

RACIAL MICROAGGRESSIONS

A distinguished Asian American psychologist was traveling with an African American colleague on a small regional jet with 1 + 2 seating. When they boarded the uncrowded plane, the (White) flight attendant told them that they could sit wherever they wished, so they sat across the aisle from each other toward the front. Later, three White men in suits boarded the plane and sat in the row in front of them. Before takeoff, the flight attendant scanned the plane and asked the Asian American and African American men to move to the back of the plane to distribute weight evenly.

The two psychologists did as they were told, but they felt resentful and angry. Why were they the ones who had to move to the back of the bus (plane)? Finally, the Asian American spoke to the flight attendant and said, "Did you know that you asked two passengers of color to step to the rear of the 'bus'?" Her response: "Well, I have never been accused of that! How dare you? I don't see color! I only asked you to move to balance the plane." Needless to say, the flight attendant's response did little to appease the two psychologists.

This incident is an example of what Derald Wing Sue calls a **racial microaggression** (Sue, 2010; Sue et al., 2007). Racial microaggressions are subtle insults directed at people of color that may be done consciously or nonconsciously. Just like modern sexism, there is modern racism; microaggressions are an expression of modern racism in the United States today. Part of the power of these microaggressions is that they are often invisible to the perpetrator, as they were to the White flight attendant.

Racial microaggressions can take different forms. They may be *microinvalidations*, such as being told that all members of your racial/ethnic group look alike. Or they may be *microinsults*, such as being teased for being different from White people. *Microassaults* tend to be more explicit, such as name-calling. Each of these examples, on their own, may seem insignificant to many White people. But research indicates that these kinds of racial microaggressions happen frequently (e.g., Ong et al., 2013), raising concerns about the cumulative effects of being "othered" and treated differently because of one's racial/ethnic heritage.

Racial microaggressions create psychological dilemmas both for the White perpetrator and for the person of color. According to Sue's analysis, there are four principal dilemmas:

Dilemma 1: Clash of Racial Realities. The psychologists of color and the White flight attendant had different perceptions of the reality of what happened on the plane. The psychologists believed that they had been subjected to subtle racial discrimination. The White flight attendant believed that she was an unbiased person and that race had nothing to do with her behavior. Both sides were convinced of the reality of their own views, but they were in opposition to each other. Data indicate that most White people believe they do not engage in racist behavior, whereas the majority of African Americans report experiencing racial discrimination in the past year. How is that possible? Whose perception of reality is right? And, perhaps more importantly, what kind of psychological toll does it take on the person of color when they feel discriminated against and their perceptions are not believed by others?

Dilemma 2: The Invisibility of Unintentional Expressions of Bias. To White people who believe they aren't biased, their own biased behaviors are invisible. How, then, can the person of color prove that a racial microaggression occurred? White people's claims that they are "color-blind" serve only to invalidate the experiences of people of color.

Dilemma 3: Perceived Minimal Harm of Racial Microaggressions. Microaggressions are typically so subtle that it is difficult to convince others that they do serious harm. In the case of the plane passengers, what difference did it make if they rode at the back of the plane? They still got to their destination safely and at the same time. But what if these microaggressions happen every day for years and years? Research evidence indicates that being the object of racial microaggressions can result in serious psychological distress, sometimes for a long period of time, and such distress can have a negative impact on health (Ong et al., 2013).

Dilemma 4: The Catch-22 of Responding to Microaggressions. One of the problems with microaggressions is that the person of color loses whether they respond or not. In the case with the flight attendant, the Asian American psychologist spoke up and was rewarded with an antagonistic response from the flight attendant. If, instead, he had done nothing, he would have stewed and felt angry for the rest of the flight and perhaps long afterward. The experience of a microaggression is distressing, whether one speaks up or tries to ignore it.

Can we use an intersectional approach and see how racial microaggressions may also be gendered? Researchers have developed the Gendered Racial Microaggressions Scale to measure the frequency and stress of gendered racial microaggressions experienced by Black women (Lewis & Neville, 2015). The scale measures nonverbal, verbal, and behavioral racial and gender microaggressions. Some of the items include "imitated the way they think Black women speak," "I have felt unheard," and "Perceived to be an 'angry Black woman.'" Participants respond to these items regarding how often they happened (from 0 [never] to 5 [once a week or more]) and how stressful they are (from 0 [not at all stressful] to 5 [extremely stressful]). Black women's frequency and stress of these gendered racial microaggressions is linked to their experience of psychological distress (Lewis & Neville, 2015).

Similarly, trans and queer people of color also experience such intersectional microaggressions. Research indicates that racist microaggressions that are experienced within LGBT communities and in dating and close relationships are common at this intersectional location, for example (Balsam et al., 2011).

4. *Subcultural variations*: Be aware of subcultural variations. For example, while many Asian American groups have common or shared experiences, they also have some important differences. Thus, we should be attentive to differences between, say, Chinese Americans and Japanese Americans.

5. *Cultural heritage*: Do the researchers understand the cultural heritage of the group being studied, including the values of the culture of origin (e.g., Japan for Japanese Americans) and the history of that ethnic group in the United States? Researchers need to be culturally competent.

6. *Deficit interpretations*: Do not assume that differences between two ethnic groups reflect a deficit within one of those groups. In particular, differences between European Americans and people of color do not imply deficits among people of color.

7. *Race/ethnicity versus social class*: In many research designs, race and social class are confounded, largely because many racial/ethnic groups in the United States are overrepresented among lower income people. When racial/ethnic differences are found in research, it is often unclear (and perhaps impossible to tell) whether such differences are due to race or social class (or both). Researchers should remove this confound from their research designs or at least be very cautious in interpretations of findings of any ethnic group differences.

Racial microaggressions: Subtle insults directed at people of color, consciously or nonconsciously.

Cultural Heritages of People of Color in the United States

Before we can consider contemporary gender roles and issues for people of color, we must first understand the cultural and historical heritage of these groups. This heritage includes the cultures in the lands of origin (Africa, Asia, Latin America), the impact of the process of both forced and voluntary migration to the United States, and the impact of the dominant European American culture of the United States.

The Cultural Heritage of Asian American Persons

Asian Americans make up nearly 6% of the U.S. population (U.S. Census Bureau, 2015). Overall, Asian Americans come from 40 distinct ethnic groups that speak 40 languages and are from more than 20 countries (Chan, 2003). The largest Asian ethnic groups in the United States are Chinese (22%), Indian (20%), Filipino (18%), Vietnamese (11%), Korean (10%), and Japanese (5%; U.S. Census Bureau, 2010a).

People from these different ethnic groups arrived in the United States for different reasons and at different points in history. For example, Chinese people—almost all of them men—were recruited first in the 1840s to come to America as laborers in the West and later in the 1860s to work on the transcontinental railroad (for excellent summaries of the cultural heritage of Asian Americans, see Chan, 2003; Root, 1995). In response to growing racist sentiment against the Chinese, there was a shift toward recruiting Japanese and Korean immigrants, and then Filipinos. An immigration control law passed in 1924 virtually ended the immigration of Asian Americans until the act was revoked in 1965. Then, during the Vietnam War era of the late 1960s and 1970s, there was a mass exodus of refugees from war-torn Southeast Asia to the United States.

Across these diverse groups, research indicates that Asian Americans tend to share five core values (Kim et al., 2005):

1. *Collectivism*: Others' needs, especially those of the family, should be considered before one's own needs.

2. *Conformity to norms*: Individuals should conform to the expectations of their family and society.

3. *Emotional control*: Emotions should be controlled and not openly expressed.

4. *Family recognition through achievement*: One's educational success brings honor to the family, and one's educational failure brings shame.

5. *Humility*: One should be humble and never boastful.

For Asian Americans, the family is a great source of emotional nurturance and support. For them, the family includes not only the nuclear family but ancestors and the family of the future as well. One has an obligation to the family, and the needs of the family take precedence over the needs of the individual. Maintaining harmonious relations with others, especially one's family, is important. Shame and the threat of loss of face, which can apply both to the individual and to their family, are powerful forces shaping good behavior. Often what may appear to be passivity in Asian American persons actually reflects conscientious efforts to maintain dignity and harmony.

Asian American women often marry individuals from different ethnic groups, having a high interracial marriage rate relative to Asian American men and to women of other ethnic groups (Jacobs & Labov, 2002; Wang, 2015). This pattern began when White and African American U.S. servicemen married Asian women in World War II, the Korean War, and the Vietnam War. Today that pattern continues: 37% of the Asian American women who were married in 2013 wed someone of a different racial/ethnic group (Wang, 2015).

There are numerous examples of racism directed against Asian American groups. Perhaps the most flagrant was the internment of Japanese Americans during World War II. Over 100,000 Japanese Americans (most of whom were American citizens) had their property confiscated and were forcibly relocated and incarcerated in prison camps in the United States.

Subcultural Variations

Although Asian Americans share some similarities in culture, great variations also exist. One Asian American woman is a Chinese American who is a physician and a fourth-generation descendant of a man brought to work on the transcontinental railroad. Another is a woman who dramatically escaped from Vietnam in a leaky boat in 1975 and lived in poverty as she adapted to a new language and host culture. There are substantial *subcultural variations* among Asian American women.

Research on these diverse cultures is increasingly found in mainstream psychology journals. One example is research on Khmer refugee women (e.g., Marshall et al., 2005; Thompson, 1991). The Khmer are an ethnic group from Cambodia in Southeast Asia. From 1975 to 1979, more than 1.5 million Cambodians were killed by the genocidal regime known as the Khmer Rouge. Many Khmer people fled to the United States around that period. Today, more than 275,000 Cambodian Americans (most of whom are Khmer) live in the United States. Researchers have studied Khmer refugee women, beginning with understanding their roles in Cambodia before the war, the culture in which these women had grown up and been socialized.

Khmer refugee women have experienced many forms of war-related and refugee-related trauma, including rape, abduction, and torture. The ethics of feminist research posed a dilemma for the researchers interviewing the refugee women. While researchers wanted to learn more about the traumatic experiences, it seemed that questioning the women about those topics reactivated traumatic memories and caused further pain. The researchers tried to achieve a balance between the goals of giving voice to these women's experiences and not traumatizing the women further (Thompson, 1991).

Among Cambodians who lived during the Khmer Rouge regime, prevalence rates of posttraumatic stress disorder (PTSD; see Chapter 14) are high (Sonis et al., 2009). In the United States, researchers estimate that up to 62% of Khmer refugees have PTSD (Marshall et al., 2005). In addition, most experienced near-death due to starvation and had a family member murdered by the Khmer Rouge (Marshall et al., 2005).

Alain Nogues/Sygma/Getty Images.

PHOTO 4.4
Khmer refugee women show high rates of posttraumatic stress disorder.

Today, many of those people who survived the Khmer Rouge regime are parents. Researchers have begun to study the intergenerational transmission of trauma to the children of Khmer women (e.g., Field, Myong, et al., 2013; Field, Om, et al., 2011). For example, one study with Khmer refugee women living in California found that mothers' PTSD symptoms were linked to their children's experiences of anxiety and depression. The evidence suggested that PTSD shaped the mothers' parenting, which then shaped their children's anxiety and depression symptoms. While humans are very resilient, it can take a great deal of support and time—perhaps even generations—to overcome severe trauma.

The Cultural Heritage of Latinx Persons

According to the U.S. Census Bureau (2015), nearly 18% of the population in the United States identifies as Hispanic. Of those living on the mainland, their backgrounds are as follows: 63% Mexican, 9% Puerto Rican, 4% Cuban, 3% Dominican, and 13% from other Central and South American countries (U.S. Census Bureau, 2010a). Some Latinx identify as White and some identify as Black, and many identify as neither. Nonetheless, most have both European and indigenous ancestors and therefore may identify as *mestizo* (de las Fuentes et al., 2003).

In understanding Latinx culture, two factors are especially significant: bilingualism and the importance of the family. *Bilingualism*, or knowing two languages, is important because Latinx children often grow up with two languages and thus two cultures. Often, Spanish is the language of home and family, and English the language of school and job. Latinx immigrants may know no English at first, and this language barrier is a problem in finding employment and in other areas of daily life.

Familismo: In Latinx culture, a sense of obligation and connectedness with both one's immediate and extended family.

Latinx daily life is focused on the family, demonstrating *familismo*. **Familismo** is defined as a sense of obligation to and connectedness with both one's immediate and extended family (Hernández et al., 2010). Thus, traditional Latinas tend to place a high value on family loyalty and on warm, mutually supportive relationships. Family solidarity and ties to the extended family are vital (de las Fuentes et al., 2003). As a result, a young Latina is likely to be "mothered" not only by her own mother, but by her aunts or grandmothers as well. In many ways, familismo can seem at odds with dominant U.S. culture, which places a high value on individualism. And for employed Latinas, this emphasis on family can be especially stressful, as they are expected to be the preservers of family and culture and must juggle multiple roles to do so.

As with Asian American women, the process of migration is also critical in understanding the background of Latinx women. While the majority of Latinx were born in the United States, approximately 35% are foreign born (U.S. Census Bureau, 2016b). These differences in migration contribute to diversity in the experiences and needs of Latinx.

The Cultural Heritage of American Indian Persons

American Indians and Alaska Natives make up 1.2% of the population of the United States (U.S. Census Bureau, 2015). Just as we have recognized subcultural variations for people of other ethnic groups, we must do the same for American Indians, this time recognizing tribal variations. American Indians come from 550 different federally recognized tribes, as well as other tribes, and 220 Alaska native villages (Trimble, 2003). Indian societies were invaded by European Americans, so many current Indian practices resemble European American culture as a result of forced acculturation, Christianization, and economic changes (LaFromboise et al., 1995).

Historical trauma: Cumulative psychological wounding over generations resulting from massive group trauma.

Historical trauma is an important concept in discussions of American Indians (Brave Heart, 2003; Gone, 2009). **Historical trauma** refers to cumulative psychological wounding over generations resulting from massive group trauma. For American Indians, historical trauma occurred with the invasion of and colonization by Europeans in the 1700s and 1800s, the murder of countless Native people, and being forced onto reservations. Women were sterilized without their consent and their children were forcibly abducted from them. The children were sent to institutions, where they were mistreated and punished for speaking their Native languages, so that they could be assimilated into White culture (Native American Rights Fund, 2013). These practices persisted into the mid-20th century. As one woman reported,

> [The residential school] is where I encountered all forms of abuse. . . . The form of discipline (the priest) used to give us was physical discipline. Used to get strapped. . . . We used to run away, too. I was trying to run away from that pain. We were trying to run away from the way we were treated. But when we . . . were caught, they used to shave our head. . . . I'm the victim of sexual abuse, too, by the priest. . . . I couldn't study and I couldn't concentrate across all that pain I carried there. (quoted in Gone, 2009, p. 755)

This historical trauma continues to affect American Indians today. Efforts by coalitions of American Indian tribes, such as the National Native American Boarding School Healing Coalition (www.boardingschoolhealing.org/), continue to seek reparations for these abuses against Native children and culture. While American Indians display resilience in the face of historical trauma (LaFromboise et al., 2006), their experiences of oppression and marginalization continue.

The Spirit World is essential to Indian life, and especially to the life of Indian women. Women are seen as extensions of the Spirit Mother and as keys to the continuation of their people (LaFromboise et al., 1994). Another important part of American Indian life is a harmonious relationship with the Earth. The Earth is referred to as Mother Earth, and women are seen as connected with this important part of existence.

Thus American Indian women see themselves as part of a collective, fulfilling harmonious roles in the biological, spiritual, and social realms: Biologically, they value being mothers; spiritually, they are in tune with the Spirit Mother; and socially, they preserve and transmit culture and are the caretakers of their children and relatives (LaFromboise et al., 1990).

The Cultural Heritage of African American Persons

Over 13% of Americans identify themselves as Black or African American (U.S. Census Bureau, 2015). As with each of the ethnic groups discussed in this chapter thus far, considerable subcultural variations exist. One concerns whether the individual was born in the United States and descended from people brought here involuntarily as slaves, compared with those who are voluntary immigrants from the Caribbean or Africa.

Multiple factors shape the cultural heritage of African American persons, including the heritage of African culture and the experience of slavery and continued racial oppression in America (Staples, 2006). These factors have varied somewhat by gender, although there are also differences. Today, two characteristics of the African woman's role are maintained: an important economic function and a strong bond between mother and child (Greene, 1994). African women have traditionally been economically independent, functioning in the marketplace and as traders. Black women in the United States continue to assume this crucial economic function in the family to the present day. Mother–child bonds also continue to be extremely important in the structure of Black society.

The concept of historical trauma, discussed earlier for American Indians, is also important for African American people (Williams-Washington, 2010). For African Americans, the massive group trauma began with the period of slavery and continued with Jim Crow laws and then mass incarceration. The repercussions of these forms of oppression persist today.

African American culture, like that of other people of color, and in contrast to European American society, emphasizes the collective over the individual (Fairchild et al., 2003). It recognizes the important connections between generations, and it is concerned with the individual's harmonious relationship with others (Myers et al., 2000), in contrast to the individualism of contemporary White culture and contemporary White psychology.

In the 1800s, when it was popular in the United States to put White women on a pedestal, Black women were viewed as beasts of burden and subjected to the same demeaning labor as Black men (Dugger, 1988). Angela Davis (1981) argued that this heritage

Ulf Andersen/Hulton Archive/Getty Images.

PHOTO 4.5
The author and activist Mary Crow Dog (also known as Mary Brave Bird and Mary Ellen Moore-Richard) was a Lakota Sioux woman who grew up attending the St. Francis Boarding School on the Rosebud Sioux Reservation in South Dakota, where she was taught to practice Christianity and not to speak her native Sioux language. She was punished for speaking out against the abuses she and other children experienced at the boarding school.

created an alternative definition of womanhood for Black women, one that includes a tradition of "hard work, perseverance and self-reliance, a legacy of tenacity, resistance, and an insistence on sexual equality" (p. 29). This is also an example of intersectionality: Womanhood is constructed differently across different racial/ethnic groups. Some researchers have found that this construction of Black womanhood contributes to the stereotype of the "strong Black woman," which can be both aspirational and constricting for Black women (Abrams et al., 2014; Etowa et al., 2017).

FOCUS 4.2

WOMEN AND ISLAM

©iStockphoto.com/Juanmonino.

PHOTO 4.6

Around the world, there is diversity in the practice of veiling among Muslim women.

The Prophet Muhammad founded Islam around 610 CE (Common Era, or AD). Muhammad advocated more equal treatment for women than could be found in the cultures of the time. For example, female infanticide was practiced widely in those cultures, but was prohibited under Muhammad. After Muhammad's death, conditions for women worsened. Women were increasingly confined to the private sphere of the home. This seclusion of women ensured that they would not participate in the public sphere of government and business.

Islam, much like other religions such as Christianity and Judaism, is not uniform. Islamic law and religion and their implications for women are interpreted differently across various Muslim cultures. For example, two major divisions within Islam are the Sunni and the Shi'a; Sufi is a third, smaller branch. Worldwide, the majority of Muslims are Sunni.

Similarly, there is diversity in the practice of veiling or wearing *hijab*. Today, three nations mandate that women be covered: Iran, Sudan, and Saudi Arabia. In contrast, in Turkey, a secular state, women are forbidden from wearing headscarves in, for example, driver's license photos. In Afghanistan, Pashtun women wore the *chadri* (a full-body covering that also covers one's face, except for mesh fabric over one's eyes) prior to the time of Muhammad and most continue that practice today. Yet this type of veiling is illegal in some countries such as France, where Muslims are a religious minority.

The Qur'an, or Koran (Islam's holy scripture, revealed to the Prophet), is clear that women should participate equally with men in religious observances. Over time, though, this principle has been lost. The Qur'an gives women the right to inherit property and to divorce, revolutionary ideas at the time. Although several Islamic cultures today practice the stoning of women if they commit adultery, this practice is not stated in the Qur'an. In short, many of the practices that oppress women in Islamic nations are the result of culture, not Islam. Female circumcision is a good example; it is not mandated in the Qur'an.

There are about 3.3 million Muslims in the United States today. Many Muslim women are immigrants or descendants of immigrants from Arab nations. In addition, some African American women practice Islam.

Today, Islamic women in many nations struggle for equal rights, but they do so in the context of intense and sometimes violent religious and political conflict. Terrorist organizations such as ISIL (the Islamic State of Iraq and the Levant) and Boko Haram claim to be representative of Islam, but they are rejected by the vast majority of Muslims around the world.

Sources: Mohamed (2016); Sechzer (2004); Wyche (2004).

Gender Roles and Ethnicity

A basic tenet of intersectionality is that gender and race/ethnicity are interconnected. Gender roles are constructed within the cultural context of a particular ethnic group and the broader political system, so it is not surprising that both similarities and differences exist in gender roles across diverse racial/ethnic groups. Moreover, we should keep in mind that strict gender roles rooted in the gender binary may create a particularly challenging developmental context for queer and trans persons. Yet very little research on this topic is available.

In the context of the cultural heritages of people of color in the United States, let us consider the gender roles that have evolved within these diverse communities.

Gender Roles Among American Indian Persons

Today it is clear that the early work of anthropologists misrepresented women's roles in American Indian culture (LaFromboise et al., 1990). Their work demonstrates how gender bias and race bias can easily affect research in the social sciences. For starters, the researchers were men and non-Indian. As such, they focused on male activities and had greater access to male informants. A stereotyped dichotomy of American Indian women as either princess or squaw emerged, much like the saint/slut dichotomy that was drawn for Victorian White women. In addition, because the anthropologists were not Indian and thus were outsiders, they were able to observe only the public sphere and how Indians interacted with outsiders. Since, in some tribes, dealing with outsiders was an activity assigned to men, researchers overestimated men's power within the tribe. They were not witness to women's interactions and powerful roles within the private sphere. And some tribes had a matrilineal system of inheritance, meaning that women could own property, which would be passed from mother to daughter. After a long legacy of White violence against American Indians, Indian women were unlikely to share their intimate rituals or feelings with these outsiders. In sum, researchers had only a vague and imprecise sense of American Indian women's roles.

For example, it was reported that, during their menstrual periods, American Indian women were isolated from their tribe and its activities and kept in a secluded menstrual hut, based on the Native view that women were contaminated at this time (e.g., Stephens, 1961). Yet firsthand accounts from Indian writers provided a different interpretation (LaFromboise et al., 1990). Menstruating women were not shunned as unclean, but rather were considered extremely powerful, with tremendous capacities for destruction. Women's spiritual forces were thought to be especially strong during menstruation, and women were generally thought to possess powers so great that they could counteract or weaken men's powers. The interpretation matters—shifting from a view of a shunned, powerless woman to that of a too-powerful woman.

While there are considerable variations across tribes, there were also shared values. For example, an American Indian woman's spirituality, extended family, and tribe were central to her identity and gender role (LaFromboise et al., 1990). Collectivity and harmony with the spiritual world, the world of one's family and tribe, and the natural world were emphasized. In addition, women's status increased with their age. Older women were respected for their wisdom and for their knowledge of tribal history, healing, and the sacred (LaFromboise et al., 1995). Some American Indian women advocate a return to these traditional values associated with women's roles, while at the same time cultivating the skills of the dominant European American culture—a combination known as *bicultural competence* (LaFromboise et al., 1995).

The evidence shows that some American Indian tribes had a system of egalitarian gender roles, in which separate but equally valued tasks were assigned to men and women (Blackwood, 1984). While some tribes, such as the Klamath, had these egalitarian patterns, it is important to keep tribal variations in mind.

In addition, some tribes, such as the Canadian Blackfeet, had institutionalized alternative female roles. In these roles, women might be expected to express "masculine" traits or participate in male-stereotyped activities while continuing to live and dress as a woman. For example, there was the role of the "manly hearted woman," a role that an independent and aggressive woman could adopt. There also was a "warrior woman" role among the Apache, Crow, Cheyenne, Blackfoot, and Pawnee tribes (e.g., Thomas, 2000). In some cases, we might understand these alternative female roles as reflecting a third gender or a transgender identity.

In Chapter 1, we introduced the Two Spirit, a third or fourth gender category found within some American Indian tribes. Two Spirits are people who feel they possess both male and female spirits. Traditionally, Two Spirit people performed important and unique roles in their communities, such as serving as medicine people or community leaders or bestowing sacred names (Robinson, 2017). For example, the Zuni Pueblo Two Spirit We'wha served as a cultural ambassador to the U.S. federal government for her tribe. In some cases, Two Spirit people might also be involved in masculine or feminine tasks, such as hunting, fighting, preparing food, or making pottery or baskets. Today, Two Spirit people may be found performing a variety of tasks and working in diverse careers, much like other members of their tribes.

Gender Roles Among African American Persons

As noted earlier, research on African Americans and other people of color tends to be limited by a critical methodological issue. The issue is that race/ethnicity and social class are often confounded. Black people tend to be overrepresented among the poor and White people tend to be overrepresented among the middle class and wealthy, so it is often unclear whether differences between Black and White Americans should be attributed to race/ethnicity, social class, or both. In general, research techniques have not been powerful enough to completely address this confound. As we review the material on gender and ethnicity, keep in mind that much of what seems to be ethnic group differences may have much to do with social class differences as well.

For African American women, the multiple roles of parent, worker, and spouse/partner have been a reality for generations. This stands in contrast to the situation for White middle-class American women, for whom these multiple roles are more recent (this issue is discussed more generally in Chapter 9). Motherhood remains a primary definer of the female gender role, but African American women have typically taken on additional roles, such as worker and head of household. Black women generally expect that they must hold paying jobs as adults (Greene, 1994), and this expectation has important consequences for their educational and occupational attainments, as we shall see later.

An intersectional approach demonstrates that, across racial/ethnic groups, women have different experiences. For example, in 2015, 49.5% of Black family households (that is, households with children under age 25) were maintained by single women, compared with 16.3% of White families (U.S. Census Bureau, 2016b). This discrepancy has increased over time. For example, only 25% of Black families were headed by women in 1965 (Dickson, 1993). A number of factors contribute to the greater rates of female-headed households among African Americans.

1. *Lower heterosexual marriage rates among African Americans.* Among Black women in 2015, 26% were married (U.S. Census Bureau, 2016a). At the same time, 18% were divorced or separated and 48% had never been married. For comparison, among White women, 51% were married, 15% were divorced or separated, and 24% had never been never married. This pattern of lower marriage rates is a result of many of the factors listed below.

2. *The obstacles African American men have encountered in seeking and maintaining jobs necessary to support their families* (Harknett & McLanahan, 2004). Since World War II, the number of manufacturing jobs in the United States has declined dramatically. These jobs were a major source of employment for working-class Black men. The result has been a decrease in working-class jobs and an increase in joblessness among Black men (Byars-Winston et al., 2015).

3. *The unequal gender ratio among African Americans* (Stockard et al., 2009). The most recent census found that, among adults, there were only 83 Black men for every 100 Black women, compared with 95 White men per 100 White women (U.S. Census Bureau, 2010a). This gender ratio is driven by two factors: Black men's higher incarceration rates and early death rates (Wolfers et al., 2015).

4. Interracial dating and marriage patterns of Black men. For example, Black men are far more likely to marry White women than Black women are to marry White men (Wang, 2015).

Among older adults as well, the role of Black women differs from that of White women. The feelings of uselessness and the lack of roles experienced by White women in their youth-oriented culture are less common among African Americans. The extended-family structure among African Americans provides a secure position and role for older women. The "granny" role—helping to care for young grandchildren, giving advice based on experience—is a meaningful and valued role for the older Black woman (Greene, 1994). Older Black women have a more purposeful and respected role than elderly White women do. This respect for older women and their wisdom is also found among American Indians.

Gender Roles Among Asian American Persons

It is common to think of Asian Americans as the "model minority." In 2015, for example, the median annual income was $48,313 for Asian American women, higher than for women of any other ethnic group, including European Americans (U.S. Census Bureau, 2015). At the same time, over 49% of Asian American women graduated from college, also higher than for women of any other ethnic group (see Table 4.1; U.S. Census Bureau, 2016a). Nonetheless, feminist Asian Americans note that Asian American women are victims of both racism and sexism. For example, the model minority stereotype hides the trauma and struggle of

©iStockphoto.com/monkeybusinessimages

PHOTO 4.7
The "granny" role is a meaningful and valued role for older Black women, who are respected within the family.

refugees, as the earlier discussion of Khmer refugee women illustrated. And distorted stereotypes remain in the mass media (Marchetti, 1993), such as the Asian man as the violent Kung Fu warrior.

At least five stereotypes about Asian American women are widespread (Root, 1995). The first is female subservience, deriving in part from women's lower status in countries such as China and Japan. The second stereotype is that Asian American women are exotic sex toys. The third is the Dragon Lady stereotype, in which Asian American women are depicted as diabolical wielders of power. A variation on this stereotype is of the cold and demanding Tiger Mother. The dichotomy between the subservient stereotype and the Dragon Lady stereotype reinforces good girl/bad girl dualities, and the Asian American woman who fails to be subservient may be quickly cast as a Dragon Lady. The fourth stereotype is the sexless worker bee, which includes women who work as domestics or garment workers. The fifth stereotype is the China doll, the idea that Asian American women are fragile and innocent.

The expectations from traditional Asian culture—for family interdependence, preservation of group harmony, and stoicism—are closely connected to Asian American women specifically. As part of their bicultural existence, Asian American women experience gender role conflict between the gender roles of their traditional Asian culture and modern American culture, which prioritizes independence and individuality.

Gender Roles Among Latinx Persons

Gender roles are strictly defined in traditional Latin American cultures (Raffaelli & Ontai, 2004). Gender roles are emphasized early in the socialization process for children and are reiterated across development (Umaña-Taylor et al., 2009). For example, Latino boys are given greater freedom, encouraged in sexual exploits, and not expected to share in household work. By contrast, Latina girls are expected to be passive, obedient, and feminine, and to stay in the home caring for the needs of others.

Machismo: The ideal of manliness in Latinx culture.

These traditional roles are epitomized in the cultural ideals of *machismo* and *marianismo* (Miville et al., 2017). **Machismo**, or macho, refers to the mystique of manliness or male gender norms, literally meaning "maleness" or "virility." The cultural ideal of machismo among Latin Americans assumes heterosexual marriage and, in that context, mandates that the man must be the provider and the one responsible for the well-being and honor of his family (Glass & Owen, 2010). Men hold a privileged position and are to be treated as authority figures.

There are both positive and negative sides of machismo (Arciniega et al., 2008). *Caballerismo*, rooted in the Spanish word *caballero*, is an ideal of a Spanish gentleman with good manners and ethics. It is much like the English chivalric code for knights. As the positive side of machismo, it emphasizes chivalry and the centrality of the family. Yet the negative side of machismo tends to be overemphasized in research and popular culture. It has come to include sexist or chauvinistic attitudes and behaviors, including the glorification of sexual conquests and even violent physical domination of women. Of course, such hypermasculinity is also common among European Americans.

Marianismo: The ideal of womanliness in Latinx culture.

Marianismo is the female complement to male machismo (Castillo et al., 2010; Miville et al., 2017). The ideal of marianismo is rooted in the Catholic worship of the Virgin Mary and holds that women must emulate her. That is, women are expected to be chaste, obedient, modest, and pious, and thus capable of enduring the suffering inflicted by men. Latin American cultures attribute high status to motherhood, and higher status is given to Latinas who are mothers. Women are expected to be self-sacrificing in relation to their children and the rest of their family. On the surface, the machismo and marianismo roles may seem to endorse male domination and female subordination, but the situation is complex. Women who excel in the marianista role come to be revered as they grow older and their children feel strong loyalty and deference to them, such that they wield considerable power within the family.

In sum, the traditional gender roles for Latinos and Latinas are complementary but complex. Machismo includes both positive and negative sides, emphasizing both dominance and chivalry. And marianismo involves passivity and subservience, but this generalization masks the powerful roles that women play within the family.

Immigration

A topic that is of personal significance to many people, including people of color, is immigration. In the United States today, one-quarter of the population is either first- or second-generation American, meaning that they or one of their parents were born in another country (U.S. Census Bureau, 2013). In general, three broad factors drive migration. People migrate from one country to another because the want to reunite their family, to find work, or to seek humanitarian refuge or asylum (American Psychological Association [APA] Presidential Task Force on Immigration, 2012).

While the United States and Canada both have rich histories of immigration, the topic has also been controversial in large part because of perceived racial, ethnic, and religious differences, as well as perceptions that immigrants will receive valuable jobs or threaten public safety (Murray & Marx, 2013). For example, in the United States, Italian immigrants were once discriminated against, in part, because they were perceived as not White. Today, immigrants from many Middle Eastern and Muslim-majority countries experience similar discrimination. Here we briefly introduce some of the psychological aspects of immigration. We focus on immigrant experiences in the United States but note that experiences elsewhere are both similar and different.

Broadly, people moving into the United States from other countries can be grouped according to their status as (a) legal immigrants, (b) undocumented immigrants, and (c) refugees. *Legal immigrants* are people who have legal authorization (e.g., a green card or visa) to live in the United States. *Undocumented immigrants* are people who lack such authorization. *Refugees* are people who have been forced to flee their home countries because of persecution, war, or violence.

For any of these three groups, the process of migration can be extremely stressful and risky (Lueck & Wilson, 2011; Yakushko & Espín, 2010). For a woman who leaves her homeland and friends, acute feelings of loss and grief are to be expected. Among refugees, girls and women are considered the most vulnerable (UNHCR, 2017). As described earlier, refugee women (such as those fleeing the Khmer Rouge regime) are particularly at risk for severe stress and PTSD.

According to the UNHCR (2017), there are 21.3 million refugees in the world, the vast majority of whom are never able to resettle or find safe, permanent homes to rebuild their lives. As people fleeing persecution, war, or violence, most refugees have experienced considerable trauma, possibly including unexpected and sudden loss of friends and family members, sexual violence, and torture, as well as witnessing violence. As they flee their home countries, they may encounter additional stressors such as lack of access to basic necessities like food, clean water, and physical safety, as well as unemployment. If refugees do not speak the language of their postmigration host country, and/or if the citizens of that country are not welcoming, they may face continued stress and feelings of isolation, sadness, and fear. One study with Syrian refugees found that 33.5% have PTSD, with women's rates being four times higher than men's (Alpak et al., 2015). A review of such research showed that stress-related symptoms such as sleep disturbances, changes in appetite, dizziness, migraine headaches, and repeated vomiting are common (Ghumman et al., 2016). Making psychological services available to refugees is important for their well-being and reducing PTSD and depression within this vulnerable population.

When we speak of immigration for any of these groups, a critical psychological concept is acculturation. **Acculturation** is the process of psychological and behavioral change that one undergoes as a result of long-term contact with another culture, including the adoption of values, customs, norms, attitudes, and behaviors from that culture (APA Presidential Task Force on Immigration, 2012; Yoon et al., 2013; Zea et al., 2003). For example, because of acculturation, the culture of Mexican Americans is different from both the culture of Mexico and the dominant European American culture of the United States. Mexican American culture is based on the Mexican heritage, modified through acculturation to incorporate European American components. Similar diversity is seen with other immigrant groups in the United States. Acculturation includes multiple dimensions, such as language use, norms, and attitudes. The process may vary based on age, in that, relative to older immigrants, younger immigrants tend to adopt and incorporate the host culture more quickly and may not retain their origin culture (APA Presidential Task Force on Immigration, 2012).

Acculturation can be a stressful process, particularly if there is conflict between one's native culture and host culture. **Acculturative stress** refers to the stress of acculturation and may happen because of the pressure to both maintain values from one's native culture and adopt behaviors and norms of one's host culture (APA Presidential Task Force on Immigration, 2012). Still, in general, acculturation is associated with positive outcomes.

Acculturation: A multidimensional process of psychological and behavioral change one undergoes as a result of long-term contact with another culture, including the adoption of that culture's values, customs, norms, attitudes, and behaviors.

Acculturative stress: Specific stress of the acculturation process.

Education

Education has long been a valued path for people of color and immigrants to the United States seeking to improve their job success, their status, and their standard of living.

PHOTO 4.8
A Syrian refugee family. There are 21.3 million refugees in the world, most fleeing persecution, war, or violence in their home countries.

Anadolu Agency/Getty Images.

Worldwide, education and literacy are critical issues for women: Two-thirds of the illiterate adults in the world are women (UNESCO, 2008). Therefore, as we examine women's achievements, it is important to look at education.

Table 4.1 shows the educational attainments of Americans broken down by gender (as a binary) and ethnicity, as the U.S. Census Bureau reports. Focusing first on the section of the table that deals with high school graduation, you can see that although there is some problem with high school dropouts among Whites, African Americans, and Asian Americans, basically about 80% to 90% of each group does graduate from high school. Graduation rates are considerably lower for Hispanic men and women, but many are immigrants from countries with little access to education. Another interesting pattern is that, across ethnic groups, the graduation rates for women and men are similar.

TABLE 4.1   **School completion rates for women and men across ethnic groups.**

Ethnic Group	Less than high school		High school graduate		Some college		College graduate or higher	
	W	M	W	M	W	M	W	M
White	7.8%	8.7%	28.3%	28.4%	31.2%	29.1%	32.7%	33.8%
Black	15.0%	17.7%	28.3%	34.6%	35.1%	30.7%	21.6%	17.0%
American Indian	19.4%	22.5%	29.0%	34.1%	36.7%	30.8%	14.9%	12.5%
Asian American	15.7%	12.0%	16.0%	14.5%	19.1%	19.4%	49.2%	54.1%

Source: U.S. Census Bureau (2016a).

The section on those who graduate from college indicates a pattern of gender similarities in these recent years. That is, women's rates of graduating from college are similar to men's. The ethnic differences in college graduation rates, however, are stark.

Beyond these statistics are also important issues regarding the intersection of race discrimination and sex discrimination in the schools. Even elementary school children can identify race discrimination by teachers toward students in stories read to them (Brown, 2006). A study of gender and racial discrimination in high schools investigated both discrimination by peers and classroom discrimination by teachers in a sample of Black youth (Chavous et al., 2008). In general, the study found that Black boys were stereotyped more negatively than Black girls or White youth and that Black boys reported more peer discrimination and classroom discrimination than Black girls did. These experiences of discrimination can affect school performance and students' sense of the importance of school. Boys' experience of discrimination was negatively associated with their GPA; in other words, boys who reported more discrimination had lower GPAs. Yet the same pattern did not hold for girls. In sum, racist stereotypes are gendered and they seem to affect boys and girls differently.

In predominantly White colleges and universities, women of color may experience the paradox of underattention and overattention. On the one hand, their comments may be ignored or they may not receive the help they need in a lab. On the other hand, if the discussion focuses on women of color, they may be called on to represent the views of all women of their ethnic group. They are "othered" and treated differently based on their race.

FOCUS 4.3

AFFIRMATIVE ACTION

In 2016, the U.S. Supreme Court ruled in *Fisher v. University of Texas at Austin* that universities could include race as a factor in admissions decisions to promote student diversity on campus, bolstering the constitutionality of affirmative action programs. Affirmative action is a controversial topic in the United States, with some arguing that it is absolutely necessary to achieve diversity and make up for historic wrongs and others arguing that it is unfair and runs counter to American principles of succeeding purely on one's merit. The treatment of both women and people of color is at the center of the debate.

Affirmative action can be defined as "voluntary and mandatory efforts undertaken by federal, state, and local governments; private employers; and schools to combat discrimination and to promote equal opportunity in education and employment for all" (American Psychological Association, 1996, p. 2). Affirmative action is generally considered to have two goals: eliminating discrimination against women and ethnic minorities and righting the effects of past discrimination.

Can psychological data shed any light on whether affirmative action is a beneficial policy? Psychologist Faye Crosby and her colleagues analyzed the potential costs and benefits, as judged by the available data, as follows (Crosby, Iyer, Clayton, et al., 2003; Crosby, Iyer, & Sincharoen, 2006).

POTENTIAL BENEFIT: ENHANCED DIVERSITY AND ACHIEVEMENT

The idea here is that affirmative action increases diversity—whether in the workplace or in the student body—and that

PHOTO 4.9

In diverse classrooms and schools, prejudice is reduced and cross-racial friendships are fostered.

this diversity is itself beneficial. The first question, then, is whether affirmative action actually increases diversity. Analyses by economists indicate that affirmative action has been very effective at increasing the numbers of women and people of color at all organizational levels. As for benefits in the workplace, research shows that diversity introduces more points of view into an organization, which can enhance the organization's problem-solving capacity. Laboratory studies show that ethnically diverse workgroups generate a wider range of ideas of higher quality, compared with homogeneous workgroups. A diverse workforce also helps firms create and market products to new populations.

Turning to diversity in colleges and universities, one benefit is that students learn more and think more critically when they are exposed to more heterogeneous learning environments, whether the learning environment is other students or faculty (Bowman, 2010). A second benefit is that a diverse student body helps prepare all students for the multicultural interactions they will have in modern American society. Third are benefits to society as a whole; meta-analytic evidence indicates that, compared with their White peers, students of color are more likely to become civic leaders later in life (Bowman, 2011).

Enhanced diversity also promotes a better climate for students of color. In nondiverse educational settings, students of color experience higher rates of microaggressions (McCabe, 2009). By contrast, in diverse educational settings, prejudice is reduced and cross-racial friendships are fostered (Levine & Ancheta, 2013).

POTENTIAL COST 1: VIOLATION OF PRINCIPLES OF MERIT AND JUSTICE

Opponents of affirmative action argue that decisions about hiring or college admissions should be made on merit alone and that American principles of justice are violated when factors such as gender or ethnicity are taken into account. Crosby and her colleagues concluded, however, that almost all measures of merit are flawed and/or somewhat subjective and therefore influenced by decision makers' prejudice. As an example of a flawed measure, the SAT generates much lower scores for Black and Latinx test takers and some Asian Americans (Cambodian, Filipino), yet those students with much lower scores go on to earn only slightly lower grades and graduate at only slightly lower rates, compared with their White peers. Similar findings, discussed in Chapter 8, indicate that women score lower than men on the SAT Math, but then earn better grades in college. And a large data set from the University of California indicates that SAT scores do not predict grades if socioeconomic status is controlled in the analysis. In short, the argument that decisions should be made on merit alone assumes that we have perfect measures of merit, but we do not.

The other issue with merit is that, often, subjective judgments are made by people such as the person doing the hiring, the supervisor evaluating the employee for promotion, or the college admissions officer. A massive amount of data from social psychology indicates that Americans—including supervisors and college admissions officers—hold sexist and racist prejudices, but the prejudices are implicit so the person thinks that they are being entirely fair. Again, these individuals may think that they are making decisions based purely on merit, but the data indicate that they are at least in part responding to implicit gender and ethnic stereotypes.

POTENTIAL COST 2: UNDERMINING THE SELF-CONFIDENCE OF THE BENEFICIARIES

Another argument is that if people know they are affirmative action hires or affirmative action admissions, that will undermine their self-confidence, making them feel inferior to their coworkers or classmates. Contrary to this argument, social psychologists' research shows that people have a number of self-protective psychological processes that buffer them from undermining. When they encounter negative treatment, women and people of color may attribute it to sexism or racism and their self-confidence remains intact. All this assumes, of course, that the hiring was based not only on affirmative action but also on qualifications, which is almost invariably the case. As one Black woman said,

> I believe in Affirmative Action. My view of Affirmative Action is that it is long overdue. . . . And my thing is (picking up the audio recorder and placing it close to her mouth), I don't care how I got here, dammit! Move over! I'm coming for that seat. What really throws people is that they say, "You just got here." So! I'm here now! And I'm doing just as good or even better than most of the folks here. They let a whole lot of White folks in this school that had no business being in here and they always want to throw up GPA and SAT scores and all this crap. How did Bush go to Yale? (quoted in Gutter, 2002, p. 100)

Crosby and her colleagues concluded that, on balance, affirmative action policies have far more benefits than costs. In addition, these findings affirm that rulings such as *Fisher v. University of Texas at Austin,* in allowing race-conscious admissions decisions at universities, promote more diverse educational settings, which in turn foster higher achievement and a more positive climate across contexts.

As we consider the educational experiences of women of color, it is important to recall the important research on stereotype threat, discussed in detail in Chapter 3 (e.g., Spencer et al., 2016; Steele, 1997; Steele & Aronson, 1995). According to that research, every time a Black woman takes a calculus test, she is likely to experience double stereotype threat because women—and Black people—are stereotyped as bad at math. Even if she is academically talented, she may be seized with worries that she will confirm stereotypes, and as a result, her performance suffers. The same is true for Latinas and American Indian women. Stereotype threat poses a serious barrier to educational attainment for women of color, and meta-analysis shows that the effects of stereotype threat on math performance are greater for women of color (Spencer et al., 2016).

In summary, in this section on education we have examined the intersection of race and gender at two levels: the microlevel (classroom interactions and stereotype threat) and the macrolevel (statistics on degrees awarded to people of color in the United States). Two important points emerge from this discussion:

1. Gender and race are powerful factors in classroom dynamics, whether in elementary school or college. Women of color may receive stereotypical responses that encourage neither their academic achievement nor their sense of their own academic competence.

2. With the exception of Asian Americans, women of color in the United States are not graduating from college or pursuing graduate education at a rate comparable to that of Whites. This lack of education in turn precludes many occupations and limits earnings. Therefore, the recruitment and retention of women of color in higher education need to be top priorities.

Mental Health Issues

Racism pervades the history of clinical psychology and its treatment of people of color in the United States. For example, the census of 1840 reported that African Americans in the Northern states had far higher rates of psychopathology than African Americans in the slave states. Psychiatrists of the day interpreted this finding as indicating that the supervision and control that slavery provided were essential to African Americans' well-being. In other words, the data and methods of social science were used to defend slavery as beneficial for African Americans (Deutsch, 1944). While that part of the census data was later found to have been fabricated, the official record remained uncorrected and the damage was done.

In the early 1900s, psychologists advanced theories that perpetuated racial stereotyping. For example, it was theorized that African Americans were innately happy-go-lucky and therefore immune to depression (Landrine, 1988; A. Thomas & Sillen, 1972). This bias persisted through the 20th century, when depressed African Americans were likely to be misdiagnosed, often as schizophrenics (Landrine, 1988; Simon et al., 1973).

Today, research clearly demonstrates that experiences of oppression based on gender, race/ethnicity, and sexual orientation can be a source of both short-term and long-term stress, and stress undermines mental and physical health (e.g., Russo, 2010; Spencer et al., 2010). For example, in a study with Asian Americans, Hispanic Americans, and African Americans, researchers found that individuals' perceptions of racist discrimination were linked to depression, PTSD, and substance abuse, as well as other mental health issues (Chou et al., 2012). Researchers have identified the experience of *race-based traumatic stress* among people of color (Carter, 2007). Race-based trauma occurs when a person experiences a sudden, unexpected, and emotionally painful encounter, such as being racially profiled by police. In turn, the person's reaction may include arousal or hypervigilance, intrusion or reexperiencing, and avoidance or numbing, which are characteristic of PTSD (discussed further in Chapter 14). The person may also experience depression, anger, physical symptoms, and low self-esteem.

Still, contemporary psychology may not be a good fit for all racial/ethnic groups. For American Indians, the definition of well-being and the method of treating disturbances are at odds with mainstream psychotherapy in the United States (Gone, 2009). In most American Indian cultures, a person is considered to be well psychologically when they are peaceful and exuding strength through self-control and adherence to their cultural values (LaFromboise et al., 1990). Yet when a person is unwell, traditional healing systems are used, which involve a community process that helps the individual while also reaffirming the norms of the community; the process is holistic and naturalistic (LaFromboise et al., 1995).

Whether on the reservation or off, American Indian women experience intense stressors, but they appear to be reluctant to use mental health services (LaFromboise et al., 1995). In part, this reluctance is caused by the fact that they view the existing services as unresponsive to them and their needs. American Indians who do use mental health services often express concern that these services guide their behavior in a direction that is at odds with their Native culture.

At another corner of the gender-ethnicity intersection, Asian American women also experience stresses from racism and sexism. Yet, compared with European Americans, Asian Americans underutilize mental health services (Abe-Kim et al., 2007; Kimerling & Baumrind, 2005). For a long time, the explanation was that Asian Americans simply have a low rate of mental disturbance. Today, it seems more accurate to say that, while mental illness is stigmatized broadly, the stigma and shame are especially strong within Asian American cultures, so individuals are reluctant to seek help until a true crisis has developed. And when Asian Americans do seek therapy, they often find that it is not sensitive to the values of their culture (Root, 1995).

As these studies demonstrate, an important task for clinical psychology is to develop culturally sensitive methods of psychotherapy (American Psychological Association, 2003). An additional, related task is to increase the number of psychologists of color, who can bring valuable cultural sensitivities and competence to therapeutic and research settings. Guidelines on providing affirmative care to transgender and gender nonconforming people of color are also available (Chang & Singh, 2016). Such guidelines include examining the intersectionality of race/ethnicity and gender identity, reflecting on one's own race/ethnicity and gender identity, and assessing client strengths and resilience in coping with multiple oppressions.

Feminisms of Color

As members of multiply marginalized groups, women of color have unique perspectives on sexism and racism. Women of color have emerged as powerful forces in the feminist movement, shaping feminism to be more inclusive of the diversity of experiences and priorities among women (Comas-Diaz, 1991; Hurtado, 2010; Sinacore & Enns, 2005). *Women of color feminism* or *feminisms of color* tend to be critical of White feminists who have focused exclusively on "universal" female experiences (e.g., reproductive freedom) while ignoring both the diversity in women's experiences and their own privileged status as Whites (Bryant-Davis & Comas-Díaz, 2016; Enns & Sinacore, 2001).

Womanism: Feminism rooted in the lived experience of Black women and women of color; also Black feminism.

At the same time, some people of color have been critical of civil rights and other social justice activist groups for marginalizing the voices and experiences of women of color. For example, the #SayHerName movement emerged in response to the Black Lives Matter movement's tendency to focus on anti-Black violence and police brutality against Black men while ignoring similar violence against Black women (African American Policy Forum, 2015). The explicitly intersectional perspective of #SayHerName emphasizes how racism and sexism contribute to the marginalization of and violence against Black women and girls.

New York Daily News/Getty Images

PHOTO 4.10
The #SayHerName movement is an explicitly intersectional activist movement focused on ending violence against Black women and girls.

Womanism (or *Black feminism*) is a feminist perspective grounded in the experience of Black women in the United States (Boisnier, 2003; Collins, 1989; James & Busia, 1993; Ransby, 2000; Walker, 1983). Although womanism formally emerged in the context of mainstream feminism dominated by White women in the 1970s and 1980s, its historical origins go back much further. It is evident in the activism of Sojourner Truth, Ida Wells-Barnett, and Fannie Lou Hamer, among others, and also in the actions of common Black women and their everyday acts of resistance, beginning in the days of slavery (Collins, 1989). Womanism explicitly considers the intersecting oppressions of racism and sexism, forming the foundation of intersectionality theory (Else-Quest & Hyde, 2016). In her writing about womanism, the author Alice Walker (1983) described the commitment to the survival and wholeness of people of color—not just women of color—and emphasized how sexism, racism, and classism are important.

Womanism is considered a holistic and interdisciplinary feminism, respecting and honoring women's spirituality and multiple ways of knowing (Bryant-Davis & Comas-Díaz, 2016). The emphasis on spirituality—which is largely absent from mainstream White feminism—is especially noteworthy.

Feminisms of color, such as womanism, tend to be *strengths-based*. That is, these perspectives emphasize strengths, agency, resilience, and other positive traits of women of color (Bryant-Davis & Comas-Díaz, 2016). Thus, in light of a history characterized by, among other things, oppression based on both gender and race, womanism pivots from victimization to resilience and the collective power of communities of color. Womanist theorists have proposed a positive womanist psychospirituality, which integrates Black psychology and womanism within a positive psychology approach. It includes six positive life principles: (1) Black women's extended ways of knowing and contextualized knowledge; (2) spirited and inspired living, including hope and faith in God; (3) interconnected love and compassion; (4) balance and flexibility, including responsibility and adaptation; (5) liberation and inclusion, as well as resistance against oppression; and (6) empowered authenticity, including courage and the importance of speaking truth to power (Harrell et al., 2014). Each of these principles is consistent with the womanist and Black feminist emphases on strengths, agency, resilience, and spirituality.

Black feminist thought also holds that viewpoints and opinions are personal rather than objective (see our discussion of social constructionism and the feminist critique of objectivity in Chapter 1) and that individuals are also personally accountable for their beliefs. Thus, a psychologist whose theorizing perpetuates racial stereotypes or racism is held responsible for those effects and cannot hide behind the mask of scientific objectivity.

Mujerismo: Feminism rooted in the lived experience of Latinas; Latina womanism.

Similarly, **Mujerismo** developed among Latinas who felt marginalized by White feminism. Mujerismo comes from the Spanish word *mujer*, meaning *woman*. Translated literally, mujerismo means Latina womanism. Mujeristas seek to promote the liberation, self-definition, and self-determination of Latinas (Bryant-Davis & Comas-Díaz, 2016). A related feminism of color is *Chicana feminism* (see, e.g., Hurtado, 2003). In the 1960s, at much the same time as the Black Power movement was very active, a Chicano liberation movement was a vital force. Probably the best-known facet of this movement was the unionization of the United Farmworkers. Chicanas were an important part of this movement. Like African American women in the Black liberation movement, they gained experience with activism, but at the same time they became disturbed by the male dominance and sexism within the Chicano movement. Chicana feminism grew from these roots. Chicana feminists thus have the dual goals of cultural nationalism (liberation for Chicanas/os) and feminism (liberation for women).

A more recent development is transnational feminism (see Chapter 1), which is consistent with some but not all aspects of feminisms of color in the United States. Both perspectives note that definitions of feminism need to be broadened, but transnational feminism also emphasizes colonization and globalization as contributing systems of oppression (Grabe & Else-Quest, 2012; Lugones, 2010). In particular, transnational feminism focuses on political and economic oppression, especially the oppression of Global South or Third World women by people (including women) from wealthy Western nations.

Colonization is also at the heart of American Indian feminism, which provides another feminist perspective at the intersection of gender and ethnicity. American Indian feminism theorizes that the sexism experienced by American Indian women is inextricably linked to the colonization of the indigenous peoples of North America (Smith, 2005). That is, European gender roles, norms, and hierarchies have been imposed on American Indians through colonization, stripping Indian women of their autonomy both as women and as tribal members. In turn, decolonization and sovereignty are understood as a rejection of both gender- and ethnic-based systems of oppression. The rights to land, self-governance, an economic base, and identity, as well as to one's own body, are all central to American Indian feminism.

The topic of feminisms of color is a delicate one. There is much evidence that American feminism has been dominated by White middle-class women who have put their issues at the top of the agenda while ignoring issues that are more important to people of color and low-income people. At the same time, many women of color may feel that feminism divides their loyalties within their own community and that they should put their energies into fighting racism. A Black woman who seeks to be engaged in both Black Lives Matter and the contemporary feminist movement may find that her particular perspective is not always recognized within each activist movement. This tension demonstrates the importance of an intersectional feminism that promotes equity and equality for all people. When the perspectives and scholarship of diverse feminisms and related social justice movements are integrated, an effective and inclusive feminist movement is achieved.

Experience the Research

Gender Roles and Ethnicity on Prime Time

Identify three current television series (i.e., not reruns) that focus on an African American family. Then identify three comparison series that focus on a European American family. Ideally, choose comparison series that air at the same time as, or perhaps are shown immediately following, the shows about the African American families but on a different station. Observe each program twice. As you observe the programs, answer the following questions:

1. How are gender roles portrayed on the program? Does the main female character have a paying job? What kind of job is it? Does the main male character have a paying job? What is it? Who does the cooking? Who does the grocery shopping?

2. How is the family portrayed on the program? Is it a traditional heterosexual married couple with children, a single parent and their children, a queer couple, or some other kind of family?

3. How is emotional expressiveness portrayed on the program? What emotions do women express? What emotions do men express?

After you have completed your observations, compare the results for the African American family shows and the European American family shows. What are the differences? What are the similarities? What impact do you think these programs have on African American and European American viewers?

Finally, locate three comparable programs that focus on Asian American families, Latinx families, and American Indian families. Were you able to do it? If so, how are gender roles portrayed on those programs?

CHAPTER SUMMARY

One of the fundamental points of feminist theory is that we must examine not only gender but also ethnicity as powerful forces in people's lives. To do this, we must go far beyond acknowledging race differences, although we should recognize them when they exist. Similarities across ethnic groups—and there are many—deserve recognition as well. Most importantly, each ethnic group has its own cultural heritage, including its own definitions of gender roles and feminism, and all such heritages exert profound influences on the people from those cultures.

This chapter reviewed the cultural heritages of people of color in the United States, including Asian American persons, Latinx persons, American Indian persons, and African American persons. A recurring theme in the cultural heritages of these groups is subcultural variations. Gender roles across these diverse ethnic groups were also discussed. Reflecting the theme of intersectionality, the experience of gender is both similar and different across ethnic groups.

Immigration is an important force in the lives of many people of color. Experiences may differ across legal immigrants, undocumented immigrants, and refugees. Nonetheless, these groups all share the experiences of leaving one's home country, sometimes in the context of trauma, and acculturation within the new host culture. Acculturative stress can be exacerbated when immigrants and refugees face discrimination.

Education has long played a powerful role for people of color as a means to improve socioeconomic status and develop opportunities. Still, ethnic/racial disparities in educational attainment persist today.

Research on mental health issues at the intersection of gender and ethnicity finds that depression, PTSD, substance abuse, and other mental health problems can result from sexist and racist oppression. Clinical guidelines for providing culturally informed care to people of color and affirmative care to trans people of color have been developed.

Feminisms of color, such as womanism and mujerismo, are often strengths-based. These perspectives emphasize strengths, agency, resilience, and other positive traits of women of color in the face of sexist and racist oppression.

SUGGESTIONS FOR FURTHER READING

African American Policy Forum. (2015). *Say her name: Resisting police brutality against Black women*. New York, NY: Center for Intersectionality and Social Policy Studies. This report builds upon the work of activists and scholars and demonstrates the need for a more intersectional approach to racial justice.

Bryant-Davis, Thema, & Comas-Díaz, Lillian. (2016). *Womanist and Mujerista psychologies: Voices of fire, acts of courage*. Washington, DC: American Psychological Association. This book provides an excellent interdisciplinary review of womanist and mujerista perspectives.

Gender and Communication

Verbal and nonverbal communication are at the core of human psychology, essential to our social interactions and relationships as well as to our thoughts and understanding of the world. In this chapter we will explore the evidence on the differences between how women and men communicate verbally and nonverbally, and on how women and nonbinary people are treated in language. We will also provide practical guidance on using inclusive, nonsexist language.

Verbal Communication

Suppose you found the following caption, torn from a cartoon: "That sunset blends such lovely shades of pink and magenta, doesn't it?" If you had to guess the gender of the speaker, what would you say? Most people would guess that the speaker was a woman. Many people have ideas about what is typical or "appropriate" speech for men and women, and *lovely* and *magenta* just don't sound like things a man would say. Are those ideas just inaccurate gender stereotypes, or is there some kernel of truth to them? Do women and men actually differ in their verbal communication?

Tentativeness

The study of gender differences and similarities in language was sparked by Robin Lakoff (1973, 1975), who theorized that gender differences in communication stem from gender roles and the relative power those roles have. In other words, women and men don't differ in communication because they are innately different from one another, but because the social hierarchy makes them different. She argued that men use more assertive speech because they have power, whereas women use more tentative speech because they lack power.

What does tentative speech look (or sound) like? According to Lakoff, *tentative speech* has four forms or patterns: expressions of uncertainty, hedges, tag questions, and intensifiers. Expressions of uncertainty include **disclaimers**, like "I may be wrong, but . . ." or "This is just my opinion, but. . . ." **Hedges** are expressions such as "sort of" or "kind of." A **tag question** is a short phrase at the end of a declarative sentence that turns it into a question, such as "This is a great class, isn't it?" And **intensifiers** include adverbs like *very*, *really*, and *vastly*, such as "The governor is really interested in this proposal." Lakoff maintained that intensifiers add little content to a sentence and actually reduce the strength of the statement, so they contribute to tentativeness.

Lakoff's theorizing gained popularity as well as criticism in part because it highlighted a tension within feminism regarding gender differences and gender similarities. That is, if women and men are equal, does that mean that women and men are exactly the same? If women and men are different, how does patriarchal culture create those differences? Thus, it's not surprising that critics said Lakoff exaggerated and overemphasized gender differences without giving adequate attention to power and status. Similarly, some criticized her theory because it seemed to reflect gender stereotypes rather than empirical evidence. Her theory also implies, for some, a female deficit interpretation in labeling women's communication as deficient in respect to men's communication, which is held up as the standard. That is, maybe tentative speech can be more effective speech, reflecting interpersonal sensitivity.

What do the data show? Campbell Leaper and Rachael Robnett (2011) conducted a meta-analysis to examine the evidence for gender differences in the four forms of tentative speech. Overall, they found that women used more tentative speech but that the gender differences were small. For expressions of uncertainty, such as disclaimers, $d = -0.33$, and for hedges, $d = -0.15$. For tag questions, $d = -0.23$, and for intensifiers, $d = -0.38$. In sum, the pattern of gender differences in tentative speech supports Lakoff's claim, but those differences are small.

In addition, Leaper and Robnett (2011) interpreted the results of their meta-analysis to mean that women display greater interpersonal sensitivity, not that they lack assertiveness. If gender differences in tentative speech reflect issues of power and assertiveness, then they should be largest in mixed-gender groups, with men dominating and women being tentative. Yet gender differences in tentative speech were actually larger in same-gender groups ($d = -0.37$) than in mixed-gender groups ($d = -0.21$). Thus, we might say that the tag question is intended to encourage communication rather than to shut things down with a simple declarative statement. The tag question helps maintain the conversation and encourages the other person to express an opinion.

Affiliative Versus Assertive Speech

As the data evaluating Lakoff's theory accumulated, linguist Deborah Tannen popularized the belief that women's and men's communication patterns are vastly different

Disclaimers: Phrases such as "I may be wrong, but . . ."

Hedges: Phrases such as "sort of" that weaken or soften a statement.

Tag question: A short phrase added to a sentence that turns it into a question.

Intensifiers: Adverbs such as very, really, and vastly.

©iStockphoto.com/kali9 & ©iStockphoto.com/digitalskillet.

and that these differences create problems when women and men communicate with one another. In her widely read books, including *You Just Don't Understand: Women and Men in Conversation* (Tannen, 1991), she proposed that gender differences in communication are so substantial that it is as though women and men come from different linguistic communities or cultures. Thus, communication between women and men is as challenging as communication between people from different cultures—say, a person from the United States and a person from Japan. Tannen's position is called the **different cultures hypothesis**.

Tannen's perspective differed from Lakoff's in an important way: Whereas Lakoff theorized that gender differences develop because of men's power over women, Tannen claimed that gender differences in communication stem from the different goals that men and women have when they communicate. These different communication goals are rooted in gender roles. The female role emphasizes nurturing and relationships, whereas the male role emphasizes dominance and power. Thus, these roles require that women aim to establish and maintain relationships, whereas men aim to exert control, preserve their independence, and enhance their status (Tannen, 1991; J. T. Wood, 1994). Women try to show support or empathy by matching or mirroring experiences ("I've felt that way, too"), whereas men try to display their knowledge, avoid disclosing personal information, and avoid showing the slightest vulnerability. Women engage in conversation maintenance, trying to get a conversation started and keep it going ("How was your day?"), whereas men engage in conversational dominance (e.g., interrupting). Tannen claimed that women display tentative and affiliative speech, whereas men display assertive and authoritative speech.

Thus, another perspective on gender differences in verbal communication is Tannen's different cultures hypothesis. To evaluate it, we can examine gender differences in affiliative and assertive speech. **Affiliative speech** is speech that demonstrates affiliation or connection to the listener and may include praise, agreement, support, and/or acknowledgment. By contrast, **assertive speech** is speech that aims to influence the listener and may include providing instructions, information, suggestions, criticism, and/or disagreement. Note that some speech could be both assertive and affiliative, such as when someone gives instructions that are supportive (e.g., "You seem tired; go and get some rest").

Leaper and his colleagues have conducted two meta-analyses that examine gender differences in affiliative and assertive speech, one with children and one with adults. Let's first consider affiliativeness. In general, girls and women are somewhat more affiliative relative to boys and men. Among children, the gender difference is small, $d = -0.26$

PHOTO 5.1
According to the theorist Robin Lakoff, we should expect these two social groups to differ in the amount of disclaimers, hedges, and tag questions. Do you interpret that gender difference as evidence of women's greater tentativeness or interpersonal sensitivity?

Different cultures hypothesis: Tannen's perspective that gender differences in communication are so different that it is as though women and men come from different linguistic cultures.

Affiliative speech: Speech that demonstrates affiliation or connection to the listener and may include praise, agreement, support, and/or acknowledgment.

Assertive speech: Speech that aims to influence the listener and may include providing instructions, information, suggestions, criticism, and/or disagreement.

©iStockphoto.com/Wavebreakmedia.

PHOTO 5.2

According to linguist Deborah Tannen, women and men have different goals when they speak. Women aim to establish and maintain relationships, whereas men aim to exert control.

(Leaper & Smith, 2004). That gender difference shrinks in adulthood, $d = -0.12$ (Leaper & Ayres, 2007).

With regard to assertiveness, the gender differences are tiny. Among children, boys engage in more assertive speech than girls do, but the difference is very small, $d = 0.10$ (Leaper & Smith, 2004). Among adults, men are slightly more assertive than women, $d = 0.09$ (Leaper & Ayres, 2007). Thus, evidence suggests that male speech patterns are only marginally more assertive than female speech patterns.

In sum, the gender differences in affiliative and assertive speech are just too small to support the different cultures hypothesis. Apparently, cross-cultural communication is possible—girls and women can and do use assertive speech, just as boys and men can and do use affiliative speech!

Interruptions

Early researchers found that men interrupt women considerably more often than women interrupt men (e.g., C. West & Zimmerman, 1983; Zimmerman & West, 1975). For example, one important and widely cited study found that gender differences in interruptions are found only in mixed-gender conversation pairs (McMillan et al., 1977). That is, women interrupted women about as often as men interrupted men. However, women very seldom interrupted men, whereas men frequently interrupted women. How should we interpret this pattern of gender differences and similarities? The typical interpretation made by feminist social scientists involves the assumption that interruptions are an expression of power or dominance. That is, the interrupter gains control of a conversation, and that is a kind of interpersonal power. The gender difference, then, is interpreted as indicating that men are expressing power and dominance over women. This pattern may reflect the subtle persistence of traditional gender roles; it may also help to perpetuate traditional roles.

Yet one recent study found slightly different results (see Table 5.1; Hancock & Rubin, 2015). Across conversational pairs, women were more likely to be interrupted than men were, regardless of who was doing the interrupting. One interpretation of this finding, consistent with the feminist perspective, is that women are generally perceived as lower status and, thus, can be interrupted. Men, because they have higher status, are less likely to be interrupted.

TABLE 5.1   **Mean number of interruptions per 3-minute conversation in same- and mixed-gender pairs.**

Gender of Interrupter	Gender of Interruptee	
	Woman	Man
Woman	2.9	1.0
Man	2.1	1.8

Source: Data from Hancock & Rubin (2015).

Some researchers have suggested that interruptions can have multiple meanings, which complicates the interpretation of these gender differences (Aries, 1996; McHugh & Hambaugh, 2010). Some interruptions are requests for clarification. Others express agreement or support, such as an *mm-hmm* or *definitely* murmured while the other person is speaking. Some interruptions express disagreement with the speaker, and other interruptions change the subject. These last two types of interruptions are the ones that express dominance. Most interruptions in fact turn out to be agreements or requests for clarification and have nothing to do with dominance. Some researchers have found that women engage in more of this supportive interrupting, particularly when they are in all-female groups (e.g., Aries, 1996).

A meta-analysis of gender differences and similarities in conversational interruption provides us with some clarity on this controversy. Anderson and Leaper (1998) found that the gender difference in interruptions was $d = 0.15$, indicating that men interrupt more often than women. However, moderator analyses told a more complex story about interruptions. Effect sizes for *intrusive interruptions* (i.e., interruptions that display dominance, such as a change in subject or expression of disagreement) were considerably larger, $d = 0.33$.

Overall, then, to say that men interrupt more than women do, and that this indicates men's expression of dominance, is not entirely accurate (Aries, 1996; McHugh & Hambaugh, 2010). Patterns of gender differences in interruption may vary depending on context (mixed-gender group vs. same-gender group, natural conversation vs. laboratory task), and interruptions can have many meanings besides dominance. For intrusive interruptions, however, men interrupt more often than women do.

The Gender-Linked Language Effect

As you've seen, many of the gender differences in verbal communication are unimpressive. Anthony Mulac (2006) proposed that, while many features of verbal communication show very small gender differences, it is the clustering of these features that matters. That is, there are feminine and masculine patterns of speech, each with multiple features that show subtle differences on their own but, in combination, are perceived as distinctly gendered. The verbal communication of girls and women tends to be rated as more socially intelligent and aesthetically pleasing, whereas the verbal communication of boys and men is rated as more dynamic and aggressive. Mulac calls these patterns of gender differences the *gender-linked language effect*.

Mulac (2006) conducted a series of studies in which the speech of men and women (or boys and girls) is transcribed, masked as to the identity of the speaker, and then presented to university students to see whether they can tell whether the speaker was male or female. If Tannen's hypothesis is correct, the task should be a snap and students should be able to identify the gender of the speaker with a high degree of accuracy. In fact, though, students perform no better than chance on the task. These findings support the notion of gender similarities in communication.

Other studies, though, find significant differences between women's and men's speech when highly trained coders look for specific details such as intensifiers, tag questions, and references to emotions (Mulac, 2006). The differences must therefore be subtle, detectable by scientifically trained coders but not by the average person.

Mulac and his colleagues (2013) found some evidence of the gender-linked language effect in a recent study of written language. In the first task, participants wrote descriptions of landscape photographs and the research team coded those descriptions for

13 features of language that have been shown to differ between men and women. Only six of those features showed gender differences. For example, men tended to make more references to quantity (e.g., "60 feet tall") and use elliptical sentences (e.g., "great picture"), whereas women tended to write more words overall and make more references to emotion (e.g., "a somber scene"). Many features of tentative language, such as hedges and intensifiers, showed gender similarities.

In the second task, the researchers asked the participants to write descriptions of more photographs, this time under the guise of specific genders. That is, participants were asked to describe the photographs "as a man" and "as a woman." This task was used to indicate participants' gender-linked language schemas. The results showed that schemas were somewhat consistent with the actual gender differences found in the first task: Gender differences in the second task matched four of the six features that showed gender differences in the first task, including references to quantity and emotion. In other words, participants had clear gender schemas about language, and these schemas were fairly accurate. These findings demonstrate that the gender-linked language effect exists but that the effect is subtle.

Clinical Applications

You might be wondering: How are the gender-linked language effect and other gender differences in verbal communication relevant? Well, there are at least two reasons that these findings matter. One reason is that language is often used to persuade, solve problems, and connect with people. Doing these things effectively requires using our language well. As discussed earlier, in some cases tentative language is more interpersonally sensitive and, therefore, more effective. As the old saying goes, you can catch more flies with honey than with vinegar.

Another reason the gender-linked language effect is relevant is in its clinical application, such as in the case of *communication therapy*. For transgender people, communication therapy is often a component of their transition. This therapy might include working with a speech-language pathologist to change such speech features as vocal pitch, resonance, intonation, volume, articulation, and others so that their speech is more aligned with their gender identity (Adler et al., 2012; Hancock et al., 2015). For example, a transgender woman might work with a therapist to speak in a higher vocal pitch and to alter her intonation so that some of her declarative statements end with a rise in pitch. Even if the differences in speech are subtle, they can improve the quality of social interactions and may help to prevent painful misgendering experiences in which others misidentify their gender identity.

Nonverbal Communication

Nonverbal communication is just as important as verbal communication. Imagine saying to someone "How nice to see you" while standing only 6 inches from them or while actually brushing up against them. Then imagine saying the same sentence while standing 6 feet away from them. The sentence conveys a much different meaning in the two instances. In the first, it will probably convey warmth and possibly sexiness. In the second case, the meaning will seem formal and perhaps cold. As another example, a sentence coming from a smiling face conveys a very different meaning from that of the same sentence coming from a stern or frowning face.

FOCUS 5.1

GENDER AND ELECTRONIC COMMUNICATION

How we communicate with one another has changed dramatically in the last two decades. Today, much of our communication is via e-mail, text messaging, social media, and other online platforms. Do we see gender differences in electronic communication?

Let's first consider texting. Research on texting has been mixed with regard to whether there are gender differences in the quantity of texts sent (e.g., Forgays et al., 2014; Tossell et al., 2012). When we look at the qualities of text messages, women tend to use more emoticons, but men tend to use a greater variety of emoticons (Tossell et al., 2012). This pattern may have more to do with gender roles than actual gender, though; another study found that femininity (on the Bem Sex Role Inventory, discussed in Chapter 3) was more strongly linked to emoticon usage than gender (Ogletree et al., 2014). Men are somewhat more permissive about the range of contexts in which they feel texting is appropriate, such as while sharing a meal with someone or being at church (Forgays et al., 2014). While there are gender similarities in the amount of sexually explicit text messages (i.e., "sexts") sent, men report receiving more of such messages (Ogletree et al., 2014).

To explore gender differences and similarities in language use online, researchers may analyze language used in e-mail messages and posts to blogs and comment boards, for example.In one study, researchers examined the language used by men and women in postings to electronic bulletin boards as a function of whether the topic was gender stereotyped or gender neutral (Thomson, 2006). When topics were female stereotyped (e.g., fashion) or male stereotyped (e.g., sports), findings were similar to those found in face-to-face interactions. Women used more hedges and intensifiers, and they expressed more emotion and disclosed

©iStockphoto.com/m-imagephotography.

PHOTO 5.3
Researchers have found evidence of gender differences and gender similarities in electronic communication.

more personal information. Men, in contrast, issued more directives,disagreed more, and boasted more. These differences, however, were not found when the topic was gender-neutral.

In another experiment by the same team, participants conducted e-mail correspondence with two fictitious netpals and received responses that, in actuality, came from the experimenter (Thomson et al., 2001). For each participant, one netpal responded with female-linked language (more emotion references, more intensifiers, etc.) and the other netpal responded with male-linked language (more opinions, fewer emotions, etc.). Interestingly, participants—whether male or female—responded differently depending on the gendered content coming from the netpal, shifting their e-talk to be like that of their netpal. This is a great illustration of how gender is constructed in social interactions and how gender patterns depend heavily on social context.

Gender stereotypes generally hold that women are more nonverbally expressive than men are (Briton & Hall, 1995). Are these stereotypes accurate? Here we will review the evidence on gender differences in nonverbal communication and what those differences mean (for meta-analyses, see Hall, 1998; McClure, 2000).

PHOTO 5.4
According to gender stereotypes in most Western cultures, two adult men hold hands only if they are romantically involved. By contrast, in some cultures, this nonverbal behavior merely conveys friendship. Images of President George W. Bush holding hands with Saudi Crown Prince Abdullah went viral when the two men met to discuss oil prices in 2005.

Jim Watson/AFP/Getty Images.

Encoding and Decoding Nonverbal Behavior

Effectively encoding (i.e., sending or conveying) and decoding (i.e., perceiving or reading) nonverbal behaviors are important for social interaction. Are men and women equally accurate in encoding and decoding nonverbal messages?

Meta-analysis tells us that women convey nonverbal messages or cues more accurately than men do (Hall, 1984). Is this because men are not very expressive in general or because their expressions are difficult to read? Some evidence indicates that men tend to suppress their nonverbal expressions, beginning around adolescence, whereas women tend to amplify their expressions (LaFrance & Vial, 2016). Women are also more accurate at decoding or reading others' nonverbal cues. The gender difference in decoding exists even in childhood (McClure, 2000), though it is somewhat larger in adults (Hall, 1984; LaFrance & Vial, 2016).

These patterns of gender differences in encoding and decoding suggest that men and women differ not because they are inherently or innately different, but because they face pressure to adhere to different gender roles. In particular, the female role entails communality, or establishing and maintaining social relationships, which requires interpersonal sensitivity.

Smiling

Around the world, women smile more than men (LaFrance et al., 2003). According to meta-analyses, this gender difference fluctuates across the lifespan. In infancy and childhood, for example, it is nonexistent, $d = -0.01$ (Else-Quest et al., 2006), but in adolescence, the gender difference swells to $d = -0.56$ (LaFrance et al., 2003). The gap then declines, such that $d = -0.30$ in middle adulthood and $d = -0.11$ in older adulthood (LaFrance et al., 2003). In addition, some evidence suggests that gender differences seem to vary as a function of ethnicity; the pattern is more characteristic of White women than African American women (LaFrance et al., 2003).

Understanding the meaning of these gender differences in smiling requires thinking about why people smile. Sometimes, it indicates positive affect, such as happiness. Other times, its meaning is more complicated. Smiling has been called the female version of the

"Uncle Tom shuffle"—that is, rather than indicating happiness or friendliness, it may serve as an appeasement gesture, communicating, in effect, "Please don't hurt me or be mean." A person who is smiling is not likely to be perceived as threatening.

Smiling may also be a status indicator: Dominant people smile less and subordinate people smile more, so women's smiling might reflect their subordinate status (Henley, 1977, 1995). A number of studies, however, contradict this status interpretation. Although women consistently smile more than men in these studies, lower-status people (e.g., employees in a company) do not smile more than higher-status people (e.g., supervisors; Hall & Friedman, 1999; Hall et al., 2001).

PHOTO 5.5
Artist Tatyana Fazlalizadeh's work, Stop Telling Women to Smile (http://stoptellingwomentosmile.tumblr.com/)

Smiling is also a part of the female role, which requires being warm, nurturant, and physically attractive. Most women can remember having their faces feel stiff and sore from smiling at a party or some other public gathering at which they were expected to smile. The smile, of course, reflected not happiness, but rather a belief that smiling was the appropriate thing to do. Women's smiles, then, do not necessarily reflect positive feelings and may even be associated with negative feelings and pressure to adhere to the female role and "put on a happy face."

Consistent with this view that smiling is part of the female role and therefore important in social situations, a meta-analysis found that the gender difference was more than twice as large when participants knew that they were being observed ($d = -0.46$) than when they did not know they were being observed ($d = -0.19$; LaFrance et al., 2003).

Most women can recall being told by men to smile, regardless of how they might be feeling. Popular media has even created an unfortunate term for women's neutral (i.e., nonsmiling) facial expressions: *resting bitch face*. Indeed, when women violate the role requirement of smiling, others react negatively. For example, in one study, participants were given a written description of a person, accompanied by a photograph of a man or woman who was smiling or not smiling (Deutsch et al., 1987). The results indicated that the women who were not smiling were given more negative evaluations: They were rated as less happy and less relaxed in comparison with men and in comparison with women who were smiling.

Interpersonal Distance

In many countries, including the United States, it seems that men tend to prefer a greater distance between themselves and another person, whereas women tend to be comfortable with a smaller distance between themselves and others. This is particularly evident in same-gender pairs. For example, when two women interact, they tend to sit or stand closer to one another than two men do (e.g., Gifford, 1997). Similarly, people tend to prefer to maintain greater interpersonal distance from unfamiliar men than they do from unfamiliar women. Regardless of our own gender, we tend to need greater interpersonal space with men than with women in order to feel comfortable (e.g., Iachini et al., 2016).

What do we make of such differences? There are several possibilities. Our interpersonal space preferences may, at least in part, reflect concerns about falsely signaling that we are sexually or romantically interested in someone. It is a significant gender role violation for a heterosexual man to signal sexual interest in another man. Another possibility is that men are perceived as a threat or considered potentially dangerous, so we try to stay out of their "territory" to avoid conflict. By contrast, women are perceived as nonthreatening and considered safe, so we may feel less wary of getting in their space. Indeed, some have suggested that women have a small interpersonal distance as a result of, or in order to express, warmth, caring, or friendliness (Mast & Sczesny, 2010). Each of these possibilities is plausible; researchers who study interpersonal distance theorize that our interpersonal space preferences are shaped by sexual attraction, self-protective, and affiliative forces (Iachini et al., 2016). Also, each of these interpretations suggests that gender differences in interpersonal distance have more to do with gender roles than with gender. That is, how we position ourselves relative to other people is one way that we perform our gender roles.

One study compared the effects of gender, gender role identification, and sexual orientation on interpersonal distance (Uzzell & Horne, 2006). The researchers first administered the Bem Sex Role Inventory (see Chapter 3) to a sample of British college students who were diverse in terms of their sexual orientation (but not in terms of race/ethnicity; all were White). Then they assigned participants to interact with one another in a structured conversational task: Every 2 minutes, participants moved around to different stations or zones in the research lab. The researchers videotaped the interactions and marked the floor of the stations with a grid so that they could measure the distance between the feet of the conversational pairs. Results indicated significant effects of gender: Female-female pairs stood significantly closer to one another than did male-male or female-male pairs.

However, the effects of gender were completely eliminated when the researchers considered gender role identification. That is, self-reported femininity and masculinity were far more important than gender in determining interpersonal distance: Feminine people stood closer to their conversational partner, and masculine people stood farther away from their conversational partner. Sexual orientation had minimal effects on interpersonal distance. Although we don't know if we can generalize these findings to other cultures or ethnic groups, it is clear that just examining differences between men and women is too simplistic. Gender roles are important!

Eye Contact

Eye contact between two people when speaking to each other can reflect patterns of power and dominance. Although the meaning of eye contact varies across cultures, in North American cultures higher-status people tend to look at the other person while they (the dominant people) are speaking. Lower-status people tend to look at the other person while listening. Researchers in this area compute a **visual dominance ratio**, defined as the ratio of the percentage of time looking while speaking relative to the percentage of time looking while listening (Dovidio et al., 1988; Mast & Sczesny, 2010).

Visual dominance ratio:
The ratio of the percentage of time looking while speaking relative to the percentage of time looking while listening; an indicator of social dominance.

Research on the connection between visual dominance and social power indicates, for example, that patterns of visual dominance are expressed across different levels of military rank and different levels of educational attainment (e.g., Dovidio et al., 1988). One study found that gender differences in visual dominance aligned with gender differences in knowledge about a gendered task, such as changing a tire versus changing a diaper (Brown et al., 1992). When researchers trained participants and eliminated gender differences in knowledge, the gender difference in visual dominance was also eliminated.

Another experiment investigated visual dominance as a function of both gender and power (Dovidio et al., 1988). College students were assigned to mixed-gender dyads.

Each pair discussed three topics in sequence. The first discussion was on a neutral topic, and there was no manipulation of power (control condition). For the second topic, one member of the pair evaluated the other member and had the power to award extra-credit points to that person. For the third topic, the roles were reversed, and the person who had been evaluated became the evaluator.

In the control condition, men were visually dominant: Men looked at their partners more while speaking, and women looked more while listening. This was as predicted, given that men tend to have greater status or power relative to women. However, in the second and third discussions, when women were in the powerful role, they looked more than men while speaking, and men looked more while listening. That is, when women were given social power, they became visually dominant. These results again support a power or status interpretation of gender differences in eye contact and visual dominance. And as women gain more power in society, such patterns may well change.

Posture: Expansive or Contractive?

Another relevant aspect of nonverbal communication here is posture. People who are sitting or standing with their legs together and their arms close to their body are displaying a closed or **contractive posture**. By contrast, people who are sitting or standing with their limbs extended away from their body are displaying an open or **expansive posture** (see Photo 5.6). Expansive posture, sometimes referred to as *power posing*, takes up more space with one's body and conveys social dominance and confidence, whereas contractive posture makes a person seem smaller and conveys submissiveness (LaFrance & Vial, 2016). In one study, participants were randomly assigned to conditions in which they were instructed to position their bodies in specific expansive or contractive poses (Carney et al., 2010). Relative to participants in the contractive pose condition, those in the expansive pose condition felt more powerful, were more willing to gamble their payment for participation, and even showed hormonal changes that are usually associated with power. The experimenters found these effects in male and female participants alike. Since then, over 30 experiments have replicated some of these effects (Carney et al., 2015), but they generally link expansive posture to feelings of power and dominance.

With all this discussion of power and dominance conveyed with nonverbal behaviors, it's probably not surprising that we see gender differences in posture. Women are more likely than men to sit or stand in contractive poses (Hall, 1984). The gender difference in expansive posture is large, with men more likely than women to sit or stand in expansive poses (Hall, 1984). In one study, researchers observed passengers on the subway in Amsterdam and found that men more often displayed an expansive posture whereas women more often displayed a contractive posture (Vrugt & Luyerink, 2000). Indeed, some feminists have coined the term *manspreading* to refer to men's expansive posture on public transit (Jane, 2016; see Photo 5.7).

Why do women tend to have more contractive posture? In some cases, it may be a strategy to avoid being perceived as threatening. In other cases, it may be a strategy

Contractive posture: Sitting or standing with legs together and arms close to the body.

Expansive posture: Sitting or standing with limbs extended away from the body; also referred to as power posing.

©iStockphoto.com/drbimages.

PHOTO 5.6
What information do these people convey with their expansive and contractive postures?

Dude . . .
Stop the Spread, Please
It's a space issue.

PHOTO 5.7
The Metropolitan Transportation Authority in New York City launched a campaign in 2015 to stop manspreading on subways and buses. http://web.mta.info/nyct/service/CourtesyCounts .htm#DUDESTOPTHESPREAD

to protect or shield one's body from scrutiny and the male gaze (Kozak et al., 2014). So we might think of contractive posture as a protective strategy for women, which they've developed as an adaptation to objectification.

In summary, displaying expansive (vs. contractive) postures makes people feel more powerful and more willing to take risks, and men are more likely than women to display expansive postures.

How Women and Nonbinary People Are Treated in Language

Up to this point we have discussed gender differences and similarities in both verbal and nonverbal forms of communication. Another aspect of communication that needs to be considered is how gender issues are treated in our language. That is, how are women and people who do not fit within the gender binary treated in language? For example, trans and nonbinary people are often described with language that is inadequate, incomplete, or inaccurate, which can make them feel invisible and alienated (Langer, 2011). For genderqueer people, in particular, neither of the standard English language options *he* or *she* is an appropriate pronoun, but the alternative *it* is dehumanizing. Feminists have sensitized the public to the issue of *sexist language*, which includes inappropriate or irrelevant reference to gender, the use of masculine generics and male-as-normative/female-as-exception word choices, as well as the use of misgendering speech. Objectifying, sexualizing, or infantilizing euphemisms are also examples of sexist language. Here we will discuss patterns of sexist language and why they matter for the psychology of women and gender.

Misgendering

Misgendering: A form of sexist language in which gendered language that does not match a person's gender identity is used or when a person's gender identity is misidentified by some other means.

One form of sexist language that can be particularly harmful is misgendering. **Misgendering** occurs when we use gendered language that is inconsistent with a person's gender identity or when a person's gender identity is misidentified by some other means. Misgendering occurs in a variety of circumstances and is particularly common among women working in stereotypically male professions, who may be referred to using masculine pronouns (e.g., Stout & Dasgupta, 2011). Transgender people are frequently misgendered (McLemore, 2014, 2016), such as when medical and mental health professionals label them by the gender they were assigned at birth rather than by their gender identity (Ansara & Hegarty, 2014; Hagen & Galupo, 2014). When people are misgendered, they may feel ignored, devalued, stigmatized, and hurt, or worse.

Using incorrect gendered pronouns to refer to transgender people has clearly harmful effects. When a person is misgendered in this way, their personal identity has not been affirmed, which threatens their sense of a strong and coherent identity (McLemore, 2014, 2016). Surveys of transgender men and women show that their experiences of being misgendered are linked to negative moods (such as anxiety and depression), feeling negatively about their identity and appearance, and feelings of stigmatization (McLemore, 2014, 2016).

Euphemisms

Generally, when there are many euphemisms for a word, it is a reflection of the fact that people find the word and what it stands for to be distasteful or stressful. For example, consider all the various terms we use in place of *bathroom* or *toilet*. And then note the great variety of terms that we substitute for *die*, such as *pass away*.

Feminist linguists have argued that we similarly have a strong tendency to use euphemisms for the word *woman* (Cralley & Ruscher, 2005; Lakoff, 1973). That is, people have a tendency to avoid using the word *woman* and instead substitute a variety of terms that seem more polite or less threatening, the most common euphemisms being *lady* and *girl*. Other euphemisms objectify or sexualize women, such as *chick*, *shorty*, *honey*, or *ho*. Another euphemism for woman is *bitch*, which has a hostile connotation.

How common are these different euphemisms? In one study, undergraduates were asked to list as many slang terms as they could for either woman or man (Grossman & Tucker, 1997). Fully 93% of men listed *bitch* as a term for woman! But then, so did 73% of the women. Overall, the euphemisms listed for *woman* were more likely to carry a sexual meaning than those listed for *man*; roughly 50% of the slang terms for *woman* were sexual, compared with 23% of the terms for *man*.

In contrast to the word *man*, which is used frequently and comfortably, *woman* is used less frequently and apparently causes some discomfort or we wouldn't use euphemisms for it. However, the tendency to use euphemisms for *woman* can be changed by becoming sensitive to this tendency and by making efforts to use the word *woman* when it is appropriate.

Infantilizing

A 25-year-old man wrote to an advice columnist, depressed because he wanted to get married but had never had a date. Part of the columnist's response was "Just scan the society pages and look at the people who are getting married every day. Are the men all handsome? Are the girls all beautiful?"

This is an illustration of the way in which people, rather than using *woman* as the parallel to *man*, substitute *girl* instead. As noted in the previous section, this in part reflects the use of a euphemism. But it is also true that *boy* refers to male children, and *man* to male adults. Somehow *girl*, which in a strict sense should refer only to female children, is used for female adults as well. Women are called by a term that seems to make them less mature and less powerful than they are; women are thus infantilized in language. Just as the term *boy* is offensive to Black activists, *girl* is offensive to feminists.

There are many other illustrations of this **infantilizing** theme. When a ship sinks, it's "Women and children first," putting women and children in the same category. Other examples in language are expressions for women, such as *baby* or *babe*. The problem with these terms is that they carry a meaning of immaturity and lack of power.

Infantilizing: Treating people—for example, women—as if they were children or babies.

Male as Normative and Female as the Exception

One of the clearest patterns in the English language is the male as normative, or androcentrism, a concept discussed in Chapter 1 (Smith et al., 2010). The male is regarded as the normative (standard) member of the species, and this is expressed in many ways in language, for example, the use of *man* to refer to all human beings and the use of *he* for a neutral pronoun (as in the sentence "The infant typically begins to sit up around 6 months of age; he may begin crawling at about the same time"). The male-as-normative principle in language can lead to some absurd statements. For example, there is a state law that reads, "No person may require another person to perform, participate in, or undergo an abortion of pregnancy against his will" (Key, 1975).

At the very least, the male-as-normative usage introduces ambiguity into our language. When someone uses the word *men*, is the reference to male adults or to people in general? When Dr. Karl Menninger writes a book titled *Man Against Himself*, is it a book about people generally, or is it a book about the tensions experienced by male adults?

Masculine generics: The common usage of masculine forms (e.g., he, his, him) as generic for all people.

Masculine generics—that is, using masculine nouns and pronouns to refer to all people in a gender-neutral sense—have long been used in English. Some people excuse masculine generics and say they aren't an example of male as normative speech. However, this explanation is problematic and inadequate. To illustrate the flaw in the "generic" logic, consider the objections raised by some men who joined the League of Women Voters. They complained that the name of the organization should be changed, for it no longer adequately describes its members, some of whom are now men. Suppose in response to their objection they were told that *woman* meant "generic person," which of course could include a man. Do you think they would feel satisfied? Why are masculine generics acceptable but feminine generics aren't?

For some time, feminist linguists have theorized that the masculine generic is an example of sexism in language (e.g., Lakoff, 1973; Stahlberg et al., 2007; Swim et al., 2004). And the use of masculine generics in English has been linked to the status of women in the United States. For example, Jean Twenge and her colleagues (2012) analyzed the ratio of male to female pronouns (e.g., *he/she, his/hers, him/her*) in the full texts of about 1.2 million U.S. books in the Google Books database. They found that when women's status was higher, such as when women had greater educational attainment and labor force participation, the proportion of female pronouns was also higher. By contrast, when women's status was lower, the use of female pronouns was less frequent.

Female-as-the-exception phenomenon: If a category is considered normatively male and there is a female example of the category, gender is noted because the female is the exception; a by-product of androcentrism.

The male-as-normative principle is also reflected in the **female-as-the-exception phenomenon**. This phenomenon occurs when a category that is considered normatively male has a female example; in those cases, gender is noted because it is a deviation from the norm. A newspaper reported the results of the Bowling Green State University women's swimming team and men's swimming team in two articles close to each other. The headline reporting the men's results was "BG Swimmers Defeated." The one for the women was "BG Women Swimmers Win." As another example, in the wake of Hurricane Katrina, which destroyed much of New Orleans, federal officials referred to the governor of Louisiana, Kathleen Blanco, as the "female governor" (Lipton, 2005). At the same time, the governor of Mississippi, Haley Barbour, was never referred to as the "male governor." His maleness would not have been considered newsworthy. We assume that athletes and governors are male, so in cases where they are female, this exception is often noted.

Many parallel words also reflect the male-as-normative, female-as-exception pattern. Some nouns can be qualified by adding a suffix—such as *ess, euse, ette,* or *ix*—that indicates female gender. For example, *actor* can be modified to *actress, adulterer* can be modified to *adulteress*, and *comedian* can be modified to *comedienne*. With such words, the masculine form is clearly the norm and the feminine form is a deviation from that norm.

Sometimes, noting a person's gender in this way can be a strategy to increase visibility of an underrepresented gender group, but other times it's just not relevant to the situation and may even stigmatize the person as the exception to the norm.

Gendering of Language

Natural gender language: A type of language in which most personal nouns are gender-neutral (e.g., student) but pronouns are differentiated for gender; examples include English and Swedish.

Languages vary with regard to how they handle gender. Some languages are gendered and others are genderless (Stahlberg et al., 2007). Languages such as English and Swedish are **natural gender languages**, which means that although personal pronouns are differentiated by gender (as in *she, he, her, him*, etc.), most personal nouns are gender neutral. So, for example, *student* is gender neutral, but you would use the subject pronoun *she* to refer to a female student.

By contrast, languages such as Spanish, German, Hindi, and Hebrew are **grammatical gender languages**, such that various parts of speech (including nouns, pronouns, verbs, adjectives, etc.) that would not naturally be considered masculine or feminine are inflected with gender. For example, in German the word for the noun *student* is masculine, as in *der Student*, but the word for the noun *university* is feminine, as in *die Universität*. Young children whose first language is a grammatical gender language, such as Spanish, quickly learn this information as they learn to speak correctly (Lew-Williams & Fernald, 2007).

Languages such as Finnish, Mandarin, and Turkish are **genderless languages**, in that neither personal nouns nor pronouns are differentiated for gender. For example, in Turkish the word for the noun student is *öğrenci*, which is gender neutral, and you would use the subject pronoun *o* for that student, regardless of their gender.

Researchers have demonstrated that these different language types reflect societal gender equality. In a study of 111 countries with different language types, researchers found that a country's level of gender equality (as described in Chapter 1) was associated with its language type (Prewitt-Freilino et al., 2012). Countries with grammatical gender languages tend to have less gender equality relative to countries with natural gender languages or genderless languages. In addition, masculine generics are more prominent in grammatical and natural gender languages (Vainapel et al., 2015).

Does Sexist Language Actually Matter?

You might be asking yourself: Does any of this stuff—such as the use of masculine generics and gendered languages—actually matter? It's good to be skeptical, but it's better to examine the data and weigh the evidence.

Sexist language and sexist attitudes go hand in hand. The use of masculine generics reflects not only the cultural or societal status of women (Twenge et al., 2012), but also personal attitudes about gender. For example, Janet Swim and her colleagues (2004) conducted two studies on sexist beliefs and the use of sexist language. In the first study, participants completed measures of sexist beliefs and were asked to mark a list of sentences for grammatical and sexist language errors. Swim et al. found that participants who endorsed modern sexist beliefs (discussed in Chapter 1) were less able to detect sexist language, in part because they had narrower definitions of sexist language. In the second study, participants completed measures of sexist beliefs and wrote responses to how they would respond to several moral dilemmas. Swim et al. then coded participants' responses for the use of sexist language, such as masculine generics. Participants who held modern sexist beliefs used sexist language more often.

Some research finds gender differences in attitudes toward sexist language: Men are generally more supportive of sexist language, and women are more supportive of non-sexist language (e.g., Douglas & Sutton, 2014; Parks & Roberton, 2004). Karen Douglas and Robbie Sutton (2014) conducted a study to explore why this gender difference exists. Participants completed a questionnaire measuring their general preference for social hierarchy and inequality over equality (known as *social dominance orientation*; Sidanius & Pratto, 1999) and their tendency to think gender inequality is fair and legitimate (or *system-justifying beliefs*). Douglas and Sutton found that gender differences in attitudes toward sexist language were explained by social dominance orientation and system-justifying beliefs. In other words, the finding that men are more supportive of sexist language was explained by men's preference for social inequality and belief that gender inequality is fair. These findings are in line with the argument that sexist language is caused by sexist beliefs, but, because the data are quasi-experimental, we can't actually infer causation.

Grammatical gender language: A type of language in which parts of speech (including nouns, pronouns, verbs, adjectives, etc.) are gender-inflected; examples include Spanish, German, Hindi, and Hebrew.

Genderless language: A type of language in which gender is expressed only lexically and neither personal nouns or pronouns are differentiated for gender; examples include Finnish, Mandarin, and Turkish.

Some argue that sexist language is a symptom of sexist attitudes and societal gender inequality. The generic use of *man* and *he* reflects the fact that we think of the male as the norm for the human species and that we carry gender stereotypes and biases in our thoughts (Cralley & Ruscher, 2005; Stahlberg et al., 2007). That is, we use sexist language because we think in sexist terms. The practical conclusion from this is that if we change our thought processes, language will change with them.

An alternative perspective comes from one of the classic theories of psycholinguistics, the **Whorfian hypothesis** (Whorf, 1956). The Whorfian hypothesis states that the specific language we learn influences our mental processes. If that is true, then gendered language doesn't just reflect gender inequality; gendered language perpetuates gender inequality. Similarly, some experts have argued that language encodes inequalities in a culture and that language can normalize bias by making it part of everyday speech (Ng, 2007).

In one study, researchers examined how using a natural gender language or a grammatical gender language influenced people's self-reported sexist attitudes (Wasserman & Weseley, 2009). Participants who were native English speakers and bilingual were randomly assigned to respond to the survey in either a natural gender language (English) or a grammatical gender language (Spanish or French). Participants who completed the survey in a grammatical gender language reported more sexist attitudes than participants who completed the survey in the natural gender language. These findings suggest that using a grammatical gender language may actually promote sexist attitudes. Yet feminists need not despair—another study found that, even in a grammatical gender language such as German, nonsexist language can still be used (Koeser et al., 2015).

In another study, researchers randomly assigned research participants in Israel to complete a survey measuring aspects of academic motivation in Hebrew (a grammatical gender language) using either masculine generics or a gender-neutral form (i.e., using both masculine and feminine forms; Vainapel et al., 2015). They found gender differences in self-efficacy when the survey used masculine generics but gender similarities when gender-neutral forms were used. That is, women's self-efficacy scores were lower than men's scores only when masculine generics were used.

In addition, the Whorfian hypothesis would predict that practices like the use of masculine generics actually make us think that the male is normative and the female is the exception. The process by which language encodes inequality and influences how we think about gender might start with very young children when they are just beginning to learn their first language. As we develop, then, cultural linguistic practices become deeply ingrained and form the foundation for how we think about gender.

In fact, many studies show that the use of masculine generics shapes how we think (e.g., Braun et al., 2005; Foertsch & Gernsbacher, 1997; Gastil, 1990; Hamilton, 1988; Moulton et al., 1978; Vervecken & Hannover, 2015). We highlight a few of these studies here.

One of us (JSH) conducted a series of studies to investigate the effects of sexist language on children (Hyde, 1984a). First, she generated an age-appropriate stimulus sentence and asked first-, third-, and fifth-grade children to tell stories in response to it. The children were divided into three groups. The stimulus sentence was as follows:

When a kid goes to school, ___ often feels excited on the first day.

One-third of the children received *he* for the blank, one-third received *they*, and one-third received *he or she*. When the pronoun was *he*, only 12% of the stories were about women, versus 42% when the pronoun was "he or she." Interestingly, when the pronoun was *he*, not a single elementary school boy told a story about a girl. Clearly, then, when children hear *he* in a gender-neutral context, they think of a boy or man. Hyde also asked

Whorfian hypothesis:
The theory that the language we learn influences how we think.

the children some questions to see if they understood the grammatical rule that *he* in certain contexts refers to everyone, both men and women. Few understood the rule; for example, only 28% of the first graders gave answers showing that they knew the rule.

Hyde also had the children fill in the blanks in some sentences, for example:

If a kid likes candy, ___ might eat too much.

The children overwhelmingly supplied *he* for the blank; even 72% of the first graders did so.

This research shows two things. First, the majority of elementary school children have learned to supply *he* in gender-neutral contexts (as evidenced by the fill-in task). Second, the majority of elementary school children do not know the rule that *he* in gender-neutral contexts refers to both men and women and have a strong tendency to think of men in creating stories from neutral *he* cues. For them, then, the chain of concepts is as follows: (1) The typical person is a "he." (2) *He* refers only to boys and men. Logically, then, might they not conclude that (3) the typical person is male? Language seems to contribute to androcentric thinking in children.

In a final task, Hyde created a fictitious, gender-neutral occupation: wudgemaker.

Few people have heard of a job in factories, being a wudgemaker. Wudges are made of plastic, are oddly shaped, and are an important part of video games. The wudgemaker works from a plan or pattern posted at eye level as ___ puts together the pieces at a table while ___ is sitting down. Eleven plastic pieces must be snapped together. Some of the pieces are tiny, so ___ must have good coordination in ___ fingers. Once all eleven pieces are put together, ___ must test out the wudge to make sure that all of the moving pieces move properly. The wudgemaker is well paid and must be a high school graduate, but ___ does not have to have gone to college to get the job.

One-quarter of the children received *he* in all the blanks, one-quarter received *they*, one-quarter received *he or she*, and one-quarter received *she*. The children then rated how well a woman could do the job on a 3-point scale: 3 for very well, 2 for just okay, and 1 for not very well. Next, they rated how well a man could do the job, giving ratings on the same scale. The results are shown in Figure 5.1. Which pronoun the children were given didn't seem to affect their ratings of men as wudgemakers, but the pronoun had a big effect on how women were rated as wudgemakers. Notice in the graph that when the pronoun *he* was used, women were rated at the middle of the scale, or just okay. The ratings of women rose for the pronouns *they* and *he or she*, and finally were close to the top of the scale when children heard the wudgemaker described as *she*. These results, then, demonstrate that pronoun choice does have an effect on the concepts children form; in particular, children who heard *he* in the job description thought that women were significantly less competent at the job than children who heard other pronouns did.

Other experiments show that when job titles are marked for gender (e.g., *policeman*), children are more likely to view those occupations as being appropriate for only one gender, relative to when job titles are unmarked for gender (e.g., *plumber*; Liben et al., 2002). There is also reason for concern about the effect on broader issues, such as girls' self-efficacy in male-stereotyped jobs (Vervecken & Hannover, 2015). Research demonstrates that men and boys remember material better when it is written with masculine generics, but girls and women remember it better when it is written with gender-neutral or feminine generics (Conkright et al., 2000).

FIGURE 5.1 Children's ratings of the competence of women and men as wudgemakers, as a function of the pronoun they heard repeatedly in the description of the wudgemaker.

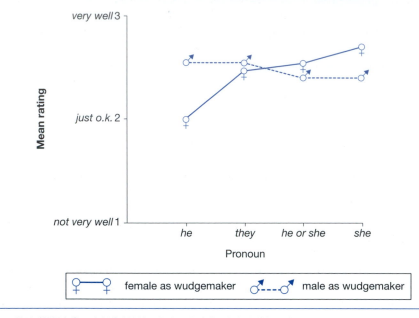

Source: Hyde (1984a). Copyright © 1984 by the American Psychological Association.

In answer to the original question of whether this language business is really important, the data show that it is. We need to be concerned about the effects that sexist pronoun usage has on children as their attitudes about gender and aspirations for themselves are developing. Of course, social learning theory would tell us that, if we want children to use nonsexist language, we adults should model it for them!

Some people believe that in theory it would be a good idea to eliminate sexism from language, but in practice they find themselves having difficulty doing this in their speaking or writing. Next we discuss some practical suggestions for avoiding sexist language (American Psychological Association, 2010; Miller & Swift, 1995) and for dealing with some other relevant situations.

Toward Nonsexist Language

Our review of the evidence indicates that sexist language reflects societal gender inequality and has harmful effects on how we think. Not surprisingly, feminists advocate for nonsexist language in order to reduce sexist stereotyping and discrimination (e.g., Sczesny et al., 2016; Stahlberg et al., 2007). Nonsexist language might include omitting inappropriate or irrelevant references to gender, replacing masculine forms of words (e.g., nouns such as *policeman*, pronouns such as *he*) with gender-unmarked forms (e.g., *police officer, they*), and increasing the use of feminine forms (e.g., using *he or she* instead of only *he*) to make female referents more visible.

A common solution is to use *he or she* instead of the generic *he*, *him or her* instead of *him*, and so on. Therefore, the generic masculine in sentence 1 is modified as in sentence 2:

1. When a doctor prescribes birth control pills, he should first inquire whether the patient has a history of blood clotting problems.

2. When a doctor prescribes birth control pills, he or she should first inquire whether the patient has a history of blood clotting problems.

Some believe that the order should be varied so that *he or she* and *she or he* appear with equal frequency. If *he or she* is the only form that is used, women still end up second!

In addition, the problem with using a phrase such as *he or she* is that, while it makes women more visible, it also reaffirms the gender binary and, therefore, makes nonbinary people invisible. So another possibility is to switch from the singular to the plural, because plural pronouns do not signify gender, at least in English. Therefore, the generic masculine in sentence 1 can be modified as follows:

3. When doctors prescribe birth control pills, they should first inquire whether the patient has a history of blood clotting problems.

Another possibility is to reword the sentence so that there is no necessity for a pronoun, as in this example:

4. A doctor prescribing birth control pills should first inquire whether the patient has a history of blood clotting problems.

Another solution to this problem in English is the singular use of *they* and *their*. Singular *they* was standard usage in English until the late 1700s, when a group of grammarians decided it was wrong (Bodine, 1975). Today, there is increasing acceptance of the use of singular *they* in written English, and its use has long been widespread in spoken English. Singular *they* is especially useful when someone's gender is not known or identified.

As consciousness of sexist language and critiques of the gender binary have become more visible, new gender-neutral pronouns have been created. For example, one set that has been proposed is *tey* for *he* or *she*, *tem* for *him* or *her*, and *ter* for *his* or *her*. Thus one might say, "The scientist pursues ter work; tey reads avidly and strives to overcome obstacles that beset tem." Entire books have been written with this usage. These new pronouns have a great deal of merit, but they are not widely used yet. If the *New York Times*, the *Washington Post*, the *Wall Street Journal*, and the president all started using *ter*, *tey*, and *tem*, these terms would certainly have a better chance of widespread use.

Making a conscious effort to avoid misgendering people is also important for using more inclusive and nonsexist language. When in doubt of the correct pronouns to use for a person, sometimes the best solution is to politely ask that person. Still, if you make a mistake and misgender someone, a simple apology and correction will do.

Space does not permit a complete discussion of all possible practical challenges that may arise in trying to avoid sexist language and be more inclusive with our word choices. Usually, however, a little thought and imagination can solve most problems. For example, the salutation in a letter, "Dear Sir," can easily be changed to "Dear Colleague" or simply "To Whom It May Concern." Salutations such as "Dear Madam or Sir" and "Dear Sir or Madam" reaffirm the gender binary and are therefore best avoided.

Another aspect of nonsexist language is to avoid irrelevant reference to a person's gender and gender identity. When a person's gender isn't relevant, it's best not to identify it (Dumond, 2014). Likewise, if a person's transgender or cisgender status isn't relevant, it shouldn't be identified (National Lesbian & Gay Journalists Association, 2016).

Honorific titles such as *Mr.*, *Miss*, *Mrs.*, and *Ms.* can be problematic for several reasons. First, these titles necessarily identify gender even when gender may not be relevant. In turn, using these titles carries the risk of misgendering people. In addition, looking just at *Miss* and *Mrs.*, these terms are considered by many to be outdated and condescending to women. How often is it necessary to identify a woman's marital status in her title? Moreover, *Miss* is often used in an infantilizing manner. *Ms.* addresses both of these concerns and affords the same status to a woman as to a man, regardless of marital status. But is there a title that is more inclusive of nonbinary people, a title that avoids misgendering? In fact, more people have begun to adopt the use of the gender-neutral title *Mx.* (pronounced *mix*; Corbett, 2015). Like *Ms.*, this title isn't an abbreviation of an existing word in English. Its use isn't yet widespread, but neither was *Ms.* until quite recently!

Institutional Change

A number of institutions have committed themselves to using and encouraging nonsexist language. For example, most textbook publishers have guidelines for nonsexist language and refuse to publish books that include sexism. (Two examples are Scott, Foresman and McGraw-Hill, which initiated this policy in 1972 and 1974, respectively.) The American Psychological Association (2010) requires the use of nonsexist language in articles in the journals it publishes. And Webster's Dictionary has a policy of avoiding masculine generics and other forms of sexist language ("No Sexism Please," 1991). In general, these are good sources for the reader wanting more detail on how to reduce sexist language.

Nonetheless, some forms of sexism—particularly *cisgenderism*, which privileges cisgender people—have not yet been adequately addressed by most institutions. For example, although the American Psychological Association's (2010) *Publication Manual* instructs authors to avoid masculine generics when referring to groups of people, it also instructs authors to "be clear about whether you mean one sex or both sexes" (p. 73). The problem with such statements is that it reaffirms the gender binary and makes transgender, intersex, and nonbinary people invisible.

The use of gender-neutral pronouns is increasing at public and private universities in the United States, some of which now offer incoming students the option to register their gender pronouns. For example, in the fall of 2015, Harvard University gave new students the following options: *he, she, they, e,* and *ze*. Notice that three of these pronouns—*they, e,* and *ze*—are gender-neutral!

In Sweden, a new gender-neutral pronoun (*hen*) has been incorporated into the official Swedish language and is used in Swedish media and government settings. Recall that Swedish is a natural gender language, like English.

Many occupational titles, particularly in government agencies, have also changed. It is worth noting that some of the changes introduce definite improvements. For example, *firemen* has been changed to *firefighters*. In addition to being nonsexist, the newer term makes more sense, because what the people do is fight fires, not start them, as one might infer from the older term.

Language and Careers

Our discussion of gender and language raises important practical questions for gender and the workplace. Though we discuss gender and work in detail in Chapter 9, there are two issues regarding language that are relevant in this chapter.

One issue is how the use of sexist language in job descriptions may contribute to a lack of gender diversity in the workplace. For example, the use of sexist language in a job ad might signal that only men should apply. A series of experiments explored the psychological effects of using sexist language during a mock job interview (Stout & Dasgupta, 2011). Under the guise of a career development program, researchers invited undergraduate participants to the lab to do mock job interviews. In the first part of the interview, participants read a job description that used sexist language (e.g., masculine generics such as *he, him, guys*), "gender-inclusive" language (e.g., *he or she*), or gender-neutral language (e.g., *one, the employee*). Both male and female participants reported the job description in the sexist language condition to be sexist. Among women only, the type of language used affected their feelings about the job. Women in the sexist language condition expected lower sense of belonging in the job, reported lower motivation to get the job, and identified less with the job, relative to the other two language conditions. In a follow-up study with only female participants, the researchers also observed the participants' nonverbal behavior and found that, in the sexist language condition, women displayed less interested and more negative nonverbal behaviors. If an employer wants a diverse workforce, they shouldn't use sexist language!

For women aspiring to careers in male-dominated occupations, consider the implications of gender differences in verbal communication. Which styles of speaking will work best for such women? One interesting experiment assessed the impact of women using stereotyped patterns of tentative speech compared with assertive speech (Carli, 1990). Participants listened to an audiotape of a persuasive speech delivered by either a woman or a man. On one of the tapes, the woman used many tag questions ("Great day, isn't it?"), hedges ("sort of"), and disclaimers ("I'm no expert, but . . ."), indicating tentativeness. On another tape, she used no tag questions, hedges, or disclaimers, thus indicating assertiveness. In the third tape, a man used tentative speech, and in a fourth tape, a man used assertive speech. The results indicated that the female speaker who used tentative speech was more influential to men than the assertive female speaker. For female listeners, the effect was just the reverse: They were more influenced by the woman using assertive speech than by the woman with tentative speech. Interestingly, men were equally influential whether their speech was tentative or assertive. Apparently, men acquire their status and influence simply by being male; speech style makes little difference. But to return to the implications for women and careers, the results of this study indicate that changing from tentative to forceful speech for women is likely to have different effects, depending on whether the woman is speaking to a man or a woman. Tentative speech seems to work best with men, and assertive speech works best with women. Other research shows that some people react negatively to gender-norm violations in women's speech (Lindsey & Zakahi, 2005). Women have to strike a delicate balance as they try to advance their careers without evoking the ire of gender traditionalists.

In Conclusion

In this chapter, we began by considering the evidence on gender differences in verbal and nonverbal communication. We think it is important to remember that verbal and nonverbal communication, like many other forms of human behavior, are regulated by cultural norms and gender stereotypes. Violations of gender stereotypes are sometimes perceived as evidence that a person is queer. Indeed, people often rely on both verbal and nonverbal behaviors for cues regarding a person's sexual orientation (e.g., Ambady et al., 1999; Van Borsel & Van de Putte, 2014). Although many people believe that they can rely on particular gestures, styles of speech, and other nonverbal behaviors as cues to sexual orientation—often referred to as *gaydar*—evidence indicates that gaydar is inaccurate (Cox et al., 2016). In other words, it is often difficult to interpret violations of gender stereotypes of verbal and nonverbal behavior.

Gendered patterns of verbal and nonverbal behaviors—whether tentativeness in speech or interpersonal distance—always develop in cultural contexts. As such, we should be mindful of the intersectionality of gender and culture when interpreting gender differences and similarities.

Experience the Research
Gender and Conversational Styles

Recruit four students, two who identify as men and two who identify as women (and who are not in this class), to participate. Pair one man and one woman together alone in a room and tell them that you are going to give them a topic to discuss and that you want to record their discussion to analyze it for a class. Be sure to obtain their permission to record the conversation, and assure them that you will not reveal to anyone the identities of your participants. Then give the pair a controversial topic to discuss—perhaps a current controversy on your campus or in national politics. Be sure that the topic is not gender stereotyped so that one person will feel superior to the other. For example, "How good is the new quarterback on the football team?" would probably not be a good topic. By contrast, "Would you vote for the new health care bill before Congress and why?" is a good topic. Tell them that you will record their discussion for about 10 minutes. You should remain in the room and note any observations you have of their discussion. Specifically, count the number of times each person nods in response to what the other is saying.

Repeat this procedure with the second male-female pair. You now have two audio recordings for data. Analyze the recordings in the following ways:

1. Count the number of times the man interrupted the woman and the woman interrupted the man. Did men interrupt women more than the reverse?

2. Count the number of tag questions (see text for explanation). Did women use more tag questions than men did? Having listened to their conversation, how would you interpret the difference you found? Were the women indicating uncertainty, or were they trying to encourage communication and maintain the relationship?

3. Count the number of hedges (e.g., "sort of"). Did women use more hedges than men?

4. Did women nod more in response to what men were saying or the reverse?

CHAPTER SUMMARY

Tannen's different cultures hypothesis holds that gender differences in speech patterns stem from the different goals that men and women have when they communicate, such that women use more affiliative speech, whereas men use more assertive speech; meta-analyses provide limited support for this position, as the gender differences found are very small. Mulac proposed that the verbal communication of girls and women tends to be rated as more socially intelligent and aesthetically pleasing, whereas the verbal communication of boys and men is rated as more dynamic and aggressive. While data show these differences to be subtle, this research may be used to inform *communication therapy* for transgender women and men.

Many gender differences in nonverbal communication—including encoding and decoding communication, smiling, visual dominance, interpersonal distance, and posture—are tied to gender roles and power.

Analyses of the way women are treated in language reveal patterns in which the male is normative, as in the use of masculine generics. Research with adults as well as children shows that masculine generics are not psychologically gender neutral, but rather evoke images of men. In addition, such sexist language appears to both reflect and perpetuate gender inequalities. Sexist language may contribute to the early social construction of gender for children.

Nonsexist language involves omitting inappropriate or irrelevant references to gender, using gender-unmarked forms, and avoiding misgendering language. While many efforts to reduce sexist language have become standard, some forms of sexism, such as cisgenderism, persist.

Gender and Emotion

> "When I get upset, I can't express myself at all, but if my wife's upset, you'd think you were hearing poetry. She can express exactly what she's feeling inside."

> James, age 47 (quoted in Brody, 1999, p. 1)

James's description of the difference between him and his wife resonates with many of us. It reflects not only ubiquitous gender stereotypes about emotional expression and emotional competence, but also why those stereotypes matter. The ability to accurately express one's emotions is important for intrapersonal and interpersonal reasons, and social relationships can be strained when this ability is lacking. In this chapter we explore gender stereotypes about emotions and evaluate their accuracy. We also examine how real gender differences in emotional experience, expression, and competence might develop.

Gender Stereotypes About Emotions

Emotionality

Women have long been stereotyped as more emotional than men (Brody et al., 2016; Broverman et al., 1972; Shields, 2005). That is, stereotypes hold that, compared with men, women experience and express more emotions and do so more intensely. This stereotype is among the most pervasive of gender stereotypes: It is found in the United States and across most other cultures (Brody, 1999; Fischer & Manstead, 2000).

The stereotype that women are emotional can hurt women as they try to succeed in education and in the workplace. Since it was founded, Virginia Military Institute (VMI), a state university supported by taxpayers' money, had been for men only. VMI is very prestigious within Virginia, setting up networks for its graduates that lead them into the halls of power. Women were denied access to all this. When the men-only policy was challenged in the 1990s, the case went all the way to the Supreme Court. The interesting aspect for us is the argument made by VMI in the courts defending its policy (Shields, 2000). One expert gave testimony that VMI "was not suitable for most women, because, compared with men, women are more emotional, less aggressive, suffer more from fear of failure, and cannot withstand stress as well" (Greenberger & Blake, 1996, p. A52). If that expert were right, women would have difficulty succeeding at any competitive university or demanding job. Fortunately, the expert was wrong and was only parroting gender stereotypes, and the Supreme Court ruled that women must be allowed admission. Still, it is clear that stereotypes about emotions can have a huge impact on our lives.

Specific Emotions

Gender stereotypes hold that not only are women more emotional than men, but there are specific emotions that are appropriate based on one's gender. In one study, psychologists gave a list of 19 specific emotions to participants (including undergraduates as well as adults from the community) and asked them to rate how much men and women are expected to experience each emotion in our culture (Plant et al., 2000). The findings of this study are shown in Table 6.1.

You will notice several important patterns in the table. First, the vast majority of the emotions—13 out of 19—are stereotyped as appropriate for women. This echoes the stereotype of women being generally more emotional than men. Second, those 13 female-stereotyped emotions encompass positive emotions (love, happiness, sympathy) as well as negative emotions (embarrassment, fear, guilt). Third, all three male-stereotyped emotions—anger, contempt, and pride—are associated with dominance and power. Those three emotions are consistent with men's dominant position in society (Brody, 1999; Hess et al., 2004). By contrast, most of the female-stereotyped emotions (such as sadness, distress, and shame) convey vulnerability and powerlessness. Fourth, there are only six emotions that men can experience without violating a gender stereotype: In addition to the three male-stereotyped emotions, men are expected to experience amusement, interest, and jealousy about as much as women. That's not much of an emotional range for men, is it? In Chapter 16 we will explore the consequences of restricting the expression of vulnerable emotions in men and boys.

The stereotypes listed in Table 6.1 reflect what participants said when asked about stereotypes in "American" culture, and most of the participants were White. Might those same stereotypes ring true across other ethnic groups in the United States? Different cultures hold quite different views on the experience and expression of emotion. Asian

TABLE 6.1	Americans' gender stereotypes of emotions.

"Female" Emotions	"Male" Emotions	Gender-Neutral Emotions
Awe	Anger	Amusement
Disgust	Contempt	Interest
Distress	Pride	Jealousy
Embarrassment		
Fear		
Guilt		
Happiness		
Love		
Sadness		
Shame		
Shyness		
Surprise		
Sympathy		

Source: Data from Plant et al. (2000). Table created by Nicole Else-Quest.

cultures, for example, value great restraint in the expression of emotion. Might we see different stereotypes at the intersection of ethnicity and gender?

To answer this question, Amanda Durik and I (JSH) asked African Americans about gender stereotypes of emotion among African Americans, Hispanic Americans about gender stereotypes of emotion among Hispanic Americans, European Americans about gender stereotypes of emotion among European Americans, and Asian Americans about gender stereotypes of emotion among Asian Americans (Durik et al., 2006). The results demonstrate that gender stereotypes vary across ethnic groups, which suggests that the social construction of gender hinges, in part, on ethnicity. For example, we found that African Americans stereotype African American women as expressing almost as much anger as African American men, and anger stereotypes for African American women are about the same as for European American men. Of the four groups, European American women are the ones who are stereotyped as not expressing anger. The expectations for women, then, depend on those women's ethnicity. This is a key point of intersectionality.

In Figure 6.1, we show Durik et al.'s (2006) findings on stereotypes of pride and love within each of the four ethnic groups. Notice that European Americans are highly gender stereotyped about pride, whereas African Americans are not; the findings show that African American women express about as much pride as African American men do. European Americans and African Americans reported considerable gender stereotypes about love, whereas Asian Americans' ratings were less gender differentiated, probably because of the cultural norm of nonexpression of emotions, which results in restraint in women's expression of love. Interestingly, Asian Americans rate women from their group as expressing about as much love as Hispanic Americans (a far more emotionally expressive

FIGURE 6.1   Gender stereotypes of emotions in four ethnic groups.

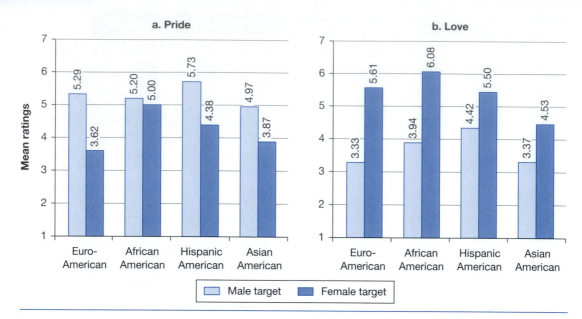

Source: Durik et al. (2006). Figure created by Nicole Else-Quest.

group) rate Hispanic men as expressing. The larger point is that there is substantial variation from one ethnic group to the next in their expectations about which emotions are expressed by women and which are expressed by men.

What are the practical implications of the findings on ethnicity and gender stereotypes? Consider the case of African American women and anger. In African American culture, it is acceptable for women to express anger about as much as men do. This norm is caricatured by the "angry Black woman" stereotype. Among White Americans, it is not acceptable for women to express anger; expressing anger violates the female gender role requirement to be warm and submissive. At work, an African American woman might express anger over some issue in a way that is completely appropriate in her culture, but her White male boss may react to her as being completely inappropriate because, to him, women are not supposed to express anger. He may see her as a problem employee, or he may find confirmation of his stereotype that African American women are angry. Gender stereotypes of emotion, then, can have a powerful impact on interpersonal interactions in highly important situations.

While intersectionality involves examining how gender is constructed differently across ethnic groups, it also involves identifying similarities. Indeed, many similarities were found across ethnic groups as well. All ethnic groups, for example, expect women to express more embarrassment and guilt relative to men (Durik et al., 2006).

Some Consequences of Gender Stereotypes About Emotion

In previous chapters we discussed how stereotypes factor into how we process information about people. In general, our stereotypes make us see all the confirmations of them and filter out exceptions to the stereotypes (see Chapter 3). When a really major stereotype violation that we cannot ignore occurs, we are likely to respond negatively to the stereotype violator. All these processes occur with gender stereotypes of emotion. Consider the emotions of anger and sadness: Anger is male-stereotyped and sadness is female-stereotyped.

Because we don't expect women to express anger, we may inaccurately perceive and explain their anger.

For example, in one study, researchers showed participants slides of two men's and two women's faces displaying specific emotions (Plant et al., 2000; see also Plant et al., 2004). In some of the slides, the poser displayed anger, in others they displayed sadness, and in some they displayed an ambiguous blend of anger and sadness (see Photo 6.1). The posers were experts, graduate students who were emotion researchers and had been trained to contract exactly the right facial muscles to display particular emotions. Participants were asked to rate how much sadness and anger were being expressed by the posers in each of the slides.

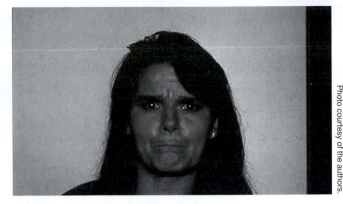

Photo courtesy of the authors.

PHOTO 6.1

What emotion is this woman expressing? When women display an ambiguous blend of anger and sadness, as observed in this photo, people believe that women are sad, not angry, whereas a man with a similar ambiguous expression is seen as angry (Plant et al., 2000).

The researchers hypothesized that gender stereotypes would influence participants' ratings most when the emotional expressions were ambiguous. That is, in the anger-sadness blend, a man would be rated as angry (a male-stereotyped emotion) and a woman would be rated as sad (a female-stereotyped emotion). The results were consistent with this hypothesis: Participants rated men's blends as significantly angrier than women's and women's blends as significantly sadder than men's. Gender stereotypes affect the emotions we see people displaying, even when the facial expressions are identical.

What happened when the emotional expression was clear and unambiguous? Participants rated women's unambiguous anger poses as significantly less angry than men's unambiguous anger poses. The raters simply saw less anger in women's anger than in men's anger. And as if that weren't enough, participants saw sadness in women's anger poses but not in men's. Anger just isn't an acceptable emotion for women. People fail to see it in women's faces, or they misinterpret it as sadness. How difficult for women not to have their anger be perceived, much less taken seriously. Gender stereotypes of emotions are harmful, in part, because they can lead us to inaccurately perceive another person's feelings.

Gender stereotypes of emotions may also lead us to inaccurately explain or attribute another person's feelings. In one study (Barrett & Bliss-Moreau, 2009), participants viewed pictures of faces expressing sadness, fear, anger, and disgust paired with descriptions of situations that explained the emotions. For example, the experimenters paired a picture of a man expressing sadness with the description "Attended the funeral of a grandparent," or a picture of a woman expressing anger was paired with "Argued with a coworker." Participants viewed 32 such face–description pairings four times; the experimenters were careful to make sure that an equal number of each emotional expression was displayed by both genders. Next, the participants viewed the faces again, but without the descriptions explaining them. This time, they were asked to describe the person in the picture as either "emotional" or "having a bad day."

For expressions of sadness, fear, and anger, participants attributed women's emotions to their being more emotional; that is, they made dispositional, *internal* attributions for women's emotions. Yet when men expressed the same emotions, participants made situational, *external* attributions, attributing men's emotions to their simply having a bad day. In other words, men's emotions were judged as being justified by the situation, but women's emotions were judged as being due to their more emotional nature. In sum, gender stereotypes can lead us to ignore information about the situational causes and overemphasize the dispositional causes of women's emotions or exaggerate the situational causes and minimize the dispositional causes of men's emotions.

FOCUS 6.1

GENDER AND THE POLITICS OF EMOTION

As we consider the consequences of gender stereotypes of emotion, a feminist analysis would propose that emotions are political (Shields, 2005, 2013). Emotion stereotypes regulate people's behavior and help to preserve the organization of social groups. For example, in the South before the Civil War, enslaved Black people were forbidden to express anger, and that worked very well for their White masters, maintaining the power of master over the enslaved. In the 19th century, women were stereotyped as emotional and therefore weak and incapable of rational thought; the essence of this stereotype persists today. When a culture tells men or women what emotions they may or may not express, the culture is preserving one group as more powerful and the other as less powerful.

Social psychologist Victoria Brescoll (2016) has proposed that gender stereotypes of emotion create emotional minefields for women in leadership roles. She points to the gender stereotype about emotionality, explaining that men are believed to have better control over the expression of their emotions compared with women. That is, the stereotype holds that men and women differ in their emotional expression but not in their actual emotional experience. Because of this perception about men's ability to control their displays of emotion, people infer that men are therefore more rational and less likely to let emotion sway their decision making. This emotional restraint is stereotyped as masculine and reflective of good

judgment (MacArthur & Shields, 2015). Effective leadership requires a calm, cool-headed, and dispassionate nature, but these traits don't mesh with the stereotype of women as emotional. In turn, Brescoll notes, women are perceived to be less competent as leaders. It might seem, then, that the solution for women is to control their emotional expression and to demonstrate that they are capable of rational decision making. However, Brescoll argues that this alternative is also risky, because they might be perceived as cold, calculating, or dishonest if they don't display enough emotion. That is, too much emotional expression violates their leadership role, but too little emotional expression violates their gender role. This double bind was echoed by Hillary Rodham Clinton during the 2016 presidential campaign, when she explained to a reporter that she wanted to acknowledge and express her feelings, but knew she had to be cautious about it:

> As a woman in a high public position or seeking the presidency, as I am, you have to be aware of how people will judge you for being, quote, emotional. It's a really delicate balancing act—how you navigate what is still a relatively narrow path—to be yourself, to express yourself, to let your feelings show, but not in a way that triggers all of the negative stereotypes. (quoted in de Cadenet, 2016)

Chip Somodevilla/Getty Images News/Getty Images & Robyn Beck/AFP/Getty Images.

PHOTO 6.2

How much emotion can a female leader express? Former U.S. secretary of state and Democratic presidential candidate Hillary Rodham Clinton.

Do the data support Brescoll's (2016) theorizing? One recent study examined how people perceive men and women who control or restrain their emotional expression (Hess et al., 2016). The results demonstrated that, when men showed emotional restraint, they were perceived as more emotionally competent and more intelligent than when they expressed their emotion immediately, yet the opposite finding was true for women. When women showed emotional restraint, they were perceived as less emotionally competent and less intelligent. Thus, women seeking leadership roles must walk a fine line between expressing and restraining their emotions lest they violate the expectations for their leadership role and gender role. We will return to this dilemma in Chapter 9.

Gender and Emotional Experience and Expression

Just how accurate are these gender stereotypes of emotion? What do we know about the real emotional lives of women and men and how similar or different they are?

Emotional Expression and Display Rules

Emotion researchers distinguish between the experience of emotion and the expression of emotion. Every day you may experience some emotions that you express and others that you do not express. You may mask socially inappropriate emotions to be polite, for example. **Display rules** are a culture's rules for which emotions can be expressed or displayed. In American culture, for example, it is acceptable for people to express happiness; in fact, they are encouraged to do so. In contrast, expressions of grief are discouraged. Gender stereotypes contribute to display rules, so some emotions are acceptable for men but not women and vice versa. Have you heard the expression "Boys don't cry"? The restriction on boys and men crying is an example of a gendered display rule of emotion. Another example is that it is acceptable for men, but not women, to express anger. Can you think of other gendered display rules of emotion?

In light of display rules, we need to ask two distinct questions: Do women and men differ in their *experiences* of emotion? Do they differ in their *expressions* of emotion? Before those questions can be answered, though, you need to know how psychologists go about measuring emotion.

Measuring Emotion

Emotion researchers have measured emotional experience and expression in a variety of ways. There is no one best way to measure emotion. Instead, the different methods tap into different aspects or modalities of emotions.

One approach is to measure physiological aspects of emotion. In addition to being governed by display rules, gender roles, and other cultural factors, emotions have biological foundations. You have no doubt noticed that, in a situation that provokes intense fear, your heart pounds and your palms sweat. A pounding heart can also go with anger. Different regions of the brain are active depending on the emotion a person is experiencing. Emotional stimuli trigger the firing of neurons in the amygdala (a small region deep within the temporal lobes of the brain), which activates neurons in the brain stem, which in turn triggers the autonomic nervous system—reflected, for example, in changes in heart rate. The prefrontal cortex (the very front of the brain) and hippocampus (a small structure lying close to the amygdala) are activated as well. All of these physiological phenomena are part of the experience of emotion.

Display rules: A culture's rules for which emotions can be expressed or displayed.

Modern neuroscientists are miles away from saying that, because brain regions are activated with the experience of emotions, emotions are "hardwired" or biologically determined. Rather, neuroscientists studying emotion emphasize the plasticity of the brain (Davidson & McEwen, 2012). Activation of a certain brain region may create a particular psychological state, but the reverse process occurs as well: Behavior and experience can create changes in the brain. The brain is plastic and capable of change.

Thus, emotion researchers use a variety of techniques to measure these physiological aspects of emotions. These measures may include blood pressure, heart rate, and skin conductance, which assess autonomic nervous system activation, or arousal. Researchers may also include neuroendocrine components of emotions by measuring levels of epinephrine and norepinephrine, or they may measure electrical activity in the brain by using an EEG (electroencephalogram). Neuroimaging techniques, such as fMRI (functional magnetic resonance imaging) and PET (positron emission tomography), are used to explore and identify the areas of the brain associated with specific emotions. Many of these techniques continue to be refined to be more precise, and researchers are learning more about the physiological aspects of emotions every day.

An alternative approach is to examine people's own subjective experience of emotion, typically with self-reports. The reports may take a variety of forms, from checklists on which respondents identify the emotions they have experienced in the past week to daily diary methods in which participants record their emotional responses to events at the time they occur. Self-report measures assume that people recognize and are aware of the emotions they experience, yet it seems likely that some people are better than others at recognizing their emotions. Of course, emotional experience is inherently internal and subjective, and self-reports are able to capture that aspect in a way that physiological measures cannot.

Researchers might also choose to focus on emotional expression. The pattern of facial muscles that contract when a person expresses anger, or disgust, or happiness is present from infancy and is universal across cultures (Ekman & Oster, 1979). Facial expressions of emotion may be measured with visual observations as well as with facial EMG (electromyography), which assesses patterns of electrical activity associated with facial muscle contractions. And verbal expressions of emotion may be captured in measures such as the number and kind of emotion words that people use in their language, for example, in a conversation or diary entry.

An important point to remember here is that no single measure of emotional experience or expression is perfect. Each measure has costs and benefits, depending on the needs or aims of the researcher. For example, some physiological techniques are very informative when participants are not aware of their emotional experiences or are motivated to mask their emotions because of display rules, but those techniques are also quite expensive and sometimes imprecise. Ideally, researchers can use multiple measures of emotion (for example, using skin conductance, EMG, and self-report) to get a clear picture of participants' emotions.

Experience Versus Expression

One study provides a particularly nice example of research on gender differences in these multiple aspects of emotion and demonstrates why it's ideal to use multiple measures (Kring & Gordon, 1998). Undergraduates viewed brief film clips designed to stimulate happiness, sadness, or fear. While the participants viewed the film, their skin conductance was measured and their facial expressions were videotaped. At the end of each clip, they rated how much they had experienced each of four emotions: sadness, fear, disgust, and happiness. In short, the researchers used physiological, facial expression, and self-report measures.

The results showed both similarities and differences between women and men. For all emotion clips, women were significantly more facially expressive than men. While men and women reported similar emotional experiences, men showed significantly higher skin conductance reactivity to the fear films than women did (contrary to the stereotype that fear is unmanly!). Men also showed more skin conductance reactivity to the happy clips, as did women to the sad clips, although the differences were not quite significant. In short, patterns of gender differences can reverse themselves depending on the aspect of emotion that is measured. Women tend to be more facially expressive than men (except perhaps in the expression of anger). But men, at least for some emotions, show more autonomic nervous system reactivity.

How do we make sense of these complex patterns of gender differences and similarities in emotional experience and expression? This study found that women were more likely to be *externalizers*, in that they were facially expressive but had a low skin conductance response (Kring & Gordon, 1998). By contrast, men were more likely to be *internalizers*, being facially inexpressive but having a higher skin conductance response. Other researchers argue that, although men are more likely to show the internalizer pattern, women are more likely to be *generalizers*—that is, to express emotions on all measures (Brody et al., 2016). The internalizer pattern of men corresponds, of course, to the gender role requirement that men restrain or control their emotional expression (MacArthur & Shields, 2015).

In a follow-up experiment by the same group, the first experiment was replicated but with different film clips and, in addition, the measurement of participants' gender role identity using the Bem Sex Role Inventory, discussed in Chapter 3 (Kring & Gordon, 1998). Again, women were more facially expressive than men across all film clips. In terms of skin conductance, men showed more reactivity to the anger and fear films and women showed more reactivity to the sadness and disgust films. Interestingly, gender role identity showed larger effects on emotion responses than gender did: Androgynous people were more facially expressive than masculine people. This finding provides evidence of the importance of gender roles in determining which emotions we express or do not express. It also reminds us that gender is much more complex than the gender binary would suggest.

Specific Emotions

Recall that most emotions are stereotyped as feminine, whereas only a few are stereotyped as masculine or gender-neutral (Plant et al., 2000). Are these gender stereotypes accurate? Many studies have been conducted on the experience of specific emotions, and meta-analysis helps us find patterns among those studies. Here we'll describe three meta-analyses of gender differences in emotion.

We conducted a meta-analysis of gender differences and similarities in child **temperament,** which includes traits such as emotionality and the tendency to express specific emotions like anger and fear (Else-Quest, 2012; Else-Quest et al., 2006). Parent and teacher reports of children's behaviors were the primary source of data for the meta-analysis. In contrast to gender stereotypes, boys were not more prone than girls to express anger ($d = 0.04$), and girls were not more emotional than boys ($d = 0.01$). Girls were only slightly more prone than boys to express fear ($d = -0.12$) and sadness ($d = -0.10$).

Temperament: Constitutionally based individual differences in reactivity and self-regulation, such as emotional intensity, inhibitory control, activity level, and distractibility.

Another meta-analysis examined gender differences and similarities in children's expression of specific emotions (Chaplin & Aldao, 2013). Among the female-stereotyped emotions, such as happiness, surprise, sadness, fear, and disgust, gender differences were generally close to zero or very small, with the exception of shame (which was higher in girls). Among the male-stereotyped emotions, findings were mixed. Girls actually expressed more contempt than boys did, and boys expressed only slightly more anger than girls did.

My (NEQ) students and I conducted a meta-analysis of gender differences and similarities in a subset of emotions known as **self-conscious emotions** (Else-Quest et al., 2012). Self-conscious emotions are emotions about the self, such as guilt, shame, pride, and embarrassment, and often have to do with morality or adhering to social norms. Gender stereotypes hold that women experience more guilt, shame, and embarrassment but that men experience more pride (Plant et al., 2000). Our meta-analysis found that, while women and girls reported experiencing more guilt ($d = -0.27$) and shame ($d = -0.29$), gender similarities were the rule for embarrassment ($d = -0.08$) and pride ($d = -0.01$).

In sum, meta-analyses of gender differences in emotional experience and expression indicate that gender stereotypes about emotions tend to be exaggerated or, in some cases, just plain wrong.

Another important pattern has emerged across studies of gender and emotion. That is, just as gender stereotypes of emotion may vary across ethnic groups (Durik et al., 2006), so can gender differences in actual emotional experiences. For example, we found that for guilt and shame experiences, people of color displayed gender similarities but White people displayed gender differences (Else-Quest et al., 2012). Similarly, in a study of low-income, primarily African American adolescents, gender similarities were the rule for expressions of anger (Panjwani et al., 2016). These patterns remind us to take an intersectional approach to gender.

Self-conscious emotions: Emotions about the self, which often have to do with morality or adhering to social norms; includes guilt, shame, pride, and embarrassment.

© iStockphoto.com/Steve Debenport

PHOTO 6.3

While gender stereotypes suggest that girls don't experience as much pride as boys do, empirical data show a pattern of gender similarities in pride experience.

Emotional Intensity

Researchers have found gender differences in self-reported intensity of emotional experience and expression, with women reporting the greater intensity (Brody et al., 2016). And, whether in conversations or in writing samples, girls and women use more emotion words and talk about emotions more than boys and men do (Brody et al., 2016; Goldschmidt & Weller, 2000). But does this mean that women are actually more emotional than men? A feminist analysis—which suggests that emotions are political—can help us make sense of these findings.

Consistent with the feminist analysis of gender and emotion discussed earlier, emotions that function to display one's power and dominance and encourage competition—such as anger, contempt, and pride—can be considered *powerful* emotions. By contrast, emotions that function to display one's vulnerability and maintain harmony within a relationship—such as fear, sadness, shame, and guilt—can be considered *powerless* emotions. We know that powerful emotions are stereotyped as masculine and that powerless emotions are stereotyped as feminine, but do men and women actually differ in their expression of these emotions?

©iStockphoto.com/drbimages &
©iStockphoto.com/Juanmonino

PHOTO 6.4
Cultural display rules of emotion prohibit women from expressing anger, yet these rules may not apply equally to people of color. An intersectional approach to gender and emotion reveals ethnic variations in gender differences in emotional expression.

Analyzing data from 37 cultures, Fischer and her colleagues (2004) tested the cultural universality of gender differences in the experience of powerful and powerless emotions. They found gender similarities in the experience of powerful emotions; that is, men and women reported experiencing the same intensity of anger and disgust, regardless of culture. However, compared with men, women reported experiencing significantly more intense powerless emotions. In other words, men's experience of fear, sadness, shame, and guilt was less intense than women's experience of these emotions. Women's emotional intensity did not vary across cultures, but men's did. Men's experience of powerless emotions depended, in part, on gender equality: Men in more gender-egalitarian countries tended to report less intense fear, sadness, and so forth, compared to men in less gender-egalitarian countries. How might societal gender equality be linked to gendered display rules for powerless emotions?

Gender roles may account for the gender difference in intensity of emotion (M. Grossman & Wood, 1993). For women, endorsement of gender stereotypes and reports of intensity of personal emotional experiences are positively correlated: The more that women believe in stereotypes, the more intense they report their own emotions to be. For men, the correlation between endorsement of gender stereotypes and reports of emotional intensity is negative: The more that men believe in gender stereotypes, the less intense their emotions. Stereotypical men don't express emotions and stereotypical women do.

In a related experiment, researchers removed gender role pressures by exerting pressure for both men and women to be emotionally expressive—specifically, by telling participants that research showed a positive correlation between emotional responsiveness and psychological adjustment (M. Grossman & Wood, 1993). In the control condition no such instructions were given, and presumably gender role pressures were in force as usual. Under the control condition, women gave more extreme emotional responses to negative slides than men did, but under the instructions encouraging emotional expressiveness, men's responses were the same as women's. Women's greater emotionality is thus not a biologically determined Natural Law. This study shows powerfully that it is determined by gender roles.

Emotional Competence

Emotional competence:
The ability to perceive, appraise, and express emotions accurately and clearly; to understand, analyze, and use knowledge about emotions to think and make decisions; and to regulate the emotions of oneself and others.

Being able to perceive, appraise, and express emotions accurately and clearly, to understand, analyze, and use knowledge about emotions to think and make decisions, and to regulate the emotions of oneself and others is known as **emotional competence** (sometimes *emotional intelligence*). On most of these abilities, women score higher than men (Brody et al., 2016). For example, compared with men, women tend to display more complex emotion knowledge when describing how others might feel in hypothetical situations (Ciarrochi et al., 2005). Elementary school teachers report that girls are better at regulating their emotions than their male classmates (Rogers et al., 2016). One meta-analysis found that women are more skilled than men at recognizing the emotions of others, whether in photographs, films (with or without audio), or audio recordings, $d = -0.27$ (Thompson & Voyer, 2014). Women also demonstrate more awareness of their own emotions and seem to encode their emotional experience in more detail in memory than men do (Barrett et al., 2000; Gohm & Clore, 2000; Seidlitz & Diener, 1998).

Similarly, women are generally more accurate than men at what psychologists call *decoding nonverbal cues*—that is, at reading other people's body language (Guerrero & Jones, 2006; McClure, 2000; see Chapter 5). For example, women are better than men at reading facial expressions of emotion (Hall & Matsumoto, 2004). The evidence indicates that this gender difference develops early in the lifespan and persists into adulthood. In adolescence, girls are able to read facial expressions of emotions faster and more sensitively than boys (Lee et al., 2013). Even as young as 3½, girls are better at identifying emotions than boys are (Bosacki & Moore, 2004; Nelson & Russell, 2015).

Emotionally competent behavior sometimes includes masking socially inappropriate emotions and feigning polite ones. For example, cultural display rules dictate that when children are presented with a disappointing gift, they should not show how disappointed they feel and they should instead express happiness and gratitude. By elementary school, girls are better than boys at controlling their emotions and displaying socially appropriate emotions. For example, first- and third-grade girls, when presented with a disappointing gift, display less negative emotion and more positive emotion than their male peers (Davis, 1995). Should we take these findings as evidence that men and boys cannot read others' emotions or understand their own emotions? Are men destined to be emotionally incompetent? Thank goodness, no! In fact, several studies have indicated that, when motivated, men can be just as emotionally competent as women are (Ciarrochi et al., 2005; Klein & Hodges, 2001).

It seems that, unlike the female gender role, the male gender role does not entail many aspects of emotional competence. Given that emotional competence is associated with social and emotional well-being (Salovey et al., 2008), wouldn't it be better if everyone were emotionally competent? For example, it is often an asset to be able to read others' emotions accurately, whether those emotions are expressed by one's boss, one's employee, or one's romantic partner. Indeed, emotional competence even appears good for one's physical health (Mikolajczak et al., 2015). Thus, an important question for psychology is this: How do we encourage and socialize all aspects of emotional competence for children during development, regardless of their gender?

There is one area of emotional competence in which women do not seem to do as well as men, and that is in some aspects of emotion regulation. We will return to this issue in Chapter 15, when we discuss gender differences in rumination and depression.

Emotions Beyond the Binary

As you've probably noticed, much of the research on gender and emotion is firmly planted in the gender binary. Studies have generally focused on differences between cisgender men and cisgender women in emotional experience, expression, and competence. When psychologists have studied emotions in transgender men and women, the focus has been on their experience of negative emotions and psychological distress (Budge et al., 2015). Consequently, psychologists do not know enough about the full range of emotional experience, expression, and competence of trans people.

As more and more researchers begin to incorporate new knowledge about gender diversity, we expect that research on gender and emotion will flourish. New questions about gender and emotion are being asked, and researchers are discovering new knowledge about the emotional world of trans people. For now, much of this research is in its infancy. Some lines of research have begun to shift focus away from gender assigned at birth. For example, several studies demonstrate that gender role identification plays a larger role than binary gender in shaping emotional expression (e.g., Fischer & LaFrance, 2015). Other lines of research specifically examine the emotional experiences of trans people. For example, one study of transgender men and women examined how changes in levels of testosterone and estrogen during medical transition might shape emotional competencies such as the ability to recognize emotions (Spies et al., 2016).

Another study with transgender men, conducted by Stephanie Budge and colleagues (2015), explored how masculinity and trans identity may shape the experience of positive emotions across the transition process. The men described the experience of emotions such as pride, happiness, awe, and love, as well as a lack of shame and fear. For example, one participant described pride in his identity: "I'm proud that I'm myself now, that I'm being myself. You know? And that I wasn't like that before, and now I am. I'm me. And I'm proud to be me" (p. 418). Another participant described the change in his emotions across the transition process: "I've had people say, my friends say, you know, you're so much more relaxed. You're so calm. You know, much more easygoing and happy. That I look happy" (p. 419).

These are exciting times for the study of gender and emotion, and we are on the brink of many new discoveries.

The Socialization of Gendered Emotions

An 18-month-old, frustrated at not being allowed to play with a captivating toy that is in plain view, will not say, "I'm angry." Instead, the child experiences frustration and rage and expresses these emotions facially and in other ways. The parent may respond by saying, "You're angry, aren't you?" or "You seem sad," or "Don't get mad." The child learns differently depending on the parent's response—in the first case, learning to label their feelings as anger; in the second, to misinterpret them as sadness; and in the third, to restrain or regulate their feelings. Between the ages of 2 and 5, children rapidly learn to identify their own emotions and those of others (Saarni, 1999). Parents guide this process, socializing their children about how to label and interpret their feelings and what to do with them (Eisenberg et al., 1998). In the process, parents are likely to impose gender stereotypes. Here we consider both the family and peers as early socializers of gendered emotions.

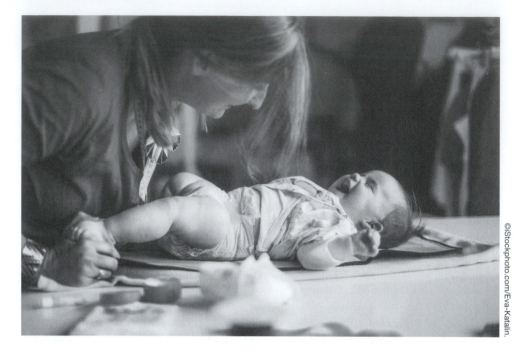

©iStockphoto.com/Eva-Katalin.

PHOTO 6.5
The socialization of emotion: Mothers display more intense facial expressions of emotion to infant daughters compared with infant sons.

Socialization in the Family

In general, the family is an important source of gender socialization. With regard to the socialization of gendered emotions, several patterns emerge from the research. One pattern in the data is that parents sometimes treat sons and daughters differently. A number of studies demonstrate that parents talk about emotions differently with sons compared with daughters (Denham et al., 2010; Fivush & Buckner, 2000). For example, mothers talk about emotions more with daughters than with sons (Brody, 2000; Fivush et al., 2000). And when parents do talk about emotions with their children, it's often in a way that conveys gender stereotypes (van der Pol et al., 2015).

In a classic experiment, a videotape was made of a baby's emotional responses to a jack-in-the-box popping open (Condry & Condry, 1976). The baby stared and then cried. The videotape was shown to adults, half of whom were told the baby was a boy and half of whom were told it was a girl. Those who thought the baby was a boy labeled the emotions "anger"; the other half, who thought the baby was a girl, called the emotions "fear." In short, the adults read the emotions differently depending on the baby's gender. This partly explains why parents socialize children's emotions in gender-stereotyped directions: The parents, viewing a child's behavior through the lens of gender stereotypes, perceive the child to be experiencing gendered emotions.

Have things changed since this classic study was conducted? Recent attempts to replicate Condry and Condry's (1976) findings have produced more complex results. For example, raters who tend not to endorse gender stereotypes rate the emotions of boy and girl infants similarly. Raters, especially male ones, who tend to endorse gender stereotypes are the most likely to perceive a baby boy's reaction as angry (Plant et al., 2000). In other words, it seems that some adults may still see the baby's behavior through the lens of gender stereotypes. As gender stereotypes change and people become more vigilant about stereotyping, we might expect gender socialization of emotions by parents to change, too.

Another pattern in the research is that mothers and fathers differ in emotion socialization behaviors. For example, mothers are more emotionally expressive than fathers (Dunsmore et al., 2009). Compared with fathers, mothers talk about emotions more often with their children (Zaman & Fivush, 2013) and are more supportive and less unsupportive of their children's negative emotions (Nelson et al., 2012). Other research suggests that, while fathers are more likely to play the role of a playmate, mothers are more likely to serve as *emotional gatekeepers* for children (Aznar & Tenenbaum, 2013; Denham et al., 2010). Being an emotional gatekeeper involves taking on the work of regulating children's emotions and fostering children's emotional competence.

Moreover, differences between mothers' and fathers' emotion socialization behaviors may depend on how involved they are in caring for their children. That is, when fathers become more involved with their children, patterns of gendered emotions are different (Brody, 1999). Girls with more involved fathers express less fear and sadness, compared with girls whose fathers are less involved. Boys with more involved fathers express more warmth and fear. Consistent with Nancy Chodorow's theory (see Chapter 2), fathers' involvement in the family seems to be crucial to breaking down stereotypes in the next generation.

In addition, both parent gender and child gender interact in the socialization of gendered emotions; that is, they both matter. Mothers actively encourage boys, more than girls, to respond to angry situations with anger and retaliation (Brody, 1996). Boys get the message and expect their mothers to react more warmly to them when they express anger than when they express sadness (Brody, 1996). Fathers pay more attention to their daughters when they are displaying sadness or anxiety and to their sons when they are displaying anger (Chaplin et al., 2005). This attention probably encourages more expression of those emotions.

How mothers and fathers respond to their children's expression of negative emotions may depend on the child's gender and also differ across ethnic groups. For example, one study examined how mothers and fathers of three ethnic groups (European American, Lumbee American Indian, and African American) responded to their children's expressions of negative emotions (Brown et al., 2015). For responses to their daughters' negative emotions, mothers were more supportive than fathers across each group. In responses to their sons' negative emotions, European American mothers were more supportive than European American fathers, Lumbee mothers and fathers were equally supportive, and African American mothers were less supportive than African American fathers. Some of these patterns are consistent with gender stereotypes within those specific racial/ethnic groups.

Why do parents socialize children's emotions in stereotypical ways? Parents' patterns of socialization likely reflect the roles that they anticipate sons and daughters will hold in adulthood (Brody, 1999). Men's roles focus on employment, where competition, power, and control are thought to be functional. Boys are therefore shaped not to express their emotions, especially emotions that would reveal vulnerability. The exceptions are anger, contempt, and pride, which boys and men are allowed to express and which seem consistent with high-status work roles. Women's roles focus on caregiving, whether as mothers or in occupations such as teacher or nurse. Girls are therefore socialized for qualities such as warmth and empathy. At the same time, in their anticipated lower-status roles, they can express vulnerability by revealing fear and sadness.

Importantly, these differences in emotional expression then serve to perpetuate power and status differences between women and men. An openly fearful person is ill-suited to be the CEO of a corporation, and a person who is too ready to express anger and contempt is ill-suited to be a preschool teacher.

Socialization by Peers

A college student recalled to one of us how, around fifth grade, his expressions of sadness were literally beaten out of him by other boys. Some sad events happened in his family that year, and that in turn made him more emotional at school. He learned that if he cried in front of his peers, they would ridicule him and engage in dominance behaviors such as punching him. That only made him feel sadder and more like crying. But he learned, painfully yet quickly, never to cry, no matter how much he was hurting, emotionally or physically. This is a clear example of how peers may socialize one another and enforce gendered display rules of emotion.

Data suggest that this student's experience isn't unusual. One study asked adolescents to imagine how their friends would react if they expressed negative emotions like anger in response to a negative event, such as getting bad news or discovering that someone had done something unfair to them (Klimes-Dougan et al., 2014). Girls reported that their friends were likely to engage in behaviors such as asking questions about the situation, rewarding or magnifying the emotions, or overriding the emotions and telling the girl to cheer up. By contrast, boys reported that their friends would likely ignore or neglect their negative emotions or engage in physical, verbal, or relational victimization.

Other studies also find that, when it comes to expressing negative emotions such as sadness, boys and girls are socialized differently by their peers. Boys and girls differ not only in how much sadness they express to their peers, but also in how their peers respond to that emotional expression (Perry-Parrish & Zeman, 2011). In turn, boys who do express sadness in front of peers are less accepted and popular, and more likely to be teased (Perry-Parrish & Zeman, 2011).

In sum, these studies tell us that peers are active gender socializers who enforce gendered display rules about negative emotions such as anger and sadness.

Brody's Transactional Model

Feminist psychologist Leslie Brody (1999) has proposed a comprehensive model for the development of gender differences in emotional expression, building on the work of Chodorow (1978; see Chapter 2) and emphasizing the complex interactions among biological, social, and cultural factors. Brody's model is a *transactional* model in that it emphasizes the bidirectional influences of children and parents, interacting and shaping each other's behaviors. That is, the process begins in infancy with subtle differences in temperament between girls and boys. While boys are more physically active than girls, girls are more sociable than boys. Girls also have better and earlier language skills than boys, and they develop self-control earlier than boys. Parents respond to the temperamental traits that they perceive in their children, such as by reinforcing girls' sociability and empathy with more opportunities to develop their social skills and emotional competence. Parents also socialize their children in socially acceptable gender-stereotyped ways, preparing them for their adult gender roles. In turn, the subtle gender differences in activity, sociability, language, and self-control develop into meaningful gender differences in emotional expression.

As children continue to develop, peers play an increasingly important role in gender role socialization. According to Brody, peers enforce gender stereotypes and gendered display rules of emotion, especially in the context of gender-segregated groups. That is, within same-gender peer groups, gendered patterns of social interaction and emotional expression are reinforced, such that girls continue to hone their skills for warm and intimate dyadic interactions and boys continue to develop their capacity for intense competitive interactions. Because those who violate these norms are socially excluded, children and adolescents are motivated to adhere to their gender role and follow the display rules. The result, according to Brody, is social acceptance in the short term but decreased mental and physical well-being in the long term.

Experience the Research
The Gender Socialization of Emotions

In this exercise, you are going to investigate the differences in two mothers' emotion words, comparing the conversations of a mother with her daughter and a mother with her son. Find two mothers with kindergarteners, one a boy and one a girl. Get their permission to record a conversation between them and their children. Ask each mother to think of two specific events her child has experienced and would be likely to remember and then to engage the child in conversation about first one event and then the other. Record the conversations, which should last between 5 and 10 minutes.

After you've completed the data collection, transcribe the tapes—that is, type up exactly what was said in each conversation. Count the number of positive emotion words and negative emotion words that each mother used. As you do this, consider these questions: How are you going to define which words count as emotion words? Did the mother of the daughter use more emotion words than the mother of the son? Were there any other differences in patterns? For example, was anger discussed with the son but not the daughter?

CHAPTER SUMMARY

Women are stereotyped as expressing a wide variety of both positive and negative emotions, including fear, sadness, sympathy, happiness, and love. Men, in contrast, are supposed to express only anger, contempt, and pride. Such stereotypes not only reflect women's and men's roles in adulthood, but also help to perpetuate these differentiated roles.

Although there is great similarity across U.S. ethnic groups in gender stereotypes of emotion, there are also some notable differences. African Americans, for example, believe that African American women express anger nearly as much as African American men do. Gender

stereotypes of emotions can have important consequences, leading people to misread others' emotions and evaluate people based on different standards.

Beyond the stereotypes, the issue of gender differences in actual emotional experience and expression is complex. Emotion manifests itself in many ways, including facial expressions, subjective feelings captured in self-reports, and arousal of the autonomic nervous system. Patterns of gender differences may be inconsistent across these various modalities, thus highlighting how oversimplified the stereotypes are. With regard to gender differences in the experience of specific emotions, the evidence suggests

(Continued)

(Continued)

that gender stereotypes are often exaggerations or just plain inaccurate. Gender differences in emotional expression are complex and enforced by gendered display rules of emotion.

Emotional competence is important for social, emotional, and even physical well-being. Consistent gender differences in most aspects of emotional competence demonstrate that boys and men lag behind girls and women in this aspect of emotion. Still, emotional competence is socialized and learned, which indicates that these gender differences can be eliminated.

Much of the research on gender and emotion rests on the assumption of a gender binary. Emerging lines of research examine emotional experiences of transgender individuals and emphasize the importance of gender identity over gender assigned at birth.

Gender socialization shapes emotional expression, beginning with parental socialization from infancy. As children grow older, peers play a larger role in gender socialization, including the socialization of emotional expression. We have just seen that peers from preschool to middle school exert powerful pressures in favor of gender-stereotyped expressions of emotion. Gender-segregated patterns of play are influential as well. Boys play with other boys, and girls play with other girls. In those same-gender groups, gendered display rules and gender roles are honed. Relative to boys and men, girls and women are more facially expressive of emotion and talk more about emotions. Brody's developmental model ties these diverse findings together and proposes that subtle differences in infancy grow into real gender differences in emotional competence because of family and peer socialization practices within a cultural context.

It is important to remember the cultural context in which we develop. The media, for example, portray women and men displaying different emotions. And, as we have seen, different cultures and ethnic groups have different expectations about gendered emotions. These cultural norms shape our gender development.

SUGGESTION FOR FURTHER READING

Barrett, Lisa F., Lewis, Michael, & Haviland-Jones, Jeannette M. (Eds.). (2016). *Handbook of Emotions* (4th ed.). New York, NY: Guilford. This handbook, with chapters written by leading emotion researchers, reviews the diverse empirical research on emotional experience, expression, and development.

Lifespan Development

In May 2011, reporters revealed that a Toronto couple was hiding the gender of their 4-month-old baby, hoping that the child would receive more gender-neutral treatment and not be stereotyped (Blackwell, 2011). They named the baby Storm.

Meanwhile, on television there was a series called *Toddlers and Tiaras*, in which girls as young as 4 were thrust into elaborate dresses and "dolled up" with heavy makeup and pouffy hairdos to compete in a beauty pageant for tots. No gender neutrality for them.

These two cases represent the extremes of the gender development questions facing parents and their children growing up today. Some parents want their kids to be treated equally and without the constraints of gender roles and gender stereotypes. By contrast, others think that the best thing to do is to teach their daughters how to be feminine and their sons how to be masculine. Parents of transgender and gender nonconforming kids face similar questions about gender, often with an additional level of complexity.

The decisions parents make about how to raise their children are often rooted in personal and cultural values, which can make questions about gender development very controversial.

In this chapter we will consider gender development over the lifespan and the extensive cultural forces that act to shape that development. Although most of the available research focuses on the development of cisgender individuals, we discuss research on trans individuals whenever possible. We focus our discussion on key developmental issues within the broad stages of infancy, childhood, adolescence, emerging adulthood, adulthood, and later adulthood.

Infancy

Developmental psychologists have spent an extraordinary amount of time studying children, particularly preschoolers and infants. Investigations of infant gender differences generally have involved two primary lines of reasoning. First, some have reasoned that, if gender differences are found in newborns, then those differences must surely be innate and the result of biological factors, because gender role socialization can scarcely have had time to have an effect. The idea, then, is to try to discover which gender differences are innate by studying newborns.

Second, many investigators think it is important to study the way parents and other adults treat infants, to discover the subtle (and perhaps not-so-subtle) differences in the way adults treat boy babies and girl babies, beginning the process of socialization at a tender age. The logic in this line of reasoning is that boys and girls are socialized to be different. We review research in these two areas below and also discuss what infants appear to know about gender.

Gender Differences in Infant Behavior

Most infant behaviors do not show gender differences. That is, gender similarities are the rule for most behaviors and traits, such as infant temperament. As noted in Chapter 6, researchers use the term *temperament* to refer to biologically based emotional and behavioral traits that appear early in life and predict later behaviors, personality, and psychological problems. A meta-analysis of studies of temperament in infancy and childhood found evidence of gender similarities as well as gender differences (Else-Quest et al., 2006). For example, male and female infants display equal amounts of sociability, shyness, soothability, and adaptability (Else-Quest, 2012; Else-Quest et al., 2006). Boys and girls also do not differ in how intense their moods are or how easy or difficult they are to care for. Nonetheless, a few notable gender differences in temperament exist.

One significant gender difference in temperament is in activity level. In small infants, this may be measured by counting the number of times they swing their arms or kick their legs. In older babies, it might be measured by counting the number of squares the baby crawls across on a playroom floor. Researchers may also ask parents how much a baby moves their limbs during activities such as having a bath. Meta-analyses have reported small but consistent gender differences in infants' activity level, $d = 0.13$ to 0.29 (D. W. Campbell & Eaton, 1999; Else-Quest et al., 2006). That is, male infants are more physically active than female infants. However, this gender difference changes across development. Effect sizes of gender differences in activity grow larger as children mature but then shrink in adolescence and become negligible in adulthood (Else-Quest, 2012).

Girls do better on tests of inhibitory control, $d = -0.41$, which is a medium-sized difference. This means that girls are better at controlling impulsive or inappropriate behaviors, which is definitely an asset in situations such as school. Similarly, girls also display better regulation of their attention; they can focus and shift their attention when they need to. Gender differences in attention focusing ($d = -0.15$) and purposeful attention shifting ($d = -0.31$) are small. Girls show greater perceptual sensitivity than boys, $d = 0.38$, a medium-sized difference. Perceptual sensitivity refers to awareness of subtle changes in the environment. Essentially, girls notice more about what is around them than boys do. While all these differences may make the transition to school a bit more challenging for boys, who are more active, less able to regulate their attention, and less perceptually sensitive, there is evidence that boys eventually catch up to girls and the differences become negligible (Else-Quest, 2012). That is, boys may mature a bit later than girls.

Adults' Treatment of Infants

The other area of interest in infant gender differences research concerns whether parents and other adults treat female and male babies differently. In one clever study, mothers of 11-month-old babies were asked to estimate how steep a slope their infant could successfully crawl down (Mondschein et al., 2000). Mothers of boys estimated that they would be successful at steeper slopes than mothers of girls did. Thus, even in infancy, parents have different expectations for their sons than for their daughters, and parents' expectations do have an impact on their children. It's important to bear in mind, however, that not only do parents influence infants, but infants also influence parents. Therefore, if differences exist in the behavior of boys and girls, these may cause the differences in parental treatment rather than the reverse. In the study described above, though, the boy and girl babies did not differ significantly in their crawling performance.

Some researchers have proposed that, if adults treat baby girls and baby boys differently, they do so in subtle and complex ways. For example, one longitudinal study examined how mothers handled and touched their babies, arguing that complex combinations of simple behaviors create a pattern of gender-differentiated treatment and ultimately foster gender differences in children's behaviors (Fausto-Sterling et al., 2015). The researchers observed a group of mother–infant dyads on a weekly basis starting at 3 months and ending at 12 months. The researchers videotaped the dyads and measured the frequency and duration of the behaviors of both the mothers and the babies. Although the babies showed no gender differences in their behaviors (e.g., crying, grasping, rolling), the mothers appeared to touch their sons and daughters differently. That is, the mothers not only touched their infant sons more than their infant daughters overall, but also touched them in different ways. For example, mothers tended to use more affectionate and caretaking touch with their daughters, such as cleaning and snuggling. With sons, mothers used more stimulatory touch, such as jiggling or rocking the infant and moving their limbs, and instrumental touch, such as shifting the infant's position or assisting with locomotion. The differences were especially pronounced in the early months, when

PHOTO 7.1
Research by Anne Fausto-Sterling and her colleagues (2015) indicates that mothers touch their infant sons more than their infant daughters and in different ways.

mothers tend to touch their infants the most. The authors proposed that these early gender-differentiated behaviors may underlie eventual gender differences in motor activity and play behaviors, such as girls' preference for play-grooming and boys' preference for rough-and-tumble play.

Gender Learning in Infancy

Infants begin learning about and categorizing gender at surprisingly young ages. Infancy researchers use several clever techniques to ascertain how and what infants perceive or know, and these techniques have been applied to the study of infant gender learning. One technique is the *habituation* paradigm, in which an infant is shown the same stimulus (e.g., a picture of a face) repeatedly until the infant habituates or gets used to it. If a new stimulus is presented, the infant responds with interest and a change in heart rate. Thus, for example, a researcher could habituate a baby to a set of pictures of different female faces. When a new female face is presented, the baby still acts habituated because the stimulus belongs to the same category (i.e., female). But if a male face is presented, the infant shows interest and a change in heart rate. Such a pattern of responding would show that the baby responds to male faces as being in a different category than female faces. While newborn infants do not appear to distinguish between male and female faces, this ability develops sometime between birth and 3 months of age (P. C. Quinn et al., 2008).

A similar technique is the *preferential looking* paradigm, in which researchers measure how long babies look at particular stimuli to assess which stimuli the baby prefers to look at. Research using this technique has found that, by 3 to 4 months, infants who have female caregivers prefer to look at female faces instead of male faces (P. C. Quinn et al., 2002).

And by 5 months, infants are sensitive to the distinction between typical male bodies and typical female bodies (Hock et al., 2015). For example, one study showed infants pairs of photographs and measured their looking direction and duration. The photographs were of people who were gender *congruent* (either a masculine body with a masculine face or a feminine body with a feminine face) and gender *incongruent* (modified photographs of either a feminine body with a masculine face or a masculine body with a feminine face). These images are shown in Figure 7.1. While 3.5-month-olds showed no preference for photographs of gender congruent or gender incongruent people, 5-month-olds preferred to look at the gender incongruent photographs. Presumably, the older babies preferred looking at the gender incongruent people because they were novel or more interesting than gender congruent people.

An important implication of these studies on babies' gender learning is that humans do not appear to innately categorize gender as a binary system. Rather, we learn to understand gender as having two categories that do not overlap. So as gender nonconformity becomes more common and children see greater gender diversity in their social world, might we expect this preference for gender incongruent people to change? This is a question that future researchers may want to pose.

Childhood

Gender Differences in Child Behavior

Already by the early preschool years, several reliable gender differences have appeared. One is in toy and game preference. Preschool children between the ages of 2 and 3 tend to have a strong preference for gender-typed toys and same-gender playmates (Blakemore et al., 2009). In the United States and many other nations, girls prefer dolls and doll

FIGURE 7.1 **Images used by Hock and colleagues (2015) to ascertain infants' knowledge of gender categories.**

A

Gender Congruent   Gender Incongruent

B

Gender Congruent   Gender Incongruent

Source: Hock et al. (2015).

accessories, arts and crafts, and fashion, whereas boys prefer guns and transportation toys. Boys are particularly resistant to playing with girl-stereotyped toys (Green et al., 2004; Leaper, 2015). The result is strong gender segregation in childhood, a point we will explore in more detail below.

Another difference that appears early is in aggressive behavior. About as soon as aggressive behavior appears in children, around the age of 2, gender differences are found; boys are more aggressive than girls. This difference persists throughout the school years (see Chapter 3). It is also found in a wide variety of cultures, from North America to Africa (Best & Thomas, 2004).

Gender Learning in Childhood

If you ask a typically developing 3-year-old girl whether she is a boy or a girl, she will likely answer that she is a girl. But if you ask her whether she can grow up to be a daddy, she may answer yes. A 6- or 7-year-old girl will probably answer this question differently. The 3-year-old understands some aspects of the concept of gender, but has not yet developed **gender constancy**—the understanding that gender is a stable and consistent part of oneself—which develops in three stages, according to Kohlberg's cognitive developmental theory (introduced in Chapter 2). The first stage is the development of **gender identity**, in which children can identify and label themselves, as well as others, as boys or girls; gender identity develops around 18 months to 2 years (Kohlberg, 1966; Zosuls et al., 2009). However, at this stage a girl may feel strongly that when she grows up she can be a boy if she wants to. (We think it's worth remembering that, while most people today believe that their gender is permanent, a critique of the gender binary questions this assumption.)

The second stage of gender constancy is the development of **gender stability**, which happens around 3 to 4 years of age and refers to the understanding that gender is stable over time. Yet a 4-year-old girl with a firm grasp of gender stability may still insist that if she wears pants she will no longer be a girl. Once kids understand that gender is generally stable over time, they go through a period of rigidity in adhering to gender norms. One example of this behavior is **appearance rigidity** (that is, rigid adherence to gender norms in appearance), such as wearing highly masculine or feminine clothing and avoiding clothes typical of another gender.

There is some evidence that appearance rigidity is higher in girls than in boys. One study of ethnically diverse 4-year-olds found that appearance rigidity was widespread (Halim et al., 2014). A few interesting patterns emerged in the comparisons across gender and ethnic groups. First, gender differences in appearance rigidity were found among Chinese American, African American, and White children. This difference was largest in White children: Only a minority (11%) of White boys exhibited appearance rigidity, compared with a majority (68%) of White girls. By contrast, among the Latinx (specifically, Mexican American and Dominican) children, boys and girls were equally likely to exhibit appearance rigidity. The salience of gender and the importance of adhering to gender norms differs across the intersection of gender and ethnicity in the United States.

In the third stage of gender constancy development, between 5 and 7 years of age, gender consistency develops and kids become more flexible about gender stereotypes. **Gender consistency** is the understanding that gender remains consistent despite superficial changes in appearance (such as wearing dresses instead of pants). After gender constancy is fully developed, then, children become more flexible because they know that playing with gender-stereotyped toys or wearing gender-typed clothing won't have any effect on their gender (Leaper, 2015). Yet this potential for flexibility doesn't mean that children start engaging in cross-gender-typed behaviors en masse. Kohlberg theorized that the acquisition of gender constancy is critical for the acquisition of gender roles. That is, once the little girl knows that her gender is a constant part of herself,

Gender constancy: The understanding that gender is a stable and consistent part of oneself.

Gender identity: The first stage of gender constancy development, in which children can identify and label their own gender and the gender of others.

Gender stability: The second stage of gender constancy development, in which children understand that gender is stable over time.

Appearance rigidity: Rigid adherence to gender norms in appearance, such as wearing highly masculine or feminine clothing and avoiding clothes typical of another gender.

Gender consistency: The third stage of gender constancy development, in which children understand that gender remains consistent despite superficial changes in appearance.

gender becomes much more important to her. Motivated to have a positive sense of self, the girl comes to see femininity as good and then associates this valuation with cultural stereotypes and roles, so the female role becomes attractive and important to her. Thus, children are motivated to adopt gender roles as part of their attempt to understand their world and develop a stable and positive sense of self.

In short, preschoolers rapidly become little gender essentialists, believing that differences between women and men are large and unalterable, and that there can be no behavioral overlap between the categories (Gelman et al., 2004).

Transgender and Gender Nonconforming Child Development

For transgender and gender nonconforming children, gender development may progress differently. Their gender identity does not match the gender label that adults have given them, so conflict can arise. This **gender dysphoria**, and the social conflicts that may ensue, can be very distressing for children; like anyone else, children want to feel confident and sure of themselves as well as accepted and understood by others. Adults may respond with concerns that there is something wrong with the child or that the child isn't developing "normally" (Edwards-Leeper et al., 2016; Olson et al., 2015). What do we know about gender development for transgender and gender nonconforming children?

Historically, transgender children have been met with skepticism (Olson et al., 2015). That is, others have viewed transgender kids as being confused about their gender identity, delayed in their gender constancy development, oppositional, or just plain pretending. How do we know if a child's expression of their gender identity is the "true" one? While there isn't a wealth of research on the gender development of transgender children specifically, or even gender nonconforming children generally, there are a handful of well-designed studies that help us understand these children and how best to support them and promote their healthy development.

For example, one study recruited three groups of 5- to 12-year-old children and compared them on implicit and explicit measures of gender identity and preferences (Olson et al., 2015). The first group was composed of transgender children who presented themselves consistent with their gender identity (i.e., they did not appear to match the gender assigned at birth); the second group was composed of their cisgender siblings; the third group was composed of cisgender children who were of the same gender identity, age, verbal IQ, and socioeconomic status as the transgender kids. The researchers measured the children's explicit gender identity and preferences, such as whether they preferred to play with same- or other-gender peers and whether they preferred toys appropriate for a particular gender. Implicit measures of gender identity and preferences were also included, using the Implicit Association Test (discussed in Chapter 3). The researchers reasoned that, if transgender children were confused, delayed, oppositional, or pretending when it came to their gender identity, their responses to the implicit and explicit

©iStockphoto.com/tbrengel.

PHOTO 7.2
Gender essentialists? Young children's thinking about gender changes as they develop gender constancy.

Gender dysphoria:
Discomfort or distress related to incongruence between a person's gender identity, sex assigned at birth, and/or primary and secondary sex characteristics.

PHOTO 7.3
Much more research with gender nonconforming children is needed in order to support their development and well-being.

measures would be inconsistent or maybe even random. Yet the pattern of results was striking and unambiguous: The transgender children were indistinguishable from two groups of cis-gender children when matched on gender identity. When matched on gender assigned at birth, the transgender children differed significantly from the two groups of cisgender children. In other words, the evidence indicated that the transgender children were not confused, delayed, oppositional, or pretending. The children's gender identity was deeply felt and true to themselves, and it was clearly inconsistent with their gender assigned at birth.

Nonetheless, not all gender nonconforming children will go on developing with a gender identity that doesn't match their gender assigned at birth (Edwards-Leeper et al., 2016). The evidence suggests that for many gender nonconforming children, their gender dysphoria will abate and their gender identity will eventually become consistent with the gender they were assigned at birth (Drummond et al., 2008; Steensma et al., 2013; Wallien & Cohen-Kettenis, 2008). Somewhere between 12% and 50% of children diagnosed with gender dysphoria will continue to identify their gender as inconsistent with their gender assigned at birth, but there is controversy about these estimates (American Psychological Association [APA], 2015). How do we know which kids will continue to be transgender? It seems that gender nonconforming children whose gender identity is very intense in childhood are more likely to continue with that gender identity and are less likely to identify with their gender assigned at birth (Steensma et al., 2013). In addition, kids whose gender dysphoria continues or intensifies in adolescence are also more likely to identify their gender as different from their gender assigned at birth (APA, 2015).

For these reasons, researchers have concluded that there is no "one size fits all" approach and have advocated that we approach the care of each transgender or gender nonconforming child individually (Edwards-Leeper et al., 2016). More broadly, the American Psychological Association (2015) has provided guidelines for providing trans-affirmative care for transgender and gender nonconforming people. **Trans-affirmative practice** (also called *gender-affirming care*) is care that is respectful, aware, and supportive of the identities and life experiences of transgender and gender nonconforming people (APA, 2015). For prepubescent children, trans-affirmative care might include *socially transitioning*—that is, changing one's name, pronoun, clothing, and so on to be consistent with one's gender identity—though this would depend on the child and their family. When children reach puberty, there are additional aspects of care and development to consider. We return to this issue later in the chapter.

Trans-affirmative practice: Care that is respectful, aware, and supportive of the identities and life experiences of transgender and gender nonconforming people; also called gender-affirming care.

From Gender Identity to Gender Roles: Self-Socialization

One of Kohlberg's arguments was that once children have a concept of gender identity, and especially a concept of gender constancy, they essentially self-socialize. That is, children want to adopt the characteristics of their gender based on their knowledge of the characteristics of the people they see in the world around them.

A more contemporary version of these ideas is the **gender self-socialization model** (Tobin et al., 2010). According to this model, children's gender identity ("I am a girl"),

Gender self-socialization model: A theoretical model that children's gender identification makes them want to adopt gender-stereotyped behaviors.

their gender stereotypes ("Boys are good at math"), and their gender self-perceptions ("I am good at math") all influence each other as children develop. One of the processes linking these three aspects is *stereotype emulation*; the more that children identify with their gender, the more they view themselves as having the qualities specified by stereotypes about their gender ("I am a girl. I want to wear dresses."). A second process is *identity construction*; the more that children engage in gender-stereotyped activities, the more identified with their own gender they become ("I love playing with dolls. I am such a typical girl."). In short, the culture provides plenty of information about acceptable behavior for girls and for boys, but children do not always have to be forced to conform. In many ways, they self-socialize.

Children are learning not only about gender categories and gender roles, but also about gender discrimination (C. S. Brown & Bigler, 2005). In one study, elementary school children were read scenarios about teachers' evaluations of students; in some of the scenarios, information was included suggesting that gender discrimination was likely (for example, "Mr. Franks almost always gives boys higher grades than girls"; C. S. Brown & Bigler, 2005). Even first and second graders recognized discrimination some of the time, and older children (fourth and fifth graders) were even more likely to recognize it.

Gender Role Socialization

One of us (NEQ) took her preschool-age daughter Raeka to the pediatrician's office. Raeka was playing with a model space shuttle that she had gotten at the air and space museum. She showed it to the nurse and said, "This is my spaceship. Blast off!" The nurse replied, "Wow, I've never seen a girl play with a spaceship before!" This event illustrates how the forces of gender socialization are all around children. It occurred not in the 1950s, but in 2010.

As we develop across childhood, the forces of gender role socialization become more prominent. **Socialization** refers to the ways in which society conveys to the individual its expectations for their behavior. Parents are a major source of gender socialization (Epstein & Ward, 2011). Parents influence their children's development in four ways: channeling, differential treatment, direct instruction, and modeling (Blakemore et al., 2009). With **channeling** (also called shaping), parents create a gendered world for their child through the toys they purchase, the activities they choose (for example, ballet lessons for girls but not boys), the way they decorate their bedroom, and so on. Essentially, they channel their child in certain directions and not others. With **differential treatment**, parents behave differently toward sons compared with daughters. For example, in some countries a parent may give more food to a son than to a daughter when resources are scarce (United Nations, 2015). The example of Raeka and her space shuttle also is an example of differential treatment; the nurse would not have made such a comment to a boy. **Direct instruction** involves parents telling children how they should behave. For example, fathers may tell sons that boys don't cry, or mothers may teach daughters how to care for babies. Finally, parents, often without knowing it, also engage in **modeling** behaviors for their children, who then form ideas about how women and men should behave.

Parents talk differently with their daughters compared with their sons. Mothers talk more and use more supportive speech with daughters than with sons, perhaps creating a greater emphasis for daughters on verbal interactions and relationships (Leaper et al., 1998). And, as we saw in Chapter 6, parents talk differently about emotions with daughters and sons. Much of the gender teaching in parents' talk is subtle

Socialization: The ways in which society conveys to the individual its expectations for their behavior.

Channeling: Selection of different toys, activities, and so on for boys and girls; also called shaping.

Differential treatment: The extent to which parents and others behave differently toward boys and girls.

Direct instruction: Telling boys and girls to behave in different ways.

Modeling: Demonstrating gendered behavior for children; also refers to the child's imitation of the behavior.

and implicit rather than obvious and explicit (Gelman et al., 2004). That is, today parents don't say that girls cannot grow up to be doctors. Instead, their talk emphasizes the categories of gender and assigns gender even to animal characters that are portrayed as gender neutral in books. In many ways, this corresponds to the subtlety of modern sexism discussed in Chapter 3.

Parents also play differently with sons compared with daughters in the preschool years. Parents engage in more pretend play with girls than with boys, and fathers in particular engage in more physical play with sons than with daughters (Lindsey & Mize, 2001; Lindsey et al., 1997). What is unclear, however, is whether parents engage in these different types of play because of their own gender-stereotyped ideas or because they are responding to the lead of the child and boys and girls initiate different kinds of play.

Not all families are the same, of course. Parents with traditional gender role attitudes have different expectations for sons compared with daughters (Pomerantz et al., 2004). Parents with liberal or egalitarian attitudes tend to treat sons and daughters similarly.

The research on gender socialization within the family has been based almost exclusively on White middle-class samples (Reid et al., 1995). Yet, as we saw in Chapter 4, there is good reason to think that gender role socialization varies across different ethnic groups in the United States. For example, gender roles are less differentiated among Black Americans, and Black children are exposed to Black women who are assertive, express anger openly, and are independent (Reid et al., 1995). The version of the woman that these children observe and model differs from the version displayed by many White, middle-class women.

As children grow older, schools, the media, and peers become increasingly important sources of gender socialization.

The *schools*, whether purposely or unwittingly, may transmit the information of gender role stereotypes. Research based on classroom observations in preschools and elementary schools indicates that teachers treat boys and girls differently. For example, teachers, on average, pay more attention to and interact more with boys (DeZolt & Hull, 2001; S. M. Jones & Dindia, 2004). Teachers also hold gender-stereotyped expectations for children's behavior, expecting better academic performance from girls than from boys and more misbehavior from boys than from girls (S. Jones & Myhill, 2004). These gender-stereotyped expectations may be especially strong among teachers of African American children (Wood et al., 2007). Fortunately, when teachers are given gender-equity training to sensitize them to these issues, they respond with more equitable treatment (DeZolt & Hull, 2001).

Children also receive implicit messages from teachers about how important the categories of gender are. In one field experiment in preschool classrooms, researchers began by measuring children's gender attitudes and preferences (Hilliard & Liben, 2010). Then, for a 2-week period, teachers either did or did not make gender salient in the classroom. Teachers in the gender salience condition did this in numerous ways, such as by saying, "Good morning, boys and girls" rather than "Good morning, children," by lining children up separately by gender, and by having different bulletin boards for boys and girls. At the end of the 2 weeks, children were tested again. Those in the high gender salience condition showed significantly increased gender stereotypes, less positive ratings of other-gender peers, and decreased play with other-gender peers. Teachers make choices about how much they emphasize gender in the classroom, and these choices have an impact on children. Yet so many of these choices have become habitual, and it takes conscious effort to create a classroom in which gender isn't salient.

The *media* are powerful socializing agents as well. Many people assume that things have changed dramatically since the 1970s and that gender stereotypes are a thing of the past. The evidence indicates that some change has occurred, yet the same stereotyped gender roles are in plentiful supply. An analysis of toy commercials shown on the Nickelodeon network showed continued stereotyping (Kahlenberg & Hein, 2010). Almost all the toys were gender specific and showed only one gender playing with them. Mixed-gender groups of children were shown in only 19% of the commercials, and everything else was gender segregated.

Even supposedly nonsexist children's books, which show girls and women in some nonstereotypic roles, still portray the female characters as having feminine personality characteristics (e.g., they are affectionate, sympathetic), performing household chores, and engaging in female-stereotyped leisure activities such as shopping (Diekman & Murnen, 2004).

Video games are also a source of gender role socialization. The average eighth- or ninth-grade boy plays computer games 13 hours per week, compared with 5 hours for the average girl (Gentile et al., 2004). Video games show patterns of extreme gender stereotyping, including violence against women. Female characters are generally portrayed as submissive and often serve as rewards or prizes for the male characters. For example, in the game *Duke Nukem Forever*, players can play "Capture the Babe," in which they compete to catch a woman who, dressed as a schoolgirl, utters only sexually suggestive phrases (Stermer & Burkley, 2015). Boys' exposure to such sexist video games is substantial. There is increasing evidence that the games encourage and reinforce sexist attitudes in adults (e.g., Stermer & Burkley, 2015). How might such games affect children, whose gender role ideologies are still developing?

The stereotyping of media messages has been demonstrated to have an effect on children's gender role attitudes and behaviors and on girls' body dissatisfaction (L. M. Ward & Harrison, 2005). For example, in one study first and second graders were exposed to television commercials in which all boys were playing with a gender-neutral toy (traditional condition), all girls were playing with it (nontraditional condition), or the commercial was not about toys (control; Pike & Jennings, 2005). After the viewing, children were asked to sort six toys into those that were for boys, those that were for girls, or those that were for both boys and girls. Among the six toys was the toy they had seen in the commercial. Children in the traditional condition were more likely to say that the toy was for boys, whereas children in the nontraditional condition were more likely to say that it was for both boys and girls. These results show not only the power of stereotyped television images, but also that children can respond positively to nonstereotyped messages.

Despite the pressures of gender socialization, not every child conforms. Although many social critics emphasize the restrictiveness of girls' socialization, stereotype-inconsistent behavior is in fact far less tolerated for boys than it is for girls. Many parents tolerate their daughters climbing trees and playing soccer but get upset at a son playing with dolls. It is seen as far worse to be a sissy than to be a tomboy.

©IStockphoto.com/lmtmphoto.

PHOTO 7.4
The media—including video games, television, and books—are a source of gender role socialization for children.

Peers and the Gender Segregation Effect

The eminent developmental psychologist Eleanor Maccoby (1998), in her book *The Two Sexes: Growing Up Apart, Coming Together*, concluded that gendered patterns of behavior are not solely the result of socialization by forces such as parents and the media. By 3 years of age, children have a tendency to seek out and play with other children of their own gender and to avoid playing with children of the other gender. The tendency grows stronger by the time children are in elementary school. It occurs regardless of the gender socialization principles in their families, and it occurs in villages in developing nations as much as in the United States. The all-girl and all-boy groups differ in terms of their activities (Fabes et al., 2003). Boys' play is rougher and involves more risk, confrontation, and striving for dominance. The members of all-girl groups are more likely to use conflict-reducing strategies in negotiating with each other and to engage in more self-disclosure. Girls' groups also tend to maintain communication with adults, whereas boys separate themselves from adults, test the limits, and seek autonomy.

The gender segregation and the different play styles in these groups essentially egg each other on. Boys are attracted to boy groups in part because they adore the rough play, and girls avoid boy groups because they dislike rough play. Once in a boy group, boys are encouraged to play roughly. Boys may be attracted to rough, active play by their higher activity level, which, as we have seen, is present from infancy and may have a biological basis. Engaged in rough play, they become even more active. Girls are attracted to girl groups because they like the positive social network and the self-regulated style of play. Once they are in the group, self-regulation is encouraged.

Much of the gender segregation of childhood, then, results from forces within the child—whether biological or psychological. (An example of the latter is the child's desire to maintain a positive gender identity by engaging in gender-typed activities.) Peer play groups rapidly create the next generation of gender-typed children (Maccoby, 2002).

Interestingly, as Maccoby noted, when children play alone, gender differences in behavior are minimal. When in their same-gender group, the gender differences are large and striking. Again we see evidence of the importance of context in shaping gender differences in behavior.

With all this gender segregation in childhood, how do men and women get back together in adulthood to form relationships, work cooperatively, and so on? The answer is that, in some cultures, they don't. That is, in some cultures even the adult world is highly gender segregated, leaving contact between husbands and wives as the only intergender contact. In societies that do allow open contact between men and women, sexual attraction helps bring the sexes together. The process is not without pitfalls, though, as boys' much-practiced dominance style meshes with girls' conflict-reducing style. As men and women come together, whether in romantic relationships or at work, they pursue common goals and their behavior becomes more similar.

Is this gender segregation in childhood, and the male dominance it encourages, inevitable? Maccoby suggests that as long as we allow children the freedom to choose their playmates, the pattern will continue. Nonetheless, schools could take steps to ensure that children have multiple experiences of working cooperatively in mixed-gender groups in the classroom. Such practices reduce the extreme gender differentiation of childhood and should foster better mixed-gender relationships in adulthood.

The Sexualization of Girls

Sexualization: The process of valuing a person only for their sex appeal, sexually objectifying a person, or inappropriately imposing sexuality on a person.

In 2007 the American Psychological Association released the report of its Task Force on the Sexualization of Girls. **Sexualization** occurs when a person is valued only for sex appeal or is sexually objectified, or when sexuality is inappropriately imposed on the person. The report strikingly documented the multiple ways in which the culture sexualizes girls. In the media and in beauty contests, little girls are groomed to look like sexy adults. Products for girls contribute to sexualization, including the Bratz dolls (who wear sexy and provocative clothing and makeup) and Barbie. One experiment with 5- to 8-year-old girls, in fact, showed that just 15 minutes of exposure to Barbie images lowered girls' body esteem compared with girls in a control condition (Dittmar et al., 2006).

Sexualization also occurs when girls are treated like sexual objects by family, friends, teachers, or other adults. The most extreme examples occur with child sexual abuse, but milder examples occur in the daily lives of girls. For example, some parents convey to their daughters that being attractive to boys should be their top priority.

The sexualization of girls raises many concerns. Sexualization may cause reduced self-esteem when girls cannot meet the standards for sex appeal. Sexualization may also lead to reduced cognitive performance and even lowered career aspirations. In one study, undergraduate women and men received an objectifying gaze during an interaction with a person of another gender, who was actually a confederate of the experimenter (Gervais et al., 2011). The objectifying gaze involved looking from the participant's head to the waist and back to the head and then, at several other times during the interaction, looking briefly at the chest. The objectifying gaze led to decrements in math performance for the women in the experiment but not for the men. No one has done such an experiment with younger girls, but surely incidents like these occur, and it is highly likely that they have similar negative effects.

The APA report suggested many ways to counteract sexualization. Within the schools, we could provide media literacy training programs so that girls can learn to analyze when they are being sexualized by the media. Girls can empower themselves by engaging in activism and resistance, such as campaigning against companies that use sexualized images to sell products.

Adolescence

If the behavior and development of girls and boys are similar for about the first 10 years of life, how do the gender differences in adulthood arise? In the early years, girls do better in school and have fewer adjustment problems than boys. Yet adult women, on average, have lower-status jobs than men (see Chapter 9) and have a higher incidence of depression (see Chapter 15). Although the groundwork for these differences is prepared in childhood, the real precipitating factors occur in adolescence.

Puberty for Cisgender and Transgender Youth

When we think of our adolescence, many of us remember the seemingly dramatic changes of puberty. Our bodies changed in ways we may or may not have appreciated at the time, we felt increasingly self-conscious about our appearance, and adults' and peers' expectations for us changed. Puberty can seem awkward, exciting, scary, and just plain bizarre to adolescents, particularly if they don't have age-appropriate information about what to expect as they develop. For cisgender youth, feelings about puberty often depend on their gender: While boys often eagerly relish the transformations that their bodies go through, girls tend to dread the change their bodies experience. Why this difference?

For one thing, boys' pubertal changes bring them closer to the masculine ideal of having a muscular build and greater athletic ability. The increased testosterone secreted by their testes makes it easier to build muscle mass, and muscular men are deemed more masculine. By contrast, girls' bodies start to change in ways that actually take them further away from the contemporary feminine ideal. This feminine ideal is hyper-thin and waif-like, complete with a "thigh gap." Yet this shape is a genetic anomaly for the vast majority of healthy women and has been criticized by many for promoting highly restricted eating and self-objectification (see Chapter 2).

The timing of puberty matters, too. For boys, early puberty tends to make them more popular because their taller and more muscular bodies make them more athletic, though the effects are not uniformly positive (Mendle & Ferrero, 2012). But for girls, early puberty is clearly detrimental to several other aspects of their development (Blumenthal et al., 2011; Ge & Natsuaki, 2009). Girls who develop breasts and feminine curves earlier than their peers tend to get harassed and sexualized. Their mature bodies make them look more like women than like girls, and this fact gets noticed by peers as well as by adults. And because these girls are socially and emotionally less mature than they look, the harassment and sexual attention can be very difficult to cope with. Still, early puberty is a risk factor for adolescent mental health, regardless of gender. Early puberty increases girls' and boys' risk of developing internalizing disorders, such as depression, anxiety, and eating disorders (Ullsperger & Nikolas, 2017; we return to these topics in Chapter 15).

For trans kids, puberty can be especially difficult if their body is changing in ways that don't align with their gender identity. A transgender boy who starts growing breasts may feel self-conscious and deeply distressed about the feminine body he is developing. Trans-affirmative care for adolescents may include **pubertal suppression** (or *puberty blockers*), in which the adolescent takes medication that suppresses endogenous (that is, originating from within the body) pubertal changes (Edwards-Leeper et al., 2016). Essentially, pubertal suppression can be helpful because it buys kids some extra time to explore and feel confident about their gender identity before irreversible pubertal changes (e.g., deepening voice or changes in bone structure) take effect, either through endogenous puberty or as a result of undergoing gender-affirming hormone treatment, or before initiating invasive and permanent surgeries or procedures (e.g., mastectomy, also called *top surgery*). Given that gender dysphoria does not persist past adolescence for a substantial proportion of gender nonconforming kids, this extra time can be precious.

After a few years of pubertal suppression, if gender dysphoria continues for a child, gender-affirming hormone treatment may be initiated. This would involve taking hormones that promote the development of secondary sex characteristics, such as facial hair or breasts (see Chapter 10). Health care providers often encourage kids to wait until around age 16 to begin these hormones because their effects are less reversible and may have implications for the teen's later fertility. Still, the long-term effects of these medical treatments—both pubertal suppression and gender-affirming hormone treatment—have not been thoroughly examined among individuals who received them in childhood. We need high-quality research so that we can provide the safest and most effective care to transgender youth.

Gender Intensification

Pubertal development changes how we are perceived by others, often making our gender more salient. Adolescence researchers have argued that pressures for gender role conformity increase dramatically at the beginning of adolescence, a process known as **gender intensification** (Crouter et al., 1995; McHale et al., 2009). The pressure, then, is

Pubertal suppression: Medical suppression of endogenous pubertal changes in adolescents; also called puberty blockers.

Gender intensification: Increased pressures for gender role conformity, beginning in adolescence.

for girls to become more feminine and less masculine, beginning around 11 or 12 years of age. A recent study of youth who entered adolescence in the 21st century, however, questioned whether gender intensification is as strong as it once was (Priess et al., 2009). Girls did not increase in femininity scores from age 11 to 15, and girls actually scored as high as boys on masculinity. Pressures for gender conformity may not be as strong today as they once were, or perhaps they have simply become more subtle, like modern sexism.

Identity Development

The eminent developmental theorist Erik Erikson (1950) proposed that adolescence is the stage in which the primary developmental crisis is a quest for identity. As we prepare for the autonomy of adulthood, we must explore and commit to a coherent identity to guide us. Erikson's theory was androcentric: He focused on boys and their identity development, which has long been defined largely in terms of work. Thus, vocational identity, such as "I am a doctor," takes center stage in this model. Adolescence becomes a time to prepare for this adult identity, as in "I must start taking science courses and become a responsible student in order to become a doctor." The emphasis for boys, therefore, is on developing autonomy and a separate identity that is grounded in an occupation. Once that identity is achieved, they can move on to the next stage, which focuses on intimacy and marriage.

What happens to girls? Originally, Erikson and others said that girls were in a state of identity suspension, postponing identity formation until marriage, which in itself created identity for them. Additionally, they were thought to shape their identity to the husband's and therefore had to remain flexible before that. In other words, a young woman can't have an identity until she knows her husband's identity. For much of American history, girls simply did not anticipate that work outside the home would be a major source of identity.

Researchers later began to question this cramming of female identity development into an Erikson-shaped box. They suggested, instead, that girls and women define their identities more in interpersonal terms, in a sense of self that is connected to others (Douvan & Adelson, 1966).

Research indicates that adolescent girls progress by developing both an *interpersonal* identity and an *autonomous* identity, whereas boys' identity development focuses mainly on autonomous identity (Fivush & Zaman, 2015; Lytle et al., 1997). In short, adolescent girls balance the two sources of identity, whereas boys grow in autonomous identity considerably more than in interpersonal identity. It seems likely that girls today develop both aspects of identity because real career options are available to them that simply were not there 40 or more years ago.

Girls in late adolescence also vary considerably among themselves in what components they believe will shape their identities. A study of women at a southern U.S. university found that 22% anticipated a balanced identity with equal emphasis on career, marriage, and parenthood; 57% anticipated a family-oriented identity, with little emphasis on career and much on marriage and parenthood; 9% anticipated a career-oriented identity with less emphasis on marriage and parenthood; and 12% anticipated a

istock.com/Mixmike.

PHOTO 7.5

In early adolescence, gender intensification occurs and girls learn that their status will be determined by their attractiveness, not their achievements.

career-and-marriage-oriented identity, with little emphasis on motherhood (Kerpelman & Schvaneveldt, 1999). Even today, then, the majority thought that career would not be the major definer of their identity. Yet substantial numbers held other views, in which career was a major definer. In this study, women and men did not differ in their ratings of the salience of career in defining their identity, nor did they differ in their ratings of marriage, but women anticipated, more than men, that parenthood would be salient in their identity.

Erikson's original theory, despite its androcentrism, continues to spur psychological research (e.g., Koepke & Denissen, 2012; McLean & Syed, 2015; Merrill & Fivush, 2016). For example, there is a vast literature on ethnic identity development originating from Erikson's work (e.g., Huang & Stormshak, 2011; Meeus, 2011). Interestingly, some of that research has found variation among youth from different ethnic groups in terms of their exploration of and commitment to a coherent sense of ethnic identity (Else-Quest & Morse, 2015). There remains much to learn about identity development in adolescence, and Eriksonian theory has provided a starting point for that work.

In sum, girls' identity development in adolescence is more complex than Erikson theorized, with aspects of autonomy as well as deep connections to others. The elevated importance of interpersonal relationships, particularly in the context of gender intensification, means that appearance and the opinions of others can be especially powerful.

Friendship and Dating

It has been said that, in their friendships, girls and women stand "face to face" and boys and men stand "shoulder to shoulder" (Winstead & Griffin, 2001). That is, girls are face to face as they talk and self-disclose, whereas boys are shoulder to shoulder, engaged in some common activity such as a sport.

The origins of these different friendship styles certainly lie in early childhood and the gender-segregated play groups with their different play styles. By fourth or fifth grade, gender differences in same-gender friendships have appeared that resemble those found in adulthood (Winstead & Griffin, 2001). Girls are more likely than boys to talk and self-disclose. And girls' talk is more often about personal concerns or other people, whereas boys' talk is more likely to be about sports and leisure activities. Not wanting to overemphasize gender differences, though, we should note that girls' and boys' friendships are similar in qualities such as honesty, straightforwardness, mutual activities, and loyalty (Buhrmester, 1998). And friendship networks become less gender-segregated across adolescence (Poulin & Pedersen, 2007).

Adolescent dating is the stage for the enactment of heterosexual, gendered scripts (O'Sullivan et al., 2001). Girls are valued for their appearance, boys for their athleticism. Around 10 to 12 years of age, girls begin paying more attention to their hair, clothing, and makeup, in efforts to make themselves more attractive to boys.

Despite plentiful research on adolescent sexuality, there are few studies on romantic relationships in adolescence. Yet we know that these relationships touch off strong emotions including love, jealousy, anger, and anxiety (O'Sullivan et al., 2001). These relationships also serve a developmental function in the transition to adulthood. They provide a context for learning about the self, including a consideration of one's gender identity and sexual orientation. Heterosexual dating relationships typically involve power differentials between the boy and the girl (O'Sullivan et al., 2001). Girls may be more invested in maintaining the relationship, giving boys more power. Often, too, boys assume decision-making authority. How might these early romantic relationships prepare us for adult romantic relationships?

FOCUS 7.1

PEER SEXUAL HARASSMENT IN THE SCHOOLS

Although we consider sexual harassment in detail in Chapter 14, we discuss it here briefly because it is such a widespread experience during adolescence. The U.S. Department of Education Office for Civil Rights (2010, p. 6) defines sexual harassment as "unwelcome conduct of a sexual nature, which can include unwelcome sexual advances, requests for sexual favors, or other verbal, non-verbal, or physical conduct of a sexual nature," including sexual touching, comments, jokes, or gestures, calling students sexually charged names, spreading sexual rumors, rating students on sexual activity or performance, and circulating, showing, or creating e-mails or websites of a sexual nature. Note that behaviors must be unwelcome to be considered harassment.

Peer sexual harassment is common in adolescence. In a national survey of students in seventh through twelfth grades, the American Association of University Women (AAUW; 2011) found that nearly half (48%) of the students had experienced some form of sexual harassment by peers. Rates were similar across socioeconomic and racial groups.

The AAUW (2011) report included findings of important gender differences. For example, 56% of girls said they'd been sexually harassed in the past year, compared with 40% of boys. This was the case for harassment in person and for harassment via text, e-mail, Facebook, or other electronic means. Moreover, compared with boys, girls reported being more negatively affected by this harassment. Gender differences in perpetration were also evident: 14% of girls admitted to sexually harassing a peer, compared with 18% of boys.

There were also gender similarities in the report. For example, 18% of girls and 18% of boys reported being called gay or lesbian in a negative way (AAUW, 2011). However, this particular form of harassment was reported by boys to be the most upsetting. Heterosexist phrases such as "that's so gay" and "no homo" are commonly heard in middle schools and high schools in the United States (Kosciw et al., 2014). In short, the school climate is, for many youth, both sexist and heterosexist.

Indeed, gender nonconforming and sexual minority adolescents experience especially high rates of peer sexual harassment. The Gay, Lesbian & Straight Education Network (GLSEN) regularly conducts national school climate surveys of sexual minority youth, focusing on discrimination and victimization based on sexual orientation and gender expression. In its most recent survey of lesbian, gay, bisexual, transgender, and queer adolescents in Grades 6 through 12, 74% said they'd been verbally harassed because of their sexual orientation and 55% said they'd been verbally harassed because of their gender expression (Kosciw et al., 2014). Thirty-six percent of the adolescents reported experiencing physical harassment such as being pushed or shoved because of their sexual orientation, and 11% reported experiencing it because of their gender expression.

Peer sexual harassment is a threat to adolescent development and well-being. Students who experience harassment report negative effects like having trouble sleeping, not wanting to go to school and even missing school, and changing the way they go to or from school (AAUW, 2011; Kosciw et al., 2014). Peer sexual harassment is also linked to worse educational outcomes, such as lower GPA, and poorer psychological well-being, such as higher levels of depression and lower levels of self-esteem (Kosciw et al., 2014).

Across both of these studies of peer sexual harassment, the majority of incidents went unreported to the schools (AAUW, 2011; Kosciw et al., 2014). Indeed, two-thirds of public school districts in the United States reported zero incidents of such harassment during the 2013–2014 school year (U.S. Department of Education, 2016). Fifty-seven percent of students in the AAUW study said that allowing students to report harassment anonymously would be helpful. While the LGBT students in this sample were more likely than the students in the AAUW sample to report these incidents of peer sexual harassment, nearly two-thirds said that school staff did nothing in response to the incidents.

Body Dissatisfaction

Many studies have found that adolescent girls have poorer body esteem than adolescent boys (Mendelson et al., 2001; Polce-Lynch et al., 2001). This gender difference is large compared with many others we have seen, $d = 0.58$ (Feingold & Mazella, 1998). Body esteem or body image has many components, of course, including feelings about one's weight, face, hair, and shape. Beginning in late elementary school, girls are more dissatisfied with their weight than boys are (Smolak & Striegel-Moore, 2001). One longitudinal study found that nearly one-third of girls reported dieting by age 11; more than three-quarters reported dieting by age 15 (Balantekin et al., 2014).

The emphasis on thinness is so strong, and the dissatisfaction with weight so great among American girls and women, that it has been termed a *normative discontent*. Three decades after this term was coined, meta-analysis indicates that women's body dissatisfaction has lessened somewhat (Karazsia et al., 2017). Yet many women of diverse ethnic groups continue to feel they don't meet the feminine beauty standard, which idealizes a thin, light-skinned body and straight hair. Body dissatisfaction remains a serious and pervasive problem.

It's also dangerous. Dissatisfaction with weight and shape can lead adolescent girls to a number of unhealthy and potentially dangerous behaviors such as dieting and cosmetic surgery, including liposuction and breast enlargement (Smolak & Striegel-Moore, 2001). Girls' weight worries are no small thing—they can actually become life-threatening.

There is little doubt that girls' dissatisfaction with their bodies is powerfully shaped by the media and their displays of hyper-thin models (Grabe et al., 2008). Experimental research shows that as little media exposure as viewing 10 slides from women's magazines such as *Glamour* increases weight concerns (Posavac et al., 1998; see also Lavine et al., 1999). This effect holds true only for women with more initial body dissatisfaction, though.

At the intersection of gender and ethnicity, we see diversity in women's experiences. In regard to ethnicity, White, Latina, and Asian American women generally express more weight concern compared with Black women, who express less (Grabe & Hyde, 2006). Consistent with this finding, Black adolescent girls are more likely to be proud of their bodies (60%) than White (38%), Hispanic (45%), and Asian American (50%) girls (Story et al., 1995). And viewing Black-oriented television is associated with a healthier body image for Black female adolescents (Schooler et al., 2004).

There is very little empirical research on body image among trans and nonbinary women. Yet these women experience pressure to adhere to the feminine beauty standard much as cisgender women do, in addition to experiencing cisgenderist harassment and discrimination (Hendricks & Testa, 2012). For some trans women, adhering to the feminine beauty standard may be critical to being perceived and treated as women (Sevelius, 2013). One qualitative study with an ethnically diverse sample of transgender women found that three-quarters of the women had engaged in disordered eating behaviors in efforts to control their body shape (Gordon et al., 2016).

A social process that helps keep body dissatisfaction alive is *fat talk* between girls (Salk & Engeln-Maddox, 2011). One girl says she is fat. Her friend tells her that she isn't, but that she herself is, and the conversation cycles round and round. Fat talk both reflects and encourages body dissatisfaction. Meta-analysis of fat talk and body image suggests that fat talk is actually a risk factor for body dissatisfaction (Mills & Fuller-Tyszkiewicz, 2017).

Emerging Adulthood

A new phenomenon has appeared in the United States and other Western nations: emerging adulthood (Arnett, 2004). This developmental period spans the late teens through the early 20s. In earlier decades, people felt that they were adults either when they graduated from high school (if they weren't going to college) or when they graduated from college. Today, neither of these ages seems to be true adulthood for many people. Instead, there is a kind of suspended state of not being a teenager anymore and not yet being an adult that extends through the early 20s. Marriage is delayed until the mid- to late 20s, and the emerging adult years are spent in self-focused exploration of career or work and intimate relationships. Financial independence from one's family is occurring at later ages as well. Interestingly, this pattern is typical of both young men and young women. As one 24-year-old woman said, "I mean, this is cool for now. I'm just going to hop around for a while" (quoted in Arnett, 2004, p. 29).

Adulthood

Gender and Work

The work role is increasingly important for adults, and there are unique challenges for women and trans individuals in the workplace. For that reason, we have devoted an entire chapter to the topic of gender and work (Chapter 9) and will postpone discussion of that topic until then.

Romantic Relationships and Marriage

Marriage has undergone dramatic transformation over the past 50 years. For example, people marry at considerably older ages now than in the past. In 1960, the average age of first marriage for women was 20.3 years, whereas today it is 27.4 (U.S. Census Bureau, 2016d). For men, the average age of first marriage is now 29.5, up from 22.8 in 1960. Another major historical change in marriage in the United States is that two consenting adults can marry each other, regardless of their genders. In 2015, the U.S. Supreme Court ruled in *Obergefell v. Hodges* that the right to marry is guaranteed to same-gender couples. Of course, not all couples choose to marry. Cohabitation is much more common today than it was a generation ago. Today, 7.2% of couples in the United States cohabit, up from 0.4% in 1967 (U.S. Census Bureau, 2016d).

Is marriage good or bad for women? That turns out to be a more complex question than it seems. In 1972, the eminent sociologist Jessie Bernard published a book in which she coined the phrase *his and hers marriage*, meaning that heterosexual marriage has different consequences for husbands and wives. She concluded that marriage was definitely good for men. The evidence came from comparisons of married men and never-married men on mental health and physical health outcomes. The married men consistently scored better. Married women scored worse than married men, yet never-married women scored better than never-married men. She concluded that marriage benefits men but hurts women. This idea became popularized with the general public and persists today. Yet much has changed. For example, when Bernard conducted her research, the majority of married women were home full time, but today the majority of married women are employed. Do modern data support Bernard's idea?

PHOTO 7.6

Will this marriage last? Statistics indicate that 40% to 50% of today's heterosexual marriages will end in divorce. One implication is that women need to acquire the education and skills necessary to support themselves.

Although many studies show that heterosexual marriage provides health benefits to both husbands and wives, the benefits are not equal. For example, one large study of adults in Britain found that marriage was positively associated with a variety of health indicators in middle age, but that this effect was greater for men than for women (Ploubidis et al., 2015). In addition, the data indicated that the health of women and men who cohabited was similar to that of married couples. In sum, marriage benefits both women and men, although it benefits men more.

Most research on marriage has focused on heterosexual marriage. Before *Obergefell v. Hodges*, some states had laws permitting same-gender marriage, whereas others had constitutional amendments outlawing it. Research comparing the well-being of same-gender couples living in states with or without legal same-gender marriage sheds light on the impact of marriage equality policies. For example, one study with a nationally representative sample found that same-gender couples living in states with marriage equality had better health than same-gender couples living in states without it (Kail et al., 2015). In the coming years, new data will help us understand more about the psychological aspects of marriage for same-gender couples.

Not all marriages are alike, though. Some are happy, characterized by mutual support, good communication, equality, and respect. Others are miserable, with the partners having little in common, intentionally degrading each other, and perhaps committing abuse. Research consistently shows that the quality of marriage is far more important to people's mental and physical health than simply whether one is married (Barnett & Hyde, 2001; Gallo et al., 2003; Steil, 2001b). Equality between husband and wife in decision making is an important aspect of the quality of heterosexual marriage (Steil, 2001a). Good marriage is good for women. Bad marriage isn't.

Divorce

Another historical shift regarding marriage is divorce rates. The divorce rate in the United States increased by 136% between 1960 and 1996, and then dropped steadily through 2006 (Amato, 2010). Among marriages today, approximately 40% to 50% will eventually end in divorce, with somewhat higher rates for Whites and African Americans and lower rates for Latinx and Asian Americans (Kreider & Ellis, 2011). It is also true that remarriage rates are high; 70% to 75% of divorced women remarry (Amato, 2000). Longitudinal research indicates that couples divorce because of a variety of factors, including intimate partner violence, conflict, infidelity, and a lack of commitment to marriage (Amato, 2010).

Is divorce harmful to one's psychological or physical well-being? Most research indicates that divorced individuals have poorer psychological and physical well-being compared with married individuals (Amato, 2010). Yet two important factors can contribute to these effects. One factor that influences the psychological outcomes of divorce is one's

©iStockphoto.com/pixdeluxe.

history of depression; that is, divorce can be a significant stressor for people who are already at higher risk for developing depression (Sbarra et al., 2014). If you have a history of depression, getting divorced might trigger a depressive episode.

Another important factor influencing outcomes following divorce is marital quality. That is, if the marriage is stressful and difficult, maybe even abusive, it might actually be beneficial to end it. This is particularly true for women. One study with a nationally representative sample of adults in the United States found that the psychological effects of divorce depend on both marital quality and gender (Bourassa et al., 2015). For women, ending a poorer quality marriage resulted in a greater increase in life satisfaction than ending a higher quality marriage. For men, there was no association between marital quality and life satisfaction after divorce.

The economic consequences of divorce are also important to consider. A study of women and divorce by sociologist Lenore Weitzman (1986) attracted a great deal of attention. She found that divorced women and their children are becoming the new underclass: Whereas divorced men experience a 42% increase in their standard of living, divorced women experience a 73% decrease. These are the unintended consequences of no-fault divorce, which in the 1970s was thought to be positive for women. The problem is that divorce settlements often make the liberated assumption that women will go out and become self-sufficient earners, ignoring the great disparity between women's wages and men's wages in the United States (see Chapter 9). In short, no-fault divorce has been an economic disaster for those women who do not have professional training, job skills, or strong work experience. We don't mean to suggest, of course, that no-fault divorce is all bad for women. For example, it makes it easier for a woman to get out of a marriage in which she is abused. Weitzman's statistics have also been criticized for exaggerating divorced women's economic decline (Faludi, 1991; Peterson, 1996). A decline of 35%—not 73%—is probably more accurate (Amato, 2000). Nonetheless, a 35% decline in standard of living is still a dramatic loss.

Divorced women also may experience role strains and role overload. They may have to manage a household by themselves, including doing tasks such as repairs that the husband may have done previously. Divorced women with children may feel that their social life has become extremely limited and that they are socially isolated from other adults. Social support from family and friends is extremely important during the divorce transition.

Black women tend to fare less well than White women following divorce (McKenry & McKelvey, 2003). Compared with their White counterparts, divorced Black women are less likely to receive child support and more likely to live in poverty.

Single Women

Today, 28.6% of American women are single, never married (U.S. Census Bureau, 2013). By ethnicity, the never married comprise 23.4% of White women, 46.3% of Black women, 26.4% of Asian American women, and 35.4% of Latinas. These statistics are up from 1960, a result of trends toward not marrying and toward marrying later.

Two advantages are typically mentioned in discussions of being a single woman. One is freedom. There is no necessity to agree with someone else on what to have for dinner, what TV program to watch, or how to spend money. There is the freedom to move when doing so is advantageous to one's career—or to stay put and not to move to follow a husband's career. The other advantage is a sense of self-sufficiency and competence. The single woman has to deal with the irritation of fixing the leaky faucet herself, but having done so, she gains a sense that she is competent to do such things.

Women who are satisfied by long-term single status tend to have (a) satisfying employment that provides economic independence, (b) connections to the next generation through extended family or by mentoring younger people, and (c) a strong network of family and friends who provide support when it is needed (Trimberger, 2005).

Motherhood

Just as women are delaying marriage today, they are also delaying childbearing. Whereas in the 1960s the average age of first giving birth was 21, today it is 26 (Costello et al., 2003; Hamilton et al., 2015). This varies somewhat by ethnicity; the average age of first birth is 24.3 for Hispanic women, 24.2 for Black women, 27.0 for White women, 23.1 for American Indian women, and 29.5 for Asian American women (Hamilton et al., 2015). In this section we discuss the experience of motherhood, but we save our discussion of pregnancy and childbirth for Chapter 11.

Research shows that although marriage and employment are both generally associated with positive adjustment for women, parenthood is generally associated with mixed emotions. Having children can increase parents' experiences of positive emotions and finding meaning in life, but it can also increase their experiences of negative emotions and magnify or exacerbate financial problems or relationship problems (Nelson et al., 2014). One meta-analysis found that parents have lower marital satisfaction than non-parents, but the effect is small ($d = -0.19$; Twenge et al., 2003). Following the birth of a child, married women tend to experience a decline in marital satisfaction (Shapiro et al., 2015). The transition to motherhood can be very difficult and stressful. It requires that a woman rapidly acquire new skills, develop a new interpersonal relationship, and integrate a new role into her identity, all while experiencing considerable disruptions in her sleep patterns.

Motherhood is so basic an assumption of the female role that it is easy to forget that society pressures women to be mothers; indeed, the pressure is so strong that the situation has been called the **motherhood mandate** (Meyers, 2001). And, in fact, 84% of American women have at least one child by age 50 (Monte & Ellis, 2014).

Motherhood mandate: A cultural belief that women must become mothers.

Psychology has a history of mother blaming—that is, of holding mothers responsible for everything from schizophrenia to eating disorders (Caplan, 2001). Psychologists have been slow to ask what role fathers might play in their offspring's problems or about the role of peers and other social forces. In particular, much research attention has been devoted to the potential harm that children experience when mothers work outside the home, but scant attention has been paid to the negative impact that fathers' employment might have. We return to this topic in Chapter 9.

Today, women are expected to be not only mothers, but exceptional mothers—a norm called *intensive mothering* (Arendell, 2000). Mothering should be emotionally involving, time-consuming, and completely child-centered, according to this norm. These ideals are impossible for real women to achieve, leaving them feeling that they're not doing a very good job (Douglas & Michaels, 2004).

The so-called mother wars make matters worse (Johnston & Swanson, 2004). The mother wars, created by the media, pit working mothers against stay-at-home mothers. The polarizing rhetoric portrays stay-at-home mothers as dimwits on Prozac running organic vegetables through the blender to feed the baby. Employed mothers are characterized as being stressed beyond human endurance and spending almost no time with their children, leaving them in dangerous day care. Neither of these images is accurate, but they contribute to a rift between the two groups of mothers, leaving neither one feeling good.

Despite all of this, most women gain satisfaction from motherhood. The degree of satisfaction depends on a number of factors; women report more satisfaction with motherhood when they are in a happy marriage and when they have strong social support (Thompson & Walker, 2004).

Of course, not all women accept the motherhood mandate. The birthrate in the United States has declined in recent decades (U.S. Census Bureau, 2015), much as it has in other countries such as Germany and Japan (CBS/AP, 2014). More and more women are choosing to be *child-free*, or opting for *voluntary childlessness*. Terminology makes a difference here. Some reject the term *childless*, which may seem to imply some sort of deficit, in favor of *child-free*.

While the evidence indicates that women who are voluntarily childless do not feel guilty, regretful, or distressed by their choice (DeLyser, 2012; McQuillan et al., 2012), they remain a highly stigmatized group. Child-free women are perceived as less warm and less psychologically fulfilled than women with children (Ashburn-Nardo, 2017; Bays, 2016). They may also be viewed as selfish or deviant (Mollen, 2006). Why are child-free women perceived so harshly? There is a great deal of social pressure for women to have children, which probably has to do with the fact that motherhood is so central to the female gender role (McQuillan et al., 2012).

Still, many women are *in*voluntarily childless. About 6% of married women experience **infertility**, or an inability to become pregnant despite having carefully timed, unprotected sex for one year; about 12% of American women experience *impaired fecundity*, or difficulty getting pregnant or carrying a pregnancy full-term (National Center for Health Statistics, 2016). Infertility and impaired fecundity can be very distressing to those who wish to become pregnant and have a child. The motherhood mandate can compound this distress because it contributes to a woman's sense that she has failed as a woman if she cannot have children (Ceballo et al., 2015). Some women may pursue *assisted reproductive technologies* (ARTs), such as *in vitro fertilization* (IVF), in order to become pregnant. ARTs like IVF are very expensive and may not be covered by one's health insurance. The financial strain and low success rate of ARTs adds to the distress experienced by women experiencing infertility.

An intersectional analysis of infertility uncovers an unsettling pattern of inequity sometimes referred to as **stratified reproduction** (Ceballo et al., 2015; Greil et al., 2011). Essentially, White women's childbearing is more highly valued and promoted than the childbearing of women of color. Women of color and poor women are more likely to experience infertility. To make matters worse, these women are less likely to have access to the fertility treatments that White women and wealthier women have. Economic constraints, lack of health insurance, and discrimination from medical professionals all contribute to this disparity in access. In addition, the majority of research on fertility treatments has relied on wealthy White women as participants. Meanwhile, racist

Infertility: Not getting pregnant despite having carefully timed, unprotected sex for one year.

Stratified reproduction: A systematic pattern of inequity in which women of color are overrepresented among women with infertility but are underrepresented among those who receive treatment for infertility.

©iStockphoto.com/monkeybusinessimages

PHOTO 7.7
Intersectional analysis of fertility issues indicates that White women's childbearing is more highly valued and promoted than the childbearing of women of color.

stereotypes of Black mothers as lazy "welfare queens" who are inadequate and selfish persist. The motherhood mandate, it seems, applies only to wealthy White women.

Queer and trans people who wish to become pregnant face additional challenges with regard to their fertility (dickey, Ducheny, et al., 2016; Hayman et al., 2015; Jones et al., 2016). While there are more options available to these folks today than ever before, several obstacles may stand in their way. For example, to become pregnant, some couples may opt for ARTs with donated sperm. This is more challenging than it might seem. First, for many queer and trans people, some ARTs are financially out of reach. Second, finding a sperm donor can be complicated—should the donor be someone who is known to the couple, or should they be anonymous? Third, for trans people in particular, fertility is shaped in part by their history of gender-affirming care (namely, whether they've had particular hormone treatments or surgical procedures). Some trans women may still produce sperm and some trans men may still ovulate, but other trans people will not be able to biologically parent a child because they have undergone treatments that have made them infertile. In the face of infertility, some couples may wish to adopt a child, but discrimination against queer and trans people adopting children remains a barrier for many. Despite these challenges, many queer and trans people become parents of a biological, step, or adopted child at some point in their lives. Research indicates that 48% of LGBT women and 20% of LGBT men in the United States have at least one child under age 18 (Gates, 2013).

An Empty Nest

Empty nest: The phase of the family life cycle following the departure of adult children from the family home; also known as the postparental period.

During middle adulthood, children may leave home—to go to work, to go away to college, to get married. This phase of the family life cycle is known as the **empty nest**, or the *postparental period*. Traditional stereotypes held that, because motherhood is a major source of identity, the empty nest promotes depression in middle-aged women. Yet research shows this not to be true. Indeed, many women find rewards during the empty nest phase.

For example, a study of 60- to 65-year-old women found that 70% described their lives currently as better than when they were younger (Burns & Leonard, 2005). In some cases, the gains they reported were due to the women's own actions. In other cases, women reported that changes in roles or simply the passage of time provided stress relief. And one woman in a comparison group of 40- to 50-year-olds said,

> I've just thought that all my life I've worried about the girls leaving home and growing up. I love my girls so much I thought I can't deal with them growing up. And then a couple of years ago, it was almost as if God tossed them out of the nest or something. Because I'm getting to the stage where I want them to leave so that my husband and I can just have our own life. I never thought I could feel like that! (Burns & Leonard, 2005, p. 275)

Of the remaining women who felt differently about this phase of life, 20% reported continued, consistent contentment and only 10% characterized their lives as dominated by losses.

What should we conclude, then? A review of the research on the empty nest revealed several patterns in the data (Bouchard, 2014). First, most couples experience an increase in marital quality during the empty nest, especially for women. There is also some evidence of an increase in marital equity reported by women, presumably because child-related responsibilities have been lessened. Second, some women experience loneliness or a sense of loss, but most experience an increase in well-being.

Later Adulthood

Ageism, or negative attitudes toward older adults, is a pervasive problem (Levy & Macdonald, 2016). Ageist stereotypes describe older adults as forgetful, incompetent, and depressed, living only in the past. Yet research on aging indicates that older adulthood is not nearly as pathetic as ageism suggests.

And yet, an intersectional perspective on aging indicates unique challenges for older women. In particular, there is a **double standard of aging** (Calasanti, 2005; Chonody & Teater, 2016). That is, as a man reaches middle age and beyond, he may appear more distinguished and handsome, but a woman of the same age is considered less beautiful or even invisible. As we saw in a previous section, a woman's value in her youth is often judged by her appearance; as women age, their appearance tends to change in ways that move them further away from mainstream standards of beauty. The media helps to perpetuate this double standard. Older women are underrepresented as television characters, and when they do appear, they are portrayed negatively or stereotypically, as victims, dependent, or poor (Kjaersgaard, 2005). Here we will examine some of the research on older women.

Ageism: Negative attitudes toward older adults.

Double standard of aging: Cultural norms by which men's status increases with age but women's decreases.

Grandmotherhood

The stereotype of a grandmother is of a white-haired lady baking cookies for the little ones. Of course, grandmothers are a much more diverse group. Women can become grandmothers at vastly different ages. One woman becomes a grandmother at age 35, and another does so at age 65. Some are retired, but many may still be employed.

Grandmothers often play an important role in the lives of their grandchildren (Barnett et al., 2010). For example, they often provide emotional and financial support, as well as information, to parents and grandchildren. When grandmothers are more involved in the lives of their grandchildren, it can enhance the children's adjustment and protect them from risk factors for poor adjustment (Barnett et al., 2010).

The grandmother role is likely to vary for different ethnic groups as a result of different family structures and cultural traditions. African American grandmothers, for example, are disproportionately likely to raise their own grandchildren in the absence of the mother or father (Conway et al., 2011; Kelch-Oliver, 2011). This situation can create emotional and physical strain as well as rewards for the grandmother.

©iStockphoto.com/real444.

PHOTO 7.8
Cultural values of filial piety and respect for elders shape grandmotherhood.

One study of Chinese American immigrant grandmothers found that traditional Chinese values of filial piety and respect for elders shaped the grandmother experience (Nagata et al., 2010). Grandmothers had frequent contact with their grandchildren, and the contact was hierarchically structured, with the grandmother having an authoritative, respected role. The grandmothers' goals for their grandchildren emphasized moral character, good manners, and achievement.

There is even a grandmother effect, a term coined by evolutionary theorists (Herndon, 2010). Compared with other species, female humans experience far more years of vigorous life after ovulation ceases and they can no longer reproduce. Why is this adaptive, in an evolutionary sense? According to the grandmother effect, older women who are healthy and active enhance their own fitness by providing care for their grandchildren, who carry their genes, thereby enhancing the survival of those offspring. According to this hypothesis, natural selection occurred among early humans, favoring women who lived longer, were vigorous, and helped to care for their grandchildren.

Gender and Cognitive Aging

A lifespan perspective reminds us that there are gains as well as losses in development. In older adulthood, it is common to experience some changes in our cognitive functioning. While some cognitive changes may be signs of disease or dementia, other changes are normal parts of aging that result from a general slowdown or reduced efficiency in our brain processes. For example, older adults tend to experience declines in some aspects of executive functioning, such as mental flexibility (Phillips & Henry, 2008) and inhibitory control (von Hippel & Dunlop, 2005). However, our long-term memory remains generally well intact, and we can continue acquiring new knowledge and skills throughout our lives. An important question to pose in the psychology of women and gender, then, is whether there are gender differences or similarities in cognitive aging.

As we discuss in Chapter 8, a handful of cognitive abilities show some mean gender differences, and these differences vary in magnitude. Researchers have also explored whether women and men experience similar cognitive changes as they age. That is, researchers were interested in the cognitive trajectories of older adults, or how their cognitive abilities changed over time. One review found that, across 13 longitudinal studies, men and women tended to show similar rates of cognitive changes over time, with similar cognitive trajectories between 60 and 80 years of age (Ferreira et al., 2014). However, those studies had inconsistent findings and varied in quality, which makes our conclusions tentative.

A recent long-term longitudinal study of aging examined changes in multiple cognitive abilities among a sample of adults who showed no signs of cognitive impairment or dementia (McCarrey et al., 2016). In general, they found that participants' cognitive abilities declined with age, as expected. With regard to gender, a few patterns in their results are noteworthy. First, women tended to outperform men on most, but not all, of the abilities. For example, women scored higher on tests of reasoning, verbal learning, verbal memory, fluent language production, and episodic memory. They also found that, although men outperformed women in visual memory and visuospatial abilities, men also showed steeper decline in those abilities over time. That is, men's mean levels were higher but they declined at a faster rate. By contrast, there was no cognitive ability in which women showed steeper decline than men did.

The authors concluded that women may be less vulnerable to age-related changes in brain functioning and cognition. Yet they also cautioned that the gender differences were subtle. Considered alongside the previous mixed findings about gender differences in cognitive aging, it seems that women may experience slower rates of cognitive aging but that the effects may not be large enough to be detected consistently.

Widowhood and Gender Ratios

Gender ratios become more and more lopsided with advancing age. Among Americans between the ages of 60 and 69, there are 110 women for every 100 men. By 80 to 89 there are 162 women for every 100 men, and for those 90 and older, there are 259 women for every 100 men (Howden & Meyer, 2011). As a result, older women stand a good chance of living alone. Among women 65 and older, 32% live alone (Stepler, 2016).

What drives these lopsided gender ratios? One factor is widowhood. Women are far more likely to be widowed than men are (Elliott & Simmons, 2011). This is the result of two trends: the longer life expectancy of women and the tendency of women to marry men older than themselves. Opportunities for remarriage are limited because there are so few men compared with women in the "appropriate" age-group. Therefore it is fairly common for women to face the last 15 years or so of their lives alone. The evidence indicates that recently widowed individuals have higher levels of depressive symptoms compared with married individuals but that these levels decrease after 2 to 3 years (Monserud & Markides, 2017).

A number of factors affect how women respond following the death of a spouse, including whether the death was anticipated or unexpected and her financial and social resources (Antonucci et al., 2010). Widows who had been caring for an ill spouse for a long time may be grateful that their spouse is no longer suffering and that they are relieved from exhausting caregiving responsibilities. The consequences of widowhood for a woman's depressive symptoms can depend on her spouse's health status before death as well as the woman's age and how long she's been widowed (Sasson & Umberson, 2014). In addition, widows may draw on their faith and religious practices for comfort and support during the transition to widowhood. A longitudinal study with Mexican American older adults found that more frequent church attendance slowed the development of depressive symptoms when a spouse died (Monserud & Markides, 2017).

Financial strain for widows can be severe (Hungerford, 2001). There is loss of the spouse's income, and the couple's savings may have been depleted by medical expenses associated with the spouse's illness. Older women are more likely than older men to live in poverty, and older minority women are even more likely to be poor than White women.

The death of a spouse seems to be harder on men than it is on women, whether measured by depression, illness, or death (Shor et al., 2012; Stroebe et al., 2001). Put another way, women tend to cope better with widowhood. One possible reason for this is that women are more likely to have deep friendships that they have developed over the years and from which they can draw social support. Another possibility is that women are better than men at "grief work"—that is, at expressing their emotions and then going on to cope and readjust (Stroebe, 2001).

Experience the Research

Older Women

For this exercise, interview an older woman, over the age of 65. You might choose a female relative, a woman from your place of worship, or a family friend. Record her age, marital status, and ethnic group. Ask her the following questions, and either audiotape or take notes on her answers:

1. What does she feel were the three major events in her life? Why?

2. Did she spend most of her life as a homemaker or having a job or career? Reflecting back on that role, what were the good things about it? What were the negative things?

3. If she is single, is she lonely? Why or why not?

CHAPTER SUMMARY

This chapter has traced aspects of development across the lifespan, focusing especially on girls, women, and transgender persons. Most infant behaviors do not show gender differences. While boys are more active, girls regulate their impulses and attention better; these differences may contribute to challenges at the transition to kindergarten. Parents generally treat boy and girl babies similarly, although mothers appear to touch their infants in subtly different ways, which may promote gender differences in motor activity and play behaviors, such as girls' preference for play-grooming and boys' preference for rough-and-tumble play.

Infants begin processing information by gender early on, categorizing male and female faces, bodies, and voices. Yet evidence also suggests that we learn to categorize gender as a binary system.

Gender differences in toy and game preferences emerge in the preschool years. By age 3, children's play is highly gender segregated. Appearance rigidity also becomes more common during the preschool years. The cognitive process of gender constancy development may play a role in these behaviors.

For transgender children during the process of gender constancy development, their gender identity does not match their gender assigned at birth, known as gender dysphoria. Transgender children have long been met with skepticism, perceived as being confused, delayed, oppositional, or pretending. Yet scientific research indicates that such children's gender identity is authentic and deeply felt. Trans-affirmative practice provides guidance for sensitive, respectful, and individualized care of transgender children.

Parents continue to socialize gender-appropriate behavior, and the media and peers gain influence during childhood. Parents exert their influence through channeling, differential treatment, direct instruction, and modeling. In addition, children self-socialize. Gender segregation of peer groups also contributes to gender socialization.

Girls are also sexualized from an early age. In late adolescence, girls move toward an adult identity, balancing an autonomous identity with an interpersonal identity.

Puberty offers dramatic changes for cisgender and transgender kids. While cisgender boys may look forward to puberty, cisgender girls are often less positive; girls' negative feelings often have to do with the contrast between cultural ideals and actual body shapes and sizes. Timing of puberty also matters. For transgender adolescents, pubertal suppression may be included as a part of trans-affirmative practice, as it gives those kids more time to decide before long-term or permanent physical changes occur. Pubertal changes in adolescence may contribute to gender intensification.

Peer harassment based on gender and gender expression is widespread during adolescence. This form of victimization is especially common for gender nonconforming and sexual minority youth. Peer sexual harassment is linked to poorer educational and psychological outcomes. Negative body esteem and weight worries become issues for girls in adolescence, and fat talk may contribute to body dissatisfaction.

In adulthood, marriage and romantic relationships are important. Most research on marriage has focused on heterosexual marriage; in the coming years, new data will help us understand more about the psychological aspects of marriage for same-gender couples. Marriage—at least good marriage—benefits women's mental and physical health. Likewise, divorce can offer benefits to a woman if her marriage is very poor in quality.

Motherhood is a valued role for most adult women. Voluntary childlessness remains stigmatized. Research on the empty nest and depression in middle age indicates that, in fact, most women fare well during this time, and some researchers believe that the early 50s are the prime of life for women.

In older adulthood, the grandmother role is an important and meaningful one for many women. Development in older adulthood includes cognitive aging. Women may be less vulnerable than men to cognitive aging, but these gender differences are subtle. Men on average die younger than women do, resulting in lopsided gender ratios in the population. The gender ratio becomes more lopsided with each passing decade, as widowhood becomes increasingly common. While losing a spouse is among the most distressing and difficult events in a person's life, widows psychologically rebound from this loss within a few years. Social support, faith, financial stress, and the circumstances around the spouse's death all contribute to the psychological outcomes of widowhood.

SUGGESTIONS FOR FURTHER READING

Brown, Christia Spears. (2014). *Parenting beyond pink and blue: How to raise your kids free of gender stereotypes*. Berkeley, CA: Ten Speed Press. A developmental psychologist, Brown provides a parenting guide for those who want gender stereotypes to take a backseat in their children's lives.

Levin, Diane, & Kilbourne, Jean. (2008). *So sexy so soon: The new sexualized childhood and what parents can do to protect their kids*. New York, NY: Ballantine. Drawing on the APA Task Force report on the sexualization of girls, Levin and Kilbourne offer guidance to parents and schools on promoting healthy development in kids.

McLean, Kate C., & Syed, Moin. (Eds.). (2015). *Oxford handbook of identity development*. New York, NY: Oxford University Press. This handbook thoroughly reviews the psychological research on the many aspects of identity development.

Orenstein, Peggy. (2011). *Cinderella ate my daughter: Dispatches from the front lines of the new girlie-girl culture*. New York, NY: HarperCollins. Journalist Orenstein exposes the cultural forces—from Disney princesses to beauty pageants—that are making little girls into girlie-girls.

Abilities, Motivation, and Achievement

> ❝ Which man, which woman? ❞

Samuel Johnson, when asked whether man or woman is more intelligent

In 2005, then-president of Harvard University Lawrence Summers speculated, at a professional meeting, that women were underrepresented at the highest levels of achievement in mathematics and science because they lack the necessary mathematical ability (Dillon, 2005). Is there any scientific evidence that women are less intellectually competent than men? In this chapter we will explore empirical evidence regarding the abilities and achievements of women and whether they differ from those of men. Of course, it is important to remember that the finding of a gender difference does not say anything about what causes it—that is, whether biological or environmental factors are responsible. After a consideration of gender differences and similarities in abilities, we will examine motivation, framed by expectancy-value theory. Next we will look at data on girls' and women's achievements in school and occupations. And finally, we will consider the gender gap in STEM (science, technology, engineering, and mathematics), what causes it, and what might be done about it.

Abilities

General Intelligence

There is no evidence to support the hypothesis that girls and women are less intelligent than boys and men. In fact, research has consistently shown that there are no gender differences in general intelligence (Maccoby & Jacklin, 1974).

These results need to be interpreted carefully, though, because of the nature of IQ test construction. It became clear to the early test constructors that boys would do better on some kinds of items, whereas girls would do better on others. They decided to balance these subtests so that there would be no gender differences in overall measured intelligence. Therefore, saying that there are no gender differences in tested intelligence essentially means that the test constructors succeeded in their goal of eliminating gender differences. Rather than looking at global assessments, it is more informative to analyze patterns of specific abilities by gender, such as mathematical ability or verbal ability.

For years, psychology textbooks have told students that there were gender differences in three basic abilities: verbal ability, spatial ability, and mathematical ability, with female test takers scoring higher on verbal tests and male test takers scoring higher on spatial and mathematical tests. However, we now have meta-analyses to give us a more accurate and detailed understanding of whether there are gender differences in these abilities and, if so, how large the differences are.

Verbal Ability

Although the stereotype is that girls and women show better verbal ability than boys and men, a meta-analysis found that the gender difference in verbal ability is so small as to be trivial (Hyde & Linn, 1988). Overall, $d = -0.11$, indicating a slight female superiority, but one that is so small that it can be called zero. The analysis also looked at different types of verbal ability, such as vocabulary, analogies, reading comprehension, and essay writing. The gender difference was small for all types of verbal performance.

Another interesting finding emerged: The evidence indicated that gender differences had grown smaller over time. For studies published earlier than 1973, $d = -0.23$, whereas for studies published after 1973, $d = -0.10$. That is, the gender difference was cut approximately in half. We can't be certain what caused this narrowing of the gender gap. One possibility is that gender role socialization practices became more flexible over those decades, and a result is a reduction in the size of gender differences. Another possibility is that those who produce standardized tests have become more sensitive about gender equity issues, resulting in tests that show reduced gender differences.

Spatial Ability

Several major meta-analyses of gender differences in spatial performance are available. An early meta-analysis found that there are actually at least three types of spatial ability, each showing a different pattern of gender differences (Linn & Petersen, 1985). The first type, *spatial visualization*, involves finding a figure in a more complex one, like the hidden figures games you may have played as a child. This type of spatial ability shows only a slight gender difference favoring boys and men, $d = 0.13$ (Linn & Peterson, 1985). The second type of spatial ability, *spatial perception*, requires a person to identify a true vertical or true horizontal line when there is distracting or misleading information around it. This type of spatial ability showed a somewhat larger gender difference favoring boys and men. The third type of spatial ability, *mental rotation*, requires the test taker to mentally rotate an object in three dimensions in order to obtain the correct answer. A sample of one of these items is shown in Figure 8.1. In the most recent meta-analysis, male participants outperformed female participants in 3-D mental rotation by a moderate amount, $d = 0.57$ (Maeda & Yoon, 2013).

An important point is that 3-D mental rotation skills are not just something that you're born with, something that is hardwired in the brain. In fact, spatial skills improve with training and practice, just like mathematical knowledge is learned. For example, in one experiment, college students were given 10 hours of training on an action video game, Medal of Honor: Pacific Assault; controls played a puzzle game (Feng et al., 2007). Both women and men in the experimental group improved their performance on a mental rotation test. The women improved more than the men, and experimental group women performed as well as control group men.

A meta-analysis of spatial skills training studies found that, on average, training improved scores by $d = 0.47$ compared with controls (Uttal, Meadow, et al., 2013). The effects of training lasted, too, even when tested weeks later. Notice that the training effect is about as large as the gender gap.

The problem is that, unlike the extensive language arts curriculum and math curriculum in the schools, there is no curriculum to train spatial skills in most schools (Uttal, Miller, et al., 2013). As a matter of gender equity, this skill in which girls are disadvantaged should be part of the school curriculum. Research also indicates that training in spatial skills leads to better performance in STEM courses, so a spatial skills curriculum should have multiple benefits to both girls and boys (Uttal, Miller, et al., 2013).

An intersectional approach is informative here, with a focus on the intersection of gender and social class. In one study, elementary school children were tested in two areas of spatial performance: mental rotation and map reading (Levine et al., 2005). No gender

---

FIGURE 8.1 **Sample item and solution from a test of spatial ability.**

The test below is made up of pictures of blocks turned different ways. The block at the left is the reference block, and the five blocks to the right are the answer blocks. One of these five blocks is the same as the reference block, except that it has been turned and is seen from a different point of view. The other four blocks could not be obtained by turning the reference block. For example:

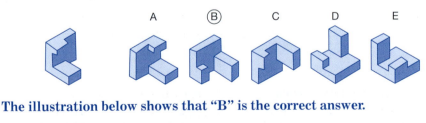

The illustration below shows that "B" is the correct answer.

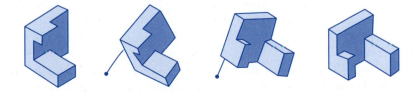

Source: From R. E. Stafford, *Identical Blocks*, form AA, 1962. Reprinted with the permission of R. E. Stafford and Harold Gulliksen.

difference was found among the low-income children, but the usual gender difference was found for middle- and upper-income children. The researchers concluded that boys in low-income environments do not have access to the activities (such as computer games, puzzles, and building toys) that give boys in more affluent environments the chance to improve their spatial skills and improve them relative to girls. These findings speak to the importance of environment and experience in creating or erasing gender differences.

Mathematics Performance

The stereotype is that boys and men have the edge over girls and women in math. What do the data say? A major meta-analysis compiled data on the mathematics performance of 7 million U.S. children in Grades 2 through 11, using data from well-sampled state assessments (Hyde et al., 2008). Contrary to the stereotype that boys and men are the smart ones in math, averaged across all ages, $d = 0.0065$, meaning that there is exactly no gender difference. Gender differences were uniformly close to zero at all grade levels.

Another meta-analysis synthesized data from 242 studies representing the testing of 1.2 million people of all ages (Lindberg et al., 2010). Overall, $d = 0.05$. Consistent with the first meta-analysis, there was no gender difference in mathematics performance. Stated a different way, female test takers scored as high as male test takers.

Similar results have been found in many other nations. The Trends in International Mathematics and Science Study (TIMSS) involves testing 15-year-olds in 46 countries (Else-Quest et al., 2010). Results for six of these countries are shown in Table 8.1. Notice that the effects fluctuate slightly from one country to another, but all are close to 0.

The odd thing is that, despite all the evidence of gender similarities in actual math performance, stereotypes about male math superiority persist. As we saw in Chapter 3, implicit stereotypes measured by the Implicit Association Test (IAT) link mathematics to males (Nosek et al., 2002). As early as second grade, children show the implicit stereotype that math is for boys (Cvencek et al., 2011).

Why is the gender difference in math performance—or its absence—so important? One reason is that mathematical skills are essential to a number of high-status, lucrative occupations that are male-dominated, such as engineering and the physical sciences.

TABLE 8.1   **The magnitude of gender differences in mathematics performance in other nations: Trends in international mathematics and science study, 15-year-olds.**

Country	(d)
Norway	−0.04
New Zealand	−0.03
Israel	0.09
Korea	0.07
Sweden	0.00
United States	0.06

Source: Data from Else-Quest, Nicole M., Hyde, Janet S., & Linn, Marcia C. (2010). Cross-national patterns of gender differences in mathematics: A meta-analysis. *Psychological Bulletin, 136,* 103–127. Table created by Janet Hyde.

Women's underrepresentation in these fields has been attributed to their lack of mathematical ability (Ceci & Williams, 2010), but, as we have just seen, that explanation is bogus. Measured in a number of different ways, and based on large meta-analyses, women have as much mathematical ability as men do. The implication is that other factors must explain women's underrepresentation, a point to which we will return later in this chapter in the section on the gender gap in STEM. It is important that women have equal access to these high-paying, prestigious careers.

Physical Performance and Athletics

Gender differences in physical and athletic performance provide a contrast to the findings for cognitive abilities. For example, $d = 2.0$ for physical height in humans (Niewenweg et al., 2003), a difference that is about four times greater than the gender difference in spatial ability.

Large gender differences in some kinds of athletic performance tend to emerge in adolescence (Eaton & Enns, 1986). For example, for speed in the 50-yard dash, $d = 0.63$, when averaged over all ages, but $d = 2.5$ for adolescence and beyond. For throwing distance, $d = 1.98$. For some other aspects of athletic performance, though, gender differences are small or zero; for example, on tests of balance, $d = 0.09$.

Athletic performance is also strongly responsive to training and diet, as we have seen in the past 25 years with the great advances made in these areas. Figure 8.2 shows gold medal performance in the Olympics over the years for men and women in the 100-meter dash. As you can see, the women who win today run faster than the record-breaking men of 1928, and the gender gap has narrowed.

FIGURE 8.2   **Gold medal performances of men and women in the 100-meter dash in the Olympic Games. Women were not permitted to compete in track and field events until 1928.**

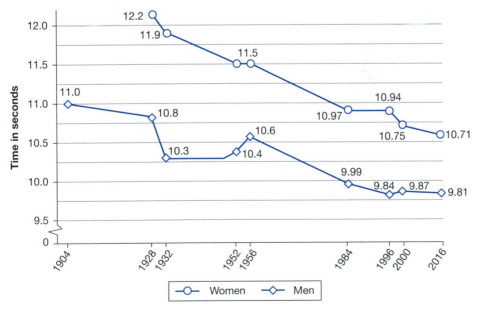

Source: Created by the authors.

FOCUS 8.1

GENDER DIVERSITY AND ATHLETICS

Dutee Chand is a woman sprinter from India who grew up in a low-income family (Padawer, 2016). At 5'3'' tall and 110 pounds she holds the national championship in the 100 meters and qualified for the 2016 Olympics. She found herself at the center of a controversy in 2014, at age 18, when she was about to compete in the Commonwealth Games (for Britain and the former colonies). Pregame biological testing indicated that she has unusually high levels of testosterone for a woman; her level is in the range more typical for men. The condition is known as **hyperandrogenism**. Officials ruled that she was ineligible to compete. The Indian government appealed the decision and it was eventually reversed, but not until Chand had been the object of intense scrutiny.

In another case, Maria José Martinez-Patiño, from Spain, was a rising star in women's track and field, but in 1985 sex testing revealed that she had a Y chromosome and she was ruled ineligible to compete as a woman (Sánchez et al., 2013). She has complete **androgen-insensitivity syndrome (AIS)**, so, despite her XY chromosomes, her body does not respond to androgens and she has the body of a woman and the identity of a woman. Eventually she was reinstated, but the incident left long-lasting marks on her.

One thing to notice is that, in both these cases and all others in which athletes' sex has been called into question, women are the only ones tested and the only ones whose sex is disputed. Sex verification testing of female athletes began in the 1930s and, in the past, included such indignities as appearing naked before judges and even physical exams (Vilain & Sánchez, 2012).

Advocates for sex testing of female athletes say that their goal is to "level the playing field." Critics point out that this kind of testing mainly has the effect of humiliating the woman who has some atypical gender feature, such as chromosomes or hormone levels. Moreover, many other biological factors contribute to individuals becoming elite athletes. For example, there are actually genes for muscularity (ACTN3 and MSTN; Vilain & Sánchez, 2012). Yet no one claims that people with those genes have an unfair advantage in athletics.

In the end, we realize that athletic competitions are stuck in the concrete of the gender binary. A college has a men's basketball team and a women's basketball team. Yet contemporary understandings of gender indicate that the binary is completely inadequate. We have people who are female (based on gender assigned at birth) and who identify as women (cisgender women) yet have high testosterone levels. There are people who are male (based on gender assigned at birth) but who identify as female (transgender women) and may undergo some medical gender reassignment. How will sports organizations deal with these complexities?

Photo of Chand by Athletics Federation of India—Odisha2017.games, CC BY-SA 4.0.

PHOTO 8.1
Dutee Chand (left) and Maria José Martinez-Patiño (right)

Summary

A number of conclusions emerge from this discussion of gender differences in abilities.

1. There are no gender differences in verbal ability.

2. There are no gender differences in mathematical performance.

3. There are gender differences in one type of spatial ability, mental rotation—an ability that is important in career fields such as engineering. However, spatial skills can be improved by training.

4. Gender differences in cognitive abilities are so small as to be irrelevant in practical situations such as job counseling. It would be a great mistake, for example, to urge a high school girl not to pursue an engineering career just because girls on average score lower than boys on tests of mental rotation. There is too much variability from one girl to the next to predict that an individual woman will not have adequate spatial ability for such a career. A far better indicator would be her score on a mental rotation test. And even if her score is mediocre, we could suggest that she take a spatial training program.

5. Gender differences in some kinds of athletic performance are large beginning in adolescence.

Motivation: Expectancy-Value Theory

What motivates a person to take physics in high school? To study hard for a math exam? To declare an engineering major in college? In many cases, what we achieve in life is more a matter of motivation than it is of abilities. Psychologists have studied motivation extensively. Here we will focus on one major theory of motivation, Jacquelynne Eccles's **expectancy-value theory** (e.g., Eccles, 1994; Meece et al., 1982). Literally hundreds of studies have been based on this theory, and it has much to say about gender.

A diagram of Eccles's model is shown in Figure 8.3. The final outcome that the model seeks to predict is achievement behavior (such as taking a physics course in high school), and it is shown in box K on the far right of the figure. The multiple factors feeding into the choice of a course are shown in the other boxes in the diagram.

The model is an expectancy-value theory of achievement motivation. That is, any particular achievement behavior is a product of the person's *expectations for success* and the person's *values*. Several types of values are involved (box J), but we will focus on two of them: *utility value* (How useful is this course to me, now and in the future?) and *interest-enjoyment value* (Will I find this course intrinsically interesting or enjoyable?). Marika is a high school junior who is contemplating taking an optional course in physics. The theory says that she will sign up for physics only if she has positive expectations for success in the course (if she thinks she'll get an F, she won't sign up) and positive values with respect to the course (if she thinks the course will be valuable to her now and in the future; for example, she might think that having physics on her transcript will help her get into college). The values part of the model is shown in the bottom half of Figure 8.3 (box J) and the expectancies part is show in the top half (box I).

Hyperandrogenism: A condition in which the body produces very high levels of androgens. Typically, it is noticed only in women. It can result from a variety of medical conditions, including polycystic ovary syndrome and Cushing syndrome.

Androgen-insensitivity syndrome (AIS): A genetic condition in which the cells of the body are unresponsive to androgens. In genetic males (XY chromosomes), the result is genitals that appear female (complete AIS) or intersex, somewhere in between typical males and typical females (partial AIS).

Expectancy-value theory: A theory of motivation that posits that a person will take on a challenging achievement task if they expect that they can succeed at it and if they value it (find it useful or interesting).

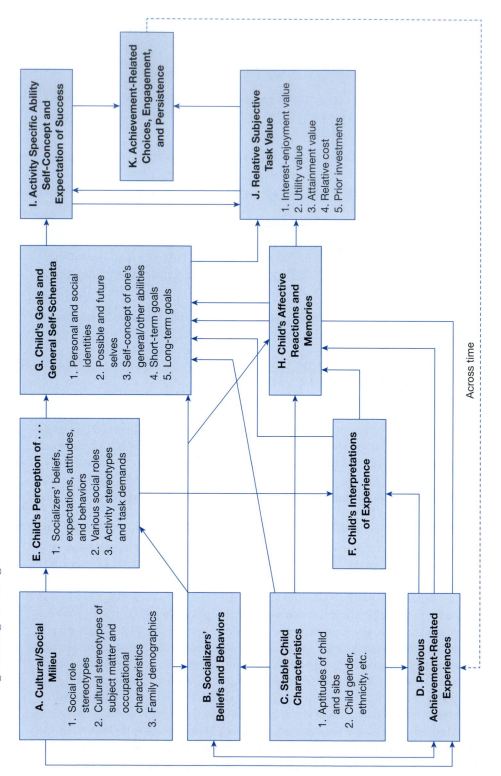

FIGURE 8.3 Eccles's model of academic course choice and achievement shows how girls' expectations and values may be shaped such that they do not take as many science courses in high school as boys do or might not major in engineering in college.

I. Activity Specific Ability Self-Concept and Expectation of Success

K. Achievement-Related Choices, Engagement, and Persistence

J. Relative Subjective Task Value
1. Interest-enjoyment value
2. Utility value
3. Attainment value
4. Relative cost
5. Prior investments

G. Child's Goals and General Self-Schemata
1. Personal and social identities
2. Possible and future selves
3. Self-concept of one's general/other abilities
4. Short-term goals
5. Long-term goals

H. Child's Affective Reactions and Memories

E. Child's Perception of . . .
1. Socializers' beliefs, expectations, attitudes, and behaviors
2. Various social roles
3. Activity stereotypes and task demands

F. Child's Interpretations of Experience

A. Cultural/Social Milieu
1. Social role stereotypes
2. Cultural stereotypes of subject matter and occupational characteristics
3. Family demographics

B. Socializers' Beliefs and Behaviors

C. Stable Child Characteristics
1. Aptitudes of child and sibs
2. Child gender, ethnicity, etc.

D. Previous Achievement-Related Experiences

Across time

Source: © Jacque Eccles. Reprinted with permission.

According to the theory, many factors shape Marika's values regarding science courses, including the following:

1. Her *goals* (box G): Marika has some tentative occupation goals. Perhaps she plans to go premed in college and knows that physics is a premed requirement. Therefore, she should take physics in high school to prepare. Alternatively, perhaps she plans on becoming a high school English teacher. She perceives no usefulness or relevance of physics for her future career.

2. Her *socializers' beliefs* (box B) and her *perceptions of those socializers' beliefs and expectations* (box E): These factors shape her goals. Perhaps her mother is a physician and has encouraged or even expects Marika to go that route, too. Perhaps her father loves (is intrinsically interested in) literature and has conveyed that love to Marika so that she wants a career as an English teacher.

Many factors also shape *expectancies for success*, including the following:

1. Her *aptitudes and grades* (boxes C and D): Marika has a pretty good idea of her aptitudes for math and science from a variety of sources, including her grades in past courses and her scores on standardized tests.

2. Her *interpretations or attributions* (box F): It isn't always the objective outcomes (grades and test scores) that influence us, but instead our subjective interpretations of them. Marika may have gotten A's and B's in all her math and science courses, but she may not attribute the good grades to her own abilities. Instead, she may think that the courses so far have just been easy. As a result, she has low expectations for success in a difficult physics course.

Eccles and others have conducted numerous studies testing various links in the model. Space does not permit us to review all of this research, but, in brief, the evidence supports the model. As one example, research has documented the links between parents' beliefs and their child's sense of competence and achievement in math and science. In one remarkable longitudinal study, mothers' estimates of their sixth-grade child's likelihood of success in mathematics predicted the child's actual math career choice at 24 years of age, even after controlling for measures of the child's ability (Bleeker & Jacobs, 2004). Importantly, mothers' sixth-grade estimates of their child's math career success were significantly higher for boys than for girls. Parents' belief in their children is a powerful force.

Other studies, including experimental research, show that, when students perceive more utility value in their courses, they work harder, develop more interest in the material, and perform better in the course (e.g., Hulleman et al., 2010). These findings support key points in the expectancy-value model.

As an interesting exercise, you might trace through Eccles's model, thinking of yourself, trying to see how it predicts why you did or did not continue taking math and science courses in high school and college.

What are the practical implications of Eccles's model? Suppose that our goal was to get more girls enrolled in science courses to expand their career options. How would we do that, according to the theory? We could work on the expectancy side of the model, on the value side, or both. On the expectancy side, we would try to get high school girls to have higher expectancies for success in math and science courses. This could be done in a number of ways: by stressing that no average gender differences exist in math ability, by pointing to a pattern of success in math and science courses for an individual girl, and by encouraging girls to attribute their previous good grades in math and science to their own abilities. On the value side, we would need to increase the utility value that girls attach to math and science courses. Most girls are probably not aware of the wide variety of careers (such as nursing) that require math and science. Individual counseling sessions might examine each girl's anticipated career and the math and science required for it. We will return to these ideas in the section on the gender gap in STEM later in this chapter.

Achievement

We can think about gender and achievement in many areas. Here we will focus on school achievement and occupational achievement.

School Achievement

In terms of school achievement, girls earn better grades than boys at all grade levels. And they earn better grades in all subjects, including those stereotyped as showing male superiority, such as math and science. A meta-analysis found that, overall, $d = -0.23$ (Voyer & Voyer, 2014). When broken down by subject, the female advantage was greatest in language arts and smallest (but still an advantage) in math.

The media have proclaimed news of a "boy crisis" in education, implying that boys have recently fallen behind girls to an alarming extent. The findings from a meta-analysis contradict those claims (Voyer & Voyer, 2014). The meta-analysis covered data from 1914 to 2011, and girls have been getting better grades than boys the whole time.

We can also take an intersectional approach to school achievement, examining the intersection of gender and ethnicity. Table 8.2 shows the gender gaps in students' grades in 10th grade in math and science for four ethnic groups in the United States (Else-Quest et al., 2013). Several results are worth noting. First, all of the gender gaps (d values) are small, pointing to gender similarities. Second, the gaps can be reversed for math compared with science. For example, among Whites, boys had better grades than girls in math, but girls had the better grades in science. Third, the gaps can be reversed from one ethnic group to another. For example, among Latinx, girls had better grades than boys in science, but among Asian Americans, boys had better science grades. All of this cautions against universalizing statements about gender differences. Boys aren't better than girls at science in all ethnic groups, nor do girls always perform better.

Occupational Achievement

We will take up the topic of women and work in detail in Chapter 9. Here we will briefly summarize a few patterns in women's occupational achievements.

Over the past several decades, women have moved strongly into a number of high-status, challenging occupations that were formerly dominated by men. The best examples are medicine, veterinary medicine, and law. Other occupations have not seen such an influx of women and remain male-dominated. The best example is engineering. Earlier in the chapter, using expectancy-value theory, we considered some of the motivational factors that might contribute to women choosing to achieve in some occupations and not others. Later in this chapter, we will consider explanations specifically for the gender gap in STEM.

One researcher analyzed data from the National Education Longitudinal Study, which followed a large, representative sample of U.S. students longitudinally into adulthood (Mello, 2008). In high school, boys and girls had similar educational expectations, on average expecting to attend college. Girls actually had higher expectations of a

TABLE 8.2	School achievement: The intersection of gender and race. These data are based on grades for 10th graders in Philadelphia schools.

	Gender Gap d
Whites	
Math	.25
Science	−.25
African Americans	
Math	.10
Science	−.18
Latinx	
Math	−.24
Science	−.29
Asian Americans	
Math	.15
Science	.20

Note: Positive values of *d* represent better grades for boys, and negative values represent better grades for girls.

Source: Else-Quest et al. (2013). Table created by Janet Hyde.

professional occupation than boys did, from high school through age 26. This pattern was the same across all ethnic groups. By age 26, the women had attained more education than the men had. Remarkably, given patterns in the 1950s and earlier, by age 26 women were more likely to be in a professional occupation than men were. Now, of course, professional occupations include female-dominated occupations such as teaching and social work, but they also include doctors, lawyers, and engineers. With these data, we can see the remarkable progress that women have made in entering the professions.

The Gender Gap in STEM

STEM refers to science, technology, engineering, and mathematics. Women tend to be underrepresented in some—but not all—of these fields. We can look at the underrepresentation at multiple levels: undergraduate majors, PhD degrees, and workforce representation. Data on these points are shown in Table 8.3.

As you can see, women are actually not underrepresented in all STEM areas. Women earn roughly half of the undergraduate degrees in biology and in mathematics. If women can't do math and science, how can this be? Even at the PhD level, women earn half the degrees in biology and a substantial fraction in chemistry. In other areas, though, women are severely underrepresented: computer science, engineering, and physics. That is true whether we look at PhDs awarded to women or women in the workforce in those areas. And those numbers aren't budging. They have been at that level for more than a decade

STEM: An acronym for science, technology, engineering, and mathematics.

FOCUS 8.2

ACHIEVING WOMEN: ELLEN OCHOA

Dr. Ellen Ochoa is the director of the Johnson Space Center in Houston. And she was an astronaut before that, making her the first Latina in space. How did she get to her prestigious position in a very nontraditional field for women?

By NASA - spacelight.nasa.gov, Public Domain.

PHOTO 8.2
Ellen Ochoa

Born in 1958, she grew up with her four siblings in La Mesa, California. While she was a child, she displayed great interest in math and science. She went on to earn her BS in physics from San Diego State University, graduating at the top of her class. She was also dedicated to music and, for a time, she considered pursuing a career as a professional flutist. However, she decided in favor of continuing in science, earning her PhD in electrical engineering at Stanford in 1985.

She went to work as a research engineer at the Sandia National Laboratory and later went to NASA's Ames Research Division. The systems that she developed in these positions made important contributions to aerospace technology, and she was accepted into NASA's astronaut training program. In 1993, she traveled on the Discovery space shuttle mission.

She has been honored with many awards, too numerous to list, including NASA's highest award, the Distinguished Service Medal, and the Hispanic Heritage Leadership Award. In addition, four schools have been named for her.

Source: NASA (2015).

TABLE 8.3   Women's representation in STEM.

	% of Undergraduate Degrees Awarded to Women	% of PhDs Awarded to Women	Women as % of Workforce
Biology	59	53	53
Chemistry	N/A*	39	36
Computer science	18	21	24
Engineering	19	23	15
Mathematics and statistics	46	28	42
Physics	N/A	20	12

Source: National Science Foundation (2017, Tables 5-1, 7-2, and 9-5). Table created by Janet Hyde.

*N/A. For some reason, the National Science Foundation combines chemistry, physics, and astronomy into physical sciences for undergraduate degrees, so the numbers for chemistry and physics are not available separately.

and are not increasing, despite the efforts of many. What we need to do, then, is explain the underrepresentation of women in computer science, engineering, and physics, not in all of STEM. Once we have the explanation(s), we can devise interventions that will close the gap.

But first, let's consider this question: Why do we care about the underrepresentation of women in STEM? What would you say? Here are some reasons. First, we want women to have equal opportunities in all areas of life, and the data seem to indicate that they don't have equal opportunity in some of these fields. Second, these are jobs that pay very well and where there is much demand for workers. They definitely beat unemployment or some of the low-wage jobs that women are stuck in. For many women, STEM jobs represent real opportunities for themselves and their families and, as we will see in Chapter 9, many women are the sole support or the major supporter of their family. These are not just puzzling academic questions; they are important to people's lives.

Explanations for the Gender Gap in STEM

Numerous explanations have been proposed for the gender gap in STEM—or more accurately, in computer science, engineering, and physics (Cheryan et al., 2017). Let's call that CEP. We will consider seven of those explanations here.

Women lack interest: According to this explanation, women simply lack interest in CEP and don't pursue it. It's not that they face discrimination or a chilly climate in those fields; it's just that they don't find them interesting. It is a matter of free choice.

A meta-analysis of research on gender differences in interests found that, in general, men are more interested in things (robots, computers, race cars) and women are more interested in people (Su et al., 2009). If we look at the specifics, men showed more interest in engineering ($d = 1.11$), science ($d = 0.36$) and mathematics ($d = 0.34$), whereas women were more interested in social ($d = -0.68$) and artistic (-0.35) areas.

Some of these effect sizes are enormous compared to ones we have seen previously, such as gender differences in math performance. Does that mean that gender differences in interests explain gender gaps in CEP? Not so fast.

First, finding these large gender differences in interests tells us nothing about why the differences are there in the first place. It does not mean that they are biologically determined or hardwired in the brain. It seems likelier that boys are encouraged to be interested in fields like engineering and girls are not. We could change the environment so that girls would find engineering interesting.

Second, people who are in the CEP fields tend to portray them in a certain way that will be more interesting to men than to women. Engineering, for example, is portrayed as designing bridges or a better computer chip. If, instead, engineering advertised itself in the biomechanical engineering area (for example, designing better prostheses for people with damaged limbs), women might well find it more interesting and want to be part of it.

Women can't do the necessary math: The areas in which women are underrepresented require a high level of mathematical skills. They are termed math-intensive fields. If women are weak in math, they will not be able to succeed in those fields. However, as we saw earlier in this chapter, today girls are scoring as well as boys on mathematics tests, at least in the United States, and women are earning 46% of the undergraduate degrees in mathematics, so weak math ability cannot be the explanation for women's underrepresentation in CEP.

Hostile environment and discrimination: According to this explanation, women continue to be discriminated against in CEP, perhaps not in the crude, obvious ways that occurred in the past (old-fashioned sexism), but in more subtle ways (modern sexism), including implicit attitudes held by those in power. In the face of this discrimination, women would be likely to switch to other fields that they find more hospitable.

What is the evidence of continuing discrimination against women in CEP? First, as noted in Chapter 3, research shows that implicit attitudes link men and science, but not women and science (Carli et al., 2016). In one clever experiment, science faculty from research universities rated the materials of an applicant for a laboratory manager position (Moss-Racusin et al., 2012). All faculty saw the same materials, but half saw them with a male name for the applicant and half saw them with a female name. Faculty rated the male applicant as significantly more hirable and competent than the female applicant (who had identical qualifications to the male). The faculty also offered the male applicant a higher starting salary. Interestingly, both male and female faculty members showed this pattern. This study provides evidence of continuing discrimination against women in science.

Other research has sought to assess women's own experiences of discrimination in STEM fields. One study surveyed high school girls who wanted STEM careers, women in undergraduate STEM majors, and women in STEM PhD programs (Robnett, 2016). Overall, 61% of the respondents reported having experienced gender bias in the past year alone. Consistent with patterns of women's underrepresentation, experiences of gender bias were most common for those in math-intensive STEM fields (computer science, physics, engineering), and male peers were a major source of the bias. For example, among those in math-intensive graduate programs, 41% had experienced bias from male peers and 42% had experienced it from a professor. All of these numbers were much lower for women in the biological sciences—that is, they experienced much less bias. So women are underrepresented in areas (CEP) where they experience more bias.

A related idea is that the CEP fields are characterized by a masculine culture (Cheryan et al., 2017). The culture is masculine in several ways: There are few women in the field and stereotypes of people in the field are dominated by nerdy men. Women therefore feel that they don't belong there. That brings us to the issue of role models.

Role models: The conventional wisdom is that girls don't aspire to CEP careers because of the absence of role models, specifically female role models. As shown in Table 8.2, women are only 15% of the engineering workforce, so girls look at people in those jobs—perhaps in TV programs or brochures about engineering careers—and think, "I don't belong here." End of story, end of aspirations.

Following from this reasoning, many programs have been launched to expose girls to female role models in the sciences. The programs include presentations to middle school and high school girls, camps for girls, and websites targeted at encouraging girls (Cheryan et al., 2013). Many of the initiatives involve one-time exposure to a female role model. As scientists, we must ask: Are these programs effective? Many are not evaluated rigorously, so it is difficult to tell. But if the interventions were effective, we would have seen an increase in women in CEP majors and jobs over the last 10 to 15 years and we haven't, so there is reason to suspect that these well-intentioned efforts are not working.

One of the flaws in these interventions may be that they expose girls to stereotypical role models, and girls (and many boys as well) are turned off by those role models, not by the field itself. For example, computer scientists are stereotyped as being socially awkward, lacking in relationship skills, and obsessed with technology (Cheryan et al., 2013). In one study, undergraduate women who were not computer science majors met a role model who they were told was a computer science major. With a 2-by-2 experimental design, the role model was either a man or a woman and was either stereotypical for computer science or not stereotypical. The stereotypical role model reported hobbies such as video games, watching anime, and programming, and favorite magazine as *Electronic Gaming Monthly*. The nonstereotypical role model reported hobbies such as playing sports, hanging out with friends, and listening to music, and favorite magazine as *Rolling Stone*. After the participant and role model interacted, the participant completed a number of rating scales; they also completed the scales again 2 weeks later. The results indicated that exposure to the stereotypical role model reduced women's interest in computer science and their sense of belonging in the field, and the effects lasted for 2 weeks. Interestingly, gender of the role model made no difference—it was the stereotypicality that had the effect.

Overall, then, women may be less interested in CEP fields in part because they do not see women in those fields, but also because of unattractive stereotypes about people who work in the fields, regardless of gender. This research also connects to the lack-of-interest explanation described earlier.

Self-expressive value systems: This explanation puts the underrepresentation of women in CEP into a cultural, cross-national context. In the United States, we believe that you should work at a job that you love and feel passionate about. This approach is termed a *self-expressive value system* (Charles & Bradley, 2009). In a global context, that's a very privileged approach. In many other, less wealthy nations, the goal is to find a job that will support you (and your family). Love for the work would be a remote luxury.

In a study of 44 nations, the results indicated that there was actually more gender segregation in the workforce in the more economically developed nations (Charles & Bradley, 2009). That is, women were in more gender-stereotypical occupations in wealthier nations than in less wealthy nations. For example, women are found more often in engineering in Bulgaria and Colombia than they are in the United States and Canada. Engineering pays well, and in nations such as Bulgaria and Colombia, pay and job security may be far more important than whether you find it interesting or you love it.

Ironically, our American emphasis on individual preferences and finding a job that you love may be a factor in keeping women in traditional, female-dominated jobs and out of CEP jobs.

Stereotypic attribution bias: How do we explain setbacks that a person may experience in their career? To what do we attribute the setback? When people are told about a situation in which a woman has a setback in a STEM field, they tend to attribute it to internal causes such as her lack of ability; when people hear about a man encountering a setback in a STEM field, they tend to attribute it to external factors such as not getting enough sleep (LaCrosse et al., 2016). The problem is that the internal attributions imply that the woman is probably not going to make it in STEM (she just doesn't have the ability), whereas the external attributions for men mean that they can make it; they just have to try again. This attribution bias can be held both by women in STEM fields and by powerful others in their environment. If a woman in a STEM field has this bias, she is likely to give up on STEM when she encounters a setback—and everyone encounters setbacks. And if powerful others, such as her graduate school adviser or her boss, have this attribution bias, if she has a setback, they are likely to believe that she won't be successful in STEM. These attribution biases need to be identified and questioned.

The belief in geniuses: In some fields, the top people are considered geniuses. We think of math geniuses, for example, but perhaps not biology geniuses. Women are underrepresented in the "brilliance-required" STEM fields: math and physics. There is another field in which women are seriously underrepresented, and it is in the humanities: philosophy. Interestingly, it is also a field in which there is a belief that brilliance or genius is necessary for success. One study found that the belief in field-specific brilliance among people in the field correlated, across 30 fields, with female representation in the fields, and the correlation was substantial and negative, $r = -0.60$ (Leslie et al., 2015). That is, the more that people in the field believe that brilliance (raw, innate talent) is required in their field, the smaller the number of women. This same study also found a substantial negative correlation between beliefs in brilliance in fields and African Americans' representation. Just as women are stereotyped as not brilliant, so, too, are African Americans.

Distressingly, these stereotypes about gender and brilliance appear early. At age 6, girls are less likely than boys to believe that members of their gender are "really, really smart" (Bian et al., 2017).

This "brilliance required" effect might reduce the representation of women in those fields in two ways. First, it might discourage women themselves from entering the field, because women are less likely to see themselves as brilliant geniuses than men are. Second, powerful people in the field may not encourage aspiring women students because the powerful people believe that women don't have the necessary brilliance.

Which explanation is correct? The answer is that probably all of these factors play a role except the belief that women can't do math, which isn't supported by the data showing gender similarities in math performance. The cumulative effects of all these factors can produce big effects. And it may be that some women, along their career paths, encounter one or several of these obstacles and other women encounter others.

An Intersectional Approach to the Gender Gap in STEM

Much of the research on gender and STEM has been done with college samples, and therefore with mainly White samples. Let's consider the intersection of gender and ethnicity. Are the same gender–STEM patterns found with other ethnic groups? In one large study of college students across multiple universities, African American women had a higher rate of participation in STEM majors than European American women did (O'Brien et al., 2015). In another study, implicit stereotypes about gender and STEM were weaker among African American college women than they were among European American college women (O'Brien et al., 2015). We need research of this type with other U.S. ethnic groups, but the study suggests that some of our thinking about gender and STEM could be limited to Whites.

Interventions to Close Gaps in STEM

Based on research and theories, social psychologists have pioneered a number of interventions designed to close gender gaps, as well as race and social class gaps, in STEM fields. Here we will consider two categories of interventions: values affirmation and utility value.

One set of interventions is based in stereotype threat theory (discussed in Chapter 3). These interventions are called *values affirmation interventions* and are based on the idea that if an underrepresented or at-risk group feels threatened about underperforming in an academic setting, that sense of threat can be offset by having the students affirm their own personal values through writing assignments (Lazowski & Hulleman, 2016). In one study on gender gaps, students in a college physics course were randomly assigned to the affirmation condition or control (Miyake et al., 2010). Those in the affirmation condition selected their most important values from a list provided by the researchers (e.g., relationships with friends and family, gaining knowledge) and wrote an essay about why those values were important to them. They repeated the exercise again 2 weeks later. Those in the control group wrote an essay about their least important value. On exam scores in the physics course, the gender gap in the control condition was substantial, with men performing better ($d = 0.93$); in the affirmation condition, the gender gap was small ($d = 0.18$). That is, the intervention was successful in reducing the gender gap in performance in a college physics class. It also suggests that stereotype threat is a major factor in producing the gender gap in physics.

Another approach is based in Eccles's expectancy-value theory, discussed earlier in this chapter. The interventions, called *utility-value interventions*, tackle the value part of expectancy-value theory. The idea is that, by writing about the utility value or usefulness of the material they are studying, students will become more motivated (Lazowski & Hulleman, 2016). One study focused on social class and race gaps in performance in a college biology course (Harackiewicz et al., 2016). The social class gap refers to the gap in performance between first-generation college students (FG; neither parent has a college degree) and continuing-generation college students (at least one parent has a college degree). The race gap refers to the gap in performance between White students and those who are from underrepresented minority groups (URM: African American, Latinx, and American Indian). Students in the utility-value condition wrote essays about the relevance or usefulness of course material, whereas those in the control condition wrote essays simply summarizing the material. In the control condition, the gap between FG-URM students and continuing-generation White students was large ($d = 0.98$). The good news is that the intervention reduced the gap substantially, by 61%. Why didn't the intervention erase the gap completely? Doubtless there are many other factors that contribute to the gap in performance between FG-URM students and continuing-generation majority students, such as high school quality and preparation. We may not be able to close these gaps completely by the time students reach college, but we can at least reduce the size of the gap and help more students be successful.

Overall, then, researchers can use theories such as stereotype threat (Chapter 3) and expectancy-value (this chapter) to design interventions to close gender gaps in STEM as well as race and social class gaps.

Experience the Research
Gender and Computers

This exercise has two parts:

1. Visit a local store that sells computer games. Examine 10 games that are currently being sold. Based on the information on the packages and what you know about the games, classify each game as male oriented, female oriented, or neutral. To do this, you will have to specify your criteria for each of these categories. For example, you might decide that any game that involves violence is male oriented. Or you might say that any game that has only boys on the packaging is male oriented. Specify your criteria clearly and write them down. If there is not enough information on the package to classify a game, ask a salesperson in the store to give you more details about it.

Overall, what were your findings? What percentage of the games were male oriented? Female oriented? Neutral? What are the implications of your findings?

2. Find out whether the local high school has an after-school computer lab. If it does, visit the lab twice to make observations. On each occasion, count the number of male-appearing students, female-appearing students, and trans-appearing students who are there. Next, observe the computer activity in which each student is engaging, such as playing a game (what kind of game?) or programming.

Do the boys' computer activities differ systematically from the girls'? What about the trans-appearing students? Do there seem to be power dynamics in the lab, with some people dominating over others? What is the gender pattern of those power dynamics?

CHAPTER SUMMARY

There are no gender differences in general intelligence. When we look at more specific abilities, we find no gender difference in verbal ability or mathematical ability, but a moderate gender difference favoring boys and men in 3-D spatial ability. Some aspects of athletic performance show large gender difference beginning in puberty.

Eccles's expectancy-value theory posits that, to be motivated to take on a challenging task (for example, majoring in engineering in college), a person needs to have an expectancy of success and needs to value the task (for example, seeing it as useful or interesting). The expectancies and values that a person has about a particular task are, in turn, shaped by many forces, such as socializers' beliefs and feedback that the student has received in the form of standardized test scores or grades in school.

Gender may enter into any of these processes. For example, parents have higher expectancies of math scores for sons than for daughters.

For school achievement, girls get better grades than boys at all grade levels and in all subjects. Some of these patterns of similarities and differences vary by ethnic group in an intersectional analysis.

For occupational achievement, women have gained much in the last several decades in entry into some prestigious occupations such as medicine, veterinary medicine, and law. However, women remain a small minority in engineering.

There is a gender gap in STEM, particularly in computer science, engineering, and physics, where women are seriously underrepresented. Explanations for the gap include women lacking interest, women being unable to do the necessary math (not supported by the data), hostile environments and discrimination in these fields, lack of role models, self-expressive value systems, stereotypic attribution bias, and the belief in geniuses combined with the belief that geniuses are men.

SUGGESTION FOR FURTHER READING

Rivers, Caryl, & Barnett, Rosalind C. (2015). *The new soft war on women: How the myth of female ascendance is hurting women, men—and our economy.* New York, NY: Penguin. Journalist Rivers and psychology researcher Barnett team up to document the subtle biases and barriers to women that persist, despite the great strides that women have made in recent decades.

Gender and Work

The majority of American women hold paying jobs. Among women between the ages of 25 and 54, 71% of White women and 69% of Black women hold jobs (Bureau of Labor Statistics, 2010). The working woman, then, is not a deviation from the norm; she *is* the norm. Women today constitute 47% of the American labor force—very close to half—compared with 29% in 1948 (White House Council of Economic Advisers, 2016).

Pay Equity and the Wage Gap

In 1960, American women earned about 61 cents for every dollar American men earned (U.S. Census Bureau, 2016d). While that gap has decreased in the decades since, we have not yet achieved pay equity: today, women earn about 80 cents for every dollar men earn (U.S. Census Bureau, 2016d). This gender gap in wages is larger in the United States than it is in many developed nations, including Norway, Hungary, Italy, and New Zealand (White House Council of Economic Advisers, 2016). And this gap gets larger over the course of women's careers. The wage gap occurs despite the fact that, on average, women are actually better educated compared with men.

An intersectional perspective demonstrates that the gender gap in wages is also linked to ethnicity. Table 9.1 shows median annual earnings as a function of both gender and ethnicity as well as the gender gap in wages within each ethnic group. These statistics clearly demonstrate that, within every ethnic group, women earn less than men. Yet the size of the wage gap varies across ethnic groups: It is largest among White Americans, and smallest among African Americans. Note, also, the highest paid group—Asian American men—earns nearly twice as much as the lowest paid group—Hispanic/Latina women. In sum, pay inequity exists in each group, but it's most severe among Hispanic Americans.

Wages also vary at the intersection of age and gender, such that the wage gap is smallest among younger adults and largest among older adults (Joint Economic Committee Democratic Staff, 2016). What appears to happen is that, over time, small or minor discrepancies in wages accumulate, such that they are negligible among younger adults but grow over decades of work. The wage gap is significant beginning at about age 35. This wage gap is a serious concern for older adults, who are often on fixed retirement and social security income (which are determined largely by how much they earned in previous years). Older women are more likely than older men to live in poverty.

The Motherhood Penalty

Motherhood penalty:
The reduction in women's lifetime earnings that result from having children.

What is behind the wage gap? One factor that seems to contribute to the wage gap is women's family roles and responsibilities. Although heterosexual marriage and children raise the amount of household work for both women and men, the effect is much greater for women (a point we will return to in the section on work and family issues). In particular, there is a **motherhood penalty** in wages, such that women's lifetime earnings are reduced by having children, typically by about 5% to 10% for each child (Budig & Hodges, 2010; J. R. Kahn et al., 2014). By contrast, fatherhood generally does not carry such a wage penalty; indeed, there is evidence of a fatherhood bonus (e.g., Budig, 2014; Evers & Sieverding, 2014)!

The reduction in women's earnings is partly due to behaviors such as taking time off from work after the birth of a child, cutting their education short, working jobs with more flexible hours, and working fewer hours because of caregiving responsibilities. These are all things that women are more likely than men to do.

TABLE 9.1 **Median annual earnings as a function of gender and ethnicity in the United States.**

	Women	Men	Wage Gap*
White or European American	$43,063	$57,204	75.3%
Black or African American	$36,212	$41,094	88.1%
Asian American	$48,313	$61,672	78.3%
Hispanic	$31,109	$35,673	87.2%
Total	$40,742	$51,212	79.6%

Source: Data from U.S. Census Bureau (2016c). Table created by Nicole Else-Quest.

*The wage gap is women's earnings as a percentage of men's earnings.

For example, to be a successful partner in a law firm or to earn tenure as a college professor requires considerably more than 40 hours of work per week—often 60 to 80 hours. Some (though certainly not all) women in this situation may choose not to commit to the extra hours, because they want to spend them with their family or because family commitments simply prevent working beyond 40 hours per week. These women then work in the less well-paid and less prestigious levels of their occupations— lawyer but not partner, lecturer but not tenured professor. There is much questioning of why women's family responsibilities should interfere with their job advancement when men's do not.

©iStockphoto.com/monkeybusinessimages.

PHOTO 9.1

A motherhood penalty for her and a fatherhood bonus for him? Family roles and responsibilities, as well as child care and family leave policies, contribute to the wage gap.

The motherhood penalty is greatest for women who have three or more children and for women who have their children at younger ages (Kahn et al., 2014). An intersectional analysis suggests that women in low-wage work may also experience a more severe motherhood penalty (Budig & Hodges, 2010).

What can be done to reduce the motherhood penalty? Cross-national research suggests that affordable child care is crucial. A study of women in 13 European countries found that the motherhood penalty in wages was reduced in countries with publicly funded child care (Abendroth et al., 2014). The researchers concluded that, when women have improved access to child care, there is less of a need for them to leave their jobs or work fewer hours in order to take care of their children.

Of course, the motherhood penalty in wages may also stem from discrimination in the workplace. Employers might discriminate against mothers, something that is illegal but difficult to prove. We will return to the topic later in this chapter.

Occupational Segregation

Another clear factor contributing to the wage gap is occupational segregation. Most occupations are segregated by gender. Very few jobs are held by equal proportions of men and women. Table 9.2 lists women's share of a variety of occupations in the United States and how that share has changed in recent decades. Notice that most occupations are highly segregated by gender, with 90% or more of the workers coming from one gender. Men dominate as airline pilots, auto mechanics, carpenters, and welders. Women dominate as child care workers, dental hygienists, and registered nurses. Only a few occupations come close to a 50-50 gender ratio: bus drivers, editors and reporters, and college and university teachers.

Beyond the problem of the wage gap, occupational segregation remains a critical issue for other reasons. The stereotyping of occupations severely limits people's thinking about work options. A man might think himself well suited to being a registered nurse or a woman might love carpentry, but they are discouraged from following their passions because certain occupations are not considered appropriate for them because of their gender (see Chapter 8).

Occupations are segregated by race/ethnicity as well, and this segregation has numerous consequences. For example, in one study Black children 6 to 7 years of age were told about fictitious occupations, and people with those jobs were shown as either only Black, only White, or some from each (Bigler et al., 2003). The children then rated the status

TABLE 9.2   Occupational segregation: Women as a percentage of all workers in selected occupations in the United States, 1975–2015.

Occupation	Women as Percentage of Total Employed		
	1975	1989	2015
Airline pilot	0.0	3.8	7.9
Auto mechanic	0.5	0.7	2.2
Bus driver	37.7	54.8	42.7
Carpenter	0.6	1.2	1.2
Child care worker	98.4	97.1	96.6
Dentist	1.8	8.6	33.9
Dental hygienist	100.0	98.9	93.0
Editor	44.6	49.2	46.3
Elementary and middle school teacher	85.4	84.7	80.6
College/university teacher	31.1	38.7	43.7
Lawyer	7.1	22.3	37.4
Librarian	81.1	87.3	78.5
Physician	13.0	17.9	38.2
Registered nurse	97.0	94.2	88.3
Social worker	60.8	68.1	81.1
Telephone installer, repairer	4.8	10.8	5.7
Welder	4.4	6.6	4.0

Sources: Data from Bureau of Labor Statistics (2016); Costello & Stone (2001).

of the occupations. Jobs that had been shown as being done only by White people were rated as higher in status than jobs shown as being done only by Black people, with ratings for mixed-race jobs rated in between. This experiment provides powerful evidence that Black children have learned that Black adults generally hold lower-status occupations, and they generalize this principle even to fictitious occupations.

Economists estimate that about 51% of the wage gap is due to occupational segregation (White House Council of Economic Advisers, 2016). Occupations that are predominantly held by women are almost invariably low paying.

Yet even when men and women work side by side in similar jobs, the wage gap persists (White House Council of Economic Advisers, 2016). For example, about equal numbers of men and women work as financial managers, but women in those jobs make only 65 cents for every dollar men make (Bureau of Labor Statistics, 2016). So occupational segregation is only one part of the puzzle.

It was the recognition of the gender gap in wages, and the fact that it was partly due to occupational segregation, that led to the concept of **comparable worth**. Comparable worth is the principle that people should be paid equally for work in comparable

Comparable worth: The principle that people should be paid equally for work that is comparable in responsibility, educational requirements, and so forth.

PHOTO 9.2
Many jobs are segregated by gender.

jobs—that is, jobs with equivalent responsibility, educational requirements, level in the organization, and required experience. As an illustration of the importance of comparable worth, in one state both liquor store clerks and librarians are employed by the state government. Liquor store clerks are almost all men, and the job requires only a high school education. Librarians are almost all women, and the job requires a college education. But in this state, liquor store clerks are paid more than librarians. The principle of comparable worth argues against this pattern. It says that librarians should be paid at least as much as, and probably more than, liquor store clerks because librarians must be college graduates. Several states have enacted comparable worth legislation, stating that at least all government employees must be paid on a comparable worth basis. This requires extensive job analyses by industrial/organizational psychologists to figure out which jobs have equivalent requirements in terms of responsibilities, education, and so on, regardless of gender. Preliminary results in states that have legislated this principle are promising, and it turns out not to be terribly expensive for employers to pay on a comparable worth basis. Federal laws have also been passed to ensure equal pay for equal work (see Focus 9.1).

Compensation Negotiation

Another cause of the wage gap that has been proposed has to do with wage negotiation; that is, maybe women are paid less because they don't negotiate for higher pay as well as men do. This proposal may strike you as yet another female deficit explanation that blames women for being paid less than men, but let's consider the evidence.

A recent meta-analysis examined gender differences in economic negotiation outcomes, analyzing data from studies that measured how successful people were at negotiating different economic outcomes, including salary (Mazei et al., 2015). Participants included undergraduate and graduate students as well as businesspeople. The overall effect size was $d = 0.20$, a small gender difference, indicating that men achieved somewhat better economic outcomes than women in negotiation situations. As is often the case, however, the size of the gender difference depended on context. Moderator analyses showed that gender differences were reduced when negotiators had experience with negotiation or when the negotiators were given information about the bargaining range (for example, information about the aspects of the situation that were negotiable). In other words, the more negotiators knew about negotiation generally and about the situation specifically, the smaller the gender difference in outcomes.

FOCUS 9.1

PSYCHOLOGY AND PUBLIC POLICY: EMPLOYMENT DISCRIMINATION IN THE UNITED STATES

Several important pieces of federal legislation prohibit employment discrimination in actions such as unfair hiring, promotions, wages, termination, and layoffs. Title VII of the Civil Rights Act of 1964 prohibits employment discrimination based on "race, color, religion, sex, or national origin." Title VII also called for the creation of the Equal Employment Opportunity Commission (EEOC), which has the authority to investigate and, when appropriate, file lawsuits against employers for violations of these and subsequent prohibitions against employment discrimination, including discrimination on the basis of disability, genetic information, and age (i.e., being 40 or older).

What is particularly relevant for the psychology of women and gender is the meaning of *sex* in Title VII. Initially, *sex* referred primarily to the status of being female (or male) and included protections for women during pregnancy and childbirth. Since then, the EEOC has clarified that *sex* includes pregnancy, gender identity, and sexual orientation. Thus, Title VII affirms that, for example, a qualified job applicant cannot be denied a job because they are pregnant, a transgender woman cannot be denied access to the women's restroom at work, and a lesbian woman cannot be denied a promotion for

not conforming to the employer's gendered expectations or stereotypes. Although the EEOC defines sex in this way, legal precedent has not yet been set in the federal courts. In other words, federal protections against discrimination on the basis of gender identity (rather than gender assigned at birth) and sexual orientation exist only in theory, not in practice. Thus, it is uncertain the extent to which trans and nonbinary people are legally protected from employment discrimination under Title VII. Some states provide protections, but in most it is perfectly legal to fire someone for being trans, queer, or gender nonconforming.

Other legislation has focused specifically on the issue of pay equity between women and men. For example, the 1963 Equal Pay Act requires that people be paid the same wages for the same job, regardless of their gender. Yet it falls short of the standards set by the principle of comparable worth because it requires that, for gender-equal pay, the jobs must be identical, not merely comparable.

More recently, the Lilly Ledbetter Fair Pay Act of 2009 made it easier for targets of wage discrimination to sue their employers for violating Title VII, in that it clarified that the 180-day statute of limitations for employees to sue for wage discrimination resets at each paycheck. The law was named after Lilly Ledbetter, who filed a pay discrimination claim with the EEOC and sued her employer, Goodyear Tire Company, for being paid less than her male counterparts. Ledbetter worked as a manager at Goodyear for 19 years and filed her lawsuit 6 months before her retirement in 1998. Initially, her pay was similar to that of men in her position, but over time a substantial wage gap developed, which also negatively affected her social security and eventual retirement income. Her claim was ultimately denied in 2007 by the U.S. Supreme Court in *Ledbetter v. Goodyear Tire and Rubber Co.* solely on the grounds that more than 180 days had passed since the discrimination started. In other words, before this law was passed, a person might be discriminated against for many years but have no grounds for legal action because the statute of limitations had run out 180 days after the first unfair paycheck. This statute of limitations is unrealistic in most cases. In the dissenting opinion, Justice Ruth Bader

Retrieved from the White House Archives.

PHOTO 9.3

President Barack Obama signed the Lilly Ledbetter Fair Pay Act of 2009 into law. The law states that the 180-day statute of limitations for employees to sue for wage discrimination resets at each paycheck.

Ginsburg acknowledged that it is often difficult for employees to identify when pay discrimination has occurred:

> Pay disparities often occur, as they did in Ledbetter's case, in small increments; cause to suspect that discrimination is at work develops only over time. . . . It is only when the disparity becomes apparent and sizable, e.g., through future raises calculated as a percentage of current salaries, that an employee in Ledbetter's situation is likely to comprehend her plight and, therefore, to complain. (pp. 2–3)

That is, discrimination in pay might occur in small increments, with minor raises here and there that accumulate to a major disparity over time. Moreover, in most jobs, people don't know how much their coworkers make, so it may not be immediately obvious to a woman when she is being paid less than her male counterpart.

The EEOC also handles claims of sexual harassment in the workplace, a topic we discuss in Chapter 14. For more information about the EEOC and employment discrimination, visit https://www.eeoc.gov/.

In one field experiment, researchers published two versions of a job ad: both versions offered the same wage, but one version said the wage was negotiable and the other version was ambiguous about the possibility of negotiation (Leibbrandt & List, 2015). The researchers measured how many men and women applied for the job and whether the applicants initiated wage negotiations. When ads were ambiguous about whether wages were negotiable, fewer women applied for the jobs and, when they did, they were less likely to initiate wage negotiations. By contrast, when ads explicitly said that wages were negotiable, more women applied and the gender difference in initiating wage negotiation was eliminated. Again, the context of having more information—such as whether a salary is negotiable—can significantly change outcomes related to the wage gap. Employers would be wise to consider this information when writing their job ads.

In sum, the evidence indicates that, while men tend to negotiate better, this difference is small and, well, negotiable. A logical extension of these findings, then, would seem to be this: We need to teach girls and women how to negotiate for higher pay. But before we jump into salary negotiation workshops, let's reconsider the concern about female deficit interpretations and dig deeper into this pattern. Why do women, on average, negotiate for higher pay less effectively than men do?

There is evidence suggesting that, for women, salary negotiation comes with a price that goes beyond wages. Negotiating for higher pay involves expressing confidence about one's ability to do the job well and advocating for one's financial worth. These behaviors are consistent with the male role, which demands self-confidence, personal agency, and being a breadwinner. By contrast, these behaviors are at odds with the female role requirements of being modest and putting the needs of others ahead of one's own needs. Thus, women tend to be more reticent to negotiate for higher pay because of the **social backlash** for doing so (Amanatullah & Morris, 2010; Bowles & Babcock, 2012; Rudman & Glick, 1999). Suppose Alicia is offered a job and she negotiates for higher pay, violating her gender role and others' expectation that she should be modest and simply grateful for whatever is offered to her. The social backlash to Alicia's effective self-advocacy would involve negative evaluations of her interpersonal qualities. In short, Alicia's new boss and colleagues may perceive her as aggressive, out for herself, and overconfident. Who wants to start a new job under those conditions? For many women, the risk of alienating coworkers is greater than the benefit of higher pay, particularly if the opinions of those coworkers are important for job advancement.

Social backlash: Negative evaluation of someone for violating the norms of their gender role.

Women aren't imagining this risk: The research evidence supports the existence of a social backlash in the workplace (e.g., Bowles et al., 2007). A meta-analysis of the social backlash examined penalties for expressions of dominance, assertiveness, or agentic behavior and found that expressing dominance reduces women's hirability considerably more than it does men's, $d = -0.58$ (M. J. Williams & Tiedens, 2016). Moreover, making explicit or direct demands for a raise or better job benefits has a more negative effect on women's likability than on men's, $d = -0.28$. In many cases, then, it seems that women (but not men) must choose between better pay and being liked by their coworkers.

Remember that a feminist perspective always involves finding a path forward, a way to make things more equitable and just. Therefore, feminist researchers have focused their efforts on devising strategies that improve women's pay negotiation effectiveness while avoiding the social backlash for gender role violations (e.g., Bowles & Babcock, 2012; Heilman & Okimoto, 2007). These strategies often involve women conveying their communal traits—such as interpersonal warmth and concern for the well-being of others—during the negotiation process, which reduces the perception that they are violating their gender role.

Entitlement

Entitlement: An individual's sense of what they should receive (e.g., pay) based on who they are or what they've done.

A related factor that may contribute to gender differences in salary negotiation is entitlement. **Entitlement** refers to the individual's sense of what they should receive (e.g., pay) based on who they are or what they've done. If a woman thinks she is entitled to better pay, she's more likely to ask for it. A number of studies have demonstrated that, relative to men, women have a lower sense of entitlement to pay for their work (Hogue & Yoder, 2003; Major, 1994).

What drives this gender difference in entitlement? Social psychologist Brenda Major (1994) developed a theory that explains how social structural factors and psychological factors interact to perpetuate the wage gap. The process begins with inequalities in the social structure in the United States, such as occupational segregation by gender, the chronic underpayment of women and of women's work, and the lack of equal opportunities for women. These inequalities in the social structure then lead women and men to have different standards of comparison—that is, standards against which they compare their own pay when deciding whether it is equitable. The result is that women compare their pay with that of other women and with others in their typically female-dominated occupation. Women see other women and those in their own occupation as the appropriate comparison group because of a proximity effect—that is, those are the people who are around them and about whom they have information. The average administrative assistant is unlikely to have information on what electricians earn. Self-protective factors may also play a part. An underpaid female librarian who is a college graduate may not want to know what a male high school graduate working in a skilled trade earns. It will just make her feel bad. Her tendency will be to compare her pay with that of other female librarians, and then she won't be doing so badly.

These gender differences in standards of comparison then have a great impact on women's and men's perceptions of their

CARTOON 9.1

Oh, so that explains the difference in our salaries!

entitlement to pay. Many women do not feel entitled to high pay for their work in the way that men do because (a) their pay is reasonable relative to those with whom they compare themselves, (b) their pay is reasonable compared with their own past pay, and (c) their pay is reasonable according to what is realistically attainable given restricted job opportunities for women.

The result is that women have less of a sense of entitlement to high pay than men do. This in turn leads them to tolerate wage injustice. Another consequence is that others come to believe that women will settle for less in pay, precisely because many women do, leading to further bias in setting wage rates. And so the cycle continues.

What evidence is there to support this theory? Many experiments have been conducted testing various aspects of it, and virtually all of them support it. In one study (O'Brien et al., 2012), female and male undergraduates were given 20 minutes to circle every letter *e* they could find in a legal document. In a self-report measure of entitlement, participants were asked to report how much they thought they deserved to be paid for their work. The researchers also measured entitlement by observing the participants' behavior. Participants were initially paid $8 for the work, and they were also given the option of awarding themselves bonuses. Participants paid themselves bonuses privately from an envelope containing $5. The gender differences were striking: Not only did men report that they deserved higher pay than did women ($d = 0.75$), but they also paid themselves higher bonuses ($d = 0.63$). Yet, compared with men, women actually completed more work and did so with greater accuracy! Thus, men's greater entitlement couldn't possibly have resulted from doing superior work.

As we noted in Chapter 1, we must be careful of interpretations of these phenomena, so that this theory does not become another female deficit model. One interpretation is that women have a low sense of personal entitlement compared with men—that is, that women have a deficit in their sense of entitlement. The other possible interpretation is that men have an inflated sense of entitlement— a sense that they are entitled to more than they are worth. An inflated sense of entitlement characterizes many dominant groups, including men, White people, and people from upper social classes (O'Brien & Major, 2009). In an interesting twist, researchers have been able to manipulate men's (but not women's) sense of entitlement by priming their belief in meritocracy (O'Brien et al., 2012). That is, members of dominant groups feel more entitled when they're reminded of beliefs that justify or seem to legitimize the systems of inequality that perpetuate their dominance. Yet this effect does not occur for members of subordinate groups.

©iStockphoto.com/asiseeit.

PHOTO 9.4

How can women feel entitled to higher pay and effectively negotiate for a fair wage while avoiding the social backlash for violating their gender role?

The research on entitlement is an excellent example of the ways in which social structural factors, such as the gender segregation of occupations, are linked to psychological processes, like sense of entitlement, to create gender bias.

Implicit Stereotypes

New research points to another factor that may be behind the wage gap: implicit stereotypes. In Chapter 3 we discussed implicit stereotypes, or learned, automatic associations, and how they are measured with the Implicit Association Test (IAT). Researchers have used the IAT and uncovered automatic associations between the category of "male" and the category of "rich" (Williams et al., 2010). That is, people may possess implicit stereotypes that men (not women) may be rich. Moreover, when the participants in this study were asked to estimate the salaries of men or women in different occupations, they tended to estimate higher salaries for men than for women. This tendency to overestimate men's salaries was linked to the participant's implicit stereotypes.

Other studies have found that implicit stereotypes about gender and leadership are linked to the evaluation of women's and men's work (e.g., Latu et al., 2011). This research points to another layer of psychological factors that may contribute to the wage gap. Recall that implicit stereotypes are not conscious; thus, a manager may believe they are fair and equitable in determining salaries or wages, but their implicit bias may still lead them to make unfair decisions. Still, conscious forms of bias and discrimination may also contribute to the wage gap.

Gender Discrimination and Workplace Climate

Gender discrimination in the workplace may take several forms, including gender discrimination in job ads, in hiring decisions, in pay, and in the evaluation of work, as well as phenomena such as the glass ceiling. Sexual harassment is also a tool of sexism in the workplace, but we will discuss that in the context of gender-based violence in Chapter 14.

Gender Discrimination in Job Advertisements

Often, the first step in the employment process is the job ad. There is a long history of gender discrimination at that initial stage. For many years, newspapers published job ads in two sections distinguished by gender: *Jobs for Men* and *Jobs for Women*. The Jobs for Women were largely clerical and invariably low-paying. Women were explicitly told that they should not bother applying for the higher-paying jobs reserved for men. It was old-fashioned sexism, and today it's shocking. The courts then ruled that it was illegal to advertise jobs for just one gender and newspapers switched to having a single section of job ads.

Yet today we grapple with the subtle ways of modern sexism, which is just as inequitable yet often more difficult to identify. For example, job ads often include gendered wording. One study found that ads for male-dominated occupations contained significantly more masculine words (e.g., *leader, competitive, dominant*; Gaucher et al., 2011). In follow-up laboratory experiments, the researchers asked participants to read job ads that were identical except for masculine or feminine wording. For example, in the ad for a real estate agent, the feminine wording said, "We support our employees with an excellent compensation package," whereas the masculine wording said, "We boast a competitive compensation package." When the ads included more masculine words, participants estimated that there were more men in the occupation. In addition, female participants found such jobs less appealing, largely because they felt less sense of belonging in jobs advertised with masculine wording. That is, with masculine wording, women felt less like they belonged in that job, compared with feminine wording. This research demonstrates how subtle forces can maintain occupational segregation by gender and discourage women from applying for certain occupations. If we don't think we belong in a job, why would we apply for it?

Gender Discrimination in the Evaluation of Work

Psychologists have made important contributions to the study of gender discrimination in the evaluation of work over many years. For example, a classic experiment demonstrated that even when a woman's work was identical to a man's, her work was judged to be inferior to his (Goldberg, 1968; replicated by Pheterson et al., 1971). Participants read and evaluated essays written either by a male author (e.g., John T. McKay) or a female author (e.g., Joan T. McKay). The essays were identical except for the names of the authors. Results showed that essays by male authors were rated more highly than essays by female authors, even when the topic of the essay was traditionally feminine (e.g., dietetics). In other words, the work of a man was judged better than that of a woman, even when the work was identical in quality.

Since that classic experiment, several meta-analyses of similar experiments have been conducted (e.g., Davison & Burke, 2000; Koch et al., 2015; Swim et al., 1989). In general, these meta-analyses have found little evidence of bias in the evaluation of women's work. For example, the most recent meta-analysis reported an average effect size of $d = 0.08$, indicating that men's work was given slightly higher ratings than women's work, but the d was so small that we could say it was zero (Koch et al., 2015). Notice that—in contrast to other meta-analyses we have reported, in which d reflected the difference between the performance of men and the performance of women—here the effect is for the difference between evaluations of work with a man's name on it and evaluations of work with a woman's name on it. The effect size d, in this instance, is a measure of the extent of gender bias or discrimination.

Wouldn't it be satisfying to say that women's work is evaluated fairly and that gender bias is no longer a problem? Yet, as is often the case, the moderator analyses reveal complexities in the data and tell us that there is much more to this story (Koch et al., 2015). For example, the gender bias was greater in jobs that were male-dominated (e.g., police officer) than in jobs that were female-dominated (e.g., teacher), $d = 0.13$ versus $d = -0.02$. That is, gender bias depended on whether the job appeared congruent with the gender role of the applicant or employee. In addition, men tended to have more gender-biased ratings than women did.

Another layer of complexity in the data was that gender bias depended on how much information the rater had about the applicant or employee. For example, when raters were given only a small amount of information—maybe just a male or female name—there was more gender bias (favoring men) than when raters were given more information (Koch et al., 2015). This is consistent with a general finding in social psychology that people stereotype others less the more they know about them.

Yet an important limitation in these meta-analyses was that nearly all the studies reviewed were laboratory experiments with college students serving as the raters. In short, the studies do not directly measure what really matters: Gender discrimination in the actual evaluations of real work done by real people. Such experiments don't tell us about gender bias and discrimination in the evaluations conducted by supervisors, by people actually making hiring decisions, or by other powerful persons. The laboratory experiments in these meta-analyses provide only analogies to the real situation, and for that reason they are called analog studies. We are left wondering how much gender bias shapes real hiring decisions and whether it contributes to the wage gap.

In Chapter 8 we described an experiment using a similar design with science faculty rating job applications for a lab manager position (Moss-Racusin et al., 2012). That experiment demonstrated that the equally qualified man not only was rated as more competent and hirable but also was offered a higher starting salary and more career mentoring. Studies like this provide more reliable evidence of gender discrimination in the evaluation of women's work and have alarming implications for the wage gap. In addition, because this study was conducted with people with the power to make hiring decisions, it addressed the limitation of previous laboratory experiments conducted with students.

Workplace Climate

The problems of discrimination and harassment have much to do with the climate of a workplace. For example, is the climate or general environment and culture of a workplace one that promotes fair and equitable treatment of all employees? Or is it one that permits and fosters microaggressions, indirect aggression, and feelings of exclusion or anxiety?

Workplace climate matters for everyone's job satisfaction, productivity, and well-being, of course, but it is a particular concern for individuals from marginalized groups, such as sexual and gender minority groups. While U.S. federal laws currently do not provide clear protections for members of such groups in the workplace (see Focus 9.1), corporate America has led a shift toward more inclusive nondiscrimination policies. For example, 91% of Fortune 500 companies explicitly include sexual orientation in their non-discrimination policies, and 61% include gender identity (Fidas & Cooper, 2015). In addition, many employers have extended benefits to members of sexual and gender minority groups in an effort to recruit and retain the most talented and qualified employees, no matter their sexual orientation or gender identity. Simply put, it's good business to make all employees feel valued and protected at work!

Still, more subtle aspects of the workplace climate, such as coworkers' implicit stereotypes and microaggressions, remain problematic for many individuals from sexual and gender minority groups. For example, one national study surveyed lesbian, gay, bisexual, and transgender (LGBT) people and found that more than half reported hiding their sexual orientation or gender identity in the workplace, and more than one-third reported feeling compelled to lie about their personal lives at work (Fidas & Cooper, 2015). Yet it is the norm across workplaces for coworkers to discuss personal topics such as their weekend plans, children, or romantic relationships. So, while coworkers have such non-work-related conversations, members of sexual and gender minority groups feel compelled to keep quiet or closeted. Their concerns are well founded: The same national study found that 70% of non-LGBT respondents said it was "unprofessional" to talk about sexual orientation or gender identity at work. A workplace climate that tolerates only cisgender, heterosexual employees talking openly and honestly about their personal lives is one that excludes members of sexual and gender minority groups. Whereas a workplace climate that is inclusive and accepting retains its LGBT employees, 9% of LGBT employees surveyed said they'd left a job because the workplace climate was not accepting. Of course, not everyone has the means to leave a job because of workplace climate.

Leadership and the Glass Ceiling

On November 9, 2016, after losing the U.S. presidential election, Hillary Rodham Clinton stated in her concession speech, "I know we have still not shattered that highest and hardest glass ceiling, but some day, someone will, and hopefully sooner than we might think right now." Throughout Clinton's presidential campaigns in 2008 and 2016, the **glass ceiling** was discussed in the popular media. The term is a metaphor used to describe the barrier or ceiling that prevents women from advancing to the highest-level jobs, including the presidency. Women may be promoted and move up the ranks in their company, but there is a point past which they can't seem to rise any further. For example, some women make it to the upper levels of management, but don't break into executive positions in the C-suite—they can see the highest levels through the glass ceiling, but they can't break through it.

What evidence is there that a glass ceiling exists? A study of S&P 500 companies found that although 44.3% of all employees in these companies were women, women made up only 25.1% of executives and managers (see Figure 9.1). At the highest level of the company, less than 5% of CEOs were women. These data indicate that the higher one goes in corporations, the fewer women (and, often, people of color) one will find. This pattern clearly demonstrates the glass ceiling.

The glass ceiling hurts everyone. Corporations with more women at the top actually perform better than other corporations. One study examined a sample of 353 Fortune 500 companies and found that those with the highest representation of women in top management showed better financial performance than the companies with the lowest representation of women (Catalyst, 2004). Breaking the glass ceiling isn't just good for women; it's good for business.

PHOTO 9.5

In the 2016 presidential election, Hillary Rodham Clinton won the popular vote but lost the election, and the "highest and hardest glass ceiling" remained intact.

Glass ceiling: Invisible barriers to the promotion of women and ethnic minorities into upper management and executive levels.

Leadership Effectiveness and Gender Role Congruity

We've discussed how discrimination can lead to a shortage of women in leadership positions, but we should also explore whether and how women can be successful when they reach those leadership positions. In real-world job situations, women might be perceived as ineffective leaders, managers, and supervisors for various reasons. One possibility is that women are truly lacking in the abilities, personality traits, interpersonal skills,

FIGURE 9.1 | **Statistics on the glass ceiling: As the level at S&P 500 companies increases, the percentage of women decreases.**

Category	Percentage
CEOs	4.6%
Top Earners	9.5%
Board Seats	19.9%
Executive/Senior-Level Officials and Managers	25.1%
First/Mid-Level Officials and Managers	36.4%
Total Employees	44.3%

Source: Catalyst (2016). Figure created by Nicole Else-Quest.

and so on that are necessary to be successful in the leadership role. Another possibility is that, regardless of whether women are actually effective in leadership roles, they are judged or evaluated unfairly; that is, people are biased in their evaluations of female leaders.

Let's consider the evidence for these possible explanations. In regard to the first hypothesis—whether women can do the job—research generally shows no gender differences in the actual effectiveness of leaders. Eagly and her colleagues (1995) conducted a meta-analysis of studies of the effectiveness of leaders and found that the magnitude of the gender difference in leadership effectiveness was $d = -0.02$. In other words, there was no gender difference. Leadership effectiveness can be measured either subjectively, as when a manager's skills on relevant dimensions are rated by other managers, or more objectively, as when the productivity of a leader's group is assessed. The results were similar with subjective measures ($d = 0.05$) and objective measures ($d = -0.02$). Still, in some situations, female leaders may be more effective than male leaders, and vice versa. When the leadership position was consistent with the female gender role, female leaders were judged as more effective. Similarly, when the leadership position was consistent with the female gender role, female leaders were more effective.

The second hypothesis is that people are biased in their evaluation of female leaders. A meta-analysis of laboratory studies evaluating women and men in leadership roles generally found little evidence of gender bias when all other factors were controlled (Eagly et al., 1992). That is, female and male leaders were given similar evaluations ($d = 0.05$). Yet this finding was qualified by leadership style: Under certain conditions women received notably poorer evaluations. If women used an autocratic or dictatorial leadership style rather than a more democratic and nurturant style, they received lower evaluations ($d = 0.30$). It may be, then, that it is not so much a question of bias against women leaders as bias against women leaders who do not behave in a style consistent with their female gender role. The female gender role requires that women be gentle, nurturant, and cooperative, not assertive, confrontational, or bossy. People have trouble with autocratic, pushy women, while men who engage in the same behaviors are not judged as harshly. This is the social backlash discussed earlier; women's dominant behavior is perceived negatively because it violates their gender role. These are important findings for women as they assume leadership roles and consider the management style they adopt.

Role congruity theory: A theory that holds that people tend to perceive an incongruity between leadership behaviors and the female role, and therefore are prejudiced against female leaders.

Social psychologist Alice Eagly has proposed a **role congruity theory** of prejudice toward female leaders (Eagly & Karau, 2002). The theory holds that people tend to perceive an incongruity or incompatibility between leadership behaviors and the female gender role. This perceived incongruity in turn leads to two forms of prejudice. First, people perceive women less favorably than men as potential occupants of leadership positions. This gives women less access to leadership opportunities. Second, when women engage in leadership behavior, the behavior is evaluated less favorably than the same behavior enacted by a man. One implication is that female managers who engage in behaviors that, objectively, represent effective leadership may nevertheless be ineffective as leaders because subordinates react negatively to that kind of behavior coming from a woman.

Taking an intersectional approach to gender and leadership, we must consider how race or ethnicity can shape the evaluation of women and men in leadership positions. In some cases, being marginalized or lower status on multiple social categories—such as being both Black and a woman—means facing double jeopardy, in which the multiple disadvantages are combined or amplified. By contrast, sometimes the effects of low status in one category might cancel out the effects of low status in another category. For example, we might ask what happens when a woman of color displays agency or dominance. Is the role incongruity and social backlash to her behavior similar to or different from that faced by White women? One study compared evaluations of leaders at the intersection of race and gender, asking participants to rate leaders who were (a) Black or White, (b) female or male, and (c) dominant and assertive or communal and compassionate (Livingston et al., 2012). The participants rated the effectiveness and expected salaries of the leaders. The researchers found that White men and Black women were rated similarly regardless of their behavior, while Black men and White women were penalized for expressing dominance. In short, the gender role incongruity, and subsequent social backlash, was defined differently based on race. Reflecting on the complexity of these findings, the researchers cautioned that Black women and White women likely face some unique barriers and bias in the workplace as well as some similar ones. In addition, because gender and racial stereotypes are intertwined, the perceived gender role incongruity of dominance or assertiveness depends on gender as well as race (Rosette et al., 2016). This is an exciting and important area of research as we continue to use an intersectional approach to explore how the glass ceiling impacts women from diverse backgrounds.

Are We Making Any Progress?

Feminists have been talking about the glass ceiling for decades now. Have things gotten better? Yes and no. Social psychologists Alice Eagly and Linda Carli (2007) have argued that barriers to women's advancement today are more permeable than the rigid, impenetrable barrier suggested by the glass ceiling metaphor. Instead, they propose that a labyrinth is a more apt metaphor for women's advancement in corporations. That is, today women can make it to the top, but they often have to do it by navigating complex and sometimes indirect paths, much like maneuvering through a labyrinth. Improved opportunities for women have been created by several trends. One of these is changing definitions of leadership in corporations. The old image of the dictator boss has, in many sectors, been replaced by an ideal of transformational leadership in which the leader motivates and mentors employees. The dictator boss model did not work well for many women, but the transformational leader model does. Moreover, women are rated more highly than men on many of the characteristics of transformational leadership (Eagly et al., 2003).

©iStockphoto.com/kali9.

Nonetheless, the data are clear that there remain barriers preventing or hindering women's advancement in corporations. Progress has been slow in this area. Still, in certain fields, women have quickly risen to earn substantial numbers of professional degrees. Some statistics from professions in which women have made some of the greatest advances are shown in Table 9.3. Now that women are earning so many of the professional degrees in these areas, occupational segregation will surely decrease. It is particularly interesting to note that all of these are high-paying, high-status occupations. Education can be one of the most important solutions to the problems women face in the workforce.

PHOTO 9.6
Women aspiring to nontraditional careers may face various forms of bias and discrimination; for example, some people have difficulty recognizing a woman—especially a Black woman—in a leadership role. This photograph shows a woman attorney and her client. When you saw the picture, did you perceive him as being her boss?

TABLE 9.3   **Percentages of professional degrees awarded to women in selected professions in which there have been substantial advances, 1970–2014.**

Field	1970	1980	1990	2000	2014
Dentistry	0.9%	13.3%	30.9%	40.1%	47.5%
Medicine (MD)	8.4%	23.4%	34.2%	42.7%	47.6%
Law	5.4%	30.2%	42.2%	45.9%	46.8%

Source: Data from the National Center for Education Statistics (2016).

You may be interested in which jobs pay the best for women. The top four are pharmacists, lawyers, computer software engineers, and physicians (Bureau of Labor Statistics, 2011b).

Work and Family Issues

Scarcity hypothesis:
In research on women and multiple roles, the hypothesis that adding a role (e.g., worker) creates stress, which has negative consequences for mental health and physical health.

The female gender role has always centered on maintaining the family and providing care to children. During the second wave of feminism in the 1970s and 1980s, women marched into the paid workforce, adding the responsibilities of paying jobs to their workload. Yet this all happened while women maintained their family responsibilities. In turn, the issue of combining work and family emerged. It remains one of the most important social issues in the 21st century, especially for women. Work and family issues rank high on the feminist agenda, and corporate executives realize their importance. Even the U.S. government has recognized the centrality of this issue for families; legislation on parental leave went into effect in 1993 (see Focus 9.2).

Work and Women's Psychological Well-Being

The average American woman today holds a full-time job while managing a household and a marriage and raising a child or caring for an elderly relative. Is she on overload, stressed out with all her responsibilities, prone to physical and mental illness? Or is she Supermom, able to have it all and be happy? The answer is somewhere in between these extremes, often complicated by structural and political factors.

Social scientists have asked important questions about the effects of multiple roles (e.g., worker, spouse, parent) on well-being. Broadly speaking, researchers in this area have taken two major theoretical approaches(Barnett & Hyde, 2001).

One approach proposes the **scarcity hypothesis**, which assumes that each person has a fixed amount of energy and that any role makes demands on this pool of energy. Therefore, the greater the number of roles, the greater the strain on their energy and the more negative the consequences on well-being. The conclusion from this view, then,

PHOTO 9.7
Work/family issues are among those at the top of the feminist agenda. Does combining work and motherhood serve as a source of stress, or does it enhance women's well-being?

©iStockphoto.com/monkeybusinessimages.

is that as women take on increased work responsibilities in addition to their family responsibilities, stress and negative mental and physical health consequences must result.

An alternative approach proposes the **expansionist hypothesis**, which assumes that people's energy resources are not limited and that multiple roles can have benefits for well-being. That is, just as a regular program of physical exercise makes one feel more energetic, not less energetic, multiple roles can be beneficial. According to this approach, the more roles one has, the more the opportunities for enhanced self-esteem, stimulation, social status, and identity (Barnett & Hyde, 2001). Indeed, one might be cushioned from a traumatic occurrence in one role by the support one is receiving in another role.

Expansionist hypothesis: In research on women and multiple roles, the hypothesis that multiple roles are good for mental health because they provide more opportunities for stimulation, self-esteem, and so on.

If the scarcity hypothesis is correct, then Maria is likely to feel stressed and overwhelmed by the demands of multiple roles when she takes on a paying job while her child is at day care or school. By contrast, if the expansionist hypothesis is correct, Maria is likely to feel greater self-esteem and personal fulfillment from her multiple roles. Alternatively, it might also be true that both of these theoretical approaches have some validity.

Actual research on the effects of paid employment on women's health paints a generally positive, but also complex, picture (Barnett & Hyde, 2001; Perry-Jenkins et al., 2000). In general, employment does not appear to have a negative effect on women's physical and mental health. Actually, employment seems to improve the health of both unmarried women and married women who hold positive attitudes toward employment. By being employed, Maria might gain social support from her colleagues and supervisors, as well as opportunities for success or mastery. She can develop and use different skills at work that she might not use at home, and vice versa. Factors such as opportunities for mastery and social support seem to be important to the health-enhancing effects of employment for women.

Of course, many women are not in such ideal situations. If Maria is underpaid relative to her male colleagues or if she is sexually harassed by her supervisor, she probably won't experience positive health benefits from employment. And, as income inequality persists and grows in today's economy, many work-family issues are highlighted at the intersection of gender and class. For example, poor or low-income families have few choices when it comes to finding sustainable work-family arrangements. If Maria's job has little flexibility in hours or a stingy leave policy, she'll have few options when her child gets sick and needs to stay home from school. Moreover, if Maria lacks a college education or a skilled trade, she may not have access to a better job. These factors make it less likely that poor or low-income women will find benefits from multiple roles.

A critical factor in the relation between employment and women's well-being is child care. If a mother cannot find child care, or if she feels that the available sources do not offer high-quality care for her child or are so expensive that she cannot afford them, then combining work and motherhood becomes stressful. Maria might question the value of working if the bulk of her wages go to child care or if the child care is of poor quality. Alternatively, if the child care she can afford is excellent, and she feels that her child is thriving while she's at work, then work and family roles are more likely to enhance each other.

These complexities demonstrate the importance of the *quality* of roles, not simply the quantity of them. Clearly, combining multiple low-quality roles isn't likely to help anyone. But a high-quality role that elicits joy, pride, or happiness can make a big difference in one's life, especially if other roles are less satisfying.

Researchers have proposed two processes by which multiple roles might contribute to our well-being in both positive and negative ways. One such process is **spillover**, in

Spillover: A process in which positive or negative feelings in one role carry or spill over into another role.

FOCUS 9.2

PSYCHOLOGY AND PUBLIC POLICY: FAMILY LEAVE

In 1993, the United States passed the Family and Medical Leave Act (FMLA). Prior to that legislation, the United States was one of only two industrialized nations in the world (the other being South Africa) that did not have a nationally legislated policy on parental leave. *Parental leave* refers to leave from work for purposes of recovering from childbirth and/or caring for a newborn, adopted, or foster child. An even broader term, *family leave*, also includes caring for a family member (such as an ill spouse or parent). *Medical leave* refers to attending to one's own medical condition. FMLA covers family and medical leave. Until FMLA was passed, in all but a handful of states a woman could give birth to a baby and return to work quickly—say, a month later—only to find that she had lost her job, and it was perfectly legal for her employer to have fired her for not working. There was an urgent need for legislation that ensured parents the right to care for a newborn infant and know they had their jobs waiting for them; among other things, they obviously need the income to support the baby.

FMLA requires that employers allow employees a minimum of 12 weeks of job-guaranteed, unpaid leave at the time of a birth or adoption. FMLA has several important features to note. First, it is *gender fair*—that is, all parents have equal rights to take the leave, regardless of their gender, and some couples might choose to take the leaves back to back so that the child has a parent at home with them for a total of 24 weeks, or nearly 6 months. Yet, for most families, this isn't feasible (as we explain below). A second feature is that the leave is *job guaranteed*, which means that the employee has a right to return to the same or a comparable job (in terms of pay and responsibilities) after their leave. A third feature is that the leave can be *unpaid*, at least as a minimum standard. Most couples cannot afford to lose one member's income for very long, if at all, and even fewer couples can afford to lose both members' income for any period of time. Thus, most families find it's not feasible to take back-to-back leaves totaling 24 weeks. A fourth feature is that the legislation sets a *minimum standard*. Employers can choose to be more generous. It's like the minimum wage—if it is $7.25 per hour, employers are perfectly free to pay a highly skilled person $20 per hour; they just can't pay anyone less than $7.25. In the same way, employers can be more generous with parental leave. They can allow more than 12 weeks and they can provide paid leave. Some progressive corporations have realized that it is beneficial to provide paid leave and are already doing so.

This legislation could be improved in a number of ways to support parents. Providing paid leave is a major necessary improvement. Several states—including California, Rhode Island, New Jersey, and (starting in 2018) New York—have passed additional family leave legislation mandating paid leave. Employers worry about how costly this would be to them, but these states have solved this problem as Canada has, using a small payroll tax paid by employees and then administered by their disability programs. A second improvement that is needed is to expand coverage to employees at small businesses. FMLA applies only to employers with 50 or more employees. Women work disproportionately for small businesses, and it is important to extend the coverage to all parents.

Psychology played an important role in developing and passing FMLA. Often, as Congress considers legislation, it calls on expert witnesses, such as psychologists, who can provide evidence on the need for the legislation and the potential impact that it might have. Developmental psychologists had a wealth of knowledge to share. For example, decades of research with families led to the consensus among psychologists that infants need to spend at least the first 4 months of life with a stable caregiver who can provide consistent, sensitive, and responsive care (Brooks-Gunn et al., 2010; Zigler & Frank, 1988). This stability helps infants establish a predictable routine with a reliable caregiver, regulate body processes like sleeping and eating, and ultimately form secure attachments to their caregiver. Therefore, psychologists testified before Congress that legislation should provide 4 months of parental leave to meet the important developmental needs of an infant. This expert testimony on psychological research was influential in the passage of the bill.

If parental leave is beneficial for babies, what effects might it have for parents? Feminist psychologists immediately noticed that the well-being of mothers was invisible in the parental leave debate. So they conducted a large-scale research project that adds a second focus to the psychological research: the effects of parental leave, or the lack of it, on mothers and fathers (Hyde & Essex, 1991; Hyde et al., 1993; Hyde et al., 1995). The researchers found that, in that sample, fathers took an average of 5 days of leave and mothers took an average of 8 weeks. The researchers studied the impact of taking a short leave (6 weeks or less) compared with a long leave (12 weeks or more) on women's mental health. They found that a short leave can act as a risk factor for mental health problems: When a short leave is combined with some other risk factor such as a stressful marriage or a stressful job, problems such as depression result. For example, women who took short leaves and had many concerns about their marriages had elevated levels of depression, compared with women who took longer leaves or who took short leaves but had happy marriages. They also found that many of the women in the sample wished they could have taken a longer leave than they did. The leading reason why they didn't take a longer leave was that they could not afford to do so. Parental leave also affected whether and how long mothers breastfed their babies. In short, many families wanted to take parental leave, and longer leave was beneficial for families.

This research and the research of developmental psychologists on infants' attachment needs illustrate how important psychological research can be in framing legislation that will have an impact on most of us at some time in our lives.

Sources: Berger et al. (2005); Brooks-Gunn et al. (2010); Gale (2006); Kamerman (2000); Waldfogel (2001).

which positive or negative feelings in one role might carry or spill over into another role. For example, if Maria has a productive day at work, she might bring feelings of accomplishment and satisfaction home with her, being in a generally positive mood when she interacts with her child. Spillover could also be negative, such as when her child has a tantrum at preschool drop-off, putting Maria in a bad mood just as she starts her workday. Another possible process is **compensation**, in which positive aspects or rewards from one role compensate or make up for the stresses or costs in another role. For example, Maria's supportive and loving relationship with her partner might compensate for the stresses she's been enduring at work.

Compensation: A process in which positive feelings or rewards from one role compensate or make up for stresses or costs in another role.

The Second Shift

In her book *The Second Shift: Working Parents and the Revolution at Home*, sociologist Arlie Russell Hochschild (1989, 2012) wrote about the rewards and challenges of working while raising a family. The book is based on her qualitative research with *dual-earner couples* with children—that is, two-parent households in which both parents work. And, as with nearly all of the research on dual-earner couples, all of the couples in Hochschild's sample were cisgender and heterosexual. She found that most employed mothers put in a full day of work on the job and then return home to perform a second shift of house and family work. By contrast, employed fathers did not work a second shift.

She also described studies from the 1970s concluding that, if "work" is defined as including work for pay outside the home plus work done in the home, then women worked, on average, 15 hours more per week than men did (Hochschild, 1989, 2012). Thus, over the course of a year, women worked an extra month of 24-hour days!

The problem of multiple roles for women is more than just a question of hours and quantity of roles. Hochschild found that women were also more emotionally torn between the demands of work and the demands of family. In addition, the second shift creates a struggle in some marriages. The wife, in many cases, struggles to convince the husband to share the housework equally; alternatively, she does almost all of it and resents the fact that she does. And even when husbands contribute to some of the housework, women are still responsible for all of it. In addition, much of the work the women were doing—in particular, caring for children and other relatives—was undervalued.

Hochschild concluded that we are living in a time of transition amid a social revolution in which gender roles are in flux. She described this as a "stalled revolution" in which women have been catapulted into the world of paid work even as men have not shown an analogous move into caring for children and the home environment. In this period of transition, we have not yet arrived at stabilized new social structures that promote and maintain gender equality.

While Hochschild's arguments were challenged by some researchers (e.g., Gilbert, 1993; Pleck, 1992), other research supports her conclusions. One question is whether Hochschild adequately took account of changes over the last few decades. Men's contributions to family work have increased from 1970 to the present, yet the change has been gradual and there is still not gender equity. Women have adapted, in large part, by altering the way they spend their time. In particular, women today spend as much time with their children as they did in the 1960s (Bianchi & Milkie, 2010). The dramatic change has been in the amount of time spent in housework. Today, survey data show employed married women spend only 1.6 hours per day on housework, compared with 1 hour per day spent by husbands (White House Council on Women and Girls, 2011). That is unequal, but it hardly seems like a second shift. Overall, the gender gap in housework and child care appears to have narrowed substantially over the past few decades (Bianchi & Milkie, 2010).

Yet these studies have largely relied on survey data, in which researchers ask people to estimate how much time they typically spend on housework and child care each week. Such surveys are problematic for at least two reasons: They don't take into account multitasking (i.e., doing more than one activity at a time), and people's estimates of their time use in the past week are often unreliable. Another measure is to ask participants to complete *time diaries*, in which they record how they use their time throughout a given day. Time diaries are more reliable and accurate because they include more detail, can take multitasking into account, and ask participants to remember only one day at a time.

In one longitudinal study, researchers asked heterosexual dual-earner couples to complete both surveys and time diaries of their time spent in paid work, housework, and child care (Yavorsky et al., 2015). The researchers were interested in how the division of labor within couples changed after having a baby, so they asked couples to complete the measures during the third trimester of pregnancy and then again when the baby was 9 months old. Results showed that having a baby didn't change how much time wives and husbands spent in their paid jobs: Before and after the birth, husbands spent about 2.5 hours more per week at work (see Figure 9.2). However, time diaries told a different story when it came to housework and child care. Prior to the birth, husbands and wives shared equally in their housework; after the baby arrived, wives spent 4 hours more than husbands did on housework each week. And, compared with their husbands, wives spent nearly 8 hours more on child care each week. In other words, the birth of a child resulted in a greater workload at home for wives and husbands, but wives did a greater share of that work. This isn't exactly a second shift, but it amounts to nearly 2 hours more work at home each day for women.

Some researchers have pointed out that the type of housework husbands and wives tend to do differs in terms of when it needs to be done and how often (Hook, 2010). Routine housework is more demanding of time and energy than nonroutine housework, and routine housework is more likely to be done by women. For example, dinner needs

FIGURE 9.2 The division of household labor changes after the birth of a child in heterosexual dual-earner couples.

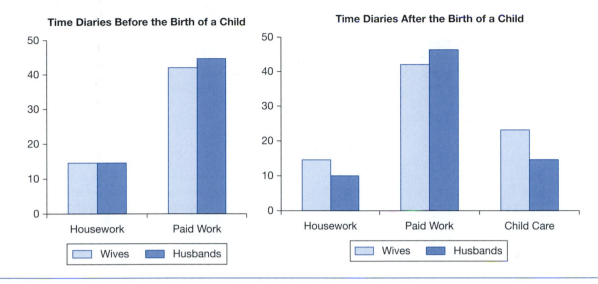

Source: Yavorsky et al. (2015). Figure created by Nicole Else-Quest.

to be made every night and within a particular window of time, but mowing the lawn or changing the oil in the car can be done less often and when it's convenient.

Attitudes about gender roles and the importance of women's paid employment have also changed since Hochschild's original work. Today, many couples aspire toward an egalitarian division of labor. Yet only about one-third of dual-earner couples share in the paid work, housework, and child care equally (Gilbert & Dancer, 1992). An important factor for the marital satisfaction of dual-earner couples is the perception of fairness in the division of labor (Coltrane & Shih, 2010). For some couples, equity in work does not necessarily require equality in work.

Overall, work–family arrangements in the 21st century have continued to evolve and are shaped by two trends: increasing diversity in families and increasing diversity in the nature of work and workplaces (Bianchi & Milkie, 2010). Heterosexual married couples have long been described as the norm, but there are increasing numbers of single parents with children, cohabiting couples, queer couples, and divorced parents with children. The research on the division of household labor in lesbian and gay couples indicates that these couples tend to have more egalitarian arrangements than heterosexual couples (Goldberg, 2013). That is, household tasks are divided more equally between same-gender partners, who also tend to be more attentive and sensitive to issues of equality within their relationships. Finding the right work–family arrangements is likely challenging across each of the diverse family arrangements in America today, but work–family researchers have not yet studied each of these in equal depth.

In parallel, work arrangements have become more complex, in part because of the trend toward a 24/7 economy, in which some businesses are expected to be open at all hours. That trend puts increasing pressure on employees to work in nonstandard arrangements, such as teleworking and evening shifts. And communication and information technologies, including e-mail and texting, often presume that workers, even when at home, are constantly available. In many of these cases, the boundaries between work and home have become blurred, which makes spillover more likely.

Experience the Research
Entitlement

In this exercise you will investigate Brenda Major's notion of entitlement and how it is related to the gender gap in wages.

Interview four psychology majors, two men and two women, preferably seniors. In each case, read them the following paragraph:

> Imagine that you have just graduated with your degree in psychology. You want to get some research experience before deciding whether to go to graduate school. You manage to land a job as a full-time research assistant in the laboratory of a professor at the University of Wisconsin. What do you think your pay would be for your first year at that full-time job? How did you come up with that number—that is, what factors did you take into account?

Write down the gender of your respondent, their estimate of pay (be sure to get it in terms of an annual salary, not an hourly wage), and their reasoning about the pay.

Were your results consistent with Major's theory of entitlement? Did the men estimate higher salaries than the women? What factors did the women take into account in deciding on the salary? Were these factors different from the men's?

CHAPTER SUMMARY

This chapter reviewed the research on how, across ethnic groups, the gender gap in wages persists and what factors might contribute to that gap, including occupational segregation, compensation negotiation, and implicit bias. Discrimination and the climate are also important considerations in gender equity in the workplace. The glass ceiling continues to prevent women from serving in leadership positions, as the leadership role seems incompatible with femininity. Moreover, federal laws regarding gender discrimination and family leave do not provide adequate protection and support for women and individuals from gender and sexual minority groups. What directions do we need to take for the future?

A combination of private change and public change is needed to foster gender equity and help all people find productive and satisfying work. In the private realm, gender roles must continue to change so that men contribute equally to and feel equal responsibility for household and child care tasks. In the public realm, some states and corporations have led the way in protecting gender and sexual minority groups against workplace discrimination, but federal protections are long overdue. We must have pay equity so that all people are paid fairly for the work they do. In addition, we need new social policies planned by the government that provide real support for dual-earner families—policies that are truly pro-family. The U.S. government urgently needs to promote high-quality, affordable child care. It also needs to devise a system to provide paid parental leave for new mothers and fathers, and opportunities for part-time work, flextime, telework, and job sharing so that working parents can successfully manage their multiple roles.

SUGGESTIONS FOR FURTHER READING

Eagly, Alice H., & Carli, Linda L. (2007). *Through the labyrinth: The truth about how women become leaders*. Boston, MA: Harvard Business School Press. Psychologists Eagly and Carli assembled the evidence about women climbing the career ladder, concluding that a labyrinth is a better metaphor than the glass ceiling.

Slaughter, Anne-Marie. (2015). *Unfinished business*. New York, NY: Random House. The first female director of policy planning at the U.S. State Department writes about the importance of caregiving and how public policy can promote gender equality in work and family responsibilities.

Biology and Gender

“ An extraordinarily important part of the brain necessary for spiritual life, the frontal convolutions and the temporal lobes are less well developed in women and this difference is inborn. . . . If we wish a woman to fulfill her task of motherhood fully, she cannot possess a masculine brain. If the feminine abilities were developed to the same degree as those of the male, her maternal organs would suffer, and we should have before us a repulsive and useless hybrid. ”

Moebius (1907), *Concerning the Physiological Intellectual Feebleness of Women*

The human brain is a spectacular organ, containing over 100 billion neurons. It is constantly rearranging its more than 100 trillion connections between neurons in response to learning and exposure to new stimuli. Spectacular though the human brain is, scientists have wondered for more than 100 years whether men's brains weren't more spectacular than women's. Women[1] have also been thought to be the victims of their "raging hormones." In this chapter, we examine what is known about genes, hormones, and the brain in women compared with men and in transgender individuals.

Genes

Typically, a human has a set of 46 chromosomes in each cell of the body. Because chromosomes occur in pairs, there are 23 pairs, classified as 22 pairs of autosomes (non-sex chromosomes) and one pair of sex chromosomes. Typically, women have the sex chromosome pair XX and men have the sex chromosome pair XY. Thus there are no genetic differences between men and women except for the sex chromosomes and the genes on them.

Traits that are controlled by genes on the sex chromosomes are called **sex-linked traits.** For such traits, a woman will have a pair of genes controlling a particular sex-linked trait, but a man will have only one gene for that trait, because he has only one X chromosome. The Y chromosome is small, containing fewer than 50 genes, compared with the X chromosome, which contains between 1,000 and 2,000 genes (Wizemann & Pardue, 2001).

Rapid advances in genetic research, including the Human Genome Project, have given us much better information about what's happening with the X and Y chromosomes. The Y chromosome contains a few especially interesting genes. One is the SRY (Sex-determining Region Y chromosome) gene, which during the prenatal period directs the fetus's gonads to differentiate in a male direction, forming testes, which then produce testosterone. It also contains a few genes related to male fertility (Lahn & Page, 1997).

The X chromosome, with its large number of genes, influences many aspects of the functioning of cells, growth, and development. It contains several genes responsible for differentiation of the ovaries during fetal development. But there is a difference between men and women in "gene dosage" from the X chromosome. Women have twice as many genes because they have two X chromosomes. This extra gene dosage is compensated for by a process called **X-chromosome inactivation**, in which one of the X chromosomes in female fetuses is inactivated or silenced in almost all cells, so only one X chromosome

Sex-linked trait: A trait controlled by a gene on the X chromosome (and occasionally on the Y chromosome).

X-chromosome inactivation: In female fetuses, the process in which one of the two X chromosomes is inactivated or silenced in nearly every cell, so only one X chromosome functions.

©iStockphoto.com/adogslifephoto.

PHOTO 10.1

X-chromosome inactivation: A tortoiseshell cat such as this one is always female (carries XX chromosomes). The pattern of coat colors results from having one X chromosome carrying the gene for black coat color and the other X chromosome with the gene for orange coat color. Different X chromosomes were inactivated in different parts of the coat, causing patches of different colors. The patches of white coat are due to a different gene.

---

[1] This chapter focuses on biology, and we use *women* throughout as shorthand to refer to people with all or some of these biological characteristics: XX chromosomes, a uterus, vagina, clitoris, and so on. Here, *women* is not used to refer to people's gender identity. Thus, this chapter focuses on the biology of cisgender women, a subset of transgender men who have female organs, nonbinary individuals who were assigned a female gender at birth, and some intersex individuals.

functions (Okamoto et al., 2004; Percec et al., 2002). A gene on the X chromosome, called "Xist," causes the inactivation (McCarthy & Arnold, 2011). The same X chromosome is not inactivated in every cell—in some cells the X chromosome from the mother is silenced, and in other cells it is the X chromosome from the father that is silenced.

Epigenetics

One of the hottest topics in genetics today is **epigenetics**, which refers to changes in gene expression caused by factors others than DNA (Bird, 2007; Salk & Hyde, 2012). (If you're interested in the details, one mechanism involves methylation—attachment of a methyl group—to cytosine in the DNA sequence.) What is meant by gene expression? All of us carry genes that are expressed at some times and not others—perhaps depending on how old we are or what our levels of sex hormones are. For example, men carry genes for beard growth, but those genes were not expressed when they were 5 years old. They aren't expressed until puberty, with its surge in testosterone levels. The bottom line with epigenetics is that environmental experiences can modify whether certain genes are expressed in an individual.

It is tough to conduct epigenetic research with humans, so researchers have used animal models instead. As an example, mother rats lick their pups a lot; it stimulates the pups and helps them grow. Some rat mothers, though, engage in more licking than other mothers do. Female pups born to high-licking mothers are themselves high lickers when they become mothers, whereas female pups who don't get much licking grow up to be low lickers (Champagne, 2008). Genetics cannot account for the effect, though, because if a pup born to a low-licking mother is given to a high-licking mother to raise, that pup is a high licker in adulthood. The explanation lies in epigenetics. The licking or care that pups receive leads to long-term effects on gene expression, which then show up when the females become mothers themselves (Champagne, 2008, 2010, 2013).

Epigenetics represents a real breakthrough, not just for geneticists, but for gender researchers as well. Epigenetic research shows that genes (DNA) are not destiny—that even the effects of genes are modified by the environment that the individual experiences over the lifespan (Salk & Hyde, 2012).

Epigenetics: Changes in gene expression caused by factors other than DNA.

Are There Genes for Being Transgender?

Scientists have searched for genes that are associated with transgender and gender dysphoria. The research has focused specifically on transsexuals, who are a subset of trans persons; transsexuals have a clear gender identity as male or female, which does not match their gender assigned at birth, and they want to undergo a social transition and medical treatments so that their body aligns with their gender identity (see Chapter 1). The term *transsexual* is not used much anymore. Instead, the terms used are *trans woman* (who has a birth-assigned male gender and female gender identity) and *trans man* (who has a birth-assigned female gender and male gender identity).

According to early research, the genes seem to be different for trans women compared with trans men (Bentz et al., 2008; Hare et al., 2008; Henningsson et al., 2005). In one study, trans women were more likely than cisgender men to have a mutation in the androgen receptor gene (Hare et al., 2008). However, not all the trans women had this mutation. Later studies that have tried to replicate the results for specific genes have often failed to find the same results, though (Zucker et al., 2016). Therefore, at least right now, there is no solid evidence of a particular gene or genes that create a tendency to becoming transgender. If there are genes for being transgender, we don't yet know what they are.

FOCUS 10.1

FEMINIST BIOLOGY

By Michal Klajban (Hikingisgood.com)—Own work, CC BY-SA 4.0.

PHOTO 10.2

Dr. Marlene Zuk, a feminist biologist at the University of Minnesota

To some people, "feminist biology" sounds like an oxymoron. Biology is a science. It's objective. Feminism is political. The two can't mix.

In fact, feminist biology has been around for a while and is rapidly gaining momentum. Feminist biology involves two goals: (1) to identify gender bias in traditional biology and (2) to create new biological research that corrects these biases. In many ways, it is like feminist psychology. Here we present three feminist biologists and their research.

Dr. Marlene Zuk is a professor at the University of Minnesota specializing in animal behavior and evolution. In her book *Sexual Selections,* Zuk (2002) documents how, in animal research, males are most often the subjects; we saw the same pattern in human research in Chapter 1. That is, there is gender bias in the choice of subjects, even with animal research. Some of that research involves early-stage drug studies that will lead to new drugs for humans, and if the drugs work differently in females, it would be important to know it. Even at the level of cells, bias can occur. For example, much research and theory has focused on males and what their sperm do to achieve fertilization of eggs, but

in fact females control much in mating. They control the frequency of mating, and they choose to mate with some males and not with others. And here is an example that's actually funny. The concept of dominance hierarchies and the "alpha male" that is so popular actually originated in research with chickens and the pecking order of hens, who can be quite ruthless! Yet the translation to "alpha males" implies that females have no dominance hierarchies or tendencies to dominate.

Dr. Sari van Anders is a professor of psychology and women's studies at the University of Michigan. She specializes in social neuroendocrinology in research with humans. That is, she studies the interplay between hormones and social behavior. In one study of hers, the experimental condition involved the masculine behavior of wielding power in a competitive situation, compared with a control condition that involved watching a travel documentary (van Anders et al., 2015). In the power condition, the participant acted out firing a subordinate in the workplace. They were directed to do it in a masculine way, for example, taking up space, infrequent smiling, and interrupting (see Chapter 5 for a discussion of these gendered behaviors). Participants provided a saliva sample both before and after the experience, and testosterone was assayed from the saliva samples. The results indicated that the experience of wielding power increased testosterone levels in women compared with the control condition. The same effect did not occur in men, probably because their testosterone levels were in a much higher range already. The bigger point here is that, although people (including biologists) usually think of hormones as influencing behavior, the reverse process also occurs. That is, behavior—in particular, gendered behavior (wielding power)—can have an effect on hormones.

Dr. Caroline VanSickle (2014) is a biological anthropologist who studies female fossils. It turns out that most of the people who have studied fossils were focusing on male skeletons. She was also part of the team that recently discovered a new species of prehumans in South Africa, *Homo naledi*. The feminist archaeologists and geologists have a website: www.trowelblazers.com.

All three of these researchers exemplify the goals of feminist biology, identifying sex bias in traditional research and then creating innovative new research on women and gender.

Basic Physiological Processes

Men and women differ in a few basic physiological processes, including metabolism and drug absorption (Hornstein & Schwerin, 2013; Wizemann & Pardue, 2001). After puberty, men have more muscle mass and, on average, a lower percentage of body fat than women. Muscle tissue metabolizes faster than fat tissue, so men have larger energy requirements—they need more food. Stated another way, women add fat if they consume the same food as that eaten by a man who does not gain fat—even if the two have the same body size. Biology can be very unfair.

Other differences between men and women in metabolism can create differences in risk for metabolic diseases and certain blood cancers, such as multiple myeloma (Petrosino et al., 2014).

Quite a bit of work has been done on differences between women and men in the immune system. In general, girls' and women's bodies mount a stronger immune response to infections than boys' and men's bodies do (World Health Organization, 2011). That said, women are more vulnerable to a few diseases than men are; one example is influenza (the flu; Klein et al., 2012). Also, being in the biological state of pregnancy has an impact on immune functioning. For example, during the H1N1 pandemic of 2009, women in the third trimester of pregnancy were especially vulnerable to infection (World Health Organization, 2011). Sex hormones appear to play a role in both phenomena, that is, why women usually have a stronger immune response and why they can be more vulnerable to infection during pregnancy (Robinson & Klein, 2012). Physiological processes such as these are important as we consider women and health issues (see Chapter 11).

Although these gender differences in basic physiological processes are important to health, there is little evidence that they have behavioral or psychological effects. Yet there are exceptions. For example, meta-analyses show that women are more sensitive to pain than men are, an effect that is found across many species (Berkley & Holdcroft, 1999; Riley et al., 1998). And it is thought to be related to gender differences in levels of testosterone and estrogen (Wizemann & Pardue, 2001). This brings us to another biological factor that may influence gender differences.

Sex Hormones

Hormones are powerful chemical substances manufactured by the various endocrine glands of the body. Endocrine glands secrete hormones into the bloodstream so that they have effects throughout the body, including effects on target organs far from the endocrine gland that secreted them. Among the endocrine glands are the gonads (ovaries and testes) and the pituitary, thyroid, and adrenal glands.

Testosterone is one of a group of "male" hormones called **androgens**, which are manufactured by the testes. The "female" sex hormones are **estrogen** and **progesterone**, which are manufactured by the ovaries. If these hormones influence behavior, then they could create gender differences.

But actually it is a mistake to call testosterone the "male" sex hormone and estrogen and progesterone "female" hormones. Testosterone, for example, is found in women as well as men. The difference is in amount, not presence or absence. In women, testosterone is manufactured by the adrenal gland and the ovaries, and the level in women's

Testosterone: A sex hormone manufactured by the testes and, in lesser amounts, by the ovaries; one of the androgens.

Androgens: A group of "male" sex hormones, including testosterone, produced more abundantly in men than in women.

Estrogen: A sex hormone produced by the ovaries; also produced by the testes.

Progesterone: A sex hormone produced by the ovaries; also produced by the testes blood is about one-tenth or less than that in men's (Janowsky et al., 1998). Estrogen and progesterone are also found in men's blood.

The differences in levels of sex hormones may affect behavior at two major stages of development: prenatally (the time between conception and birth) and during and after puberty (adulthood). Endocrinologists refer to the effects that occur prenatally or very early in development as *organizing effects* because they cause a relatively permanent effect in the organization of some structure, whether in the reproductive organs or the nervous system. Hormone effects in adulthood are called *activating effects* because they activate or deactivate certain behaviors. To understand the **prenatal** effects, we need to examine the process of prenatal gender differentiation.

Prenatal: Before birth.

Prenatal Gender Differentiation

Male–female differences exist at the moment of conception. If the fertilized egg contains two X chromosomes, then the genetic sex is female; if it contains one X and one Y chromosome, the genetic sex is male. The single cell then divides repeatedly, becoming an embryo and then a fetus. Interestingly, during the first 6 weeks of human prenatal development, the only differences between male and female fetuses are in genetic sex. That is, anatomically and physiologically, male and female fetuses develop identically during this period. Beginning approximately during the sixth week of pregnancy, and continuing through about the sixth month, the process of prenatal gender differentiation occurs (Figure 10.1). First, the sex chromosomes direct the differentiation of the gonads. Here's how that happens. As we saw earlier in the chapter, a Y chromosome contains the SRY gene, and it directs the synthesis of a substance called TDF (testis-determining factor). It causes the neutral gonads to turn into testes. If there is no Y chromosome and no SRY gene, there is no TDF and the neutral gonads turn into ovaries. The gonads then begin secreting sex hormones. That means that the internal environment becomes different for female fetuses and male fetuses because of the differences in levels of hormones that are present.

The sex hormones then influence the course of fetal differentiation. The testes produce testosterone. If testosterone is present, a penis forms. If testosterone is not present, a clitoris and vagina differentiate. Research indicates that the presence of estrogen is also critical for the development of female sexual organs (Fausto-Sterling, 1992). In addition to influencing gender differentiation of the sex organs, the sex hormones influence the rapidly developing brain (McCarthy & Arnold, 2011). The structure most affected seems to be the hypothalamus. The importance of this differentiation will be discussed later in the chapter.

Prenatal Sex Hormone Effects

Male fetuses and female fetuses, then, live and develop in different hormonal environments. Does this have any effect on later behavior?

Most of the evidence in this area is based on experiments done with animals. It may be that the effects on humans would not be the same. But let us consider the animal experiments and then see what is known about similar processes in humans (for reviews, see Hines, 2004, 2011).

Prenatal sex hormone exposure seems to affect mainly two behaviors in animals: *sexual behavior* and *aggressive behavior*. The organizing effects of sex hormones on sexual behavior have been well documented. In a classic experiment, testosterone was administered to pregnant female guinea pigs (Phoenix et al., 1959). The female offspring that

The sequences of typical prenatal differentiation in female and male humans.

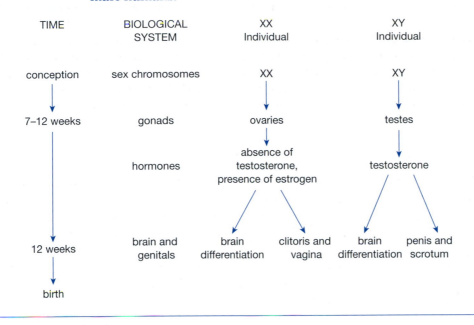

Source: Created by the authors.

had been exposed to testosterone prenatally were, in adulthood, incapable of displaying female sexual behavior (in particular, lordosis, which is a sexual posture involving arching the back and raising the hindquarters so that the male can insert the penis). It is thought that this occurred because the testosterone "organized" the brain tissue (particularly the hypothalamus) in a male direction. These female offspring were also born with masculinized genitals, so their reproductive systems had also been organized in the male direction. But the important point here is that the prenatal doses of testosterone had masculinized their sexual behavior. Similar results have been obtained in experiments with many other species as well (Hines & Collaer, 1993).

In adulthood, these hormonally masculinized females displayed mounting behavior, a sexual behavior typical of males. When they were given testosterone in adulthood, they showed about as much mounting behavior as males did. The testosterone administered in adulthood *activated* male patterns of sexual behavior.

The analogous experiment with males would be castration at birth (removing the testes, the source of testosterone) followed by administration of "female" sex hormones in adulthood. When this was done with rats, female sexual behavior resulted. These male rats responded to mating attempts from normal males the way females usually do, with lordosis (Harris & Levine, 1965). Apparently the brain tissue had been organized in a female direction during an early critical period when testosterone was absent, and the female behavior patterns were activated in adulthood by administration of ovarian hormones.

Similar effects have been demonstrated for aggressive behavior (Beatty, 1992). Early exposure to testosterone increases the fighting behavior of female mice (Edwards, 1969). Female rhesus monkeys given early exposure to testosterone show a higher incidence of rough-and-tumble play (Young et al., 1964). Thus early exposure to testosterone also organizes aggressive behavior in a "masculine" direction.

What relevance do these studies have for humans? (For a review, see Collaer & Hines, 1995.) It would be unethical, of course, to do experiments like the ones described above on human participants. Nonetheless, a number of "natural" experiments and "accidental" experiments of this sort occur. The natural experiments are the result of a few genetic conditions that cause atypical hormone functioning prenatally. The accidental experiments have occurred when pregnant women were given drugs containing hormones. (These drugs are no longer administered during pregnancy.) We will consider one of the genetic conditions as an example.

Congenital adrenal hyperplasia (CAH) is a rare recessive genetic condition that causes the fetus's adrenal glands to produce unusually large amounts of androgens beginning about 3 months after conception. CAH is most interesting in genetically female individuals, for whom the testosterone exposure is particularly atypical. Researchers have studied the behavior of CAH girls (Collaer & Hines, 1995; Hines, 2011). CAH girls are significantly more likely, compared with a control group of non-CAH sisters, to choose male-stereotyped toys for play and to prefer active, rough play. These outcomes with humans, then, look much like the experiments with animals, although the effects with humans seem to be smaller and more subtle.

Some cautions must be sounded about the research with humans. First, CAH girls are born with masculinized or ambiguous genitals—the kind of pattern that is called *intersex*. Some of them were given surgeries to correct the "problem," particularly in previous decades. We have no idea how traumatic that might have been, nor whether that trauma would have an effect on behavior. Second, the girls' parents know about the genetic condition. Might parents of CAH girls treat them differently than they would typical daughters?

Congenital adrenal hyperplasia (CAH): A rare genetic condition that causes the fetus's adrenals to produce unusually large amounts of androgens. In XX individuals, the result may be a girl born with masculinized genitals so that she has an intersex condition.

Hormone Effects in Adulthood

The effects of sex hormones in adulthood that are of interest to us fall into two categories. First, sex hormones in women fluctuate over the menstrual cycle. This raises the question of whether these hormone fluctuations cause fluctuations in mood or other psychological characteristics. (See Chapter 11 for a detailed discussion of this topic.) Second, levels of sex hormones differ in men and women. For example, as noted earlier, women have about one-tenth the level of testosterone in the blood that men do. Could it be that these different levels of hormones activate different behaviors in men and women?

As noted above, studies done with animals indicate that sex hormones in adulthood have effects on both aggressive behavior and sexual behavior. Are there similar effects in humans? Testosterone has well-documented effects on libido, or sexual desire, in humans (Bancroft & Graham, 2011; Everitt & Bancroft, 1991). For example, men deprived of their main source of testosterone by castration show a dramatic decrease in sexual behavior in some, but not all, cases. Testosterone therefore has an activating effect in maintaining sexual desire in adult men.

Research indicates that androgens, not estrogen, are related to sexual desire in women (Bancroft & Graham, 2011). If all sources of androgens in women (the adrenals and ovaries) are removed, women lose sexual desire. Women who have undergone oophorectomy (surgical removal of the ovaries, typically because of cancer) report marked decreases in sexual desire. If they are treated with testosterone, their sexual desire increases (Shifren et al., 2000). Women who seek sex therapy for low sexual desire have,

FOCUS 10.2

ENDOCRINE DISRUPTERS

A preschool girl begins growing pubic hair (Sanghavi, 2006). Frogs are born hermaphroditic, with mixed male and female organs (Hayes et al., 2002). The pesticide residues in fruits and vegetables are linked to lower sperm counts in men (Chiu et al., 2015). These cases and many others have appeared in the news in the 21st century. Are they unrelated bizarre occurrences or is there a common link that explains them?

Scientists believe that underlying such troubling cases are **endocrine disrupters**, or endocrine-disrupting chemicals (EDCs), which are chemicals found in the environment that affect the endocrine system as well as other aspects of biological functioning and behavior of animals, including humans. Evidence of the effects of endocrine disrupters comes both from studies of animals in the wild and from carefully controlled laboratory experiments. For example, a carefully controlled study showed that pregnant women with high exposure to phthalates (found in plastics) are more likely to give birth to baby boys with undescended testes or with hypospadias, a rare condition in which the urethral opening is not at the tip of the penis but somewhere else (Sathyanarayana et al., 2016).

What chemicals are the culprits? Some are pesticides and herbicides such as atrazine and DDT, used by farmers and others to kill unwanted insects and weeds. Bisphenol A (BPA) is used in making plastics such as baby bottles. PCBs, which were banned in the United States in 1976, were used in making products such as paints, plastic, and printing ink. Some of these chemicals have a half-life of over 1,000 years and therefore are still abundant in the environment even though they were banned many years ago.

These chemicals exert their effects on sexual biology and behavior by affecting the endocrine system and, specifically, the sex hormone system. Many have multiple effects. Atrazine, for example, affects both estrogen and testosterone and inhibits their binding to estrogen receptors and androgen receptors. Atrazine also depresses the LH surge that triggers ovulation, described in the next chapter in the discussion of the menstrual cycle. The insecticide DDT affects estrogen, progesterone, and testosterone by mimicking estrogen and binding to estrogen receptors as well as by altering the metabolism of both progesterone and testosterone. PCBs are both anti-estrogens and anti-androgens. These chemicals are in the food we eat and the water and milk we drink.

Even though the age of menarche (first menstruation) has changed little in the past several decades, the very early stages of pubertal development—specifically, the first development of breast tissue—is occurring nearly a year earlier than it used to. This trend is thought to be explained by EDCs in the environment. It seems likely that some chemicals are having an estrogen-like effect, and many EDCs have such effects (Mouritsen et al., 2010). Scientists are concerned that the effects of environmental contaminants may be particularly severe on children because they eat more, drink more, and breathe more than adults, relative to body weight (Trentacosta et al., 2016).

Scientists see these cases as examples of the proverbial canary in the coal mine—that is, they are small signs that something terribly dangerous is happening. The European Union is beginning to take steps to regulate these chemicals, but we have seen little action on the issue in the United States.

---

on average, lower androgen levels than age-matched controls (Guay & Jacobson, 2002). Interestingly, these androgen effects in women were overlooked for decades. Perhaps researchers had trouble believing that "male" sex hormones existed in women, and it would have been a huge stretch to imagine that such hormones actually had effects.

One innovative study examined the behavior of both trans women and trans men before and after they began hormone therapy as part of their gender-affirming treatments (Van Goozen et al., 1995; see Chapter 11 for more on health issues for transgender persons). When androgens were administered to the trans men, their aggression proneness and sexual arousability increased. When anti-androgen drugs were given to the trans women, their aggression proneness and sexual arousability decreased. The

Endocrine disrupters: Chemicals in the environment that affect the endocrine system as well as other aspects of biological functioning and behavior in animals, including humans.

results are consistent with the broader point that sex hormones have activating effects on aggressive and sexual behaviors in humans.

To summarize, sex hormone levels probably do have some effects on behaviors in adult humans, particularly aggressive and sexual behaviors. It is also likely that these effects are not as strong as they are in animals and that they are more complex and interact more with environmental factors.

Better Hormone Models

The traditional model in psychology has maintained that "hormones influence behavior"—in other words, that the influence goes in one direction only. Feminists have criticized this model. Recall from Chapter 1 that feminist scientists urge researchers to consider bidirectional models, in which A influences B, but B also influences A. As it turns out, hormone researchers have been working on exactly these sorts of effects. For example, if women engage in resistance exercise, it raises their testosterone levels (Nindl et al., 2001). Testosterone levels rise in both men and women following an interpersonal competitive victory (Schultheiss et al., 2005). (For another example, see the research of Van Anders in Focus 10.2.) That is, behavior and experience influence hormones! We shouldn't settle for simple, biologically deterministic models that assume that hormones determine behavior or that biological factors such as hormones are fixed and unchanging. Nor should we ignore hormones completely. In short, we need more complex models that will help us understand how hormones and behavior influence each other.

The Brain

In this section we will consider various hypotheses that have been proposed about differences between male and female brains and what effects those differences might have on behavior.

Brain Size

In the late 1800s, scientists discovered that men had somewhat larger brains than women. In the culture of the time, they concluded that this brain difference was the cause of the well-known lesser intelligence of women. The hypothesis was later discredited when other scientists found that men's larger brain size was almost entirely accounted for by their greater body size. Men have larger kidneys and livers than women do, too, but that doesn't mean that it gives them an advantage. The organs are just proportional to body size.

Amazingly, this same brain-size hypothesis resurfaced in the 1990s. Two scientists separately found that men's brains were larger in volume and weighed more than women's, and they argued that this brain difference had an impact on gender differences in intelligence (Ankney, 1992; Rushton, 1992). Interestingly, the same scientists also claimed that Caucasian Americans had larger brains than African Americans and that Asian Americans had larger brains than either group (Rushton, 1992)—so the argument had racial aspects as well, but here we will focus on the argument about gender.

We now have a meta-analysis on brain size. It indicates that, on average, men's total brain volume is 11.5% larger than women's (Marwha et al., 2017). That is roughly the same as the overall size difference between men and women. And there is no evidence that, among humans, brain size is correlated with intelligence.

The Hypothalamus

Gender differences do exist in the **hypothalamus**, a tiny but powerful region of the brain on its lower side (McCarthy & Arnold, 2011). These differences are the result of differentiation of brain tissue in the course of fetal development, much as is the case for the reproductive organs (Figure 10.1). Additional differentiation occurs in the days immediately after birth. Recall that the sequence of typical development consists of the sex chromosomes directing the differentiation of gonadal tissue into ovaries or testes. The gonads then secrete sex hormones, which cause further reproductive system differentiation. The fetal sex hormones, as well as several genes, also cause gender differentiation of the hypothalamus (McCarthy & Arnold, 2011). Basically, then, hypothalamus differentiation in the fetus is a process much like reproductive system differentiation.

One of the most important organizing effects of prenatal sex hormones is the determination of the estrogen sensitivity of certain cells in the hypothalamus, which contain *estrogen receptors* (Choi et al., 2001; McEwen & Milner, 2017, argue that there are also subtle organizing effects in other regions beyond the hypothalamus). If testosterone is present during fetal development, certain specialized receptor cells in the hypothalamus become insensitive to estrogen; if estrogen is present, these cells are highly sensitive to levels of estrogen in the bloodstream. This is important because of the hypothalamus-pituitary-gonad feedback loop (see Chapter 11). In this process, gonadal hormone output is regulated by the pituitary, which is in turn regulated by the hypothalamus. The hypothalamus responds to the level of gonadal hormones in the bloodstream. Hypothalamic cells in men are relatively insensitive to estrogen levels, whereas hypothalamic cells in women are highly sensitive to them. We also know that estrogen (and progesterone as well) lowers the threshold of central nervous system excitability in adults. Therefore, the estrogen sensitivity effect amounts to a greater increase in central nervous system excitability in response to estrogen in women than it does in men. The estrogen sensitivity effect is a result of the organizing effect of hormones. Hormones administered in adulthood activate male and female nervous systems differentially depending on early determination (organizing effects) of estrogen sensitivity.

What are the consequences of these gender differences in the hypothalamus? One consequence is the determination of a cyclic or acyclic pattern of pituitary release of hormones beginning with puberty. The hypothalamus directs pituitary hormone secretion. A hypothalamus that has undergone differentiation in the female direction will direct the pituitary to release hormones cyclically, creating a menstrual cycle, whereas a hypothalamus differentiated in the male direction directs a relatively steady, acyclic production of pituitary hormones.

The gender differences in the hypothalamus may have some consequences for behavior, too (Ngun et al., 2010). As discussed earlier, the organization of the hypothalamus in a male or a female direction may have some influence on both sexual and aggressive behavior.

Hypothalamus: A part of the brain that is important in regulating certain body functions, including sex hormone production.

Other Brain Regions

Researchers have claimed that other regions of the brain show gender differences. Here we consider the evidence.

The *amygdala* is a structure in the central part of the brain that is highly involved in processing emotions. There has been much speculation about whether men have larger amygdalae than women and whether that might account for the gender imbalance in some disorders such as depression (more women than men) and autism (more men than women; Marwha et al., 2017).

A meta-analysis found that amygdala volume was about 10% larger in men than women (Marwha et al., 2017). However, that is roughly the same discrepancy as in overall brain volume. If studies correct for total brain volume, gender differences in amygdala volume are nonsignificant.

The *hippocampus*, located close to the amygdala, is important in memory. Research shows that the volume of the hippocampus is reduced in people with depression (Tan et al., 2016), although what isn't clear is whether the reduced volume is the result of the depression or whether it existed before the depression and predisposed the person to it. Because more women than men become depressed, researchers have wondered whether women have smaller hippocampi than men. Again, we have a helpful meta-analysis to settle the question. It showed that, when corrected for total brain volume, there is no gender difference in hippocampal volume (Tan et al., 2016).

Some researchers have claimed that there are differences between men and women in the *corpus callosum* (CC), a region in the central part of the brain containing fibers that connect the right hemisphere and the left hemisphere. The original report, based on research with nine male and five female humans, documented a larger CC—actually, one larger subsection of the CC, the splenium—in women than in men (Delacoste-Utamsing & Holloway, 1982). But these findings were disputed (Fausto-Sterling, 2000), and later studies found inconsistent results. When a meta-analysis was conducted, it revealed that men have a slightly larger CC overall ($d = 0.21$), but again probably because men have a somewhat larger brain volume. Moreover, there were no gender differences in the size or shape of the splenium (Bishop & Wahlsten, 1997). Once again, gender similarities are the rule, even when it comes to brain anatomy.

To make matters more complicated and interesting, certain regions of the corpus callosum increase in size in women through their 50s, whereas for men the size peaks in their 20s to 30s and then declines (Cowell et al., 1992). These findings defy the notion that brain anatomy is fixed and unchanging. They also challenge simple characterizations of gender differences. For the CC, the gender difference might go in one direction or the other, depending on the age of the sample.

Right Hemisphere, Left Hemisphere

The brain is divided into two halves, a right hemisphere and a left hemisphere. These two hemispheres carry out somewhat different functions. In particular, in right-handed persons, the left hemisphere is specialized for language and verbal tasks and the right hemisphere for spatial tasks. The term **lateralization** refers to the extent to which a particular function, such as verbal processing, is handled by one hemisphere rather than both. For example, if verbal processing in one person is handled entirely in the left hemisphere, we would say that that person is highly lateralized or completely lateralized for verbal tasks. If another person processes verbal material using both hemispheres, we would say that that person is bilateral for verbal functioning.

Lateralization: The extent to which one hemisphere of the brain organizes a particular mental process or behavior.

Based on the old belief that there are gender differences in both verbal ability and spatial ability (see Chapter 8), various theories have been proposed using gender differences in brain lateralization to account for the supposed differences in abilities (for a detailed review, see Halpern, 2000).

Psychologists typically use two types of tasks to measure brain lateralization. One is the dichotic listening task, in which the researcher presents different stimuli to each ear through headphones. As it turns out, people have ear—or hearing—dominance on the same side as hand dominance. If you are right-handed, you are also right-eared! That is, your right ear is more ready, willing, and able to process stimuli than your left ear is. This ear dominance, in turn, relates to the hemispheres of the brain. Researchers in this field believe that the more dominant your right ear is (in accuracy and speed of processing stimuli), the more lateralized you are; the same would be true if you were very left-ear dominant. The other task used to measure lateralization is the split visual field, in which different stimuli are presented to different sides of your eyes, much like the different stimuli to different ears.

What does the evidence say about gender differences in brain lateralization? A meta-analysis based on 266 studies showed that—whether measured in the visual or auditory mode and whether verbal or nonverbal tasks are used—gender differences in lateralization are close to zero, $d = 0.06$ (Voyer, 1996). Clearly, then, statements such as "women are left-brained, men are right-brained" are far from the truth.

Another serious criticism of the brain lateralization hypotheses about gender differences is that they were designed to explain gender differences in verbal abilities and spatial abilities, yet the results of meta-analyses indicate currently there are no gender differences in verbal ability, and there are gender differences in only one type of spatial ability (see Chapter 8). Moreover, a meta-analysis of studies of gender differences in lateralization for language indicated no gender difference (Sommer et al., 2008).

Brain lateralization is an active area of research, and there are often flashy newspaper or magazine articles on a scientist who has discovered *the* cause of gender differences in abilities based on right-hemisphere/left-hemisphere differences. It is therefore worthwhile for you to know the kinds of ideas that have been proposed and the meta-analytic results showing no gender differences in brain lateralization (Voyer, 1996).

Neural Plasticity

You won't hear a modern neuroscientist say something like "Gender differences in the brain are hardwired" or "The brain is hardwired." The reason is that a major theme in

FOCUS 10.3

SINGLE-SEX SCHOOLING AND THE BRAIN

Single-sex public schools are the latest fad in the United States. To be clear from the outset, we are talking only about public schools, not private schools such as Catholic schools, which are free to make whatever choices they wish. The question we address here is this: Should taxpayer dollars be used to support single-sex schools because they yield better student outcomes than coed schools do?

One argument by the advocates for single-sex schooling concerns boys' brains and girls' brains. According to the website of the National Association for Single-Sex Public Education (NASSPE; 2017), single-sex schools break down gender stereotypes and are geared to the "facts" that "the brains of girls and boys differ in important ways. These differences are genetically programmed and are present at birth."

(Continued)

(Continued)

Yet as we have seen in this chapter, differences between girls' brains and boys' brains are at most small, and what neuroscientists know about neural plasticity implies that any differences could be due to differences in experience, not anything that was genetically programmed.

In their book *The Boys and Girls Learn Differently Action Guide for Teachers,* Michael Gurian, a major advocate for treating boys and girls differently in the classroom, and Arlette Ballew (2003) claim, "Boys use the right hemisphere of the brain more, girls the left" (p. 11). Yet as discussed in this chapter, a meta-analysis of studies of gender differences in lateralization found no gender difference. So a bogus scientific claim is used to make the case that boys and girls learn differently and must be segregated into different classrooms and even different schools.

Neuroscientist Lise Eliot (2009) reviewed all the available evidence on gender differences in the brain and concluded, "What I found, after an exhaustive search, was surprisingly little solid evidence of sex differences in children's brains" (p. 5). She then went on to emphasize neural plasticity.

A second claim from advocates of single-sex education is that it is needed to accommodate girls' and boys' different learning styles. Boys are "thrilled" and "aroused" by energetic teachers who talk loudly, whereas girls are intimidated to the point of nausea; thus boys should be taught through loud confrontation, whereas girls must be treated delicately (Sax, 2006). The idea of learning styles has captured the popular imagination. "I'm a visual learner" or "I'm an auditory learner," people say. In fact, though, a blue-ribbon panel commissioned by the Association for Psychological Science concluded that there is no evidence that people with one preferred learning style actually benefit more from one instructional method than from another (Pashler et al., 2009). So the argument for the importance of learning styles in education, much less gender differences in learning styles, fails the test of science.

The third argument by proponents of single-sex schools is that they break down stereotypes and allow kids to excel in counter-stereotypic areas. Developmental psychologists, however, have much evidence to indicate that, when social groupings—for example, boys versus girls or Blacks versus Whites—are made salient to children,

stereotyping and prejudice toward the other group increase (Bigler & Liben, 2007). Researchers can even get some of these effects by putting some of the kids in a classroom in red T-shirts and others in blue T-shirts and having the reds and blues line up separately. The reds start preferring other reds and feeling negative about the blues. Single-sex education does exactly that—it makes gender very salient by saying that girls and boys are so different that they cannot be educated in the same classroom. This sets the stage for increases, not decreases, in stereotyping.

Does single-sex schooling actually produce better outcomes for children? The background is that many studies on this question have weak designs. They may compare a private single-sex school against a nearby public coed school, but the children in the single-sex school come from wealthier families and their parents have more education. To use the language of Chapter 1, it is a quasi-experimental design. If the kids in the single-sex school perform better on a standardized math test, for example, it is impossible to know whether it is because of the single-sex schooling or whether the kids started out with a lot of advantages.

A large meta-analysis, with data from 1.6 million children, separated the studies into those that were uncontrolled and used weak designs like the one described above and controlled studies that used strong designs involving random assignment of children to single-sex versus coed (true experimental designs) or designs that controlled for preexisting differences between children (Pahlke et al., 2014). The results indicated a few advantages for single-sex schooling in the uncontrolled studies, but in the high-quality, controlled studies, there were no advantages for single-sex schooling on outcomes such as math performance, science performance, and self-concept. In short, single-sex schooling does not produce better outcomes.

In 2011, NASSPE changed its name to the National Association for Choice in Education. That shifted the argument from whether single-sex schooling is actually better than coed schooling to whether public schools should provide parents with a choice of single-sex schooling for their children. That would be extremely costly for schools to do, of course. How has the change in the name of the organization co-opted the feminist principle of choice?

Neural plasticity:
Changes in the brain in response to experience.

neuroscience today is **neural plasticity**, which refers to the fact that the brain changes in response to experience (Eliot, 2009). The brain simply is not hardwired (Jordan-Young, 2010). New connections between neurons are constantly being made to register learning, and other, unnecessary connections are pruned away.

The implication for gender–brain research is profound. If a researcher uses brain scanning methods (such as fMRI) with a sample of college students and finds that region X "lights up" more for men doing math problems than for women doing math problems, there is no way of telling whether it is because there are innate, hardwired, unchangeable

FIGURE 10.2

FIGURE 10.2 **Neural plasticity: If a researcher uses fMRI and finds that a region "lights up" more for men doing math problems than for women, we can't infer that those differences are hardwired. They might be due to differential experiences that caused men to use that region more than women.**

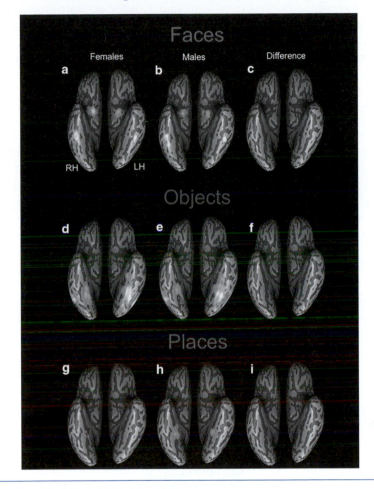

Source: Adapted from Scherf, Elbich, & Motta-Mena (2017).

male–female differences in region X or because men have had more experiences that use region X (see Figure 10.2). As an example, 10-year-old Ahmad and his father spend about a half hour every evening out in the backyard tossing a baseball back and forth. They both enjoy it. Katie, the 10-year-old who lives next door, does not toss a baseball with her father at all. He never suggested it. Neural circuits are forming in Ahmad's brain that are not forming in Katie's, and it isn't because they were born that way; it's because they are having different experiences.

Feminist Criticism

Books such as Louann Brizendine's (2007) *The Female Brain* become best sellers. Brizendine claims that there are hardwired differences between male and female brains that create all sorts of psychological effects such as men's purported inability to understand emotions and women's purported innate skill at doing so. These arguments, of course, fly in the face of modern neuroscience and the concept of plasticity, but these books sell like hotcakes. Why?

Neurosexism: Claims that there are fixed differences between male and female brains and that these differences explain women's deficits in performance or why they should occupy certain roles and not others.

Cordelia Fine (2008) has coined the term **neurosexism** for what is going on. Somehow, neuroscience research using measures such as fMRI seems more real and authoritative than other research (Beck, 2010). It has become the new way to dignify old-fashioned sexism and stereotypes, for example, that women are emotional and men are unemotional and very rational. The average reader is not a neuroscientist, hasn't heard of neural plasticity, doesn't know the limitations of fMRI research, and doesn't know how ridiculous these claims are, so they accept the ideas gladly and find their stereotypes confirmed.

The Brain Mosaic

Feminist neuroscientist Daphna Joel, based on research with thousands of human brains, has discovered an entirely different way to think about male and female brains. She calls the human brain a *gender mosaic* (Joel et al., 2015). Her research uses MRI scans of multiple brain regions, assessing the volume of each. Each region is then classified as *female-leaning* if, on average, it is larger in women, and *male-leaning* if it is larger in men. Regions that don't show a male–female difference are termed *intermediate*. Her discovery is that most people have brains that are a mosaic of female-leaning, male-leaning, and intermediate regions (see Figure 10.3). Very few women have brains with all female-leaning regions, and very few men have brains with all male-leaning regions. This research contradicts beliefs that there is a "male brain" and a "female brain." Most brains are gender mosaics or, to use a term usually used for genital structures, most brains are intersex. As Daphna Joel says, there is not a male brain and a female brain; there are human brains.

FIGURE 10.3   **A brain mosaic.**

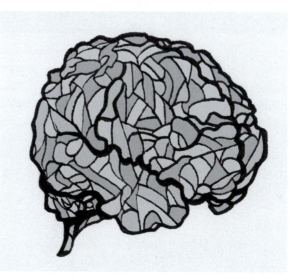

Source: Image courtesy of Ann Fink.

Transgender and the Brain

Scientists have wondered whether there might be brain differences between transgender individuals and cisgender individuals that would, at least in part, account for the psychological differences. Like the genetic research described earlier in the chapter, this research has focused specifically on trans men and trans women, who are a subset of trans persons.

The background for the research is that it has been based on the assumption that there are clear differences between human male and female brains and it has tried, for example, to see whether trans women have brains that are more male-like or female-like. The problem with these assumptions, as we have seen, is that differences between men's and women's brains are not all that clear or pronounced. But let's continue with this strain of research.

Research that looks at brain volume in untreated (have received no hormone or surgical treatments) trans women shows that their brain volume does not differ from that of cisgender men (for a review of this and the points that follow, see Guillamon et al., 2016). That is, their brain volume matches their gender assigned at birth. Similar research on trans men is in short supply, so we can't reach strong conclusions.

When considering specific brain regions, the idea behind the research is that, for some regions of cisgender brains, men have the larger region, denoted M > F ("masculine" regions), and for other regions, women on average have the larger region, denoted F > M ("feminine" regions). The major review on the question concluded that trans women have brains that are a complex mixture of masculine, feminine, and neutral regions (Guillamon et al., 2016; see also Smith et al., 2015). But, of course, that is exactly what Daphna Joel concluded about the brains of cisgender men and women, and the findings of gender mosaic brains. As of now, it is not clear that there are major differences between the brains of trans women and cisgender men, and there is little research on trans men. This pattern is true in many other areas of transgender research—trans women have been studied much more than trans men. Why do you think this has occurred?

What happens, then, when transgender folks receive hormone treatments to make their transition? Trans women receive estrogen plus anti-androgens, and trans men receive testosterone. Longitudinal studies of trans women find that, pretreatment, their brain volume matches their natal gender, male. After 4 months or more of hormone treatment, brain volume decreased and was more in the female range (Guillamon et al., 2016).

This research is very new and is generally based on small samples. It certainly does not warrant a conclusion such as "The difference between transgender women and cisgender men is in brain region X." Moreover, the research we have seen in this chapter on the similarities between cisgender women's and cisgender men's brains should make us skeptical about whether there will be clear brain markers in transgender persons.

Experience the Research

Biology and Gender Differences in the Media

Search through back issues of *Time,* the *New York Times, U.S. News & World Report*, or news websites such as *Huffington Post* to find at least two articles that report on gender differences. Do the articles report on a psychological gender difference or a biological one? If it is a psychological gender difference, what explanation does the author of the article offer? Does the author imply that it is biologically caused or environmentally caused, or is there a balanced discussion of both possibilities? If the article is about a biological gender difference, what is it? Is the information consistent with what you have learned in this chapter?

CHAPTER SUMMARY

Sex-linked traits are controlled by genes on the X chromosome and, occasionally, on the Y chromosome, which is smaller and contains relatively few genes. The SRY gene is on the Y chromosome. The field of genetics is much less deterministic than it was previously because of the discovery of epigenetics—changes in gene expression caused by factors other than DNA.

To date, despite research attempts, genetic differences between transgender and cisgender individuals have not been identified.

Men and women differ in a few basic physiological processes including, especially, metabolism and drug absorption, and these differences have implications for health. There are also differences between women and men in the immune system.

Testosterone (produced at higher levels in male bodies) and estrogen and progesterone (produced at higher levels in female bodies) may have organizing effects (due to prenatal exposure) or activating effects (due to exposure in adulthood). The process of prenatal gender differentiation begins with XX or XY chromosomes. The Y chromosome contains the SRY gene, which causes the production of TDF, which directs the gonads to become testes. In the absence of a Y chromosome, ovaries result. The gonads then secrete sex hormones, which cause additional differentiation of reproductive structures.

Congenital adrenal hyperplasia is a condition in which genetic female fetuses are exposed to high doses of androgens prenatally, creating genital structures that are intersex.

In adulthood, sex hormones can have activating effects on aggressive behavior and sexual behavior, although the effects are probably weak in humans compared with animals. Feminist scientists encourage more complex hormone models in which hormones influence behavior but behavior and experience also influence hormone levels.

Gender differences in brain size are proportional to gender differences in body size. The same is true of specific regions, such as the amygdala and the hippocampus. The hypothalamus does differ between men and women, particularly in estrogen sensitivity due to estrogen receptors. Despite hypotheses about gender differences in brain lateralization, research shows no gender difference.

Neural plasticity refers to the fact that the brain changes in response to experience. It is not "hardwired."

New research shows that the brain is a gender mosaic; each person has a mixture of regions that are male-leaning, female-leaning, and intermediate. This research defies the notion of a "male brain" or "female brain."

Neuroscientists have attempted to identify differences between the brains of transgender and cisgender individuals but, at this point, they have not succeeded.

SUGGESTIONS FOR FURTHER READING

Eliot, Lise. (2009). *Pink brain, blue brain: How small differences grow into troublesome gaps—and what we can do about it.* Boston, MA: Houghton Mifflin. Eliot, a respected neuroscientist, reviews the evidence on male-female brain differences and other possible biological influences on behavioral gender differences.

Fine, Cordelia. (2017). *Testosterone rex: Myths of sex, science, and society.* New York, NY: Norton. Fine is a wonderful writer, and this book provides a feminist critique of many biological explanations for gendered behavior.

Zuk, Marlene. (2002). *Sexual selections: What we can and can't learn about sex from animals.* Berkeley: University of California Press. This book is a great example of feminist biology by animal behaviorist Zuk. With an enjoyable writing style, she considers what biology and feminism have to offer each other, and gives detailed examples of how scientists' observations of animal behavior have been biased by gender stereotypes.

Psychology, Gender, and Health

An important component of the feminist movement has been the women's[1] health movement. The basis for the women's health movement has been a belief that when women know more about their bodies, they are empowered by that knowledge and can make well-informed health choices. One of the best books to come out of that movement is *Our Bodies, Ourselves*, written and regularly updated by the Boston Women's Health Book Collective (1972, 2011).

In this chapter we discuss some of the health topics that are specific to women. These include the menstrual cycle and reproductive health topics such as contraception,

---

[1] This chapter focuses on physical health, and we use *women* throughout to refer to people with any combination of the following organs: a uterus, vagina, clitoris, and so on. Here, *women* is not used to refer to people's gender identity. Thus, this chapter generally focuses on the health of cisgender women, a subset of transgender men who have female organs, nonbinary individuals who were assigned a female gender at birth, and a subset of transgender women who have sought medical or surgical transition.

pregnancy, childbirth, abortion, miscarriage, and infertility, as well as breast cancer and cervical cancer. We also review several health topics that are specific to transgender people, such as pubertal suppression and gender-affirming surgery. We give brief information on the physical and medical aspects of each of these topics and concentrate on the relevant psychological research that has been conducted. Ideally, we would also include research on health topics for nonbinary people, such as those who identify as genderqueer. However, almost no research has been conducted with these individuals. Of course, some nonbinary people were assigned a female gender at birth and may have a vagina, uterus, or other female reproductive organs. In certain cases, it may be possible to generalize very cautiously from some research on individuals with female reproductive organs (e.g., cisgender women), but not always. It is important that the experiences of nonbinary people be included in medical and psychological research.

First, let's review the overall statistics on gender and health and how women and transgender persons fare in the health care system.

Gender and Health

Women and the Health Care System

Feminists have long been critical of the treatment of women in the health care system (Landrine & Klonoff, 2001; Travis, 1988a, 1993; Travis & Compton, 2001). Among those criticisms are the following:

1. The physician–patient relationship reflects the subordinate status of women in society, with the physician (usually male) having power and control over the female patient.

2. Historically, the medical profession actively discriminated against women as practitioners (Walsh, 1977). And while women now earn 48% of MD degrees (Association of American Medical Colleges, 2011), they still often receive their medical training in an atmosphere that is hostile to women. The status of nurses (over 90% of whom are women) in relation to physicians also reflects the higher status of male-dominated professions and the lower status of female-dominated professions (World Health Organization, 2011). Moreover, among academic physicians, women are paid less than men, even after taking age, experience, specialty, rank, and research funding and productivity into account (Jena et al., 2016). Yet a recent analysis indicates that mortality and hospital readmission rates are lower for elderly hospitalized patients with female physicians (Tsugawa et al., 2017).

3. Medical care offered to women is often inadequate, irresponsible, or uncaring. As many as 70% of **hysterectomies** (surgical removal of the uterus) are unnecessary (Broder et al., 2000). Women are 55% more likely than men to receive a prescription for an anti-anxiety drug or an antidepressant during an office visit with a physician (Simoni-Wastila, 1998; Svarstad et al., 1987), leading some to conclude that women's physical health problems are likely to be misdiagnosed as psychological.

4. Medical research conducted on women is often irresponsible or simply missing. For example, far more contraceptives have been developed for women

Hysterectomy: Surgical removal of the uterus.

than for men, and thus the health risks associated with them have been borne disproportionately by women. One notorious example is the Dalkon Shield, an intrauterine device (IUD) that was withdrawn from the market after 17 women died of pelvic inflammatory disease directly traceable to the IUD (Travis, 1988a). Class and ethnicity are also factors relating to irresponsible medical research. For example, the initial field trials for the birth control pill, whose risk was unknown at the time, were conducted among poor women in Puerto Rico. Yet women often have not been included in clinical trials of drugs or other medical interventions, and even when they have been, gender has not been analyzed, so it is impossible to tell whether the drug is as effective in women as it is in men (Harris & Douglas, 2000; Melloni et al., 2010).

©iStockphoto.com/Peopleimages.

PHOTO 11.1
Women now earn 48% of MD degrees but are paid less than their male counterparts.

Regarding the last point, these problems with clinical trials were documented in a scathing 1992 report by the U.S. government's General Accounting Office. A number of women in Congress successfully introduced legislation, passed in 1993, requiring that clinical trials involving a disease found in both women and men be carried out in a way that allows the researchers to determine whether the treatment affects women or members of ethnic minority groups differently from others. Efforts such as this demonstrate how the women's health movement has fostered tremendous changes in health care policy (Helmuth, 2000).

Transgender Persons and the Health Care System

An important issue in gender and health is the treatment of transgender persons in the health care system. Transgender women and men have unique health needs, many of which can be complicated by their experience of marginalization, prejudice, and discrimination. The following are some of the issues regarding the treatment of transgender persons in the health care system:

1. Research on transgender health issues is limited (Stroumsa, 2014). Large-scale studies that assess the risk for particular diseases or clinical trials of treatments within the transgender population remain scarce. In particular, there is a serious need for evidence-based research on pubertal suppression (see Chapter 7) and **gender-affirming therapies** for transgender persons, including hormonal therapy and surgical therapy. Research on transgender health is necessary so that transgender persons can make informed choices about their health care in consultation with their health care providers.

2. Of the existing medical research, transgender persons are often objectified and/or misgendered (Stroumsa, 2014). In particular, medical research has long prioritized gender assigned at birth.

Gender-affirming therapies: Medical care designed to assist individuals in adjusting their primary and secondary sex characteristics to align with their gender identity. May include hormonal therapy, surgical therapy, or both.

3. Structural factors—such as poverty, incarceration, and gaps in insurance coverage—limit access to health care for multiply marginalized groups. For example, many insurance plans do not cover expensive gender-affirming therapies, and transgender persons who are also low-income, incarcerated, or people of color are especially likely to lack access to affordable and adequate health care. Indeed, a large-scale national survey of transgender persons' health needs, funded by the Network for LGBT Health Equity, found that 19% of respondents lacked insurance coverage (Grant et al., 2011).

4. Discrimination and prejudice create barriers to health care for many transgender persons. The Network for LGBT Health Equity study found that 19% of respondents reported that they'd been denied health care because of their gender identity and that 28% had experienced verbal harassment in a medical setting (Grant et al., 2011).

5. Access to gender-affirming therapy is limited by the shortage of medical doctors who are knowledgeable about and comfortable providing care to transgender persons. One national survey found that nearly two-thirds of transgender persons reported that their doctors were unaware of transgender health needs. Currently, most medical school curricula do not address transgender health issues (Obedin-Maliver et al., 2011).

For the health needs of transgender persons to be treated appropriately and sensitively, these concerns will need to be addressed. The trans activist movement has fueled many recent changes in health care policy, some of which were written into the Affordable Care Act—often referred to as Obamacare—which was signed into law by President Barack Obama in 2010. For example, the health care law prohibits discrimination against LGBT patients.

Health Issues at the Intersection of Gender, Ethnicity, and Class

Feminist theory and intersectionality emphasize the importance not only of gender, but of ethnicity and social class as well. That principle is important as we consider the health care system.

Around the world, being born female is dangerous to your health, especially if you are also poor. For example, although pregnancy and childbirth are relatively safe in the United States—only 1 woman in 3,700 dies from them—an African woman's chance of dying from pregnancy or childbirth is 1 in 16 and an Asian woman's is 1 in 65. Many of these deaths are due to poverty and lack of access to medical care. Malnutrition is a major factor in pregnancy-related deaths and many other conditions as well. In many areas, when food is scarce, men and boys receive the best and the most.

In the United States, boys and men have a higher death rate than girls and women at every age, from conception to old age. More male than female fetuses are conceived, yet more male fetuses also die before birth. At age 100, women outnumber men by a 5:1 ratio. A baby born in the United States today is expected to live approximately 79 years (Arias et al., 2017). However, life expectancy varies considerably at the intersection of gender and race/ethnicity. For example, the average life expectancy is approximately 81 years for White women and 77 years for White men, but 78 years for Black women and 72 years for Black men.

Data on the 10 leading causes of death for women and men are shown in Table 11.1. You'll notice striking gender differences as well as gender similarities. Suicide and homicide are more common among men than women, yet heart disease and cancer are the top two causes of death for both women and men in all ethnic groups.

TABLE 11.1 Ten leading causes of death for women and men, by racial/ethnic group (percentage of deaths within each group).

	Women					Men				
	White	Black	American Indian	Asian/Pacific Islander	Hispanic	White	Black	American Indian	Asian/Pacific Islander	Hispanic
Cancers	21.3	22.5	17.4	27.3	22.6	23.8	22.3	17.6	26.4	20.6
Heart disease	22.4	23.2	16.8	20.0	19.7	25.0	24.1	19.5	23.0	20.4
Accidents/injuries	4.0	3.0	8.1	3.3	4.5	6.2	6.0	13.6	5.3	9.7
Cerebrovascular diseases	5.9	6.2	4.3	8.1	6.0	4.0	4.9	3.0	6.1	4.4
Diabetes	2.2	4.6	5.4	3.8	4.7	2.8	4.1	5.1	3.9	4.5
Respiratory diseases	6.7	3.2	5.2	2.6	3.1	5.8	3.2	3.7	3.4	2.6
Alzheimer's disease	5.4	3.1	2.7	3.9	4.3	2.3	*	*	1.6	*
Liver diseases	*	*	5.7	*	2.3	*	*	4.9	1.2	4.2
Pneumonia and influenza	2.2	*	2.7	3.0	2.5	2.0	1.7	2.0	*	2.1
Kidney diseases	1.6	3.0	2.1	2.0	2.0	1.7	2.6	*	2.1	2.0
Suicide	*	*	*	1.2	*	2.6	*	3.7	2.6	2.8
Assault (homicide)	*	*	*	*	*	*	4.3	2.1	*	2.3
Septicemia	1.5	2.3	*	1.2	*	*	1.9	*	1.2	*
Hypertension	*	1.9	*	*	*	*	*	*	*	*

* Cause is not in the top 10 for that group.

Source: Data from Kochanek et al. (2016).

Note: The U.S. government continues to categorize by race and Hispanic origin separately, such that Hispanic persons may also identify as belonging to another racial/ethnic group. Data for White and Black persons are for persons of non-Hispanic origin only. Data for American Indian and Asian/Pacific Islander persons include persons of Hispanic and non-Hispanic origins.

Women of color have several special health concerns (Ro, 2002; Travis & Compton, 2001; Walters & Simoni, 2002; Williams, 2002). For example, women of color experience higher rates of infant mortality than White women. This in turn is related to higher rates of low-birth-weight babies among women of color. And this in turn is related to more frequent adolescent childbearing among people of color. That is, adolescent mothers are more likely to have low-birth-weight babies, who have a higher death rate.

Chronic diseases are more prevalent among women of color than among White women. Examples include diabetes, high blood pressure, and heart disease.

Women of color are overrepresented among the poor. We have, then, a combination of sexism, racism, and poverty contributing to reduced access to necessary health care. This in turn creates more health problems for these women. There is an urgent need for equal access to health care.

In addition, research evidence demonstrates another health risk for multiply marginalized women: stereotypes and discrimination. In one study, researchers used Claude Steele's stereotype threat manipulation (discussed in Chapter 3). African American and White college students were placed in either a stereotype threat condition or a control condition and then worked on some difficult tests (Blascovich et al., 2001). African American students under stereotype threat not only performed worse but also exhibited larger increases in blood pressure compared with White or with African American students not under stereotype threat. And high blood pressure is a major risk factor for heart disease.

In another study, African American and White women were asked to imagine that they had been wrongfully accused of shoplifting in a department store and then to speak in their own defense (Guyll et al., 2001). African American women, but not White women, reacted with elevated blood pressure. Stereotype threat and incidents of discrimination may be chronic, repeated stressors that pose serious risks to one's health, particularly for women of color and poor women.

Menstruation

Biological Aspects of the Menstrual Cycle

Follicle: The capsule of cells surrounding an egg in the ovary.

Ovum: An egg.

Follicular phase: The first phase of the menstrual cycle, beginning just after menstruation.

Ovulation: Release of an egg from an ovary.

Luteal phase: The third phase of the menstrual cycle, after ovulation.

Menstruation: A bloody discharge of the lining of the uterus; the fourth phase of the menstrual cycle.

The average female person is born with about 400,000 **follicles** in her ovaries, each containing an **ovum**. During a menstrual cycle, one egg is released from a follicle, traveling down the fallopian tube for possible fertilization and implantation in the uterus. Figure 11.1 shows a diagram of female reproductive anatomy.

We can separate the menstrual cycle into four phases, each describing the state of the follicle and ovum within that phase (see Figure 11.2). The first phase is the menstrual phase, beginning on day 1. Yet, physiologically speaking, it actually represents the end of the cycle. Next, extending from about day 4 to day 14 is the **follicular phase**. During the follicular phase, a follicle matures and swells. The follicular phase ends when the follicle ruptures and releases the egg; this marks **ovulation** and the beginning of the ovulatory phase. The next phase is the **luteal phase**, during which a group of reddish-yellow cells, called the corpus luteum, forms in the ruptured follicle. Then, the menstrual phase begins again, marked by **menstruation**, when the endometrium (i.e., the inner lining) of the uterus, which had built up in preparation for nourishing a fertilized egg, is sloughed off. The days we provide are approximate, because every person's menstrual cycle (more specifically, their menstrual and follicular phases) varies in length. In general, if an egg is not fertilized, menstruation begins 14 days after ovulation.

FOCUS 11.1

GENDER AND INFECTIOUS DISEASE

Infectious diseases—such as HIV, diarrheal diseases, influenza and other respiratory diseases, and Ebola—are among the top 10 causes of death worldwide (World Health Organization [WHO], 2017). In lower-income countries, these diseases have especially high and devastating death tolls. So what's gender got to do with any of this?

Researchers at WHO (2011) provided a detailed framework for analyzing how gender and gender roles impact infectious disease transmission and outcomes. They noted how it is crucial to consider not only biological aspects of gender but also psychological aspects of gender when analyzing gender and infectious disease. For example, biological aspects of gender can influence immune responses (see Chapter 10). Pregnancy is also included here; for example, during the 2009 H1N1 (swine flu) pandemic, pregnant women in their third trimester were especially vulnerable to the disease (WHO, 2009). Psychological aspects of gender can also influence infectious disease transmission and outcomes; these aspects include gender norms and behaviors, gendered division of labor, and gendered access to and control over resources and decisions.

The WHO researchers described how these biological and psychological aspects of gender can influence disease transmission and outcomes at four levels:

1. *Vulnerability to infectious disease*. Gender can affect our risk and vulnerability to specific infectious diseases, particularly through the gendered division of labor. Consider, for example, how women are typically responsible for meal preparation. In lower-income countries, solid fuels (e.g., wood, coal) are often used for cooking, which makes women in those contexts more vulnerable to pneumonia and lower respiratory diseases (WHO, 2006).

2. *Exposure to pathogens*. Gender can influence our exposure to infectious disease. For example, because the female role typically includes caring for sick relatives, women are more often exposed to pathogens. During the 2014–2016 Ebola outbreak in West Africa, women's traditional roles in caregiving, performing funeral rites, and cross-border trading resulted in more women than men contracting and dying from the disease (Manivannan, 2015).

3. *Response to illness*. Gender can impact how individuals respond to illness, especially in obtaining access to health care. Here, gender inequality has life-or-death consequences. For example, in many parts of the world, sons are more valued than daughters and are thus given better access to health care. One study in India found that parents are more likely to vaccinate boys than girls against diseases such as measles (Corsi et al., 2009). Similarly, gender inequality in household decision-making power extends to health care; 54% of married women in South Asia do not have the ability to make decisions about their own health (UNIFEM, 2009).

4. *Effectiveness of public health interventions*. To be effective, public health interventions must be targeted and communicated in a way that is sensitive to gender. For example, if women are expected to be responsible for carrying out aspects of a public health intervention—such as changes in cleaning the home, preparing food, or caring for children—then public health officials need to communicate directly with those women. In some countries, this may involve taking into account restrictions on women's access to public spaces as well as their lower literacy rates.

Of course, good science is essential to our understanding of how the biological and psychological aspects of gender apply at each level of analysis. That means we need to collect data and compute statistics on gender and infectious diseases. However, many communities and organizations responsible for such statistics do not take the psychological aspects of gender into account.

FIGURE 11.1   Schematic cross-section of the female pelvis, showing sexual and reproductive organs.

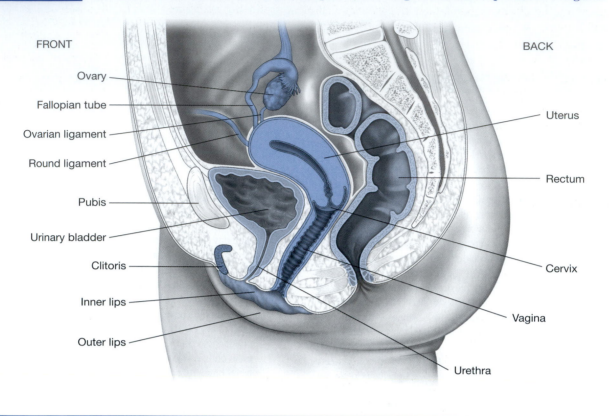

FIGURE 11.2   Changes in levels of estrogen and progesterone across the phases of the menstrual cycle.

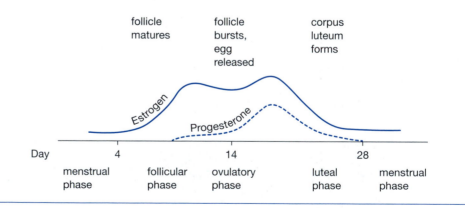

© Cengage Learning 2013.

These cyclic phases are regulated by hormones that act in a negative feedback loop with one another (Figure 11.3), so the production of a hormone increases to a high level, producing a specific physiological change. The level is then reduced through the negative feedback loop. Here we are concerned with two basic groups of hormones—those

produced by the ovaries, most importantly estrogen and progesterone, and those produced by the pituitary gland, most importantly **follicle-stimulating hormone** (**FSH**)
and **luteinizing hormone** (**LH**). We also need to consider regulation of the pituitary by
the hypothalamus, an important region of the brain on its lower side (Figure 11.3), by
gonadotropin-releasing hormone (**Gn-RH**). The overall pattern of the negative feedback loop is that the activity of the ovary, including its production of estrogen and progesterone, is regulated by the pituitary, which in turn is regulated by the hypothalamus,
which is sensitive to the levels of estrogen produced by the ovaries.

The regulation of the menstrual cycle involves interactions among the levels of these
hormones. The pituitary secretes FSH, which signals the ovaries to increase production

**Follicle-stimulating
hormone (FSH):** A
hormone secreted by the
pituitary that stimulates
follicle and egg development.

**Luteinizing hormone
(LH):** A hormone secreted
by the pituitary that triggers
ovulation.

**Gonadotropin-releasing
hormone (Gn-RH):** A
hormone secreted by the
hypothalamus that regulates
the pituitary's secretion of
hormones.

FIGURE 11.3   **Schematic diagram illustrating the negative feedback loops
controlling hormone levels during the menstrual cycle. FSH
and LH are produced by the pituitary gland and influence
production of estrogen and progesterone in the ovaries. The
hypothalamus is sensitive to levels of these hormones and, in
turn, regulates levels of FSH and LH.**

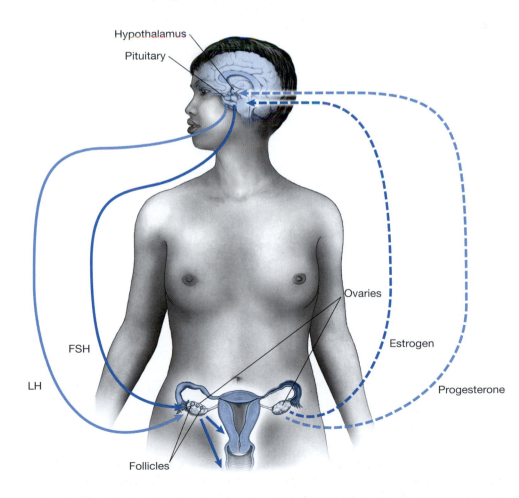

Hypothalamus

Pituitary

Ovaries

Estrogen

FSH

Progesterone

LH

Follicles

of estrogen and to bring several follicles to maturity, thus initiating the follicular phase. The resulting high level of estrogen, through the feedback loop, signals the pituitary to decrease production of FSH and to begin production of LH, whose chief function is to trigger ovulation. Temporarily, FSH and LH induce even more estrogen production, which further lowers the amount of FSH. At this point the level of LH spikes, causing the follicle to rupture and release the egg. The corpus luteum then forms in the ruptured follicle. The corpus luteum is a major source of progesterone. When progesterone levels are sufficiently high, they will, through the negative feedback loop, inhibit production of LH and simultaneously stimulate the production of FSH, beginning the cycle over again.

Estrogen has a number of functions and effects in the body. It maintains the lining of the vagina and uterus and provides the initial stimulation for breast growth. Its nonreproductive functions include increasing water content and thickness of skin and slowing growth rate. At the beginning and the end of the menstrual cycle, estrogen is at a low level. In between these two times, it reaches two peaks, one immediately prior to and during ovulation, the other in the middle of the luteal phase (Figure 11.2).

Progesterone is especially important in preparing the uterus for implantation of the fertilized ovum and maintaining pregnancy. Because the corpus luteum is a major source of progesterone, progesterone level peaks during the luteal phase and is otherwise low.

Dysmenorrhea

Dysmenorrhea: Painful menstruation; cramps.

Painful cramps during menstruation are called **dysmenorrhea**. Some women get menstrual cramps regularly, some women get them some of the time, and some women don't get them at all. For those who do experience dysmenorrhea, the menstrual phase can be a challenging time. It is very difficult for a person who does not experience severe dysmenorrhea to understand precisely how it feels to those who do experience it. Traditional medical remedies have not been completely successful in treating the problem. Over-the-counter drugs such as Midol help some people some of the time, but they do not help everyone. For some, healthy habits—such as adequate sleep, exercise, and a healthy diet—and managing stress may be helpful in limiting the pain.

Prostaglandins: Hormone-like biochemicals that stimulate the muscles of the uterus to contract.

Menstrual cramps are caused by **prostaglandins**, hormone-like substances produced by many tissues of the body, including the lining of the uterus (Deligeoroglou, 2000). Prostaglandins cause smooth muscle to contract and can affect the size of blood vessels. Women with severe menstrual pain have unusually high levels of prostaglandins. The high levels cause intense and painful uterine contractions; these contractions in turn choke off some of the uterus's supply of oxygen-carrying blood, which only increases the pain. Prostaglandins may also cause greater sensitivity in nerve endings. The combination of the uterine contractions, lack of oxygen, and heightened nerve sensitivity produces cramps.

As a result of this analysis of the causes of cramps, antiprostaglandin drugs are now used in treatment. The drug is mefanamic acid and is sold under brand names such as Ponstel. Other, similar drugs are Motrin, Naprosyn, and Anaprox.

Psychological Aspects of the Menstrual Cycle

The perception that girls and women experience personality or mood changes depending on the phase of their menstrual cycle is common. Yet, do empirical data support this notion? Here we will examine the evidence on the nature and extent of these moods and behavior shifts and their relationship to the hormone cycles occurring during the menstrual cycle.

One approach to this question is to ask women to report retrospectively their symptoms and moods at various phases of the cycle. Unfortunately, such studies are largely useless because retrospective accounts, particularly of such subjective phenomena as moods in relation to one's menstrual cycle, are notoriously unreliable and have not been demonstrated to correlate with other indicators of premenstrual symptoms (Haywood et al., 2002; Marván & Cortés-Iniestra, 2001).

Another approach is to ask women to complete daily diaries throughout the cycle. Ideally, this is done across several menstrual cycles in a diverse sample of women. For example, one well-designed study followed a random sample of Canadian women between the ages of 18 and 40 for 6 months (e.g., Romans et al., 2013; Romans et al., 2017). Participants were given smartphones and completed surveys on their moods, health, stress, and social support at the same time each day. The researchers also asked the women each day if they had gotten their period, and then determined women's menstrual phases based on that information. The results showed that fluctuations in some of the women's moods (e.g., sadness, irritability) were greater during the menstrual and premenstrual phases than during midcycle. Yet these effects were very small. By contrast, women's reports of stress, health, and social support had much larger correlations with their mood fluctuations. And while women's reports of feeling like they wanted to cry were higher during the premenstrual and menstrual phases, there were no differences in actual crying. In sum, the results of the research suggest that there are small fluctuations in mood corresponding to the phases of the menstrual cycle, at least in some women, but that factors such as stress, health, and social support are more important.

Might these mood changes somehow be linked to changes in hormone levels occurring during the menstrual cycle? For example, it seems that high levels of estrogen (at ovulation) might be associated with positive moods, but low levels of estrogen and progesterone premenstrually might be associated with negative moods. Yet, this conclusion has long been criticized on a number of counts (Hardie, 1997; Parlee, 1973; Stanton et al., 2002). First, virtually all of the data (with some exceptions discussed below) presented to support this conclusion are correlational; correlation does not imply causation. In other words, the data simply demonstrate a correlation between cycle phase or hormone levels and mood, but they cannot tell us that hormones actually cause or influence mood. Indeed, we could just as easily conclude from these data that the direction of causality is the reverse—that psychological factors affect hormone levels and menstrual cycle phase.

One approach in responding to the issue about correlational data involves examining how oral contraceptives—which involve altering the monthly cycles of estrogen and/or progesterone—might shape the links between moods and menstrual phase. Oral contraceptives may be *monophasic* (pills that provide a steady high dose of both estrogen and progestin, a synthetic progesterone, for 20 or 21 days) or *triphasic* (pills that provide 15 days of estrogen, followed by 5 days of estrogen-progestin, similar to the natural cycle, but at higher levels). A review of such studies found that women taking triphasic pills show the same kinds of mood changes as women not taking any oral contraceptives (Oinonen & Mazmanian, 2001). Because triphasic pills produce an artificial hormone cycle that parallels the natural one, these findings suggest that monthly hormone fluctuations may be linked to mood fluctuations. Moreover, monophasic pill women tend to show greater mood stability compared with triphasic pill and nonpill women. Therefore, it appears that the steady high level of both hormones leads to a steady level of mood.

Premenstrual syndrome (PMS): A combination of severe physical and psychological symptoms (such as depression) occurring in some women for a few days before menstruation.

A second criticism of this area of research is that the term **premenstrual syndrome (PMS)** is poorly defined. For example, the range of symptoms is broad, including a variety of physical, psychological, and behavioral features. In addition, which days of the cycle count as "premenstrual"? It would be worthwhile to know what proportion of women experience premenstrual symptoms, but because the concept is so poorly defined, estimates of this proportion vary from 25% to 80% (Stanton et al., 2002). In view of the vagueness of the definition, it is not surprising that these estimates are not consistent, and until the "syndrome" is more clearly defined, we can have no really accurate estimate of its incidence. At least from these data it seems fair to conclude that premenstrual syndrome is far from universal among women.

A third problem with this area of research has to do with participants' expectations. Many women are socialized by various forces (e.g., menstrual drug ads) to expect to feel more negative feelings premenstrually. In turn, those expectations may shape how women perceive or attribute their moods (Romans et al., 2017).

A subtle problem of interpretation exists in menstrual cycle research. A typical conclusion is that symptoms increase or that mood is negative premenstrually. Perhaps, however, the premenstrual state is the usual one, and what occurs is really a decrease in symptoms, or a positive mood shift, at ovulation. This is essentially a problem of establishing a baseline of behavior—and what should that be? Should it be the average for men? Or are men irrelevant to this research? These are complex questions.

Also noteworthy are the tremendous cultural influences on menstrual cycle mood shifts (Woods et al., 1995). In many societies and religions, a menstruating woman is seen as unclean, and many taboos arise to prevent her uncleanness from spreading to others (Golub, 1992). For example, she may not be permitted to cook while menstruating, or she may even be isolated from the rest of the community in a separate hut outside the village. Such superstitions become subtler in modern America, but they still persist. For example, many women abstain from sexual activity during their periods. There is also considerable evidence of cultural influences on menstrual distress. An analysis of over 200 advertisements for menstrual products in popular women's magazines indicated that the common theme was heightening insecurities (Simes & Berg, 2001). The ads talk about the possibility of "accidents," embarrassment, "getting caught" having

PHOTO 11.2
Does advertising for menstrual drugs contribute to the social construction of PMS?

your period (i.e., others find out), feeling dirty or unclean, and odor. Drug ads, of course, emphasize pain and their products' ability to relieve PMS. The sign over the aisle in Walgreen's calls them "feminine hygiene" products—"hygiene" meaning practices such as cleanliness that preserve health. If a menstruating woman has to use hygiene products, she must be unclean. Is all this so different from the menstrual hut?

Just as feminist approaches to science often highlight alternative interpretations of phenomena, the perspectives of different ethnic groups can suggest new interpretations. For example, many American Indian women believe that menstruation is a time of centering and balancing oneself (Hernandez, 1990). The menstrual flow out of the body washes away impurities and the negative things that have occurred during the month. Reflecting their close connection to nature, American Indian women refer to the menstrual period as being "on the moon," which is considered a positive time.

The Social Construction of PMS

The diversity of women's premenstrual experiences across cultures and history supports a feminist interpretation that premenstrual syndrome is socially constructed. As we discussed in Chapter 6, the expression of emotions is carefully regulated by gendered display rules. For most emotions—love, sadness—it is far more acceptable for women to express them than for men. Anger is an exception. The expression of anger by men is tolerated; it is not for women. The expression of anger by women is socially unacceptable in large part because it interferes with the performance of their gender role, which requires nurturance and emotional support to others. Nonetheless, many women have plenty to be angry about—lower status jobs, unequal pay for equal work, and gender-based violence, for example.

So, while many women feel angry or irritable, expressing or even feeling these emotions is a serious deviation from social norms. This creates the need for a socially acceptable explanation for their emotions. Enter PMS.

From a psychological or social constructionist point of view, PMS can be seen as an attribution for particular emotions (attributions for emotions were discussed in Chapter 6). A woman experiences or expresses a particular emotion. To what does she attribute it? If the emotion is a socially unacceptable one, such as anger or irritability, she and others seek a socially acceptable attribution, and society makes PMS a readily available attribution. Magically, she isn't really angry; she is just in that temporary state of insanity, PMS. With a single stroke of attribution, her emotion no longer violates social norms, but at the same time, any real feelings of true anger she may have, perhaps toward her husband or her boss, are also brushed away. So, while her anger becomes temporarily acceptable, it remains impotent and ineffectual.

Practical Implications

In assessing the practical implications of research on mood shift and menstrual phase, some important considerations should be kept in mind. First, the magnitude of the mood shift depends on the individual woman. Certainly in practical situations, the magnitude of the mood shift is most significant. For instance, it is much more essential to know that a particular woman experiences mood shifts so small as to be unnoticeable in her work and interpersonal relations than it is to know that she experiences slight mood shifts detectable only by sensitive psychological tests. Hence the most important characteristics are individual ones, just as they are for men.

Second, in making practical decisions about hiring people, performance is certainly more crucial than mood. Research on performance—such as intellectual or athletic performance—generally shows no fluctuations over the cycle (Golub, 1992; Stanton et al., 2002). Research has found no fluctuations in academic performance, problem solving, memory, or creative thinking (Golub, 1992). Thus there is no evidence of cycle fluctuations in the kinds of performance that are important on the job.

In one particularly interesting study, female pilots were tested in a flight simulator to assess their performance in the mid-luteal and menstrual phases (Mumenthaler et al., 2001). The results indicated no significant difference between performance in the two phases and no significant correlation between performance and estradiol (an estrogen) or progesterone levels. The flying public should be happy to know about this one.

There's one exception to this pattern, however. Some studies have found menstrual cycle fluctuations in three-dimensional spatial ability (Hausmann et al., 2000; McCormick & Teillon, 2000; see Chapter 8 for more on spatial abilities). Spatial test performance is highest during menstruation, when estradiol and progesterone levels are low. Interestingly, spatial performance is positively correlated with women's testosterone levels and negatively correlated with their estradiol levels (Hausmann et al., 2000). In addition, one study found that women's spatial scores during the menstrual phase did not differ significantly from men's (McCormick & Teillon, 2001).

In summary, the research suggests that menstrual cycle changes in hormone levels are linked to mood fluctuations in at least some women. Women show substantial variability in these menstrual cycle–mood relationships (Kiesner, 2011). Importantly, there is no evidence of fluctuation in performance. The existing research has many problems: Most of it is correlational in nature, and expectations complicate interpretations. Cultural factors may also contribute to mood shifts.

Menopause

Physical and Psychological Changes

Amenorrhea: The absence of menstrual periods.

Menopause: The cessation of menstruation.

As women age, their ovaries also age and reduce their production of estrogen. In turn, ovulation and menstruation ceases. After 12 months of **amenorrhea** (the absence of menstrual periods), a woman is considered to be menopausal. On average, **menopause** (the cessation of menstruation) begins around age 51. A number of symptoms may occur at this time, including vasomotor symptoms (e.g., "hot flashes," night sweats), vaginal dryness, and sleep difficulties (Al-Safi & Santoro, 2014).

How common are these symptoms? The Study of Women's Health Across the Nation studied over 16,000 American women from diverse racial/ethnic groups during the menopausal transition. About 60% to 80% of those women reported experiencing vasomotor symptoms, peaking just before actual menopause (Gold et al., 2006). While vasomotor symptoms are experienced across racial/ethnic groups, the rates are highest among African American women (Gold et al., 2006). In addition, the study found that sleep difficulties occur in nearly 40% of women during the menopausal transition (Kravitz et al., 2003). For most women, these symptoms subside within a few years.

Just as there is a stereotype that the menstrual cycle affects mood, there is a stereotype that menopausal women are depressed and irritable. Yet the evidence indicates that depression incidence is no higher during menopause than at other times in a woman's life (Avis, 2003). For women who do experience depression during the transition to menopause, vasomotor symptoms and sleep difficulties appear to be responsible (Bromberger et al., 2007; Shifren & Schiff, 2010).

In general, the evidence indicates that menopause does not bring on an avalanche of problems, whether one looks at well-sampled studies of middle-aged women or compares middle-aged women with other age-groups. A few limited symptoms do appear, particularly hot flashes and sleep difficulties.

Treating Menopausal Symptoms

Estrogen replacement therapy (ERT): Doses of estrogen given to some women to treat menopausal symptoms.

Hormone replacement therapy (HRT): Doses of estrogen and progesterone and possibly testosterone given to some women to treat menopausal symptoms.

Some menopausal symptoms appear to be related either to low estrogen levels or to hormonal imbalance. Evidence for this point of view comes from the success of **estrogen replacement therapy** (**ERT**, such as Premarin) and **hormone replacement therapy** (**HRT**, such as Prempro), which involves both estrogen and progesterone, and possibly testosterone as well. HRT is successful in relieving low-estrogen menopausal symptoms such as hot flashes, night sweats, osteoporosis (brittle bones), vaginal discharges, and vaginal dryness (Shifren & Schiff, 2010; Wright et al., 2002). Osteoporosis increases the risk of broken bones, such as hip fractures, which may lead to death. Also, 80% of people with osteoporosis are women (Shifren & Schiff, 2010), so this is a serious women's health issue.

Yet each woman must weigh the possible benefits of HRT against the dangers. HRT increases the risk for heart disease, breast cancer, and endometrial cancer, particularly for older women or after extended use (Chen et al., 2002; Shifren & Schiff, 2010; Wright et al., 2002).

In a startling move in 2002, the National Institutes of Health (NIH) stopped a clinical trial of the HRT drug Prempro with menopausal women (Enserink, 2002). The NIH did not stop the other treatment group in the study, who were taking ERT only. The reason for the dramatic action was that women in the HRT group had a higher incidence of heart attack, stroke, breast cancer, and blood clots, compared with the placebo control group. That is, HRT was increasing rather than decreasing the rates of heart attack and stroke.

Does this mean that all women should stop HRT? Not necessarily. The ERT group was doing well, so no concerns were raised about receiving only estrogen. The study was investigating long-term use of HRT and stopped the HRT group at 5 years. Short-term use of HRT for 1 or 2 years is probably safe for most women. Moreover, the increase in risk from HRT might seem small to women who are having serious difficulty with menopausal symptoms. For example, women who become depressed after many months of hot flashes and trouble sleeping show improvements in mood with HRT (Soares et al., 2001).

The picture on ERT and HRT is complex and speaks to the importance of individualized evaluation and treatment for each woman, taking into account her particular pattern of symptoms and how distressed she is by them. Women who are otherwise at risk for heart disease, stroke, or endometrial or breast cancers—for example, women who are overweight or who have a family history of one of these diseases—are generally advised to consider alternatives to HRT (Shifren & Schiff, 2010). In sum, each woman must make this decision for herself, in consultation with her health care provider.

We have a strong cultural bias toward expecting menopausal symptoms. Any quirk in a middle-aged woman's behavior is attributed to "the change." It simultaneously becomes the cause of, and explanation for, all the problems and complaints of the middle-aged woman. Given such expectations, it is not surprising that the average person perceives widespread evidence of menopausal symptoms. Ironically, idiosyncrasies in women of childbearing age are blamed on menstruation, whereas problems experienced by women who are past that age are blamed on the lack of it.

Reproduction and Health

Contraception

Detailed information on the various methods of contraception is available elsewhere (e.g., Hyde & DeLamater, 2017). Here our focus is on the psychological aspects of contraceptive use.

Each year in the United States more than 600,000 teenage girls become pregnant. About 2 in 10 White women and about 4 in 10 Black and Latina women become pregnant by age 20. Nearly all of these pregnancies are unintended. Although the rate of unintended pregnancies in the United States is down overall, it is highest among poor women (Finer & Zolna, 2016). Contraception can be prohibitively expensive, around $600 per year for oral contraceptives (i.e., the pill). We will return to this point shortly.

Even though many highly effective contraceptives are available, about 10% of women at risk of unintended pregnancy (i.e., sexually active and not wanting to get pregnant) use no method of contraception (Daniels et al., 2014). Among 15- to 19-year-olds, this proportion is 18% (Jones et al., 2012).

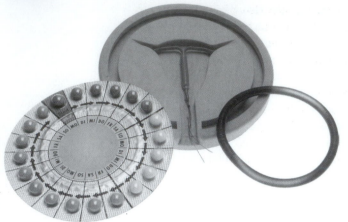

©iStockphoto.com/EdnaM.

PHOTO 11.3
Today, many highly effective contraceptives are available, but they can be costly.

Around the world, contraception is a crucial women's health issue. When women can plan their pregnancies and space them farther apart, everyone is better off: Infant mortality declines and women's physical and mental health benefit (Guttmacher Institute, 2011; Sonfield et al., 2013). In addition, some contraceptive methods (e.g., the pill, IUD) have numerous benefits beyond avoiding unintended pregnancy, such as reducing dysmenorrhea, excessive menstrual bleeding, and acne (Jones, 2011).

Unfortunately, millions of women who do not want to become pregnant do not use contraceptives, either because they lack access or because they fear side effects or health risks (Sedgh, Ashford, et al., 2016). Many of these fears are unfounded and stem from a lack of education about contraceptives. Cost can also be an issue. Many contraceptive methods are expensive—especially when added up over many years of use. In the United States, the Affordable Care Act originally required that private health insurance plans cover contraceptives. However, the requirement for contraception coverage was eliminated by President Trump in October 2017.

Pregnancy

The 9 months of pregnancy are divided into three trimesters of 3 months each, and each has its own set of physical and psychological developments. In the first trimester, the first issue is finding out that one is pregnant. Home pregnancy tests—which work by detecting human chorionic gonadotropin hormone (hCG) in urine—are widely available and generally accurate if done correctly. They are most accurate if done with undiluted urine and after a period has been missed.

The first trimester is the time of morning sickness (feelings of nausea and sometimes vomiting, which actually occur at any time of day), yet about 25% of women do not experience it. Fatigue is very common at this stage and is often intense. The levels of estrogen and progesterone sharply increase as the developing placenta vigorously produces both hormones. Although cultural myths describe pregnant women as either radiantly happy or exceptionally moody, research in fact shows that pregnancy is a time of neither heightened well-being nor heightened emotional turmoil (Striegel-Moore et al., 1996). Many women, though, feel anxious about miscarriage.

As pregnancy progresses, most women feel an increasing attachment to the developing fetus. They may do much to promote the health of the baby, such as eating well, not smoking, and maintaining a drug-free lifestyle. They also imagine what their baby will be like and spend time preparing for the baby's arrival. These are all signs of maternal–fetal attachment (Salisbury et al., 2003).

During the second trimester, the woman's belly begins to expand noticeably. She can also feel the fetus's movements; this experience of quickening can promote maternal–fetal attachment. Morning sickness has probably disappeared, but the woman may experience edema—water retention and swelling—in areas such as the ankles, feet, and hands. Psychologically, the second trimester tends to be relatively calm, with worries about miscarriage past.

By the third trimester the belly—and the uterus inside it—are large, causing some women to feel awkward or uncomfortable. The expanded uterus puts pressure on the lungs, causing shortness of breath, and on the stomach, causing indigestion.

The physical and psychological changes of pregnancy are strongly influenced by many contextual factors in a woman's life: whether she wanted to become pregnant; whether she can afford to have a child; whether she can afford adequate, nutritional food for herself prenatally; and whether she has a supportive cohabiting partner or spouse (Zimmerman-Tansella et al., 1994).

A feminist analysis of the experience of pregnancy is captured by one author: "I am not a patient, and I am not a child" (Rudolfsdottir, 2000). In the United States and other Western nations, pregnancy has been medicalized. As part of the process of **medicalization**, the physician is cast as the knowledgeable authority, and the woman may be treated as a child, lacking the knowledge and ability to make good decisions herself.

Medicalization: The process by which normal life events or situations are defined and treated as medical conditions in need of diagnosis and treatment.

Childbirth

Childbirth, too, has been medicalized, with an emphasis on giving birth in a hospital equipped with fancy instruments and monitors. When one of us (JSH) was born in 1948, her mother had a general anesthetic and missed the whole event. She was kept in the hospital for 2 full weeks afterward—partly because that was typical for the time and partly because she was an "old" mother at age 35.

Since then, women have engaged in resistance against the medicalization. Beginning in the 1960s the Lamaze method of childbirth became popular. It allows women to control the pain of childbirth and to give birth while fully awake, with little or no use of anesthetics. Since then, other approaches to childbirth (e.g., the Bradley method) have emerged. Home births and being under the care of a midwife rather than a physician are also increasingly popular options today as women seek a less medicalized childbirth and more control over their experience. With home birth, rates of obstetrical interventions are lower and rates of vaginal birth are much higher than with hospital birth (Snowden et al., 2015). Planned home births can be a safe option for women and their babies when their risk of complications is low (de Jonge et al., 2015). For the best outcomes, each woman should make the many choices about childbirth methods and setting in consultation with her health care provider.

Cervix: The lower part of the uterus, forming a passageway to the vagina.

Every birth is unique and shaped by multiple factors, including the woman's health, her psychological and emotional resources, the setting, the health care providers and social support that are present, and so on. The goal is to have not just a healthy baby, but also a healthy mother. Each woman needs to discuss her options with her health care provider and have the information to make childbirth choices that are the best fit for her and her baby.

Childbirth occurs in three stages. In the first stage, the **cervix** must dilate to 10 centimeters. It is important to remember that there is much variability from one birth to the next; just as every woman is unique, so is every birth. Some women may take a few days to dilate the first 2 to 3 centimeters, perhaps feeling nothing, while others may dilate more quickly. Getting from 3 to 10 centimeters is more intense, however, and can often take 8 hours or longer. This happens as uterine contractions are fueled by the release of the hormone oxytocin. At the start of labor, these contractions typically feel like menstrual cramps, until they begin to rise and fall at regular, predictable intervals. The pain of the

Karl Gehring/Denver Post/Getty Images.

PHOTO 11.4
A doula provides continuous physical, emotional, and informational support to a woman before, during, and shortly after childbirth. Having a doula can improve birth outcomes.

contractions becomes intense and can be made worse by anxiety and dehydration. For some women, medical pain management is helpful at this stage.

Having a doula present can be helpful with pain management, too, and may help reduce complications (Hodnett et al., 2013). A **doula** provides continuous physical, emotional, and informational support to a woman before, during, and shortly after childbirth. This might entail providing massage, reassurance, and social support, as well as information about a woman's options in childbirth. During this physically demanding process, it's especially important for the woman to feel supported and relaxed, and to stay as hydrated and nourished as possible. A doula typically assists with those needs as well.

The second stage of labor involves the actual delivery of the baby. This can take a few minutes to a couple of hours, depending on a variety of factors, including the position of the mother and the size and position of the baby. After the baby has been born, the third stage—delivery of the placenta—occurs. This usually takes only a few minutes and involves much less effort than the previous two stages.

In the postpartum period, many new mothers may feel overwhelmed by the immense responsibilities of the maternal role; the physical changes of pregnancy, childbirth, and perhaps breastfeeding; and the sudden deprivation of sleep. For women with adequate social support and financial resources to provide care for themselves and their newborn, the stress and anxiety of the postpartum period are lessened. For women who don't have supportive partners or family members, or who must quickly return to work, the challenges of this transition are exacerbated. While some degree of emotional ups and downs is common at this stage, more severe experiences of irritability, anxiety, and sadness may be symptoms of postpartum depression. Postpartum depression occurs in up to 19% of mothers, and women with a history of depression are at highest risk (O'Hara & McCabe, 2013). The prevalence is higher among lower-income women, who also have reduced access to treatment (Zlotnick et al., 2016). Postpartum depression can interfere with a mother's ability to care for herself and her newborn and, like depression at any stage in life, can be very dangerous if left untreated.

Abortion

In the United States, 42% of unintended pregnancies end in abortion (Finer & Zolna, 2016). Each year, about 56 million abortions are performed worldwide (Sedgh, Bearak, et al., 2016). In the United States, the abortion rate continues to decline; there were 926,200 abortions performed in 2014 (Jones & Jerman, 2017). About three-quarters of the American women who choose abortion are low-income (Jerman et al., 2016). Yet, because federal (and most state) Medicaid funds cannot be used to pay for an abortion, low-income women often struggle to find the cash to pay for an abortion, which is typically around $500 during the first trimester. Here we briefly discuss two methods: surgical abortion and medical abortion (see Hyde & DeLamater, 2017, for a more complete discussion).

The most commonly used abortion method is surgical abortion (more specifically, **vacuum aspiration**). It is done on an outpatient basis with a local anesthetic. The procedure itself takes only about 10 minutes and the woman stays in the doctor's office, clinic, or hospital for a few hours. The woman is prepared as she would be for a pelvic exam, and an instrument is inserted into the vagina (Figure 11.4) to open her cervix. Next, a tube is inserted through the cervical opening until one end is in the uterus. The other end is attached to a suction-producing machine, and the contents of the uterus, including the

Doula: A trained professional who provides continuous physical, emotional, and informational support to a woman before, during, and shortly after childbirth.

Vacuum aspiration: A method of surgical abortion that is performed in the first trimester.

FIGURE 11.4   **In a vacuum aspiration abortion, a tube is inserted through the vagina and the cervix into the uterus. The uterine contents are then suctioned out.**

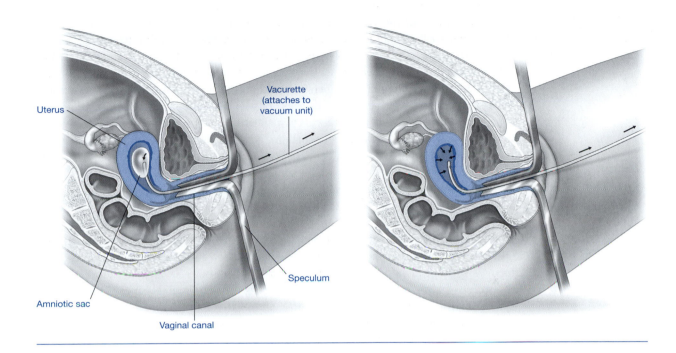

fetal tissue, are sucked out. Vacuum aspiration is a very safe procedure and is safer than pregnancy (Hatcher et al., 2004).

Within the first 10 weeks of pregnancy, a woman may choose a medical abortion. This involves taking a medication (typically, mifepristone). The medication causes the lining of the uterus to be sloughed off. About 31% of abortions in the United States are medical abortions (Jones & Jerman, 2017). Medical abortion can be done at home and is very safe (Ngo et al., 2011).

Women choose abortion for a variety of reasons. The most common reasons reported by women are that they cannot afford financially to have a baby, that it is not the right time to have a baby, and that their partner is not supportive of the pregnancy or that the relationship with their partner is unhealthy (Rocca et al., 2013). In short, women consider multiple aspects of their situation and take the decision seriously.

It is a commonly believed myth that having an abortion is an extremely stressful event that causes mental health problems. Yet this myth has no scientific evidence supporting it. Reviews of research on the psychological outcomes of legal abortion indicate that mental health problems are rare and that, in fact, most women are more distressed before the abortion than after it (Adler et al., 1990, 1992; Adler et al., 2003; Major et al., 2009). One large study found that the risk for psychiatric disorder did not increase in the year following abortion, but did increase following childbirth (Munk-Olsen et al., 2011).

When evaluating the evidence about the psychological consequences of abortion, it is important to disentangle women's emotions about an abortion from those about an unwanted pregnancy. A well-conducted study of ethnically diverse women obtaining an abortion found that women felt more regret, sadness, and anger about the pregnancy than they did about the abortion (Rocca et al., 2013). Moreover, those women reported feeling more relief and happiness about having an abortion than about having an unwanted pregnancy. Still, a mix of negative and positive emotions was common. Recall that a feminist analysis reminds us to examine the social context of women's emotions. Among women who had made efforts to avoid getting pregnant (e.g., using contraception), who had difficulty making the decision, or who felt their partner was not supportive of their choice, there were higher levels of negative emotions after the abortion (relative to other women who'd obtained an abortion). Nonetheless, 95% of the women reported feeling that having an abortion was the right choice for them, even if they also felt some negative emotions.

Political bias has fueled abortion myths and plagued the research on women's post-abortion mental health (Joffe, 2013). The most widespread methodological flaws in abortion research have to do with finding an appropriate comparison group, using valid measurement of psychological outcomes, studying diverse populations of women, and accounting for women's pre-abortion mental health. A review of the research on the long-term psychological outcomes of abortion found that the poorest quality studies reported the worst outcomes for women, while the highest quality studies reported better outcomes (Charles et al., 2008).

In the United States, many state legislatures have restricted women's access to legal abortion, such as by requiring waiting periods, mandating that women view fetal ultrasounds or hear fetal heartbeats, and lowering the gestation limit (that is, denying access to legal abortion after a particular point in pregnancy). One analysis found that, in 23 out of 33 states with laws requiring pre-abortion counseling, the laws required conveying medically inaccurate and blatantly false information that, in turn, interfered with women's ability to give informed consent (Gold & Nash, 2007).

Thus, it is also important to consider the possible consequences of restricting abortion. What are the implications for women who are denied abortion? One study compared women who obtained a legal abortion just before the gestational limit in their state to women who were denied an abortion for seeking one after the limit (Biggs et al., 2017). It found that women who were denied an abortion experienced more mental health problems (such as depression and low self-esteem) initially, but that the two groups were comparable 5 years later.

We should also consider the psychological consequences for children whose mothers sought an abortion but were denied one. In some countries, access to abortion requires obtaining official approval. In Czechoslovakia, for example, researchers followed 220 children born to women who were denied abortion (the study group) and 220 children born to women who had not sought an abortion (David, 1992; David & Matejcek, 1981; David et al., 2003). The researchers followed the children from childhood through adolescence and into early and middle adulthood. By age 14, 43 children from the study group, but only 30 from the control group, had been referred for counseling. Although there were no differences between the groups in measured intelligence, children in the study group did less well in school and were more likely to drop out. At age 16, the boys (but not the girls) in the study group more frequently rated themselves as feeling neglected or rejected by their mothers and felt that their mothers were less satisfied with them. When in their early 20s, the study group reported less job satisfaction, more conflicts with coworkers and supervisors, and fewer and less satisfying friendships. Several other studies have found results similar to the Czechoslovakian study (e.g., David et al., 1988). These results point to the serious long-term psychological consequences for children whose mothers would have preferred to have an abortion.

Abortion myths are linked to abortion stigma and the social judgment of women who have abortions. Out of fear of judgment, many women keep their abortions secret (Harris, 2012), which can further fuel the stigma. A review of studies on abortion stigma found that women who had abortions were afraid of social judgment and felt a need for secrecy (Hanschmidt et al., 2016). In turn, keeping their abortion secret was linked to increased psychological distress and social isolation.

In sum, scientific evidence indicates that legal abortion is safe for women. Yet there appear to be long-term negative consequences for children born to women denied access to abortion. Abortion myths and stigma may contribute to restrictions in abortion access and to women's distress about abortion.

Miscarriage

Much like abortion, miscarriage is common but often kept a secret. **Miscarriage** refers the spontaneous demise of a fetus before the 20th week of pregnancy; after 20 weeks, this is referred to as a **stillbirth**. About half of all fertilized eggs die, but most of those miscarriages happen before a woman has missed a period. About 20% of known pregnancies end in miscarriage, most often during the first trimester. Depending on how early in pregnancy the miscarriage occurs, symptoms vary but may include painful cramping and unusually heavy bleeding. In some cases, it may take weeks or require surgical or medical intervention to help the woman's body pass the fetal tissue. Although many women blame themselves for miscarrying, miscarriage is most often the result of a genetic defect or chromosomal abnormality that prevents the fetus from developing normally. Most women who miscarry go on to carry a healthy pregnancy to term.

Miscarriage: Spontaneous demise of a fetus before the 20th week of pregnancy.

Stillbirth: Spontaneous demise of a fetus after the 20th week of pregnancy.

Miscarriage is a potentially devastating experience; anxiety, depression, and even posttraumatic stress disorder are common and may last for 6 to 12 months or longer (Lok & Neugebauer, 2007). For many, a miscarriage is experienced as the death of one's child or a future child (Séjourné et al., 2010). Many women search for deeper meaning in the experience (Nikčević & Nicolaides, 2014). Nonetheless, women's psychological experiences of miscarriage are diverse and depend on contextual factors, such as whether the pregnancy had been planned or wanted (Shreffler et al., 2011). For women who do not want to be pregnant, a miscarriage may come as a relief.

A review of qualitative research on women's experiences of miscarriage revealed four major themes (Radford & Hughes, 2015):

1. *What I feel.* Women described a need for recognition and acknowledgment of their emotions and physical symptoms. Many women reported intense and deep feelings of isolation, loneliness, grief, shock, denial, and bereavement. While others' expressions of empathy were described as helpful, many women felt abandoned by their health care providers after the miscarriage.

2. *Care for me, communicate with me.* Women described a need for communication and information about the physical and emotional aspects of miscarriage and what to expect. They reported that the lack of information made them feel helpless and that the situation was out of their control.

3. *Me, my baby, and others.* A loss of the rights and identity associated with motherhood and a sense of personal failure were described. Women felt that others didn't respond sensitively to the miscarriage, so they were reluctant to discuss it.

4. *Help me cope with the future.* Women wanted guidance on how to move forward after the loss and reported that the most helpful support came from other women who had miscarried.

In sum, miscarriage is common and yet rarely talked about. It can be a deeply distressing experience for women and may be accompanied by physical trauma. The psychological consequences for some may last many months or even years and depend on women's social context.

Infertility

Having a sense of control over one's childbearing is important to women. Just as the woman with an unwanted pregnancy may feel distress about the options available to her, a woman who struggles to become pregnant feels distress about her limited options. And just as abortion and miscarriage are rarely talked about openly, infertility is often kept secret. See Chapter 7 for more discussion of infertility.

Breast Cancer

About one out of every nine women in the United States has breast cancer at some time in her life; it is the most common form of cancer in this population. While it is rare in women under 25, a woman's chances of developing it increase every year after that age. Every year, about 41,000 women die of breast cancer in the United States (U.S. Cancer Statistics Working Group, 2016). Although it is extremely rare for men to develop breast cancer, about 450 men die of it each year.

Research on breast cancer among transgender men and women is scarce. The limited available research indicates that, while the occurrence of the disease in transgender people is very rare (Brown, 2015; Brown & Jones, 2015), evidence-based screening guidelines are sorely needed (Pivo et al., 2017). It is unclear how the risk for transgender men and women compares with that of cisgender women. Factors such as hormone therapy (i.e., receiving testosterone or estrogen) may increase risk for both transgender men and women. For transgender men, risk may also depend on whether and how much breast tissue patients have had removed (Pivo et al., 2017). Conducting large-scale studies to estimate breast cancer risk and describe breast cancer experiences among transgender men and women is crucial. Most of the available research has used samples of cisgender women; thus, that research comprises our review.

Given that breast cancer is fairly common, doctors recommend that women should do a breast self-exam monthly. For some transgender men, similar recommendations may be appropriate (Pivo et al., 2017). Given that breast tissue changes across the menstrual cycle, premenopausal women should do the breast exam midcycle (not during one's period). Fear may prevent some people from doing a self-exam or from seeing a doctor immediately when they discover a lump. This is unfortunate because the chances of recovery improve when breast cancer is detected and treated early. Today, the majority of people who get breast cancer will survive it, especially if it is discovered at an early stage.

FOCUS 11.2

HEALTH AT THE INTERSECTION OF GENDER AND DISABILITY

The U.S. government describes *disability* as including hearing difficulty, vision difficulty, cognitive difficulty, ambulatory difficulty (e.g., having serious difficulty walking), self-care difficulty, and independent living difficulty. At the intersection of gender and disability, there are considerable persistent inequities.

Over 20 million American women and girls live with a disability (U.S. Census Bureau, 2013). In nearly every racial/ethnic group, women have higher rates of disability (Miles-Cohen & Signore, 2016). Moreover, relative to men with disabilities, their rates of poverty are more severe (Nosek, 2016), which can contribute to and exacerbate health disparities.

Women with disabilities are more likely than nondisabled women to have inequitable and inadequate access to health care, increased prevalence of complications, and diminished quality of life (Miles-Cohen & Signore, 2016). Relative to nondisabled women, women with disabilities have reduced physical activity, higher rates of obesity, higher rates of chronic diseases such as asthma and diabetes, and higher smoking rates (Parish et al., 2016). These are serious health disparities.

In many ways, women with disabilities experience *double jeopardy* in that they are marginalized because they are both women and persons with disabilities. Similarly, queer or trans women with disabilities or women of color with disabilities may face triple jeopardy. Their experiences as individuals belonging to multiply marginalized groups mean that, in many instances, they face considerable barriers to adequate health care.

Women with disabilities may face architectural barriers to health care, such that health care facilities are not accessible. For example, many women with ambulatory disabilities do not get regular Pap tests (discussed later in this chapter) because examination tables are not accessible to them (Signore, 2016).

©iStockphoto.com/simonkr.

PHOTO 11.5

More research on the health and health care needs of women with disabilities is needed.

Women with disabilities may also face attitudinal barriers, including discrimination and stereotyping from health care providers (Saxton, 2016). Doctors and nurses might tell a patient that her health care needs are too excessive and cannot be met. This is illegal; health care providers cannot deny care to someone because they have a disability.

Researchers agree that there are at least two things we need to do to reduce these barriers for women. First, we need to conduct much more research to learn about the health and health care needs of women with disabilities. There is scant research on the health of queer or trans women with disabilities (Tarasoff, 2016) or women of color with disabilities (Correa-de-Araujo, 2016). Second, we need to provide patient-centered, integrated care to women with disabilities. This refers to health care that is characterized by a great deal of collaboration and communication among doctors, nurses, and psychologists.

Most breast lumps are benign. For example, some lumps may be cysts (fluid-filled sacs, also called fibrocystic disease or cystic mastitis) or fibroadenomas. Thus, while the fear of cancer is understandable, it's important to remember that most lumps are not cancerous.

Radical mastectomy: A surgical treatment for breast cancer in which the entire breast, as well as underlying muscle and lymph nodes, is removed.

Lumpectomy: A surgical treatment for breast cancer in which only the lump and a small bit of surrounding tissue are removed.

If breast cancer is diagnosed, what is the best treatment? Most often, some form of *mastectomy* (i.e., surgical removal of breast tissue) is performed. In **radical mastectomy**, the most aggressive form of this treatment, the entire breast as well as the lymph nodes and underlying muscles are removed. This method is more likely to be used if the cancer has spread to the muscle and lymph nodes. In modified radical mastectomy, the entire breast and lymph nodes, but not the muscles, are removed. In simple mastectomy, only the breast, and possibly a few lymph nodes, is removed. In partial mastectomy, or **lumpectomy**, only the lump and some surrounding tissue are removed.

Breast cancer rates, diagnoses, and treatment differ at the intersection of gender, race/ethnicity, and social class. For example, while breast cancer is more common among higher-income women, lower-income women and women of color have higher rates of mortality from it (Harper et al., 2009; Ward et al., 2004). White and higher-income women have greater access to diagnostic tools, such as mammography, which aids in early diagnosis and is key to survival. By contrast, for lower-income women and women of color, who have reduced access to mammography, breast cancer is diagnosed at later stages, resulting in increased mortality. Although clinics like Planned Parenthood provide free or reduced rates for mammography, women in rural communities are often geographically isolated from such facilities.

With regard to the psychological consequences of breast cancer diagnosis and treatment, about 30% to 40% of women report feeling increased depression and anxiety around the time of diagnosis (Compas & Luecken, 2002). It is important to note that there is great variation from one woman to the next. While the majority of studies show good adjustment after mastectomy (Helgeson et al., 2004), lumpectomy is associated with better body image and sexual functioning postsurgery than more radical surgeries (Moyer, 1997).

Many women experience considerable psychological distress during the time from discovery of a lump through diagnosis and treatment. It is important for them and their partners to have counseling available. In many towns, the American Cancer Society organizes support groups for breast cancer patients. Today, support groups are popular for dealing with just about every situation. As psychologists, we must raise this question: Are support groups effective for breast cancer patients? One study compared the effects of peer support groups for women with breast cancer with the effects of educational classes focused on relevant information (Helgeson et al., 2000, 2001). While the peer support groups provided no benefits to quality of life (compared with no intervention), the education intervention provided both immediate and long-term benefits with quality of life. Peer support groups may be helpful to some women but may actually be harmful to others so that, averaged over everyone, they appear to provide no benefit (Helgeson et al., 2000).

Breast cancer survivors are at increased risk for depression. For women who become depressed, cognitive behavioral therapy with a trained therapist is very effective (Antoni et al., 2001; Antoni et al., 2006). This form of therapy has been shown to result in lower depressive symptoms even 5 years later (Stagl et al., 2015).

©iStockphoto.com/choja.

PHOTO 11.6
Lower-income women and women of color tend to have reduced access to mammography, which can aid in early diagnosis of breast cancer.

One study compared breast cancer survivors with matched controls (Cordova et al., 2001). The cancer survivor group did not differ from the controls on measures of depression and well-being, indicating good overall adjustment. The researchers went beyond studying possible problems of adjustment, also considering the possibility of **posttraumatic growth**. Posttraumatic growth refers to positive life changes following highly stressful experiences and appears to develop soon after a breast cancer diagnosis (Danhauer et al., 2013). Breast cancer survivors showed significantly more posttraumatic growth than the controls, particularly in relationships with others, appreciation of life, and spiritual growth. Humans are resilient, and we must remain open to the potential for growth in the midst of trauma.

Posttraumatic growth: Positive life changes following highly stressful experiences.

HPV and Cervical Cancer

Cervical cancer (i.e., cancer of the cervix) is far less common than breast cancer in the United States. For example, in 2013, there were 11,955 new diagnoses of cervical cancer but 230,815 new diagnoses of breast cancer (U.S. Cancer Statistics Working Group, 2016).

What is remarkable about cervical cancer is that doctors know what causes it. Cervical cancer is caused by the human papillomavirus (HPV). There are multiple strains of HPV that are sexually transmitted, some of which cause genital warts. Here we focus on the strains that cause cervical cancer; these strains are considered high risk. While nearly all women will have an HPV infection at some point in their lives, most will not develop cancer. This is because most HPV infections do not involve the high-risk strains.

It can be difficult to know if you or your partner is infected with HPV, but a simple, painless screening technique can be used to detect HPV infection in women. The Pap (short for Papanicolaou) test involves scraping cells from the opening of the cervix and examining those cells for abnormalities (see Figure 11.5). Anyone with a cervix should have a Pap test done annually, up to age 65. If HPV is detected, it is typically advised simply to monitor the infection, since most infections will clear up on their own. If the infection does not go away on its own, gynecologists can treat the infection with a variety of procedures to prevent it from developing into cervical cancer (National Cancer Institute, 2009).

Despite the availability of this highly effective screening technique, many women and transgender men with cervixes do not routinely get screened for HPV (Agénor et al., 2014). Discrimination by health care providers is one barrier to routine HPV screening. For example, one study found that lesbian, bisexual, and queer women as well as transgender men who reported being discriminated against because of their gender expression were more than three times less likely to get regular Pap tests (Johnson et al., 2016).

In addition, doctors may not perform Pap tests on lesbian women, mistakenly thinking that women need this test done only if they have sex with men (Marrazzo, 2004). And some lesbian women think they don't need to be tested for sexually transmitted infections if they aren't having sex with men (Marrazzo et al., 2005; Polek & Hardie, 2010). In fact, being sexually active with anyone, regardless of their gender, increases risk for HPV infection. Health care providers must also be welcoming and sensitive to the needs of transgender men and nonbinary people who may have a cervix and who may feel uncomfortable or embarrassed requesting cervical cancer screening (Johnson et al., 2016). If you have a cervix, you need to have regular Pap tests.

At the intersection of gender and class, financial barriers may limit access to Pap testing. Women of lower socioeconomic status are less likely to be screened for HPV and cervical cancer (Selvin & Brett, 2003). Poor women and women without health

FIGURE 11.5   **Tools for a pap test, which detects HPV infection. Anyone with a cervix needs a regular pap test, regardless of gender identity.**

Source: © iStockphoto.com/JodiJacobson.

insurance may skip their annual Pap test because of the cost. Some clinics, such as Planned Parenthood, offer free or reduced rates for cervical cancer screening. Yet if a person does not live near such a clinic, they may not be able to access this health care.

Cervical cancer risk is higher among women of color than among White women (Rositch et al., 2014). The incidence of cervical cancer is highest among Latinas (Ward et al., 2004), and the death rate from it is highest among Black women (Beavis et al., 2017). These racial/ethnic disparities may also stem from the cost of HPV screening.

Like all sexually transmitted infections, HPV carries a stigma. HPV stigma can be internalized, leading to self-consciousness, shame, and embarrassment. Some women feel ashamed or embarrassed for having HPV (Daley et al., 2010; Kahn et al., 2007). In turn, these emotions can prevent women from getting their annual Pap test or from monitoring an existing infection. The stigmatization of HPV may also prevent some infected people from telling their sexual partners about the infection, which increases the spread of HPV.

HPV is preventable. In 2006, the U.S. Food and Drug Administration approved two vaccines—Gardasil and Cervarix—to prevent infection with two strains of HPV that cause 70% of cases of cervical cancer (Koutsky et al., 2002). The Centers for Disease Control and Prevention recommends that all children (regardless of gender) be vaccinated against HPV beginning at age 11 or 12. While public health efforts to vaccinate boys and men were initially weaker than the efforts to vaccinate girls and women, this trend appears to be changing. Men can develop oral, anal, or genital cancers from high-risk HPV, but their risk of developing cancer from HPV is lower than women's. Nonetheless, if men are not vaccinated against high-risk HPV, they may transmit the virus to other unvaccinated partners.

The United States has very low HPV vaccination rates, with only 37.6% of girls and 13.9% of boys getting vaccinated (Elam-Evans et al., 2014). There is controversy over vaccinating adolescents against a sexually transmitted infection because some parents worry that the HPV vaccine may encourage youth to be sexually active. There is no evidence that vaccination increases sexual activity.

Trans Health Issues

Transgender people need health care for many of the same health problems that cisgender people have: tobacco use, alcohol abuse, reproductive health, and cancer, as well as mental health issues (to be discussed in Chapter 15). As discussed earlier, health care provided to transgender people in the United States is lacking. Major barriers to adequate health care for trans people include social barriers such as the experience of discrimination from health care providers (who need better education about trans issues), structural barriers such as insufficient insurance coverage, and geographical barriers such as living in a rural community with reduced access to adequate health care.

In addition, many transgender people desire gender-affirming therapies to make their body and presentation match their gender identity. These and other components of health care are medically necessary for the well-being of transgender people (Coleman et al., 2012). For example, voice and communication therapy may be provided to help the person speak in the range typical for their gender identity and communicate nonverbally in ways that match their gender identity (see Chapter 5). For some transgender women, facial hair removal by electrolysis or other methods may be desirable. Supportive therapy for the transgender person and their family may also be beneficial for reducing stress. Medical and surgical transition are also options. We briefly review some of the interventions that may be used in medical and surgical transition for transgender women and men.

Medical Transition

The medical and surgical transition, in which a person's body undergoes a range of medical and surgical interventions designed to match their gender identity, are important to many, but not all, transgender people. A range of interventions is now possible, and different individuals will choose different interventions. The World Professional Association for Transgender Health (WPATH) has set standards of care for transgender people, including standards for medical treatment (Coleman et al., 2011; see also Hembree, 2009). Before medical treatments can occur, assessment and referral by a mental health professional are required.

For early adolescents, *pubertal suppression* is a medical option that delays the onset of pubertal changes. As discussed in Chapter 7, pubertal suppression buys some time for an adolescent to mature and make a well-informed decision about whether to go through medical or surgical transition before endogenous puberty starts. If the adolescent decides not to pursue transition, the pubertal suppression treatments can be stopped and the effects reversed. However, if the adolescent decides to transition, the process will be simpler after having prevented pubertal changes. For example, for a transgender man, mastectomy wouldn't be necessary because pubertal suppression would have prevented breast development. Preliminary evaluations of pubertal suppression indicate that, in young adulthood, transgender individuals treated in this manner function as well psychologically as cisgender individuals do, in contrast to the strong gender dysphoria they had before treatment (de Vries et al., 2014).

Medical transition involves *hormone therapy* with estrogen (to feminize the body) or testosterone (to masculinize the body) and may also include hormone blockers (e.g., to block the secretion of endogenous testosterone in transgender women). This type of therapy is only partially reversible and is typically applied only with older adolescents (i.e., after age 16) and adults who are capable of making a definite decision about wanting to transition. Transgender men may choose hormone therapy with testosterone, which can lead to a deeper voice, growth in facial hair, growth of the clitoris or phallus, and a decrease in body fat percentage. The testosterone, which is usually injected, typically causes menstruation to stop. For transgender women, hormone therapy with estrogen results in breast growth, fewer erections, and increased body fat that creates feminine curves.

While additional high-quality research on the effects of hormone therapies is needed, evidence suggests they are beneficial for the well-being of transgender persons who receive them (White Hughto & Reisner, 2016). In-depth discussion of the effects and experiences of hormone therapy and medical transition are available elsewhere (e.g., Deutsch, 2014, 2016).

Surgical Transition

Surgical transition can include several types of surgical treatments. These treatments are irreversible and should be chosen only by a mature adolescent over the legal age of consent or an adult. The typical requirement is that the individual lives as a member of the gender with which they identify for at least 12 months, to ensure that the transition is truly workable and desirable. We introduce some of these treatments here; in-depth discussion of the effects and experiences of surgical transition are available elsewhere (e.g., Chyten-Brennan, 2014; Deutsch, 2016).

"Top surgeries" involve surgical treatments to alter the chest. Some transgender men choose to undergo *reconstructive chest surgery*, which involves the removal of breasts. Some transgender women choose to undergo breast augmentation.

"Bottom surgeries" involve surgical treatments to alter the genitals or internal reproductive organs. For transgender women, these surgeries may include penectomy (removal of the penis), orchiectomy (removal of the testes), vaginoplasty (creation of a vagina from the skin of the penis), clitoroplasty (creation of a clitoris), and vulvoplasty (other surgery to create a female-appearing vulva). For transgender men, bottom surgeries might include removal of the uterus (hysterectomy), fallopian tubes, and ovaries; metoidioplasty or phalloplasty (to create a penis); and scrotoplasty (creation of a scrotum and insertion of artificial testes). Metoidioplasty involves releasing the clitoris, which enlarges with hormone therapy, to create a penis, whereas phalloplasty involves creation of a penis from tissue such as the forearm. These penis-creating surgeries are difficult and often not completely successful, so many transgender men decide against them.

According to research, the adjustment of transgender people who choose surgical transition is significantly better following surgery. A review of studies of vaginoplasty in transgender women found that results vary in terms of the functionality of the vagina, concluding that sexual function and patient satisfaction were "acceptable" (Horbach et al., 2015). In one study, 86% of transgender women were satisfied with their surgery to create a vagina, and 89% of transgender men were satisfied with their surgery to create a penis (De Cuypere et al., 2005). Another study of transgender men and women found that none expressed regret about having chosen surgery (Johansson et al., 2010). In that sense, then, these gender-affirming surgeries are successful.

Still, it is important to note that many transgender people do not seek the full range of these medical and surgical interventions. Some may choose to undergo some treatments but not others. For some, a social transition seems to be all that is needed or wanted. And to the extent that people do not feel forced to fit into one of the two gender binary categories, surgery may feel unnecessary.

Experience the Research
Women's Experience of PMS

Interview four female friends on the topic of PMS. Ask each the following questions and record their answers:

1. Do you experience PMS?

   [Continue with questions 2 through 7 if the answer is yes; use questions 8 through 11 if the answer is no.]

2. How do you define PMS?

3. What symptoms of PMS do you experience? Include both physical symptoms and psychological symptoms.

4. About how frequently do you experience PMS? That is, out of 10 menstrual periods, for how many of them do you experience PMS?

5. About how long do the symptoms of PMS last for you? How many days before your period do they begin? For how many days do they last?

6. How much does the PMS interfere with your functioning? Do you continue pretty much as you normally would, or do you have to stay in bed for a while?

7. How do you treat the PMS? Do you take any medication for it? If so, what? Is it effective? What symptoms does it relieve? If you do not take any medication, how do you try to relieve the PMS symptoms?

   [This ends the questions for those with PMS.]

8. How do you define PMS?

9. Do you have any ideas about why you don't have PMS?

10. Do you experience any symptoms or changes throughout your menstrual cycle? Do you experience any symptoms during your menstrual period, such as cramps?

11. How do you feel about women with PMS?

What can you conclude from your interviews? How common is PMS? What are its symptoms? How do women cope with it? How do they define it?

CHAPTER SUMMARY

This chapter examined how women and trans people are treated by the health care system. At the intersection of gender, ethnicity, and social class, health and health care are affected.

The evidence on whether women experience menstrual cycle fluctuations in mood and whether these shifts are caused by fluctuating hormone levels was considered. Although many studies have been conducted on these

(Continued)

(Continued)

questions, there are fundamental problems with the research. Our conclusion is that some, though not all, women experience menstrual cycle fluctuations in mood. Moreover, culture plays an important role in the construction of these experiences.

At menopause many women experience hot flashes, but research on psychological symptoms such as depression and irritability indicates no increases compared with other stages of life. The physical symptoms such as hot flashes are related to declines in estrogen levels.

Several topics under the broad umbrella of reproduction and health were reviewed. Worldwide, contraception is a major public health issue for women. The ability to plan and space one's pregnancies is crucial to one's health. Pregnancy and childbirth are highly medicalized health experiences. Feminists have advocated for women having greater autonomy and decision-making power during these points in the lifespan.

Research on the psychological consequences of having an abortion indicates that it is generally not a traumatic experience. However, children born to women who were denied an abortion do show problems of adjustment.

Miscarriage is very common, yet rarely talked about. Many women experience miscarriage as the death of a future child, which can be psychological and physically traumatic. We need to provide more sensitive care to women who miscarry.

Two types of cancer, breast and cervical, were discussed. Women with breast cancer are at increased risk for depression. Cognitive behavioral therapy is effective for treating depression. Following treatment, most women do well psychologically, and there is some evidence of posttraumatic growth.

Regular Pap tests and vaccination can help to prevent cervical cancer, which is caused by HPV. The stigma of sexually transmitted infections can present a barrier to the screening and treatment of HPV as well as to disclosure to partners. Regardless of gender identity, people with cervixes need regular Pap tests to screen for HPV and cervical cancer.

There are major barriers to adequate health care for trans people. Some trans people seek gender-affirming therapies to make their body align with their gender identity. Medical transition and surgical transition are important to many, but not all, trans people.

In all of these cases, individuals should learn more about the functioning of their bodies to make informed choices about their health care. It is also important to inform oneself about the psychological aspects of one's health issues.

SUGGESTIONS FOR FURTHER READING

Boston Women's Health Book Collective. (2011). *Our bodies, ourselves: A new edition for a new era*. New York, NY: Touchstone. This is the latest edition of the classic and best book on women's health.

Erickson-Schroth, Laura. (2014). *Trans bodies, trans selves: A resource for the transgender community*. New York, NY: Oxford University Press. This is an accessible and detailed resource on health and sexuality written for transgender persons.

Hatcher, Robert A., Trussell, James, Nelson, Anita L., Cates, Willard, Jr., Kowal, Deborah, & Policar, Michael S. (2011). *Contraceptive technology* (20th ed.). New York, NY: Bridging the Gap Communications. This is the authoritative book on contraceptive methods, updated regularly.

Miles-Cohen, Shari E., & Signore, Caroline. (2016). *Eliminating inequities for women with disabilities*. Washington, DC: American Psychological Association. This comprehensive book uses an intersectional approach to reviewing the research on women with disabilities.

Gender and Sexuality

It is not coincidental that the women's movement and the sexual revolution grew up together in the 1960s and 1970s. Historically, sex for women always meant pregnancy, which meant babies and a life devoted to motherhood. For the first time in the history of our species, because of the development of highly reliable methods of contraception, we are now able to separate sex from reproduction both in theory and in practice. In the 1970s, because of advances in contraception, women came to see themselves as free to enjoy sex without incurring a surprise pregnancy. The AIDS and herpes epidemics that began in the 1980s and 1990s have complicated the picture of sexual freedom. Nonetheless, female sexuality has been let out of the bag and shows no signs of returning.

Physiology

Much of our contemporary knowledge of female sexual physiology is due to the pioneering work of William Masters and Virginia Johnson (1966), which has been followed up by even more sophisticated research (Meston et al., 2004).

We can think of sexual response as occurring in four phases, although these stages actually flow together. The first phase is *excitement*. In women,[1] the primary response is **vasocongestion**, which means that a great deal of blood flows to the blood vessels of the pelvic region. A secondary response is the contraction of various muscle fibers termed **myotonia**, which results, among other things, in erection of the nipples.

Perhaps the most noticeable response in the excitement phase is the moistening of the vagina with lubricating fluid. This seems quite different from the most noticeable response in men, erection of the penis. In fact, the underlying physiological mechanism is the same: vasocongestion. The lubrication that appears on the walls of the vagina during sexual excitation results from fluids that have seeped from the congested blood vessels in the surrounding region, through the semipermeable membranes of the vaginal wall. The physiological underpinnings are the same in men and in women, although the observable response seems different.

In the excitement phase, a number of other changes take place, most notably in the clitoris. The clitoris, located just in front of the vagina (see Figures 12.1 and 12.2), has, like the penis, a shaft with a bulb or glans at the tip. The glans is densely packed with highly sensitive nerve endings. The clitoris is the most sexually sensitive organ in the female body. In response to further arousal, the clitoral glans swells, and the shaft increases in diameter, due to increasing vasocongestion. The clitoris is interesting because it is the only exclusively sexual organ in the human body; all the others, such as the penis, have both sexual and reproductive functions. The clitoris is purely for sexual pleasure.

The structure of the clitoris extends beyond the externally observable part (see Figure 12.3). Two crura—longer, spongy bodies—extend from the shaft and run along either side of the vagina, under the major lips (Clemente, 1987). Some refer to the entire structure as having a wishbone shape. These spongy bodies enlarge during arousal.

The vagina also responds in the excitement phase. Think of the vagina as an uninflated balloon in the unaroused state, divided into an outer third (or lower third, in a woman standing upright) and an inner two-thirds (or upper two-thirds). During the successive stages of sexual response, the inner and outer portions react in different ways. In the latter part of the excitement phase, the inner two-thirds of the vagina undergoes a dramatic expansion or ballooning (see Figure 12.4).

In the second phase of sexual response, the *plateau phase*, the major change is the appearance of the *orgasmic platform*. This refers to the outer third of the vagina, where there is a tightening of the bulbospongiosus muscle around the vaginal entrance (Figure 12.4). Whereas the upper portion of the vagina expands during excitement, the lower or outer portion narrows during the plateau phase. Therefore, if there happens to be a penis in the vagina at that point, the orgasmic platform grips it.

The other major change occurring during the plateau phase is the elevation of the clitoris. The clitoris retracts and draws into the body, but continues to respond to stimulation. A number of autonomic responses also occur, including an increase in pulse and a rise in blood pressure and in rate of breathing.

Once again, these complex changes are the result of two basic physiological processes, vasocongestion and increased myotonia or muscular tension, which occur similarly in both men and women. Readiness for orgasm occurs when these two processes have built up sufficiently.

Orgasm, the third phase of sexual response, consists of a series of rhythmic contractions of the muscles circling the vaginal entrance. Generally there is a series of 3 to 12

Vasocongestion: An accumulation of blood in the blood vessels of a region of the body, especially the genitals; a swelling or erection results.

Myotonia: Muscle contraction.

Orgasm: An intense sensation that occurs at the peak of sexual arousal and is followed by the release of sexual tensions.

---

[1] Here, again, we use *women* as shorthand for female-bodied persons.

FIGURE 12.1   Female sexual and reproductive anatomy viewed from the side.

FIGURE 12.2   The vulva, or external genitals, of the human female.

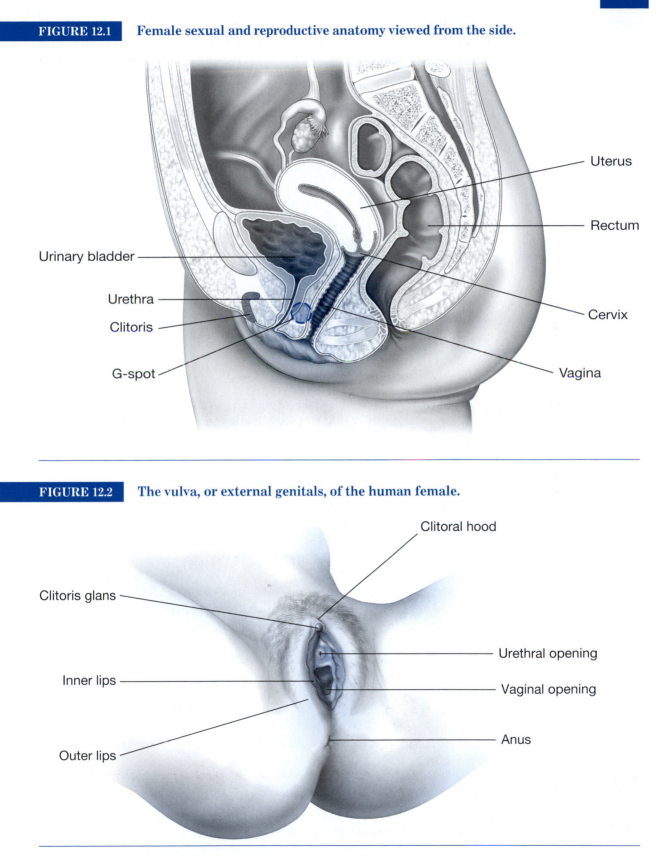

FIGURE 12.3   Beneath the surface: structure of the clitoris.

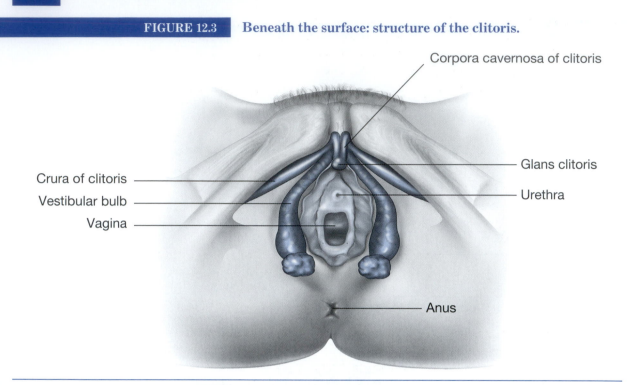

Corpora cavernosa of clitoris

Glans clitoris

Urethra

Crura of clitoris

Vestibular bulb

Vagina

Anus

FIGURE 12.4   Female sexual and reproductive organs during the plateau phase of sexual response. Notice the ballooning of the upper part of the vagina, the elevation of the uterus, and the formation of the orgasmic platform.

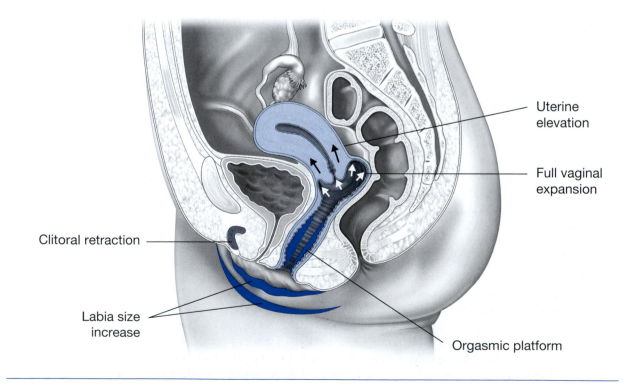

Uterine elevation

Full vaginal expansion

Clitoral retraction

Labia size increase

Orgasmic platform

contractions at intervals of slightly less than a second. The onset of the subjective experience of orgasm is an initial spasm of the muscles preceding the rhythmic contractions.

What do women's orgasms feel like? The main feeling is an intensely pleasurable spreading sensation that begins around the clitoris and then spreads outward through the whole pelvis. There may also be sensations of falling or opening up. The woman may be able to feel the contractions of the muscles surrounding the vaginal entrance. The sensation is more intense than just a warm glow or a pleasant tingling.

In the fourth phase, or *resolution phase*, of sexual response, the processes of excitement are reversed. The major physiological changes are a release of muscular tensions throughout the body and a release of blood from the engorged blood vessels. In women, the breasts, which were formerly enlarged with nipples erect, return to the unaroused state. The clitoris returns to its unaroused, unretracted position and shrinks to normal size. The muscles around the vaginal entrance relax, and the ballooned upper portion of the vagina shrinks. The return of a woman to the unstimulated state may require as long as a half-hour following orgasm. If the woman reaches the plateau phase without having an orgasm, the restoration process takes longer, often as much as an hour.

Criticisms of the Masters and Johnson Model

Criticisms of Masters and Johnson's work have been raised (e.g., Tiefer, 1991; Zilbergeld & Evans, 1980). One of the most important of these criticisms is that Masters and Johnson's model focuses exclusively on physiological processes and ignores cognition and affect— that is, what we are thinking and feeling emotionally during sexual response. In the wake of these criticisms, researchers have proposed other models.

Alternative Models

One alternative model to address this criticism, the **triphasic model**, was proposed by the eminent sex therapist Helen Singer Kaplan (1979). According to her, there are three components to sexual response: sexual desire, vasocongestion, and the muscle contractions of orgasm. The vasocongestion and orgasm components are consistent with Masters and Johnson; the new component is sexual desire, which refers to an interest in or motivation to engage in sexual activity. Without this psychological component of desire, sexual activity is not apt to take place, or if it does, it is less likely to be pleasurable. The desire component is also important in understanding some sexual disorders (discussed later in this chapter).

Triphasic model: A model that there are three components to sexual response: sexual desire, vasocongestion, and myotonia.

John Bancroft, Erick Janssen, and their colleagues have introduced a **dual control model** of sexual response (Bancroft et al., 2009). The model proposes that two basic processes underlie human sexual response: excitation (responding with arousal to sexual stimuli) and inhibition (inhibiting sexual arousal). These researchers argue that almost all sex research has focused on the excitation component, which is true of the Masters and Johnson model. The dual control model asserts that the inhibition component is equally important to understand. Inhibition of sexual response is adaptive across species; sexual arousal can be a powerful distraction that could become disadvantageous or even dangerous in certain situations.

Dual control model: A model that two basic processes underlie human sexual response: excitation and inhibition.

According to the dual control model, people vary widely in the strength of their tendencies toward sexual excitation and inhibition. Most people fall in the moderate range on both and function well. At the extremes, however, problems can occur. People who are very high on excitation and low on inhibition may engage in risky sexual behaviors. People who are very high on inhibition and low on excitation may be more likely to develop problems such as a disorder of sexual desire (discussed later in this chapter).

Researchers have developed scales to measure individuals' tendencies toward sexual excitation and sexual inhibition (Graham et al., 2006). Examples of *excitation* items include the following:

> When I think of a very attractive person, I easily become aroused.

> When a sexually attractive stranger accidentally touches me, I easily become aroused.

The following are examples of *inhibition* items (female version):

> I need my clitoris to be stimulated to continue feeling aroused.

> If I am masturbating on my own and I realize someone is likely to come into the room at any moment, I will lose my sexual arousal.

The dual control model recognizes that, although excitation and inhibition both have biological bases, early learning and culture are critical factors because they determine which stimuli the individual will find exciting and which will set off sexual inhibition. Most heterosexual men in our culture, for example, have been exposed to pornography, which shapes their idea of the type of female body that should be arousing (Dines, 2010).

Wouldn't evolution have selected purely for sexual excitation? It is the engine that drives reproduction and the passing of one's genes to the next generation. Why would inhibition exist? According to the dual control model, inhibition is highly functional in some situations. First, sexual activity in certain situations would be downright dangerous—say, when a predator is about to attack. Second, sometimes the environment is not conducive to reproduction and it is adaptive to wait for a better day or a better season. For example, in conditions of drought and famine, women's fertility is usually sharply reduced because any baby born would likely die, and the mother might die as well in the attempt to provide food. Inhibiting sexual response and waiting until conditions improve would be the best strategy.

Research typically shows gender differences, with men scoring somewhat higher on sexual excitation and women somewhat higher on sexual inhibition (Bancroft et al., 2009).

Clitoral and Vaginal Orgasm

Freud believed that women can experience two different kinds of orgasm: clitoral and vaginal. According to his view, little girls learn to achieve orgasm through stimulation of the clitoris during masturbation. However, in adulthood they have to learn to transfer the focus of their sexual response from the clitoris to the vagina and to orgasm from penis-in-vagina intercourse. Because some women fail to make this transfer, they can experience only clitoral orgasm and are therefore "vaginally frigid." Freud thought that the only mature female orgasm was vaginal.

Masters and Johnson dispelled this myth by showing convincingly that, physiologically, there is only one kind of orgasm. The major response is the contraction of the orgasmic platform. That is, physiologically an orgasm is the same whether it results from clitoral stimulation or from vaginal stimulation. Some women are even able to have orgasms through breast stimulation—and the physiological response is identical to that occurring from vaginal intercourse (Masters & Johnson, 1966).

Multiple Orgasms

Traditionally, it was thought that women, like men, experience only one orgasm, followed by a *refractory period* of minutes or even hours when they are not capable of arousal and orgasm. Research shows that this is not true and that in fact women can have multiple orgasms. Alfred Kinsey and his colleagues (1953) discovered this more than half a century ago, reporting that 14% of the women they interviewed experienced multiple orgasms. The scientific establishment dismissed these reports as unbelievable, however.

Observations from the Masters and Johnson laboratory provided convincing evidence that women do indeed experience multiple orgasms within a short time period. Moreover, these multiple orgasms do not differ from single ones in any significant way except that there are several. They are not minor experiences.

Physiologically, after an orgasm, the vaginal region loses its engorgement of blood. However, in women, but not in men, this process is immediately reversible. That is, under continued or renewed erotic stimulation, the region again becomes engorged, the orgasmic platform appears, and another orgasm is initiated. This is the physiological mechanism that makes multiple orgasms possible in women.

Most frequently, multiple orgasms occur through masturbation rather than vaginal intercourse, because it is difficult for a man to postpone his orgasm for such long periods. As Natalie Angier (1999) put it, regarding the clitoris, penis, and multiple orgasms, "Who would want a shotgun when you can have a semiautomatic?" (p. 58).

Sexuality and Aging

It is a popular belief that a woman's sexual desire is virtually gone by the time she is 60 or so, and perhaps ceases at menopause. Some people believe that sexual activity is a drain on their health and physical resources, and they deliberately stop all sexual activity in middle age to prevent or postpone aging. These, too, are myths that research has exploded.

A major survey of people over 50, conducted by the American Association of Retired Persons (1999), found that 24% of the women between 60 and 74 had sexual intercourse at least once a week. That declined to 7% for women over 75, but about 80% of them had no sexual partner, so the problem is mainly one of lack of a partner.

It is true that certain physiological changes occur as women age that influence sexual activity. The ovaries sharply reduce their production of estrogen at menopause, causing the vagina to lose much of its resiliency, and the amount of lubrication is substantially reduced. Use of lubricants can be helpful. Sexual functioning depends much more on the opportunity for regular, active sexual expression and physical and mental health than it does on hormone levels (Masters & Johnson, 1966).

A study of healthy women in their 60s, all with a male partner, found differences between those who were sexually active and those who were not (Bachmann & Leiblum, 1991). Those who were sexually active reported intercourse an average of five times per month. A pelvic exam by a physician who was unaware of which women were sexually active found less atrophy of the genitals in the women who were sexually active. If you don't use it, you lose it.

The G-Spot

The **G-spot** (short for **Gräfenberg spot**, named for a German obstetrician-gynecologist who originally discovered it in 1944, although his work was overlooked) is the popularized term for the *Skene's gland* or *paraurethral gland*. It lies between the wall of the urethra and the wall of the vagina (Zaviačič et al., 2000). Its ducts empty into the urethra, but the gland itself can be felt on the front wall of the vagina. Anatomically, it is the *female prostate* (see Figure 12.1). It may be that some women have a G-spot and others do not; a study using MRI scans identified a female prostate in six of the seven women studied (Wimpissinger et al., 2009).

G-spot (Gräfenberg spot): A small gland on the front wall of the vagina, emptying into the urethra, which may be responsible for female ejaculation.

There are two reasons that the G-spot is important. First, the researchers who have investigated it believe it is the source of *female ejaculation* (Addiego at al., 1981; Belzer, 1981; Ladas et al., 1982; Perry & Whipple, 1981). Traditionally, it was thought that men ejaculate and women don't. However, sex researchers John Perry and Beverly Whipple (1981) discovered fluid spurting out of the urethra of some women during orgasm. According to one study, the fluid is chemically similar to the seminal fluid of men, but contains no sperm. Perry and Whipple estimated that 10% to 20% of women ejaculate during orgasm. This is an important discovery, because given the old wisdom that women don't ejaculate, many women who did ejaculate suffered extreme embarrassment and anxiety, thinking they were urinating during sex.

There is a second reason that the G-spot might be important. Based on its discovery, Perry and Whipple theorized that there is a *uterine orgasm*. They believe that there are two kinds of orgasm: vulvar (the kind studied by Masters and Johnson, produced by clitoral stimulation and named for the vulva, or external genitals, of the female) and uterine (felt more deeply and produced by stimulation of the G-spot). This sounds like the old argument about clitoral versus vaginal orgasm, and certainly we should withhold judgment on the uterine orgasm until there can be independent replication by other scientists.

Psychological Aspects of Gender and Sexuality

Gender Differences in Sexuality

It is a traditional stereotype in our culture that female sexuality and male sexuality are quite different. Women were reputed to be uninterested in sex and slow to arouse. Men, in contrast, were supposed to be constantly aroused. What is the scientific evidence on gender differences in sexuality?

Jennifer Petersen and Janet Hyde (2010) conducted a meta-analysis of studies reporting data on gender differences in sexuality. Two gender differences were substantial: the incidence of masturbation and attitudes about casual sex. Women are less likely to have masturbated than men are ($d = 0.53$), and women are less approving of sex in a casual or uncommitted relationship than men are ($d = 0.45$). Notice that the sizes of these gender differences, 0.53 and 0.45, are large compared with some of the other gender differences we have examined, such as gender differences in abilities (see Chapter 8).

Let's first consider the gender difference in masturbation. Kinsey, based on his massive survey conducted in the 1940s, found that 92% of the men in his sample reported having masturbated to orgasm at least once in their lives, compared with 58% of the women (Kinsey et al., 1953). More recent surveys have found percentages very close to those (Laumann et al., 1994). That is, this gender difference doesn't seem to have disappeared in recent years with the sexual revolution.

One question we must ask, however, is whether this is a real gender difference or just an inaccuracy resulting from the use of self-reports. In our culture, particularly in previous decades, more restrictions have been placed on female sexuality than on male sexuality. It might be that these restrictions have discouraged girls and women from ever masturbating. On the other hand, they might simply lead women not to report masturbating. That is, perhaps women do masturbate but are simply more reticent to report it on a sex survey than men are. We tend not to believe this argument. On today's sex surveys, women report all kinds of intimate behaviors, such as fellatio and cunnilingus. More of them report having engaged in fellatio and cunnilingus than report having masturbated. It is hard to believe that these women honestly report about oral-genital sex and suddenly get bashful and lie about masturbation.

Another substantial gender difference was in attitudes about casual sex, such as sex in a "one night stand," $d = 0.45$ (Petersen & Hyde, 2010). Men are more approving and women are more disapproving. In one well-sampled national study, 76% of White women, but only 53% of White men, said that they would have sex with someone only if they were in love (Mahay et al., 2001). This gender difference is consistent across U.S. ethnic groups: The comparable statistics were 77% for Black women and 43% for Black men, 78% for Mexican American women and 57% for Mexican American men. This gender difference can be a source of great conflict between women and men.

Consistent with their attitudes about casual sex, men report a larger number of sex partners than women report. Once again, though, it is important to remember that these data are based on self-reports, which can sometimes be inaccurate. It could be that men and women actually have roughly the same number of sex partners, but men exaggerate their number and/or women underreport their number.

A clever study used the *bogus pipeline method* to test this possibility (Alexander & Fisher, 2003; see also Jonason & Fisher, 2009). College students were brought to the lab to fill out questionnaires about their sexual attitudes and behaviors. They were randomly assigned to one of three experimental conditions. In the bogus pipeline condition, the student was hooked up to a fake polygraph (lie detector machine) and told that the machine could detect false answers. People should respond very honestly in this condition. In the anonymous condition, the student simply filled out the questionnaire anonymously, as is typical of much sex research, and placed the questionnaire in a locked box when finished. In the exposure threat condition, respondents had to hand their completed questionnaires directly to the experimenter, who was an undergraduate peer, and the experimenter sat in full view while the respondents completed their questionnaires, serving as a reminder that this other person would easily be able to see their answers. Figure 12.5 shows the results for reports of the number of sexual partners the respondent had had.

FIGURE 12.5   **Number of sex partners reported by men and women in the bogus pipeline study.**

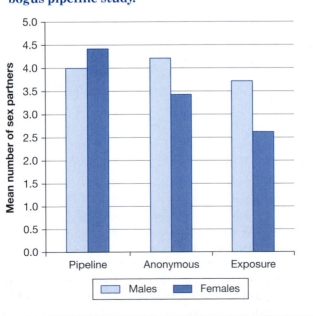

Source: Based on data from Alexander, Michele G., & Fisher, Terri D. (2003). Truth and consequences: Using the bogus pipeline to examine sex differences in self-reported sexuality. *Journal of Sex Research, 40,* 27–35. Figure created by Janet Hyde.

In the anonymous condition and the exposure threat condition, the usual gender difference appeared, with men reporting more partners than women did. The fascinating result is that, in the bogus pipeline condition, when people were presumably being most truthful, there was no significant gender difference in the number of sexual partners reported. The other interesting point in Figure 12.5 is that men's reports of number of partners did not vary significantly with experimental condition. It was women's reports that varied. The implication is that men feel free to report their number of partners regardless of whether others will find out. Women, in contrast, underreport their number when it may become known. This finding is powerful evidence of the ways in which women believe that the culture tells them to suppress their sexuality.

Another stereotype is that a gender difference exists in interest in and arousal to erotic materials, men being much more interested in and responsive to them than women are. Is there any scientific evidence that this is accurate?

The Petersen and Hyde (2010) meta-analysis found that reported use of pornography was one of the largest gender differences ($d = 0.63$), with men engaging in the behavior more than women. A meta-analysis of laboratory studies on gender differences in arousal to erotic materials found that men are more aroused, but the difference is not large, $d = 0.31$ (Murnen & Stockton, 1997). Interestingly, the difference was largest among college students ($d = 0.38$) but was nonexistent among adults beyond the college years ($d = -0.04$). This finding points to the importance of looking at changing patterns of gender differences in sexuality across the lifespan.

An interesting study by Meredith Chivers and colleagues provides insight into the responses of women and men to erotic materials (Chivers et al., 2007; for a meta-analysis of similar research, see Chivers et al., 2010). Participants were heterosexual and lesbian women, and heterosexual and gay men. They watched a series of 90-second video clips from seven stimulus categories: control (landscapes), nonhuman sexual activity (bonobos), female nonsexual activity (nude exercise), male nonsexual activity (nude exercise), female–female sexual expression, male–male sexual expression, and female–male sexual expression. The researchers not only obtained people's self-ratings of their arousal during each segment, but also got objective measures of their physiological levels of arousal. To do this, they used two instruments: a penile strain gauge and a photoplethysmograph. The penile strain gauge is used to obtain a physiological measure of arousal in men; it is a flexible loop that fits around the base of the penis and measures its circumference. The photoplethysmograph measures physiological arousal in women; it is an acrylic cylinder that is placed just inside the vagina. Both instruments measure vasocongestion in the genitals, which is the major physiological response during sexual arousal.

Several interesting findings emerged from this study.

1. For both men and women, genital responses were strongest for partnered sexual activity.

2. Actor gender was more important for men than it was for women. That is, heterosexual men were turned on by heterosexual sex and women's sex, and gay men were turned on by sex between men. However, for women, the gender of the actors made less of a difference. Many studies have found this effect, that women respond to a wider range of stimuli, regardless of gender.

3. The correlations between physiological measures of arousal and self-report of arousal were larger for men than for women. This means that women are sometimes unaware that they are physiologically turned on.

In sum, then, this research indicates that men and women are similar in their responses to erotic materials, except that women are less particular about the gender of the actors. The research also indicates that women can sometimes be unaware of their own physical arousal.

An additional gender difference in sexuality is found in *orgasm consistency*. According to one major survey, 91% of men but only 64% of women had an orgasm during their most recent sexual encounter (Herbenick et al., 2010). The gap is narrower for orgasm consistency during masturbation, but even here men seem to be more effective: 80% of men, compared with 60% of women, reported that they usually or always have an orgasm when masturbating (Laumann et al., 1994, p. 84).

Sexual Development

Sexual development in childhood and adolescence involves a complex interplay between the developing body, early experiences with masturbation, and messages from the media, parents, and peers (Hyde & DeLamater, 2017).

The earliest sexual experiences many people have are in masturbation. But as we have seen, the data indicate that substantial numbers of girls and women never masturbate, and many of those who do, do so later in life than boys and men do. This may have important consequences in other areas of sexuality as well. As one sex educator said, "I talk to so many girls where the first person to actually touch their clitoris is somebody else" (Orenstein, 2016, p. 205).

Childhood and adolescent experiences with masturbation are important early sources of learning about sexuality (Kaestle & Allen, 2011). Through these experiences we learn how our bodies respond to sexual stimulation and what the most effective techniques for stimulating our own bodies are. This learning is important to our experience of adult, two-person sex. Perhaps the women who do not masturbate, and who are thus deprived of this early learning experience, are the same ones who do not have orgasms in sexual intercourse. This is exactly what Kinsey's data suggested: 31% of the women who had never masturbated to orgasm before marriage had not had an orgasm by the end of their first year of marriage, compared with only 13% to 16% of the women who had masturbated (Kinsey et al., 1953, p. 407). Girls' lack of experience with masturbation in adolescence, then, may be related to their problems with having orgasms during heterosexual intercourse. And research with adult women shows that masturbation can be a source of feelings of sexual empowerment (Bowman, 2014).

Boys and girls seem to learn about masturbation in different ways. Most boys report having heard about it before trying it themselves, and a substantial number observe others doing it. Most girls, in contrast, learn to masturbate by accidental discovery of the possibility. Both boys and girls may learn about it from the media (Kaestle & Allen, 2011). And there seems to be a real double standard (see below), in which masturbation is more taboo for girls than it is for boys. As a result of these different experiences, it appears that most boys have learned to associate the genital organs with pleasure by the time of puberty, whereas many girls have not.

An illustration of the way in which masturbation can expand female sexuality is given by what one young woman student wrote in an essay:

> At twelve years old, I discovered masturbation. . . . I was almost relieved to have, quite by accident, discovered the practice. This actually was one of the nicest discoveries that I've ever made. I feel totally comfortable with this and have actually

discussed it with some of my friends. One of my favorite theories centers around this. When men have asked me to have intercourse with them and I felt that I was basically going to only serve the purpose of being an instrument to produce their orgasm, I usually tell them that I'm sure that they'd "have a better time by themselves." Masturbation does produce a better, more controlled, orgasm for me. I'm not saying that it's better than sexual contact with a man for me but I do think it's more satisfying than waking up next to someone I don't care about and feel comfortable with. I'm surprised that according to Kinsey, only 58 percent of women masturbate at some time in their lives. I thought everyone did. It's very creative for me. I've tried several techniques and it certainly helps me in my sexual experiences. I know a great deal about my sexual responses and I think that in knowing myself, some of it relates to men and their sexual responses.

Experiences with masturbation—or lack of such experiences—then, may be very important in shaping female sexuality and making it different from male sexuality.

Of course, socialization forces on girls' developing sexuality are also important. Our culture has traditionally placed tighter restrictions on women's sexuality than it has on men's, and vestiges of these restrictions linger today. These restrictions have acted as a damper on female sexuality, and thus they may help to explain why some women do not masturbate or do not have orgasms. In an essay, one woman student recalled one of her childhood socialization experiences:

> A big part of my childhood was Catholic grammar school. The principal and teachers were nuns of the old school. . . . I remember one day the principal called all of the girls (third grade to eighth) to the auditorium. "I can't blame the boys for lifting your skirts to see your underwear," she scolded, "you girls wear your skirts so short it is temptation beyond their control." I had no idea what she was talking about, but throughout school the length of our skirts was of utmost importance. Nice girls did not show their legs.

Double standard:
The evaluation of male behavior and female behavior according to different standards, including tolerance of male promiscuity and disapproval of female promiscuity; used specifically to refer to holding more conservative, restrictive attitudes toward female sexuality.

The differences in restrictions on female and male sexuality are encoded in the **double standard** (Crawford & Popp, 2003; Fasula et al., 2014). The double standard says, essentially, that the same sexual behavior is evaluated differently depending on whether a man or a woman engages in it (see Chapter 2). An example is casual sex, which can be a status symbol for a man but a sign of being a slut for a woman (Bogle, 2008). The media play a role in subtly maintaining the double standard. One analysis of teen girl magazines, for example, found that negative consequences of sex were associated more often with girls than with boys (Joshi et al., 2011).

Sexuality is an area of ambivalence for girls and women (Orenstein, 2016; Tolman, 2002). This ambivalence results from the kind of mixed messages that they get from society. Beginning in adolescence, they are told that popularity is important for them, and being sexy—being "hot"—increases one's popularity. But actually engaging in intercourse, especially with many partners, can lead to a loss of status. The ambivalence-producing message is "Be sexy but don't be sexual."

This ambivalence is writ large with media celebrities. In 2013, Miley Cyrus "twerked" (a kind of dancing with suggestive hip thrusts) on stage in a televised performance and generated enormous media coverage. For her, was that performance a display of empowerment and agency? Or was she the victim of powerful media herself? One might make either argument from a feminist point of view.

Adolescent Girls, Desire, and First Intercourse

Most discussions of teenage girls' sexuality focus on topics such as teen pregnancy and date rape—that is, on the negatives. Missing from such discussions is any recognition that adolescent girls may actually experience sexual desire. Psychologist Michele Fine (1988) has called this the "missing discourse of desire."

A study of 11th-grade girls, some urban and some suburban, representing multiple ethnic groups, gives us insight into these girls' experience of sexual desire (Tolman, 2002). This study is part of a broader trend among researchers to see adolescents' sexual experiences as a normative part of development (Tolman & McClelland, 2011). About two-thirds of the sample said that they felt desire. As they described it, the desire had a power, intensity, and urgency. It was grounded in the body, challenging beliefs that girls' sexuality is purely relational. At the same time, the girls questioned their entitlement to their own sexual feelings.

Differences emerged between the urban and suburban girls in how they responded to feelings of desire. The urban girls expressed agency (feelings of confidence) with a goal of self-protection. They exercised self-control and caution about their body's feelings, recognizing their own vulnerability to AIDS, pregnancy, and getting a bad reputation. The suburban girls, in contrast, expressed agency with a goal of pleasure. They were curious about sex and were less restrained by feelings of vulnerability, although cultural messages about appropriate female sexuality still exerted controls. One suburban girl expressed her complicated feelings:

> I don't like to think of myself as feeling really sexual. . . . I don't like to think of myself as being like someone who needs to have their desires fulfilled. . . . I mean I understand that it's wrong and that everybody has needs, but I just feel like self-conscious when I think about it, and I don't feel self-conscious when I say that we do these things, but I feel self-conscious about saying I need this kind of a thing. (quoted in Tolman & Szalacha, 1999, p. 16)

A content analysis of teen magazines for girls in the United States (*Seventeen*, *CosmoGirl!*, and *Teen*) gives us some insight into the cultural factors that create these dilemmas of desire for adolescent girls (Joshi et al., 2011). Boys' sexual desire received more attention than girls' sexual desire, whereas sexual risks and negative consequences were portrayed more often for girls than for boys. The researchers also conducted the same analysis for comparable magazines in the Netherlands, with some differences in results. For example, in the Dutch magazines, sexual desire was portrayed as much for girls as for boys. Compared with the United States, Dutch culture is more open about sexuality and has more of a commitment to gender equality.

These national variations, too, provide evidence that cultural factors play a major role in the socialization of girls' sexuality.

Many girls have their first experience of heterosexual intercourse during high school or the early college years. Girls tend to experience less pleasure at first intercourse than boys do. In a large sample of college students, women reported significantly less pleasure ($d = 1.08$) and significantly more guilt ($d = -.55$) about first intercourse than men did (Sprecher, 2014). On a pleasure scale ranging from 1 (*not at all*) to 7 (*a great deal*), women gave an average rating of only 3.01 for first intercourse. Despite, or perhaps because of, our culture's romanticized version of first intercourse, adolescent girls typically find it disappointing. Nonetheless, they persist.

Hooking Up

The dating scene and casual sex now have more options—and more terminology. **Hooking up** is a poorly defined term—which is part of its problem—but it generally means any kind of casual sexual contact, ranging from making out to intercourse, between two people who are strangers or only casually acquainted, with no strings attached, that is, with no commitment to a future relationship (Bogle, 2008).

Sociologist Kathleen Bogle (2008) conducted a qualitative study of hooking up on college campuses, interviewing students and recent alumni from two eastern U.S. universities. According to her findings, college campuses provide an ideal environment for hookup culture to flourish. There is plenty of access to same-age peers. In recent years, students have come to believe that college is a time to party and no one seems to be in a hurry to marry. Developmental psychologists note that the period of adolescence has become extended. College students do not view themselves as adults—adulthood comes a few years after college. For many, real dating and building a long-term relationship does not begin until after college.

Bogle found that a sexual double standard exists in hookup culture. Despite sexual liberation and women's participation in hookups, women cannot have too many partners, and those who do can be ostracized and labeled "sluts." For men, there are no rules. As the college years progress, women increasingly want a relationship because it is one way to avoid being labeled a slut, but men have less motivation to begin a relationship. Even in this very contemporary form of sexual expression, a double standard still exists.

Other studies have also found evidence of a double standard, as well as gendered power dynamics, in hookups. In one, women were more likely than men to feel judged for hooking up (Kettrey, 2016). Feeling judged was related to a sense of lack of power in the interaction. And lack of power meant that a woman might perform a sexual act just to please the man or give in to pressure for intercourse.

The Sexuality of Transgender Persons

The sexuality of transgender persons is a complex topic. Some experts like to categorize transgender people as either heterosexual or homosexual (Blanchard, 1985). The terminology is complicated, though. Let's say we have a trans woman, whose natal gender was male and whose identity is as a woman. Is she heterosexual because she prefers female sexual partners and her natal gender was male? Or is she heterosexual because her identity is woman and she prefers male sexual partners? And why do we have to use a binary categorization of sexual orientation anyhow? To this is added the complexity of whether the person is undergoing hormonal treatments and possibly surgical interventions. Importantly, sexuality is so fundamentally about the body. Yet for so many trans persons, the body is the problem, because the sex of the body does not align with the person's gender identity.

In one qualitative study, 25 trans men were interviewed about their sexuality (Williams et al., 2013). The men ranged in age from 20 to 65 and were ethnically diverse. All but one of them were taking testosterone. Most had had top surgery (see Chapter 11). Only two of them had had bottom surgery. For most of the men, the testosterone treatments had a big effect, both physically and psychologically. The clitoris grew considerably for them so that they could consider it more as a penis. And they developed a sense of sexual urgency that is so associated with masculinity in our culture. As one man said, "I had a pea-sized clit before I started T (testosterone) and it grew 10-fold, and now I have a dick that's the size of a gherkin" (Williams et al., 2013, p. 726). Another man said that his sexuality had "gone through the roof. I never had an orgasm before.... Now I jack off two to four times a day" (Williams et al., 2013, p. 728). Yet some regretted their loss of multiple orgasms. And for those who had not had bottom surgery, the vagina could seem like an unwelcome reminder of their female body.

The researchers also found generational shifts in patterns of identity development. For the older generation of trans men, many had decided first that they were lesbian. That was an available category and identity at that time. Trans was not. Only later did they conclude that they were trans. In more recent generations, the trans identity develops earlier and first, because it is now better known to the general public.

The same research team also interviewed 25 trans women (Williams et al., 2016). Almost all of the women were on estrogen, and the majority had had cosmetic surgery so as to appear more feminine. The majority had not had bottom surgery, though. The cosmetic surgery was successful to varying degrees, depending on how masculine the person's body type was to begin with (e.g., whether they had very broad shoulders). For most of the women, it was very important to feel sexually attractive and feminine. When they were asked what the most serious problem was for a trans person in a love relationship, the most common response was that it was being truly accepted for who they are.

The Intersection of Gender and Race in Sexuality

The topic of the intersection of gender, race, and sexuality is a large and complex one that could easily fill several books. Many historical issues are involved. For example, during the period of slavery in the United States, White masters assumed that they had the right to sexual intercourse with African American slave women. In sharp contrast, the reverse—an African American slave man having sex with a White woman—was not only forbidden but grounds for death.

Here we will focus on contemporary data collected by social scientists that allow us to compare the sexual behavior of girls and women of various ethnic groups. Some of these data are summarized in Table 12.1. The data show evidence of both differences and similarities. Among 15- to 19-year-olds, Whites, African Americans, and Latinx are about equally likely to have had heterosexual intercourse. Yet the sequence of sexual behaviors can vary by ethnic group. For example, Whites are the most likely to have oral sex before first vaginal intercourse, and African Americans are the least likely. When asked about their feelings about the first time they had sex, nearly half of both Whites and Latinx really wanted it to happen, but the percentage was much smaller for African Americans. Also striking in Table 12.1 is the fact that data on these questions were not available for Asian Americans in these well-sampled, large studies. Clearly, we need much more research on the sexuality of Asian Americans.

Earlier in the chapter we noted that girls tend to begin masturbating at later ages than boys do. When the data are broken down by ethnicity, however, it becomes clear that this statement is true for Whites but not for African Americans. On average, Black women begin masturbating at an earlier age than Black men do and considerably earlier than White women do (Belcastro, 1985). This finding is a good reminder that we shouldn't look simply at gender differences, but should remember the intersection of gender and ethnicity.

The media portray women's sexuality differently depending on their ethnicity. In magazine advertisements, White women's sexuality is portrayed as submissive and dependent on men, whereas Black women's sexuality is portrayed as independent and dominant (Baker, 2005). Asian American women have been stereotyped in the media as exotic sex toys (Reid & Bing, 2000). American Indian women and their sexuality are essentially invisible, except for some representations in the magazine *Latin Girl* (Sanchez-Hucles et al., 2005).

TABLE 12.1   A comparison of the sexuality of American women of different ethnic groups.

	Whites	African Americans	Latinx	Asian Americans
Had intercourse, among 15- to 19-year-olds*	42%	45%	42%	NA
Oral sex experience with a man, among 15- to 24-year-olds**	69%	63%	59%	NA
Oral sex occurred before first vaginal intercourse**	49%	27%	37%	NA
Relationship with partner at first sex: just met or just friends*	16%	21%	9%	NA
Feelings about first sex: I really wanted it to happen*	44%	29%	42%	NA

Sources: *Martinez et al. (2011); **Copen et al. (2012).

NA = not available in that study.

Sexual socialization by the family can also vary by ethnic group. Asian American women, for example, report that sexuality is a taboo topic of discussion within the family (Kim, 2009). Nonetheless, Asian American parents implicitly convey their attitudes and expectations, which are conservative and restrictive about sexuality. One woman, commenting about her mother, said,

> She's very, very hush hush about it. . . . I have mostly Asian friends and we all don't know. . . . Our moms and our parents, we just grew up never hearing. . . . I have never heard the word "sex" come out of my mom's mouth (Amanda, Korean American, age 19). (quoted in Kim, 2009, p. 339)

There was also evidence of a double standard in fathers' treatment of daughters compared with sons. As one woman said,

> My dad always implies to me things that I should do and I shouldn't do. Like, I shouldn't have a boyfriend and things like that. But when he talks about my brother, he's like, "I'm going to buy your brother a car. I'm going to give him all this money to go on dates.". . . I've told him, "You treat us differently." And he's like, "Yeah." He admits it. . . . He thinks it's appropriate (Naomi, Filipina American, age 19). (quoted in Kim, 2009, p. 342)

Sexual Disorders and Therapy

Sexual disorder: A problem with sexual responding that causes a person mental distress; examples are erection problems in men and orgasm problems in women.

The term **sexual disorder** (or sexual dysfunction) refers to various disturbances or impairments of sexual functions, such as inability to have an orgasm (orgasmic disorder) or premature ejaculation. Here we will look at some specific examples of sexual disorders in women. The disorders are grouped into the categories of desire disorders, arousal disorders, orgasmic disorders, and pain disorders.

Desire Disorders

Sexual desire, or libido, refers to a set of feelings that lead the individual to seek out sexual activity or to be pleasurably receptive to it. When sexual desire is inhibited, so that the individual is not interested in sexual activity, the disorder is termed *low sexual desire*, or **hypoactive sexual desire** (Basson et al., 2004). The defining characteristic is lack of interest in sex or sharply reduced interest, or a lack of responsive desire. Many people's desire occurs before sexual activity begins and leads them to initiate sex, whereas in other cases they begin to feel desire as sexual activity starts; this latter pattern is called *responsive desire*. Responsive desire is particularly common in women.

Hypoactive sexual desire: A sexual disorder in which there is a lack of interest in sexual activity; also termed inhibited sexual desire or low sexual desire.

Roughly 10% to 15% of women report no sexual desire, with the percentage increasing as women age (West et al., 2004). Men, too, experience lack of desire; it is just less common in men than it is in women.

As with other dysfunctions, disorders of sexual desire entail complex problems of definition. There are many circumstances when it is perfectly normal for a person's desire to be inhibited. For example, one cannot be expected to find every potential partner attractive. Sex therapist Helen Singer Kaplan (1979) recounted an example of a couple consisting of a shy, petite woman and an extremely obese (350 pounds, 5 feet 3 inches tall), unkempt man. He complained of her lack of desire, but one can understand her feelings and would certainly hesitate to classify her as having a sexual disorder. One cannot expect to respond sexually at all times, in all places, with all persons.

It is also true that an individual's absolute level of sexual desire is often not the problem; rather, the problem is a **discrepancy of sexual desire** between the partners (Zilbergeld & Ellison, 1980). That is, if one partner wants sex less frequently than the other partner wants it, there is a conflict.

Discrepancy of sexual desire: A sexual disorder in which the partners have considerably different levels of sexual desire.

In the latest edition of the *Diagnostic and Statistical Manual of Mental Disorders* (DSM-5), the American Psychiatric Association (2013) did some odd things in regard to gender and sexual disorders. The prime example is hypoactive sexual desire disorder. In the DSM-5, it is split into two disorders, male hypoactive sexual desire disorder and *female sexual interest/arousal disorder*. Why is it that hypoactive sexual desire disorder had to be split into male and female versions? And what does that do for trans individuals? Moreover, why should desire (called interest in DSM-5) be merged with arousal for women (Balon & Clayton, 2014; Basson, 2014)? Those favoring this new category say that it is appropriate because interest or desire problems so frequently co-occur with arousal problems in women. The new classification system reinforces the gender binary in striking ways.

The following have been implicated as determinants of low sexual desire: hormones, antidepressant medications, psychological factors (particularly anxiety and/or depression), cognitive factors (not having learned to perceive one's arousal accurately or having limited expectations for one's own ability to be aroused), and sexual trauma such as sexual abuse in childhood (Ashton, 2007; Pridal & LoPiccolo, 2000).

A closely related phenomenon is asexuality, which today is an available sexual identity with an Internet presence. **Asexuality** is usually defined as a lack of interest in or desire for sex or as a lifelong lack of sexual attraction (Brotto & Yule, 2011; Prause & Graham, 2007). Research with asexual people shows that the defining feature is low sexual desire. Still, it's important to note that asexuality is not a sexual disorder.

Asexuality: A lack of interest in or desire for sex.

Arousal Disorders

Sex therapists do not use the term *frigidity* because it has a variety of imprecise, negative connotations.

Female sexual arousal disorder: A lack of response to sexual stimulation, including a lack of lubrication.

Female sexual arousal disorder refers to a lack of response to sexual stimulation, including a lack of lubrication (Graham, 2010). The disorder involves both the subjective, psychological component and a physiological element. Some cases are defined by the woman's own subjective sense that she does not feel aroused despite good stimulation, and others are defined by difficulties with vaginal lubrication.

Difficulties with arousal and lubrication are common, reported by roughly 10% of women (Mitchell et al., 2013). These problems become particularly frequent among women during and after menopause. As estrogen levels decline, vaginal lubrication decreases. The use of lubricants is an easy way to deal with this problem. The absence of subjective feelings of arousal is more complex to treat.

Orgasmic Disorders

Anorgasmia: The inability to have an orgasm; also called orgasmic disorder.

Orgasmic disorder (also termed **anorgasmia,** orgasmic dysfunction, female orgasmic disorder, or inhibited female orgasm) is the condition of being unable to have an orgasm. In *lifelong orgasmic disorder* the woman has never experienced an orgasm. In *situational orgasmic disorder,* the woman has orgasms in some situations, but not in others. Clearly, in this case there is no organic (physical) impairment of orgasm, because the woman is capable of experiencing it. One example of situational orgasmic disorder is the case of women who are able to have orgasms through masturbation but not through penis-in-vagina intercourse. This pattern is so common, however, that it probably shouldn't be classified as a disorder (Hyde & DeLamater, 2017).

Orgasmic disorders in general are common among women. Roughly 20% of women report difficulties with anorgasmia (West et al., 2004).

Pain Disorders

Dyspareunia: Painful intercourse.

Painful intercourse, or **dyspareunia,** can trigger other problems with sexual functioning (Farmer & Meston, 2007). Too often, a woman's complaints of pain are dismissed, particularly if the physician cannot find an obvious physical problem. However, this is a serious condition and should be treated as such. When pain is felt in the vagina, it may be due to failure to lubricate, to infection, to special sensitivity of the vagina (such as to the contraceptives being used), or to changes in the vagina due to age. Pain may also be felt in the region of the vaginal entrance and clitoris or deep in the pelvis. In this latter case, the causes may be infection or tearing of the ligaments supporting the uterus, particularly following childbirth.

Vaginismus: A strong, spastic contraction of the muscles around the vagina, perhaps closing off the vagina and making intercourse impossible.

Vaginismus involves a tightening or spasm of the outer third of the vagina, possibly to such an extent that the opening of the vagina is closed and intercourse becomes impossible (Basson et al., 2001; Leiblum, 2000). Factors in the woman's history that seem to cause this condition include family background in which sex was considered dirty and sinful, a previous sexual assault, and long experience of painful intercourse due to a physical problem.

Behavioral Therapy for Sexual Disorders

Masters and Johnson pioneered modern sex therapy (Masters & Johnson, 1970; for a critique, see Zilbergeld & Evans, 1980). Their approach can be seen basically as behavior therapy, grounded in learning theory, although they themselves did not frame it that way.

The major objective in therapy is abolishing goal-directed sexual performance. Most people think that certain things should be *achieved* during sexual activity—for example, that the woman should achieve or attain orgasm. This emphasis on achieving leads to a fear of failure, which spells disaster for sexual enjoyment. The therapist therefore tries to remove the individual from a spectator role in sex—observing their own actions, evaluating their success. Instead, the emphasis is on the enjoyment of all sensual pleasures. Clients use a series of *sensate focus* exercises in which they learn to touch and to respond to touch. They are also taught to express sexual needs to their partners, which people generally are reluctant to do. For instance, the woman is taught to tell her partner in which regions of her body she enjoys being touched most and how firm or light the touch should be. Beyond this basic instruction, which includes lessons in sexual anatomy and physiology, the therapist simply allows natural sexual response to emerge. Sexual

FOCUS 12.1

WOMEN'S SEXUAL PROBLEMS: A NEW VIEW

Feminist psychologist and sex therapist Leonore Tiefer, together with a large group of experts, has proposed a new view of women's sexual problems (Kaschak & Tiefer, 2001; Tiefer, 2001). Tiefer argues that the classification of sexual problems has, for decades, been based on men's problems and the increasing medicalization of their problems encouraged by drug companies that have made billions on Viagra. A new view is needed, Tiefer argues, that focuses on women's sexual experiences. The new view proposes four broad categories for women's sexual problems:

1. *Sexual problems due to sociocultural, political, or economic factors.* These include ignorance and anxiety about sexuality resulting from inadequate sexuality education. In the absence of education, women may lack information about the biology of sexual functioning. And in the absence of information about the impact of gender roles, women may experience sexual avoidance or distress because they feel they cannot meet cultural standards of ideal female sexuality.

2. *Sexual problems relating to partner and relationship.* These include discrepancies in desire or in preferred behaviors between the partners, distress about sexuality because of dislike or fear of the partner, and problems created by poor communication about sex.

3. *Sexual problems due to psychological factors.* These include sexual aversion and inhibition of sexual pleasure due to past experiences of physical, sexual, or emotional abuse; problems associated with attachment issues; and depression and anxiety.

4. *Sexual problems due to medical factors.* These include pain or lack of response during sex that is not due to any of the factors listed above. Problems in this category can result from specific medical conditions such as diabetes, or they may involve side effects of medications.

This classification scheme starting from women's point of view is strikingly different from the traditional one reflected in the American Psychiatric Association's *Diagnostic and Statistical Manual* (DSM-5). What would happen if we now imposed these categories on men's sexual experience?

Source: Tiefer (2001). Reprinted with permission of the Society for the Scientific Study of Sexuality.

pleasure is natural; sexual response is natural. After removing artificial impediments to sexual response, most people quickly begin joyful, "successful" participation in sex.

Many sex therapists require that both partners participate in therapy. Masters and Johnson maintained that there is no such thing as an uninvolved partner in cases of sexual disorders, even if only one person displays overt symptoms. For instance, a woman who does not experience orgasm is anxious and wonders whether there is anything wrong with her or whether she is unattractive to her partner. The partner, at the same time, may wonder why they are failing to stimulate her to orgasm. Both partners are deeply involved.

Masters and Johnson evaluated the success of their therapy, both during the 2-week therapy session and in follow-up studies 5 years after couples left the clinic. Their research indicated that therapy was successful in approximately 75% of the cases (although their results have been disputed; see Zilbergeld & Evans, 1980).

Today many sex therapists use a combination of the behavioral exercises pioneered by Masters and Johnson and cognitive therapy (Heiman, 2002). This is termed *cognitive-behavioral therapy*. The cognitive approach involves restructuring negative thoughts about sexuality to make them positive.

Additional Therapies for Women's Sexual Disorders

The prevalence of women who have problems having orgasms, particularly in heterosexual intercourse, is so high that it seems that this pattern is well within the range of normal female sexual response. It is questionable whether it should be called a disorder, except insofar as it causes unhappiness for the woman. With the growing awareness of the frequency of this problem have come a number of self-help sex therapy books for women, one of the best being Emily Nagoski's (2015) *Come as You Are*. Reading and working through the exercises in these self-help books actually has a fancy name—bibliotherapy—and it has been demonstrated to produce significant gains in women's frequency of orgasm (Van Lankveld, 1998).

A common recommendation from Nagoski and other therapists (LoPiccolo & Stock, 1986; Meston et al., 2004) is that preorgasmic women practice masturbation to increase their capacity for orgasm. The idea is that women must first explore their own bodies and learn how to bring themselves to orgasm before they can expect to have orgasms in heterosexual intercourse. As noted earlier in this chapter, many women have not had this kind of practice, and sex therapists recommend that they get it.

Kegel exercises: Exercises to strengthen the muscles surrounding the vagina; also called pubococcygeal muscle exercises.

Kegel exercises or *pubococcygeal muscle exercises* are also recommended (Kegel, 1952). The pubococcygeal (PC) muscle runs along the sides of the entrance to the vagina. Exercising this muscle increases women's sexual pleasure by increasing the sensitivity of the vaginal area. This exercise is particularly helpful to women who have had the PC muscle stretched in childbirth or who simply have poor tone in it. The woman is instructed first to find the PC muscle by sitting on a toilet with her legs spread apart, urinating, and stopping the flow of urine voluntarily. The muscle that stops the flow is the PC muscle. After that, the woman is told to contract the muscle 10 times during each of six sessions per day. Gradually she can work up to more.

Feminist Sex Therapy

Sex therapist Leonore Tiefer has pioneered models of feminist sex therapy (Tiefer, 1996, 2001). Tiefer questions the medicalization of sexual disorders that results from therapists using the DSM "diagnoses" (for further discussion of the DSM, see Chapter 15).

She argues that these diagnoses are based on Masters and Johnson's exclusively physiological model of sexual response and that they oversimplify sexuality and ignore the social context of sexuality and sex problems (see Focus 12.1). The advent of Viagra has only increased the medicalization of sex problems, and the search for a "female Viagra" channels the medicalization toward women's problems.

Tiefer recommends that feminist sex therapy for women include the following components:

1. *Education about feminism and women's issues:* This can be liberating as a woman realizes that her individual problem is common and often rooted in the culture's negative attitudes about sexuality and women.

2. *Anatomy and physiology education:* Because sexuality education in the United States—whether from parents or schools—is so inadequate, many women have fundamental misunderstandings about their sexual anatomy and its functioning. Education can be a simple solution in many cases.

3. *Assertiveness training:* Women need to learn to be assertive in asking a partner for what they need in a sexual interaction, just as in other areas of life.

4. *Body image reclamation:* Women need to make a substantial shift away from seeing their bodies as objects to be evaluated (as we saw in the discussion of objectified body consciousness in Chapter 2) to seeing their bodies as sources of sensations and competencies.

5. *Masturbation education:* As noted earlier, many women do not masturbate and some do not even know about masturbation. Masturbation education has proven to be successful in sex therapy for women. From a feminist point of view, it can be seen as empowering women.

Where's the Female Viagra?

Men have Viagra for their erections. Why isn't there a pill for women's sexual problems? Is this another case of gender bias in the medical establishment? It turns out to be a complicated story.

The drug company Pfizer, which produced Viagra, hoped that it would also work for women. After many failed clinical trials, Pfizer announced in 2004 that it would give up on testing Viagra for women (Harris, 2004). The problem is that Viagra is good at producing erections, but women's sexual problem is not lack of erections—it's lack of desire and difficulty with orgasms.

In another attempt at a female Viagra, the German pharmaceutical company Boehringer developed the drug flibanserin (trade name Addyi). It had originally been developed to be an antidepressant, but it didn't work very well. Its effect is to reduce levels of the neurotransmitter serotonin and increase levels of dopamine and norepinephrine. To use terms from the dual control model (discussed earlier in this chapter), serotonin seems to have an inhibitory effect on sexual desire, and dopamine and norepinephrine seem to have excitatory effects. All of that sounds good in theory, but in 2010 the U.S. Food and Drug Administration (FDA) refused to approve flibanserin, based on clinical trials that showed no actual increase in sexual desire in women taking it, compared with controls. Boehringer decided not to pursue it further.

In 2014, the plot thickened (Moynihan, 2014). The drug was bought by a new company, Sprout Pharmaceuticals. A feminist campaign materialized, pressuring the FDA to approve flibanserin because of the need for a "pink Viagra" and arguing that the FDA was discriminating against women by not approving it. As it turned out, the "feminist" campaign was actually created and funded by Sprout. And flibanserin still didn't work. But the FDA approved it in 2015 because of the pink Viagra campaign. This whole episode is a salient example of the co-optation of the women's movement by big business, in this case, Big Pharma.

Gender Similarities

In previous chapters we stressed gender similarities in psychological processes. There are also great gender similarities in sexuality. In earlier generations, at the time of the Kinsey research, there were marked gender differences in several aspects of sexuality. However, more recent research shows that these differences are greatly decreased, or even absent, now.

For example, according to Kinsey's data collected in the 1940s, 71% of men but only 33% of women had premarital intercourse by age 25 (Kinsey et al., 1953). There was, at that time, a marked gender difference in premarital sexual activity. By the 1990s, though, 78% of men and 70% of women had engaged in premarital sexual intercourse (Laumann et al., 1994), representing a clear trend toward gender similarities. In the meta-analysis discussed earlier in this chapter, a number of variables showed no gender difference, including incidence of same-gender sexual behavior and attitudes about masturbation (Petersen & Hyde, 2010). Although there are some large gender differences in sexuality (incidence of masturbation, use of pornography, and attitudes about casual sex), there are many gender similarities.

Experience the Research

Gender Differences in Sexuality

Administer the questionnaire below to 10 students: 5 cis women and 5 cis men. If you are able to recruit some trans folks or non-binary people, their responses will be interesting, too. Because the information you will collect is sensitive, be sure to explain to each participant that the answers will be anonymous. You must devise some method to ensure anonymity, such as having respondents mail the questionnaire back to you, or having them place it into a large brown envelope that already contains others' questionnaires. If you have only one trans person in your sample, how can you guarantee their anonymity? Assure your respondents that the questionnaire will take less than 5 minutes to complete.

SEXUALITY QUESTIONNAIRE

1. Age: _____

2. Gender: ___ Woman ___ Man ___ Trans woman ___ Trans man ___ Nonbinary
   Other: Specify _____

3. Ethnic heritage (check the one that applies):

   ___ Black/African American

   ___ Hispanic/Latinx

   ___ Asian American

   ___ American Indian

   ___ White (not Hispanic)

   ___ Biracial or multiracial

For each of the questions below, circle the letter that best reflects your response. Remember that your answers will be kept completely anonymous.

4. What is your attitude about a heterosexual couple engaging in sexual intercourse when they are engaged?

   a. Strongly disapprove

   b. Disapprove somewhat

c. Neutral

d. Approve somewhat

e. Strongly approve

5. What is your attitude about a heterosexual couple engaging in sexual intercourse when they are only casually acquainted (i.e., a "one-night stand" or hookup)?

   a. Strongly disapprove

   b. Disapprove somewhat

   c. Neutral

   d. Approve somewhat

   e. Strongly approve

6. Have you ever masturbated to orgasm?

   a. Yes (Go to question 7)

   b. No (Skip question 7 and go to question 8)

7. In the past month how many times did you masturbate to orgasm? Number: _____

8. Have you ever engaged in heterosexual intercourse?

   a. Yes (Go to question 9)

   b. No (Skip question 9 and go to question 10)

9. With how many different partners have you engaged in heterosexual intercourse?

   Number: ____

10. Have you ever engaged in sex to orgasm with someone of your own gender?

   a. Yes

   b. No

CHAPTER SUMMARY

Physiologically, sexual response involves vasocongestion and myotonia, as people pass through four stages of response: excitement, plateau, orgasm, and resolution. This analysis results from the research of Masters and Johnson, which has been criticized for omitting psychological aspects of sexuality. Alternative models have been proposed, including Kaplan's triphasic model, which adds sexual desire, and the dual control model, which emphasizes processes of sexual excitation and inhibition.

Contemporary sex research challenges Freud's assertion that women can have either clitoral or vaginal orgasms. Research also lends support to the contention that some women possess a G-spot, which may be responsible for ejaculation in some women.

According to meta-analysis, there are moderate-sized gender differences in the incidence of masturbation, attitudes about casual sex, and use of pornography. There is also a gender difference in reported number of sex partners, although the bogus pipeline study questions whether that is a true difference or just a bias in reporting.

Across child and adolescent development, girls are less likely to masturbate than boys are. That means that girls get less experience with their body's sexual response. To that is added the double standard and forces of socialization that also discourage girls' sexual responding. Despite this, research shows that adolescent girls do experience sexual desire. First intercourse is a significant event, but girls experience substantially less pleasure in it than boys do. Hooking up is a contemporary form of sexual interaction, yet even here, a double standard is found.

The sexuality of transgender persons is a new topic for research. The issues are poignant, because sexuality is so much about the body, and yet for transgender people, the body can be exactly the problem, because it does not align with the person's gender identity. Trans men tend to be pleased with the effects of testosterone administration, which can enlarge the size of the clitoris and increase sexual desire. For trans women, issues often center on feeling feminine and sexually attractive.

In considering the intersection of gender and ethnicity in sexuality, research shows some similarities for women of different ethnic groups, but also some differences.

Sexual disorders for women include hypoactive sexual desire, female sexual arousal disorder, anorgasmia, dyspareunia, and vaginismus. Therapy for sexual disorders includes behavior therapy, bibliotherapy, and directed masturbation. Feminist sex therapy has also been developed.

Even though gender differences in sexuality are often emphasized, there are many gender similarities.

SUGGESTIONS FOR FURTHER READING

Dines, Gail. (2010). *Pornland: How porn has hijacked our sexuality.* Boston, MA: Beacon Press. Dines presents a feminist analysis of contemporary pornography and how it has distorted both male and female sexuality.

Hyde, Janet S., & DeLamater, John D. (2017). *Understanding human sexuality* (13th ed.). New York, NY: McGraw-Hill. Clearly, we have a prejudice in favor of this book, but we would like to recommend it if you want more information on sexuality than we could provide in one brief chapter here.

Nagoski, Emily. (2015). *Come as you are.* New York, NY: Simon & Schuster. This is a great book on sexual techniques and how to think about one's own sexuality in healthy ways, with all of the information based solidly in science.

Gender and Sexual Orientation

> " After I graduated from college . . . I found myself not necessarily only attracted to both sexes, but also slightly more open-minded to the notion that . . . maybe I can find something in just a person, that I don't necessarily have to be attracted to one sex versus the other. . . . Since then I've been in . . . a couple of different long-term relationships with women and I've had lots of sex with men and currently I'm in a long-term relationship with a man that I find very, very, very enjoyable and . . . fulfilling so it's hard for me to identify so therefore I kind of prefer

> to not identify or just kind of . . . kind of joke about it and say, 'I'm not bisexual or homosexual, I'm just sexual.'

A woman respondent quoted in Diamond (2005, p. 126)

With the sexual revolution and the feminist movement has also come the rise of gay liberation. The gay liberation movement can be counted as dating from June 1969, when, in response to police harassment, gays and trans people rioted in Greenwich Village in New York. A discussion of women and gender today would be incomplete without a discussion of lesbian and bisexual women.

It is important to bear in mind that "lesbian" is not a homogeneous category. Lesbians vary tremendously from one another, just as heterosexual women do. Some are professors and some work on assembly lines. Some are fat and some are thin. Some are White and some are African American.

Sexual orientation is defined as a person's erotic and emotional orientation toward members of their own gender or members of another gender (Hyde & DeLamater, 2017). Sexual orientation is not just an issue of eroticism or sexuality, but also an issue of the direction of one's emotional attachments. It is not just a matter of whom one has sex with, but whom one loves. A **lesbian**, then, is a woman whose erotic and emotional orientation is toward other women. A **bisexual** is a person whose erotic and emotional orientations are toward both women and men (note that this term reflects the gender binary). With the proliferation of possible sexual identities, the term **sexual minority** is used as an umbrella term for all people with nonheterosexual sexual identities and behaviors. The term **queer**, which has been used as an anti-gay insult, has been reappropriated by some gay activists and theorists to cover all sexual minorities. Queer theory is prominent in lesbian-gay-bisexual (LGB) studies.

Sexual orientation encompasses three components: attraction, identity, and behavior (Katz-Wise & Hyde, 2015). *Attraction* refers to whether one is sexually attracted to one's own gender, the other gender, or both. *Identity* refers to how one thinks of oneself—I'm straight, I'm lesbian, I'm bisexual, I'm queer, I'm mostly heterosexual. *Behavior* refers to whom one engages in sexual behavior with—members of one's own gender or another gender. For example, some men have a heterosexual identity yet occasionally have sex with other men. That is why some researchers refer to *men who have sex with men* (MSM) rather than *gay men*, because they are studying behavior, not identity.

How does gender diversity intersect with sexual orientation? Some trans women are attracted to women and have a lesbian identity (Tate & Pearson, 2016). Therefore, a trans-inclusive definition of *lesbian* includes both cis women and trans women who are attracted to women. In this chapter, we use *lesbian* to include both cis women and trans women, although most of the research done with lesbians has focused just on lesbians who are cis women.

Sexual orientation: A person's erotic and emotional orientation toward members of their own gender or members of another gender.

Lesbian: A woman whose sexual orientation is toward other women.

Bisexual: A person who is erotically and emotionally attracted to both women and men.

Sexual minority: An umbrella term for all people with a sexual orientation other than heterosexual.

Queer: An epithet that has been reappropriated by gay activists and theorists to refer to sexual minorities.

Queer Theory

Queer theory was introduced in Chapter 2. Recall the important arguments in this theory: (1) Binaries should be challenged, whether the gender binary (male, female) or the sexual orientation binary (heterosexual, homosexual); (2) sexual orientation and gender are not essential, fixed, biologically based characteristics. Instead they are fluid and dynamic over time and in different situations. Queer theory also challenges other binaries such as normal versus deviant (Tolman & Diamond, 2014). Moreover, queer theory asserts that these binary categories themselves exert power over people and their interactions. These binaries exert regulatory force and create privilege as well as marginalization. In particular, heterosexuality is privileged and normalized, and all other sexual orientations are marginalized.

Performativity, a concept originated by philosopher Judith Butler, is another key concept in queer theory (Butler, 1990; Tolman & Diamond, 2014). The idea here is that gender is performed, as is sexual orientation. Women perform gender through their clothing, makeup, and jewelry, as well as through their interactions with others. Likewise, sexual orientation is performed. For example, heterosexuality is performed constantly in male–female interactions, such as a male–female couple holding hands as they stroll down the street. And heterosexuality can be performed in male–male interactions such as the "bro hug," in which men half hug each other to signal friendship but clarify that there is no sexual attraction.

Performativity: The idea that gender and sexual orientation are constructed through a constant set of performances by people (actors).

Queer theory and its assertions have an uneasy relationship with psychology. Traditional psychology, and even some feminist psychology, loves to categorize people and then look at differences between the categories—whether gender differences or differences between gays and straights. Because this textbook is based in science, we report research of that kind while being mindful of the critique of it posed by queer theory. It is also true that some psychology is consistent with queer theory. Perhaps the best example is Lisa Diamond's work on sexual fluidity (discussed later in this chapter).

Stereotypes and Discrimination

Some experts believe that many Americans' attitudes toward lesbians and gay men can best be described as homophobic. **Homophobia** may be defined as a strong, irrational fear of sexual minority persons. Some scholars dislike the term *homophobia* because, although certainly some people have antigay feelings so strong that they could be called a phobia, what is more common is negative attitudes and prejudiced behaviors. Therefore, some prefer the term **antigay prejudice** or *sexual prejudice* (Herek, 2000a). A related term is **heterosexism**, which refers to discrimination or bias against people based on their sexual orientation, and nonheterosexuality in particular.

Homophobia: A strong, irrational fear of sexual minority persons.

Antigay prejudice: Negative attitudes and behaviors toward gay men and lesbians. Also called sexual prejudice.

Results of a well-sampled 2012 survey of Americans' attitudes are shown in Table 13.1, along with comparable data from 1973. Notice that Americans' attitudes have become substantially more accepting over roughly 40 years. Four times as many Americans in 2012, compared with 1973, believed that same-gender sexuality is not wrong at all. Nonetheless, 46% still believed that it is always wrong.

Heterosexism: Discrimination or bias against people based on their nonheterosexual orientation.

Many tangible instances of antigay prejudice exist. There are numerous documented cases of women being fired from their jobs or dishonorably discharged from the armed forces upon disclosure of their sexual orientation (Shilts, 1993), and in 1993 there was a great debate between President Bill Clinton and military leaders about whether the military should continue this practice of dishonorable discharge. The result was a "don't ask, don't tell" policy, in which it was all right to be gay or lesbian as long as one was secretive about it (this policy was repealed in 2011 by President Barack Obama). Until recent Supreme Court cases, most states did not recognize lesbian partners in matters of health insurance, inheritance, or marriage. The most extreme expressions of antigay prejudice occur in *hate crimes* against sexual minorities (Cogan & Marcus-Newhall, 2002).

TABLE 13.1   **Attitudes of adult Americans toward same-gender sexuality, 1973 and 2012.**

Questions and Responses	1973	2012
Are sexual relations between adults of the same sex . . .?		
Always wrong	74%	46%
Almost always wrong	7%	3%
Wrong only sometimes	8%	7%
Not wrong at all	11%	45%

Source: Data gathered via *General Social Survey, 1972–2012* (2012).

A meta-analysis assessed the extent of victimization of LGB individuals (Katz-Wise & Hyde, 2012). The results indicated that substantial numbers had experienced one or another kind of victimization. For example, 56% had experienced verbal harassment and 28% had experienced a physical assault on account of their sexual orientation.

Some victimization, then, is obvious, such as physical assault. Yet some is more subtle. Derald Wing Sue's (2010) concept of *microaggressions,* introduced in Chapter 4, is relevant here as well. In Chapter 4, we discussed racial microaggressions, which are subtle insults directed at people of color and often done automatically or nonconsciously. Sexual orientation microaggressions occur as well (Nadal, 2013). They can occur in many forms, such as heterosexist jokes or not inviting a same-gender partner to a family holiday gathering. Other examples include heterosexist language (for example, the popular expression "That's so gay") and denial that individual heterosexism exists. Assumptions that gay people are deviant continue and can be manifested in subtle ways. For example, in a PowerPoint presentation at one college, a slide read, "LGBT people are six times more likely to attempt suicide than normal people" (Nadal, 2013, p. 57).

Microaggressions based on gender identity or expression are also abundant (Nadal, 2013). One common occurrence is the misgendering of a person—for example, calling a trans person "she" (the natal gender) instead of the pronoun they prefer, which might be "he" or "they" (see Chapter 5).

Perhaps the most subtle and simultaneously most powerful discriminatory belief is the assumption that heterosexuality is universal. As a result, lesbians must tolerate coworkers asking if they have a boyfriend or mothers asking if a husband is on the horizon yet. Just as we saw in previous chapters that the male is normative, so, too, is heterosexuality normative. The term **heteronormativity** was coined to refer to this pervasive cultural belief that heterosexuality is the norm.

Heteronormativity: The belief that heterosexuality is the norm.

Lesbian Culture

Lesbian Community

Today there is a lesbian community or culture with its own norms and values. Even for lesbians who are in the closet, this culture has a profound impact on identity and behavior—such as the books they read or the way they define sex. As one woman put it,

I have seen lesbian communities all over the world (e.g., South Africa, Brazil, and Israel) where the lesbians of that nation have more in common with me (i.e., they play the same lesbian records, have read the same books, wear the same lesbian jewelry) than the heterosexual women of that nation have in common with heterosexual women in the United States. (E. Rothblum, personal communication, 2007)

Participation in the lesbian community can then become a major force in the lives of lesbians, at least for those who are out of the closet.

Lesbian Relationships

With the 2000 census, the U.S. Census Bureau made an unprecedented change. It allowed as a category in the count of household types same-sex, unmarried-partner households. Previously these households and the relationships that they imply had been literally invisible in the census. In fact, in the 1990 census, if a same-gender couple reported that they were married, the Census Bureau changed the gender of one of the partners and counted them as a heterosexual married couple (Smith & Gates, 2001). The 2000 census counted 600,000 same-gender partner households in the United States, although this is likely an undercount (Smith & Gates, 2001). These households were about evenly split between gay male households and lesbian households, and they were found in 99% of all counties in the United States. The 2015 Supreme Court decision on gay marriage, discussed in a later section, recognized and at the same time changed the cultural climate on many of these issues.

What is known psychologically about the relationships in these households? Across numerous surveys, between 8% and 21% of lesbian couples have been together for 10 or more years (Kurdek, 2005). In 2000, same-sex civil unions became legal in Vermont. Research on the first year of couples entering into these unions showed that two-thirds were female (Solomon et al., 2004). The lesbian couples had been living together for an

David A. Smith/Getty Images Entertainment/Getty Images.

PHOTO 13.1
The Riff Raff Band, with lead singer queer-identified Alynda Lee Segarra, trans fiddler Yosi Perlstein, bassist Callie Millington, and drummer David Jamison. One important feature of lesbian culture is music.

average of 9 years and 34% had children (15% from the current relationship and 19% from a prior relationship, typically heterosexual).

Lesbian couples—like heterosexual couples—must struggle to find a balance that suits both persons. Three aspects of the relationship typically have to be negotiated and can be sources of conflict: money, housework, and sex (Solomon et al., 2005). Lesbian couples tend to have more equality in housework than heterosexual couples do (Gotta et al., 2011).

What is striking about the research on gay and lesbian relationships is how similar they are—in their satisfactions, loves, joys, and conflicts—to heterosexual relationships (Holmberg & Blair, 2009; Patterson, 2000). For example, one study compared lesbian and gay couples with heterosexual couples who were engaged or married (Roisman et al., 2008). Lesbian couples did not differ from heterosexual couples in the reported quality of their relationship, nor did they differ on laboratory measures of relationship quality. The one exception was that, compared with heterosexual couples, lesbians were somewhat more skilled at working harmoniously with their partners on a laboratory task.

Lesbians tend to value an equal balance of power in their relationships, although they don't always achieve it (Patterson, 2000). When there is an imbalance, the woman who has more income and more education tends to be the more powerful member of the couple.

Doubtless the 2015 Supreme Court decision legalizing same-sex marriage will have an impact on these relationships, but it is too early for research to have emerged.

Gay Marriage

In 2000 Vermont became the first U.S. state to provide formal, legal civil unions to same-gender couples, with all the benefits—such as health insurance—that are normally provided to heterosexual spouses. The term *civil union* was used at the time to make the idea more palatable to those who opposed gay marriage and said that marriage was only between a man and a woman. After 2000, it was a state-by-state battle. By 2011, same-gender *marriage* was legal in the United States in California, Connecticut, Massachusetts, Iowa, New York, and Vermont, as well as in Belgium, Canada, Spain, and the Netherlands.

The state-by-state battles were slow and uneven, though, and matters of principle were involved. Many people felt that this was an important issue of equal rights. Several cases made their way through the courts. Finally, in 2015, the U.S. Supreme Court issued a decision in the case of *Obergefell v. Hodges*. The question was whether states must allow gay marriage, and the court ruled that they must. The legal basis was the equal protection clause in the U.S. Constitution, which asserts that all citizens have a right to equal protection under the law. That principle was extended to equal rights to marriage. Many activists prefer to say that the issue is not gay marriage, but *marriage equality*.

Research shows that, prior to *Obergefell v. Hodges*, the implementation of state-level marriage equality policies was associated with reductions in suicide attempts among sexual minority youth (Raifman et al., 2017). And same-gender couples in legally recognized relationships show better mental health than other LGBs (Riggle et al., 2010), so the right to gay marriage may represent a victory on many fronts.

Sexual Orientation Development and Fluidity

Developmental psychologists have studied the process by which people develop a sexual identity, that is, an identity that one is lesbian, heterosexual, bisexual, or something else.

Bloomberg/Getty Images.

PHOTO 13.2
As of 2015, gay marriage was legal in the United States.

A 5-year-old would have no sense of being lesbian or heterosexual, but sometime along the way, usually during adolescence or early adulthood, sexual minority individuals acquire a sense of sexual identity. Heterosexuals, of course, have the privilege of simply assuming theirs, consistent with what the culture expects.

Lisa Diamond (2008b) has conducted extensive research on the process of the development of women's sexual orientation. She began with a sample of college women and women recruited from LGB community events and followed them for more than 10 years. Her research led her to conclude that a defining feature of women's sexual orientation (leaving open the question of men's sexual orientation) is **sexual fluidity**, that is, situation-dependent flexibility in women's sexual responsiveness. Many women, of course, have a sexual orientation that is fixed and stable across their lives. But others find their orientation and attractions shifting over time, sometimes because of a particular person—regardless of gender—to whom they are attracted. Diamond also notes that the concept of a fixed sexual orientation and identity is a Western notion that is not shared by some other cultures.

Sexual fluidity: Situation-dependent flexibility in women's sexual responsiveness to women or men.

In her longitudinal study, Diamond found that women changed in all directions over time, for example, from lesbian to bisexual, from bisexual to lesbian, and from lesbian to heterosexual. These findings contradict the idea of a fixed sexual identity, at least for some individuals.

Physiological research also supports these ideas. In these studies, both subjective arousal and physiological arousal are measured using techniques like those in the Chivers study described in Chapter 12. Participants are shown videos of either male–female, male–male, or female–female sexual activity. Heterosexual women show the same amount of genital arousal to female–female activity as they do to male–male activity and male–female activity (Chivers et al., 2004). (Heterosexual men, in contrast, show strong arousal to the female–female video, somewhat less to the male–female video, and almost none to the male–male video.) These results, then, show that, consistent with Diamond's work, many women are flexible about which gender arouses them.

Stage theories of the development of gay sexual identity have been popular (e.g., Cass, 1979). They posit that individuals begin in a stage of identity confusion and gradually move to identity acceptance and identity pride. The most recent research, though, questions these step-by-step, linear models. They may be accurate for some people, perhaps especially men. However, for many others, sexual identity and behavior may shift back and forth depending on the situation and the potential partner.

Coming out: The process of acknowledging to others that one is lesbian, gay, bisexual, or queer.

Another developmental process for sexual minority women involves **coming out**. Women can be very vulnerable in the process of coming out, whether in the sexual minority community, to their old friends, or to their coworkers. Whether they experience acceptance or rejection can be critical to self-esteem. There may also be fears of losing one's job or custody of one's children. Many lesbians make a decision to be selectively out—that is, to be out with people they know they can trust, and not with others.

Lesbians who are selectively out may face a distinct set of stresses. Consider a common situation in which a woman is not out at work, but is out in the lesbian community. At work, she must take care not to reveal her secret, be careful about the pronoun she uses when referring to her date, or worry that a worker will phone her at home and her partner will answer. On the other side, she may be pressured by the lesbian community to be completely out.

Coming out to one's family is one of the most significant events for gays and lesbians. In one sample of LGB adults, roughly 73% of both the men and the women had talked with a parent about being LGB (Rothman et al., 2012). Typically, they disclosed to their mother first. There were also links between disclosure and mental health. Those who had not come out to their parents were more likely to be depressed than those who had. Among those who had disclosed to their parents, those whose parents reacted unsupportively were also more likely to be depressed. Parents' responses are important to the mental health of LGB people.

Many lesbians function with essentially a *dual identity*. That is, they identify and have ties with the sexual minority world and at the same time they identify and have ties with the majority heterosexual world (Fingerhut et al., 2005). In many ways this is like being bilingual or bicultural. Both the strength of lesbian identity and the strength of mainstream identity are positively associated with psychological well-being.

Mental Health Issues

Lesbians' Adjustment

Prior to 1973, *homosexuality* was a diagnosis in the American Psychiatric Association's *Diagnostic and Statistical Manual*. That is, homosexuality per se was seen as a mental disorder. In 1973 the American Psychiatric Association decided to remove homosexuality from the diagnostic list, reflecting new research and changing understandings of sexual orientation.

Current research comparing lesbians and heterosexual women on measures of mental health finds many similarities between the two groups, but also some differences (Balsam et al., 2015; Cochran et al., 2003; Meyer, 2003; Wichstrøm & Hegna, 2003). Lesbian and heterosexual women are roughly equal on measures such as self-esteem and current psychological distress. Compared with heterosexual woman, however, lesbians are more likely to have had suicidal thoughts, to have attempted suicide, and to have used psychotherapy.

Researchers debate the meaning of these findings. Almost certainly they reflect the stress of being a sexual minority person. And how large are the differences? In one study, 4.4% of heterosexual women, compared with 7.9% of lesbians, had attempted suicide after age 18 (Balsam et al., 2005). We could focus on the finding that lesbian women were nearly twice as likely as heterosexual women to have attempted suicide. Alternatively, we could note that it is only a 3.5 percentage point difference and that 92.1% of the lesbians had not made suicide attempts. Should we view the glass as half full or half empty? These questions reflect the issue of interpretation of results explained in Chapter 1 for gender differences, applied here to sexual orientation differences.

Rather than seeing lesbian identity as automatically causing adjustment problems or not causing problems, it is preferable to understand that being lesbian may be a risk factor for some mental health problems. In social psychological terms, being a sexual minority is associated with stigma. This stigma is a source of stress for the individual (Hatzenbuehler, 2009). This stress can in turn lead to emotional distress, interpersonal problems, and/or negative cognitive style (see Chapter 15). Any of these can make a person vulnerable to psychological problems such as depression and anxiety. *Minority stress theory* was developed to describe these stresses and their impact on mental health (Meyer, 2003). Many sexual minority women display resilience in the face of these stresses. Social support from parents and friends can help offset the effects of minority stress. In addition, according to stress inoculation theory, exposure to some stress makes people more resilient in the future (Hatzenbuehler, 2009).

Therapy

Some lesbians seek psychotherapy for psychological distress, just as some heterosexuals do. Unfortunately, however, many psychotherapists are not well educated about sexual orientation issues and may provide inappropriate or inadequate care. In response to this problem, the American Psychological Association has adopted guidelines for psychotherapy with gay, lesbian, and bisexual clients. These guidelines emphasize issues such as the following (Division 44, 2000):

1. It is important for psychologists to understand that having a homosexual or bisexual orientation does not automatically mean that the person is psychologically disturbed. Psychologists, of course, grow up in the same culture as everyone else and learn the same kinds of myths that laypersons learn.

2. Psychologists need to probe their own attitudes about sexual orientation issues as well as their knowledge about these issues. If they discover limitations in their expertise or attitudes that might have a negative impact on the client, they should refer the client to another therapist.

3. Lesbians, gays, and bisexuals are stigmatized in dozens of ways, ranging from subtle prejudice to outright violence, and psychologists must gain a deep understanding of the impact this may have on the mental health of their client. They should also understand that these experiences may affect the client's behavior in therapy.

4. Psychologists should be knowledgeable about relationship issues for sexual minority persons. This includes respecting lesbians', gays', and bisexuals' romantic relationships and understanding how disclosure of sexual orientation may have an impact on the client's relationship with their family of origin—and how nondisclosure places a psychological burden on the client.

5. Lesbian, gay, and bisexual persons who are members of ethnic minority groups may face particular challenges because of cultural norms against homosexuality within their group, and psychologists must be sensitive to these issues.

Children of Lesbian Mothers

Increasingly, lesbian couples are creating families that include children. These children may have resulted from a previous heterosexual marriage, assisted reproduction (e.g., artificial insemination), or adoption. Lesbians raising children is a controversial practice to some heterosexual people in the United States, who view a lesbian household as a damaging setting for children to grow up in. The courts have often assumed that lesbians were unfit mothers. Lesbian mothers have lost custody of children they had when heterosexually married, and being a lesbian has been grounds for being denied the possibility of adoption (Patterson, 2009). The underlying psychological assumption has been that lesbians are bad mothers, in the sense that they will not do a good job rearing their children and the children will grow up poorly adjusted. There also is an assumption that these children will be stigmatized, teased by their peers, and so on. How well adjusted are the children of lesbian mothers?

Research has compared children of lesbian mothers with children of heterosexual parents on measures such as sexual identity, personal development, and social relationships. This research has found that the children of lesbian mothers develop as well as children reared by heterosexual couples (Farr, 2017; Golombok et al., 2003; Patterson, 2017). Research has also shown that the child-rearing practices of lesbian mothers and heterosexual mothers are quite similar (Farr et al., 2010). Some research has even found that lesbian couples show better parenting skills than heterosexual couples (Farr & Patterson, 2013).

The U.S. National Longitudinal Lesbian Family Study initially recruited 154 prospective lesbian mothers who were going to have a baby through artificial insemination (Gartrell & Bos, 2010). The researchers then followed up with the families, collecting data when the children were 10 years old and again when they were 17. The bottom line: At both ages, the children of lesbian mothers scored as well as or better than an age-matched normative sample from the general population on measures such as academic performance, rule-breaking, and aggressive behavior.

Another concern is that lesbian parents might work to "convert" their children to being lesbian or gay or that children might model their mother's lesbian relationship. In fact, the data indicate that the great majority of children growing up with a gay or lesbian parent become heterosexual (Patterson, 2009).

In summary, the evidence indicates that there is no cause for concern about the adjustment of children growing up in a lesbian household.

©iStockphoto.com/flySnow.

PHOTO 13.3

An important political issue for lesbian couples is the right to have children.

Why Do Women Become Lesbian, Bi, or Straight?

A fascinating psychological question is this: Why do people become heterosexual, lesbian, or bisexual? Older theories and research took it as their task to explain homosexuality.

They operated under the assumption that everyone should turn out heterosexual unless some "accident" occurs that shifts the person in a homosexual direction. Newer theories and research take it as their task to explain sexual orientation—not only why people become lesbian or gay, but why people become heterosexual as well.

Biological Explanations

Three biological explanations have been proposed: genetics, brain factors, and hormones.

Some have suggested that sexual orientation is genetically determined or influenced (see review by Hyde, 2005b). To test this hypothesis, one research team recruited lesbian women who were either members of an identical twin pair or members of a nonidentical twin pair, or had a sister by adoption (Bailey et al., 1993; for a critique, see Byne & Parsons, 1993). The concordance rate for lesbian orientation was 48% for identical twins (*concordance* means that if one member of the twin pair is lesbian, so is the other). This was compared with a concordance rate of 16% for nonidentical twins and 6% for adoptive sisters. The finding that identical twins have a much higher concordance rate than nonidentical twins provides evidence for a genetic basis. At the same time, the 48% concordance rate means that 52% of the identical twins pairs were *dis*cordant—one was lesbian and the other heterosexual. If sexual orientation were completely genetically determined, the concordance would be 100%. Therefore, environmental factors must also exert an influence.

The same researchers conducted a second study using improved methodology (Bailey et al., 2000). This time the concordance rate among women was 24% for identical twins and 11% for nonidentical twins. This finding suggests some possible genetic contributions, but the results are not as strong as in the earlier study.

This is the era of the Human Genome Project, and it is now possible to scan people's DNA to check for linkages to many different traits. One genome scan has been done for sexual orientation but—this will sound all too familiar—it looked at men only (Mustanski et al., 2005).

In regard to brain factors, a highly publicized study by neuroscientist Simon LeVay (1991) identified differences in the hypothalamus between heterosexuals and homosexuals. The three study groups were gay men, heterosexual men, and heterosexual women; there was no lesbian group, giving us no information about their brains. Much research and theory on sexual orientation have had this problem—lesbians have been invisible.

Investigating the possibility that endocrine imbalance is the cause of same-gender orientation, researchers have tried to determine whether testosterone levels of gay men might be low compared with those of heterosexual men and whether lesbians might have higher testosterone levels or perhaps lower estrogen levels than heterosexual women. Research testing these hypotheses has consistently found no differences between lesbian and heterosexual women on a variety of hormones (Byne, 1996; Downey et al., 1987). This hypothesis is not taken seriously anymore.

Others have wondered whether prenatal hormone exposure might be influential. They have, for example, studied girls with congenital adrenal hyperplasia (discussed in Chapter 10). None of these studies has yielded definitive evidence either.

Environmental Factors

Learning theory fares no better when tested against the data. For example, children who grow up with a gay parent are not themselves more likely to become gay (Bailey et al., 1995; Golombok & Tasker, 1996; Patterson, 2009). Modeling therefore does not seem to play a role. In addition, lesbians are no more likely than heterosexual women to have been heterosexually raped (Bell et al., 1981). This counters a hypothesis from learning theory that an unpleasant heterosexual experience should channel sexual orientation in a lesbian direction.

The Bottom Line

The bottom line, simply put, is that scientists do not know what causes sexual orientation. But there may be a good theoretical lesson to be learned from that somewhat frustrating conclusion. It has generally been assumed not only that lesbians are a distinct category, but also that they form a homogeneous category, that is, that all lesbians are fairly similar. Not so. Moreover, queer theory leads to a questioning of the sexual orientation binary—that women are either lesbian or heterosexual. The data in fact indicate that many women fall outside that binary because they are bisexual, queer, mostly heterosexual, or sexually fluid. Theories about simple causes of women being lesbian or heterosexual may be doomed to failure.

Differences Between Lesbians and Gay Men

Theorists frequently refer to homosexuals or gays as if there were no differences between gay men and lesbians (or else as if gay men were the only phenomenon of interest). How different are lesbians and gay men?

Some differences between the two groups do emerge. First, lesbians place more emphasis on the emotional intimacy of their relationship than gay men do (Peplau & Garnets, 2000).

Second, many gay men have numerous different sexual partners, whereas lesbians more typically form long-term, exclusive relationships and therefore have fewer different partners. In a well-sampled national study, men who had had at least one same-gender sex partner reported, on average, 44 different sex partners since age 18 (Laumann et al., 1994). This compares with an average of 20 different partners for women in that same category. Gay men are also more likely than lesbians to have sex outside the relationship (to "cheat"); in one study, 59% of gay men had done so, compared with 8% of lesbians (Gotta et al., 2011).

Third, men with a male partner have sex (defined as genital sex) considerably more frequently than women with a female partner do (Peplau, 1993).

Fourth, women tend to be more bisexual than men do (Lippa, 2006). In the same well-sampled survey, among people who reported having had at least one same-gender sexual partner, 38% of the women had had both male and female partners, compared with 28% of the men (Laumann et al., 1994). And, as we saw earlier in the chapter, women are more likely to be aroused by both female and male stimuli than men are (Chivers et al., 2004). Similarly, women are more likely to display sexual fluidity than men are (Katz-Wise & Hyde, 2015).

Finally, lesbians and gay men are the objects of somewhat different attitudes from the predominantly heterosexual American population. People hold negative attitudes toward both gay men and lesbians, but, on average, they are more negative toward gay men (Herek, 2000b; Petersen & Hyde, 2010). This trend is driven by men's more negative attitudes toward gay men than toward lesbians. Women's attitudes toward lesbians and gay men are similar.

In sum, gay men and lesbians are similar in the sense of same-gender attraction. The differences between the two are logical consequences of psychological differences between the genders and differences in their developmental experiences. Sexual minority women are probably more like heterosexual women than they are like gay men. It will be interesting to see whether these patterns of gender differences change with the legalization of gay marriage.

The Intersection of Sexual Orientation and Ethnicity

From an intersectionality perspective, sexual minority women of color have three intersecting identities: as women, as people of color, and as sexual minorities. Lesbians who are women of color experience triple oppression: discrimination on the basis of gender, race, and sexual orientation (Fassinger & Israel, 2010). For the individual woman, there may be conflicts between lesbian identity and ethnic identity, because some ethnic groups in the United States have even more negative attitudes toward lesbians than Anglo society does. In one study, Whites had the lowest levels of antigay attitudes and Blacks had the highest, with Latinx and Asian Americans falling in between (Haslam & Levy, 2006).

As a first example, we will consider Latinx lesbians (Espín, 1987a, 1993). Although in Latin cultures emotional and physical closeness among women is considered acceptable and desirable, attitudes toward lesbianism are even more restrictive than in European American culture. The special emphasis on family—defined as mother, father, children, and grandparents—in Latin cultures makes the lesbian even more of an outsider.

Despite these forces—or perhaps because of them—Latinx lesbians have engaged in resistance and activism. One example is the activist group Lesbianas Unidas (Gil-Gómez, 2016). Beginning in the 1960s, the Chicano movement advocated for civil rights for Chican@s. The movement, however, was male-dominated, and Latinx lesbians were seen as a liability to the cause. In universities, Chicano/Latino Studies was also male-dominated. Latinx lesbians found more support among feminists, but that group was still dominated by Whites. Latinx lesbians then founded their own activist group, Lesbianas Unidas. It served important goals of creating community and was committed to taking action against anti-gay campaigns within the Latino community. Today, the group maintains an Internet presence.

As a second example, we will consider Asian American sexual minority women. Two features of Asian American culture shape attitudes toward same-gender sexuality and its expression: (1) a strong distinction between what may be expressed publicly and what should be kept private and (2) a stronger value placed on loyalty to one's family and on the performance of family roles than on expression of one's own individual desires (Cochran et al., 2007). Sexuality must be expressed only privately, not publicly. And having an identity, much less a sexual identity or a lesbian identity, apart from one's family is almost incomprehensible to traditional Asian Americans. As a result, a relatively smaller portion of Asian American lesbians seem to be out compared with non-Asians. Those who are out tend to be more acculturated, that is, more influenced by American culture. They echo the sentiments of the Latina lesbian just mentioned, saying that they would prefer not to have to choose between their ethnic identity and their sexual identity but that when forced to make the choice, they are more closely tied to the LGB part of their identities.

©iStockphoto.com/mauro_grigollo.

PHOTO 13.4
Lesbians who are women of color may experience multiple forms of discrimination—on the basis of gender, sexual orientation, and ethnicity.

A third example concerns African American lesbians, who regard their ethnic community as extremely homophobic (Greene, 2000). This sexual prejudice probably derives from a belief among Blacks that any sexual behavior outside the norms of the dominant culture in the United States may reflect negatively on Blacks, as they strive for respect and acceptance. In this context, Black lesbians may seem to be an embarrassment to the Black community.

That said, there may also be advantages to double or triple minority status. In one study, African American and Latina lesbians began wondering about being lesbian at an earlier age (14.5 years), on average, compared with White lesbians (17.5 years; Parks et al., 2004). The women of color also decided that they were lesbian at somewhat earlier ages (21–22 years) than the White lesbians (23 years). The researchers hypothesized

FOCUS 13.1

A QUEER WOMAN TELLS HER STORY

Despite growing up in a small midwestern town, I was exposed to homosexuality when several of my close friends came out during high school. At about the same time, I began to date a boy who was a year older than myself and we continued to date on and off for the next 3 years. By the end of high school I identified myself as bisexual but had had no sexual experiences with women. I considered sexuality to be a continuum and, perhaps idealistically, believed that gender was not a factor in determining whether I was attracted to someone. I felt that I existed on the edge of my gender, not traditionally masculine or feminine but a mixture of the two. I declined to embrace this by learning to ride a motorcycle and teaching myself to box, but kept my hair long and continued to wear makeup.

For the first 3 years of college I did not date and, instead, chose to maintain a close relationship with my family and to develop intense friendships. Even then, though, I found myself gravitating toward queer identified people. During my final year of college I began dating again and had a succession of relatively brief encounters with both men and women. Instead of feeling disappointed, I realized that a certain amount of dissatisfaction was acceptable and even inevitable; after all, the process of sifting and winnowing is exactly what dating is about. A year ago I met a woman with whom I chose to develop a long-term relationship. The beginning of our relationship was difficult as I struggled to understand how to be intimate with a woman. I found that there was little difference between relationships with men and women. I have spent the past year navigating what it means to be in a sexual-emotional relationship with a woman.

Being queer, even in a relatively progressive university community, has its ups and downs. Though personal safety is a concern, I find myself most irritated by the common assumption that women have sexual relationships with each other solely for the benefit and consumption of heterosexual men. Men have approached my girlfriend and me, only to initially assume that we are available heterosexual women (something that would not occur if a man and a woman were sitting together at a bar), and then, upon realizing we are together, ask if we are interested in engaging in group sex. When heterosexual couples talk about their relationships, people do not automatically think about them having sex. But when two women talk about being together, people often imagine various sexual permutations or assume that they are asexual, emotional companions (the **Boston marriage** theory). There is not a whole lot of room between these two stereotypes. For many people it is difficult to understand how frustrating these assumptions about sexuality can be. To put this problem in perspective, I have overheard many straight men express their discomfort with gay men, saying things like "I'm fine with him as long as he doesn't try to flirt with me." The same can be said for my girlfriend and me. I wish that it wasn't necessary to share or advertise my sexual orientation.

I am fortunate, however, to have a family that supports the choices I have made about my sexuality. My parents have taught me a great deal about how to have a healthy, satisfying relationship with an emphasis on clear and open communication. I don't know if I will even date men again; I am satisfied with the relationship I have now and I don't spend time thinking about who I will date in the future.

Source: Based on an essay written for the author's class.

that the women of color, having grown up as minorities, had already learned to negotiate minority identity and bicultural competence with the help of their families and communities. Essentially, they have already had practice and therefore are able to take on an additional minority identity more easily than their White counterparts.

We have seen many times in this book that women have been rendered invisible in everything from history to science. Lesbians who are women of color are, in a sense, triply invisible—invisible because they are women, because they are people of color, and because they are lesbian. They deserve much more attention in psychological research in the future, for their complex identities have much to tell us about the intersection of gender, race, and sexuality.

The **queer of color critique** is highly relevant here (Ferguson, 2004; Tompkins, 2015). Growing out of queer theory, feminist theory, and women of color feminism, the queer of color critique begins with tracing the historical encounters between the Christian European colonizers (British, Spanish, and French), the indigenous peoples of the Americas, and Africans who were forcibly transported there. The Europeans brought with them rigid heteronormativity and a firm belief in the gender binary. They were horrified by the alternative forms of gender expression and sexual expression that they encountered among the indigenous peoples. The European colonizers engaged in violence against the native peoples, destroying their cultures and interfering with their family structures. Alternative forms of gender expression, as well as same-sex attraction, were criminalized. Similarly, African slaves were subjected to sexual violence in multiple ways, including being treated as breeding stock and the sanctioning of White men raping African American slave women.

Despite the destructive violence directed at them, people of color survived and created culture and families (Tompkins, 2015). In particular, queer people of color survived and created their own networks. As one writer put it, "The queerness . . . of peoples of color emerges from the fire of modernity's historical forges and has an energy to survive and create that is fiercely its own" (Tompkins, 2015, p. 175).

According to the queer of color critique, we cannot understand queer people of color today without understanding the history of violence and yet survival. Moreover, this violence continues today as manifested, for example, in the Orlando nightclub shootings of 2016, in which a gunman opened fire in a gay nightclub filled with people of color, killing 49 (Healy & Eligon, 2016).

Boston marriage: A romantic but asexual lesbian relationship.

Queer of color critique: An approach that brings together queer theory, feminist theory, and women of color feminism.

Experience the Research

Lesbian Community

Does your campus have an LGBT speakers' bureau? If not, why do you think there is none? If so, contact the speakers' bureau and arrange for three sexual minority women to attend your class to lead a panel discussion. When the speakers attend your class, have them introduce themselves first and then follow a question-and-answer format with the class. Be sure that the following questions are asked of the women:

1. What is your experience of the lesbian community? Explain, for a heterosexual audience, the features of the lesbian community.

2. Have you ever been the object of a hate crime because you are a sexual minority? If so, what happened?

3. Describe the process of coming out as you experienced it.

In addition, describe at least one research finding that you learned about in this chapter, and ask the panel whether the research "rings true" to them.

CHAPTER SUMMARY

Sexual orientation encompasses three components: attraction, identity, and behavior.

Queer theory challenges binaries and sees sexual orientation as fluid. Queer theory highlights performativity (i.e., the ways in which people perform gender or sexual orientation).

Lesbians experience antigay prejudice and may be the objects of various forms of victimization, including hate crimes. A lesbian culture or community exists in cities and towns around the world.

Diamond's research on the development of women's sexual orientation indicates that, for some women, it is fluid, passing back and forth between lesbian, bisexual, heterosexual, and undecided.

Regarding mental health, research generally shows that lesbian women are as well-adjusted as straight women, with the exception that lesbian women have a higher rate of suicide attempts. This outcome can be attributed to the stress of being a sexual minority. The American Psychological Association has issued guidelines for psychotherapy with LGB clients.

Research on the development of lesbians suggests that there is probably no one single causal factor. Researchers now no longer seek to find what disturbances in development would create lesbianism; instead, they ask what developmental factors would lead a woman to develop as heterosexual or lesbian or bisexual. Gay men and lesbians are somewhat different as a consequence of psychological and developmental differences between women and men.

Women of color who are lesbians experience triple oppression: on the basis of their gender, their race, and their sexual orientation. The queer of color critique emphasizes encounters between the European colonizers and the native peoples of the Americas, in which the Europeans imposed their own notions of the gender binary and normal sexual expression, sometimes criminalizing native practices, as well as those of the Africans brought to the Americas as slaves.

Research on sexual minorities is in its infancy, and the conclusions we draw must be tentative.

SUGGESTIONS FOR FURTHER READING

Diamond, Lisa M. (2008). *Sexual fluidity*. Cambridge, MA: Harvard University Press. Diamond is one of the foremost experts on sexual minority women.

Nadal, Kevin. (2013). *That's so gay! Microaggressions and the lesbian, gay, bisexual, transgender community.* Washington, DC: American Psychological Association. Nadal explores microaggressions, as discussed in earlier chapters, against LGBT people.

Gender and Victimization

In this chapter we will review the psychological research on gender-based violence and victimization. **Gender-based violence** refers to forms of violence in which women are the predominant victims and men are the predominant perpetrators; in addition, transgender individuals are also overrepresented among victims. Such forms of violence include rape, intimate partner violence, sexual harassment, child sexual abuse, human trafficking, female genital mutilation, and child marriage. For several reasons, gender-based violence is tragically underreported. For example, victims sometimes believe that it was their fault or that they won't be believed if they report it. And, frequently, victims of gender-based violence are blamed for the violence while their perpetrators go unpunished. In sum, victims may perceive that the costs of reporting violence outweigh the potential benefits. Gender-based violence has clearly demonstrated psychological and physical health consequences for victims (United Nations, 2015).

Gender-based violence: Forms of violence in which women are the predominant victims and men are the predominant perpetrators; transgender individuals are also overrepresented among victims.

Rape

Definition and Prevalence

Rape: Penetration, no matter how slight, of the vagina or anus with any body part or object, or oral penetration by a sex organ of another person, without the consent of the victim.

In 2011, the U.S. Federal Bureau of Investigation (FBI) revised its definition of **rape** as follows: "Penetration, no matter how slight, of the vagina or anus with any body part or object, or oral penetration by a sex organ of another person, without the consent of the victim." This definition includes instances in which the victim is incapable of giving consent because of temporary or permanent mental or physical incapacity; for example, they cannot give consent due to the influence of drugs or alcohol or because of age. By contrast, the FBI's old definition of rape was "the carnal knowledge of female forcibly and against her will." In the revised definition, notice that victims and perpetrators may be of any gender and that physical force is not required. Thus, the revised definition focuses on the fact that some form of penetration occurs and that consent is not given.

Based on the FBI's (2014) revised definition, 116,645 rapes were reported in the United States in 2014; that means there were 36.6 reported rapes for every 100,000 inhabitants. It is important to note that rape is one of the most underreported crimes. It is estimated that, between 2006 and 2010 in the United States, about 65% of rapes and sexual assaults went unreported (Langton et al., 2012). Sexual assault includes rape and other forms of unwanted sexual contact, such as sexual groping or crotch grabbing. Rapes committed by an acquaintance are far less likely to be reported to the police compared with those committed by a stranger.

Moreover, most rapes are committed by acquaintances, often by an intimate partner or date. More than half of female rape victims report that they were raped by an intimate partner, while 13.8% report that they were raped by a stranger (Black et al., 2011). And in a study of adolescent girls' experiences of sexual victimization, 40% of incidents occurred with a boyfriend or date (Livingston et al., 2007).

Rape is a form of gender-based violence. According to a well-sampled national survey conducted by the Centers for Disease Control and Prevention, a woman has an 18.3% chance of being the victim of a rape in her lifetime, compared with a 1.4% chance for a man (Black et al., 2011). Nearly one in five women have been raped at some point in their lives, compared with one in 71 men. Perpetrators of rape are disproportionately male: 99% of all persons arrested for rape are men (Rozée & Koss, 2001).

While most rapes are committed by men against women, it is important to remember that rape victims and perpetrators may be of any gender. Data show that sexual violence, such as rape, is alarmingly prevalent among sexual minority and trans populations. For example, 46.4% of lesbians, 74.9% of bisexual women, 40.2% of gay men, and 47.4% of bisexual men have experienced sexual violence (Walters et al., 2013). High rates of violence have also been reported in transgender populations (Stotzer, 2009). Still, there is not enough research on sexual violence against members of gender and sexual minority groups (Turchik et al., 2016). In this chapter, we primarily discuss rape of cisgender women by cisgender men and include data about transgender people when available.

Impact of Rape

Many studies have examined the psychological responses of women following rape (see the review by Martin et al., 2011). This research shows that rape is a time of crisis for a woman and that the effects on her adjustment may persist for a year or more.

Compared with women who have not been raped, women who have been raped are more likely to experience anxiety, depression, suicide ideation and attempts, and **posttraumatic stress disorder** (**PTSD**; Martin et al., 2011). PTSD is a disorder that develops in some people after experiencing a terrifying event. While PTSD affects about 1% to 3% of the population, about half of rape victims develop PTSD. People with PTSD may have persistent and intrusive flashbacks or memories of the traumatic event, avoid anything that reminds them of the event, experience reactivity symptoms (e.g., being easily startled, having trouble sleeping), and have negative changes in their thoughts and mood (Bisson et al., 2015).

Most women who have been raped have a negative psychological response immediately. Yet many will show significant recovery within a year (Martin et al., 2011). A number of factors may worsen a woman's psychological response to rape, such as whether she had previously experienced sexual violence, how severe the violence was, and how others reacted when she disclosed the rape. For example, a woman who has been repeatedly victimized, has been victimized severely, or has not been supported or believed when she disclosed the rape is likely to have a more negative psychological response. It is important to remember that no particular psychological response to a trauma such as rape is "right" or "wrong." We humans are sensitive but also remarkably resilient.

Some women blame themselves for having been raped. A woman may spend hours agonizing over what she did to bring on the rape or what she might have done to prevent it: "If I hadn't worn that short skirt . . ."; "If I hadn't had so much to drink . . ."; "If I hadn't been stupid enough to trust that guy . . ." This is an example of a tendency on the part of both the victim and others to blame the victim. Of course, only the rapist is responsible for rape. Blaming oneself for having been raped is associated with worse psychological outcomes for women (Koss & Figueredo, 2004).

When discussing self-blame, the sociocultural context in which rape occurs is relevant. One study compared Black and White women who had been raped (Neville et al., 2004). The study found that the two groups of women were similar in many ways, such as their self-esteem and coping after the rape, but their responses differed in some systematic ways. Black women's responses echoed the Jezebel stereotype that Black women are hypersexual and promiscuous and therefore cannot be raped. Many of the Black women internalized this negative stereotype and attributed their rape to it, and this attribution was associated with lower self-esteem.

The physical effects of rape are just as serious as the psychological effects (Centers for Disease Control and Prevention, 2014; Martin et al., 2011). Some rape victims may experience physical injuries, such as cuts and bruises, head injuries, or broken bones. Victims who were forced to perform oral sex may suffer irritation or damage to the throat. Those who were anally penetrated may experience rectal bleeding and pain. Rape victims may also contract a sexually transmitted disease, such as HIV/AIDS or herpes. Some rape victims become pregnant; about 5% of rapes result in pregnancy (Holmes et al., 1996). There are also long-term health effects. In general, having a history of being sexually assaulted is linked to worse overall health and a variety of specific problems including chronic pelvic pain, menstrual disturbances, headache and other pain syndromes, intestinal disorders, and sexual disorders (Martin et al., 2011).

The effects of rape are pervasive and extend even to those who have not been raped. In particular, most women do a number of things out of fear of being raped, such as avoiding walking alone at night, holding their keys out like a weapon, or checking the backseat of a car to make sure no one is hiding there. If you are a woman, you can probably extend this

Posttraumatic stress disorder (PTSD): A disorder that develops in some people after experiencing a terrifying event. Symptoms include reexperiencing symptoms (e.g., flashbacks, bad dreams), reactivity symptoms (e.g., easily startled, trouble sleeping), and cognition and mood symptoms (e.g., distorted feelings of guilt, loss of enjoyment in activities).

list from your own experience. The point is that most women experience the fear of rape, if not rape itself. This fear controls women by restricting their activities. Moreover, these behaviors will do nothing to prevent the most likely kind of rape—acquaintance rape.

Rapists

Who is the typical rapist? The simple answer to this question is that there is no typical rapist. Rape is so widespread, and rapists vary so much in occupation, education, marital status, race/ethnicity, previous criminal record, and motivation for rape, that it becomes very difficult to make generalizations or claims about who the typical rapist might be.

Nonetheless, researchers have identified four factors that seem to make men more likely to rape women or predispose men to rape women (Abbey & McAuslan, 2004; Knight & Sims-Knight, 2011; Malamuth, 1998). These factors were identified from research with a national representative sample of male college students (Abbey et al., 2001).

One factor is growing up in a hostile or *violent home environment*. Boys who grow up in a home environment that is hostile or violent are more likely to engage in sexual aggression against women. A hostile or violent home environment may include violence between the parents (i.e., intimate partner violence) as well as childhood abuse. Children are sensitive to many aspects of the home environment, and witnessing or experiencing violence in the home—a place that is supposed to be safe and nurturing—can have profound effects on their development.

Another factor is *delinquency*. This can be related to the previous factor, as being involved in delinquency is itself made more likely by coming from a hostile home. Still, delinquency increases the likelihood of engaging in rape. Boys may rationalize their delinquent behaviors (e.g., stealing, fighting, drinking alcohol) as being part of a tough or aggressive image, and they may associate with peers who encourage this image.

Sexual promiscuity is also a factor that predisposes men to rape. Some boys and men place a high value on sexual conquests as a way to feel masculine or have high status among male peers. In turn, they may feel it is perfectly reasonable to coerce or force women into having sex. This isn't about enjoying sex and physical intimacy with women so much as it is about viewing sex and women as a means to an end. One study of college men found that over one-third reported that they would use arguments or pressure women into sex; indeed, these men were more likely than other men to perpetrate sexual aggression (Gidycz et al., 2011).

Having a *hostile masculine personality* is another factor. A hostile masculine personality involves a deep hostility toward women and a negatively defined, exaggerated masculinity that rejects anything that is feminine. Thus, a man with a hostile masculine personality is focused on power and control and avoids or rejects nurturance and vulnerability. This personality, combined with a willingness to have impersonal sexual relations without emotional intimacy, is linked to engaging in sexual aggression (Hall et al., 2005; Malamuth et al., 1995). We return to the psychological risks of this type of masculinity in Chapter 16.

By contrast, one factor seems to reduce a man's likelihood of committing rape: empathy (Hunter et al., 2007). That is, a man who has several of the risk factors listed above, but who also is sensitive to the needs and feelings of others and isn't focused solely on himself, is less likely to rape than a man who has the risk factors and lacks empathy and is self-centered.

Causes of Rape

A number of theoretical views of rape have been proposed, most of which focus on men's rape of women (Turchik et al., 2016). Many of the theories of rape fall into the following categories (Baron & Straus, 1989; Ullman & Najdowski, 2011):

1. *Victim-precipitated*. This perspective claims that a rape is always caused by a victim "asking for it." Victims, not perpetrators, are ultimately responsible for rape, according to this view. This view represents the tendency to blame victims.

2. *Psychopathology of rapists*. This view claims that rape is a deviant act committed by men who are mentally ill or disturbed. Thus, the rapist is not responsible for rape; instead, his psychopathology is to blame.

3. *Feminist*. The feminist theoretical view holds that rapists are the product of gender role socialization in our culture. Feminists emphasize that rape isn't about sex so much as it is an expression of male power and dominance over women. Thus, rape is both a cause and an effect of gender inequality, in that they perpetuate one another.

4. *Social disorganization*. The sociological view holds that crime rates, including rape rates, increase when the social organization of a community or society is disrupted. Under conditions of social disorganization—such as poverty or even war—communities cannot enforce norms against crime.

The first view, that rape is caused by victims, is illogical. Rape is, by definition, non-consensual, so no one can "ask" to be raped.

Regarding the second view—that rapists' psychopathology is to blame—there is some evidence that young men who are sexual aggressors are likely to have been sexually abused in childhood (Knight & Sims-Knight, 2011). While some rapists have a history of victimization themselves, it does not follow that this history clears rapists of responsibility for their violent behavior. Moreover, rape is too widespread a problem to be the result of only men who are mentally ill or disturbed (Koss et al., 1994).

The feminist theory and social disorganization theory were examined in classic research by sociologists Larry Baron and Murray Straus (1989). Both theories frame rape as a product of the sociocultural context. Baron and Straus collected extensive data on each of the 50 U.S. states, seeing them as representing variations in cultural context (think, for example, of the different cultures of Louisiana, New York, and North Dakota). They collected data on the extent of gender inequality in each state (for example, the gap between men's and women's wages). They also collected measures of social disorganization, such as the number of people moving into or out of the states and the divorce rate. Their data gave strong support to three conclusions: (1) Social disorganization contributes to rape (those states with the greatest social disorganization tended to have the highest rape rates), (2) gender inequality is related to rape (the states with the greatest gender inequality had the highest rape rates), and (3) pornography provides cultural, ideological support for rape (the states with the highest circulation of pornographic magazines had the highest rape rates). This sociological research shows that many complex factors in the culture may contribute to cultural values that encourage rape.

With regard to the conclusion regarding pornography, psychological research evidence has demonstrated that pornography may promote sexual violence. For example, a recent meta-analysis found that, around the world, pornography consumption is linked to engaging in sexually aggressive behaviors (Wright et al., 2016). Today's pornography is characterized by a high degree of brutal gender-based violence, including both verbal and physical aggression and objectification of women, often representing rape of women and girls as sexy or even pleasurable to victims (Bridges et al., 2010; Dines, 2015). It is likely that, especially for younger viewers, pornography may function as a kind of informal sex education. That is, from a cognitive social learning theoretical perspective, viewers may observe and learn from pornography that gender-based violence in sexual relations is expected and arousing. Experimental research evidence demonstrates that viewing even nonviolent pornography increases attitudes supportive of sexual violence, particularly for men who are low in the personality trait of agreeableness (Hald & Malamuth, 2015). In other words, men who are more antagonistic and unsympathetic to the needs of others are especially likely to become more supportive of sexual violence against women after viewing pornography.

An extreme example of social disorganization is war, in which rape of women is common (Zurbriggen, 2010). In 2008 we saw graphic examples of this in the war in Sudan's Darfur (Robertson, 2008). Humanitarian observers reported that rape was an integral part of the violence that the government of Sudan inflicted on targeted ethnic groups. Likewise, the terrorist organization ISIL (Islamic State of Iraq and the Levant) has engaged in systematic enslavement and rape of Yazidi (a religious minority group in Iraq) women and girls (Callimachi, 2015). Across history, rape has been a weapon commonly used in war.

Rape myths: False beliefs about rape, rape victims, and rapists, which support rape culture (e.g., victim precipitation, victim fabrication, victim masochism).

Some *cultural values* support or even encourage rape. For example, in the United States, research has documented widespread acceptance of **rape myths**, which are false beliefs about rape, rape victims, and rapists (e.g., Barnett et al., 2016; Edwards et al., 2011). Three broad types of rape myths have been identified and can be applied to other forms of gender-based violence, such as sexual harassment and intimate partner violence (Koss et al., 1994). These myths, shown in Table 14.1, include *victim precipitation* (i.e., women ask for or deserve rape), *victim fabrication* (i.e., women lie about the rape), and *victim masochism* (i.e., women enjoy being raped). Note that the first theoretical cause of rape described above—that rape is caused by the victim—is reflected in the rape myths described. Rape myths function to discredit victims' accounts of rape and excuse rapists' behavior. Films (even nonpornographic ones), television, video games, and music may also include content or depictions of gender and sexuality that

TABLE 14.1   **Rape myths are widely accepted and maintain rape culture.**

Type of Rape Myth	Examples
Victim precipitation	The victim seduced the perpetrator, who could not control himself; the victim dressed provocatively, invited the perpetrator into her dorm room, or led on the perpetrator; the victim had already been sexually active with the perpetrator.
Victim fabrication	The victim regretted having consensual sex with the perpetrator, so she lied and called it rape; the victim doesn't have any bruises, so the rape wasn't really harmful; the perpetrator was intoxicated/high or wasn't himself when he raped the victim.
Victim masochism	The victim likes rough sex; the victim wanted to be raped; the victim said no when she meant yes.

help to convey and promote rape myths or permissive attitudes about rape, such as when women are objectified (e.g., Beck et al., 2012; Bogle, 2008; Edwards et al., 2011; Fox & Potocki, 2016).

Ultimately, rape myths help to perpetuate a culture in which rape is considered to be normal and is accepted. **Rape culture** refers to a set of cultural attitudes and beliefs about gender and sexuality—for example, that it is natural and normal for men to be sexually aggressive and that rape is inevitable. According to the feminist perspective, rape will continue to be a widespread problem as long as we believe rape myths, objectify women, and encourage men to be sexually aggressive.

Rape culture: A set of cultural attitudes and beliefs about gender and sexuality, e.g., that it is natural and normal for men to be sexually aggressive and that rape is inevitable.

Rape myths also shape our *sexual scripts* (Ryan, 2011), which may be another factor in rape. Sexual scripts tell us what sexual behaviors are appropriate and in what order. Adolescents quickly learn gendered expectations about dating and sex through culturally transmitted sexual scripts. For example, there are sexual scripts for hooking up and for seducing someone; there are also scripts for rape. Many scripts for heterosexual sexual behavior support rape in conveying the message that men are supposed to be sexually aggressive and uncontrollable in their sexual desire and that women are supposed to be sexually passive and say no but actually mean yes.

The *peer group* can have a powerful influence encouraging men to rape. In August 2012 in Steubenville, Ohio, a 16-year-old girl who was intoxicated and unconscious was taken to parties where she was repeatedly raped by two boys (Macur & Schweber, 2012). During this time, other boys watched, recorded, and joked about the rape, supporting and encouraging it while the girl was incapable of resisting or consenting. The case gained national attention, in part, because the boys posted about the rape on social media.

In some cases, *miscommunication* between men and women may be a factor. Because many people in the United States are reluctant to discuss sex directly and frankly, they try to infer sexual interest from subtle nonverbal cues, a process that is highly prone to errors. As discussed in Chapter 5, men are less skilled than women at decoding nonverbal cues. In particular, men tend to inaccurately interpret women's friendliness or politeness as sexual interest (Abbey et al., 2001; Lindgren et al., 2008). To prevent miscommunication about sexual interest, some people advocate for *affirmative consent*, in which partners explicitly and voluntarily agree to have sexual relations with one another rather than assume or infer it based on nonverbal cues.

Prevention

How can we prevent rape from occurring? Strategies for preventing rape fall into three categories: (1) changing the culture that contributes to rape, (2) avoiding situations in which there is a higher risk of rape, and (3) if a rape is attempted, knowing some self-defense techniques. Let's consider the first category.

Feminists argue that the responsibility for preventing rape should not rest on women's shoulders but on men's. Ultimately, the best way to prevent rape is for men not to attempt it. To do this, our society would need to make a radical change in the way it socializes boys (Hall & Barongan, 1997). That would mean not pressuring little boys to be aggressive and tough, teaching boys to be more emotionally intelligent and empathetic, and not demanding that adolescent boys demonstrate hypersexuality. It would also mean challenging rape myths. This will likely take a while, but certainly it is possible and in society's best interest.

In the meantime, how can we avoid situations that have a higher risk of rape? A quick Google search of "How to avoid rape" will yield many pages, often from universities and public safety departments, giving advice to women on how to avoid hazardous

CARTOON 14.1   Blaming the victim in cases of rape has been a serious problem. This cartoon satirizes that point of view, showing how ridiculous it would be to take this stance in regard to another victim of crime, such as a man whose wallet was stolen.

Source: Marian Henley, copyright 1992.

situations. Some of this advice may help, and some of it may contribute to victim-blaming. Some colleges and universities post information on avoiding risky situations, discouraging victim-blaming, and encouraging affirmative consent (Lund & Thomas, 2015). For example, one university's police and public safety department provides the following guidance:

1. *Communicate your limits clearly.* If someone starts to offend you or cross a line that you have set for yourself, tell them firmly and early. Polite approaches may be misunderstood or ignored. If the person does not respect your wishes, remove yourself from the situation immediately. Miscommunication can be explained later. Do not give someone the chance to violate your wishes or boundaries. This can often contribute to the guilt felt following unwanted sexual advances, but it does not make it your fault.

2. *Be assertive.* Often passivity can be interpreted as permission—it is not. Be direct and firm with someone who is sexually pressuring you. Tell an acquaintance or your partner what you want—or don't want—and stick with your decision. Regardless, there must always be active consent on both sides. Consent to one thing does not imply another.

3. *Trust your instincts.* If you feel you are being pressured into unwanted sex, you probably are. If you feel uncomfortable or threatened around an acquaintance or your partner, get out of the situation immediately. If you misread someone's signals, you can always explain later.

4. *Respond physically.* Even clear communication is not always effective. Some people simply don't listen or don't care. If either person is intoxicated or high, it may also complicate the situation. However, it is not an excuse for someone to commit sexual assault. If someone is assaulting you and not responding to your objections, you have the right to respond physically or to physically defend yourself if you feel you can do so. If possible, push the person away, scream "No!" and say that you consider what the person is doing to be rape. It is understandable that most people instinctively do not respond forcefully to people they know. It is not your fault if you find that you are unable to do so. (University of North Carolina at Charlotte, 2017)

These strategies may help in some cases, but certainly not in all of them. For example, research has demonstrated that verbal and physical resistance is sometimes effective in preventing rape in the face of an attempt (Hollander, 2016; Rozée & Koss, 2001). Of course, we aren't always able to resist.

Many have noted that these strategies don't get at the real problem, which is men raping or attempting to rape women. There is a fine line between empowering women to recognize and avoid risky situations and blaming them for being raped. How can we teach strategies that might make us safer without blaming victims at the same time?

On an institutional level, many colleges and universities have started programs designed to prevent rape. Researchers have evaluated a variety of rape prevention programs, often in educational settings, such as with incoming first-year college students. Programs generally use one of the following strategies (Gidycz et al., 2011):

1. *Awareness-based* programs aim to create community change by raising people's awareness of the prevalence of rape and sexual assault.

2. *Empathy-based* programs focus on increasing the audience's empathy by improving their understanding of experiences and outcomes for rape victims.

3. *Social norms–based* programs encourage individuals to question the gendered norms that support gender-based violence such as rape.

4. *Skills-based* programs aim to empower and teach people, especially women, skills that might reduce their risk of being victimized (e.g., avoid excessive drinking).

5. *Bystander intervention* programs encourage people to intervene actively if they see violence occurring.

For example, some college campuses have implemented bystander intervention programs, such as Green Dot, which also work to improve awareness and skills (Coker et al., 2015). These programs are designed to prevent rape by increasing bystander intervention with four kinds of tactics, known as the Four Ds: direct, distract, delegate, and delay. *Direct* tactics involve directly intervening by stepping into a situation to stop violence or speaking up when sexist statements such as rape myths are repeated. *Distraction* tactics involve distracting the potential rapist and removing the potential victim from harm. *Delegation* tactics involve multiple people working together to de-escalate a potentially violent situation. For example, one person might speak with the aggressor and another might provide support to the victim. Finally, *delay* tactics, which are more reactive and are used after violence has occurred, focus on providing support and accessing resources for victims. The data indicate that these programs are promising. Men attending college campuses with Green Dot bystander intervention programs perpetrate less violence than men at other campuses, and violent victimization rates are also lower (Coker et al., 2015).

The most effective programs have participants actively practice skills (Gidycz et al., 2011). Programs in which an expert lectures to a passive class are less effective. Peer-led programs that have multiple sessions, with repeated exposure and opportunities to practice skills, and that focus on a single gender in a small group (e.g., an athletic team) seem to be most effective.

Self-defense training has been a controversial part of violence prevention. Self-defense training goes beyond "fighting back" and emphasizes the empowerment of women in multiple ways (Hollander, 2016). For example, such programs may include increasing awareness, assertiveness, and de-escalation skills, in addition to physical defense skills that build on women's strengths. Well-designed self-defense programs also foster critical consciousness of gender roles and gender inequality.

In sum, men—not women—are responsible for men's rape of women.

Nonetheless, there are some strategies that might help women avoid situations with a higher risk of rape. Studies have consistently shown that active resistance such as screaming, fleeing, or physically struggling when a man is attempting rape reduce a woman's likelihood of being raped (Ullman & Najdowski, 2011). Active resistance is not always effective and may not be possible. At that point, we must consider ways to help victims recover and prevent rapists from reoffending.

Treatment

Once a rape has occurred, how can we help the victim and treat the rapist so that he does not repeat his offense?

Treating Victims. Women respond to being raped in diverse ways, and there is no one "right" or "normal" way to respond to this kind of trauma. Some victims are severely traumatized and develop PTSD, some recover psychologically on their own, and some fall somewhere in between.

For victims who have difficulty recovering from rape, they may seek psychotherapy. Psychologists have developed therapies that are effective in treating the symptoms of PTSD in victims of sexual violence (Foa et al., 1999; Koss, Bailey, et al., 2003). Today, therapies typically use cognitive-behavioral methods that target problematic thoughts and behaviors (see Chapter 15). For example, in cognitive processing therapy, cognitive distortions (such as "I deserved to be raped") are believed to maintain PTSD symptoms. Thus, for a rape victim with PTSD, a clinician using cognitive processing therapy might focus on the client's cognitive distortions about the rape, the sequence of events that preceded and followed the rape, and the broader impact of the rape on their beliefs about themselves, other people, and the world. This cognitive-behavioral approach has been effective in reducing both PTSD and depression symptoms in rape victims (Iverson et al., 2015).

Treating Rapists. After committing rape, perpetrators are in need of treatment, not just punishment. The main goal with treatment is to reduce the risk that a rapist will reoffend. How do we treat rapists so that they do not victimize more people? The standard treatment for incarcerated sex offenders is called *risk-need-responsivity*, or RNR (Hanson et al., 2009). *Risk* refers to treating people who are likely to reoffend, and *need* refers to the strength of the person's need to commit the crime. *Responsivity* refers to applying a treatment that is best matched to the characteristics of the offender. Just as with treating rape victims, cognitive-behavioral therapy is the commonly accepted treatment for rapists (Prentky et al., 2011). For

Hyoung Chang/Denver Post/Getty Images.

PHOTO 14.1
Many experts feel that women should learn self-defense skills as a way of combating rape, but others feel that this strategy doesn't address men's role in rape.

example, therapists might help the perpetrator identify precursors to committing rape so that they can then work to intervene to change the problematic thoughts, emotions, and behaviors. To evaluate the effectiveness of such a treatment, researchers assess recidivism, or whether the person is convicted of committing the crime again. A review of studies using cognitive-behavioral treatments for male sex offenders (this includes not only rapists but also men who have committed other acts of sexual violence) found no difference in recidivism rates between treated and untreated sex offenders (Dennis et al., 2012).

There are limitations of these treatments and the research evaluating them, however. For example, most treatments for rapists are given only to arrested and incarcerated offenders. This is problematic for several reasons. First, the treatment doesn't reach the many perpetrators whose rapes went unreported and unprosecuted. Second, treatment may be court-ordered or imposed on prisoners, perhaps as a requirement for parole. Such an imposition may motivate perpetrators to participate, but only superficially. These are not perpetrators who come forward and say, "I really want to change my ways." Treatment is not likely to be effective for those who are unmotivated to really change. Third, recidivism is not a very precise measure of reoffending because it only counts the rapes that are reported to the police, and rape is an underreported and underprosecuted crime (Seidman & Pokorak, 2011). Thus, recidivism rates likely count only a fraction of these crimes.

Some courts mandate anti-androgen drugs as treatment of sex offenders. The rationale behind this treatment is that reducing testosterone levels will reduce sex drive. Despite the fact that courts may impose this treatment, the evidence on its efficacy is very poor. That is, we don't know how effective this treatment is, in large part because the research is of poor quality (Khan et al., 2015).

The literature on the treatment of rapists leaves some big questions unanswered. For example, how do we effectively stop rapists from reoffending? And what is the fate of the rapist whose victim or victims never report the rape? He remains unarrested and unjailed, and certainly untreated. What happens to him? Does he continue to rape?

An Alternative: Restorative Justice. Traditional methods of handling rape in the criminal justice system have three serious flaws: They often treat the crime as minor and do nothing to halt men who are embarking on a career of sexual offending, those rapists who are punished are not held accountable in a way that will reduce their threat of offending again in the future, and the processes traumatize victims and their families. Mary Koss and her colleagues (Koss & Achilles, 2006; Koss et al., 2014) have pioneered an alternative approach to the treatment of both rapists and victims, known as **restorative justice**. The basic premise of restorative justice is that harm has been done and that someone is responsible for repairing it. As such, restorative justice emphasizes (a) repairing harm done to victims, (b) empowering victims, (c) holding perpetrators (called "responsible persons") accountable through making reparations to victims, and (d) rehabilitating responsible persons rather than simply punishing them. Thus, restorative justice attempts to balance the needs of everyone involved. Koss's program involves *conferencing*, in which a highly structured and supervised meeting occurs between the victim, her family, and the responsible person, but no attorneys. The responsible person describes what he has done and then listens as the victim describes the impact on her. Family and friends—who experience a range of responses as members of the victim's interpersonal context—may contribute as well. Together, they make a plan for reparations, which may include elements such as the responsible person paying for medical and counseling expenses and time off work, making a formal apology, and answering the victim's question: "Why did you choose to do this?" The perpetrator is then held accountable for the next 12 months in matters such as making the reparations.

Restorative justice programs are controversial. On the one hand, there are concerns that they may trivialize rape and revictimize women. Clearly, such a program should be undertaken only if the victim agrees to it. On the other hand, it may offer the much-needed opportunity for rape victims to feel a sense of control and validation. In opening up a more holistic discussion of the rape and its context, it may reduce victim-blaming and ultimately secure some form of justice (McGlynn et al., 2012). In giving the victim voice, it may also promote perspective-taking and empathy by the responsible person.

What do the data say? Evaluations of restorative justice conferences show that they are preferred over traditional justice (e.g., trials) by 63% of victims and by 90% of responsible persons (Koss, 2014). In addition, 90% of all participants (e.g., victims, responsible persons, family, friends) reported that they felt listened to, supported, and treated fairly and with respect and that they believed that the restorative justice conference was successful (Koss, 2014).

Intimate Partner Violence

It might seem that, given the high risk of rape, women should just stay home to be safe. Yet, in many cases, women are not safer in their own home.

Definition and Prevalence

Women are more likely to be attacked, raped, injured, or killed by current or former male partners than by any other type of assailant (Garcia-Moreno et al., 2006). **Intimate partner violence (IPV)** may include any of the following components directed toward an intimate partner: (a) sexual violence, such as sexual coercion and sexual assault; (b) physical violence, such as slapping, pushing, burning, or choking; (c) stalking or harassment; (d) verbal aggression, such as name calling, insulting, or humiliating; (e) **coercive control**, which refers to behaviors meant to monitor and control or threaten an intimate partner; and (f) control of reproductive or sexual health, such as refusing to wear a condom during sex.

Restorative justice: An alternative approach to the treatment of both rapists and victims, with the basic premise that harm has been done and that someone is responsible for repairing it.

Intimate partner violence (IPV): Aggressive behaviors directed toward an intimate partner, including sexual violence, physical violence, stalking or harassment, verbal aggression, coercive control, and control of reproductive or sexual health.

Coercive control: Behaviors intended to monitor and control or threaten an intimate partner.

The following statistics give some indication of the extent of IPV as a form of gender-based violence:

- Around the world, an average of 30% of women over age 15 have experienced IPV (Devries et al., 2013).

- Globally, women are six times more likely than men to be murdered by an intimate partner (Stöckl et al., 2013).

- In the United States, about one in four women and one in seven men have experienced severe physical violence by an intimate partner (Black et al., 2011).

- More than one-third of American women have experienced rape, physical violence, and/or stalking by an intimate partner, though prevalence varies across ethnic groups, as shown in Table 14.2.

Our focus here is on IPV perpetrated by men against women. It is true that in some cases, a woman may be violent toward a man. However, when the violence is physical, the greater physical strength of the male body means that, on average, far greater damage is done in male-perpetrated IPV. Patterns of mutual violence are also common, but in these cases women show significantly worse psychological outcomes than men do (Williams & Frieze, 2005). Violence also occurs in lesbian relationships (Kaschak, 2001; Turchik et al., 2016). In addition, IPV is prevalent among transgender persons: In a community sample of transgender adults, one-third reported that they had experienced IPV (White Hughto et al., 2017). Queer and trans victims may be especially hesitant to report IPV because, as members of stigmatized minority groups, they are skeptical that their needs will be addressed.

In the context of heterosexual marriage, wife-beating has a long history. It often has been considered a legitimate form of behavior within marriage and a logical extension of men's and women's marital roles. In Russia during the reign of Ivan the Terrible, the state church supported IPV by issuing a "Household Ordinance" that detailed how a man might most effectively beat his wife (Mandel, 1975, p. 12).

TABLE 14.2 **Among U.S. women, the experience of IPV varies across ethnic groups.**

Ethnic Group	Lifetime Prevalence of Rape, Physical Violence, and/or Stalking
Hispanic	37.1%
Black	43.7%
White	34.6%
Asian or Pacific Islander	19.6%
American Indian or Alaska Native	46.0%
Multiracial	53.8%

Source: Data from Black et al. (2011).

Nonetheless, it has long been unacceptable to talk about IPV from the victim's perspective. The first contemporary book exposing the topic was *Scream Quietly or the Neighbors Will Hear*, by Erin Pizzey (1974), who opened a shelter for female IPV victims in England. And the 1994 case of the murder of Nicole Simpson, allegedly by her ex-husband, O. J. Simpson, highlighted to the public that IPV perpetrators can kill. Following that murder, domestic violence shelters were flooded with women, as many realized how dangerous their situation truly was.

Consequences of IPV for Victims

IPV can have severe physical health consequences for victims. In relationships characterized by repeated violent episodes, there is often a combination of physical assault, verbal abuse, rape, and coercive control. Physical injuries can range from bruises, cuts, black eyes, concussions, broken bones, and miscarriages to permanent injuries such as damage to joints, partial loss of hearing or vision, and even death. In a study with women from a shelter for IPV victims, nearly three-quarters had sustained brain injury and many had measurable cognitive impairments (for example, memory problems) as a result (Valera & Berenbaum, 2003). IPV can be lethal. Conservative estimates are that, across North America and South America, intimate partners commit approximately 40% of female homicides, but less than 1% of male homicides (Stöckl et al., 2013).

The psychological impact can be devastating as well (Coker et al., 2011; Walker, 2001). Reactions of shock, denial, withdrawal, confusion, psychological numbing, and fear are common. Depression and suicide attempts are also common. Chronic fatigue and tension, startle reactions, disturbed sleeping and eating patterns, and nightmares are also often found among battered women. If abuse continues over a long period of time, long-term responses include emotional numbing, extreme passivity, and helplessness.

Although the term *battered woman syndrome* was originally coined for these responses, psychologists now favor seeing them, like responses to rape, as instances of PTSD (Babcock et al., 2008; Coker et al., 2011; Walker, 1991).

Why do some women who are victims of IPV stay with the batterer? Each case is unique, but a number of reasons have been identified (Hendy et al., 2003; Walker, 2001): (a) hope that he will reform, (b) having no other place to go, (c) fear that there will be reprisals from the batterer and that he may even kill her (as we saw in the O. J. Simpson case), (d) concern about the children (they need a father, and so on), (e) lack of support from family and friends, and (f) financial dependence (the woman cannot support herself). None of these reasons justifies IPV, of course.

Consequences of IPV for Children

When IPV occurs in a household with children present, it is important to consider the impact on them as well. Men who are violent toward their intimate partners are more likely to be hostile and aggressive toward their children and display less positive parenting behaviors generally (Stover et al., 2013). It is traumatic for a child to witness their mother being beaten. Children and adolescents who are exposed to IPV show signs of trauma such as PTSD, increased aggressive behavior, depression, anxiety, and poorer school performance (Kitzmann et al., 2003; Levendosky, Huth-Bocks, & Semel, 2002; Levendosky, Huth-Bocks, Semel, & Shapiro, 2002).

The *intergenerational transmission* of IPV is also a serious concern (Ehrensaft et al., 2003; Fite et al., 2008; Fulu et al., 2017). That is, children who grow up with IPV in their home may grow up to perpetrate or be victimized by IPV. Research indicates that childhood exposure to parents' IPV triples the chances that one commits IPV in adulthood and also triples the chances that one is the victim of IPV in adulthood (Ehrensaft et al., 2003). The consequences of IPV are pervasive.

PHOTO 14.2
Witnessing IPV can have a profound effect on a child's development.

IPV Perpetrators

What kind of man beats his wife or girlfriend? As with rape, we can give no profile of the "typical" batterer. Such men are found in all social classes and in a wide variety of occupations.

Still, characteristics of the batterer are much better predictors of IPV than are characteristics of the victim (Aldarondo & Castro-Fernandez, 2011). In other words, it's something about perpetrators, not victims, that causes IPV.

For example, compared with nonviolent husbands, violent husbands are more likely to have an insecure or disorganized attachment style and to be more preoccupied with and jealous about their wives (Aldarondo & Castro-Fernandez, 2011). These men are likely to feel anxious or unsure that their partner will love them and stay with them; controlling their partners might be a strategy to make them stay. Male IPV perpetrators also have more traditional attitudes about gender roles and attitudes condoning marital violence (Stith et al., 2004). In addition, male IPV perpetrators are more likely to have experienced childhood trauma, including neglect or sexual, emotional, or physical abuse (Fulu et al., 2017).

And yet, batterers are a diverse group. To make sense of this diversity, researchers have identified three types of batterers (Holtzworth-Munroe, 2000; Holtzworth-Munroe et al., 2003). *Family-only* batterers tend to be the least violent and show little violence toward people outside their family. Aside from beating their partners, they show little psychopathology. The *dysphoric-borderline* batterer engages in moderate or severe violence toward his partner but not toward others. These perpetrators demonstrate the most psychopathology, exhibiting depression and anxiety and borderline personality characteristics such as extreme emotion fluctuations and intense, unstable interpersonal relationships. *Generally violent-antisocial* batterers are the most violent, both toward their partner and toward others, and they are likely to exhibit antisocial personality disorder.

One important implication of knowing about these three types of batterers is that the treatment that works for one of these types may not be effective for the others. We need multiple forms of treatment that are appropriate to these different types of batterers. We will return to the topic of treatment in a later section.

Causes of IPV

A number of theoretical perspectives have been proposed to explain IPV. In many ways, these perspectives parallel the theoretical perspectives on rape described earlier in this chapter. These parallels are logical, given that many IPV perpetrators rape their partners.

One perspective is that IPV occurs because of the psychopathology of the female partner. In this view, the woman is seen as a disturbed individual who brings on the attack and self-destructively stays with the man who batters her. This view blames the victim and is not supported by evidence.

Another perspective is that the man who batters his female partner is simply a rare, psychologically disturbed individual. This view does not seem plausible in light of the high incidence of IPV documented by research.

A third perspective comes from sociological theory (e.g., Straus, 1980). It emphasizes how cultural norms and attitudes condone or justify family violence generally, and IPV in particular. Sociologists call attention to the process of gender role socialization, in which girls are socialized to be passive and boys are socialized to be aggressive.

The feminist perspective holds that IPV is both a cause and an effect of gender inequality (Anderson, 1997; Dutton & Goodman, 2005; Walker, 1980, 2001). Gender inequality causes IPV because it justifies a man's (the powerful authority's) efforts to "discipline" his female partner, much as a parent may discipline a child. And gender inequality is an effect of IPV insofar as IPV is a mechanism of men's control of women. In this way, IPV perpetuates gender inequality. Feminists also point out how, across history and even today, IPV (like rape) is condoned or supported by rape myths (see Table 14.1).

Prevention and Treatment

The causes and consequences of IPV are complex, and no single measure is likely to address them all. If we could reduce violence in American society in general, that would help to a certain degree. For victims of IPV, though, their problems are special and require special solutions.

One solution involves providing shelter and refuge to victims. Domestic violence shelters address victims' immediate need of having a safe place to go, and they can also provide emotional support and possibly job counseling and legal advice. In the past four decades, domestic violence shelters have proliferated in the United States, though they still cannot meet the needs of every victim. Domestic violence shelters and the paraprofessional and peer counseling they provide are very successful treatments for victims of IPV (Sullivan, 2011). Crisis hotlines are also important so that the woman can get immediate help and access the resources she needs (e.g., finding a shelter or medical care).

Clearly, treatment for the batterer, the victim, and the children is needed. Given that children who grow up with IPV are more likely to be perpetrators and victims of IPV as adults, psychotherapy for the child is crucial (Ehrensaft et al., 2003). Therapy that helps the child develop healthier emotional regulation and relationship skills may help to interrupt the intergenerational transmission of violence.

Kathryn Scott Osler/Denver Post/Getty Images.

PHOTO 14.3
Domestic violence shelters are essential to supporting victims of IPV.

Many victims of IPV develop symptoms of PTSD and depression. For those victims, cognitive trauma therapy is available (Beck et al., 2016). Cognitive trauma therapy involves many components, including PTSD education, mild desensitizing exposures to reminders of abuse, learning to undo negative self-talk, cognitive therapy for guilt, and education on self-advocacy, assertiveness, and how to identify perpetrators. Cognitive trauma therapy has demonstrated significant and large improvements in PTSD and depression (Beck et al., 2016).

Legal and police reform are important in treating and preventing IPV (Walker, 2001). In many communities and states, activists secured a *mandatory arrest* or *shock arrest* policy in which the man must be arrested and spend a minimum of one night in jail if the police are called to respond to a case of IPV. The idea is to convey clearly to the man that what he is doing is wrong and illegal. A complementary policy is the *no-drop* policy (Goodman & Epstein, 2011). Formerly, IPV perpetrators might threaten the victim into dropping the charges, giving the perpetrators a great deal of power. Today, many states have policies that say the case must be prosecuted, regardless of the victim's wishes. It might sound like a good thing to prosecute these cases, but if the victim doesn't want to do that, these efforts may actually take power away from them when they are desperately in need of empowerment. Others have noted that these policies sound like they should work, but there are concerns about how effective they actually are (Goodman & Epstein, 2011). How can we empower victims and stop perpetrators?

Of course, at least some of the blame for IPV rests with traditional gender roles and gender role socialization. IPV is a way of expressing male dominance and exerting control over women, thereby fulfilling the traditional male role. Moreover, traditional gender roles encourage women to be submissive and stay with such a husband. In sum, reforms in gender roles, socialization, and education will also be necessary to remedy the situation fully.

Sexual Harassment

Gender-based violence includes sexual harassment, which can take a number of forms and occur in a variety of contexts. Here we will focus on sexual harassment in the workplace and education.

©IStockphoto.com/Tomwang112.

Sexual Harassment in the Workplace

Because incidents of sexual harassment differ in the degree of offensiveness and coercion, they can be difficult to define, both in a legal or scholarly sense and in a personal sense. The following is the official definition given by the U.S. government's Equal Employment Opportunity Commission (EEOC):

Harassment on the basis of sex is a violation of Section 703 of Title VII (of the United States Civil Rights Act). Unwelcome sexual advances, requests for sexual favors, and other verbal or physical conduct of a sexual nature constitute sexual harassment when

PHOTO 14.4

Sexual harassment at work may be blatant, such as making it clear that sexual activity is a prerequisite to being hired, or it may be more subtle, as is the case in this photograph. The woman cannot avoid physical contact. Yet if the man is her boss, she may think it's too risky to complain.

FOCUS 14.1

THE VIOLENCE AGAINST WOMEN ACT AND VULNERABLE POPULATIONS

Beyond supporting individual victims, what can be done on the societal level? In 1994, President Bill Clinton signed into law the Violence Against Women Act (VAWA), which was drafted by Senator Joe Biden and received bipartisan support. This law is meant to support victims and prosecute perpetrators of IPV and rape, regardless of their gender. (Although the title of the law suggests that it covers only violence against women, the language of the law is actually gender-neutral.) For example, VAWA supports the investigation and prosecution of IPV and rape, provides legal assistance to IPV and rape victims, and funds violence prevention programs as well as domestic violence shelters and rape crisis centers across the United States. It also created the Office on Violence Against Women in the U.S. Department of Justice. Previously, IPV was treated as a family problem and police were reluctant to get involved, but VAWA requires that they help victims. Since VAWA was signed into law, rates of IPV have declined (Catalano, 2015). VAWA was reauthorized in 2000 (again signed by President Clinton) and 2005 (signed by President George W. Bush). Yet, VAWA expired in 2011 because of disagreements about who should be protected by the law.

In 2011, a long battle ensued over efforts to extend VAWA protections to American Indian, immigrant, queer, and trans victims as well as victims of human trafficking. These groups of people are especially vulnerable, in some cases because they are at higher risk of being victimized by gender-based forms of violence. For example, IPV victimization rates are higher against American Indian women (see Table 14.2; Black et al., 2011; National Congress of American Indians, 2013). Many scholars and those within American Indian communities note that IPV was comparatively uncommon prior to European colonization. They argue that colonization and the introduction of alcohol contributed to the rise in IPV among American Indians (Matamonasa-Bennett, 2015).

As noted earlier, high rates of violence have also been reported against queer and transgender populations (Cantor et al., 2015; Stotzer, 2009). For example, a survey of 150,000 students at universities across the United States found that 39.1% of transgender, queer, and other gender nonconforming seniors had experienced nonconsensual sexual contact during college (Cantor et al., 2015). Relative to their cisgender siblings, transgender adults

experience higher rates of harassment and discrimination (Factor & Rothblum, 2007). Yet because gender and sexual minority groups remain so stigmatized, reporting violence or seeking help is a risky choice. For example, victims may fear revictimization by way of victim-blaming and harsh interrogation about their sexuality or anatomy.

Immigrant women are in a uniquely disadvantaged situation, in part because it is risky for them to go to the police when they are victimized. Reporting IPV or rape may put an immigrant's legal status in jeopardy. For example, if an undocumented immigrant reports that she's been raped, the police may report her to U.S. Immigration and Customs Enforcement (ICE) instead of prosecuting the perpetrator for raping her. In February 2017, an IPV victim who was also an undocumented immigrant was arrested at a Denver courthouse while seeking a restraining order against her abuser. Cases like this—which received national news coverage—have sparked fear and motivated other women in similar situations to drop their charges of IPV (Glenn, 2017). Thus, some immigrant victims face the difficult choice of reporting and seeking help, and thus risking deportation, or keeping silent to remain in the United States, thus risking revictimization. In addition, an IPV perpetrator might threaten to withhold his support for his undocumented immigrant partner or report her to ICE if she reports his violence to the police. Language barriers and financial dependence are additional barriers to help-seeking among immigrant IPV victims. One study of immigrant Latinas compared histories of sexual assault, physical assault, stalking, and help-seeking between undocumented Latina immigrants and Latina immigrants with permanent legal status (Zadnik et al., 2015). The results showed that, while the two groups of women did not differ in terms of their histories of victimization, undocumented Latinas were significantly less likely to seek formal help when they were victimized. Thus, undocumented immigrant women are especially vulnerable to IPV because they cannot simply seek help and must often choose between revictimization and deportation.

Human trafficking victims are also especially vulnerable to gender-based violence, which we will discuss in more detail later in this chapter. Quite simply, victims of human trafficking are disproportionately women and they are most frequently forced into prostitution or sexual slavery (UNODC, 2014). They often live in the shadows, without the freedom to advocate for themselves when they are victimized.

In sum, the research indicates that American Indian, immigrant, queer, and trans people are especially vulnerable to gender-based violence, as are human trafficking victims. Members of these groups are more likely to be victimized and lack the power to seek help. In 2013, VAWA was reauthorized and signed into law by President Barack Obama, with expanded protections for these vulnerable groups. For example, VAWA now funds grants to tribal governments to support anti-IPV efforts and provide services to American Indian victims. The law is up for reauthorization in 2018.

1. submission to such conduct is made either explicitly or implicitly a term or condition of an individual's employment,

2. submission to or rejection of such conduct by an individual is used as the basis for employment decisions affecting such individual, or

3. such conduct has the purpose or effect of unreasonably interfering with an individual's work performance or creating an intimidating, hostile or offensive working environment.

The EEOC definition contains two parts. The first is often termed *quid pro quo* harassment and is captured in points 1 and 2. Quid pro quo is a Latin phrase meaning "this for that," or "I'll scratch your back if you scratch mine." Quid pro quo harassment refers to exchanges such as the following: "Have sex with me and you can keep your job," or "Have sex with me and I'll see to it that you get a big raise." One recent and very public example involved Hollywood film executive Harvey Weinstein, who was ousted as the co-chairman of the Weinstein Company after the *New York Times* and the *New Yorker* reported that he had, over several decades, sexually harassed and assaulted women in the film industry and paid settlements to keep his accusers quiet (Farrow, 2017; Kantor & Twohey, 2017). After the reports were published, more than 80 women came forward with their experiences of his predatory behavior. Many described a common scenario: They were called to meet with Weinstein about a film project, and he'd make sexual advances toward them; if they rejected his advances, he'd threaten to ruin their careers. In some cases, women reported that he followed through on that threat. This pattern of quid pro quo harassment, in which sexual favors are a requirement for employment, is illegal.

The second part of the definition refers to a *hostile environment* and is captured in point 3. For this part of the definition, there does not have to be a requirement of sex in exchange for hiring, promotion, or pay. Rather, the issue is whether the behavior or environment in the workplace is so hostile to the victim that it interferes with their work performance. A classic example is the landmark Supreme Court case *Robinson v. Jacksonville Shipyards* (1991). In that case, Lois Robinson was employed at the shipyards in Jacksonville, Florida, and felt that her work was impaired by working in a hostile environment, which included prominently displayed pornographic pictures (e.g., a pinup showing a meat spatula pressed against a woman's pubic area), crude and explicit graffiti on the walls, and a dart board covered with a picture of a woman's breast with the nipple as a bull's eye. The Supreme Court found in favor of Ms. Robinson and declared this kind of hostile environment to be illegal.

Sexual harassment in the workplace is very common, probably more than most people realize. Like other gender-based forms of violence, it often goes unreported. Thus, prevalence estimates vary considerably. One meta-analysis found that 58% of women reported having experienced a behavior at work that fits the definition of sexual harassment (Ilies et al., 2003).

Sexual harassment in the workplace is a serious concern. It can mean the difference between getting a raise or promotion and getting fired. For the woman who supports her family financially, being fired for sexual noncompliance can be devastating. Because she needs her job so much, she is vulnerable and the potential for coercing her is enormous. Women who have been victimized in this way often describe the experience as being degrading and humiliating; it can make one feel trapped and powerless. Sexual harassment has been linked to anxiety, depression, sleep disturbances, nausea, headaches, and PTSD (Chan et al., 2008; Welsh, 1999). A meta-analysis examining the effects of harmful workplace experiences—including sexual harassment and discrimination—on women found significant negative effects on women's well-being, ranging from lower work satisfaction to poorer physical and mental health (Sojo et al., 2016).

Sexual Harassment in Education

In Chapter 7, we briefly discussed peer sexual harassment among adolescents. In an educational setting, sexual harassment is defined by the U.S. Department of Education Office for Civil Rights as "unwelcome conduct of a sexual nature, which can include unwelcome sexual advances, requests for sexual favors, or other verbal, nonverbal, or physical conduct of a sexual nature," including sexual touching, comments, jokes, or gestures; calling students sexually charged names; spreading sexual rumors; rating students on sexual activity or performance; and circulating, showing, or creating e-mails or websites of a sexual nature. In this section, we focus on instructors—teachers and professors—perpetrating sexual harassment against students.

We probably don't need to tell you, but instructors have power over students. At a minimum, the professor or teaching assistant holds the power of having the student's grades in their hands. This means that any sexual relations between an instructor and student are inherently unequal and problematic. Certainly, in the case of a student who is a minor, sexual harassment may cross over into the category of child sexual abuse or statutory rape. Still, even if the student is an adult, the power differential is problematic. For example, if a college student consents to a sexual relationship with their professor or teaching assistant, the student is in a position of lower power that complicates their ability to consent freely. And if they wish to end the relationship, that process is also complicated by the instructor's power over them.

How common is sexual harassment in education? The data indicate that, among undergraduates, about 62% of female students and more than 75% of transgender and queer students have been harassed in some way or another, ranging from sexual remarks and offensive jokes to persistent come-ons and requests for sex (Cantor et al., 2015). In about 95% of these cases, respondents identified fellow students as the perpetrators. In other words, undergraduate students identified instructors as the perpetrators in a small proportion of cases. Yet among graduate student respondents, faculty members are more often the perpetrators.

In cases that occur in graduate school, the instructor controls critical evaluations and recommendations that affect the course of the woman's career. A recent survey found that 38% of female graduate students and 23% of male graduate students reported that they had been sexually harassed by faculty or staff (Rosenthal et al., 2016). Women report dropping courses, changing majors, or dropping out of higher education as a result of sexual harassment. Sexual harassment is also linked to depression and symptoms of PTSD (Buchanan et al., 2009).

Perpetrators of Sexual Harassment

Psychologist John Pryor has developed a person X situation model of sexual harassment (Hitlan et al., 2009; Pryor et al., 1995). According to this model, characteristics of one's personality characteristics (namely, sexist attitudes) make some men more likely to sexually harass than others. Put those men in a situation conducive to harassment and they harass. Pryor measures men's *likelihood to sexually harass* (LSH) by asking them to imagine a series of situations in which they have the opportunity to exploit an attractive woman sexually and experience no negative consequences. For each situation, the men are asked to rate their likelihood of behaving in a sexually exploitive way.

Organizational norms play a large role in creating situations conducive to harassment (Pryor et al., 1995; Welsh, 1999). Some restaurants, for example, require the waitresses to wear short, tight skirts—and Hooters is not the only guilty one. These restaurants have created a sexualized atmosphere in which customers and coworkers are given permission to sexually harass the waitresses. Place a man who is high in LSH in that situation and he is likely to harass.

Feminist Analysis

The feminist analysis makes several points about sexual harassment. As with other forms of gender-based violence, victims are often blamed. For example, it might be argued that the victim behaved provocatively or explicitly initiated sexual activity in hopes of getting a promotion, getting a good grade, and so on. By contrast, the feminist perspective would argue that such activity is usually initiated by the man in the powerful position.

Another point made by the feminist analysis emphasizes issues of power and control. Sexual harassment happens precisely because men are so often in positions of greater power relative to women, whether at work or in education. Research indicates that women are most at risk for sexual harassment in male-dominated workplaces (Hitlan et al., 2009). Of course, harassment in male-dominated jobs has the added effect of maintaining occupational segregation (see Chapter 9). In addition, victims of sexual harassment lack power and control over the harassment and the freedom to fight back or leave. It is extremely difficult to quit one's job and find a new job without facing significant financial consequences. In this way, victims experience a lack of control over their own lives.

The feminist analysis also involves taking an intersectional approach to sexual harassment. Sexual harassment may be racist, leaving women of color especially vulnerable.

Ethan Miller/Getty Images Entertainment/Getty Images.

PHOTO 14.5
Organizational norms, such as requiring servers to dress provocatively, create a sexualized atmosphere that is conducive to sexual harassment.

For example, one study with Black women found that when harassment perpetrators were White, they tended to have more organizational power over the victim (e.g., as a work supervisor). Moreover, White perpetrators were more likely to perpetrate racist sexual harassment against the women, such as commenting on a woman's "large Black behind" (Woods et al., 2009). The researchers found that, relative to sexual harassment perpetrated by Black men, sexual harassment perpetrated by White men was perceived more negatively and, in turn, led to higher PTSD symptoms.

Human Trafficking

Human trafficking: The acquisition of people by improper means such as force, fraud, or deception, with the aim of exploiting them, most often for sexual services and forced labor or slavery.

Often referred to as "modern-day slavery," **human trafficking** is the acquisition of people by improper means such as force, fraud, or deception, with the aim of exploiting them, most often for sexual exploitation and forced labor or slavery (UNODC, 2014). The United Nations and law enforcement agencies such as the FBI have identified it as a significant and widespread human rights violation. Estimates vary, but between 21 and 26 million people are currently being trafficked (International Labor Organization, 2012; U.S. Department of State, 2013). Around the world, estimates of the incidence of human trafficking are difficult to obtain, in part because it is underreported. In addition, many countries do not collect data on human trafficking, and some don't even criminalize it. In the United States, the FBI began collecting data on human trafficking in 2013, but only a handful of state and local agencies have supported this effort.

Like the other forms of violence discussed in this chapter, human trafficking is gendered: 70% of human trafficking victims are women or girls, and about three-quarters of those prosecuted for child trafficking are men (UNODC, 2014). In light of discriminatory laws about gender and sexuality around the world, trans and queer people are especially vulnerable to human trafficking and are overrepresented among victims. Migrants, refugees, people with disabilities, and members of religious minority groups are also at increased risk of trafficking (U.S. Department of State, 2016).

About 79% of human trafficking involves sexual exploitation. For example, women and children (especially girls) may be forced into prostitution. However, because trafficking is so underreported, it may be that other forms of trafficking are more common than it seems. Forced labor and marriage, organ removal, and the exploitation of children as soldiers are other forms of human trafficking (UNODC, 2014).

Although human trafficking occurs in every country around the world, it typically involves movement from poor or less developed countries to wealthy or more developed ones (UNODC, 2014). Traffickers are often from the same country as victims. A review of research on sex trafficking of girls and women found that victims often (though not always) are poor, have low levels of education, and have a history of physical or sexual violence within their families (Meshkovska et al., 2015). Many are simply seeking a way out of poverty.

Although data are sparse, it is undeniable that victims of human trafficking are at risk for physical and mental health problems (Crawford, 2017). Researchers have documented a variety of mental health problems, including PTSD, depression, and anxiety, as well as alcohol and substance use. Physical problems include headaches, fatigue, abdominal and pelvic pain, loss of appetite, and sexually transmitted infections. Being the victim of additional forms of violence and obtaining unsafe abortions have also been reported (Meshkovska et al., 2015).

For therapists working with victims of human trafficking, feminist therapy provides some guidelines (Hopper, 2017). It is important first to build rapport and get the

PHOTO 14.6
Human trafficking is a significant and widespread crime affecting between 21 and 26 million people.

victim's informed consent before proceeding with any therapy. Next, the therapist conducts a safety assessment to determine immediate concerns about the victim's safety and a needs assessment to determine if there are basic needs (e.g., shelter, medical problems) that need to be met before addressing emotional and psychological needs. The therapist will also work with the victim to understand their narrative about being trafficked, assess their psychological symptoms, and focus on the victim's strengths to provide hope.

Child Sexual Abuse

Child sexual abuse (CSA) includes the use, coercion, or forcing of a child to engage in sexual acts or imitate sexual acts. Like other forms of gender-based violence, CSA has become more widely discussed in recent years. Whereas a few decades ago it was considered unmentionable and rare, today adult victims freely and openly share their childhood experiences of victimization on blogs and television shows.

Child sexual abuse (CSA): Behavior that includes the use, coercion, or forcing of a child to engage in sexual acts or imitate sexual acts.

Prevalence of Child Sexual Abuse

For many years, CSA was considered a rare and unusual occurrence. Early research seemed to confirm this idea, as very few CSA cases were reported and prosecuted in the United States. Yet those numbers were misleading because, like other forms of gender-based violence, the vast majority of CSA cases go unreported and unprosecuted. Recent well-sampled surveys of the general population indicate that approximately 30% of girls are victims of CSA, with 8% of girls experiencing intercourse as part of the abuse (Bissada & Briere, 2001; Kendler et al., 2000). CSA often occurs alongside other forms of child maltreatment, such as neglect or physical abuse (Pérez-Fuentes et al., 2013).

CSA is a form of gender-based violence that disproportionately affects girls. A large, nationally representative sample of adults in the United States found that 10% of adults had experienced sexual abuse in childhood, three-quarters of whom were women (Pérez-Fuentes et al., 2013). Worldwide, roughly 20% of women and 5% to 10% of men report that they experienced sexual abuse as a child (Freyd et al., 2005). Thus, about three times more girls than boys experience CSA. And approximately 91% of CSA perpetrators are men (Cortoni et al., 2010).

Further complicating the efforts to accurately assess the prevalence of CSA, there is some controversy over whether CSA may be forgotten and later remembered. That is, abuse may be so traumatic that memories of it are repressed in order to protect the child's well-being and development. Human memory is not perfect, so just as it is the case that we may forget important events, it is also the case that we may remember events inaccurately. The evidence indicates that memories of childhood sexual abuse can be forgotten for a period of time and then remembered again. For example, in one study, 100 women who were known to have been sexually abused as children—they had been brought to a hospital for the abuse and it had been medically verified—were subsequently interviewed; 38% could not remember their prior abuse (Williams, 1992, 1994). In another study with a similar design, only 10% of victims could not remember the prior abuse (Goodman et al., 2003). However, that sample was based on prosecuted cases, and it seems likely that the prosecution process increases memory of the event (Freyd, 2003). In a massive study of adults who were survivors of a variety of traumatic events, delayed recall (forgetting the event for a time and then remembering it) was reported by 20% of victims of child sexual abuse and by 16% of those who had experienced injuries in combat or witnessed others being injured (Elliott, 1997). Therefore, the evidence seems to indicate that in a significant proportion of cases, memories of CSA may be forgotten for a period of time and then remembered again.

While school-age children are most at risk of CSA, younger children are less likely to report that they've been victimized (Murray et al., 2014). Younger children are especially vulnerable in part because they may lack the cognitive and social abilities to understand what has happened and speak up for themselves. They may think the abuse is "normal," blame themselves for it, feel guilty about it, or worry that the perpetrator (who may be a family member or friend) will be punished.

Impact on the Victim

Research evidence clearly demonstrates that CSA can have serious consequences for victims, both in the short run (while they are still children) and in the long run (when they are adults).

Studies of adults who were sexually abused as children have found evidence of serious psychological consequences (Bulik et al., 2001; Testa et al., 2005). For example, one especially well-designed study focused on female adult twins (Kendler et al., 2000). The researchers were especially interested in the twin pairs who were discordant for abuse—that is, one member of the twin pair had been sexually abused but the other had not. The results showed that CSA was linked to higher rates of depression, generalized anxiety disorder, bulimia, alcohol dependence, and drug dependence. Another study, which sampled over 34,000 adults across the United States, found that those who had experienced CSA had higher rates of mood disorders (e.g., depression), PTSD, ADHD, and suicide attempts (Pérez-Fuentes et al., 2013).

CSA appears to have effects on physical health as well (Briggs et al., 2011). For example, adults who were victims of CSA are one and a half times more likely than those

By AllenS - Own work, Public Domain.

PHOTO 14.7
Feminist activism, such as the Take Back the Night campaign, seeks to raise awareness of gender-based violence and empower victims.

who weren't abused to have had health problems in the past year (Sachs-Ericsson et al., 2005). On average, victims of CSA show greater psychological distress and more health problems (Freyd et al., 2005).

The consequences of CSA vary from individual to individual. Some victims show severe distress and others seem to show little or no distress. The evidence indicates that the extent of distress is associated with a number of factors including, especially, the severity of the abuse (Kallstrom-Fuqua et al., 2004). Patterns of sexual abuse can range from 5 minutes of fondling by a distant cousin to repeated forced intercourse by a father or stepfather over a period of several years. The effects of CSA are the most severe when intercourse has been involved, when the abuse has occurred repeatedly over years, and when it was committed by someone very close, such as a father or step-father (Kendler et al., 2000; Pérez-Fuentes et al., 2013). Nonetheless, every person's experience is unique and complex, and CSA of any degree or severity has the potential to cause great harm.

Feminist Analysis

Feminists make several points about child sexual abuse. First, as with all forms of gender-based violence, they warn against victim-blaming—that is, suggesting that a victim initiated sex with her abuser by her seductive behavior and that he therefore cannot be held responsible. The evidence indicates that it is usually the perpetrator who is the initiator. And even if the child were the initiator, the perpetrator, because of his age and position of responsibility, must certainly refuse her. Second, feminists point out that, as a form of gender-based violence, this is another instance in which men exercise power and control over girls and women. Third, feminists want to alert the public to the frequency of CSA and the psychological damage it can do to girls and women.

Looking Forward

We need to acknowledge the victimization of girls and women. But we also need to move beyond that recognition to empowerment. As psychologists, our job is to improve the quality of life for everyone, but especially those who have been victimized or marginalized. How can we both acknowledge deep victimization and empower those who have been victimized to freely live their lives?

Contrast these two terms: rape victim and rape survivor. Some advocates argue that the woman who has been raped yet manages to return to a productive life is a survivor, not a victim. Even tragic situations in which women are made powerless can be a means for women to begin to discover and regain their strength and power, both at the individual level and at the level of the larger society. Throughout this chapter, we have described victims. Does using the term *victim* imply that those who've been victimized are weak or somehow deficient? We don't think so, but we do think it's important to be sensitive to this possibility. We also think it's important to be sensitive to the possibility that some feel pressured by the label *survivor* to "just get over it."

You may have heard the old saying "What doesn't kill you makes you stronger." Some psychologists have considered this possibility for severe traumas such as the ones discussed in this chapter. They study posttraumatic growth (Tedeschi et al., 2015; see Chapter 11). For example, research has found that some women report positive life changes following rape, particularly if they have strong social support and feel a sense of control over their recovery (Frazier et al., 2004). A meta-analysis of gender differences in posttraumatic growth found that women displayed somewhat more growth than men ($d = -0.27$), averaging over all types of traumas (Vishnevsky et al., 2010). Some women survive and even thrive following these traumas, and we should recognize their resiliency and learn from them in order to help others who've been victimized. It takes great courage to persist after trauma, so many have embraced the label of *survivor* to acknowledge this courage and resiliency.

Experience the Research
A Scale to Assess Views on the Causes of Rape

In this exercise, you are going to construct a scale to assess people's beliefs in the different theoretical views of the causes of rape (see discussion of causes earlier in this chapter). Generate four statements for each theoretical view; the statements should be ones that can be rated on a scale from *strongly disagree* (1) to *strongly agree* (5). For example, for the victim-precipitated theory, one statement might be "Most rapes occur because the woman really wanted it." For the feminist theory, one statement might be "Men use rape to control women." Once you've listed the 16 statements, have another person in this class check them to see whether each really reflects one of the four theoretical views. Then administer your 16-item scale to five women and five men. Compute an average score for each theoretical view for each person; that is, each of your participants will have a score on victim-precipitated beliefs, psychopathology of rapist beliefs, feminist beliefs, and social disorganization beliefs.

Do you see patterns in your data? For example, do most people seem to hold most strongly to psychopathology of rapist beliefs? Are there differences between men's and women's responses? If so, what is the pattern of those differences?

CHAPTER SUMMARY

This chapter considered five forms of gender-based violence: rape, intimate partner violence, sexual harassment, human trafficking, and child sexual abuse. These forms of violence have several characteristics in common. For example, these crimes are disproportionately perpetrated by cisgender men against women and girls. Gender and sexual minority group members are also overrepresented among the victims. All have in common the reticence of the victims to report the occurrences and a corresponding difficulty in helping the unknown victims and stopping the unknown perpetrators.

In all five, the victim traditionally has been blamed. Rape myths, which are false beliefs about rape, rape victims, and rapists, support rape culture. Feminists emphasize the basic ways in which rape, IPV, sexual harassment, human trafficking, and child sexual abuse represent male expressions of power and dominance over women.

All five of these forms of gender-based violence have significant psychological and physical health consequences for victims, including PTSD, depression, injuries from assault, and sexually transmitted infections. Feminist therapy can help victims recover from these experiences of victimization, which are traumatic in some cases. Feminist therapists encourage victims to avoid blaming themselves and instead emphasize hope and resilience.

SUGGESTIONS FOR FURTHER READING

Paludi, Michele A., Martin, Jennifer L., Gruber, James E., & Fineran, Susan. (Eds.). (2015). *Sexual harassment in education and work settings: Current research and best practices*. Santa Barbara, CA: Praeger. An interdisciplinary team of authors provide an overview of research and policy on sexual harassment in education and work settings.

White, Jacquelyn, Koss, Mary P., & Kazdin, Alan E. (Eds.). (2011). *Violence against women and children* (2 vols.). Washington, DC: American Psychological Association. This is the most up-to-date, authoritative series on violence against women.

Gender and Mental Health Issues

> I was eighteen when I started therapy for the second time. I went to a woman for two years, twice a week. She was constantly trying to get me to admit that what I really wanted was to get married and have babies and lead a 'secure' life; she was very preoccupied with how I dressed, and just like my mother, would scold me if my clothes were not clean, or if I wore my hair down; told me that it would be a really good sign if I started to wear

makeup and get my hair done in a beauty parlor (like her, dyed blond and sprayed); when I told her that I like to wear pants she told me that I had a confusion of sex roles. **99**

Phyllis Chesler (1972), *Women and Madness*

When psychologist Phyllis Chesler wrote her revolutionary book *Women and Madness* in 1972, stories like this one were not uncommon. Today, gender bias in diagnosis and treatment of mental health issues is more subtle, just as modern sexism has replaced old-fashioned sexism in many other areas of life. In this chapter, we discuss some of the mental health issues that show lopsided gender ratios in prevalence, the evidence on gender bias in psychotherapy, and feminist therapy. We also consider American Psychological Association guidelines for psychological practice with two marginalized groups: trans people and women of color.

Depression

According to the *Diagnostic and Statistical Manual of Mental Disorders, Fifth Edition* (DSM-5), at least five of the following symptoms must be present for at least 2 weeks for a diagnosis of depression:

1. Depressed, sad, empty, or hopeless mood

2. Loss of interest or pleasure in all or nearly all activities

3. Significant increase or decrease in appetite and/or weight

4. Sleeping too much or too little

5. Psychomotor agitation or retardation (e.g., restlessness, being slowed down)

6. Fatigue or loss of energy

7. Feelings of worthlessness or inappropriate guilt

8. Difficulty concentrating or making decisions

9. Thinking about death, suicidal ideation, or even attempting suicide

These are the classic, defining symptoms of depression.

Gender Differences

No matter how you count it, more women than men are depressed. The gender difference is found whether the index is diagnosable depression, people seeking therapy for depression, or even depressive symptoms in samples drawn from the general community. The lifetime prevalence of depression is 15.9% for girls and women but 7.7% for boys and men (Merikangas et al., 2010). A meta-analysis of gender differences in depression using nationally representative samples found that about twice as many women as men are depressed, or $d = -0.37$ (Salk et al., 2017). At the intersection of gender and ethnicity, these differences were found across ethnic groups in the United States. The meta-analysis included studies from 90 countries, finding that effect sizes in depression vary somewhat, but the same general pattern of gender differences is found across cultures and income levels (Salk et al., 2017).

One important finding about depression is that, across the lifespan, the gender difference changes. In childhood, there appears to be no gender difference in depression. Yet in early adolescence, girls' depressive symptoms begin to accumulate (Hankin et al., 2015; Salk et al., 2016). In U.S. community samples, a gender difference emerges between 11 and 12 years old, peaks at 16 ($d = -0.47$), and then decreases and remains stable in adulthood ($d = -0.19$ to -0.30; Salk et al., 2016; Salk et al., 2017). Adolescence is a challenging time for many youth, but it seems there's something especially difficult about it for girls.

It was once argued that these higher rates of depression in adolescent girls and women are not cause for concern because the gender difference is an "artifact" rather than a true difference. That is, it seemed possible that, in reality, men and women suffer equally from depression but that women are overrepresented in the statistics, perhaps because they are more willing to admit the symptoms or to seek help for their problems. We now know that the difference is not an artifact, but a true mental health disparity.

We also know that no single factor (for example, stress) accounts for the gender difference in depression. Multiple factors are involved, and different people may become depressed for different reasons. Newer theories of depression, such as the ABC model, must integrate multiple factors to explain gender differences in depression.

The ABC Model

The ABC model is illustrated in Figure 15.1 (Hyde, Mezulis, & Abramson, 2008). The diagram is complex, and we will break it down in the sections that follow.

The ABC model is a vulnerability-stress model. That is, people carry with them different levels of vulnerability to depression. In the presence of stress, those with high vulnerability are likely to become depressed. Someone who does not have high levels of vulnerability might encounter the same stress and not become depressed. The *A*, *B*, and *C* stand for three categories of factors that make someone vulnerable to depression: affective, biological, and cognitive. Let's consider each of them.

Affective vulnerability. The *A* stands for affective (or emotional) vulnerability. Specifically, the focus here is on temperament, which we discussed in Chapter 7. Temperament refers to constitutionally based individual differences in reactivity and regulation. It includes emotional traits that appear early in life and predict later behaviors and psychological problems, such as negative emotionality. Children who are high in negative emotionality tend to become upset, fearful, sad, or tearful more easily than their peers, and they are highly sensitive to negative stimuli. A number of studies have shown that negative emotionality predicts depression in adolescents and adults (Clark et al., 1994; Colder et al., 2002; Newman et al., 1997).

How can the affective factor of negative emotionality explain the gender difference in depression? Although meta-analysis has shown that there is no gender difference in average levels of negative emotionality, there is some evidence that, as a group, girls are somewhat more variable in this trait (Else-Quest et al., 2006). That is, girls display slightly more variability (variance) in negative emotionality so that, even though there is no average gender difference, there are more girls who score in the top 20% for negative emotionality. Those girls with higher negative emotionality are more vulnerable to depression.

Biological vulnerabilities. The *B* is for biological vulnerabilities. Here we discuss two potential biological factors—genetics and issues associated with puberty—but there are also others such as epigenetic factors and neurobiological changes.

FIGURE 15.1   **The ABC model of depression explains the emergence of gender differences in depression during adolescence.**

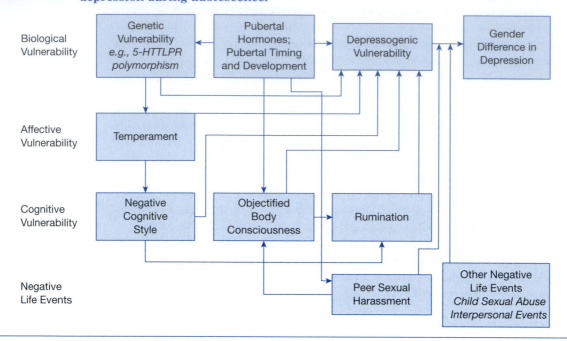

Source: From Hyde, Mezulis, & Abramson (2008).

The Human Genome Project has mapped the thousands of genes that constitute the human genome. A dozen or more of these genes have been implicated in depression, many of which have to do with coding proteins that are part of the serotonin system. Serotonin is one of the neurotransmitters involved in depression. Selective serotonin reuptake inhibitors (SSRIs) increase serotonergic activity in the brain and are effective in treating depression (Levinson, 2005).

Much research has focused on a serotonin-related gene called 5-HTTLPR, which has evidence for its importance to depression. The two alleles for this gene are called *s* (for short) and *l* (for long), so people may have an *s/s*, an *s/l*, or an *l/l* genotype. In an important study, researchers showed that *s* is the vulnerability gene and that it interacts with stress to predict depression (Caspi et al., 2003). One stressor they studied was child maltreatment, ranging from no maltreatment to severe maltreatment. The outcome was major depression occurring between ages 18 and 26. Individuals with the *l/l* genotype were unlikely to experience depression, regardless of whether they suffered maltreatment. Those with the *s/s* genotype had low rates of depression with no maltreatment, but with severe maltreatment they had high rates of depression. The results, then, show a *genotype × environment interaction*. While there are some contradictory findings, other researchers have found a similar effect (for a meta-analysis, see Karg et al., 2011). These results are also an example of a vulnerability-stress interaction. The *s/s* genotype creates a vulnerability, and in the presence of severe stress (child maltreatment), depression is a likely outcome.[1]

As discussed in Chapter 2, feminists have often been critical of biological explanations for gender differences because such explanations tend to promote biological determinism

---

[1] In case you are wondering about people with the *s/l* genotype, they fall in between the *s/s* and the *l/l*. That is, under conditions of severe maltreatment, *s/l* people have a rate of depression that is moderate, falling between the low rate for *l/l* people and the high rate for *s/s* people.

and reinforce a patriarchal status quo (Salk & Hyde, 2012). Do these criticisms apply to this research on gender and depression? For several reasons, we don't think so. Contemporary genetics research is far more sophisticated than the old-fashioned biological determinism that feminists have criticized. The research does not show, for example, that those with an *s/s* genotype absolutely will develop depression. Among *s/s* individuals, even under conditions of severe maltreatment, far less than 100% become depressed. Indeed, these findings and others in contemporary genetics research actually demonstrate the great importance of environment, including stress, in development (Salk & Hyde, 2012).

How can this gene–stress interaction help to account for gender differences in depression? It turns out that men and women are equally likely to have the vulnerable *s/s* genotype, so the answer may lie in stress. That is, if girls and women experience more stress than boys and men do, that would create a gender difference in depression among those with the *s/s* genotype. We will return to this important point later.

The sharp emergence of the gender difference in depression occurs around age 12, making puberty a suspect. In particular, researchers have examined pubertal timing, or whether kids are reaching puberty early, on time, or late relative to their peers. That is, pubertal timing is another biological vulnerability. For transgender youth, puberty is especially fraught with challenges, but there are not yet sufficient data to demonstrate precisely how pubertal timing plays a role in their well-being. We currently know much more about the effects of pubertal timing for cisgender youth. Early puberty has often been considered detrimental for cisgender girls (Ge & Natsuaki, 2009; Natsuaki et al., 2015). Consider the girl who develops sexy curves and noticeable breasts at 10 or 11: She is sexualized and teased by her peers and, compared with other girls, is less able to handle it, precisely because she is young and not mature enough to manage such social challenges (see Chapter 7). By contrast, for cisgender boys, early puberty is often welcome good news. These boys grow taller and more muscular ahead of their peers and thus perform better athletically. Nonetheless, meta-analysis indicates that early puberty is positively associated with internalizing disorders (like depression) among cisgender girls ($d = 0.19$) and boys ($d = 0.16$; Ullsperger & Nikolas, 2017). Thus, early puberty is a risk factor for depression, regardless of gender.

Cognitive vulnerabilities. C is for cognitive vulnerabilities. We consider three of them here: negative cognitive style, rumination, and objectified body consciousness.

Negative cognitive style is rooted in the **hopelessness theory** of depression, formulated by psychologist Lyn Abramson and her colleagues (1989). According to hopelessness theory, a negative cognitive style makes a person vulnerable to depression. Like the ABC model, hopelessness theory is a vulnerability-stress theory of depression.

People with a negative cognitive style tend to show a particular pattern of thinking when they experience negative life events (e.g., failing a test, losing a job, getting sick). When negative life events happen to people with a negative cognitive style, they tend to do three things: (1) They conclude that the negative event implies bad things about themselves—that is, they make an *internal* attribution. For example, after failing a math exam, a student says, "I got the F because I'm stupid" rather than "I got the F because the exam was way too difficult." (2) They attribute the negative event to global causes. In other words, they believe that whatever caused the negative event is going to generalize to many other areas of their lives (a *global* attribution). The student thinks, "I'm so stupid, I'm probably going to fail the exams in my other classes, too." (3) They believe that whatever caused the negative event is going to continue in their lives and create more negative events in the future (a *stable* attribution). The student concludes, "I'm never going to understand math. I'm just not smart enough."

Negative cognitive style: A tendency to attribute negative life events to internal, global, and stable causes.

Hopelessness theory: A vulnerability-stress theory that a negative cognitive style makes a person vulnerable to depression.

In sum, people with negative cognitive styles tend to make internal, global, stable attributions about negative life events. Someone who does this will, in turn, feel hopeless and convinced that there is nothing to be done to stop negative life events from happening.

Research with children under 11 indicates no gender difference in cognitive style (Abela, 2001; Gladstone et al., 1997). Yet research with adolescents shows that girls have a slightly more negative cognitive style (Hankin & Abramson, 2002). Adolescence, then, is when the cognitive vulnerability stage is set for the gender difference in depression to emerge.

Rumination: The tendency to think repetitively about one's depressed mood or about the causes and consequences of negative life events.

Psychologist Susan Nolen-Hoeksema (1991, 2001) introduced a second type of cognitive vulnerability to depression: **rumination**, which refers to the tendency to think repetitively about one's depressed mood or about the causes and consequences of negative life events. People who ruminate just can't seem to get these negative thoughts out of their heads, which predisposes them to depression. One meta-analysis found that gender differences in rumination are very small in childhood ($d = -0.14$) but swell during adolescence ($d = -0.36$; Rood et al., 2009). Another meta-analysis found that gender differences in rumination are significant but small in adulthood ($d = -0.24$; Johnson & Whisman, 2013). Additionally, research has demonstrated that *co-rumination*—essentially, when peers frequently discuss or rehash problems with one another—helps to explain the emergence of gender differences in depression in adolescence (Stone et al., 2011). That is, adolescent girls are more likely to co-ruminate, which then contributes to the onset, severity, and duration of depressive symptoms that they experience. Girls' and women's greater tendency to ruminate and co-ruminate, then, may help explain gender differences in depression.

A third type of cognitive vulnerability to depression is objectified body consciousness, which was described in detail in Chapter 2. The body surveillance component—a repetitive self-surveillance to make sure that one's body conforms to cultural ideals—is most relevant here. Longitudinal research shows that body surveillance predicts later depressive symptoms among adolescents (Grabe, Hyde, & Lindberg, 2007). And by age 11, girls score higher than boys on body surveillance (Grabe et al., 2007). Thus, body surveillance and the cultural forces that create it contribute to the gender difference in depression.

Negative life events. We have described the three categories of vulnerabilities to depression: affective, biological, and cognitive. But these are just vulnerabilities, and a vulnerability-stress theory such as the ABC model also requires stress for the development of a disorder like depression. Negative life events or serious stress are theorized to interact with or activate the existing vulnerabilities to depression, thereby triggering the development of depression. It is well established that negative life events predict depression including, specifically, depression in adolescence (Grant et al., 2004; Monroe & Reid, 2009; Tram & Cole, 2000).

Thus, logic follows that if boys and girls experience similar rates of negative life events but girls are more vulnerable to the effects of those negative life events, a gender difference in depression would emerge. However, it turns out that girls and women actually experience slightly more negative life events than boys and men do ($d = -0.12$; Davis et al., 1999). According to a meta-analysis of research on major and minor life events, the gender difference was not significant in childhood, but was in adolescence (Davis et al., 1999).

The gender difference in adolescence was also larger for appraisals (that is, how unpleasant or stressful the event was) of the event ($d = -0.29$) rather than just for the occurrence of the event. In other words, compared with their male peers, adolescent girls experience a greater number of negative life events *and* they report that those events are more stressful.

This meta-analysis lumped together all types of negative life events and may not have given sufficient weight to the really serious events. For example, child sexual abuse is among the most serious and detrimental of negative life events, and girls are more than twice as likely as boys to report sexual abuse in childhood and adolescence (Kendler et al., 2000; see Chapter 14).

Another category of negative life events is peer sexual harassment in the schools, as discussed in Chapter 7. More girls than boys report being victims, and girls are also more upset by such incidents (American Association of University Women, 2011). And a majority of LGBTQ youth report being verbally harassed because of their sexual orientation or gender expression (Kosciw et al., 2014). In sum, peer sexual harassment is more common for adolescents who aren't straight cisgender boys.

Violence and poverty are additional factors that contribute to depression in girls and women and help to explain the gender difference (Belle & Doucet, 2003; Cutrona et al., 2005; Koss, Bailey, et al., 2003). Gender-based violence was discussed in detail in Chapter 14, but it is clear that the experience of being victimized can lead to depression. Regarding the second factor, poverty has become increasingly gendered. An increasing proportion of those living below the poverty line are women or women and their children, a phenomenon known as the **feminization of poverty**. In turn, this pattern is related to factors such as the increased proportion of single-parent households headed by women, the inadequacy of child support payments following divorce, and the lack of decent, affordable child care that would allow these women to work at jobs that could bring them to self-sufficiency (Belle & Doucet, 2003). Abundant evidence shows a link between poverty and mental health problems (Belle & Doucet, 2003). Therefore, the feminization of poverty has mental health implications for women.

Feminization of poverty: The increasing trend over time for women to be overrepresented among the poor in the United States.

Research indicates that women who are financially stressed and have responsibility for young children experience more symptoms of depression than other women do. One study found that 40% of the low-income mothers in the sample had sufficient symptoms to be categorized as depressed (Coiro, 2001). It is clear that the higher rates of poverty among women contribute to the higher incidence of depression in women.

Summary. We have looked at the three categories of factors—affective, biological, and cognitive—proposed by the ABC model to make a person vulnerable to depression when faced with negative life events. It's important to remember that no single factor explains the emergence of the adolescent gender difference in depression. Instead, multiple pathways and multiple factors may contribute to girls' higher depression. For one girl, it may be an *s/s* genotype combined with a history of childhood abuse or other trauma. For another, it may be a high level of body surveillance combined with a comment from a boy that she looks like she's gaining weight. While humans are very adaptable and many overcome significant challenges, there are also many ways and reasons that we may develop disorders like depression.

THE POLITICS OF PSYCHIATRIC DIAGNOSIS: PREMENSTRUAL DYSPHORIC DISORDER

The American Psychiatric Association publishes a thick book called the *Diagnostic and Statistical Manual of Mental Disorders* (DSM). The latest edition, DSM-5, came out in 2013. Why is this book important? It contains the listing of all the official labels or diagnoses that psychiatrists and psychologists can give to people's mental disorders, together with a list of the criteria or symptoms that a patient must show in order to be given a particular diagnosis. Money is involved because, in order for your health insurance to pay for psychotherapy, the therapist must give you an official diagnosis from this book, which then becomes part of your medical record. In turn, a diagnosis from the DSM must be noted in situations such as an application for disability insurance and may exclude you from certain occupations or educational training. A DSM diagnosis may help you gain access to therapy, but it is also potentially stigmatizing.

The DSM-5 contains several controversial diagnoses. One such diagnosis is *premenstrual dysphoric disorder* (PMDD). (Dysphoria is the opposite of euphoria; *dysphoria* means unhappiness or depressed mood.) To be diagnosed with PMDD, a person with a female body must display at least five of the following symptoms during the last week of most menstrual cycles during the past year: mood fluctuations, irritability, anger, or increased interpersonal conflict; depressed mood, hopelessness, self-deprecation, or marked anxiety or tension; decreased interest in usual activities; subjective difficulty in concentrating; lethargy or fatigue or lack of energy; marked appetite change with overeating or food cravings; insomnia or hypersomnia; and feelings of being out of control. Somatic symptoms such as bloating, weight gain, breast tenderness, and joint or muscle pain may also be present (American Psychiatric Association, 2013). Many of these symptoms are also present in depression, but a key difference here is timing. Symptoms should improve or even disappear in the first week of the menstrual cycle, only to return again a few weeks later.

Is PMDD an attempt by the American Psychiatric Association to incorporate PMS into its diagnoses? Advocates of the PMDD diagnosis maintain that PMDD is more severe than PMS (Epperson et al., 2012). They also claim that PMDD is very rare—with only 2% prevalence, which is about the same as the prevalence of autism spectrum disorder. Yet skeptics have pointed out several problems with the PMDD diagnosis.

One reason to be skeptical about PMDD is that the scientific evidence backing it is disputed. While the DSM is supposed to contain only diagnoses that have been validated scientifically, there are many social scientists who remain critical of a PMDD diagnosis. For example, there is some concern that PMDD is culture-bound, existing only in certain cultures. If a disorder results from hormonal fluctuations in the female body, wouldn't we expect women across cultures to experience it? Most PMS research has been done in a small number of Western nations. Research conducted in Hong Kong and mainland China indicates that women there report premenstrual symptoms of fatigue, water retention, pain, and increased sensitivity to cold (Chrisler & Johnston-Robledo, 2002). American women do not report increased sensitivity to cold and Chinese women do not report depression. These findings also confirm the argument that many PMS symptoms are culturally constructed.

There is also a suspicion of drug company involvement (Ali et al., 2010). The pharmaceutical company Eli Lilly developed and owned the patent to the antidepressant Prozac. The patent was about to expire and, with it, huge profits. Eli Lilly repackaged Prozac (fluoxetine) as Sarafem, a treatment for PMDD and, miraculously, PMDD appeared in the DSM at about the same time.

A diagnosis of PMDD might be harmful to women in several ways. For example, a woman who is diagnosed with PMDD might be regarded as emotionally unstable or mentally ill and then denied insurance coverage or custody of her children. As a rule, one should be suspicious of any psychiatric diagnosis that can be applied to one gender only.

What about women who do feel depressed just before their period? Don't we need a diagnosis for them? There already is one—depression. They can be treated for it, with no need for gender-stereotyped and potentially harmful labels of PMDD.

In sum, there is serious question about the scientific validity of PMDD. Even a process as seemingly innocent as psychiatric diagnosis may involve gender stereotypes and practices that can be harmful to women.

Alcohol- and Substance-Use Disorders

Gender and Alcohol-Use Disorder

Each year in the United States, alcohol causes nearly 107,000 deaths, from car crashes to liver disease (Centers for Disease Control and Prevention, n.d.). Thirty percent of these deaths are among women. In addition to the well-known damage that alcoholism does to women's day-to-day functioning, heavy drinking increases women's mortality rates. Chronic conditions such as alcoholic liver disease and cirrhosis, as well as acute conditions such as falls, poisoning, and motor vehicle crashes, are the most common types of alcohol-attributable deaths among women.

In addition, even moderate alcohol intake is linked to an increased risk of breast cancer. About 4% of breast cancer cases are attributed to alcohol use (Collaborative Group on Hormonal Factors in Breast Cancer, 2002). Research indicates that alcohol raises the levels of specific sex hormones that are known to increase breast cancer risk (Dorgan et al., 2001). In addition, long-term alcohol abuse of the kind that occurs in alcohol-use disorder actually shrinks the brain, and the effect is larger in women than in men (Wuethrich, 2001).

We can think of drinking behavior as falling along a continuum from abstinence at one end to dependence at the other, with moderate drinking, heavy drinking, and problem drinking falling in between. As can be seen in Table 15.1, there are gender differences in any use of alcohol, with more men than women consuming alcohol. **Alcohol-use disorder** is characterized not only by excessive alcohol use, but also by the associated failure to fulfill major role obligations (e.g., work, school, home). As such, alcohol-use disorder can have pervasive and far-reaching impacts. The ratio of men to women with alcohol-use disorder is approximately 3:1. This gender difference is found across nations, although the gender ratio varies somewhat from one country to another (Wilsnack et al., 2009). The gender difference exists across ethnic groups in the United States, but overall rates differ across ethnic groups. That is, American Indians have the highest rates of alcohol-use disorder, followed by Whites, Hispanics, African Americans, and Asian Americans (American Psychiatric Association, 2013).

In short, despite the greater prevalence in men, alcohol-use disorder remains a very serious matter for women. Why did it take so long for scientists to alert us to this issue? One reason is that, as recently as 1995, all-male research samples were still common

Alcohol-use disorder: A psychological disorder characterized by excessive alcohol use and associated failure to fulfill major role obligations (e.g., work, school, home).

TABLE 15.1	Percentages of women and men age 12 and older reporting any use of substances in the past month, and the gender ratio of these rates (men to women).

Substance	Men	Women	M:W Ratio
Alcohol	57.1	47.5	1.20
Tobacco	31.1	20.2	1.54
Any illicit drug	11.5	7.3	1.58
Marijuana	9.7	5.6	1.73
Cocaine	0.8	0.4	2.00
Hallucinogens	0.7	0.3	2.33

Source: Data from Substance Abuse and Mental Health Services Administration (SAMHSA; 2014).

(Greenfield, 2002). And because alcohol-use disorder is stereotyped as a "masculine" problem, women with alcohol-use disorder stand a good chance of being overlooked.

Causes of Gender Differences in Alcohol-Use Disorder

Heavy drinking almost always precedes and often predicts the development of alcohol-use disorder, and more men than women are heavy drinkers (Dawson et al., 1995). That then leads to this question: Why are more men heavy drinkers? One possibility has to do with gender roles; in short, women's drinking is restricted and men's is encouraged. That is, heavy drinking and drunkenness are more socially disapproved for women than for men (Vogeltanz & Wilsnack, 1997). Therefore, women must limit their alcohol consumption to avoid this social disapproval. Also, men experience more social pressure to drink than women do (Suls & Green, 2003).

Another possibility has to do with how female bodies respond to alcohol. That is, alcohol has greater bioavailability in women than in men, such that, given equivalent doses of ethanol, a woman will experience a higher blood alcohol level than a man, even when body weight is controlled for (El-Guebaly, 1995; York & Welte, 1994). Partly, this has to do with metabolic differences between male and female bodies (Baraona et al., 2001). Women are therefore more sensitive to the effects of alcohol. According to this explanation, women may learn to moderate its use, thereby avoiding becoming problem drinkers.

Predictors of Alcohol-Use Disorder in Women

Many factors may contribute to the development of alcohol-use disorder in women, including genetic factors, a history of childhood adversity, having a mood disorder, and having a spouse or partner who has a drinking problem.

A substantial body of evidence indicates that genetic factors contribute to alcohol problems, although some researchers believe that genetic influence is weaker in women than in men (Hicks et al., 2007). Certainly, it is true that not everyone who has an alcoholic parent will also become alcoholic. Some factors may actually protect such people from developing alcohol use problems. For example, one study found that being in a good marriage protected women who had an alcoholic parent from also becoming alcoholic (Jennison & Johnson, 2001).

A history of childhood adversity is a strong predictor of alcohol problems in women. One especially important factor is childhood sexual abuse. For example, one study with a sample of women with alcohol- and/or substance-use disorders found that 51% had experienced childhood sexual abuse and 39% had been exposed regularly to physical abuse by a parent (Berry & Sellman, 2001). Another study examined adverse childhood experiences (such as physical, emotional, or sexual abuse; physical or emotional neglect; having household members with a history of incarceration, mental illness, and/or substance abuse; and parental discord and violence) and found that such experiences were associated with problematic alcohol and substance use (Dube, Anda, et al., 2002; Dube, Felitti, et al., 2003). Moreover, a higher number of adverse childhood experiences increased the likelihood that a participant developed an alcohol- and/or substance-use problem.

Depression and anxiety are commonly associated with alcohol problems in women (Mann et al., 2004). One question is this: Are the depression and anxiety the cause or the effect? Do they precede or follow alcohol-use disorder? In some cases, people may self-medicate their depression or anxiety with alcohol use. In others, excessive alcohol use may lead a person to make maladaptive choices (e.g., driving while drunk, missing work or school), the negative effects of which foster the development of depression or anxiety.

Substance-Use Disorder

Substance-use disorder (what many people might think of as drug abuse and addiction) has a cluster of cognitive, behavioral, and physiological symptoms that develop from a person's excessive use of a substance despite its creating significant problems in their life (American Psychiatric Association, 2013). Diagnostic criteria also include the failure to fulfill major role obligations at work, school, and home; the desire and perhaps failed efforts at stopping or cutting back on use; cravings or preoccupation with obtaining the substance; and using increasingly larger amounts of the substance over time to achieve the desired effect. These are, essentially, the same diagnostic criteria as for alcohol-use disorder. Excessive use of the substance (whether it be heroin, cocaine, methamphetamine, etc.) activates the brain's reward system, making the user feel an intense sensation of being rewarded for their behavior.

Although drug addiction is stereotyped as masculine, plenty of women suffer from addictions, and the pattern is not at all new. During the 19th century, the majority of morphine and opium addicts were women (Kandall, 1996). In 1894 Dr. Joseph Pierce proclaimed, "We have an army of women in America dying from the opium habit—larger than our standing army. The profession [medicine] is wholly responsible for the loose and indiscriminate use of the drug" (Kandall, 1996, p. 631). Addiction to prescription painkillers remains a public health problem in the 21st century.

Today, as Table 15.1 shows, substantial proportions of women continue to use illicit drugs such as cocaine, and many use the licit drugs of alcohol and nicotine (tobacco). Several historical shifts have also occurred in recent decades. For example, the decriminalization of marijuana has made its use less stigmatized and more socially acceptable.

Another historical shift is evident in the use of the illicit drug heroin and the attention it receives. In particular, the use of heroin, an opioid, has attracted considerable media attention in recent years as we've witnessed demographic shifts in the population of users. When heroin was disproportionately used by men of color in lower income communities, there was little media attention or public health funding regarding heroin addiction and treatment. Today, 90% of those who began using heroin in the last decade are White, and about half are women (Cicero et al., 2014). Most users live in rural and suburban communities and began using heroin when their use of prescription opioids such as OxyContin became too expensive (Cicero et al., 2014). While it is difficult to prove that media and public health attention for heroin use is dependent on the race, class, and gender of users, the pattern is disturbing. Moreover, an intersectional perspective would note that low-income men of color, and their well-being, have historically been marginalized.

Gender dynamics are also important in women's substance-use disorder. Men often are the gatekeepers who get women involved in illicit drug use and addiction (Collins, 2002). Straight women are more likely to have used heroin at the urging of a male sex partner, and men are more likely to have tried it due to pressure from other men. The economics of addiction also mean that many women who become addicted to illicit drugs may be drawn into prostitution to pay for their drugs (Collins, 2002).

As to the factors that increase a woman's risk of developing substance-use disorder, the list looks much like the one predicting alcohol-use disorder. It includes genetic factors, childhood sexual abuse, inadequate parenting, drug use by peers, and adult victimization by intimate partner violence (Goldberg, 1995; Hicks et al., 2007; Kilbey & Burgermeister, 2001). In one large, well-sampled study, 6.6% of women who had a history of child sexual abuse met criteria for substance-use disorder, compared with 1.4% of women with no history of abuse (MacMillan et al., 2001).

Substance-use disorder: A psychological disorder characterized by excessive use of a substance (e.g., heroin), an associated failure to fulfill major role obligations (e.g., work, school, home), failure to cut back on use, cravings, and using increasingly greater amounts of the substance over time.

In sum, while women may not abuse alcohol and other drugs to the same extent that men do, substance-use disorder is an important issue for women. Not only do they themselves suffer enormously from dependence on drugs, but also, increasingly, women are being legally charged for damage to a fetus exposed to harmful drugs during a pregnancy (Martin, 2015).

Eating Disorders

Disordered eating behaviors are common among adolescent girls and adult women. Among college women, 26% engage in dietary restraint, 21% to 32% binge eat, 9% self-induce vomiting, 6% to 9% misuse laxatives, and 7% misuse diuretics (Celio et al., 2006; Luce et al., 2008). By age 20, approximately 5% of women in the United States have developed an eating disorder (Stice et al., 2013). These disorders are noteworthy in part because they are chronic and have high relapse rates; they are also deadly. In the DSM-5, diagnostic categories for eating disorders include anorexia nervosa and bulimia, as well as binge-eating disorder and others. Here we focus on anorexia and bulimia, which are well researched and overwhelmingly more common among women, with gender ratios of 10:1 (American Psychiatric Association, 2013).

Anorexia Nervosa

When asked if she had a personal motto, the supermodel Kate Moss famously replied, "Nothing tastes as good as skinny feels" (quoted in Selby, 2014). This quote has been embraced by those with a singular focus on thinness, including pro-anorexia websites and individuals with anorexia nervosa.

Anorexia nervosa:
An eating disorder characterized by over-control of eating for purposes of weight reduction, sometimes to the point of starvation.

Anorexia nervosa is a disorder in which one essentially starves oneself. Anorexia disproportionately affects girls and women: More than 90% of people with anorexia are female. In addition, the great majority of people with anorexia are adolescents, with the usual age of onset being between 13 and 25. Anorexia is estimated to afflict 0.8% to 2.8% of young women (Stice et al., 2013).

According to the DSM-5, the following are the official criteria for a diagnosis of anorexia nervosa: (a) restriction of energy intake, leading to a body weight that is at or below the minimum normal weight for that person's age and height; (b) an intense fear of gaining weight or becoming fat, even though the person is underweight; and (c) disturbance in the experience of one's body weight or shape, an undue influence of body weight or shape on self-evaluation, or persistent denial of the seriousness of the current low body weight. Anorexia may also include recurrent episodes of binge-eating and purging, such as self-induced vomiting.

The extreme weight loss characteristic of anorexia results from the individual's compulsive dieting. Although they may begin with "normal" dieting, it soon gets out of control. They might limit their food intake to perhaps 600 to 800 calories per day or restrict their diet to only a few low-calorie foods, perhaps existing solely on cottage cheese and apples. Their thoughts become excessively focused on food and eating, and rituals develop around eating. They eat in private and generally become so preoccupied with their diet that social activities and relationships become irrelevant.

The compulsive dieting is a result of an intense fear of gaining any weight and a corresponding drive toward thinness. But their body image is severely distorted, so that they believe they are fat even though they are emaciated, perhaps 20% or more under normal body weight. Despite the low intake of calories, the individual with anorexia often undertakes overly strenuous exercise to try to burn off more calories. Only making matters worse, a person with anorexia usually engages in denial: They firmly maintain that they have no problem and that they are not underweight. They also tend to resist any treatment or psychotherapy, convinced that such efforts will only make them fat.

Bulimia Nervosa

Bulimia nervosa is an eating disorder characterized by episodes of binge-eating large amounts of food while feeling a lack of control over eating, followed by purging behaviors, such as self-induced vomiting, misuse of laxatives, diuretics, or other medications, fasting, or excessively exercising. Like anorexia, bulimia also includes an undue influence of body weight or shape on self-evaluation. An individual with bulimia may consume 4,000 to 5,000 calories per day yet continue to lose weight because they purge the food.

Bulimia nervosa: An eating disorder in which the person binges on food and then purges the body of the calories by vomiting, using laxatives or diuretics, fasting, or excessively exercising.

Prevalence estimates are that 2.6% of young women are bulimic and that 4.4% engage in bulimic behaviors but are below the threshold for diagnosis (Stice et al., 2013). The prevalence of bulimia is alarming, especially because the health consequences of it are so serious. Some of these are the result of starvation. An individual with bulimia may suffer serious damage to their teeth and esophagus, due to the acidity associated with vomiting. They may also develop problems with their stomach, heart, and bones, and may even die from complications of the disorder.

Causes of Eating Disorders

Many factors have been proposed as causes of or risk factors for eating disorders, including biological factors, personal traits such as perfectionism and low self-esteem, traumatic life events, and a culture that is obsessed with thinness (Jacobi et al., 2004; Striegel-Moore & Bulik, 2007; Tylka & Hill, 2004).

For example, it has been proposed that anorexia is a result of biological causes. People with anorexia do have some abnormalities in their biological functioning, but it's not clear whether the physiological problems are the cause of the anorexia or the result of starvation (Piran, 2001). The problem is that physicians may not identify these physiological problems until the patient is already anorexic. Many of the problematic conditions seem to be the result of starvation; that is, most of the conditions reverse and return to normal as the person gains weight. For example, electrolytes are important for the proper functioning of the nervous system, and electrolyte levels (e.g., potassium) are disturbed in people with anorexia. In people with bulimia, low potassium levels may result from vomiting and use of laxatives and diuretics. Convulsions, low blood pressure, low heart rates, and irregular heartbeats are other results of the starvation. It seems, though, that each of these physiological problems is a result, rather than a cause, of eating disorders.

Nonetheless, other biological characteristics that are not problems or abnormalities might indirectly be associated with eating disorders. For example, a large longitudinal study of young women with body dissatisfaction found that adolescent girls with a lower body mass index (BMI) had a greater risk for later developing anorexia (Stice et al., 2017). Researchers are not sure why being thin makes a woman more likely to develop anorexia.

There is also emerging evidence that eating disorders such as bulimia involve brain mechanisms like those seen in substance addiction. Research points to the possibility of dysfunction in the brain's reward system that leads individuals to engage in binge-eating (Schulte et al., 2016).

Another possible biological factor for eating disorders is genetics. Both twin studies and adoption studies show that there are significant genetic effects on eating disorders (Baker et al., 2009; Klump et al., 2009).

Personal characteristics or traits may also increase risk. For example, global self-esteem has been negatively associated with disordered eating behaviors (Zeigler-Hill & Noser, 2015). In addition, perfectionism has been identified as a risk factor for both anorexia and bulimia (Fairburn et al., 1999). Of course, not all perfectionists develop eating disorders. Perfectionism is a vulnerability that, combined with a particular stressor—like the belief that one is overweight or a comment from a gymnastics coach that one is getting too heavy to be successful in the sport—leads to the development of an eating disorder (Joiner et al., 1997).

Like many mental health issues, traumatic life events increase risk for eating disorders. Traumatic events may predispose a person to developing an eating disorder or may precipitate an eating disorder in someone who is already vulnerable. For example, compared with healthy controls, patients with eating disorders are much more likely to have a history of child sexual abuse (11% vs. 35%; Fairburn et al., 1997). Those with eating disorders are also considerably more likely (50%) to have been teased repeatedly about their weight or appearance compared with healthy controls (28%).

Finally, research indicates that a major factor in the development of eating disorders is the internalization of the thin ideal and the pressure to be thin (Stice et al., 2017). Many feminists have linked this thin-ideal internalization to objectified body consciousness and our culture's obsession with thinness.

Feminist Perspective

The feminist perspective emphasizes the socialization practices and media messages of our society over the pathology of the individual (e.g., Gilbert et al., 2005). The person with anorexia shows an extreme reaction to the socialization and thin-ideal messages that all women in American society hear while growing up. High-fashion models, Playboy centerfolds, and Miss America contestants present images of slimness that are difficult to live up to. Just as wealthy Chinese for centuries bound the feet of their daughters to achieve a culturally defined standard of beauty, so a particular standard of appearance of thinness is enforced in American society, not through physical methods but rather by socialization.

Here are some of the data on historical shifts of the past 75 years: In the 1950s, the average BMI of Miss America winners was 19.4; by the late 1980s it had declined to 18.0 (Spitzer et al., 1999). The average model, dancer, or actress today weighs less and looks thinner than 95% of the female population in the United States (Wolf, 1991). The World Health Organization's cutoff for anorexia is a BMI less than 17.5. Meanwhile, the average actual BMI of American women age 18 to 24 went from a little over 22 in 1970 to a bit over 24 in 1990 (Spitzer et al., 1999). In other words, despite decades of emphasis by the women's movement on these issues, the gap between ideal and actual women's bodies has only increased.

College women rate their ideal figure as considerably thinner than their actual figure (Lamb et al., 1993). In fact, dissatisfaction with weight is so common among adolescent girls and women that it has been termed a *normative discontent* (Rodin et al., 1985). In one study of sixth-, seventh-, and eighth-grade girls, 72% dieted (Levine et al., 1994). And in another study among fourth graders (10-year-olds), 51% of White girls and 46% of

David M. Bennett/Getty Images Entertainment/Getty Images.

PHOTO 15.1
"Nothing tastes as good as skinny feels," according to fashion model Kate Moss (pictured here). The media feature models who are unrealistically thin, which contributes to a culture that fosters eating disorders in women.

Black girls selected an ideal body size, from an array of drawings, that was thinner than their current size (Thompson et al., 1997).

Research indicates that being exposed to thin-ideal models in the media leads girls and women to feel dissatisfied with their own bodies (Grabe et al., 2008). These findings hold true in both correlational and experimental studies. That is, women who watch more thin-ideal media experience more body dissatisfaction, and women experimentally exposed to media experience more body dissatisfaction compared with women in the control group.

These standards of beauty are attached to White culture. For example, Black women tend to hold a larger body as the standard and feel more positively about their bodies, relative to White women (Grabe & Hyde, 2006). Similarly, Latinx beauty standards tend to value curves over thinness (Perez et al., 2016). Yet these ethnic differences are not as large as they once were, and women of color are often held to White standards of beauty. Immigration and acculturation may also lead to shifts in which beauty standard women of color internalize. One study with female international students from Asian nations studying in the United States found that eating disorder symptoms were correlated with the internalization of Western appearance norms (Stark-Wrobleski et al., 2005).

Psychologist Eric Stice (2001) put many of these factors into a model of the development of bulimic symptoms (see Figure 15.2) and tested the model with a sample of girls initially assessed when they were in ninth or tenth grade and then followed up 10 months and 20 months later. According to the model, the initial force is cultural pressure to be thin. This cultural pressure is internalized, leading the girl to become dissatisfied with her body. This dissatisfaction in turn leads to two outcomes: She engages in dieting, and she experiences increased negative affect (moodiness and feelings of depression). Dieting further contributes to the negative affect. The dieting and negative affect in turn lead to actual bulimic symptoms. Stice's results with the high school sample indicated significant support for every link in the model, and other studies have shown similar findings (e.g., Tylka & Hill, 2004).

Treatments for Eating Disorders

For people with eating disorders, three treatments have been used: cognitive-behavioral therapy, family-based therapy, and antidepressants (Wilson et al., 2007).

Cognitive-behavioral therapy (CBT) is a frequently used therapy for people with eating disorders such as anorexia and bulimia. Cognitive-behavioral therapy helps

Cognitive-behavioral therapy: A system of psychotherapy that combines behavior therapy and restructuring of dysfunctional thought patterns.

FIGURE 15.2   **A model of the factors that contribute to the development of bulimia.**

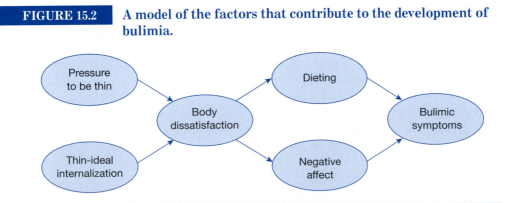

Source: Stice (2001). Copyright © 2001 by the American Psychological Association.

people change not only their behaviors but also the way they think about themselves and the world around them. People with anorexia or bulimia often have distorted perceptions of their own bodies, believing themselves to be fat when they are thin. They may believe that weight gain is a sign of indulgence or lack of control and that thinness would solve all other problems. They base their own feelings of self-worth on how well they are controlling their eating and their weight, feeling worthless or inadequate. They are preoccupied with weight control such that it distracts them from other matters. CBT targets all of these problematic thought patterns. People with eating disorders are often extremely rigid in holding onto these ideas, making any form of therapy difficult. CBT therefore also targets a patient's motivation to change.

Research evidence suggests that CBT is effective in treating anorexia, despite methodological flaws (Wilson et al., 2007). A review of studies comparing CBT to other treatments found that CBT led to improvements in important outcomes like BMI, eating disorder symptoms, and related psychopathology such as depression (Galsworthy-Francis & Allan, 2014). Still, the review concluded that CBT doesn't appear to be any more effective than other current forms of treatment, such as family therapy, in treating anorexia.

Family-based therapy (FBT) is based in family systems theory, which regards the person with anorexia not as an isolated, disturbed individual, but rather as a person embedded in a complex system that includes their family and society at large (Minuchin et al., 1978). Family events during the person's childhood may predispose the individual to anorexia. Family interaction and communication patterns trigger and then perpetuate the problem in adolescence.

The predominantly upper-middle-class families of anorexic girls tend to emphasize beauty (and therefore thinness) and tangible signs of success, such as good grades. Dieting produces external, tangible signs of "success" and simultaneously allows the girl to gain a sense of control. But the girl's problem behavior also has devastating effects on the functioning of the family. Parents feel scared and powerless about their daughter's eating disorder, which then becomes the focus of the family.

Following from family systems theory, FBT is necessary. Therapy for the girl alone is believed to be inadequate because she remains embedded in the family that maintains her illness. Thus, both the person with bulimia or anorexia and her family must participate.

Research evaluating the effectiveness of FBT on eating disorders has focused mainly on a specific form called the Maudsley model (Lock & le Grange, 2005; Schmidt et al., 2015). Data indicate that the Maudsley model of family therapy is effective for many adolescents with anorexia (Blessitt et al., 2015).

How effective is FBT with bulimia? One study randomly assigned adolescents (mostly girls) with bulimia to receive either CBT or FBT for 6 months (Le Grange et al., 2015). Researchers evaluated the patients at the end of the treatment, and then again at 6 and 12 months posttreatment. The results are shown in Figure 15.3. While both forms of therapy improved outcomes for many of the individuals with bulimia, FBT demonstrated quicker effects. The researchers also found that FBT was especially effective in families where there wasn't a high amount of family conflict.

Antidepressants—especially fluoxetine, an SSRI—have also been used in the treatment of anorexia, but there is little evidence that they are effective (Chavez & Insel, 2007; Wilson et al., 2007). Some people with anorexia also have depression, and antidepressants may be helpful with that aspect. Antidepressants are also sometimes used successfully with people with bulimia (Chavez & Insel, 2007).

Despite encouraging findings with CBT and FBT, the sad truth is that outcomes for people with anorexia and bulimia are not good enough. Successful treatment of anorexia

FIGURE 15.3 Percentage of adolescent patients who abstained from binge eating and purging at the end of 6 months of treatment with randomly assigned cognitive-behavioral therapy or family-based therapy, and at 6 and 12 months posttreatment.

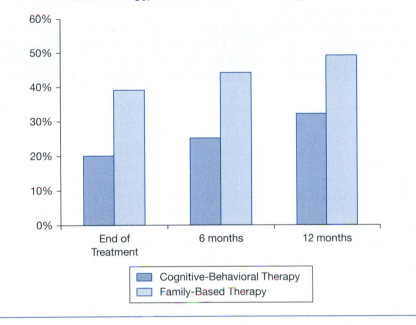

Source: Data from Le Grange et al. (2015).

and bulimia often takes many years, and some people never recover. For example, one review found that only about 50% of people with anorexia ever fully recover from their disorder, while 20% to 30% continue to experience some symptoms, 10% to 20% remain ill, and 5% to 10% die from complications of the disorder (Steinhausen, 2002). Data on outcomes of people with bulimia are only slightly better (Steinhausen & Weber, 2009).

Prevention of Eating Disorders

Of course, it would be far better to prevent eating disorders rather than to treat them after they have developed. A number of prevention programs have been created, and some show evidence that they are effective (Stice & Shaw, 2004; Stice et al., 2009). Programs that just provide education are not effective, nor are single-session workshops. Multiple sessions that actively involve participants are needed. Effective programs tend to have any or all of the following emphases: promoting self-esteem, stress management skills, healthy weight-control behaviors, and critical analysis of the thin ideal in our culture. Prevention programs are also most successful if they are targeted at high-risk girls rather than general samples of girls. Peer-led interventions for college women in sororities have also been effective (Becker et al., 2008).

Sexism and Psychotherapy

As the second wave of feminism emerged in the late 1960s, psychotherapists and the institution of psychotherapy became the object of sharp attacks for sexism (e.g., Chesler, 1972). A widely cited experiment used as evidence in support of these attacks was done

FOCUS 15.2

THE POLITICS OF PSYCHIATRIC DIAGNOSIS: GENDER DYSPHORIA

When the American Psychiatric Association published the DSM-5 in 2013, a new diagnosis was available: *gender dysphoria*. The symptoms of this disorder in adolescents and adults include at least two of the following for 6 months or more:

1. A clear incongruence between one's natal gender and one's gender identity

2. A strong desire to be rid of one's primary and/or secondary sex characteristics because they are incongruent with one's gender identity

3. A strong desire to have the primary and/or secondary sex characteristics of another gender

4. A strong desire to be treated as another gender

5. A strong conviction that one has the typical feelings and reactions of another gender

On their own, these symptoms do not indicate gender dysphoria. Instead, they must be accompanied by considerable distress or impairment in social, occupational, or other areas of functioning (American Psychiatric Association, 2013).

As you can see, this diagnosis is intended to apply to individuals who are transgender and are distressed by the experience of having a natal gender and gender identity that do not match. There are several important and complex controversies over the American Psychiatric Association's inclusion of gender dysphoria in the DSM-5.

This diagnosis reflects an important shift from the DSM-IV to the DSM-5. In the DSM-IV, the diagnosis given to most transgender people was gender identity disorder (GID). Note that gender dysphoria is not labeled a disorder, unlike GID. The GID diagnosis centered on the mismatch between natal gender and gender identity, which was framed as "cross-gender identification." Thus, the GID diagnosis rested on several problematic assumptions. First, it assumed that gender is a biological fact, not a social construction. Second, it assumed that one's natal gender was one's correct gender. Third, it assumed that one's gender identity was the "problem" to be treated. It was classic cisgenderism: To be cisgender was to be normal, but to be transgender was to be mentally ill or deviant. Trans activists pointed out that this diagnosis pathologized

gender nonconformity and stigmatized an already vulnerable group of people (Davy, 2015; Lev, 2013). Was this diagnosis really necessary? Whom did it help?

It turns out that there were also some advantages to having these diagnoses. The diagnosis of GID (and, today, gender dysphoria) legitimized and elevated transgender people's experiences, which helped to promote the development of effective treatments, including surgical and medical therapies for transition (see Chapter 11; Lev, 2013). And for many transgender people, a direct benefit of these diagnoses is that receiving one from a psychiatrist provides access to therapy. That is, access to medical and surgical therapies for transition typically requires that a patient be diagnosed with gender dysphoria. Equally important, insurance companies in North America won't reimburse or cover these expensive treatments or even psychotherapy if a patient does not have a psychiatrist's diagnosis of gender dysphoria. In short, many transgender people are desperate for the diagnosis because it provides access to the important therapies and care that will help them live healthier lives (Davy, 2015). This puts psychiatry squarely in the role of the gatekeeper to care for a marginalized group of people. Yet many insurance policies do not cover care for transgender individuals.

The shift from GID to gender dysphoria is remarkable because of the shift from pathologizing gender nonconformity to emphasizing psychological distress. Still, concerns remain that psychiatry could do more to help transgender people by removing this diagnosis altogether, thereby embracing gender diversity as part of the range of human experience. Concerns about access to therapy and medical care are important. How can that access be ensured without stigmatizing transgender people as mentally ill? Some trans advocates have suggested that medical and surgical therapies for transition, as part of gender affirming care, are part of a civil and human right to personal agency and to have one's body match one's gender identity. They note that some professional organizations around the world disagree with the American Psychiatric Association's position (Lev, 2013). Moreover, they contend that the psychological distress experienced by some transgender people stems primarily from societal intolerance of gender diversity rather than a psychopathology within transgender people.

by the psychologist Inge Broverman and her colleagues (1970). They examined the judgments of clinicians (psychiatrists, clinical psychologists, and social workers) on the criteria of mental health for men and women. Broverman and her colleagues gave the clinicians in their sample a questionnaire with a list of rating scales of gender-stereotyped personality characteristics, such as aggressive, affectionate, and tactful.

The sample of clinicians was split into three groups. One group was instructed to use the list of rating scales to describe a mature, healthy, socially competent man. Another group was instructed to do this for a woman, and the remaining group was told to do so for an adult (with no gender specified). Three interesting results emerged. First, although clinicians rated mature, healthy, socially competent men and adults as having similar personality characteristics, they rated mature, healthy, socially competent women differently. In other words, the man was indistinguishable from the adult, but the woman was a deviation from that norm. There was a double standard for mental health. As one feminist put it, the Broverman results show that "a normal, average, healthy woman is a crazy human being."

A second interesting result was that socially desirable personality characteristics tended to be used to describe men, whereas undesirable ones were used to describe women. For example, a mature, healthy, socially competent woman was supposed to be more submissive, be more excitable in minor crises, have her feelings more easily hurt, and be more conceited about her appearance than a mature, healthy, socially competent man.

A third result was that the clinician's gender was unrelated to their ratings. That is, female clinicians were just as sexist as male clinicians in their standards of mental health. Based on these findings, many concluded that psychotherapy had fundamental problems with sexism.

Yet, like any study, the Broverman study is flawed. The basic problem is that it does not provide a direct measure of the problem we are concerned with: whether therapists, in their treatment of clients, behave in a sexist manner. This study does not measure what therapists actually do in therapy, but rather what their attitudes are, based on their responses to a paper-and-pencil questionnaire. What we need are data on therapists' actual treatment of clients, but such information is in short supply.

Despite these and other flaws with the experiment, psychotherapy and training for psychotherapists have changed in response to such criticism. And later attempts to replicate the study have generally found less evidence of sexism (Widiger & Settle, 1987). The Broverman study is now more than 45 years old. Does sexism remain a problem in psychotherapy today? To answer that question, let's examine the research on gender bias in diagnosis and gender bias in treatment.

Gender Bias in Diagnosis

Clinicians' diagnoses of women seeking therapy may be influenced by gender stereotypes (Ali et al., 2010; Hartung & Widiger, 1998). For example, in one study a stereotyped description of a single, middle-class White woman was labeled by clinicians as a hysterical personality (Landrine, 1987). By contrast, clinicians who were given the same description for a married, middle-class woman labeled her depressed. As another example, a female client might be labeled as having a histrionic personality disorder, but a male client with the same characteristics might be labeled as antisocial (Ford & Widiger, 1989).

Focus 15.1 and 15.2 provide two illustrations of the ways in which the very diagnostic labels that are available in the DSM may be influenced by gender politics and stereotypes.

In short, the diagnosis of a mental disorder is not an objective, value-free process. Clinicians have stereotypes and values just like everyone else. If they are not mindful of these stereotypes and values, however, clinicians may make inaccurate diagnoses or provide therapy that is inappropriate and unhelpful. And on an institutional level, we must be vigilant about the ways that gender stereotypes and values can affect the very diagnostic categories that are officially available.

Gender Bias in Treatment

Gender bias in psychotherapy may occur in a number of forms, some of them blatant and some of them quite subtle (American Psychological Association, 2007a; Gilbert & Rader, 2001):

1. A client's concerns are conceptualized stereotypically. For example, the therapist may assume that a woman's problems will be solved by getting married to a man or becoming a better wife. Or the therapist may expect lesbian and gay relationships to mimic heterosexual relationships with regard to masculine and feminine roles.

2. The therapist uses essentialist, gender-difference beliefs in working with clients. For example, in viewing women as especially competent at relationships and less competent in the world of work, the therapist may fail to help the client construct a vision of herself that transcends traditional gender roles.

3. The therapist misuses the power of the therapist role. This may include using diagnosis as a means of categorizing and controlling a client and viewing a client who disagrees with the therapist's interpretations as being "difficult." Seduction of a female client is one of the worst abuses of a therapist's power (see Focus 15.3).

Psychoanalysis: A system of therapy based on Freud's psychoanalytic theory in which the analyst attempts to bring repressed, unconscious material into consciousness.

Gender bias in treatment may also stem from the theoretical orientation of the therapist or the system of therapy that a therapist uses. As an example, let's consider psychoanalysis. **Psychoanalysis** is a system of therapy based on Freud's theory. As discussed in Chapter 2, feminists have long sharply criticized Freudian theory as sexist. Similarly, psychoanalysis has also been criticized on similar grounds, as some of its central concepts are fundamentally sexist (e.g., American Psychological Association, 1975). For example, women's achievement strivings may be interpreted as penis envy. Women who enjoy orgasm from masturbation may be regarded as immature and thus be urged to strive for the more mature "vaginal orgasm" from penile-vaginal intercourse (see Chapter 12). The evidence indicates that women in psychoanalysis have sometimes been convinced that they are inferior, masochistic, and so on (American Psychological Association, 1975).

Can a system of therapy such as psychoanalysis be applied in an unbiased way? Some have proposed this and have even proposed feminist psychoanalysis (e.g., Eichenbaum & Orbach, 1983; Shainess, 1977). Recall from Chapter 2 that some psychoanalytic theorists, such as Nancy Chodorow, are explicitly feminist. Reflecting on how psychoanalysis has evolved in response to feminist critique, Chodorow stated, "I've learned that from my feminist medical-psychiatric colleagues, that being aware of one's body and bodily sexuality does not mean that anatomy is destiny, as Freud put it" (quoted in Chiang, 2017, p. 14).

FOCUS 15.3

SEXUAL MISCONDUCT BY THERAPISTS

One of the most serious problems for women in therapy is the possibility of a male therapist initiating sex with a female client (American Psychological Association, 2007a; Pope, 2001).

The 1978 revision of the American Psychological Association's ethical code states: "Sexual intimacies between therapist and client are unethical." This means that under no circumstances is a therapist to have a sexual relationship with a client. Although there have been vigorous efforts to educate therapists about these ethical problems, the evidence indicates that inappropriate sexual activity still occurs (American Psychological Association, 2007a).

How common is sexual misconduct by therapists? Studies from North America, Great Britain, and Australia indicate that around 4% to 9% of therapists admit to having a sexual relationship with a client (Garrett & Davis, 1998; Grenyer & Lewis, 2012; Lamb et al., 2003; Pope, 2001). A survey study with therapists found that 95% of men and

76% of women reported feeling sexually attracted to their clients at some point (Pope, 2001). Of course, feeling sexually attracted to someone and acting on that attraction are two different things. Professional training of psychotherapists is essential, and it should include guidance for therapists about how to ethically manage sexual attraction toward a client.

Experts regard this situation as having the potential for serious emotional damage to the client (Pope, 2001). Like other cases of sexual coercion, it is a situation of unequal power, in which the more powerful person, the therapist, imposes sexual activity on the less powerful person, the client. The situation is regarded as particularly serious, because people in psychotherapy have opened themselves up emotionally to the therapist and therefore are extremely vulnerable emotionally. Results from a national survey indicate that about 90% of clients who have sex with their therapist are harmed by it (Pope, 2001).

Psychotherapeutic Approaches

One of the most important factors influencing a woman's experience in therapy is the theoretical orientation of the therapist and the corresponding type of therapy they use. Below we will consider two kinds of therapy to see how they relate to women and whether they are likely to be biased.

Cognitive-Behavioral Therapy

In cognitive-behavioral therapy (discussed earlier with regard to eating disorders), the therapist and client identify not only dysfunctional behaviors, but also dysfunctional thought patterns. As an example of a problem behavior, a woman might have become so concerned that her hips are fatter than those of the models she sees on TV and in magazines that she refuses to go to the swimming pool because she will have to be seen in a swimsuit, despite the fact that she loves to swim and it's a hot summer. The therapist can help the woman confront such avoidant behaviors and substitute adaptive behaviors. In the cognitive realm, the therapist can help the client discover negative beliefs (my hips are fat and therefore no one can love me). The client can then discover how irrational those beliefs are and engage in cognitive restructuring, in which she substitutes positive beliefs (my hips are just fine, they're just fatter than those of skinny models, and I have lots of valuable qualities that people will notice, rather than staring at my hips).

While there is nothing inherently gender-biased about CBT, an individual therapist certainly could use it in a biased manner. Some feminist therapists have developed feminist cognitive-behavioral therapies (e.g., Srebnik & Saltzberg, 1994).

Feminist Therapy

Feminist therapy: A
system of therapy informed
by feminist theory.

In response to the critiques of traditional therapies, particularly psychoanalysis, feminist psychologists developed feminist counseling and psychotherapy. The basic assumptions and principles of **feminist therapy** are as follows (Enns, 2004; Worell & Johnson, 2001; Worell & Remer, 1992; Wyche & Rice, 1997):

1. Gender is a salient variable in the process and outcomes of therapy, but it can be understood only in the context of many other factors in a woman's life. Women have multiple identities defined by gender, race/ethnicity, social class, sexual orientation, and disability.

2. The personal is political: A person's experiences must be understood from a sociocultural perspective that includes an analysis of power relationships as well as intrapsychic or individual perspectives. A person's experiences of sexism and discrimination must also be addressed. "Symptoms" can be seen as a person's best attempts to cope with a restrictive and oppressive environment. Social activism can help a person gain a sense of personal strength and control over their life.

3. A major goal of feminist therapy is personal empowerment and helping people expand their alternatives and choices.

4. The therapeutic relationship is mutual and egalitarian.

5. Therapy focuses on a person's strengths rather than only on their deficits.

6. The qualities of caring and nurturing are valued and honored. Clients are encouraged to nurture themselves and to bond with others in a community of support.

Empowerment is a key feature of feminist therapy (American Psychological Association, 2007a; Enns, 2004; Worell & Remer, 2002). This process begins with the declaration that the therapist and client are equal—that is, they both are persons of equal worth—in the therapy process. Therapy cannot empower a woman or a person from a marginalized group if it begins by making them less powerful or valuable than the therapist. The client is then encouraged to develop two sets of skills, one dealing with the internal and the other with the external. They are empowered in dealing with their personal situation by developing flexibility in problem solving and by developing a wide range of interpersonal and life skills. In addition, focusing on external issues, the person is empowered by the therapist's encouragement to identify and challenge external conditions in their life that devalue them as a woman or a person of a marginalized group. Rather than "fixing" the client's problems, the feminist therapist encourages the client to discover their strengths and develop new strengths that empower them to deal with situations that have previously caused their distress.

Addressing the Mental Health Needs of People of Color

Access to mental health services has long been a privilege of middle- and upper-middle-class White people, and the services have been designed to meet their needs. Women of color and poor women have had less access to these services. Psychotherapy not only is financially inaccessible to many of these women, but also has not been sensitive to their needs (American Psychological Association, 2007; Comas-Diaz & Greene, 1994). Feminisms of color, discussed in Chapter 4, can provide some guiding principles (Enns, 2004).

An intersectional approach that is attentive to the multiple disadvantages of women of color is also helpful. In therapy with women of color, therapists must assess women's experiences as individuals of multiply marginalized groups. Women of color are likely to experience not only sexist discrimination, but also racist discrimination (American Psychological Association, 2007). Gendered racism, or other forms of intersectional disadvantage, should also be considered in the therapy setting. For example, gendered racial microaggressions (Lewis & Neville, 2015; discussed in Chapter 4) are likely to be a source of chronic stress. Each of these experiences can have a profound negative effect on psychological well-being.

For many women of color, ethnic and racial identity are important to their sense of self. Thus, in therapy with women of color, therapists need to consider the woman's degree of identification with her ethnic group. In some cases, immigrant status and degree of acculturation may also be relevant. For example, one first-generation Mexican American woman might speak Spanish almost exclusively and live in a Mexican American community in California, whereas another Mexican American woman's family might have lived in a suburb of Milwaukee for four generations, and she might speak very little Spanish. Such factors affect the cultural values the woman brings to therapy and therefore affect the goals that she and the therapist set for her. In general, therapists need to familiarize themselves with the cultures from which their clients come.

For immigrant women, challenges in maintaining relationships with family in their home country can be a unique source of stress. While they may feel lonely and miss their loved ones, returning to their home country to visit can be complicated. One study of immigrants from Latin American countries and migrants from Puerto Rico found that, for Latinas, returning to their home country was linked to later depressive episodes (Alcántara et al., 2015). By contrast, sending money home to family was linked to better mental health. Researchers believed that the trips home exacerbated Latinas' family conflicts and feelings of stress about caregiving demands, but that the financial remittances helped them feel effective in helping and caring for their families. Given the large number of immigrants living in the United States and Canada, it is important for therapists to assess these unique types of stressors that immigrant women may experience.

In addition, therapists need to be culturally competent in diagnosis. That is, mental health symptoms may vary across different ethnic and cultural groups based on cultural display rules (Brown et al., 2003). For example, *hwa-byung* is a disorder commonly found among Korean American women and involves constricted sensations in the chest, palpitations, heat sensations, a flushed face, headache, negative mood, anxiety, irritability, and difficulty concentrating (Brown et al., 2003). About half of the Korean Americans who experience *hwa-byung* meet the diagnostic criteria for major depression. A therapist working with Korean American women should be familiar with *hwa-byung*.

Most psychotherapists are White. Yet clients who are women of color may prefer to have a therapist from their own ethnic group, with whom they will feel comfortable and who will understand their cultural background better. It is critical that the field of psychology support more women of color in becoming psychotherapists. In the meantime, as White women therapists work with clients who are women of color, they will need to make extra efforts to provide culturally competent therapy.

The American Psychological Association (2003) issued guidelines for multicultural issues in therapy that are consistent with the principles of multicultural feminist therapy (Enns & Byars-Winston, 2010). Here are three key points:

1. Psychologists are encouraged to recognize that, as cultural beings, they may hold attitudes and beliefs that can have a negative influence on their perceptions of and interactions with people who are of a different ethnicity than their own. Just as in Chapter 1 we saw that there is no such thing as an unbiased researcher, so, too, there are no unbiased therapists. A first step is for them to recognize the cultural embeddedness of their beliefs and perceptions.

2. Psychologists are encouraged to recognize the importance of multicultural sensitivity and responsiveness to individuals who are of a different ethnicity. The commitment to sensitivity and responsiveness involves a commitment to acquiring knowledge about ethnicity issues; one cannot be sensitive without that knowledge.

3. Psychologists are encouraged to apply culturally appropriate skills in clinical practice. This guideline also requires that the therapist acquire the necessary knowledge and then be ready to adapt treatment methods as needed for the particular individual and their cultural context. Testing and diagnosis may require adaptation as well.

As an example, let's consider the particular needs of Asian American women (Bradshaw, 1994; Chin et al., 1993; Kawahara & Espin, 2007). A number of potential sources of stress exist in their lives. Some stresses arise from traditional Asian cultures, which are generally patriarchal and expect women to be passive and obedient. Younger, more educated Asian American women may embrace modern egalitarian values in the United States and thus may come into conflict with older family members, who hold more traditional values. Interracial dating and marriage is another potential source of stress. Although such relationships are common statistically for Asian American women, they are strongly discouraged by Asian families (True, 1990), again producing conflict and stress. On top of these stressors, there are, of course, stresses such as work–family conflicts that are commonly experienced by other women as well.

Culturally sensitive or culturally adapted therapy for Asian American women involves several features (True, 1990):

1. Use of bilingual therapists for non-English-speaking clients

2. Use of family-focused rather than individual-focused approaches, with respect for the women's family ties

3. Respect for Asian American women who are not verbally or emotionally expressive

4. Attention to the women's physical (somatic) complaints as possible reflections of psychological distress, knowing that in Asian culture it is more acceptable to have physical health problems than it is to have mental health problems

5. Recognition that there may be strong sentiment against feminism within the Asian American community

Just as we have discussed the importance of valuing women's experiences and perspectives in a feminist approach to therapy, so an ethnic validity model has been proposed in working with people of color (Chin et al., 1993; Enns & Byars-Winston, 2010). According to this model, the values and lifestyles of people of color must be valued. In addition, the deficit hypothesis, which views ethnic cultures other than European American culture to be deficient, must be abandoned and replaced by a difference hypothesis, which acknowledges differences among cultures while at the same time valuing them equally. These are important new directions for feminist therapy in the next decade.

Psychological Practice With Trans People

In Chapter 7, we introduced the topic of *trans-affirmative practice*, which is care that is respectful, aware, and supportive of the identities and life experiences of transgender and gender nonconforming people (American Psychological Association, 2015). The American Psychological Association (2015) has provided 16 guidelines for psychological practice with transgender and gender nonconforming people. We include some of those guidelines here. With regard to foundational knowledge and awareness:

1. *Psychologists understand that gender is a nonbinary construct that allows for a range of gender identities and that a person's gender identity may not align with sex assigned at birth.* Across cultures and history, there exists ample evidence of gender diversity (e.g., Nanda, 2014). Rejecting the gender binary and acknowledging gender diversity are essential to providing respectful and supportive care to trans people.

2. *Psychologists understand that gender identity and sexual orientation are distinct but interrelated constructs.* Gender identity and sexual orientation are often conflated, but they are separate aspects of an individual. Gender identity typically develops earlier in the lifespan than sexual orientation (Adelson & American Academy of Child and Adolescent Psychiatry Committee on Quality Issues, 2012). And while they are often experienced in related ways, it's important not to make assumptions about sexual orientation based on a person's gender identity, and vice versa.

3. *Psychologists seek to understand how gender identity intersects with the other cultural identities of transgender and gender nonconforming people.* Trans women of color are multiply marginalized, experiencing disproportionate discrimination and violence as trans people, as women, and as people of color. Understanding the intersectionality of social categories and identities is important in assessing the full and complex experiences of trans people (Chang & Singh, 2016).

4. *Psychologists are aware of how their attitudes about and knowledge of gender identity and gender expression may affect the quality of care they provide to transgender and gender nonconforming people and their families.* Psychotherapists, like all people, have their own biases and values that will shape their understanding and behavior toward others. Therefore, they must continually examine and reflect on these biases and values in order to provide supportive care.

And regarding stigma, discrimination, and barriers to care:

5. *Psychologists recognize how stigma, prejudice, discrimination, and violence affect the health and well-being of transgender and gender nonconforming*

people. Trans people face a disproportionate amount of marginalization and victimization that can contribute to their mental health (see Chapter 7). Discrimination related to housing, health care, employment, education, public assistance, and other social services is common.

6. *Psychologists strive to recognize the influence of institutional barriers on the lives of transgender and gender nonconforming people and to assist in developing transgender and gender nonconforming–affirmative environments.* Cisgenderism is often enacted at an institutional level. For example, transgender people have been prohibited from openly serving in the military (White House, 2017; U.S. Department of Defense, 2011), and some U.S. state laws prohibit them from using restrooms that correspond to their gender identity. These and other institutional barriers—including access to health care (see Chapter 11)—can profoundly shape trans people's daily lives.

7. *Psychologists understand the need to promote social change that reduces the negative effects of stigma on the health and well-being of transgender and gender nonconforming people.* The profession of psychology exists to improve people's psychological well-being. Advocating for trans-affirmative public policy, including legal protections for trans people, is one way that psychologists can work toward that goal.

With regard to assessment, therapy, and intervention:

8. *Psychologists strive to understand how mental health concerns may or may not be related to a transgender or gender nonconforming person's gender identity and the psychological effects of minority stress.* Given trans people's increased risk for stress and related mental health issues, careful assessment and diagnosis are essential. Still, it is important to recognize the full range of mental health among trans people and that not all mental health issues will be related to trans identity.

9. *Psychologists recognize that transgender and gender nonconforming people are more likely to experience positive life outcomes when they receive social support or trans-affirmative care.* Evidence is clear that, when trans youth and adults receive trans-affirmative care and adequate social support, they show positive mental health outcomes (e.g., Bockting et al., 2013; Olson et al., 2016).

10. *Psychologists strive to understand the effects that changes in gender identity and gender expression have on the romantic and sexual relationships of transgender and gender nonconforming people.* Much like romantic and sexual relationships between cisgender partners, such relationships with trans partners are complex and vary in quality. Respect, honesty, trust, love, understanding, and open communication are critical to the quality of romantic and sexual relationships (Kins et al., 2008). Bodily changes related to surgical or medical transition contribute to new possibilities in trans people's sexual relationships.

11. *Psychologists seek to understand how parenting and family formation among transgender and gender nonconforming people take a variety of forms.* Many trans people have and want children (Wierckz et al., 2012), and evidence suggests that children of trans parents fare as well as children of cisgender parents (White & Ettner, 2004). Trans people may encounter difficulties with legal adoption and infertility.

12. *Psychologists recognize the potential benefits of an interdisciplinary approach when providing care to transgender and gender nonconforming people and strive to work collaboratively with other providers.* Collaboration with health care providers, psychologists, psychiatrists, social workers, speech therapists, and other providers contributes to more informed and holistic care for trans people.

These guidelines are designed to help psychologists and other psychotherapists provide sensitive and effective care to trans people. The guidelines are particularly valuable because the majority of psychologists report that they feel unfamiliar with trans issues and lack training in trans-affirmative practice (American Psychological Association, 2015). Moreover, trans people have reported problematic psychotherapy experiences related to psychotherapists' lack of awareness and education about trans issues (Mizock & Lundquist, 2016). As trans people face considerable stress related to discrimination, stigma, harassment, and violence, psychologists can contribute at the institutional or structural level by cultivating a more welcoming society and advocating for trans-affirmative public policy. They can also contribute at the individual level by promoting resilience and psychological well-being among trans people. As psychologists, our goal is to promote psychological well-being among all people, and therefore it is part of our ethical responsibility to provide trans-affirmative care (Singh & dickey, 2016).

Experience the Research
Gender Stereotypes and Psychotropic Drugs

In your school's library, locate the medical journals, particularly those in the area of family medicine and psychiatry (e.g., *Archives of General Psychiatry, American Journal of Psychiatry*). If your school's library does not carry these specialty journals, it probably will at least carry the *New England Journal of Medicine* and *Journal of the American Medical Association*, and you can use those for this exercise, too. Inspect three issues. Locate all the ads for drugs for treating psychological disorders. These ads will mostly be for anti-anxiety drugs and antidepressants. For each ad, record the following: the gender of the physician in the ad, the gender of the patient, and the emotion expressed by the patient's facial expression. How does the ad signal which person is the physician and which is the patient? Also analyze the text of the ad. Does it carry a message about the expected gender of patients receiving this drug? How does it describe these patients and their problem?

Are the ads gender stereotyped? That is, do they portray physicians as men and people suffering from depression or anxiety as women? Or do the ads try to break down stereotypes, for example, by showing a woman physician? Are women of color shown in the ads? In what roles? What kinds of effects do you think these ads might have?

CHAPTER SUMMARY

Major mental health issues show lopsided gender ratios in prevalence, including depression, alcohol- and substance-use disorders, and the eating disorders of anorexia and bulimia. While women experience a disproportionate share of depression, anorexia, and bulimia, men are more likely to experience alcohol- and substance-use disorders.

Major theoretical perspectives take multiple aspects of gender into account when explaining the development of these disorders. Such theories include biological and genetic factors, cognitive factors, and sociocultural factors and take a decidedly interactionist approach.

Researchers have examined gender bias in psychotherapy, beginning with the landmark Broverman study. Today, sexism in diagnosis and treatment is more subtle. Psychotherapeutic approaches, including cognitive-behavioral therapy, family-based therapy, and feminist therapy were introduced and evaluated with regard to their equitable treatment of women.

Evidence is clear that discrimination—such as that based on gender and race or ethnicity—is destructive to mental health. The American Psychological Association guidelines for psychological practice with two marginalized groups, trans people and women of color, were introduced. The role of psychology in promoting the psychological well-being of all people is especially important in providing care to members of marginalized groups. Psychological practice extends to both institutional and individual levels, and psychologists have an ethical responsibility to advocate for groups who have historically faced discrimination and marginalization, including women, people of color, and trans people.

SUGGESTIONS FOR FURTHER READING

American Psychological Association. (2007). Guidelines for psychological practice with girls and women. *American Psychologist, 62,* 949–979. These guidelines, too extensive to include here, are a must-read for anyone considering therapy and for anyone training to be a therapist.

Enns, Carolyn Z., Rice, Joy K., & Nutt, Roberta L. (2015). *Psychological practice with women: Guidelines, diversity, empowerment.* Washington, DC: American Psychological Association. This book builds on the previous article and incorporates a more intersectional approach to providing therapy to women from diverse groups.

Singh, Anneliese A., & dickey, lore m. (2017). *Affirmative counseling and psychological practice with transgender and gender nonconforming clients.* Washington, DC: American Psychological Association. The full list of guidelines for providing psychotherapy to trans clients. Essential reading for therapists.

The Psychology of Men and Masculinity

> " Strong men, men who are truly role models, don't need to put down women for themselves to feel powerful. "
>
> First Lady Michelle Obama, October 13, 2016

We've spent 15 chapters focusing on the psychology of women, reviewing research on trans and nonbinary people when available. In this chapter, we focus on the psychology of cisgender men and the male role. You might be wondering why we include this chapter in the book. Simply put, it is impossible to understand the female role without also considering the male role because both are firmly rooted in the gender binary. The traditional view of men and women assumes the gender binary, defining the male role and female role as complementary, non-overlapping, and biologically based. Similarly, heteronormativity, or the assumption that heterosexuality is universal (see Chapter 13), considers the male and female roles to be complementary to one another. And, of course, in relation to men, women have long been referred to as the "opposite sex." Thus, because the female and male roles are defined in such terms, the psychology of women and the psychology of men are deeply interconnected.

The psychology of men and masculinity emerged from the feminist movement and feminist psychology. As a result, it is attentive to the power of gender roles, and particularly how the male role influences the lives of men. In this chapter, we review the theory and research on the psychology of men and masculinity.

PHOTO 16.1

Who is a "real" man? Traditional masculinity ideology narrowly defines the male role.

Masculinity and the Male Role

Although psychologists have long studied men, the male role has received far less attention. That is, because men have been considered the norm, they have often been studied as genderless humans (Pascoe & Bridges, 2016). But, of course, men have gender and a gender role. What does the male role look like?

Characteristics of the Male Role

Researchers have attempted to understand the male role by organizing the long list of masculine traits and identifying factors and themes. For example, early researchers described **traditional masculinity ideology**, which is a set of cultural beliefs about how men and boys should or should not think, feel, and behave (Brannon & David, 1976; Levant & Richmond, 2016). Traditional masculinity ideology includes four major components:

Traditional masculinity ideology: A set of cultural beliefs about how boys and men should or should not think, feel, and behave.

1. *No sissy stuff:* Masculinity involves the avoidance of anything feminine. Note that in this aspect of masculine stereotypes, masculinity is defined negatively; it means avoiding femininity.

2. *The big wheel:* The masculine person is a "big wheel." He is high in status, is successful, is looked up to, and makes a lot of money, thereby being a good breadwinner.

3. *The sturdy oak:* Masculinity involves exuding confidence, strength, and self-reliance.

4. *Give 'em hell:* The masculine person is aggressive (perhaps to the point of violence), tough, and daring.

Because gender ideologies are cultural beliefs and are defined by culture, there is variability across cultures in masculinity ideologies (Levant & Richmond, 2016).

Along these same lines, contemporary approaches note that the male role includes several characteristics, including aggressiveness, independence, self-confidence, and being unemotional (Spence & Buckner, 2000; Twenge, 1999). Common to each of these characteristics is a dimension of power and dominance. Research exploring gender stereotypes of emotions has revealed that, while men are stereotyped as less emotional than women, the emotions of anger, contempt, and pride are masculine and an expression of dominance (Brody et al., 2016; Plant et al., 2000; Shields, 2013; see Chapter 6). Thus, power and dominance are central to masculinity and the male role.

Cross-cultural research into masculinity has revealed how, despite cultural variations, there are commonalities. For example, Peter Glick and his colleagues (2004) examined stereotypes about men in 16 nations—including the United States, Germany, Italy, Turkey, Peru, and Taiwan—and found that men across all of the cultures are stereotyped as "bad but bold." That is, men are viewed as powerful, but that power comes with a cost of men being too powerful and using their power in negative ways. The positive aspects of their power make men well-suited for high-status jobs, but the negative aspects also make them well-suited for the role of oppressor or dictator. By contrast, women are viewed as nice but less powerful. Glick et al. argued that these views of men perpetuate gender inequality because they justify men's greater status and power. Evidence was consistent with this hypothesis, demonstrating that in countries with more gender inequality, the more men are viewed as "bad but bold" in a culture, the greater the gender inequality is in that country. This evidence supports the theory that gender stereotypes are both the cause and the effect of power inequalities between women and men in any culture. That is, gender stereotypes and gender inequality reinforce or perpetuate one another.

Looking just within American and European cultures, there are eight stereotyped types of men (Smiler, 2006; Vonk & Ashmore, 2003):

1. *The businessman:* A professional man, dressed in a suit, who is educated, money-oriented, and success-oriented

2. *The jock:* A large, muscular athlete who is a football player; he is physically fit, coordinated, competitive, and determined, and he talks sports

3. *The family man:* He is the father and the breadwinner, working full-time to support his family; he is married, responsible, and devoted to his family

4. *The nerd:* Not particularly masculine, physically weak, and unattractive, with a strong emphasis on academics

5. *The player:* This ladies' man is attractive, flirty, self-centered yet highly involved in the social scene, and irresistible to women

6. *The tough guy:* A blue-collar brawler with a quick temper

7. *The sensitive new-age guy:* This man believes in and practices gender equality and is sensitive and caring

8. *The average Joe:* A strong, simple working man who cares for his family

Again, note that dominance and power are reflected in most of these stereotypes—the businessman and family man have economic power, the jock and tough guy have physical power, and the player is powerful in his sexual prowess with women. Most types reject any hint of femininity. The least masculine type—the sensitive new-age guy—is supportive of gender equality and embraces feminine traits. The most masculine types are agentic or self-directed. These patterns echo the cross-cultural findings that gender stereotypes and gender inequality are linked, that masculinity and the male role are defined by power, dominance, and avoidance or rejection of femininity (e.g., Kimmel, 2006; Vandello & Bosson, 2013). Do these descriptions of masculinity and the male role reflect the men you know?

A recent analysis of masculinity and the male role suggests that gender roles differ not only in content (e.g., being aggressive versus nurturing, tough versus tender) but also in structure (Vandello & Bosson, 2013). According to the theory of **precarious manhood**, manhood is an elusive and achieved status, whereas womanhood is a given or assigned status. Moreover, unlike femininity, masculinity is perceived as something that is earned and hard-won, yet tenuous and easily lost. As a result, men must continue to publicly demonstrate and defend their masculinity to prove that they are "real men." Men may do this with displays of dominance and aggression and by rejecting or avoiding anything feminine.

Today, when a man is perceived as being sensitive or vulnerable, his manhood is threatened and he is told to "man up" or "grow a pair." According to the theory of precarious manhood, what we are telling men with these euphemisms is that they must earn their manhood and that they will easily lose it if they show any signs of femininity.

Precarious manhood:
The theory that manhood is an elusive and achieved social status that is hard-won and yet easily lost, and that requires constant public proof.

Historical Changes in the Male Role

Today, the male role is characterized by a number of ambiguities and conflicts. For example, men are supposed to be aggressive, yet it is increasingly unacceptable for them to rape or beat their wives. They are expected to be aggressive and even violent as soldiers and professional athletes, yet they are expected magically to transform themselves into tender, gentle partners and fathers as they walk through the door to their own homes. Men are supposed to possess great physical strength and be active, yet what is adaptive in today's society is to be able to work cooperatively with others and to interact intelligently with a computer while sitting quietly at a desk (Gee et al., 2000). What exactly are men supposed to do?

The sources of the ambiguities and conflicts in today's male role become clearer through a historical lens. Much like the female role, the male role has changed rapidly in just over a century, and such rapid changes can produce tension. Psychologist Joseph Pleck (1981, 1995) argued that, whenever roles change, ambiguities are created because of contradictions between the old role and the new role.

PHOTO 16.2
Will a gun make you a man? According to the theory of precarious manhood, being a "real man" is a hard-won and easily lost social status.

The individual feels a personal sense of conflict or strain in the contradictions between these roles, perhaps having been raised by the standards of the old role and then needing to function as an adult in the new role, and perhaps not even being aware that there is an old role and a new role.

During the Victorian era of the late 19th century in the United States and England, institutions strictly controlled the roles of men and women (Pleck, 1981). Men went to all-male colleges, lived in fraternities, worked alongside other men, voted in elections (while women remained disenfranchised), and drank at the all-male saloon. Later, men functioned in the corporate boardroom, where no woman ever entered. In short, men occupied one distinct sphere and women occupied another. Masculinity was clearly defined, and it was obvious to all what was expected and required of men.

Yet, in just a few generations, we zoomed from men and women occupying different spheres to Title IX, marriage equality, and questioning the gender binary. All-male colleges became coeducational, workplace discrimination based on gender became illegal, all-male saloons became singles' bars, and a woman won the popular vote for U.S. president by nearly 3 million votes. Some women even entered the corporate boardroom, running big corporations like Pepsi and General Motors. In short, external, institutional definition and control of masculinity declined. How, then, would masculinity be defined?

Pleck argued that as society loses one kind of control over people's lives, it increases control over other aspects. Thus, as external, institutional control of masculinity declined, emphasis shifted to internal, psychological masculinity and gender identity. And at that point the psychologists stepped in. Pleck suggested it was no accident that the first major work on psychological masculinity–femininity, Terman and Miles's (1936) *Sex and Personality*, was published at the height of the Great Depression, just when traditional definitions of masculinity—having a job and being a breadwinner—were threatened most seriously. Thus the shift was from externally defined masculinity to internally defined masculinity. That is, masculinity shifted from being defined by one's job to being defined by one's gender identity.

Paralleling these historical changes from external to internal definitions of masculinity was a shift in the traits and behaviors expected of men. That is, there was a shift from the traditional male role to the modern male role. And with increasing changes in women's roles in the last several decades, men's roles have been further destabilized (Kimmel & Messner, 2001).

In the *traditional male role*, physical strength and aggression are of primary importance. Tender emotions are not to be expressed, although anger is permitted. The traditional man likes to spend his time with other men and defines his masculinity in the male group. Although he is married, he regards himself as superior to women and does not value an egalitarian, emotionally intimate relationship with women. The traditional male role has been found in all social classes in the United States during the 19th century, in most nonindustrial societies studied by anthropologists, and in working-class communities today.

By contrast, in the *modern male role*, primary importance is given to success on the job and earning a lot of money. Thus, working successfully in a corporation and gaining power over others are far more important than physical strength. A high-quality intimate relationship with one woman, rather than numerous anonymous conquests, is considered an important goal for the modern man. Emotional sensitivity may—indeed, should—be expressed with women, but self-control and emotional restraint are still essential.

Some men find the modern male role to be oppressive and seek new options and liberation from it. Many are caught in historical change, in the ambiguities and conflicts between the traditional male role and the modern male role. Gender roles can be instructive and give us a sense of security when we don't know how to behave in new or uncertain situations, but they can also be oppressive and restrict our freedom to be authentic or honest about our identity and values. It is, in many cases, a considerable risk that men bravely take when they choose to define their gender for themselves.

Finally, we think it's worth noting that, although Pleck initially proposed these ideas several decades ago at the peak of the second wave of feminism, they are equally relevant today. As analyses of gender equality and masculinity find their ways into popular and social media—via discussions of laws about marriage equality, bathroom access, and gender-based violence, for example—we see much material for feminist analysis. The male role continues to be in flux.

The Gender Role Identity Paradigm

Gender role identity:
The psychological structure representing the individual's identification with their own gender role; it demonstrates itself in the individual's gender-appropriate behavior, attitudes, and feelings.

Gender role identity paradigm (GRIP):
Traditional psychology's perspective that optimal personality development depends on a gender role identity that matches the gender assigned at birth, consistent with the traditional masculinity ideology.

Despite the androcentric bias of traditional psychology, there have been concerns about men's **gender role identity**. Importantly, those concerns were raised when men failed to meet the expectations of the male role. As noted above, beginning in the 1930s, research into the notions of masculinity and masculine identity, continuing to the present, developed. Pleck (1981) framed this research as based on the belief in the critical importance of masculine identity, or as based on the **gender role identity paradigm (GRIP)**. Consistent with traditional masculinity ideology, the GRIP proposed that one's optimal personality development depended on a gender role identity that matched their "biological sex" (more specifically, the gender they were assigned at birth). Pleck critiqued the GRIP, analyzing the set of assumptions involved in this traditional view as well as whether the data support these assumptions. Some of the most critical assumptions are reviewed below.

One of the critical assumptions of the GRIP is that gender role identity develops through the processes of identification or modeling and, to a lesser extent, reinforcement and cognitive learning, and that cognitive learning is more important in men than in women. This assumption appears consistent with several traditional psychological theories (see Chapter 2). That is, both psychoanalytic theory and social learning theory claim that we develop our gender role identity because we identify with and learn from our same-gender parent. But psychoanalytic theory and social learning theory are at odds with each other as to which traits of the father encourage identification. Psychoanalytic theory says the boy identifies with his father out of fear of his father's wrath. Therefore, a punishing father should encourage identification. By contrast, social learning theory says it is the warm, nurturant, reinforcing father who encourages identification.

Based on his review of the evidence, Pleck (1981) concluded that research does not support the identification/modeling assumption. For example, the data do not support the punishing father idea from psychoanalytic theory. Yet there is some support for the notion that boys imitate same-gender models more than other-gender models as early as 3 years of age (Bussey & Bandura, 1999). The identification/modeling assumption also predicts that, because children should identify with and model their same-gender parent, sons should be more like their fathers than their mothers. But the data don't support this idea either—children are not necessarily more like their same-gender parent (Blakemore et al., 2009).

The other part of this first assumption is that cognitive learning of gender roles should be more important for boys than it is for girls. The reasoning goes something like this: In their formative, preschool years, boys spend most of their time with their mothers and little time with their fathers, because mothers are at home more and fathers are off at work (yes, there are a lot of problematic assumptions here!). This makes it difficult for the boy to identify with his father, so he must then look for other models for cognitive learning of masculinity. For example, he may look to cultural sources such as TV and picture books. One pair of studies supports this whole idea (McArthur & Eisen, 1976a, 1976b), but that research is quite old, and far more research on the issue is needed.

In short, we really don't know why or how boys and men develop a masculine identity. The research on this topic is often inadequate or contradictory and based on unidimensional measures of masculinity–femininity (see Chapter 3), which do not recognize the possibility of androgyny. It is likely that, as with many aspects of human psychology, many factors are involved in the process of developing a gender role identity.

Another assumption of the GRIP is that men's negative attitudes and behaviors toward women stem from men's problems with gender role identity that are caused by mothers. What could mothers be doing that causes these problems? Three possibilities have been proposed, and all three assume that fathers do not participate much in raising their sons. One possibility is that the little boy feels overwhelmed and threatened by his mother's power over him. Then, as an adult, he tries to control and subordinate women in order to defend himself against his fear that women (like his mother) will control him (this is the idea of Karen Horney, whose theories were discussed in Chapter 2). A second possibility has to do with identification. That is, the little boy mistakenly identifies with his mother because his father is not around, but he later realizes that he must shed this identification and become masculine. Therefore, men fear the feminine part of their identity and react to this fear by dominating and controlling those who are feminine (i.e., women; this is the idea of Nancy Chodorow, whose theory was also discussed in Chapter 2). A third possibility considers mothers as the primary socialization agents. Since socialization of boys frequently consists of punishing feminine behaviors, mothers punish their sons for femininity. As a result, boys come to dislike their mothers and to generalize this dislike to all women.

Any or all of these possibilities, then, could be used to explain why men have negative attitudes toward women. In extreme cases, they might be used as explanations of gender-based violence. What feminists point out, however, is that in all cases the mother is blamed and the father is uninvolved.

What do the data say? Unfortunately, there really is not enough definitive research to determine whether this second assumption of the GRIP is accurate. An alternative explanation is that men hold negative attitudes toward women because it is to their advantage to do so (i.e., negative attitudes about women justify and perpetuate men's privileged position in society). And such attitudes are so widespread in our culture that it is not surprising that each new generation of little boys picks them up.

A third assumption of the GRIP is the school feminization hypothesis, which argues that boys have academic and adjustment problems in school because schools are feminine. That is, since most teachers are female and teachers encourage femininity, boys' identity problems are made worse. These old ideas have been revived in books such as Christina Hoff Sommers's (2000) controversial *The War Against Boys*. Yet some see this trend as a backlash against advances for girls in the schools (Weaver-Hightower, 2003). The evidence, however, shows that boys' academic motivation and performance are about the same whether they have a male or female teacher (Marsh et al., 2008).

We can't ignore the sexist, cisgenderist, and heterosexist assumptions of the GRIP. Anyone can have a masculine gender identity, including women as well as trans, nonbinary, and queer people. Yet the GRIP labels men who aren't cisgender and heterosexual as having failed in the development of an appropriate gender role identity. In sum, while the GRIP was psychology's traditional view of men for many decades, none of the assumptions of the paradigm have much supportive evidence.

Why have we told you all these things about the GRIP and then told you that each of them is wrong? First, critical thinking involves understanding the assumptions of a theoretical perspective, and thus it is important to understand that the assumptions of traditional psychology's view of men are faulty. Second, based on the evidence, it is clear that traditional psychology's approach to the male role needs replacing.

PHOTO 16.3
Some have argued that boys have more problems in school than girls do because most teachers are women, with whom boys have trouble identifying. The research, however, does not support this claim; there are no differences between boys with male teachers and boys with female teachers.

The Gender Role Strain Paradigm

Gender role strain paradigm (GRSP): A feminist theory that gender roles are socially constructed by gender ideologies, which grow out of and support gender inequality, and that gender roles are a source of strain for individuals.

Contemporary feminist research on gender roles involves a new set of assumptions, collectively termed the **gender role strain paradigm** (**GRSP**; Levant, 2011; Pleck, 1995). The GRSP theorizes that the male and female roles are socially constructed by our beliefs about the roles of men and women (i.e., our *gender ideologies*), which grow out of and support gender inequality. In particular, traditional masculinity ideology determines our gender roles and helps to maintain a patriarchal system in which men have greater power than women. The GRSP has 11 assumptions (Levant & Richmond, 2016), shown in Table 16.1. Let's consider a few of them.

One important assumption is that gender roles are contradictory and inconsistent. As noted earlier in this chapter, some of these contradictions exist because of historical changes in gender roles, causing strain between the old and new norms. The more general point is that contemporary gender roles include a number of aspects that contradict one another. This is stressful for men because they may be unsure of which aspects of the male role to follow and when. Sometimes, adhering to one aspect of the male role means

TABLE 16.1	Assumptions of the gender role strain paradigm (GRSP).

1. The dominant gender ideologies in a given society define the norms for gender roles.

2. Contemporary gender roles are operationally defined by gender role stereotypes and norms.

3. Gender roles are contradictory and inconsistent.

4. The proportion of people who violate gender roles is high.

5. Violation of gender roles leads to social condemnation.

6. Violation of gender roles leads to negative psychological consequences.

7. Actual or imagined violation of gender roles leads people to overconform to them.

8. Violating gender roles has more severe consequences for men than for women.

9. Certain prescribed gender role traits (such as male aggression) are often dysfunctional.

10. Each gender experiences gender role strain in its paid work and family roles.

11. Historical change causes gender role strain.

Source: Levant & Richmond (2016).

violating another. For example, in developing emotional intimacy (which involves vulnerability and sensitivity) with his wife, a man meets one requirement of the traditional male role through heterosexual marriage, but he fails to meet another by making himself vulnerable. Note that the GRSP points to gender roles as a source of strain to individuals, compared with the GRIP, which views gender roles and masculine identity as positive goals to be achieved. Research shows that, indeed, the more conflict that men experience in the male role, the greater their psychological distress and the lower their self-esteem (Mahalik et al., 2001; Shepard, 2002).

Another assumption of the GRSP is that a substantial proportion of people violate gender roles. Gender roles are so idealized and unrealistic that most people can't possibly live up to all aspects of them on all occasions. Only a handful of people are shining examples of their gender role, and the rest bumble along in various degrees of failure to live up to it. Particularly for men who hold a traditional masculinity ideology, the discrepancy between what they think they ought to be and what they actually are can cause considerable strain.

Another assumption of the GRSP is that violating gender roles has more severe consequences for boys and men than it does for girls and women. For example, one study found that men who violated the male gender role were judged as lower status and more likely to be gay relative to women who violated the female gender role (Sirin et al., 2004). Focusing on peer interactions, boys punish other boys who violate gender roles more harshly than girls punish role-violating girls (Blakemore et al., 2009). Of course, violating one's gender role can be in one's own best interests, as when a father provides sensitive care to his children or when a woman pursues a successful career in engineering.

Related to this point, another assumption of the GRSP is that some characteristics that are prescribed by gender roles are actually maladaptive. That is, some gender role requirements may interfere with one's psychological well-being and functioning. For example, men who endorse a traditional masculinity ideology show higher levels of **alexithymia**, or difficulty identifying and describing their own and others' emotions (Levant & Wong, 2013). On average, men have higher rates of alexithymia than women ($d = 0.22$;

Alexithymia: Difficulty identifying and describing the emotions of oneself and others.

Levant et al., 2009), and it is a risk factor for some forms of mental illness. If we adopt an intersectional approach, we see how masculinity and race are interconnected. The link between masculinity ideology and alexithymia is particularly strong among White men (Levant & Wong, 2013).

Aggression is a stunning example of a maladaptive component of the male role. Right-wing militias in the United States, such as White supremacists, are bound together by an ideology of self-reliant masculinity (Kimmel, 2000). The al-Qaeda terrorists who attacked the United States on September 11, 2001, were all educated, middle-class men who were unemployed in their home countries, where economies were struggling (Kimmel, 2002). Their masculinity was threatened and al-Qaeda terrorism restored it.

Mass shootings—which occur once every week in the United States, on average (Ingraham, 2015)—are almost entirely male-perpetrated (Kalish & Kimmel, 2010). Similarly, male violence against women and girls continues to be a major public health issue (see Chapter 14). In many cases, the boys and men who commit these acts of violence have been teased and bullied. The evidence indicates that the teasing and bullying usually involves issues of masculinity and that homophobia is a motivator for it. These patterns provide dramatic evidence of the maladaptive aspects of the male role and challenge us as a society to reform our definitions and practices of masculinity.

In this section we have considered the GRSP. It shifts emphasis away from traditional psychology's concern with male gender role identity as an ideal and instead views gender roles as sources of strain for people.

Lifespan Development

In this section we review cisgender boys' and men's development using a lifespan perspective.

Infancy

As we discussed in Chapter 7, most research evidence points to psychological gender similarities during infancy. Meta-analysis has indicated that gender similarities are the rule for temperament traits such as sociability, shyness, difficulty, soothability, emotionality, and adaptability (Else-Quest et al., 2006). However, gender differences are found in physical activity level, inhibitory control, and perceptual sensitivity. Relative to girls, boys are on average more active, less able to inhibit inappropriate behaviors, and less sensitive to subtle changes in their environment. In addition, boys tend to regulate their attention less well than girls do. However, consistent with the gender similarities hypothesis (see Chapter 3), none of these gender differences is large; most are small.

Circumcision: Surgical removal of the foreskin of the penis, usually done within a few days of birth.

One experience that male infants are likely to have is circumcision. **Circumcision** (surgical removal of the foreskin of the penis, usually done within a few days of birth) is routinely done to about 59% of male infants born in hospitals in the United States (Owings et al., 2013). However, there is cultural variability in choosing this procedure for baby boys. Relative to the United States, circumcision rates are considerably lower in Europe, Canada, and Australia. Within the United States, circumcision rates are highest among White infants (91%) and lowest among Mexican-American infants (44%; Morris et al., 2014). In addition, in many states, circumcision is not covered by Medicaid, which limits poor families' access to the procedure.

Parents choose to have their sons circumcised for a variety of reasons. One has to do with religion: Circumcision is part of Jewish religious practice, symbolizing the covenant between God and God's people. Another reason has to do with public health: There is evidence that uncircumcised babies are more vulnerable to urinary tract infections (Morris & Wiswell, 2013) and that uncircumcised men have a greater risk of infection with the AIDS virus (Bailey et al., 2007). In a major shift in policy in 2012, the American Academy of Pediatrics concluded that the health benefits of circumcising newborn boys outweigh the risks. Yet, controversy exists about the procedure. For example, some physicians question the magnitude of the health benefits for boys and men in the United States (Frisch et al., 2013). And some biomedical ethicists have argued that performing nontherapeutic or medically unnecessary surgery on an infant's body is a violation of the infant's human right to bodily integrity (e.g., Svoboda, 2013).

For psychologists, one interesting question has to do with the psychological effects of this early physical trauma. Research has found no effect (Fergusson et al., 2008). That is, there appear to be no differences in behavior between circumcised and uncircumcised babies. In addition, evidence suggests that circumcised and intact men experience similar sexual functioning and satisfaction (Morris & Krieger, 2013).

Childhood

The peer group becomes an increasingly important socializing force as children develop through childhood. And school-age children spend considerably more time with their peers than they do with their parents. Given that children care deeply about gaining the approval of their peers, the peer group can be a powerful shaper of behavior through modeling, positive reinforcements, and punishments (Blakemore et al., 2009). Moreover, relative to girls, boys are more sensitive to the reactions of peers and less sensitive to those of teachers (Blakemore et al., 2009).

Children tend to be gender-segregated in their play, such that boys play with boys and girls play with girls (Maccoby, 1998). Gender-segregated play and the gender typing of toys and activities appear to have mutually reinforcing effects. In other words, the more a boy plays with other boys, the more he plays with trucks, and the more he

©iStockphoto.com/Slonov.

PHOTO 16.4
Gender-segregated play in childhood helps to perpetuate gender differences in behavior.

plays with trucks, the more playing house seems alien to him. As a result, he avoids play-ing with girls and his preference for playing with other boys grows, which means more play with trucks, which means more play with boys, and so on.

Despite many psychological gender similarities, boys tend to have more problems in school. Relative to girls, boys are more frequently put in remedial classes and referred for learning difficulties and behavior problems in school. One possible explanation has to do with gender differences in rates of hyperactivity: Boys with attention-deficit hyper-activity disorder (ADHD) outnumber girls about 3:1 (Willcutt, 2012). Hyperactivity is characterized by extremely high activity levels in situations where it is clearly inappro-priate, such as the classroom. Why are there so many more hyperactive boys than girls? Many researchers are interested in answering this question. One possibility is that boys' hyperactivity is evidence of a developmental or maturational lag; that is, children gain more control of their activity level with age, and the hyperactive child may simply be a very slow maturer. If boys generally are slower to mature than girls are, perhaps boys' greater rate of hyperactivity is a result of their slower maturation.

For children with ADHD, hyperactivity is accompanied by difficulties regulating attention. Boys' greater incidence of hyperactivity and ADHD may help to explain their problems in school as well as their higher rates of learning difficulties and referral to remedial classes. The hyperactivity itself is challenging for teachers, who must divert attention from other students to manage the behavior of the hyperactive student. These observations raise several questions about elementary education practices. For example, if there were more male elementary school teachers who themselves had been hyperac-tive as children, would outcomes for these boys improve? Perhaps male teachers would be more sympathetic or more skillful as teachers of hyperactive boys.

Adolescence

In adolescence, athleticism is an important and highly demanding aspect of the male role (Messner, 1990). Athletic participation is the single most important factor in high school boys' social status (Kilmartin, 2000). Nearly every high school has a group called the "jocks." They are dominant, highly masculine, and heterosexually successful, and they enjoy high social status in their schools (Pascoe, 2003).

Let's consider the athlete role from the perspective of the GRSP. One source of strain results from the shifting value attached to athletics at different times in the lifespan. In high school, athletics is a supreme, unquestioned value. In college, it continues to be important for some but is less important for most. At age 30, no one cares a bit about one's high school varsity letter in football, nor about the thousand hours that went into earning it. Another source of strain for athletes is the obsession with winning, expressed so eloquently by Vince Lombardi: "Winning isn't everything. It's the only thing." The problem is that in a contest between two teams, only one can win, and that means that half the players go home losers. Athletics, of course, does not have to be structured competitively, and winning does not have to be the goal. Still, the dominant reality in American athletics has been competition, and that produces losers.

For the boy who isn't athletic, the athlete role still creates strain. Athleticism contri-butes to popularity for boys (Blakemore et al., 2009). The boy who is a nonathlete is essentially flunking part of the masculinity test, and he is likely to be bullied. Remember how children choose one another to make teams for sports? The uncoordinated or unath-letic boy is chosen last. The message is clear: "Not only are you a poor athlete, but your peers don't want you on their team." Because peer relationships are so important at this age, this message can be a devastating blow, especially if it happens repeatedly.

In focusing on the psychological strains created by the athlete role, we should not forget that actual physical damage is also part of this reality. For example, repeated blows to the head—common in football and soccer—cause serious damage to the brain. New research shows that rates of brain injuries and conditions such as *chronic traumatic encephalopathy* (CTE) are alarmingly high among people who played football in high school, college, and the NFL (Breslow, 2015). Symptoms may take years to develop, by which point it may be too late to prevent memory problems, depression, and dementia. For example, Pro Football Hall of Famer Junior Seau tested positive for CTE after suffering from depression and committing suicide (see Photo 16.5). Researchers at the National Institutes of Health determined that Seau's CTE was the result of repeated head trauma during his football career.

Frazer Harrison/Getty Images Entertainment/Getty Images.

PHOTO 16.5
The athleticism of the male role can be dangerous. Pro Football Hall of Famer Junior Seau developed chronic traumatic encephalopathy after years of repeated head trauma during his football career.

In sum, the intense focus on competition and winning in athletics, particularly during high school, creates problems for the male athlete and nonathlete alike. No one actually benefits from this system. Moreover, there are serious physical dangers of some high-contact sports, such as football, which also encourage male aggression.

In Chapter 7 we discussed how, today, adolescence has been extended beyond the teenage years and a new stage of emerging adulthood extends well into the 20s. Sociologist Michael Kimmel calls these years between 16 and 26 for men *Guyland* (Kimmel, 2008). With no pressure to become an adult upon high school graduation, college and the years that follow represent an extension of adolescence. According to Kimmel, in college these not-quite-men engage in rites that define their masculinity, including binge drinking, fraternity hazing, watching porn with the guys, and hooking up with as many women as possible. None of this prepares men to be responsible, productive adults, nor is it healthy. Each year, 1,400 college students die as a result of drinking, most because of drunk driving but some from alcohol poisoning (Kimmel, 2008). Of course, not all college men behave this way. We should encourage and nurture men who are brave enough to behave responsibly and ethically. Even among those who stumble through college participating in Guyland, many come out of it after graduation, typically when faced with the demands of earning a living. But some remain long-term alcoholics or continue to think that treating women callously is just fine.

Adulthood

In this section on the developmental stage of adulthood for men, we will first consider the role of the father. Next, we will consider whether there is a male midlife crisis that is perhaps analogous to the menopause experience for women.

Fatherhood. The father role is a major part of the adult male role, and one that fathers feel is rewarding and important to their identity (Parker & Livingston, 2016). Here we will consider the transition to fatherhood and the importance of paternal influences on children's development.

The transition to parenthood is challenging and an opportunity for growth for every parent, regardless of gender. Just as with new mothers, new fathers may struggle to get adequate sleep and get to know their baby and how to care for them. For most fathers, it is not financially feasible to take paternity leave (indeed, maternity leave is not financially feasible for many mothers!), so they may experience tension or strain between caring for their baby and earning sufficient income. Since we spend a considerable amount of time and energy socializing girls and women for motherhood, but comparatively little time socializing boys and men for fatherhood, it's not surprising that some fathers feel inadequate or ill-prepared to provide care for their baby. As a result, they may instead opt to focus on the provider role, another aspect of the traditional male role (Singley & Edwards, 2015). For about 10% of fathers, the transition to parenthood is accompanied by postpartum depression (Paulson & Bazemore, 2010). Men's postpartum mental health is an important public health issue, with potentially far-reaching effects (Singley & Edwards, 2015). In short, depressed fathers (like depressed mothers) struggle to provide adequate care to their children.

Let's turn to the effects of the father on his children, technically called paternal influence (e.g., Goeke-Morey & Cummings, 2007; Marsiglio et al., 2000). We can consider two categories of effects that fathers might have on their children. *Indirect effects*, in which the father's behavior influences the child indirectly by affecting some other factor in the child's life (Goeke-Morey & Cummings, 2007), make up one category of effect. For example, consider a situation in which a father expresses unhappiness with his marriage, which may lead the mother to feel angry or depressed. In turn, she may be irritable with the child or depressed and unresponsive, either of which can affect the child.

Another category of effects consists of *direct effects*. Fathers' interactions with their children, the behaviors and attitudes they model, and so on are considered direct effects. One researcher proposed that there are at least 14 ways that fathers might be involved with their children: communicating, teaching, monitoring, engaging in thought processes, providing economic support, showing affection, protecting, supporting emotionally, running errands, caregiving, sharing interests, being available, planning, and sharing activities (Palkovitz, 2002). Based on research with families, we know that fathers can be just as sensitive and responsive to their children as mothers are (Cabrera et al., 2007). Moreover, these paternal behaviors make a real difference in their children's development: Longitudinal research shows that fathers who are warm, accepting, and loving toward their children contribute to their children's psychological well-being and to lower rates of aggression and behavior problems (Flouri & Buchanan, 2002; Rohner & Veneziano, 2001). These effects extend to other aspects of development, too: Children whose fathers are involved, nurturing, and playful tend to have higher IQs, better emotional self-regulation, and more developed language and cognitive abilities (Cabrera et al., 2007; McWayne et al., 2013).

Just as high-quality fathering is good for child development, poor quality fathering is bad for child development. For example, when fathers are more negative and less engaged during interactions with their young infants, the children are more likely to develop externalizing problems by their first birthday (Ramchandani et al., 2013).

Researchers are interested in measuring the many ways that fathers are involved with their children in order to understand the full range of paternal influence. Table 16.2 includes items from one such measure, the Paternal Involvement With Infants Scale (Singley et al., 2017). Notice that the scale has five factors, each of which may shape different child outcomes.

| TABLE 16.2 | Researchers are increasingly interested in the ways that fathers are involved with their children. Below are sample items from the Paternal Involvement With Infants Scale, which participants respond to on a scale from 1 (*not at all*) to 7 (*more than once a day*). |

Factor	Sample Items
Positive engagement	
	Feeding your baby
	Putting your baby down for nap/sleep
Indirect control	
	Arranging for child care
	Taking your baby to medical appointments
Frustration	
	Feeling jealous of your partner's connection with your baby
	Feeling frustrated when caring for your baby
Warmth and attunement	
	Feeling close to your baby
	Soothing your baby when they are crying
Control and process responsibility	
	Discussing the division of parenting responsibilities with your partner
	Choosing play activities for your baby

Source: Data from Singley et al. (2017). Created by the authors.

As noted earlier, the male role has changed in recent decades. Today, fathers are more involved with their children than ever before (Parker & Wang, 2013). Table 16.3 shows some of the ways that fathers can be involved. A related question is this: How much time do fathers spend with their children? One way to approach questions of how time is spent is the time diary method, in which individuals keep a careful record of all their activities for a 24-hour day, usually on a detailed diary form. The results of two such studies, comparing data from 1965 and 2011, are shown in Table 16.3 (Parker & Wang, 2013). Notice that, between 1965 and 2011, fathers increased the amount of time spent engaged in child care nearly threefold, going from 30 minutes per day to over 80. Still, relative to fathers, mothers continue to spend more time engaged in child care, and that amount of time has actually increased over the decades. For comparison, consider the hours spent in paid employment. In 2011, fathers spent about 1 hour less per day in paid work than they did in 1965, whereas mothers worked about 2.5 hours more per day each week. Historical changes in gender roles are reflected in how people spend their time.

Midlife Crisis? It is commonly believed that men suffer a "midlife crisis" at some point during midlife (we define this roughly as the time between the ages of 40 and 55). Countless films and television programs portray a 40-something man who, in feeling

TABLE 16.3	Hours per week spent by mothers and fathers in child care, housework, and paid work, in 1965 and 2011.		
	Child Care	**Housework**	**Paid Work**
In 1965			
Mothers	10	32	8
Fathers	2.5	4	42
In 2011			
Mothers	14	18	21
Fathers	7	10	37

Source: Parker & Wang (2013).

Midlife crisis: During men's midlife, the phenomenon of personal turmoil and sudden changes in lifestyle, touched off by a realization of aging, physical decline, and being trapped in tired roles.

anxious that his life has become monotonous and that his time is running out, buys a sports car and leaves his wife for a younger woman. Is there at least a kernel of truth to this stereotype?

Researchers have explored the phenomenon of the **midlife crisis**, which they define as personal turmoil and sudden changes in lifestyle, touched off by a realization of aging, physical decline, and being trapped in tired roles (Wethington, 2000). One author described the midlife period as follows:

> The hormone production levels are dropping, the head is balding, the sexual vigor is diminishing, the stress is unending, the children are leaving, the parents dying, the job horizons are narrowing, the friends are having their first heart attacks; the past floats by in a fog of hopes not realized, opportunities not grasped, women not bedded, potentials not fulfilled, and the future is a confrontation with one's own mortality. (Lear, 1973)

This points to the complex forces—biological, personal, and social—that converge on the middle-age man.

Andropause: A time of declining testosterone levels in middle- and older-age men.

Let's evaluate the claim about hormones. Testosterone levels gradually decline in midlife and older adulthood. Such gradual declines in androgen levels in men are sometimes called **andropause**, or ADAM (for Androgen Decline in the Aging Male; Morales et al., 2000; Tancredi et al., 2005). Some men may experience declines in libido and erectile functioning, mood changes, cognitive impairment, and vasomotor symptoms, along with decreases in muscle mass and strength and bone mineral density. Note that many of these symptoms are similar to those of menopause (see Chapter 11). Controversy remains as to whether testosterone treatments are beneficial (Tan & Culbertson, 2003).

Roles may change in midlife as well, bringing about new developmental challenges. Erik Erikson (1950) theorized that one of the major developmental tasks of adulthood is the resolution of the generativity versus stagnation stage. At this stage, according to Eriksonian theory, individuals have a desire to feel that they are contributing or creating something of value for future generations. This might be realized through parenting one's children or caring for one's grandchildren, mentoring or teaching others, or doing volunteer work that supports one's community. Generativity, then, is an important theme in midlife for all people, regardless of gender. For men with a traditional masculinity ideology, providing financially for one's family or coaching their child's sports team might meet this developmental need.

Another theme in midlife is the confrontation with death and mortality. The man is at once aware of his own aging and that of his peers and parents. He may lose peers to heart attacks or cancer, which are more common at this stage. Confronting the mortality of oneself and loved ones can be disorienting and may lead to negative outcomes such as depression. Alternatively, it may lead to a positive outcome in which the man comes to terms with the idea of his own death. Acutely aware of his limited time, he may choose to examine and reorder his priorities and make healthier choices about stress management, diet, and exercise.

Despite the physical changes and role changes in midlife, systematic, well-sampled research shows that the midlife period is far from universally stressful and that only about 10% of U.S. men undergo something that would be classified as a midlife crisis (Wethington, 2000). Like all developmental stages in the lifespan, midlife has its unique challenges.

Male Sexuality

Based on the research of Masters and Johnson (1966), we know that cisgender men go through the same phases of sexual arousal that we described for women in Chapter 12: excitement, plateau, orgasm, and resolution.

A major process during both male and female arousal is *vasocongestion*, or increased blood flow to the genitals. In men, vasocongestion produces erection of the penis. During puberty, a boy will have his first ejaculation at orgasm, in which the penis emits a milky fluid containing sperm; this is called **spermarche** (or *semenarche*). One interesting difference between men's and women's sexual functioning is that men have a refractory period after orgasm. A **refractory period** is a period of time during which one cannot be restimulated to orgasm. Whereas women have no such refractory period, and thus can have multiple orgasms, men are generally limited to single orgasms. The length of the refractory period varies in men, depending on factors such as age. For example, in younger men, the refractory period may be as short as a few minutes, whereas in men over the age of 65, it might be 24 hours.

Spermarche: The first ejaculation of seminal fluid; also called semenarche.

Refractory period: A period of time following orgasm, during which one cannot be restimulated to orgasm.

The psychology of male sexuality is even more fascinating than the biology. Sexuality—specifically, heterosexuality—is a central aspect of masculinity (Tolman et al., 2016). Men are expected to be very interested in sex, aggressive in pursuing it, and good at it. In Focus 16.1, we describe one sex therapist's analysis of the psychology of male sexuality.

Men of Color

Men of color in the United States are a diverse group of people, but they have some experiences in common. For example, Black and Latino men have generally higher unemployment rates and lower wages relative to those of White and Asian men. Data on this point are shown in Table 16.4. Economic adversity due to low wages or unemployment, as well as experiences of racial discrimination, are common for men of color.

Beyond that, we must recognize the cultural diversity in masculinity and the male role, with the understanding that traditional masculinity ideology privileges White masculinity, making masculinity for men of color especially precarious. Thus, a common stereotype among these groups is that men of color fail to live up to the ideal of traditional, White masculinity.

African American Men

There is a long history of concerns about the development of male identity among African American boys and men, particularly from White people (e.g., Frazier, 1939; Moynihan,

FOCUS 16.1

MYTHS ABOUT MALE SEXUALITY

Traditional masculinity emphasizes power, dominance, and agency; these traits extend to male sexuality. Psychologist and sex therapist Bernie Zilbergeld (1999) provided a sharp analysis of male sexuality and how to cope with it. His central thesis is that men in our culture are taught a "fantasy model of sex," which includes unrealistic and idealistic expectations that put intense performance pressures on men. In his book *The New Male Sexuality*, he provided a list of cultural myths about male sexuality, which we discuss here.

Myth 1: A real man isn't into sissy stuff like feelings and communicating. A central part of the male role is emotional restraint and toughness. Gendered display rules of emotion dictate that feelings of love, tenderness, and vulnerability are a violation of the male role and inappropriate. Yet such feelings are crucial to developing intimate relationships and enrich sexual experiences with a partner. As boys and men are socialized to the male role, they are taught that, while a sexual relationship with a woman is of great importance, they must not express emotional sensitivity or tenderness. This is tricky! Zilbergeld suggested that female partners should seek to understand this problem as a handicap and, rather than resenting men's lack of emotional expressiveness, try to help them overcome their handicap and discover the more complex and tender emotions.

In addition, Zilbergeld argued that this myth causes men to misread and mislabel their feelings. They think that what they are feeling is a sexual need for intercourse, when in fact what they are experiencing is love, or tenderness, and a need for intimacy or closeness. When men are socialized to think that they can only experience lust, they find it difficult to read and label their feelings of love or tenderness. In other words, when they want to hear someone say "I love you," they instead think they want to have intercourse.

Myth 2: A real man performs in sex. Western culture is highly achievement-oriented, and sex is often framed as yet another achievement situation. We express this in language, such as "achieving" orgasm, and in setting up achievement goals in sex, such as simultaneous orgasms for both partners. Of course, every opportunity for achievement is also an opportunity for failure.

Myth 3: A man should be able to make the earth move for his partner, or at the very least knock her socks off. Put this myth together with the preceding one, and you have a situation in which sex becomes, for the man, an impossible achievement situation. Of course, one problem with approaching sex as

an achievement situation is that it can produce performance anxiety, which interferes with the ability to have and enjoy sex. The work of Masters and Johnson (1970) and others indicates that achievement orientation and performance orientation contribute to sexual dysfunctions such as erection problems. The extent of performance pressures on men is strikingly illustrated in this account by two sex therapists:

> We'll never forget the man who called himself a premature ejaculator even though fairly regularly he lasted for forty-five minutes of vigorous thrusting. We know he lasted this long because his partner confirmed it. Actually, she had never been orgasmic in intercourse and had no desire to become so. She much preferred shorter intercourse because she sometimes became so sore through almost an hour of thrusting that she could barely sit down the next day. That had little influence on the thinking of our client, who was convinced that she would have orgasms if only he could last an hour. (quoted in Zilbergeld, 1978, p. 257)

Recent research supports the continued presence of this myth. Men—particularly those who experience greater gender role strain—feel more masculine when they imagine that a woman experiences orgasm during sex with them (Chadwick & van Anders, 2017).

It's no surprise that men experience performance anxiety—sexuality, agency, and achievement are key features of the male role.

Myth 4: A man is always interested in and always ready for sex. Men are often portrayed as constantly, incessantly interested in sex and easily arousable (if not already aroused). But that can't possibly be true. It is important for men to acknowledge and accept that sometimes and in some situations, they won't be in the mood for sex. When we are tired, stressed, or not with the right partner, sex just isn't in the cards. Moreover, men need to learn to say no to sex—something women have received more than adequate training for, but that men learned was not part of their script.

Myth 5: Sex is centered on a hard penis. We have a script for sexual interactions. The script tells us what to do and in what order to do it. Touching, kissing, and hugging progress to heavy petting, which progresses to intercourse. As a result, we have a narrow and constrained idea of what a satisfying sexual interaction can be. We do not know how to relax and enjoy sex that consists only of kissing and touching. Anything other than penis-in-vagina intercourse is not "real" sex, or is merely foreplay. For the man, this is especially problematic, because it means that an erection is absolutely essential. Erections can be nice if they happen on their own, but when they are a prerequisite for pleasure, we again arrive at an achievement situation. The stage is set for anxiety, fear or failure, and sexual dysfunction. Part of the remedy is to learn that there are many enjoyable aspects of sex that require no erection—in fact, the only thing that actually requires an erection is intercourse.

Myth 6: Good sex is spontaneous with no planning and no talking. Sure, spontaneous sex is great, but not all good sex has to be that way. One problem with the emphasis on spontaneity is that it prevents some important and valuable things from happening. For example, conversations about contraception and STD prevention are not likely to happen if sex "just happens." Indeed, some people fail to plan for and talk about birth control because they say it interferes with the spontaneity of sex. Good sex sometimes does take planning, learning, and talking.

Zilbergeld recommended that letting go of these myths and the sexual scripts we've learned is well worth the effort. For men willing to spend some time discovering what is truly pleasing to them sexually, expressing those ideas, and then trying to have sex that way, rather than the way society dictates, better and more satisfying sexual relationships are possible.

We are beginning to appreciate the complexity of male sexuality, in part by adopting a feminist perspective and examining how gender roles contribute to our sexual scripts and experiences and then considering the ways in which we all can be liberated from some of the restrictions and demands of those roles.

1965; Pettigrew, 1964). The narrative went something like this: Slavery had disrupted the patriarchal family structure, and a matriarchal subculture had developed as a high percentage of households were led by Black women, thus disempowering Black men and fostering aggression and deviance. Moreover, without their fathers in the home, how could Black boys develop into men? There are a number of problems with this logic. First, it assumes that Black women are somehow inadequate as parents. There is no evidence that children must have both a mother and a father in their home in order to develop into well-adjusted adults (Silverstein & Auerbach, 1999). Second, this logic ignores the time

TABLE 16.4   Median weekly earnings of full-time workers and unemployment rates at the intersection of gender and ethnicity, for those 16 and older, in 2016.

		Weekly Earnings	Unemployment Rate
African American			
	Men	$718	9.1%
	Women	$641	7.8%
Asian American			
	Men	$1,151	3.5%
	Women	$902	3.9%
Hispanic			
	Men	$663	5.4%
	Women	$586	6.3%
White			
	Men	$942	4.4%
	Women	$766	4.2%

Source: Bureau of Labor Statistics (2017).

PHOTO 16.6
Many African American role models are available for African American boys to identify with. President Barack Obama (left), basketball star LeBron James (center), and author Ta-Nehisi Coates (right).

fathers may spend with their sons when they don't live in the same household. Similarly, it ignores the contributions of older brothers, uncles, and grandfathers. Finally, this logic assumes that a patriarchal family is inherently better than a matriarchal one. The deficit perspective is plain to see. Note also that sexist assumptions were used to prop up racist ones, demonstrating the intersectionality of these forms of oppression.

Of course, the more adults who love, nurture, and support a child's development, the better. But that does not mean that children of single parents—in this particular case, Black children raised by Black women—are doomed. In the case of youth growing up in female-headed Black households, it's important to recognize that there are many African American heroes with whom Black youth can identify outside of their own family. Depending on their interests and concerns, African American boys may identify with different heroes or mentors within their culture (e.g., Grantham, 2004). For instance, if his passion is sports, his role model may be LeBron James, if he wants to be a writer, it may be Ta-Nehisi Coates, or if his interest is in politics and civil rights, it may be former president Barack Obama. A teacher at his school or a leader in his church or mosque can also be heroes. In sum, there are a number of Black male role models or heroes for a Black boy to identify with and look up to, beyond his own father.

Earlier in this chapter we discussed the GRIP. The concern over African American male identity is clearly part of this paradigm. Having concluded that the GRIP is not a very good approach to the male role and that concerns over gender identity are overblown, we must accept the implication that there has been too much emphasis on Black male identity.

If we shift to the GRSP, we see gender roles as sources of psychological strain for Black men, which is a more productive approach. For example, let's consider the economic status of Black men in the United States. As shown in Table 16.4, about 1 in 11 Black men is unemployed and Black men make about 76 cents for every dollar that White men make. Given that the role of breadwinner or good provider is important to the traditional male role in the United States, this high unemployment rate contributes to a gender role strain for Black men. Thus Black men may feel that they are failing to fulfill this part of their role. Consistent with the GRSP, gender roles can be a source of strain.

The stress of not fulfilling one's gender role can be expressed or manifested in a number of ways. For example, it might turn into antisocial behavior, including violence and crime. It has also been suggested that volunteering for the army becomes an alternative means of fulfilling the male role—whereas 8% of young White men intend to enlist, 18% of young Black men do (U.S. Department of Defense, 2001).

Black men may also engage in other efforts to demonstrate their masculinity, as with the **cool pose** (Majors & Billson, 1992; Rogers et al., 2015). The cool pose refers to a set of behaviors and scripts for Black men that developed in response to racial oppression. This form of masculinity emphasizes the expression of pride, strength, and control. While the cool pose is a strategy that Black men may use to maintain their sense of self-worth and resist racial oppression, it comes with a cost. Like traditional masculinity, the cool pose is demanding in its narrow construction of masculinity.

Cool pose: A set of behaviors and scripts for Black men that developed in response to racial oppression and that emphasize the expression of pride, strength, and control.

Another aspect of the male role is that of husband, which is closely tied to the breadwinner role. With elevated unemployment rates, African American men are understandably reluctant to take on the responsibility of marriage. Nonetheless, the husband and provider role are important to many Black men, particularly after they pass through young adulthood (Perry, 2013). Middle-class African American men tend to place an especially strong emphasis on the provider role and on obtaining the requisite education for that role (Diemer, 2002). One important factor in Black men's attitudes about marriage has to do with religion; marriage is of greater importance to Black men who are more religious or connected to their church (Perry, 2013).

Related to the provider role is the father role. The responsibility of supporting and raising children is enormous and can be a source of stress to any parent, but especially to one who is unemployed. Thus, for an African American man who is also unemployed, the father role might add to the gender role strain. Alternatively, it can be a means of fulfilling the male role when the provider role is elusive. In terms of parenting behaviors, relative to White men in two-parent families, Black men in two-parent families monitor their children more and exhibit more responsibility for child rearing (Hofferth, 2003). And Black fathers are as involved with their children as fathers from other ethnic groups, though they devote a smaller proportion of that time to playing with their children (McGill, 2014).

Yet, in the era of mass incarceration, fulfillment of the father role can be elusive for many Black men (Sykes & Pettit, 2014). Today, Black men are six times more likely than White men to be incarcerated (Parker & Wang, 2013). Studies have found that, in cities around the United States, people of color were more likely than Whites to be stopped and searched by police, even though they were actually less likely to be carrying illegal weapons (Cole et al., 2015). As evidence of racial discrimination in policing and the criminal justice system accumulates, scholars note that Black men are especially disadvantaged. In *The New Jim Crow*, Michelle Alexander (2010) proposed that, while racial discrimination in employment is no longer socially acceptable, Black men encounter a new, redesigned form of racial discrimination that oppresses and disenfranchises them in legal ways:

Today it is perfectly legal to discriminate against criminals in nearly all the ways that it was once legal to discriminate against African Americans. Once you're labeled a felon, the old forms of discrimination—employment discrimination, housing discrimination, denial of the right to vote, denial of educational opportunity, denial of food stamps and other public benefits, and exclusion from jury service—are suddenly legal. (p. 2)

Thus, for the Black man who has served time in prison, he will find it exceedingly difficult to fulfill many aspects of the male role, such as being a father, husband, and provider for his family.

In sum, despite the long emphasis on viewing Black men's masculinity from a deficit perspective, the GRSP is most useful in framing and understanding the experiences of Black men. Aspects of the traditional male role—particularly the breadwinner or provider role—have been denied to Black men for decades. In turn, higher unemployment rates contribute to their gender role strain and may make it more difficult to fulfill other aspects of the male role, such as the husband and father roles.

Asian American Men

Like African American men, Asian American men experience racial discrimination and prejudice in our Anglocentric society (Liu & Wong, 2016). However, Asian American men differ from African American men in some substantial ways. For example, Asian Americans do not have the heritage of slavery. And across the intersection of gender and ethnicity, Asian American men have the lowest unemployment rates and the highest earnings (see Table 16.4). This higher income—and the accompanying higher educational attainment—can shape Asian American men's experiences in important ways.

Of course, as we discussed in Chapter 4, there is tremendous diversity among Asian American groups. Some may be refugees who escaped from Vietnam or Cambodia under oppressive and traumatic circumstances, some may be Japanese Americans who lived in internment camps in the 1940s, some may be Chinese Americans who are fourth generation in the United States, and some may be recent immigrants from India. It is important to keep this diversity in mind when referring to Asian Americans.

In comparison with Asian American women, Asian American men share many of the same difficulties (see Chapter 4), including bilingualism and conflicts between Asian cultural values and the dominant cultural values of America. Yet there are also gender differences within this broad ethnic group. For example, Asian Americans' sexuality is stereotyped in gendered ways. Whereas Asian American women are stereotyped as exotic sex toys (see Chapter 4), Asian American men are stereotyped as asexual, sexually unattractive, and having small penises (Liu & Wong, 2016; Reid & Bing, 2000). Similarly, research indicates that women across diverse ethnic groups are less interested in Asian American men as potential romantic partners (Fisman et al., 2008). Asian American men are also stereotyped as introverted, socially inept, feminine and unmasculine, physically inferior and nonathletic, and perpetual foreigners (Liu & Wong, 2016). In short, they are stereotyped as not living up to the ideal of traditional White masculinity.

Another gendered aspect of Asian American men's lives in the United States has to do with gender ratios in the population. The combination of U.S. immigration policies and the circumstances under which some Asian Americans (e.g., Chinese men brought to build the transcontinental railway in the 1860s) came to the United States contributed to a lopsided gender ratio, such that there were far more Asian American men

©iStockphoto.com/TommL.

PHOTO 16.7

Asian American men are stereotyped as not living up to the ideal of traditional White masculinity, yet they earn higher median incomes relative to other men.

than Asian American women. For example, at one point in Washington state, the ratio of Filipino men to Filipino women was 33:1 (Bulosan, 1960). Given that anti-miscegenation laws prohibited Asian American men from marrying women of other racial or ethnic groups, many Asian American men were in a state of permanently enforced bachelorhood. Moreover, because marriage and parenthood are considered milestones or signs of reaching adulthood in some Asian societies, many men experienced a life of perpetual boyhood by their own cultural values (Kim, 1990).

Latino Men

Latinx culture is typically seen as highly patriarchal and gendered. Men are held to the ideal of machismo and women to the ideal of marianismo (see Chapter 4). As noted in Chapter 4, in traditional Latin American cultures, gender roles are sharply defined (Raffaelli & Ontai, 2004; Salgado de Snyder et al., 2000). And among Latino men, belief in traditional masculinity is closely tied to their identity as Latino (Saez et al., 2009). Traditional gender roles are emphasized early in the socialization process for children (Raffaelli & Ontai, 2004). Boys are given greater freedom, are encouraged in sexual exploits, and are not expected to share in the household work, whereas girls are closely monitored and expected to contribute to household work.

Yet, as with any generalization, the description of Latinx culture as highly patriarchal does not capture the rich diversity and subcultural variations across Latinx culture. For example, compared with Mexicans living in Mexico, the Mexican American family structure is less patriarchal, despite sharing the value of familismo and the strong emphasis on family (Muñoz-Laboy, 2008). The shared value of familismo also means that the father role is an important aspect of the Latino male role (Roubinov et al., 2016).

With regard to masculinity and the male role, the belief that the provider role is the man's responsibility varies according to acculturation (Taylor et al., 1999). Less acculturated Mexican immigrants hold the strongest beliefs in the man's responsibility to

©iStockphoto.com/monkeybusinessimages.

PHOTO 16.8
The father role is an important aspect of the Latino male role, consistent with the shared value of familismo.

be a provider, while highly acculturated Mexican immigrants hold less strong beliefs, and highly acculturated U.S.-born Mexican Americans hold the least strong beliefs. Still, White Americans hold this traditional belief less strongly than all three of these Latinx groups. Similar patterns have been found with regard to the importance of the father role (Cabrera et al., 2006). In sum, the aspects of being a good provider and father for one's family are important to the male role in Latinx culture, though there are subcultural variations. In the context of intense national controversy regarding the legal immigration and employment of Latinx persons in the United States, there is increased pressure on Latino men to fulfill this aspect of the male role.

American Indian Men

Like other men of color, American Indian men experience disadvantages such as discrimination and prejudice based on their ethnicity. Yet their unique cultural heritage, based on tribal diversity and hundreds of years of colonization, trauma, occupation, and enslavement by Europeans, distinguishes some of their experiences.

In considering gender roles among American Indians, it is important to note that gender is not understood as a binary construct in most American Indian languages or cultures. Traditionally, roles have been assigned not based on gender but on one's purpose (Rouse, 2016).

Some American Indian tribes, including the Cherokee, Navajo, Iroquois, Hopi, and Zuni, traditionally had relatively egalitarian gender roles (LaFromboise et al., 1990). Women had important economic, political, and spiritual roles, and there was even a matrilineal pattern of inheritance. Men tended to have more authority in the public sphere, but women's power in the private sphere of the family was great. Yet as Europeans colonized North America and cross-cultural contacts increased, this gender egalitarianism declined. Increased contact with the dominant White culture in the United States and subsequent acculturation contributed to an increase in male dominance among American Indians (LaFromboise et al., 1990).

©iStockphoto.com/RyersonClark.

Yet, paradoxically, the imposition of patriarchy and male dominance on American Indian cultures has not been very beneficial to American Indian men. Instead, American Indian men are likely to experience gender role strain, particularly as their native culture conflicts with traditional White masculinity (Whitbeck et al., 2002). For example, a Navajo man who follows his cultural tradition of wearing his hair long and tied with yarn in a bun will likely face discrimination and hostility as he is perceived as feminine. In short, his culturally defined masculinity conflicts with traditional White masculinity, which has the upper hand in mainstream U.S. society.

PHOTO 16.9
Conflicts between American Indian culture and White masculinity can contribute to gender role strain among American Indian men.

Unfortunately, there is very little psychological research on American Indian men (Wong et al., 2010), which makes it difficult to characterize the full range of their experiences. Nonetheless, researchers who study American Indians note that, despite their history of trauma, it would be a mistake to define their experiences so narrowly and think of them as victims. Instead, the indigenous peoples of North America are resilient and persistent and actively engaged in shaping their own future (Gone, 2010; Rouse, 2016).

Health Issues

A baby boy born in the United States today can expect to live 76 years if he is White and 72 years if he is Black; a baby girl can expect to live 81 years if she is White and 78 years if she is Black (see Chapter 11; Arias, 2015). In other words, men live about 5 to 6 fewer years than women do. Many researchers are interested in the causes of men's shorter life expectancy and whether biological factors or environmental factors are more important (Courtenay, 2000; Helgeson, 2009; Theorell & Härenstam, 2000). For example, are men more biologically vulnerable, more susceptible to disease, genetic defects, and so on? Or are men victims of their environment and social context, and the male role in particular? Let's examine the evidence on both sides of the issue.

With regard to biological factors, boys and men have a higher death rate than girls and women, even prenatally. At conception, the ratio of male to female zygotes is probably about 120:100. Yet, at birth, the male-to-female ratio is down to about 105:100 (Mathews & Hamilton, 2005). So, even before birth, boys have a higher death rate (Kilmartin, 2000). That disparity can't possibly be the result of the male role. What is more likely is that sex-linked recessive genetic defects or diseases such as hemophilia cause the higher male death rate.

Yet, after birth, X-linked diseases probably cause a relatively small proportion of the excess male deaths. Sex hormones are a far more important biological factor (Helgeson, 2009). While heart disease is a leading cause of death for both men and women (Mozzafarian et al., 2016), heart disease tends to strike men at much younger ages. This contributes to men's shorter life expectancy. Estrogen appears to be a protective factor against heart disease, protecting women at least until menopause.

With regard to environmental factors, an important issue is substance use, including tobacco (i.e., smoking) and alcohol. For example, lung cancer and heart attacks are among the leading causes of death in men, and cigarette smoking is implicated in both (Helgeson, 2009; Sue, 2000). Another leading cause of death in which men outnumber women is cirrhosis of the liver, and that is related to excessive drinking, a behavior that is considered more appropriate for the male role than for the female role. Men also have higher rates of illicit substance use (see Chapter 15).

Accidents—specifically vehicle accidents and gun accidents—are another cause of death in which men outnumber women. These kinds of deaths, too, can clearly be linked to masculine traits such as aggressiveness and risk taking. In sum, specific behaviors associated with the male role—smoking, drinking, aggression, and risk taking—are linked to men's higher death rates. Moreover, research indicates a link between masculinity and death, such that more masculine men die younger than less masculine men (Lippa et al., 2000).

The male role contributes to men's shorter life expectancy in other ways. For example, men are less likely than women to seek help for medical, mental health, and substance use problems (Addis & Mahalik, 2003). This gendered pattern of help-seeking is seen across ages, nationalities, and ethnic groups. Simply put, help-seeking is not masculine; the male role requires that men be self-reliant and tough. This means that men die at younger ages because they wait too long to seek treatment for problems that are preventable or treatable.

Driving is another part of the male role. Relative to women, men tend to drive more and drive faster, and they take more risks while driving (Helgeson, 2009). The result is that men account for 71% of deaths from motor vehicle crashes (Insurance Institute for Highway Safety, 2016).

In sum, neither biological factors nor environmental factors alone seem to explain gender differences in life expectancy. Clearly, there are dangerous aspects of the male

Roberto Schmidt/AFP/Getty Images.

PHOTO 16.10 The male role can be hazardous to men's health.

role, contributing to men's shorter life expectancy. Male deaths from heart disease and cirrhosis of the liver seem linked to environmental factors, specifically the male role and smoking and drinking behaviors. Nonetheless, biological factors such as genetic defects seem likely to cause the higher rate of male deaths prenatally. It is also likely that some biological factors make men more vulnerable to particular environmental factors.

We can also examine the interaction of biological and environmental factors among transgender men. Some transgender men may feel pressure to adhere to the male role in order to be seen and accepted as men. Thus, they may engage in heavier drinking or smoking, which can shorten their life expectancy. By contrast, it is unclear how much the biological factors that are linked to cisgender men's shorter life expectancy impact transgender men's health. For example, research comparing transgender men receiving testosterone to cisgender women finds no differences in cardiovascular disease (Gooren et al., 2014). Clearly, we need more research that can tease apart the biological and environmental factors contributing to cisgender and transgender men's health.

Experience the Research

Childhood Experiences of the Mother and Men's Desire to Control Women

One assumption of the gender role identity paradigm is that men's negative attitudes toward women are a result of problems of gender role identity caused by mothers. One hypothesis is that little boys experience the mother as overwhelming and therefore try to control and dominate women in adulthood. If this is the case, there should be a correlation between men's ratings of their childhood experiences of their mother and their attitudes, as adults, toward women. Men who experienced their mothers as overwhelming should want to control women, and men who did not experience their mothers as overwhelming should be less interested in controlling women. You will collect data to see whether this is true.

Use the following items to assess men's experience of their mothers in childhood:

1. When I was a child, my mother seemed overwhelming to me.

2. When I was a child, my mother tried to control me all the time.

Use the following items to assess men's attitudes toward women:

1. The husband should have the final say in family decisions.

2. In the traditional marriage vows, the wife promises to obey the husband, and there is great wisdom in that.

Participants should rate each item on a scale from (1) *strongly disagree* to (5) *strongly agree*, with (3) meaning neither agree nor disagree. To make the purpose of these items less obvious, construct at least 10 items assessing attitudes on some other topics and intersperse the four critical items among them.

Administer your 14-item scale to five men who are not in your class (men who take a psychology of women course are not a random sample of the male population). If possible, include in your sample several men who are older than traditional college age.

Take the average of the two items on experience of the mother as the man's score on Experience of Mother. Take the average of the two control of women items as the man's score on Control Women. For your five respondents, does there appear to be a correlation between Experience of Mother scores and Control Women scores? That is, do men who have high scores on one tend to have high scores on the other? If you have taken a statistics course, compute the actual correlation between the two scales. You may also put your data together with those of other students in your class to obtain a larger sample and then compute the correlation.

Do the results support or go against the hypothesis?

CHAPTER SUMMARY

In this chapter we have focused on the psychology of cisgender men and the male role. The feminist analysis of masculinity points to the link between traditional gender roles and gender inequality. In requiring men to control the public sphere and engage in dominant and aggressive behaviors while requiring women to remain in the private sphere and engage in adaptive and nurturing behaviors, traditional gender roles maintain patriarchy. Being a "real man" is a hard-won but easily lost social status. Masculinity and the male role are characterized by dominance, power, and agency, in stark contrast to femininity and the female role. Moreover, traditional gender roles are firmly rooted in the gender binary and assume that heterosexuality is the norm. As such, these roles make no space for trans or queer people. Yet some trans men feel pressure to adhere to the traditional male role in order to be seen and accepted as men by others.

An important point in this chapter was the distinction between the GRIP and the GRSP. The GRIP was traditional psychology's approach to the male role and was based on the assumption that a man must have a masculine identity in order to be psychologically healthy. Yet the GRIP is just not borne out by the evidence—boys' masculinity is not correlated with their fathers' masculinity, father absence does not necessarily produce inadequate masculinity, and so on.

An alternative model is the GRSP, which views gender roles as sources of strain. The GRSP puts masculine traits such as athleticism in context. The emphasis on athletic prowess for boys and men produces strains for both the athlete and the nonathlete alike. The father and provider roles are important aspects of the male role in adulthood.

Traditional masculinity privileges White men; men of color are stereotyped as not meeting the ideal of traditional White masculinity. For example, Asian American men are stereotyped as asexual and physically weak. Manhood seems especially precarious for men of color, and traditional masculinity contributes to gender role strain for many.

The male role involves risk taking and is often dangerous to men's health. Gender differences in life expectancy appear to be the result of an interaction of biological and environmental factors, and gendered behaviors such as drinking and smoking increase men's mortality.

SUGGESTIONS FOR FURTHER READING

Kimmel, Michael. (2015). *Angry White men: American masculinity at the end of an era*. New York, NY: Nation Books. Interviewing White supremacists, men's rights activists, and students, sociologist Michael Kimmel provides a feminist and intersectional analysis of contemporary White masculinity.

Levant, Ronald F., & Wong, Y. Joel. (2017). *The psychology of men and masculinity*. Washington, DC: American Psychological Association. This book reviews the research on the psychology of men and masculinity, with chapters written by leading researchers in the field.

Pascoe, C. J., & Bridges, Tristan. (2016). *Exploring masculinities: Identity, inequality, continuity and change*. New York, NY: Oxford University Press. Sociologists C. J. Pascoe and Tristan Bridges discuss masculinities from an intersectional perspective.

Retrospect and Prospect

> " Standing on the ground of common sense and the constitution of the human mind, I deny that anyone knows, or can know, the nature of the two sexes, so long as they have only been seen in their present relation to one another. . . . What is now called the nature of woman is an eminently artificial thing—the result of forced repression in some directions, unnatural stimulation in others. "

John Stuart Mill (1869), *The Subjection of Women*

The great philosopher and feminist John Stuart Mill, quoted here, lived in an era in which there was no science of psychology. He believed that no one could understand the true nature of women and men. Nearly 150 years—and a great deal of psychological research—later, how can one respond to Mill?

Certainly, scientists would not claim to know the "true nature" of women and men any more than Mill did. But we would argue that it is not the right question to ask. Rather than trying to establish the "true nature" of women and men, we would do better to try to understand how gender—as a construct much more complex than the male/female binary—contributes to our psychological functioning across cultures and history.

This book has focused particularly on trying to understand how gender contributes to our psychological functioning in our contemporary culture, focusing especially on women and, when data are available, trans and nonbinary people. To do this, we have reviewed the existing scientific theories and research evidence. They provide some reasonable ideas that further research will continue to refine.

Several important themes have cropped up repeatedly in this book. One is gender similarities, the notion that women and men are more similar to each other than they are different (Hyde, 2005a). A second theme is the pervasiveness of androcentrism, cisgenderism, and heteronormativity in everything from children's storybooks to psychological theories. A third theme is the inadequacy of the gender binary—it is increasingly clear to many of us that gender is much more than male/female. And a fourth theme is the importance of intersectionality and how multiple social categories (gender, ethnicity, social class, and so on) shape our identities and status.

Future Research

In 1974, when the first edition of this book was published (and NEQ was not yet born), research on the psychology of women was in its infancy. However, as we write these chapters on the heels of the most recent (2017) convention of the American Psychological Association, we feel that enormous progress has been made in the psychology of women and gender. Research and theory have become truly sophisticated and innovative. We have a deeper understanding of the ways in which sexism (as well as racism and heterosexism) can interfere with the psychological research process, and we have some ways to correct it. There are a few well-documented gender differences in psychological characteristics, we have a better sense of what those differences mean for our lives, and we know that the general pattern is gender similarities. And research is uncovering ways to make our society more equal and equitable. Principles of feminist research and therapy are more than a twinkle in some feminist's eye—they are widely practiced and, in some cases, have become conventional. And so the list goes.

Yet there is so much more to learn! What do you think are the most important questions for future research in the psychology of women and gender? Here are a few of the topics we think are most important.

Perhaps the most important need is to use an intersectional approach. This means going beyond research that studies one social category at a time—as in a study of psychological gender differences that does not consider how ethnicity or social class are simultaneously involved. It means reframing our research questions and thinking about gender in more complex ways. In particular, we must do more to study gender among people of color. The psychology of women and gender has focused too much on the psychology of White

©iStockphoto.com/monkeybusinessimages.

PHOTO 17.1
Far more research on women of color is needed in psychology.

middle-class women. We need to know far more about how gender is constructed among African American, Asian American, Latinx, American Indian, and multiethnic people. For example, how are gender roles and socialization practices shaped by ethnicity and culture? We need to know more about those who have persisted and thrived despite contexts of oppression and disadvantage, and we need to know more about how to most effectively help those who have been less fortunate. We must also remember that intersectionality isn't simply about finding all the ways in which we are different—it's also about respecting our common humanity and empowering those from marginalized groups.

And it's time for psychology to examine gender more critically and move beyond the gender binary. We all need to be willing to question what we think we know about gender. A critique of the gender binary is a logical extension of the gender similarities hypothesis; after all, if gender similarities are the rule for most psychological characteristics, what sense is there in being so fixated on essentialist notions of binary gender categories in the first place? Thinking about the steps in the research process described in Chapter 1, what does a critique of the gender binary entail? In some cases, it might mean categorizing participants not by birth-assigned gender but by gender identity or doing away with gender categories altogether. In other cases, it might mean examining sexist discrimination in more nuanced ways that incorporate attention to cisgenderism and heteronormativity. Much more psychological research is needed on the experiences of trans and nonbinary people. So much of what we think we know about gender is deeply rooted in the socially constructed gender binary. We are optimistic that psychology will figure this out, but it will take a persistent and diverse team of researchers to get it right.

The psychological study of men and masculinity has flourished in recent years, and this work needs to continue. As the male gender role continues to evolve, more research will be needed on how men adapt to these changes and perform their roles. Consider, for example, how much more time fathers spend with their children today than in previous generations (Parker & Wang, 2013; see Chapter 16). Still, new research demonstrates how fathers' parenting behaviors may still perpetuate traditional gender roles. One recent study found a number of subtle ways in which fathers treat sons and daughters differently. For example, fathers were more engaged, talked more openly about emotions, and sang more with daughters, but engaged in more rough-and-tumble play and used more achievement language with sons (Mascaro et al., 2017). In addition, fathers' brains demonstrated different neural responses to images of sons compared with images of daughters. If mothers and fathers continue to perceive and treat daughters and sons as though they are vastly different, can we ever achieve gender equality?

A deep, intersectional investigation of gender incorporates analysis of masculinity. It examines the ways in which boys' and men's psychological development and functioning are shaped by masculinity norms, which include cisgenderism and heteronormativity. Although it is true that male privilege is pervasive, the male role does not promote psychological well-being. Thus, we must be careful not to assume that, because men have more power, men are always functioning better. The male gender role, with its emphasis on power, dominance, and independence, can be isolating and limiting. In her book *Feminism Is for Everybody*, Black feminist author bell hooks (2000) articulates this tension clearly:

> Males as a group have and do benefit the most from patriarchy, from the assumption that they are superior to females and should rule over us. But those benefits have come with a price. In return for all the goodies men receive from patriarchy, they are required to dominate women, to exploit and oppress us, using violence if they must to keep patriarchy intact. Most men find it difficult to be patriarchs. Most men are disturbed by hatred and fear of women, by male violence against women, even the men who perpetuate this violence. But they fear letting go of the benefits. . . . So they find it easier to passively support male domination even when they know in their minds and hearts that it is wrong. (p. ix)

In sum, as the psychology of women and gender becomes more intersectional and moves beyond the binary, we must consider how gender matters for *everyone*.

Related to this point, we also need to know more scientifically about feminism and its place in science. What leads people to become feminists? What happens to people psychologically when they become feminists? How can feminism be more intersectional and foster positive social change for everyone? As one popular saying has it, gender equality isn't pie. Equal rights for others doesn't mean fewer rights for any of us.

Feminism Revisited

In Chapter 1, we offered a definition of feminism that deviated from the one that is often found in popular media. A feminist is "a person who favors political, economic, and social equality of all people, regardless of gender, and therefore favors the legal and social changes necessary to achieve gender equality." Your understanding of feminism is now much more complex than that. We hope that your view of feminism has been transformed in reading this book. Feminism offers a substantially different view of the world, and specifically of psychology, than the one traditional science has offered (see Focus 17.1). Feminism says that we are all of equal value and dignity, regardless of our gender, ethnicity, class, sexual orientation, religion, and so on. It says that the focus of psychology should be about more than just issues that matter to men. Issues traditionally thought of as "women's issues" (e.g., rape, sexism, reproductive health, work–family balance) should be understood as "human issues" and given research attention. Scientists must be careful in interpreting outcomes; for example, when they investigate intimate partner violence, they must not automatically blame it on the victim. We all need to be conscious of the power of gender roles in our lives. And so on. We could continue the list for pages. The point is that feminism provides a new view in psychology, a new set of questions, a fresh set of hypotheses. We find that exciting and optimistic, and we hope you do, too.

Every semester, our students tell us how their psychology of women and gender course has changed them. Some students tell us how they are thinking differently about negative events in their lives, understanding the role of the situation and context much more and blaming themselves much less. Others tell us how they are trying to be less sexist in their daily lives—for example, to stop judging women on their appearance or to stop referring to adult women as "girls." For us, the psychology of women and gender has deepened our appreciation for science as a tool that can promote gender equality and improve people's lives.

Some students develop a feminist identity through their course work. For example, in one relevant study, researchers evaluated the impact of gender and women's studies (GWS) courses on the students who take them (Bargad & Hyde, 1991; Hyde, 2002). They looked particularly at the development of feminist identity in women taking the courses compared with a group of women not taking GWS courses. According to one theory, feminist identity develops in five stages, shown in Table 17.1.

The researchers developed a scale, the Feminist Identity Development Scale, to measure women's scores on each of the stages and administered the scale at the beginning and end of the semester. The research indicated that women taking GWS courses, compared with the control group, showed significant declines in their degree of passive acceptance. That is, those in GWS courses decreased significantly in Passive Acceptance from the beginning to the end of the semester. At the same time, they increased significantly in their scores on Revelation, Embeddedness, and Active Commitment. GWS courses do seem to have an impact on students who take them.

TABLE 17.1	**Stages of feminist identity development.**
1. Passive acceptance	In this stage, the individual passively accepts traditional gender roles and discrimination and does not question either.
2. Revelation	In this stage, catalyzed perhaps by a crisis or by taking a gender and women's studies course, the individual questions gender roles and sexism. They often experience great anger and hold a negative view of men.
3. Embeddedness	The individual develops a sense of connectedness with women and receives affirmation and strength from them.
4. Synthesis	The individual develops a positive feminist identity and transcends gender roles. They no longer blame men as a group, but evaluate men on an individual basis.
5. Active commitment	Feminist identity is consolidated and the individual becomes committed to working actively to promote a nonsexist world.

Re-visioning Theory

Just as we must press forward with new research, so must we continue to revise androcentric theories in psychology. Carol Gilligan's (1982) revision of moral development theory is often trotted out as a good example, but that work is now more than 35 years old, and many, many more theories need to be revised. The process of theory revision must continue.

One of the best and most productive examples of contemporary feminist revision of theory is UCLA psychologist Shelley Taylor's major challenge to classical theories of stress and her proposed alternative (Taylor, 2006; Taylor et al., 2000). Classical stress theory, originally proposed by Walter Cannon in 1932 and taught as fact in many psychology courses today, maintains that the standard human (and animal) response to stress is the *fight-or-flight* response. The body reacts physiologically in ways that help the person stay and fight the attacker or flee with lightning speed. Specifically, the sympathetic nervous system is activated, and the HPA (hypothalamus, pituitary, adrenal) axis is stimulated, which initiates a cascade of hormone production including especially cortisol, norepinephrine, and epinephrine. Classical stress theory describes a biobehavioral response to stress: In the biological component, the sympathetic nervous system is activated, thereby facilitating the behavioral response, which is fight-or-flight.

Taylor examined the research exploring classical stress theory and noted that most of it was conducted on male rats. Moreover, in human research prior to 1995, women comprised only 17% of the participants in laboratory studies of physiological responses to stress. And yet, classical stress theory has been accepted as a theory that applies to all of us. That's a glaring example of the error of overgeneralization. While fighting or fleeing might be very adaptive for males of various animal species, it may not be for females, who are most often responsible for protecting not only themselves but also their young. The fight-or-flight response would leave vulnerable babies unprotected. That doesn't seem adaptive.

Taylor proposed an alternative to the androcentric fight-or-flight—known as tend-and-befriend—which describes females' biobehavioral response to stress. In tend-and-befriend, the female behavioral response is to tend to one's young and affiliate with

FOCUS 17.1

PARADIGMS, SCIENCE, AND FEMINISM

Thomas Kuhn's (1970) *The Structure of Scientific Revolutions* has become a modern classic in the philosophy of science. Kuhn's analysis can be used to help us understand science, and specifically how feminism fits into science.

The general public tends to view science as continually advancing in small steps by accumulating facts. Yet one of Kuhn's fundamental points is that the history of science demonstrates that science doesn't advance in this way at all. Instead, science proceeds in occasional revolutionary leaps that disrupt calm periods of data collection. Each of these revolutionary leaps involves a shift from an old paradigm to a new paradigm. As he defines it, a **paradigm** refers to the set of beliefs, underlying assumptions, values, and techniques shared by a particular community of scientists. In a sense, a paradigm is a worldview, or at least a view of the piece of the world that is the focus of the particular scientific specialty. Usually, a new paradigm is dramatically different from the old one. Scientists support the new paradigm because it solves problems that the old one couldn't handle. And paradigms are sufficiently open-ended that they create an entirely new set of questions that stimulate new scientific research.

One example that demonstrates and clarifies the concepts of a paradigm shift and revolutionary leaps in science is the Copernican revolution in astronomy. At the beginning of the 15th century in Europe, everyone, scientists included, believed that the earth was the center of the universe and that the sun revolved around the earth, a view known as the geocentric (earth-centered) or Ptolemaic view. Copernicus (1473–1543) proposed a new view, or paradigm, known as the heliocentric view—namely, that the sun was the center around which the earth rotated yearly, while the earth spun on its own axis daily. Copernicus's heliocentric view solved some problems that existed with the old, geocentric view. One of these was that in order for geocentrism to be correct, the other planets must be traveling at irregular speeds around the earth, darting ahead and then slowing down. Yet, in the Copernican view, the planets could be seen as moving at constant speed, while the earth (with the astronomer on it) moved simultaneously. Copernicus's ideas were opposed by the Catholic Church as erroneous and possibly heretical; such opposition or resistance is often the case with new scientific paradigms. As you know, eventually his ideas were widely accepted by astronomers, who then used them as the basis for their research. Kuhn's point is clear: Science proceeds in occasional revolutionary leaps as new paradigms, representing radically different ideas, arise.

The general public, as well as many scientists, tends to view science as fundamentally objective. Kuhn disputed this notion as well. He argued that there is no such thing as a pure fact in science; rather, there are only facts that exist within the context of a particular paradigm. Once a new paradigm has taken over, the old "facts" will seem wrong or downright stupid. For example, if we had lived before the time of Copernicus, we would naturally have observed the "fact" that the sun rises in the east every morning and sets in the west every evening. We would have taken this as ample evidence of the "fact" that the sun is revolving around the earth. From our modern, post-Copernican perspective, these do not seem to be facts at all. This illustrates Kuhn's argument that there are no objective facts in science; facts exist only from the point of view of a particular paradigm.

How does all this relate to psychology? Psychology has had several paradigms, the actual number depending on how broad or narrow one wants to be in identifying paradigms. For example, learning theory has been a dominant paradigm in psychology. And experimentalism has been a dominant paradigm in social psychology, within which the tightly controlled laboratory experiment has been understood as the best, and perhaps only, way to get good "facts" on people's social behavior. Yet experimentalism faces a crisis in that experimenter effects and observer effects (discussed in Chapter 1) threaten the quality of data that scientists collect in their experiments. In such situations, data are likely to conform to scientists' own biases.

Feminists point out that the paradigms of psychology have long been androcentric in coming from a male perspective and framing men's experiences as the norm or standard.

Based on Kuhn's analyses, feminism is a paradigm in the science of psychology. Feminism fits the definition of a paradigm in that it comprises a set of beliefs, values, and techniques that are shared by a community of scientists. And feminism provides a new worldview, with new questions and new tools. Traditional psychology could be viewed as seeing the world revolving around men (androcentrism), just as the pre-Copernicans saw the sun revolving around the earth. Feminists do not want to shift to viewing the world as revolving around women. Rather, the feminist desire is to view the world as revolving around our collective humanity, without sexist bias.

Kuhn noted that another characteristic of a paradigm is that it provides answers to a set of problems that could not be solved by the old paradigm and were creating a crisis. A number of such problems have not been solved by traditional psychology. For example, consider the gender role identity paradigm (Pleck, 1981; discussed in Chapter 16), which held that optimal personality development depended on a gender role identity that matches one's gender assigned at birth. The traditional view of masculinity–femininity in psychology held that gender typing was essential to mental health and that the highly masculine man and the highly feminine woman were supposed to be the most well adjusted. As we saw, the data don't actually support this paradigm. For example, highly masculine men are prone to risky behaviors and die younger than their less masculine peers (Lippa et al., 2000). Traditional psychology's paradigm cannot handle that result, but feminism provides a framework that addresses that difficulty. The feminist paradigm points out that people can be androgynous and that the androgynous person would be able to adapt to different situations and, thus, be the most well adjusted.

According to Kuhn, paradigms also create an entirely new set of research questions precisely because they offer a new perspective. The feminist paradigm has created a new set of research topics that had not been possible within the paradigm of traditional psychology: gender-based violence, sexual harassment of women in the workplace, the construction of gender roles across different ethnic groups, and sexism in psychotherapy, to name a few. And as intersectionality has been incorporated into feminism, we can see how it represents a similar shift in research questions (Else-Quest & Hyde, 2016).

Feminist psychology, then, fits Kuhn's definition of a paradigm nicely. One final comment is in order, however. It is sometimes argued that feminism has no place in scientific psychology because feminism consists merely of a set of political biases, and these biases do not permit objective research. Concerning this point, recall that Kuhn argued that science is not truly objective and that facts are facts only in the context of a particular paradigm. Thus, feminist psychology is neither more nor less objective than other paradigms in psychology. What it does is provide a set of "facts" that make sense in the feminist context.

FIGURE 17.1   Taylor's tend-and-befriend captures the female stress response and is an alternative to fight-or-flight.

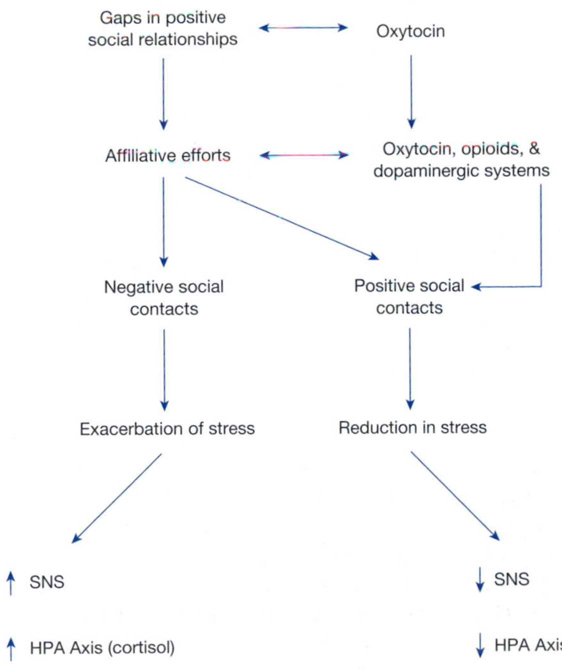

Paradigm: A set of beliefs, underlying assumptions, values, and techniques shared by a particular community of scientists.

Source: From Taylor (2006). Tend and befriend: Biobehavioral bases of affiliation under stress. *Current Directions in Psychological Science, 15,* 273–277, Figure 1, p. 274. Copyright 2006 by the Association for Psychological Science.

(befriend) a social group that, collectively, provides protection from threats. This behavioral response is facilitated by the biological response, which involves secretion of oxytocin.

In the fight-or-flight biological response to stress, the amygdala detects a threat or danger and sends signals to the hypothalamus, which secretes corticotropin-releasing hormone, which in turn stimulates the adrenal gland to secrete cortisol, epinephrine, and norepinephrine. Taylor noted that the "fight" effects of epinephrine (also called adrenaline) are magnified by testosterone, which occurs at higher levels in males and is stimulated by stress.

While females have the same sympathetic nervous system response, paired with increased cortisol, epinephrine, and norepinephrine, the hypothalamus also secretes oxytocin in response to stress. Oxytocin has two important effects. First, it interacts with estrogen to reduce epinephrine levels, which reduces fear and increases feelings of calm, thereby heading off the risky tendency to fight or flee. Second, it stimulates maternal behavior (tending) and affiliative behavior (befriending).

Taylor's revision has been productive—research on hormones and behavior continues to draw on her tend-and-befriend theory. For example, a recent field study examined the affiliative behaviors of men and women after winning or losing a competition (Sherman et al., 2017). Participants were dog handlers in a dog agility competition. The handler–dog teams were videotaped for the 3 minutes immediately following their completion of the agility course. Researchers coded video for handlers' affiliative behaviors (the behavioral response), such as playing with the dog or petting the dog on its ears, chin, and head. They also measured the handlers' cortisol secretion (the biological response) before and after the competition. Overall, male and female handlers showed the same amount of affiliative behaviors and similar changes in cortisol secretion. Yet when the researchers took into account whether handlers had won or lost the competition (that is, whether they had a score that allowed them to proceed to the next level of competition), they found striking gender differences in the biobehavioral response. Consistent with tend-and-befriend, women were more affiliative with their dogs after the stress of losing the competition. By contrast, men were more affiliative with their dogs after winning the competition. In addition, changes in cortisol levels accounted for these behavioral responses—when women's cortisol levels increased, they were more affiliative, but when men's cortisol levels increased, they were less affiliative. This is one example of innovative research that has been prompted by Taylor's feminist revisioning of theory.

Classical stress theory is fundamental in psychology and physiology. Taylor innovatively recognized that women may respond differently to stress than men do and that this different response is adaptive. She provided a coherent and plausible biological account of the response, which has prompted new research questions and findings. Her alternative approach is an exciting example of feminist revision of psychological theory.

Matt Cardy/Getty Images News/Getty Images.

PHOTO 17.2
How will this dog handler behave toward her dog if they win their agility competition? What will happen if they lose?

The Continuing Feminist Revolution and Backlash

Backlash, written by Pulitzer Prize–winning author Susan Faludi, helped to energize the third wave of feminism. The feminist movement that began in the 1960s is now referred to as the second wave (the first wave being the suffragettes who won the right to vote for women in the early 1900s), and a third wave of feminism became vigorous in the 1990s. Today we are in the fourth wave of feminism. Although Faludi's book was written in 1991, it is remarkably prescient and relevant today.

Faludi's basic argument was that these waves of feminism have fostered legal, economic, and political progress in the United States. That is, to some extent, feminists have been effective in promoting a more equal and equitable society. However, in response to this progress, a counterassault of antifeminism and modern sexism has been launched. This is the backlash against women, feminism, and gender equality.

What does this backlash look like? In some cases, it is subtle and couched in the language of modern and benevolent sexism. The backlash forces argue that women have made progress yet they are still unhappy, so their unhappiness must be the fault of feminism. The alternative explanation—that women's unhappiness may be related to continued sexism in every place from the bedroom to the boardroom—is ignored. For example, many women express their frustration and exhaustion with role overload, struggling to make ends meet as they work full-time and pay half their wages to child care providers. The backlash frames this as a sad result of feminists' fight for women to have access to paid employment, but they don't fault men's lack of involvement in child care, our country's dearth of paid family leave or child care subsidies, or the swelling inequality in today's economy.

What evidence did Faludi provide to support her argument? Much of it came from analyses of media reports of stories and flawed research that feed women's anxiety and undermine their goals to be treated as equals. For example, Faludi described the intense publicity about a study that seemed to show that a single, college-educated woman over the age of 30 had only a 20% chance of ever marrying, and a single, college-educated woman over the age of 40 had only a 1.3% chance. The messages were clear: "If you're a single woman with some education, you're going to end up a miserable old spinster!" and "There's a shortage of men! Better treat them as precious resources."

But that wasn't the full story. It turns out that the story originated when a newspaper reporter spoke to Neil Bennett, a sociologist at Yale, and got preliminary, unpublished results from recently completed data analyses. These results, which had not even been reviewed by a scientific journal, spread like wildfire. The Associated Press picked up the story, and the results were discussed in magazines ranging from *Mademoiselle* to *Cosmopolitan*. As it turned out, Bennett's statistics were seriously flawed. A better study by Jeanne Moorman of the U.S. Census Bureau indicated that the reality was far less pessimistic: at 30, a never-married college-educated woman had a 58% to 66% chance of marriage, and at 40, she had a 17% to 23% chance. Moorman's findings received only muted publicity, were in fact attacked in op-ed articles in places such as the *New York Times*, and were suppressed by her superiors at the Census Bureau under the Reagan administration.

Faludi also provided evidence that went beyond just the overpublicized, flawed research. She analyzed images of women on TV and in high fashion, the New Right, the men's movement, and much more. In all cases, the effort is to reverse the trends set in motion by the women's movement, and the messages are often quite frightening.

In laboratory experiments, social backlash (i.e., the negative evaluation of people for violating the norms of their gender role) has been documented. Social psychologist Laurie Rudman has actually been able to document and study backlash in laboratory experiments (Rudman & Fairchild, 2004). Her research shows that women who violate gender stereotypes are often sabotaged by the other person in the experiment and that this other person's self-esteem increases as a result. The sabotage, of course is a powerful force discouraging women from violating stereotypes. Whereas Faludi's research focused on the media and other institutional sources of backlash, Rudman's research documents interpersonal backlash, which is just as powerful and just as meaningful.

For example, recall that we discussed the phenomenon of social backlash in Chapter 9. Meta-analysis indicates that women's hireability and likability are substantially reduced when they express dominance, assertiveness, or agentic behavior, such as asking for a raise (Williams & Tiedens, 2016). Men aren't negatively impacted in the same way because, for them, such behaviors are in line with the norms of their gender role.

Writing in 2001 and again in 2006, Faludi updated her account of threats to feminism. She argued that the latest threat to feminism is hyperconsumerism, which has commercialized feminism. Advertisers promoted the idea that "liberation" meant earning lots of money and buying lots of stuff with it, and that this would make women feel happy and satisfied with their lives. In 2006, Faludi noted, "We have used our gains to gild our shackles, but not break them." Modern feminism as defined by popular culture involves buying designer shoes that are about as good for one's health as footbinding was. The freedom to choose became the freedom to choose expensive and risky cosmetic surgery. Feminists, according to Faludi, must challenge the commercialization of feminism and reemphasize the core values of feminism: the right of all people, regardless of gender, to act responsibly in the world, to build a society that recognizes that caring—not more "stuff"—is what's important.

Today, we are in the midst of feminism's fourth wave. It is an increasingly intersectional movement that critiques the gender binary and fights for gender equality in new and innovative ways. Feminism is not just more inclusive; it is also more accessible. The fourth wave uses Web 2.0 and user-generated content to reach more people and invite more perspectives, expanding the scope of feminist activism.

Yet, as we witnessed the stunning results of the 2016 presidential election, the precariousness of the fight for gender equality stood out in stark relief. Some have proposed that the election of Donald Trump was part of a backlash against the feminist gains of recent years (e.g., Goldberg, 2016; Moore, 2016). They point out that a man who was accused of sexual harassment by numerous women and who described his privilege to "grab 'em by the pussy" won the presidency, while his female opponent—a self-identified feminist—was routinely labeled "shrill" and a "bitch" during the campaign. If it is true that Trump's election was part of a backlash against feminist gains, what does this mean for the future of feminism? And what role does the science of psychology play in that future?

It is also possible that we are in the midst of a resurgence of feminism. The day after President Trump's inauguration, millions of people—many in pink "pussy" hats—gathered for Women's Marches across all seven continents to affirm their support for gender equality. Marchers diverse in gender, sexual orientation, ethnicity, nationality, and age demonstrated that, unified, they could resist the backlash against feminism and ultimately achieve gender equality. In that spirit, we are reminded of the persistence and courage of the women's rights activist Alice Paul, who observed, "I always feel the movement is a sort of mosaic. Each of us puts in one little stone, and then you get a great mosaic at the end." Will you put in a stone?

Mario Tama/Getty Images News/Getty Images.

PHOTO 17.3
Are we in the midst of a feminist resurgence?

Experience the Research

Feminist Identity

Think about the stages of feminist identity development described in the Bargad and Hyde (1991) study (see page 398). They go from Stage 1, Passive Acceptance, to Stage 5, Active Commitment. You have just taken a psychology of women and gender course. Do you think that you passed through one or several of those stages as the course progressed? What stage would you say you are in now?

SUGGESTIONS FOR FURTHER READING

Gay, Roxane. (2014). *Bad feminist.* New York, NY: HarperCollins. Gay provides sharp, intersectional feminist critique and humor on culture and politics.

Solnit, Rebecca. (2017). *The mother of all questions: Further reports from the feminist revolutions.* Chicago, IL: Haymarket. In this collection of essays, Solnit follows up her feminist book *Men Explain Things to Me* with humor and insight on the gender binary and the need for men to be involved in feminism.

Taylor, Shelley. (2002). *The tending instinct: Women, men, and the biology of nurturing.* New York, NY: Times Books.

Taylor expands on her tend-and-befriend theory of women's response to stress, discussed in the current chapter.

Traister, Rebecca. (2016). *All the single ladies: Unmarried women and the rise of an independent nation.* New York, NY: Simon & Schuster. Traister, a journalist who interviewed women around the United States for this book, argues that, across history, tremendous social change occurs when women postpone or forgo heterosexual marriage.

Glossary

Acculturation: A multidimensional process of psychological and behavioral change one undergoes as a result of long-term contact with another culture, including the adoption of that culture's values, customs, norms, attitudes, and behaviors.

Acculturative stress: Specific stress of the acculturation process.

Affiliative speech: Speech that demonstrates affiliation or connection to the listener and may include praise, agreement, support, and/or acknowledgment.

African Americans: Americans of African descent.

Ageism: Negative attitudes toward older adults.

Aggression: Behavior intended to harm another person.

Alcohol-use disorder: A psychological disorder characterized by excessive alcohol use and associated failure to fulfill major role obligations (e.g., work, school, home).

Alexithymia: Difficulty identifying and describing the emotions of oneself and others.

Amenorrhea: The absence of menstrual periods.

American Indians: The indigenous peoples of North America. Also called Native Americans.

Androcentrism: Male centered; the belief that the male is the norm.

Androgen-insensitivity syndrome (AIS): A genetic condition in which the cells of the body are unresponsive to androgens. In genetic males (XY chromosomes), the result is genitals that appear female (complete AIS) or intersex, somewhere in between typical males and typical females (partial AIS).

Androgens: A group of "male" sex hormones, including testosterone, produced more abundantly in men than in women.

Androgyny: The combination of masculine and feminine psychological characteristics in an individual.

Andropause: A time of declining testosterone levels in middle- and older-age men.

Anorexia nervosa: An eating disorder characterized by over-control of eating for purposes of weight reduction, sometimes to the point of starvation.

Anorgasmia: The inability to have an orgasm; also called orgasmic disorder.

Antigay prejudice: Negative attitudes and behaviors toward gay men and lesbians. Also called sexual prejudice.

Appearance rigidity: Rigid adherence to gender norms in appearance, such as wearing highly masculine or feminine clothing and avoiding clothes typical of another gender.

Asexuality: A lack of interest in or desire for sex.

Asian Americans: Americans of Asian descent.

Assertive speech: Speech that aims to influence the listener and may include providing instructions, information, suggestions, criticism, and/or disagreement.

Benevolent sexism: Beliefs about women that seem to be kind or benevolent; women are seen as pure and morally superior beings who should be protected and adored.

Bisexual: A person who is erotically and emotionally attracted to both women and men.

Boston marriage: A romantic but asexual lesbian relationship.

Bulimia nervosa: An eating disorder in which the person binges on food and then purges the body of the calories by vomiting, using laxatives or diuretics, fasting, or excessively exercising.

Care perspective: According to Gilligan, an approach to moral reasoning that emphasizes relationships between people and caring for others and the self.

Cervix: The lower part of the uterus, forming a passageway to the vagina.

Channeling: Selection of different toys, activities, and so on for boys and girls; also called shaping.

Child sexual abuse (CSA): Behavior that includes the use, coercion, or forcing of a child to engage in sexual acts or imitate sexual acts.

Circumcision: Surgical removal of the foreskin of the penis, usually done within a few days of birth.

Cisgender: A person whose gender identity matches the gender they were assigned at birth.

Cisgenderism: Prejudice against people who are outside the gender binary; also refers to bias that recognizes a person's birth-assigned gender but not their gender identity. Also termed anti-trans prejudice.

Coercive control: Behaviors intended to monitor and control or threaten an intimate partner.

Cognitive-behavioral therapy: A system of psychotherapy that combines behavior therapy and restructuring of dysfunctional thought patterns.

Coming out: The process of acknowledging to others that one is lesbian, gay, bisexual, or queer.

Comparable worth: The principle that people should be paid equally for work that is comparable in responsibility, educational requirements, and so forth.

Compensation: A process in which positive feelings or rewards from one role compensate or make up for stresses or costs in another role.

Conceptual equivalence: In multicultural research, the construct measured by a scale has the same meaning in all cultures being studied.

Congenital adrenal hyperplasia (CAH): A rare genetic condition that causes the fetus's adrenals to produce unusually large amounts of androgens. In XX individuals, the result may be a girl born with masculinized genitals so that she has an intersex condition.

Contractive posture: Sitting or standing with legs together and arms close to the body.

Cool pose: A set of behaviors and scripts for Black men that developed in response to racial oppression and that emphasize the expression of pride, strength, and control.

Critical theory: A theoretical perspective that seeks to redress power inequalities and achieve equity and equality.

Deindividuation: A state in which a person has become anonymous and has therefore lost their individual identity—and therefore the pressure to conform to gender roles.

Different cultures hypothesis: Tannen's perspective that gender differences in communication are so different that it is as though women and men come from different linguistic cultures.

Differential treatment: The extent to which parents and others behave differently toward boys and girls.

Direct instruction: Telling boys and girls to behave in different ways.

Disclaimers: Phrases such as "I may be wrong, but . . ."

Discrepancy of sexual desire: A sexual disorder in which the partners have considerably different levels of sexual desire.

Display rules: A culture's rules for which emotions can be expressed or displayed.

Double standard: The evaluation of male behavior and female behavior according to different standards, including tolerance of male promiscuity and disapproval of female promiscuity; used specifically to refer to holding more conservative, restrictive attitudes toward female sexuality.

Double standard of aging: Cultural norms by which men's status increases with age but women's decreases.

Doula: A trained professional who provides continuous physical, emotional, and informational support to a woman before, during, and shortly after childbirth.

Dual control model: A model that two basic processes underlie human sexual response: excitation and inhibition.

Dysmenorrhea: Painful menstruation; cramps.

Dyspareunia: Painful intercourse.

Electra complex: In psychoanalytic theory, a girl's sexual attraction to and intense love for her father.

Emotional competence: The ability to perceive, appraise, and express emotions accurately and clearly; to understand, analyze, and use knowledge about emotions to think and make decisions; and to regulate the emotions of oneself and others.

Empty nest: The phase of the family life cycle following the departure of adult children from the family home; also known as the postparental period.

Endocrine disrupters: Chemicals in the environment that affect the endocrine system as well as other aspects of biological functioning and behavior in animals, including humans.

Entitlement: An individual's sense of what they should receive (e.g., pay) based on who they are or what they've done.

Epigenetics: Changes in gene expression caused by factors other than DNA.

Erogenous zones: Areas of the body that are particularly sensitive to sexual stimulation.

Estrogen: A sex hormone produced by the ovaries; also produced by the testes.

Estrogen replacement therapy (ERT): Doses of estrogen given to some women to treat menopausal symptoms.

Ethnic group: A group of people who share a common culture and language.

Ethnocentrism: The tendency to regard one's own ethnic group as superior to others and to believe that its customs and way of life are the standards by which other cultures should be judged.

Eurocentrism: The tendency to view the world from a European American point of view and to evaluate other ethnic groups in reference to European Americans.

European American: White Americans of European descent; an alternative to the term Whites. Also, Euro-Americans.

Evolutionary fitness: In evolutionary theory, an animal's relative contribution of genes to the next generation.

Evolutionary psychology: A theory that humans' complex psychological mechanisms are the result of evolutionary selection.

Expansionist hypothesis: In research on women and multiple roles, the hypothesis that multiple roles are good for mental health because they provide more opportunities for stimulation, self-esteem, and so on.

Expansive posture: Sitting or standing with limbs extended away from the body; also referred to as power posing.

Expectancy-value theory: A theory of motivation that posits that a person will take on a challenging achievement task if they expect that they can succeed at it and if they value it (find it useful or interesting).

Experimenter effects: When some characteristics of the experimenter affect the way participants behave and therefore affect the research outcome.

Familismo: In Latinx culture, a sense of obligation and connectedness with both one's immediate and extended family.

Female deficit model: A theory or interpretation of research in which women's behavior is seen as deficient.

Female sexual arousal disorder: A lack of response to sexual stimulation, including a lack of lubrication.

Female-as-the-exception phenomenon: If a category is considered normatively male and there is a female example of the category, gender is noted because the female is the exception; a by-product of androcentrism.

Feminine evil: The belief that women are the source of evil or immorality in the world, as in the Adam and Eve story.

Feminist: A person who favors political, economic, and social equality of all people, regardless of gender, and therefore favors the legal and social changes necessary to achieve gender equality.

Feminist research: Research growing out of feminist theory, which seeks radical reform of traditional research methods.

Feminist therapy: A system of therapy informed by feminist theory.

Feminization of poverty: The increasing trend over time for women to be overrepresented among the poor in the United States.

Follicle: The capsule of cells surrounding an egg in the ovary.

Follicle-stimulating hormone (FSH): A hormone secreted by the pituitary that stimulates follicle and egg development.

Follicular phase: The first phase of the menstrual cycle, beginning just after menstruation.

Gender: The state of being male, female, both male and female, or neither male nor female.

Gender-affirming therapies: Medical care designed to assist individuals in adjusting their primary and secondary sex characteristics to align with their gender identity. May include hormonal therapy, surgical therapy, or both.

Gender-based violence: Forms of violence in which women are the predominant victims and men are the predominant perpetrators; transgender individuals are also overrepresented among victims.

Gender binary: A system of conceptualizing gender as having two distinct and opposing groups or kinds (i.e., male and female).

Gender consistency: The third stage of gender constancy development, in which children understand that gender remains consistent despite superficial changes in appearance.

Gender constancy: The understanding that gender is a stable and consistent part of oneself.

Gender differences: Differences between genders.

Gender dysphoria: Discomfort or distress related to incongruence between a person's gender identity, sex assigned at birth, and/or primary and secondary sex characteristics.

Gender-fair research: Research that is free of gender bias.

Gender identity: The first stage of gender constancy development, in which children can identify and label their own gender and the gender of others.

Gender intensification: Increased pressures for gender role conformity, beginning in adolescence.

Gender role identity: The psychological structure representing the individual's identification with their own gender role; it demonstrates itself in the individual's gender-appropriate behavior, attitudes, and feelings.

Gender role identity paradigm (GRIP): Traditional psychology's perspective that optimal personality development depends on a gender role identity that matches the gender assigned at birth, consistent with the traditional masculinity ideology.

Gender role strain paradigm (GRSP): A feminist theory that gender roles are socially constructed by gender ideologies, which grow out of and support gender inequality, and that gender roles are a source of strain for individuals.

Gender schema: A person's general knowledge framework about gender; it processes and organizes information on the basis of gender-linked associations.

Gender self-socialization model: A theoretical model that children's gender identification makes them want to adopt gender-stereotyped behaviors.

Gender similarities: Similarities among genders.

Gender similarities hypothesis: The hypothesis that men and women are similar on most, but not all, psychological variables.

Gender stability: The second stage of gender constancy development, in which children understand that gender is stable over time.

Gender stereotypes: A set of shared cultural beliefs about men's and women's behavior, appearance, interests, personality, and so on.

Gender typing: The acquisition of gender-typed behaviors and learning of gender roles.

Gendered racism: A form of oppression and bias based simultaneously on both gender and race/ethnicity.

Genderless language: A type of language in which gender is expressed only lexically and neither personal nouns or pronouns are differentiated for gender; examples include Finnish, Mandarin, and Turkish.

Genderqueer: A gender category that is not exclusively male or female and therefore is not captured by the gender binary.

Glass ceiling: Invisible barriers to the promotion of women and ethnic minorities into upper management and executive levels.

Gonadotropin-releasing hormone (Gn-RH): A hormone secreted by the hypothalamus that regulates the pituitary's secretion of hormones.

Grammatical gender language: A type of language in which parts of speech (including nouns, pronouns, verbs, adjectives, etc.) are gender-inflected; examples include Spanish, German, Hindi, and Hebrew.

G-spot (Gräfenberg spot): A small gland on the front wall of the vagina, emptying into the urethra, which may be responsible for female ejaculation.

Hedges: Phrases such as "sort of" that weaken or soften a statement.

Heteronormativity: The belief that heterosexuality is the norm.

Heterosexism: Discrimination or bias against people based on their nonheterosexual orientation.

Hispanic: People of Spanish descent, whether from Mexico, Puerto Rico, or elsewhere.

Historical trauma: Cumulative psychological wounding over generations resulting from massive group trauma.

Homophobia: A strong, irrational fear of sexual minority persons.

Hooking up: Casual sexual contact between two people, ranging from making out to intercourse.

Hopelessness theory: A vulnerability-stress theory that a negative cognitive style makes a person vulnerable to depression.

Hormone replacement therapy (HRT): Doses of estrogen and progesterone and possibly testosterone given to some women to treat menopausal symptoms.

Hostile sexism: Negative, hostile attitudes toward women and adversarial beliefs about gender relations.

Human trafficking: The acquisition of people by improper means such as force, fraud, or deception, with the aim of exploiting them, most often for sexual services and forced labor or slavery.

Hyperandrogenism: A condition in which the body produces very high levels of androgens. Typically, it is noticed only in women. It can result from a variety of medical conditions, including polycystic ovary syndrome and Cushing syndrome.

Hypoactive sexual desire: A sexual disorder in which there is a lack of interest in sexual activity; also termed inhibited sexual desire or low sexual desire.

Hypothalamus: A part of the brain that is important in regulating certain body functions, including sex hormone production.

Hysterectomy: Surgical removal of the uterus.

Imitation: People doing what they see others doing.

Implicit stereotypes: Learned, automatic associations between social categories (e.g., female) and other attributes (e.g., nurse but not mathematician).

Infantilizing: Treating people—for example, women—as if they were children or babies.

Infertility: Not getting pregnant despite having carefully timed, unprotected sex for one year.

Intensifiers: Adverbs such as very, really, and vastly.

Intersectionality: A feminist approach that simultaneously considers the meaning and consequences of multiple categories of identity, difference, and disadvantage.

Intersex: A variety of conditions in which a person is born with genitals or reproductive anatomy that is not typical of females or males. Also termed disorders of sex development in the DSM-5 and differences of sex development or genital diversity.

Intimate partner violence (IPV): Aggressive behaviors directed toward an intimate partner, including sexual violence, physical violence, stalking or harassment, verbal aggression, coercive control, and control of reproductive or sexual health.

Justice perspective: According to Gilligan, an approach to moral reasoning that emphasizes fairness and the rights of the individual.

Kegel exercises: Exercises to strengthen the muscles surrounding the vagina; also called pubococcygeal muscle exercises.

Lateralization: The extent to which one hemisphere of the brain organizes a particular mental process or behavior.

Latina: A Latin American girl or woman.

Latinos: Latin American people; also refers specifically to Latin American men.

Latinx: A Latin American person, unmarked by gender.

Lesbian: A woman whose sexual orientation is toward other women.

Lumpectomy: A surgical treatment for breast cancer in which only the lump and a small bit of surrounding tissue are removed.

Luteal phase: The third phase of the menstrual cycle, after ovulation.

Luteinizing hormone (LH): A hormone secreted by the pituitary that triggers ovulation.

Machismo: The ideal of manliness in Latinx culture.

Male as normative: A model in which the male is seen as the norm for all humans and the female is seen as a deviation from the norm.

Marianismo: The ideal of womanliness in Latinx culture.

Masculine generics: The common usage of masculine forms (e.g., he, his, him) as generic for all people.

Masochism: The desire to experience pain.

Medicalization: The process by which normal life events or situations are defined and treated as medical conditions in need of diagnosis and treatment.

Menopause: The cessation of menstruation.

Menstruation: A bloody discharge of the lining of the uterus; the fourth phase of the menstrual cycle.

Meta-analysis: A statistical technique that allows a researcher to combine the results of multiple research studies on a particular question.

Midlife crisis: During men's midlife, the phenomenon of personal turmoil and sudden changes in lifestyle, touched off by a realization of aging, physical decline, and being trapped in tired roles.

Miscarriage: Spontaneous demise of a fetus before the 20th week of pregnancy.

Misgendering: A form of sexist language in which gendered language that does not match a person's gender identity is used or when a person's gender identity is misidentified by some other means.

Mixed methods: Research methods that involve both quantitative and qualitative methods.

Modeling: Demonstrating gendered behavior for children; also refers to the child's imitation of the behavior.

Modern sexism: Subtle prejudiced beliefs about women; also termed neosexism.

Motherhood mandate: A cultural belief that women must become mothers.

Motherhood penalty: The reduction in women's lifetime earnings that result from having children.

Mujerismo: Feminism rooted in the lived experience of Latinas; Latina womanism.

Myotonia: Muscle contraction.

Narcissism: A personality trait characterized by an excessive focus on oneself, along with a grandiose, exaggerated sense of one's own talents, an extreme need for admiration, and a lack of empathy for others.

Native Americans: The indigenous peoples of North America.

Natural gender language: A type of language in which most personal nouns are gender-neutral (e.g., student) but pronouns are differentiated for gender; examples include English and Swedish.

Natural selection: According to Darwin, the process by which the fittest animals survive, reproduce, and pass on their genes to the next generation, whereas animals that are less fit do not reproduce and therefore do not pass on their genes.

Negative cognitive style: A tendency to attribute negative life events to internal, global, and stable causes.

Neural plasticity: Changes in the brain in response to experience.

Neurosexism: Claims that there are fixed differences between male and female brains and that these differences explain women's deficits in performance or why they should occupy certain roles and not others.

Objectified body consciousness: The experience of one's own body as an object to be viewed and evaluated; includes components of surveillance, body shame, and control beliefs.

Observational learning: Observing someone doing something and then doing it at a later time.

Observer effects: When the researcher's expectations affect their observations and recording of the data; also called rater bias.

Oedipal complex: In psychoanalytic theory, a boy's sexual attraction to and intense love for his mother and his desire to do away with his father.

Old-fashioned sexism: Open or overt prejudice against women.

Orgasm: An intense sensation that occurs at the peak of sexual arousal and is followed by the release of sexual tensions.

Overgeneralization: A research error in which the results are said to apply to a broader group than the one sampled, for example, saying that results from an all-male sample are true for all people.

Ovulation: Release of an egg from an ovary.

Ovum: An egg.

Paradigm: A set of beliefs, underlying assumptions, values, and techniques shared by a particular community of scientists.

Parental investment: In sociobiology, behaviors or other investments in the offspring by the parent that increase the offspring's chance of survival.

Performativity: The idea that gender and sexual orientation are constructed through a constant set of performances by people (actors).

Phallic stage: The third stage of development in psychoanalytic theory, around 3 to 6 years of age, during which, for boys, the pleasure zone is the penis and sexual feelings arise toward the mother and, for girls, sexual feelings arise toward the father.

Phallocentric: Male centered or, specifically, penis centered.

Posttraumatic growth: Positive life changes following highly stressful experiences.

Posttraumatic stress disorder (PTSD): A disorder that develops in some people after experiencing a terrifying event. Symptoms include reexperiencing symptoms (e.g., flashbacks, bad dreams), reactivity symptoms (e.g., easily startled, trouble sleeping), and cognition and mood symptoms (e.g., distorted feelings of guilt, loss of enjoyment in activities).

Precarious manhood: The theory that manhood is an elusive and achieved social status that is hard-won and yet easily lost, and that requires constant public proof.

Premenstrual syndrome (PMS): A combination of severe physical and psychological symptoms (such as depression) occurring in some women for a few days before menstruation.

Prenatal: Before birth.

Progesterone: A sex hormone produced by the ovaries; also produced by the testes.

Prostaglandins: Hormone-like biochemicals that stimulate the muscles of the uterus to contract.

Psychoanalysis: A system of therapy based on Freud's psychoanalytic theory in which the analyst attempts to bring repressed, unconscious material into consciousness.

Psychoanalytic theory: A psychological theory originated by Sigmund Freud; its basic assumption is that part of the human psyche is unconscious.

Psychological measurement: The processes of assigning numbers to people's characteristics, such as aggressiveness or intelligence; essential to quantitative methods.

Pubertal suppression: Medical suppression of endogenous pubertal changes in adolescents; also called puberty blockers.

Qualitative research methods: Research methods that do not use numbers or statistics, but may analyze text, in-depth interviews, participant observations, or focus groups for themes and meaning.

Quantitative research methods: Research methods that involve psychological measurement and the use of statistics to analyze data, often with the goal of generalizing from a sample to a population.

Quasi-experimental design: A research design that compares two or more groups but is not a true experiment because participants are not randomly assigned to groups; an example is a study comparing men and women.

Queer: An epithet that has been reappropriated by gay activists and theorists to refer to sexual minorities.

Queer of color critique: An approach that brings together queer theory, feminist theory, and women of color feminism.

Queer theory: A theoretical perspective that one's gender, gender identity, and sexual orientation are not stable, fixed, biologically based characteristics, but rather fluid and dynamic aspects of individuals shaped by culture.

Race: A socially constructed system of human classification, once considered a biological concept referring to discrete and exclusive groups of people with common physical features.

Racial microaggressions: Subtle insults directed at people of color, consciously or nonconsciously.

Radical mastectomy: A surgical treatment for breast cancer in which the entire breast, as well as underlying muscle and lymph nodes, is removed.

Rape: Penetration, no matter how slight, of the vagina or anus with any body part or object, or oral penetration by a sex organ of another person, without the consent of the victim.

Rape culture: A set of cultural attitudes and beliefs about gender and sexuality, e.g., that it is natural and normal for men to be sexually aggressive and that rape is inevitable.

Rape myths: False beliefs about rape, rape victims, and rapists, which support rape culture (e.g., victim precipitation, victim fabrication, victim masochism).

Refractory period: A period of time following orgasm, during which one cannot be restimulated to orgasm.

Relational aggression: Behavior intended to hurt others by damaging their peer relationships. Also termed indirect aggression.

Restorative justice: An alternative approach to the treatment of both rapists and victims, with the basic premise that harm has been done and that someone is responsible for repairing it.

Role congruity theory: A theory that holds that people tend to perceive an incongruity between leadership behaviors and the female role, and therefore are prejudiced against female leaders.

Rumination: The tendency to think repetitively about one's depressed mood or about the causes and consequences of negative life events.

Scarcity hypothesis: In research on women and multiple roles, the hypothesis that adding a role (e.g., worker) creates stress, which has negative consequences for mental health and physical health.

Schema: In cognitive psychology, a general knowledge framework that a person has about a particular topic; the schema then processes and organizes new information on that topic.

Self-confidence: A person's belief that they can be successful at a particular task or in a particular domain such as athletics or academics.

Self-conscious emotions: Emotions about the self, which often have to do with morality or adhering to social norms; includes guilt, shame, pride, and embarrassment.

Self-efficacy: A person's belief in their ability to accomplish a particular task.

Self-esteem: The level of global positive regard that one has for oneself.

Self-objectification: Perceiving and valuing oneself as an object to be viewed and evaluated.

Sex-linked trait: A trait controlled by a gene on the X chromosome (and occasionally on the Y chromosome).

Sexism: Discrimination or bias against other people based on their gender; also termed gender bias or sex bias.

Sexual disorder: A problem with sexual responding that causes a person mental distress; examples are erection problems in men and orgasm problems in women.

Sexual fluidity: Situation-dependent flexibility in women's sexual responsiveness to women or men.

Sexual minority: An umbrella term for all people with a sexual orientation other than heterosexual.

Sexual orientation: A person's erotic and emotional orientation toward members of their own gender or members of another gender.

Sexual selection: According to Darwin, the processes by which members of one gender (usually males) compete with each other for mating privileges with members of another gender (usually females), who, in turn, choose to mate only with certain preferred members of the first gender (males).

Sexualization: The process of valuing a person only for their sex appeal, sexually objectifying a person, or inappropriately imposing sexuality on a person.

Social backlash: Negative evaluation of someone for violating the norms of their gender role.

Social constructionism: A theoretical viewpoint that humans do not discover reality directly; rather, they construct meanings for events in the environment based on their own prior experiences and beliefs.

Social role theory: A theory of the origin of psychological gender differences that focuses on the social structure, particularly the division of labor between men and women; also called social structural theory.

Socialization: The ways in which society conveys to the individual its expectations for their behavior.

Sociobiology: The application of evolutionary theory to explaining the social behavior of animals, including people.

Spermarche: The first ejaculation of seminal fluid; also called semenarche.

Spillover: A process in which positive or negative feelings in one role carry or spill over into another role.

STEM: An acronym for science, technology, engineering, and mathematics.

Stereotype threat: A situation in which there is a negative stereotype about a person's group, and the person is concerned about being judged or treated negatively on the basis of that stereotype.

Stillbirth: Spontaneous demise of a fetus after the 20th week of pregnancy.

Stratified reproduction: A systematic pattern of inequity in which women of color are overrepresented among women with infertility but are underrepresented among those who receive treatment for infertility.

Substance-use disorder: A psychological disorder characterized by excessive use of a substance (e.g., heroin), an associated failure to fulfill major role obligations (e.g., work, school, home), failure to cut back on use, cravings, and using increasingly greater amounts of the substance over time.

Superego: Freud's term for the part of the personality that contains the person's conscience.

Tag question: A short phrase added to a sentence that turns it into a question.

Temperament: Constitutionally based individual differences in reactivity and self-regulation, such as emotional intensity, inhibitory control, activity level, and distractibility.

Testosterone: A sex hormone manufactured by the testes and, in lesser amounts, by the ovaries; one of the androgens.

Traditional masculinity ideology: A set of cultural beliefs about how boys and men should or should not think, feel, and behave.

Trans-affirmative practice: Care that is respectful, aware, and supportive of the identities and life experiences of transgender and gender nonconforming people; also called gender-affirming care.

Transgender: Describes a person whose gender identity differs from the gender they were assigned at birth.

Translational equivalence: In multicultural research, whether a scale written in one language and translated into another has the same meaning in both languages.

Triphasic model: A model that there are three components to sexual response: sexual desire, vasocongestion, and myotonia.

Two Spirit: Among some American Indian tribes, a gender category for individuals who feel they possess both male and female spirits.

Vacuum aspiration: A method of surgical abortion that is performed in the first trimester.

Vaginismus: A strong, spastic contraction of the muscles around the vagina, perhaps closing off the vagina and making intercourse impossible.

Vasocongestion: An accumulation of blood in the blood vessels of a region of the body, especially the genitals; a swelling or erection results.

Visual dominance ratio: The ratio of the percentage of time looking while speaking relative to the percentage of time looking while listening; an indicator of social dominance.

Whorfian hypothesis: The theory that the language we learn influences how we think.

Womanism: Feminism rooted in the lived experience of Black women and women of color; also Black feminism.

Womb envy: In Horney's analytic theory, the man's envy of the woman's uterus and reproductive capacity.

X-chromosome inactivation: In female fetuses, the process in which one of the two X chromosomes is inactivated or silenced in nearly every cell, so only one X chromosome functions.

Bibliography

In the bibliography we have largely followed the style of spelling out first names of authors. We do this to help readers become aware of the gender and ethnic diversity of researchers making scientific contributions.

Abbey, Antonia. (1991). Misperception as an antecedent of acquaintance rape: A consequence of ambiguity in communication between men and women. In A. Parrott & L. Bechhofer (Eds.), *Acquaintance rape: The hidden crime* (pp. 96–111). New York, NY: Wiley.

Abbey, Antonia D., Jacques-Tiura, Angela J., & Parkhill, Michele R. (2010). Sexual assault among diverse populations of women: Common ground, distinctive features, and unanswered questions. In H. Landrine & N. Russo (Eds.), *Handbook of diversity in feminist psychology* (pp. 391–426). New York, NY: Springer.

Abbey, Antonia, & McAuslan, Pam. (2004). A longitudinal examination of male college students' perpetration of sexual assault. *Journal of Consulting and Clinical Psychology, 72,* 747–756.

Abbey, Antonia, McAuslan, Pam, Zawacki, Tina, Clinton, A. Monique, & Buck, Philip O. (2001). Attitudinal, experiential, and situational predictors of sexual assault perpetration. *Journal of Interpersonal Violence, 16,* 784–807.

Abe-Kim, Jennifer, Takeuchi, David T., Hong, Seunghye, Zane, Nolan, Sue, Stanley, Spencer, Michael S., . . . Alegría, Margarita. (2007). Use of mental health-related services among immigrant and US-born Asian Americans: Results from the National Latino and Asian American Study. *American Journal of Public Health, 97,* 91–98.

Abela, J. (2001). The hopelessness theory of depression: A test of the diathesis-stress and causal mediation components in third and seventh grade children. *Journal of Abnormal Child Psychology, 29,* 241–254.

Abendroth, Anja-Kristin, Huffman, Matt L., & Treas, Judith. (2014). The parity penalty in life course perspective: Motherhood and occupational status in 13 European countries. *American Sociological Review, 79,* 993–1014.

Abrams, Jasmine A., Maxwell, Morgan, Pope, Michell, & Belgrave, Faye Z. (2014). Carrying the world with the grace of a lady and the grit of a warrior: Deepening our understanding of the "strong Black woman" schema. *Psychology of Women Quarterly, 38,* 503–518.

Abramson, Lyn Y., Metalsky, Gerald I., & Alloy, Lauren B. (1989). Hopelessness depression: A theory-based subtype of depression. *Psychological Review, 96,* 358–372.

Acosta-Belén, Edna, & Bose, Christine E. (2000). U.S. Latina and Latin American feminisms: Hemispheric encounters. *Signs: Journal of Women in Culture and Society, 25,* 1113–1120.

Adamsky, Catherine. (1981). Changes in pronomial usage in a classroom situation. *Psychology of Women Quarterly, 5,* 773–779.

Addiego, Frank, Belzer, Edwin G., Jr., Comolli, Jill, Moger, William, Perry, John D., & Whipple, Beverly. (1981). Female ejaculation: A case study. *Journal of Sex Research, 17,* 13–21.

Addis, Michael, & Mahalik, James R. (2003). Men, masculinity, and the contexts of help seeking. *American Psychologist, 58,* 5–14.

Adelson, Stewart L., & American Academy of Child and Adolescent Psychiatry Committee on Quality Issues. (2012). Practice parameter on gay, lesbian, or bisexual sexual orientation, gender nonconformity, and gender discordance in children and adolescents. *Journal of the American Academy of Child & Adolescent Psychiatry, 51,* 957–974.

Adler, Nancy E., & Coriell, Marilee. (1997). Socioeconomic status and women's health. In S. Gallant, G. Keita, & R. Royak-Schaler (Eds.), *Health care for women: Psychological, social, and behavioral influences* (pp. 11–24). Washington, DC: American Psychological Association.

Adler, Nancy E., David, Henry P., Major, Brenda N., Roth, Susan H., Russo, Nancy F., & Wyatt, Gail E. (1990). Psychological responses after abortion. *Science, 248,* 41–44.

Adler, Nancy E., David, Henry P., Major, Brenda N., Roth, Susan H., Russo, Nancy F., & Wyatt, Gail E. (1992). Psychological factors in abortion. *American Psychologist, 47,* 1194–1204.

Adler, Nancy E., Ozer, Emily J., & Tschann, Jeanne. (2003). Abortion among adolescents. *American Psychologist, 58,* 211–217.

Adler, Richard K., Hirsch, Sandy, & Mordaunt, Michelle. (2012). *Voice and communication therapy for the transgender/transsexual client: A comprehensive clinical guide* (2nd ed.). San Diego, CA: Plural.

African American Policy Forum. (2015). *Say her name: Resisting police brutality against Black women.* New York, NY: Center for Intersectionality and Social Policy Studies.

Agénor, Madina, Krieger, Nancy, Austin, S. Bryn, Haneuse, Sebastien, & Gottlieb, Barbara R. (2014). Sexual orientation disparities in Papanicolaou test use among US women: The role of sexual and reproductive health services. *American Journal of Public Health, 104,* e68–e73.

Alcántara, Carmela, Chen, Chih-Nan, & Alegría, Margarita. (2015). Transnational ties and past-year major depressive episodes among Latino immigrants. *Cultural Diversity and Ethnic Minority Psychology, 21,* 486–495.

Aldarondo, Etiony, & Castro-Fernandez, Michelle. (2011). Risk and protective factors for domestic violence perpetration. In J. W. White, M. P. Koss, & A. E. Kazdin (Eds.), *Violence against women and children: Mapping the terrain* (Vol. 1, pp. 221–242). Washington, DC: American Psychological Association.

Alegría, Margarita, Mulvaney-Day, Norah, Woo, Meghan, Torres, Maria, Gao, Shan, & Oddo, Vanessa. (2007). Correlates of past-year mental health service use among Latinos: Results from the National Latino and Asian American Study. *American Journal of Public Health, 97,* 76–83.

Alexander, Michele G., & Fisher, Terri D. (2003). Truth and consequences: Using the bogus pipeline to examine sex differences in self-reported sexuality. *Journal of Sex Research, 40,* 27–35.

Alexander, Michelle. (2010). *The new Jim Crow: Mass incarceration in the age of colorblindness.* New York, NY: New Press.

Ali, Alisha, Caplan, Paula J., & Fagnant, Rachel. (2010). Gender stereotypes in diagnostic criteria. In J. Chrisler & D. McCreary (Eds.), *Handbook of gender research in psychology* (Vol. 2, pp. 91–110). New York, NY: Springer.

Alink, Lenneke R. A., Mesman, Judi, Van Zeijl, Jantien, Stolk, Mirjam N., Juffer, Femmie, Koot, Hans M., . . . Van Ijzendoorn, Marinus H. (2006). The early childhood aggression curve: Development of physical aggression in 10- to 50-month-old children. *Child Development, 77,* 954–966.

Allen, Paula Gunn. (1986). Who is your mother? Red roots of white feminism. In *The sacred hoop: Recovering the feminine in American Indian traditions* (pp. 209–221). Boston, MA: Beacon Press.

Allport, G. (1954). *The nature of prejudice.* Reading, MA: Addison-Wesley.

Alpak, Gokay, Unal, Ahmet, Bulbul, Feridun, Sagaltici, Eser, Bez, Yasin, Altindag, Abdurrahman, . . . Savas, Haluk A. (2015). Post-traumatic stress disorder among Syrian refugees in Turkey: A cross-sectional study. *International Journal of Psychiatry in Clinical Practice, 19,* 45–50.

Al-Safi, Zain A., & Santoro, N. (2014). Menopausal hormone therapy and menopausal symptoms. *Fertility & Sterility, 101,* 905–915.

Amanatullah, Emily T., & Morris, Michael W. (2010). Negotiating gender roles: Gender differences in assertive negotiating are mediated by women's fear of backlash and attenuated when negotiating on behalf of others. *Journal of Personality and Social Psychology, 98,* 256–267.

Amato, Paul R. (2000). The consequences of divorce for adults and children. *Journal of Marriage and the Family, 62,* 1269–1287.

Amato, Paul R. (2010). Research on divorce: Continuing trends and new developments. *Journal of Marriage and Family, 72,* 650–666.

Amato, Paul R., & Gilbreth, Joan G. (1999). Nonresident fathers and children's well-being: A meta-analysis. *Journal of Marriage and the Family, 61,* 557–573.

Ambady, Nalini, Hallahan, Mark, & Conner, Brett. (1999). Accuracy of judgments of sexual orientation from thin slices of behavior. *Journal of Personality and Social Psychology, 77,* 538–547.

Ambady, Nalini, Shih, Margaret, Kim, Amy, & Pittinsky, Todd L. (2001). Stereotype susceptibility in children: Effects of identity activation on quantitative performance. *Psychological Science, 12,* 385–390.

American Association of Retired Persons. (1999). *Modern maturity sexuality study.* Washington, DC: Author.

American Association of University Women. (2001). *Hostile hallways: Bullying, teasing, and sexual harassment in school.* Washington, DC: Author.

American Association of University Women. (2011). *Crossing the line: Sexual harassment at school.* Washington, DC: Author.

American Psychiatric Association. (1994). *Diagnostic and statistical manual* (4th ed.). Washington, DC: Author.

American Psychiatric Association (2013). *Diagnostic and statistical manual of mental disorders* (5th ed.). Arlington, VA: Author.

American Psychological Association. (1975). Report of the task force on sex bias and sex-role stereotyping in psychotherapeutic practice. *American Psychologist, 30,* 1169–1175.

American Psychological Association. (1994). *Publication manual* (4th ed.). Washington, DC: Author.

American Psychological Association. (1996). *Research agenda for psychosocial and behavioral factors in women's health*. Washington, DC: Author.

American Psychological Association. (2003). Guidelines on multicultural education, training, research, practice, and organization change for psychologists. *American Psychologist, 58*, 377–402.

American Psychological Association. (2007a). Guidelines for psychological practice with girls and women. *American Psychologist, 62*, 949–979.

American Psychological Association. (2007b). *Report of the APA Task Force on the Sexualization of Girls*. Washington, DC: Author.

American Psychological Association. (2010). *Publication manual of the American Psychological Association* (6th ed.). Washington, DC: Author.

American Psychological Association. (2015). Guidelines for psychological practice with transgender and gender nonconforming people. *American Psychologist, 70*, 832–864.

American Psychological Association Presidential Task Force on Immigration. (2012). *Crossroads: The psychology of immigration in the new century*. Retrieved from http://www.apa.org/topics/immigration/report.aspx

Anderson, Kristin L. (1997). Gender, status, and domestic violence: An integration of feminist and family violence approaches. *Journal of Marriage and the Family, 59*, 655–669.

Anderson, Kristen J., & Leaper, C. (1998). Meta-analyses of gender effects on conversational interruption: Who, what, when, where, and how. *Sex Roles, 39*, 225–252.

Anderson, Veanne N. (2009). What's in a label? Judgments of feminist men and feminist women. *Psychology of Women Quarterly, 33*, 206–215.

Angier, Natalie. (1999). *Woman: An intimate geography*. Boston, MA: Houghton Mifflin.

Angold, Adrian, Erkanli, Alaattin, Silberg, Judy, Eaves, Lindon, & Costello, E. Jane. (2002). Depression scale scores in 8–17-year-olds: Effects of age and gender. *Journal of Child Psychology and Psychiatry, 43*, 1052–1063.

Ankney, C. Davison. (1992). Sex differences in relative brain size: The mis-measure of woman, too? *Intelligence, 16*, 329–336.

Ansara, Y. Gavriel, & Hegarty, Peter. (2012). Cisgenderism in psychology: Pathologizing and misgendering children from 1999 to 2008. *Psychology & Sexuality, 3*, 137–160.

Ansara, Y. Gavriel, & Hegarty, Peter. (2014). Methodologies of misgendering: Recommendations for reducing cisgenderism in psychological research. *Feminism & Psychology, 24*, 259–270.

Anthony, James C., Warner, Lynn A., & Kessler, Ronald C. (1994). Comparative epidemiology of dependence on tobacco, alcohol, controlled substances, and inhalants: Basic findings from the National Comorbidity Survey. *Experimental Clinical Psychopharmacology, 2*, 244–268.

Antoni, Michael H., Lechner, Suzanne C., Kazi, Aisha, Wimberly, Sarah R., Sifre, Tammy, . . . Carver, Charles S. (2006). How stress management improves quality of life after treatment for breast cancer. *Journal of Consulting and Clinical Psychology, 74*, 1143–1152.

Antoni, Michael H., Lehman, Jessica M., Kilbourn, Kristin M., Boyers, Amy E., Culver, Jenifer L., Alferi, Susan M., . . . Carver, Charles S. (2001). Cognitive-behavioral stress management intervention decreases the prevalence of depression and enhances benefit finding among women under treatment for early-stage breast cancer. *Health Psychology, 20*, 20–32.

Antonucci, Toni C., Blieszner, Rosemary, & Denmark, Florence L. (2010). Psychological perspectives on older women. In H. Landrine & N. Russo (Eds.), *Handbook of diversity in feminist psychology* (pp. 233–260). New York, NY: Springer.

Archer, John. (2004). Sex differences in aggression in real-world settings: A meta-analytic review. *Review of General Psychology, 8*, 291–322.

Arciniega, G. Miguel, Anderson, Thomas C., Tovar-Blank, Zoila G., & Tracey, Terence J. G. (2008). Toward a fuller conception of machismo: Development of a traditional machismo and caballerismo scale. *Journal of Counseling Psychology, 55*, 19–33.

Arendell, Terry. (2000). Conceiving and investigating motherhood: The decade's scholarship. *Journal of Marriage and the Family, 62*, 1192–1207.

Arias, Elizabeth. (2015). United States life tables, 2011. *National Vital Statistics Reports, 64*(11).

Arias, Elizabeth, Heron, Melonie, & Xu, Jiaquan. (2017). United States life tables, 2013. *National Vital Statistics Reports, 66*(3).

Aries, Elizabeth. (1996). *Men and women in interaction: Reconsidering the differences*. New York, NY: Oxford University Press.

Arkin, William, & Dobrofsky, Lynne R. (1978). Military socialization and masculinity. *Journal of Social Issues, 34*(1), 151–168.

Arnett, Jeffrey J. (2004). *Emerging adulthood*. New York, NY: Oxford University Press.

Ashburn-Nardo, Leslie. (2017). Parenthood as a moral imperative? Moral outrage and the stigmatization of voluntarily childfree women and men. *Sex Roles, 76,* 393–401.

Ashton, Adam K. (2007). The new sexual pharmacology. In S. Leiblum (Ed.), *Principles and practice of sex therapy* (4th ed., pp. 509–542). New York, NY: Guilford.

Association of American Medical Colleges. (2011). *Women in U.S. academic medicine: Statistics and benchmarking report 2009–2010.* Washington, DC: Author.

Astin, Helen S., & Leland, Carole. (1991). *Women of influence, women of vision: A cross-generational study of leaders and social change.* San Francisco, CA: Jossey-Bass.

Aubrey, Jennifer S. (2004). Sex and punishment: An examination of sexual consequences and the sexual double standard in teen programming. *Sex Roles, 50,* 505–514.

Avis, Nancy E. (2003). Depression during the menopausal transition. *Psychology of Women Quarterly, 27,* 91–100.

Avis, Nancy E., & McKinlay, Sonja M. (1995). The Massachusetts Women's Health Study: An epidemiological investigation of the menopause. *Journal of the American Medical Women's Association, 50,* 45–63.

Avis, Nancy E., Stellato, Rebecca, Crawford, Sybil, Bromberger, Joyce, Ganz, Patricia, Cain, Virginia, & Kagawa-Singer, Marjorie. (2001). Is there a menopausal syndrome? Menopausal status and symptoms across racial/ethnic groups. *Social Science and Medicine, 52,* 345–356.

Aznar, Ana, & Tenenbaum, Harriet R. (2013). Spanish parents' emotion talk and their children's understanding of emotion. *Frontiers in Psychology, 4,* 670.

Babcock, Julia C., Roseman, Ashley, Green, Charles E., & Ross, Jody M. (2008). Intimate partner abuse and PTSD symptomatology: Examining mediators and moderators of the abuse-trauma link. *Journal of Family Psychology, 22,* 809–818.

Bachmann, G. A., & Leiblum, S. R. (1991). Sexuality in sexagenarian women. *Maturitas, 13,* 43–50.

Backus, Faedra R., & Mahalik, James R. (2011). The masculinity of Mr. Right: Feminist identity and heterosexual women's ideal romantic partners. *Psychology of Women Quarterly, 35,* 318–326.

Bagès, Celine, Verniers, Ca, & Martinot, Delphine. (2016). Virtues of a hardworking role model to improve girls' mathematics performance. *Psychology of Women Quarterly, 40,* 55–64.

Bailey, J. Michael, Bobrow, David, Wolfe, Marilyn, & Mikach, Sarah. (1995). Sexual orientation of adult sons of gay fathers. *Developmental Psychology, 31,* 124–129.

Bailey, J. Michael, Dunne, Michael P., & Martin, Nicholas G. (2000). Genetic and environmental influences on sexual orientation and its correlates in an Australian twin sample. *Journal of Personality and Social Psychology, 78,* 524–536.

Bailey, J. Michael, Pillard, Richard C., Neale, Michael C., & Agyei, Yvonne. (1993). Heritable factors influence sexual orientation in women. *Archives of General Psychiatry, 50,* 217–223.

Bailey, Robert C., Moses, Stephen, Parker, Corette B., Agot, Kawango, Maclean, Ian, Krieger, John N., . . . Ndinya-Achola, Jeckoniah O. (2007). Male circumcision for HIV prevention in young men in Kisumu, Kenya: A randomised controlled trial. *Lancet, 369,* 643–656.

Baillargeon, Raymond H., Zoccolillo, Mark, Keenan, Kate, Côté, Sylvana, Pérusse, Daniel, Wu, Hong-Xing, . . . Tremblay, Richard E. (2007). Gender differences in physical aggression: A prospective population-based survey of children before and after 2 years of age. *Developmental Psychology, 43,* 13–26.

Baker, Christina N. (2005). Images of women's sexuality in advertisements: A content analysis of Black- and White-oriented women's and men's magazines. *Sex Roles, 52,* 13–28.

Baker, Jessica H., Maes, Hermine H., Lissner, Lauren, Aggen, Steven H., Lichtenstein, Paul, & Kendler, Kenneth S. (2009). Genetic risk factors for disordered eating in adolescent males and females. *Journal of Abnormal Psychology, 118,* 576–586.

Baker, Nancy L., & Mason, Janelle L. (2010). Gender issues in psychological testing of personality and abilities. In J. Chrisler & D. McCreary (Eds.), *Handbook of gender research in psychology* (Vol. 2, pp. 63–90). New York, NY: Springer.

Balantekin, Katherine N., Savage, Jennifer S., Marini, Michele E., & Birch, Leann L. (2014). Parental encouragement of dieting promotes daughters' early dieting. *Appetite, 80,* 190–196.

Balon, Richard, & Clayton, Anita H. (2014). Female sexual interest arousal disorder: A diagnosis out of thin air. *Archives of Sexual Behavior, 43,* 1227–1229.

Balsam, Kimberly F., Beauchaine, Theodore P., Mickey, Ruth M., & Rothblum, Esther D. (2005). Mental health of lesbian, gay, bisexual, and heterosexual siblings: Effects of gender, sexual orientation, and family. *Journal of Abnormal Psychology, 114,* 471–476.

Balsam, Kimberly F., Molina, Yamile, Beadnell, Blair, Simoni, Jane, & Walters, Karina. (2011). Measuring multiple minority stress: The LGBT People of Color Microaggressions Scale. *Cultural Diversity and Ethnic Minority Psychology, 17,* 163–174.

Balsam, Kimberly F., Molina, Yamile, Blayney, Jessica A., Dillworth, Tiara, Zimmerman, Lindsey, & Kaysen, Debra. (2015). Racial/ethnic differences in identity and mental health outcomes among young sexual minority women. *Cultural Diversity and Ethnic Minority Psychology, 21,* 380–390.

Banaji, Mahzarin R., & Hardin, Curtis D. (1996). Automatic stereotyping. *Psychological Science, 7,* 136–141.

Bancroft, John, & Graham, Cynthia A. (2011). The varied nature of women's sexuality: Unresolved issues and a theoretical approach. *Hormones and Behavior, 59,* 717–729.

Bancroft, John, Graham, Cynthia, Janssen, Erick, & Sanders, Stephanie A. (2009). The dual control model: Current status and future directions. *Journal of Sex Research, 46,* 121–142.

Bancroft, John, Long, J. Scott, & McCabe, Janice. (2011). Sexual well-being: A comparison of U.S. Black and White women in heterosexual relationships. *Archives of Sexual Behavior, 40,* 725–740.

Bandura, Albert. (1965). Influence of model's reinforcement contingencies on the acquisition of imitative responses. *Journal of Personality and Social Psychology, 1,* 589–595.

Bandura, Albert. (1986). *Social foundations of thought and action: A social cognitive theory.* Englewood Cliffs, NJ: Prentice-Hall.

Bandura, Albert, Barbaranelli, Claudio, Caprara, Gian Vittorio, & Pastorelli, Concetta. (2001). Self-efficacy beliefs as shapers of children's aspirations and career trajectories. *Child Development, 72,* 187–206.

Bandura, Albert, & Walters, Richard H. (1963). *Social learning and personality development.* New York, NY: Holt, Rinehart & Winston.

Baraona, Enrique, Abittan, Chaim S., Dohmen, Kazufumi, Moretti, Michelle, Pozzato, Gabriele, Chayes, Zeb W., . . . Lieber, Charles S. (2001). Gender differences in pharmacokinetics of alcohol. *Alcoholism: Clinical and Experimental Research, 25,* 502–507.

Barash, David P. (1982). *Sociobiology and behavior* (2nd ed.). New York, NY: Elsevier.

Barbach, Lonnie G. (1975). *For yourself: The fulfillment of female sexuality.* Garden City, NY: Anchor Press/Doubleday.

Barbaree, Howard E., & Marshall, William L. (1991). The role of male sexual arousal in rape: Six models. *Journal of Consulting and Clinical Psychology, 59,* 621–630.

Bargad, Adena, & Hyde, Janet S. (1991). Women's studies: A study of feminist identity development in women. *Psychology of Women Quarterly, 15,* 181–201.

Barlow, Tani. (2000). International feminism of the future. *Signs: Journal of Women in Culture and Society, 25,* 1099–1105.

Barnett, Melissa A., Scaramella, Laura V., Nepple, Tricia K., Ontai, Lenna L., & Conger, Rand D. (2010). Grandmother involvement as a protective factor for early childhood social adjustment. *Journal of Family Psychology, 24,* 635–645.

Barnett, Michael D., Sligar, Kylie B., & Wang, Chiachih D. C. (2016). Religious affiliation, religiosity, gender, and rape myth acceptance: Feminist theory and rape culture. *Journal of Interpersonal Violence.* Advance online publication. https://doi.org/10.1177/0886260516665110

Barnett, Rosalind C., & Hyde, Janet S. (2001). Women, men, work, and family: An expansionist theory. *American Psychologist, 56,* 781–796.

Barnett, Rosalind C., Marshall, Nancy, & Pleck, Joseph. (1992). Men's multiple roles and their relationship to men's psychological distress. *Journal of Marriage and the Family, 54,* 358–367.

Baron, Larry, & Straus, Murray A. (1989). *Four theories of rape in American society.* New Haven, CT: Yale University Press.

Barreca, Regina. (1991). *They used to call me Snow White . . . but I drifted: Women's strategic use of humor.* New York, NY: Penguin Books.

Barrett, Lisa F., & Bliss-Moreau, Eliza. (2009). She's emotional. He's having a bad day: Attributional explanations for emotion stereotypes. *Emotion, 9,* 649–658.

Barrett, Lisa F., Lane, Richard D., Sechrest, Lee, & Schwartz, Gary E. (2000). Sex differences in emotional awareness. *Personality and Social Psychology Bulletin, 26,* 1027–1035.

Barron, Kenneth E., & Harackiewicz, Judith M. (2001). Achievement goals and optimal motivation: Testing multiple goal models. *Journal of Personality and Social Psychology, 80,* 706–722.

Basow, Susan A. (2010). Gender in the classroom. In J. Chrisler & D. McCreary (Eds.), *Handbook of gender research in psychology* (Vol. 1, pp. 277–296). New York, NY: Springer.

Basson, Rosemary. (2014). On the definition of female sexual interest arousal disorder. *Archives of Sexual Behavior, 43,* 1225–1226.

Basson, Rosemary, Berman, Jennifer, Burnett, Arthur, Derogatis, Leonard, Ferguson, David, Fourcroy, Jean, . . . Whipple, Beverly. (2001). Report of the International Consensus Development Conference on female sexual dysfunction: Definitions and classifications. *Journal of Sex and Marital Therapy, 27,* 83–94.

Basson, Rosemary, et al. (2004). Summary of the recommendations on women's sexual dysfunctions. In T. F. Lue, R. Basson, R. Rosen, F. Giuliano, S. Khoury, & F. Montorsi (Eds.), *Sexual medicine: Sexual dysfunctions in men and women* (pp. 975–990). Paris, France: Editions 21.

Baulieu, Etienne-Emil, Thomas, Guy, Legrain, Sylvie, Lahlou, Najiba, Roger, Marc, Debuire, Brigitte, . . . Forette, Françoise. (2000). Dehydroepiandrosterone (DHEA), DHEA sulfate, and aging: Contributions of the DHEAge Study to a sociobiomedical issue. *Proceedings of the National Academy of Sciences of the USA, 97,* 4279–4284.

Baumgardner, Dennis J., Schreiber, Andrea L., Havlena, Jeffrey E., Bridgewater, Farrin D., Steber, Dale L., & Lemke, Melissa A. (2010). Geographic analysis of diagnosis of attention-deficit/hyperactivity disorder in children: Eastern Wisconsin, USA. *International Journal of Psychiatry in Medicine, 40,* 363–382.

Bays, Annalucia. (2016). Perceptions, emotions, and behaviors toward women based on parental status. *Sex Roles, 76,* 138–155.

Bazzini, Doris G., McIntosh, William D., Smith, Stephen M., Cook, Sabrina, & Harris, Caleigh. (1997). The aging woman in popular film: Underrepresented, unattractive, unfriendly, and unintelligent. *Sex Roles, 36,* 531–543.

Beatty, William W. (1992). Gonadal hormones and sex differences in nonreproductive behaviors. In A. Gerall, H. Moltz, & I. L. Ward (Eds.), *Handbook of behavioral neurobiology* (Vol. 11, pp. 85–128). New York, NY: Plenum.

Beavis, Anna L., Gravitt, Patti E., & Rositch, Anne F. (2017). Hysterectomy-corrected cervical cancer mortality rates reveal a larger racial disparity in the United States. *Cancer, 123,* 1044–1050.

Beck, Aaron T., & Greenberg, Ruth L. (1974). Cognitive therapy with depressed women. In V. Franks & V. Burtle (Eds.), *Women in therapy* (pp. 113–131). New York, NY: Brunner/Mazel.

Beck, Diane M. (2010). The appeal of the brain in the popular press. *Perspectives on Psychological Science, 5,* 762–766.

Beck, J. Gayle, Tran, Han N., Dodson, Thomas S., Henschel, Aisling V., Woodward, Matthew J., & Eddinger, Jasmine. (2016). Cognitive trauma therapy for battered women: Replication and extension. *Psychology of Violence, 6,* 368–377.

Beck, Victoria S., Boys, Stephanie, Rose, Christopher, & Beck, Eric. (2012). Violence against women in video games: A prequel or sequel to rape myth acceptance? *Journal of Interpersonal Violence, 27,* 3016–3031.

Becker, Carolyn B., Bull, Stephanie, Schaumberg, Katherine, Cauble, Adele, & Franco, Amanda. (2008). Effectiveness of peer-led eating disorders prevention: A replication trial. *Journal of Consulting and Clinical Psychology, 76,* 347–354.

Beijing Declaration and Platform for Action. (1995). New York, NY: United Nations Department of Public Information.

Belcastro, Philip A. (1985). Sexual behavior differences between black and white students. *Journal of Sex Research, 21,* 56–67.

Bell, Alan P., Weinberg, Martin S., & Hammersmith, Sue K. (1981). *Sexual preference: Its development in men and women.* Bloomington: Indiana University Press.

Bell, Leslie C. (2004). Psychoanalytic theories of gender. In A. H. Eagly, A. E. Beall, & R. J. Sternberg (Eds.), *The psychology of gender* (2nd ed., pp. 145–168). New York, NY: Guilford.

Bell, Margaret E., Goodman, Lisa A., & Dutton, Mary Ann. (2009). Variations in help-seeking, battered women's relationship course, emotional well-being, and experiences of abuse over time. *Psychology of Women Quarterly, 33,* 149–162.

Belle, Deborah. (1990). Poverty and women's mental health. *American Psychologist, 45,* 385–389.

Belle, Deborah, & Doucet, Joanne. (2003). Poverty, inequality, and discrimination as sources of depression among U.S. women. *Psychology of Women Quarterly, 27,* 101–113.

Belzer, Edwin G., Jr. (1981). Orgasmic expulsions of women: A review and heuristic inquiry. *Journal of Sex Research, 17,* 1–12.

Bem, Sandra L. (1974). The measurement of psychological androgyny. *Journal of Consulting and Clinical Psychology, 42,* 155–162.

Bem, Sandra L. (1975). Sex-role adaptability: One consequence of psychological androgyny. *Journal of Personality and Social Psychology, 31,* 634–643.

Bem, Sandra L. (1977). On the utility of alternative procedures for assessing psychological androgyny. *Journal of Consulting and Clinical Psychology, 45,* 196–205.

Bem, Sandra L. (1981). Gender schema theory: A cognitive account of sex-typing. *Psychological Review, 88,* 354–364.

Bem, Sandra L. (1993). *The lenses of gender.* New Haven, CT: Yale University Press.

Bem, Sandra, L., & Lenney, Ellen. (1976). Sex-typing and the avoidance of cross-sex behavior. *Journal of Personality and Social Psychology, 33,* 48–54.

Bem, Sandra L., Martyna, Wendy, & Watson, Carol. (1976). Sex typing and androgyny: Further explorations of the expressive domain. *Journal of Personality and Social Psychology, 34,* 1016–1023.

Benenson, Joyce F., Morash, Deanna, & Petrakos, Harriet. (1998). Gender differences in emotional closeness between preschool children and their mothers. *Sex Roles, 38*, 975–986.

Bentz, Eva-Katrin, Hefler, Lukas A., Kaufmann, Ulrike, Huber, Johannes C., Kolbus, Andrea, & Tempfer, Clemens B. (2008). A polymorphism of the CYP17 gene related to sex steroid metabolism is associated with female-to-male but not male-to-female transsexualism. *Fertility and Sterility, 90*, 56–59.

Bergen, David J., & Williams, John E. (1991). Sex stereotypes in the United States revisited: 1972–1988. *Sex Roles, 24*, 413–423.

Berger, Lawrence M., Hill, Jennifer, & Waldfogel, J. (2005). Maternity leave, early maternal employment, and child health and development in the US. *Economic Journal, 115*, F29–F47.

Berkley, K., & Holdcroft, A. (1999). Sex and gender differences in pain. In P. Wall & R. Melzack (Eds.), *Textbook of pain* (pp. 951–965). Edinburgh, Scotland: Churchill Livingstone.

Berli, Jens U., Knudson, Gail, Fraser, Lin, Tangpricha, Vin, Ettner, Randi, Ettner, Frederic M., . . . Schechter, Loren. (2017). What surgeons need to know about gender confirmation surgery when providing care for transgender individuals: A review. *JAMA Surgery, 152*, 394–400.

Bernard, Jessie. (1972). *The future of marriage.* New York, NY: Bantam Books.

Bernstein, A. (1988, February 29). So you think you've come a long way, baby? *Business Week.*

Berry, Raine, & Sellman, J. Douglas. (2001). Childhood adversity in alcohol- and drug-dependent women presenting to out-patient treatment. *Drug and Alcohol Review, 20*, 361–367.

Best, Deborah L., & Thomas, Jennifer J. (2004). Cultural diversity and cross-cultural perspectives. In A. H. Eagly, A. E. Beall, & R. J. Sternberg (Eds.), *The psychology of gender* (2nd ed., pp. 296–327). New York, NY: Guilford.

Betancourt, Hector, & Lopez, Steven R. (1993). The study of culture, ethnicity, and race in American psychology. *American Psychologist, 48*, 629–637.

Bettelheim, Bruno. (1962). *Symbolic wounds.* New York, NY: Collier Books.

Beyer, Sylvia. (1999). Gender differences in the accuracy of grade expectancies and evaluations. *Sex Roles, 41*, 279–296.

Bian, Lin, Leslie, Sarah-Jane, & Cimpian, Andrei. (2017). Gender stereotypes about intellectual ability emerge early and influence children's interests. *Science, 355*, 389–391.

Bianchi, JeanMarie, & Strang, Emily. (2013). Is evolutionary psychology really value-free? A reconsideration. *Journal of Social, Evolutionary, and Cultural Psychology, 7*, 304–310.

Bianchi, Suzanne, & Milkie, Melissa. (2010). Work and family research in the first decade of the 21st century. *Journal of Marriage and Family, 72*, 705–725.

Biederman, Joseph, Mick, Eric, Faraone, Stephen V., Braaten, Ellen, Doyle, Alysa, Spencer, Thomas, . . . Johnson, Mary Ann. (2002). Influence of gender on attention deficit hyperactivity disorder in children referred to a psychiatric clinic. *American Journal of Psychiatry, 159*, 36–42.

Biggs, M. Antonia, Upadhyay, Ushma D., McCulloch, Charles E., & Foster, Diana G. (2017). Women's mental health and well-being 5 years after receiving or being denied an abortion: A prospective, longitudinal cohort study. *JAMA Psychiatry, 74*(2), 169–178.

Bigler, Rebecca S., Averhart, Cara J., & Liben, Lynn S. (2003). Race and the workforce: Occupational status, aspirations, and stereotyping among African American children. *Developmental Psychology, 39*, 572–580.

Bigler, Rebecca S., & Liben, Lynn S. (2007). Developmental intergroup theory: Explaining and reducing children's social stereotyping and prejudice. *Current Directions in Psychological Science, 16*, 162–166.

Bird, Adrian. (2007). Perceptions of epigenetics. *Nature, 447*, 396–398.

Bishop, Katherine, & Wahlsten, Douglas. (1997). Sex differences in the human corpus callosum: Myth and reality. *Neuroscience and Biobehavioral Reviews, 21*, 581–601.

Bissada, Angela, & Briere, John. (2001). Child abuse, physical and sexual. In J. Worell (Ed.), *Encyclopedia of women and gender* (pp. 219–231). San Diego, CA: Academic Press.

Bisson, Jonathan I., Cosgrove, Sarah, Lewis, Catrin, & Roberts, Neil P. (2015). Post-traumatic stress disorder. *BMJ, 351*, h6161.

Black, Michele C., Basile, Kathleen C., Breiding, Matthew J., Smith, Sharon G., Walters, Mikel L., Merrick, Melissa T., . . . Stevens, Mark R. (2011). *The National Intimate Partner and Sexual Violence Survey (NISVS): 2010 summary report.* Atlanta, GA: Centers for Disease Control and Prevention, National Center for Injury Prevention and Control.

Blackwell, Tom. (2011, May 25). Toronto parents hide child's gender in bid for neutral treatment. *Montreal Gazette.*

Blackwood, E. (1984). Sexuality and gender in certain Native American tribes: The case of the cross-gender females. *Signs: Journal of Women in Culture and Society, 10*, 27–42.

Blakemore, Judith, Berenbaum, Sheri, & Liben, Lynn S. (2009). *Gender development.* New York, NY: Psychology Press.

Blanchard, Ray (1985). Typology of male-to-female transsexualism. *Archives of Sexual Behavior, 14,* 247–261.

Blascovich, Jim, Spencer, Steven J., Quinn, Diane, & Steele, Claude. (2001). African Americans and high blood pressure: The role of stereotype threat. *Psychological Science, 12,* 225–229.

Blaubergs, Maija S. (1978). Changing the sexist language: The theory behind the practice. *Psychology of Women Quarterly, 2,* 244–261.

Blechman, Elaine A. (1980). Behavior therapies. In A. M. Brodsky & R. Hare-Mustin (Eds.), *Women and psychotherapy* (pp. 217–244). New York, NY: Guilford.

Blee, Kathleen M., & Tickamyer, Ann R. (1995). Racial differences in men's attitudes about women's roles. *Journal of Marriage and the Family, 57,* 21–30.

Bleeker, Martha M., & Jacobs, Janis E. (2004). Achievement in math and science: Do mothers' beliefs matter 12 years later? *Journal of Educational Psychology, 96,* 97–109.

Blessitt, Esther, Voulgari, Stamatoula, & Eisler, Ivan. (2015). Family therapy for adolescent anorexia nervosa. *Current Opinion in Psychiatry, 28,* 455–460.

Blumenthal, Heidemarie, Leen-Feldner, Ellen W., Babson, Kimberly A., Gahr, Jessica L., Trainor, Casey D., & Frala, Jamie L. (2011). Elevated social anxiety among early maturing girls. *Developmental Psychology, 47,* 1133–1140.

Blumstein, Philip W., & Schwartz, Pepper. (1983). *American couples.* New York, NY: William Morrow.

Bockting, Walter O., Miner, Michael H., Swinburne Romine, Rebecca E., Hamilton, Autumn, & Coleman, Eli. (2013). Stigma, mental health, and resilience in an online sample of the US transgender population. *American Journal of Public Health, 103,* 943–951.

Bodine, Ann. (1975). Androcentrism in prescriptive grammar: Singular "they," sex indefinite "he," and "he or she." *Language in Society, 4,* 129–146.

Bogle, Kathleen. (2008). *Hooking up: Sex, dating, and relationships on campus.* New York, NY: New York University Press.

Boisnier, Alicia D. (2003). Race and women's identity development: Distinguishing between feminism and womanism among Black and White women. *Sex Roles, 49,* 211–218.

Bonanno, George A., Wortman, Camille B., & Nesse, Randolph M. (2004). Prospective patterns of resilience and maladjustment during widowhood. *Psychology & Aging, 19,* 269–271.

Bondas, Terese, & Eriksson, Katie. (2001). Women's lived experiences of pregnancy: A tapestry of joy and suffering. *Qualitative Health Research, 11,* 824–840.

Bootzin, Richard R., & Natsoulas, Thomas. (1965). Evidence for perceptual defense uncontaminated by response bias. *Journal of Personality and Social Psychology, 1,* 461–468.

Bosacki, Sandra L., & Moore, Chris. (2004). Preschoolers' understanding of simple and complex emotions: Links with gender and language. *Sex Roles, 50,* 659–676.

Bosselman, Beulah C. (1960). Castration anxiety and phallus envy: A reformulation. *Psychiatric Quarterly, 34,* 252–259.

Bosson, Jennifer K., & Vandello, Joseph A. (2011). Precarious manhood and its links to action and aggression. *Current Directions in Psychological Science, 20,* 82–86.

Boston Women's Health Book Collective. (1976). *Our bodies, ourselves.* New York, NY: Simon & Schuster.

Boston Women's Health Book Collective. (2011). *Our bodies, ourselves: A new edition for a new era.* New York, NY: Touchstone.

Bouchard, Genevieve. (2014). How do parents react when their children leave home? An integrative review. *Journal of Adult Development, 21,* 69–79.

Bourassa, Kyle J., Sbarra, David A., & Whisman, Mark A. (2015). Women in very low quality marriages gain life satisfaction following divorce. *Journal of Family Psychology, 29,* 490–499.

Bowker, Lee H., Arbitell, Michelle, & McFerron, J. Richard. (1988). On the relationship between wife beating and child abuse. In K. Yllo & M. Bogard (Eds.), *Feminist perspective on wife abuse* (pp. 158–174). Newbury Park, CA: Sage.

Bowles, Hannah R., & Babcock, Linda. (2012). How can women escape the compensation negotiation dilemma? Relational accounts are one answer. *Psychology of Women Quarterly, 37,* 80–96.

Bowles, H. R., Babcock, Linda, & Lai, Lei. (2007). Social incentives for gender differences in the propensity to initiate negotiations: Sometimes it does hurt to ask. *Organizational Behavior and Human Decision Processes, 103,* 84–103.

Bowman, Christin P. (2014). Women's masturbation: Experiences of sexual empowerment in a primarily sex-positive sample. *Psychology of Women Quarterly, 38,* 363–378.

Bowman, Nicholas A. (2010). College diversity experiences and cognitive development: A meta-analysis. *Review of Educational Research, 80,* 4–33.

Bowman, Nicholas A. (2011). Promoting participation in a diverse democracy: A meta-analysis of college diversity experiences and civic engagement. *Review of Educational Research, 81,* 29–68.

Brace, Laura, & Davidson, Julia O. (2000). Minding the gap: General and substantive theorizing on power and exploitation. *Signs: Journal of Women in Culture and Society, 25,* 1045–1050.

Bradshaw, Carla K. (1994). Asian and Asian-American women: Historical and political considerations in psychotherapy. In L. Comas-Diaz & B. Greene (Eds.), *Women of color* (pp. 72–113). New York, NY: Guilford.

Brady, Kathleen T., Back, Sudie E., & Greenfield, Shelley F. (Eds.). *Women and addiction: A comprehensive handbook.* New York, NY: Guilford.

Brandt, Mark J. (2011). Sexism and gender inequality across 57 societies. *Psychological Science, 22,* 1413–1418.

Brannon, Robert, & David, Deborah S. (1976). The male sex role: Our culture's blueprint of manhood, and what it's done for us lately. In D. S. David & R. Brannon (Eds.), *The forty-nine percent majority* (pp. 1–48). Reading, MA: Addison-Wesley.

Braun, Friederike, Sczesny, Sabine, & Stahlberg, Dagmar. (2005). Cognitive effects of masculine generics in German: An overview of empirical findings. *Communications, 30,* 1–21.

Brave Heart, Maria Y. H. (2003). The historical trauma response among Natives and its relationship with substance abuse: A Lakota illustration. *Journal of Psychoactive Drugs, 35,* 7–13.

Brecklin, Leanne R., & Ullman, Sarah E. (2005). Self-defense or assertiveness training and women's responses to sexual attacks. *Journal of Interpersonal Violence, 20,* 738–762.

Brescoll, Victoria L. (2016). Leading with their hearts? How gender stereotypes of emotion lead to biased evaluations of female leaders. *Leadership Quarterly, 27,* 415–428.

Brescoll, Victoria L., Dawson, Erica, & Uhlman, Eric L. (2010). Hard won and easily lost: The fragile status of leaders in gender-stereotype-incongruent occupations. *Psychological Science, 21,* 1640–1642.

Breslow, Jason M. (2015). New: 87 deceased NFL players test positive for brain disease. *Frontline.* Retrieved from http://www.pbs.org

Bretherton, Inge, Fritz, Janet, Zahn-Waxler, Carolyn, & Ridgeway, Doreen. (1986). Learning to talk about emotions: A functionalist perspective. *Child Development, 57,* 529–548.

Bridges, Ana J., Wosnitzer, Robert, Scharrer, Erica, Sun, Chyng, & Liberman, Rachel. (2010). Aggression and sexual behavior in best-selling pornography videos: A content analysis update. *Violence Against Women, 16,* 1065–1085.

Briggs, Ernestine C., et al. (2011). Psychological, health, behavioral, and economic impact of child maltreatment. In J. W. White, M. P. Koss, & A. E. Kazdin (Eds.), *Violence against women and children: Mapping the terrain* (Vol. 1, pp. 77–98). Washington, DC: American Psychological Association.

Brim, Orville G. (1992). *Ambition.* New York, NY: Basic Books.

Briton, Nancy J., & Hall, Judith A. (1995). Beliefs about female and male nonverbal communication. *Sex Roles, 32,* 79–90.

Brizendine, Louann. (2007). *The female brain.* New York, NY: Broadway Books.

Broder, Michal S., Kanouse, David E., Mittman, Brian S., & Bernstein, Steven J. (2000). The appropriateness of recommendations for hysterectomy. *Obstetrics and Gynecology, 95,* 199–205.

Brody, Leslie R. (1996). Gender, emotional expression, and parent-child boundaries. In R. D. Kavanaugh, B. Zimmerberg, & S. Fein (Eds.), *Emotion: Interdisciplinary perspectives* (pp. 139–170). Mahwah, NJ: Lawrence Erlbaum.

Brody, Leslie R. (1999). *Gender, emotion, and the family.* Cambridge, MA: Harvard University Press.

Brody, Leslie R. (2000). The socialization of gender differences in emotional expression: Display rules, infant temperament, and differentiation. In A. Fischer (Ed.), *Gender and emotion* (pp. 24–47). Cambridge, UK: Cambridge University Press.

Brody, Leslie R., Hall, Judith A., & Stokes, Lynissa R. (2016). Gender and emotion: Theory, findings, and context. In L. F. Barrett, M. Lewis, & J. M. Haviland-Jones (Eds.), *Handbook of emotions* (4th ed., pp. 369–392). New York, NY: Guilford.

Brody, Leslie R., Hay, Deborah H., & Vandewater, Elizabeth. (1990). Gender, gender role identity, and children's reported feelings toward the same and opposite sex. *Sex Roles, 23,* 363–387.

Bromberger, Joyce T., Matthews, Karen A., Schott, Laura L., Brockwell, Sarah, Avis, Nancy, Kravitz, Howard M., . . . Randolph, John F., Jr. (2007). Depressive symptoms during the menopausal transition: The Study of Women's Health Across the Nation (SWAN). *Journal of Affective Disorders, 103,* 267–272.

Brooks-Gunn, Jeanne, Han, Wen-Jui, & Waldfogel, Jane. (2010). First-year maternal employment and child development in the first 7 years. *Monographs of the Society for Research in Child Development, 75*(2), 1–142.

Brotto, Lori, & Yule, Morag A. (2011). Physiological and subject sexual arousal in self-identified asexual women. *Archives of Sexual Behavior, 40,* 699–712.

Broverman, Inge K., Broverman, Donald M., Clarkson, Frank E., Rosenkrantz, Paul S., & Vogel, Susan R. (1970). Sex role stereotypes and clinical judgments of mental health. *Journal of Consulting and Clinical Psychology, 34,* 1–7.

Broverman, Inge K., Vogel, Susan R., Broverman, Donald M., Clarkson, Frank E., & Rosenkrantz, Paul S. (1972). Sex role stereotypes: A current appraisal. *Journal of Social Issues, 28,* 59–78.

Brown, Charlotte, Abe-Kim, Jennifer S., & Barro, Concepcion. (2003). Depression in ethnically diverse women: Implications for treatment in primary care settings. *Professional Psychology: Research and Practice, 34,* 10–19.

Brown, Christia S. (2006). Bias at school: Perceptions of racial/ethnic discrimination among Latino and European American children. *Cognitive Development, 21,* 401–419.

Brown, Christia S., Alabi, Basirat O., Huynh, Virginia W., & Masten, Carrie L. (2011). Ethnicity and gender in late childhood and early adolescence: Group identity and awareness of bias. *Developmental Psychology, 47,* 463–471.

Brown, Christia S., & Bigler, Rebecca S. (2005). Children's perceptions of discrimination: A developmental model. *Child Development, 76,* 533–553.

Brown, Clifford E., Dovidio, John F., & Ellyson, Steve L. (1992). Reducing sex differences in visual displays of dominance: Knowledge is power. *Personality and Social Psychology Bulletin, 16,* 358–368.

Brown, Geoffrey L., Craig, Ashley B., & Halberstadt, Amy G. (2015). Parent gender differences in emotion socialization behaviors vary by ethnicity and child gender. *Parenting: Science and Practice, 15,* 135–157.

Brown, George R. (2015). Breast cancer in transgender veterans: A ten-case series. *LGBT Health, 2,* 77–80.

Brown, George R., & Jones, Kenneth T. (2015). Incidence of breast cancer in a cohort of 5,135 transgender veterans. *Breast Cancer Research and Treatment, 149,* 191–198.

Brown, Jane D., & Bobkowski, Piotr S. (2011). Older and newer media: Patterns of use and effects on adolescents' health and well-being. *Journal of Research on Adolescence, 21,* 95–113.

Brown, Lyn M. (1998). *Raising their voices: The politics of girls' anger.* Cambridge, MA: Harvard University Press.

Brown, Lyn M., & Gilligan, Carol. (1992). *Meeting at the crossroads: Women's psychology and girls' development.* Cambridge, MA: Harvard University Press.

Brown, Ryan P., & Josephs, Robert A. (1999). A burden of proof: Stereotype relevance and gender differences in math performance. *Journal of Personality and Social Psychology, 76,* 246–257.

Brownmiller, Susan. (1975). *Against our will: Men, women, and rape.* New York, NY: Simon & Schuster.

Bruns, Cynthia M., & Kaschak, Ellyn. (2010). Feminist psychotherapies: Theory, research, and practice. In J. Chrisler & D. McCreary (Eds.), *Handbook of gender research in psychology* (Vol. 2, pp. 187–220). New York, NY: Springer.

Bryant, Jessica A., Mealy, Linda, Herzog, Elizabeth A., & Rychwalski, Wendy L. (2001). Paradoxical effect of surveyor's conservative versus provocative clothing on rape myth acceptance of males and females. *Journal of Psychology & Human Sexuality, 13,* 55–66.

Bryant-Davis, Thema, & Comas-Díaz, Lillian. (2016). *Womanist and Mujerista psychologies: Voices of fire, acts of courage.* Washington, DC: American Psychological Association.

Buchanan, NiCole T., Bergman, Mindy E., Bruce, Tamara A., Woods, Krystle C., & Lichty, Lauren L. (2009). Unique and joint effects of sexual and racial harassment on college students' well-being. *Basic and Applied Social Psychology, 31,* 267–285.

Buchanan, NiCole T., & West, Carolyn M. (2010). Sexual harassment in the lives of women of color. In H. Landrine & N. Russo (Eds.), *Handbook of diversity in feminist psychology* (pp. 449–478). New York, NY: Springer.

Budge, Stephanie L., Orovecz, Joe J., & Thai, Jayden L. (2015) Trans men's positive emotions: The interaction of gender identity and emotion labels. *The Counseling Psychologist, 43,* 404–434.

Budig, Michelle J. (2014). The fatherhood bonus and the motherhood penalty: Parenthood and the gender gap in pay. Retrieved from http://www.thirdway.org/report/the-fatherhood-bonus-and-the-motherhood-penalty-parenthood-and-the-gender-gap-in-pay

Budig, Michelle J., & Hodges, Melissa J. (2010). Differences in disadvantage. *American Sociological Review, 75,* 705–728.

Budoff, Penny W. (1981). *No more menstrual cramps and other good news.* New York, NY: Penguin Books.

Buhrmester, Duane. (1998). Need fulfillment, interpersonal competence, and the developmental contexts of early adolescent friendship. In W. M. Bukowski, A. F. Newcomb, & W. W. Hartup (Eds.), *The company they keep: Friendship in childhood and adolescence* (pp. 158–185). New York, NY: Cambridge University Press.

Bulik, Cynthia, Prescott, Carol A., & Kendler, Kenneth S. (2001). Features of childhood sexual abuse and the development of psychiatric and substance use disorders. *British Journal of Psychiatry, 179,* 444–449.

Bulosan, Carlos. (1960). *Sound of falling light: Letters in exile.* Quezon City: University of the Philippines.

Buntaine, Roberta L., & Costenbader, Virginia K. (1997). Self-reported differences in the experience and expression of anger between girls and boys. *Sex Roles, 36,* 625–638.

Burack, Cynthia, & Josephson, Jyl J. (2002). Women and the American new right: Feminist interventions. *Women & Politics, 24,* 69–90.

Bureau of Labor Statistics. (2010). *Women in the labor force: A databook (2010 edition).* Retrieved from https://www.bls.gov/cps/wlf-databook-2010.pdf

Bureau of Labor Statistics. (2011a). Table 24. Unemployed persons by marital status, race, Hispanic or Latino ethnicity, age, and sex. Retrieved from http://www.bls.gov/cps/cpsaat24.pdf

Bureau of Labor Statistics. (2011b). *Women at work.* Washington, DC: Author. Retrieved from https://www.bls.gov/spotlight/2017/women-at-work/pdf/women-at-work.pdf

Bureau of Labor Statistics. (2016). Labor force statistics from the Current Population Survey. Retrieved from http://www.bls.gov/cps/cpsaat39.htm

Bureau of Labor Statistics. (2017). *Current Population Survey, 2016, annual average.* Retrieved from https://www.bls.gov/cps/

Burnham, Denis, & Harris, Mary. (1992). Effects of real gender and labeled gender on adults' perceptions of infants. *Journal of Genetic Psychology, 153,* 165–183.

Burns, Ailsa, & Leonard, Rosemary. (2005). Chapters of our lives: Narratives of midlife and older Australian women. *Sex Roles, 52,* 269–278.

Burt, Martha. (1980). Cultural myths and support for rape. *Journal of Personality and Social Psychology, 38,* 217–230.

Burt, Martha R., & Estep, Rhoda E. (1981). Apprehension and fear: Learning a sense of sexual vulnerability. *Sex Roles, 7,* 511–522.

Buss, David M. (1989). Sex differences in human mate preferences: Evolutionary hypotheses tested in 37 cultures. *Behavioral and Brain Sciences, 12,* 1–14.

Buss, David M. (1995). Evolutionary psychology: A new paradigm for psychological science. *Psychological Inquiry, 6,* 1–30.

Buss, David M., Larsen, Randy J., Westen, Drew, & Semmelroth, Jennifer. (1992). Sex differences in jealousy: Evolution, physiology, and psychology. *Psychological Science, 3,* 251–255.

Buss, David M., & Schmitt, David P. (1993). Sexual strategies theory: An evolutionary perspective on human mating. *Psychological Review, 100,* 204–232.

Bussey, Kay, & Bandura, Albert. (1992). Self-regulatory mechanisms governing gender development. *Child Development, 63,* 1236–1250.

Bussey, Kay, & Bandura, Albert. (1999). Social cognitive theory of gender development and differentiation. *Psychological Review, 106,* 676–713.

Butler, Judith. (1990). *Gender trouble.* New York, NY: Routledge.

Butow, Phyllis, Beumont, Pierre, & Touyz, Stephen. (1993). Cognitive processes in dieting disorders. *International Journal of Eating Disorders, 14,* 319–329.

Byars-Winston, Angela, Fouad, Nadya, & Wen, Yao. (2015). Race/ethnicity and sex in U.S. occupations, 1970–2010: Implications for research, practice, and policy. *Journal of Vocational Behavior, 87,* 54–70.

Byers, E. Sandra. (1996). How well does the traditional sexual script explain sexual coercion? Review of a program of research. *Journal of Psychology and Human Sexuality, 8,* 7–25.

Byne, William. (1996). Biology and homosexuality. In R. Cabaj & T. Stein (Eds.), *Textbook of homosexuality and mental health* (pp. 129–146). Washington, DC: American Psychiatric Press.

Byne, William, & Parsons, Bruce. (1993). Human sexual orientation: The biologic theories reappraised. *Archives of General Psychiatry, 50,* 228–239.

Cabrera, Natasha J., Shannon, Jacqueline D., & Tamis-LeMonda, Catherine. (2007). Fathers' influence on their children's cognitive and emotional development. *Applied Developmental Science, 11,* 208–213.

Cabrera, Natasha J., West, Jerry, Shannon, Jacqueline D., & Brooks-Gunn, Jeanne. (2006). Parental interactions with Latino infants: Variation by country of origin and English proficiency. *Child Development, 77,* 1190–1207.

Calasanti, Toni. (2005). Ageism, gravity, and gender: Experiences of ageing bodies. *Generations, 29*(3), 8–12.

Callimachi, Rukmini. (2015, August 13). ISIS enshrines a theology of rape. *New York Times.* Retrieved from https://www.nytimes.com/

Calogero, Rachel M., & Jost, John T. (2011). Self-subjugation among women: Exposure to sexist ideology, self-objectification, and the protective function of the need to avoid closure. *Journal of Personality and Social Psychology, 47,* 463–471.

Campbell, Anne. (2013). *A mind of her own: The evolutionary psychology of women* (2nd ed.). Oxford, UK: Oxford University Press.

Campbell, Darren W., & Eaton, Warren O. (1999). Sex differences in the activity level of infants. *Infant and Child Development, 8,* 1–17.

Campbell, Rebecca. (2008). The psychological impact of rape victims' experiences with the legal, medical, and mental health systems. *American Psychologist, 63,* 702–717.

Campbell, Rebecca, Greeson, Megan, Bybee, Deborah, & Raja, Sheela. (2008). The co-occurrence of childhood sexual abuse, adult sexual assault, intimate partner violence, and sexual harassment: A mediational model of posttraumatic stress disorder and physical health outcomes. *Journal of Consulting and Clinical Psychology, 76,* 194–207.

Campbell, Rebecca, & Paterson, Debra. (2011). Services for victims of sexual violence. In M. P. Koss, J. D. White, & A. E. Kazdin (Eds.), *Violence against women and children: Navigating solutions* (Vol. 2, pp. 95–114). Washington, DC: American Psychological Association.

Campbell, Susan M., & Collaer, Maria L. (2009). Stereotype threat and gender differences in performance on a novel visuospatial task. *Psychology of Women Quarterly, 33,* 437–444.

Cantor, David, Fisher, Bonnie, Chibnall, Susan, Townsend, Reanne, Lee, Hyunshik, Bruce, Carol, & Thomas, Gail. (2015). *Report on the AAU Campus Climate Survey on Sexual Assault and Sexual Misconduct.* Rockville, MD: Westat.

Caplan, Paula. (1995). *How do they decide who is normal?* Reading, MA: Addison-Wesley.

Caplan, Paula. (2001). Motherhood: Its changing face. In J. Worell (Ed.), *Encyclopedia of gender* (pp. 783–794). San Diego, CA: Academic Press.

Caplan, Paula J., & Caplan, Jeremy B. (2009). *Thinking critically about research on sex and gender* (3rd ed.). Boston, MA: Pearson/Allyn and Bacon.

Carani, Cesare, Zini, Dante, Baldini, Augusto, Della Casa, Luciano, Ghizzani, Anna, & Marrama, Paolo. (1990). Effects of androgen treatment in impotent men with normal and low levels of free testosterone. *Archives of Sexual Behavior, 19,* 223–234.

Carli, Linda L. (1990). Gender, language, and influence. *Journal of Personality and Social Psychology, 59,* 941–951.

Carli, Linda L., Alaway, Laila, Lee, YoonAh, Zhao, Bei, & Kim, Elaine. (2016). Stereotypes about gender and science: Women ≠ scientists. *Psychology of Women Quarterly, 40,* 244–260.

Carnes, Molly. (2001). Humor. In J. Worell (Ed.), *Encyclopedia of women and gender* (pp. 601–609). San Diego, CA: Academic Press.

Carney, Dana R., Cuddy, Amy J. C., & Yap, Andy J. (2010). Power posing: Brief nonverbal displays affect neuroendocrine levels and risk tolerance. *Psychological Science, 21,* 1363–1368.

Carney, Dana R., Cuddy, Amy J. C., & Yap, Andy J. (2015). Review and summary of research on the embodied effects of expansive (vs. contractive) nonverbal displays. *Psychological Science, 26,* 657–663.

Carpenter, Christopher J. (2012). Meta-analyses of sex differences in responses to sexual versus emotional infidelity: Men and women are more similar than different. *Psychology of Women Quarterly, 36,* 25–37.

Carr, Brandon B., Ben Hagai, Ella, & Zurbriggen, Eileen L. (2017). Queering Bem: Theoretical intersections between Sandra Bem's scholarship and queer theory. *Sex Roles, 76,* 655–668.

Carr, C. Lynn. (2007). Where have all the tomboys gone? Women's accounts of gender in adolescence. *Sex Roles, 56,* 439–448.

Carr, Priyanka B., & Steele, Claude M. (2010). Stereotype threat affects financial decision making. *Psychological Science, 21,* 1411–1416.

Carter, C. Sue. (1992). Hormonal influences on human sexual behavior. In J. B. Becker, S. M. Breedlove, D. Crews, & M. M. McCarthy (Eds.), *Behavioral endocrinology* (pp. 131–142). Cambridge, MA: MIT Press.

Carter, Robert T. (2007). Racism and psychological and emotional injury: Recognizing and assessing race-based traumatic stress. *The Counseling Psychologist, 35,* 13–105.

Caspi, Avshalom, Sugden, Karen, Moffitt, Terrie E., Taylor, Alan, Craig, Ian W., Harrington, HonaLee, . . . Poulton, Richie. (2003). Influence of life stress on depression: Moderation by a polymorphism in the 5-HTT gene. *Science, 301,* 386–389.

Cass, Vivienne C. (1979). Homosexual identity formation: A theoretical model. *Journal of Homosexuality, 4,* 219–235.

Castillo, Linda G., Perez, Flor V., Castillo, Rosalinda, & Ghosheh, Mona R. (2010). Construction and initial validation of the Marianismo Beliefs Scale. *Counseling Psychology Quarterly, 23,* 163–175.

Catalano, Shannan. (2015). *Intimate partner violence, 1993–2010.* Washington, DC: U.S. Department of Justice, Bureau of Justice Statistics.

Catalyst. (2004). The bottom line: Connecting corporate performance and gender diversity. New York, NY: Author. Retrieved from http://www.catalyst.org/knowledge/bottom-line-connecting-corporate-performance-and-gender-diversity

Catalyst. (2016). *Pyramid: Women in S&P 500 companies.* New York, NY: Author.

CBS/AP. (2014, May 7). Dropping birth rates threaten global economic growth. Retrieved from http://www.cbsnews.com/news/dropping-birth-rates-threaten-global-economic-growth/

Ceballo, R., Graham, Erin T., & Hart, Jamie. (2015). Silent and infertile: An intersectional analysis of the experiences of socioeconomically diverse African American women with infertility. *Psychoogy of Women Quarterly, 39,* 497–511.

Ceci, Stephen J., & Williams, Wendy M. (2010). Sex differences in math-intensive fields. *Psychological Science, 19,* 275–279.

Celio, Christine I., Luce, Kristine H., Bryson, Susan W., Winzelberg, Andrew J., Cunning, Darby, Rockwell, Roxanne, . . . Taylor, C. Barr. (2006). Use of diet pills and other dieting aids in a college population with high weight and shape concerns. *International Journal of Eating Disorders, 39,* 492–497.

Center for American Women and Politics. (2011). *Facts on women in Congress, 2010.* Retrieved from http://www.cawp.rutgers.edu

Centers for Disease Control and Prevention. (2005). *HIV/AIDS among women.* Retrieved from http://www.cdc.gov/hiv/pubs/facts/women.htm

Centers for Disease Control and Prevention. (2008) *HIV/AIDS surveillance report, 2006.* Atlanta, GA: Author.

Centers for Disease Control and Prevention. (2014). *Understanding sexual violence.* Retrieved from https://www.cdc.gov/violenceprevention/pdf/SV-Factsheet.pdf

Centers for Disease Control and Prevention. (n.d.). Alcohol Related Disease Impact (ARDI) application. Retrieved from http://www.cdc.gov/ARDI

Cervantes, Christi A., & Callanan, Maureen A. (1998). Labels and explanations in mother-child emotion talk: Age and gender differentiation. *Developmental Psychology, 34,* 88–98.

Chadwick, Sara B., & van Anders, S. M. (2017). Do women's orgasms function as a masculinity achievement for men? *Journal of Sex Research.* Advance online publication. http://dx.doi.org/10.1080/00224499.2017.1283484

Champagne, Frances A. (2008). Epigenetic mechanisms and the transgenerational effects of maternal care. *Frontiers in Neuroendocrinology, 29,* 386–397.

Champagne, Frances A. (2010). Early adversity and developmental outcomes: Interaction between genetics, epigenetics, and social experiences across the lifespan. *Perspectives on Psychological Science, 5,* 564–574.

Champagne, Frances A. (2013). Early environments, glucocorticoid receptors, and behavioral epigenetics. *Behavioral Neuroscience, 127,* 628–636.

Chan, Connie S. (2003). Psychological issues of Asian Americans. In P. Bronstein & K. Quina (Eds.), *Teaching gender and multicultural awareness* (pp. 179–194). Washington, DC: American Psychological Association.

Chan, Darius K.-S., Chow, Suk Y., Lam, Chun B., & Cheung, Shu F. (2008). Examining the job-related, psychological, and physical outcomes of workplace sexual harassment: A meta-analytic review. *Psychology of Women Quarterly, 32,* 362–376.

Chang, Sand C., & Singh, Anneliese A. (2016). Affirming psychological practice with transgender and gender nonconforming people of color. *Psychology of Sexual Orientation and Gender Diversity, 3,* 140–147.

Chaplin, Tara M., & Aldao, Amelia. (2013). Gender differences in emotion expression in children: A meta-analytic review. *Psychological Bulletin, 139,* 735–765.

Chaplin, Tara M., Cole, Pamela M., & Zahn-Waxler, Carolyn. (2005). Parental socialization of emotion expression: Gender differences and relations to child adjustment. *Emotion, 5,* 80–88.

Charles, Maria, & Bradley, Karen. (2009). Indulging our gendered selves? Sex segregation by field of study in 44 countries. *American Journal of Sociology, 114,* 924–976.

Charles, Vignetta E., Polis, Chelsea B., Sridhara, Srinivas K., & Blum, Robert L. (2008). Abortion and long-term mental health outcomes: A systematic review of the evidence. *Contraception, 78,* 436–450.

Charmaraman, Linda, Woo, Meghan, Quach, Ashley, & Erkut, Sumru. (2014). How have researchers studied multiracial populations? A content and methodological review of 20 years of research. *Cultural Diversity and Ethnic Minority Psychology, 20,* 336–352.

Chavez, Mark, & Insel, Thomas R. (2007). Eating disorders: National Institute of Mental Health's perspective. *American Psychologist, 62,* 159–166.

Chavous, Tabbye M., Rivas-Drake, Deborah, Glover, Ciara S., Griffin, Tiffany, & Cogburn, Courtney D. (2008). Gender matters, too: The influences of school racial discrimination and racial identity on academic engagement outcomes among African American adolescents. *Developmental Psychology, 44,* 637–654.

Chen, Chi-Ling, Weiss, Noel S., Newcomb, Polly, Barlow, William, & White, Emily. (2002). Hormone replacement therapy in relation to breast cancer. *Journal of the American Medical Association, 287,* 734–741.

Chen, Fang Fang, & Russo, Nancy F. (2010). Measurement invariance and the role of body consciousness in depressive symptoms. *Psychology of Women Quarterly, 34,* 405–417.

Cherry, Frances, & Deaux, Kay. (1978). Fear of success versus fear of gender-inappropriate behavior. *Sex Roles, 4,* 97–102.

Cheryan, Sapna, Drury, Benjamin J., &Vichayapai, Marissa. (2013). Enduring influence of stereotypical computer science role models on women's academic aspirations. *Psychology of Women Quarterly, 37,* 72–79.

Cheryan, Sapna, Ziegler, Sianna A., Montoya, Amanda K., & Jiang, Lily. (2017).Why are some STEM fields more gender balanced than others? *Psychological Bulletin, 143,* 1–35.

Chesler, Phyllis. (1972). *Women and madness.* Garden City, NY: Doubleday.

Chiang, Mengchun. (2017). "You just know it's the only thing you can think": A conversation with Chodorow. *Women & Therapy, 40,* 308–322.

Children Now. (2000). Top-selling video games "unhealthy" for girls. Retrieved from http://www.childrennow.org

Chin, Jean L., De La Cancela, Victor, & Jenkins, Yvonne M. (1993). *Diversity in psychotherapy: The politics of race, ethnicity, and gender.* Westport, CT: Praeger.

Chiu, Y. H., Afeiche, M. C., Gaskins, A. J., Williams, P. L., Petrozza, J. C., Tanrikut, C., . . . Chavarro, J. E. (2015). Fruit and vegetable intake and their pesticide residues in relation to semen quality among men from a fertility clinic. *Human Reproduction, 30,* 1342–1351.

Chivers, Meredith L., Rieger, Gerulf, Latty, Elizabeth, & Bailey, J. Michael. (2004). A sex difference in the specificity of sexual arousal. *Psychological Science, 15,* 736–744.

Chivers, Meredith, Seto, Michael C., & Blanchard, Ray. (2007). Gender and sexual orientation differences in sexual response to the sexual activities versus the gender of actors in sexual films. *Journal of Personality and Social Psychology, 93,* 1108–1121.

Chivers, Meredith A., Seto, Michael C., Lalumière, Martin L., Laan, Ellen, & Grimbos, Teresa. (2010). Agreement of self-reported and genital measures of sexual arousal in men and women: A meta-analysis. *Archives of Sexual Behavior, 39,* 5–56.

Chodorow, Nancy. (1978). *The reproduction of mothering.* Berkeley: University of California Press.

Chodorow, Nancy J. (2013). Psychoanalysis and women: A personal thirty-five-year retrospect. *Annual of Psychoanalysis, 32,* 101–129.

Choi, Eun J., Ha, Chang M., Choi, Jungil, Kang, Sang S., Choi, Wan S., Park, Sang K., . . . Lee, Buyng J. (2001). Low-density DNA array-coupled to PCR differential display identifies new estrogen-responsive genes during the postnatal differentiation of the rat hypothalamus. *Molecular Brain Research, 97,* 115–128.

Chonody, Jill M., & Teater, Barbra. (2016). Why do I dread looking old? A test of social identity theory, terror management theory, and the double standard of aging. *Journal of Women & Aging, 28,* 112–126.

Chou, Tina, Asnaani, Anu, & Hofmann, Stefan G. (2012). Perception of racial discrimination and psychopathology across three U.S. ethnic minority groups. *Cultural Diversity and Ethnic Minority Psychology, 18,* 74–81.

Chrisler, Joan C., & Johnston-Robledo, Ingrid. (2002). Raging hormones? Feminist perspectives on premenstrual syndrome and postpartum depression. In M. Ballou & L. Brown (Eds.), *Rethinking mental health and disorder: Feminist perspectives* (pp. 174–197). New York, NY: Guilford.

Chyten-Brennan, Jules. (2014). Surgical transition. In L. Erickson-Schroth (Ed.), *Trans bodies, trans selves* (pp. 265–290). New York, NY: Oxford University Press.

Ciarrochi, Joseph, Hynes, Keiren, & Crittenden, Nadia. (2005). Can men do better if they try harder: Sex and motivational effects on emotional awareness. *Cognition and Emotion, 19,* 133–141.

Cicero, Theodore J., Ellis, Matthew S., Surratt, Hilary L., & Kurtz, Steven P. (2014). The changing face of heroin use in the United States: A retrospective analysis of the past 50 years. *JAMA Psychiatry, 71,* 821–826.

Clark, LeeAnn, Watson, David, & Mineka, Susan. (1994). Temperament, personality, and the mood and anxiety disorders. *Journal of Abnormal Psychology, 103,* 103–116.

Clemans, Katherine H., DeRose, Laura M., Graber, Julia A., & Brooks-Gunn, Jeanne. (2010). Gender in adolescence: Applying a person-in-context approach to gender identity and roles. In J. Chrisler & D. McCreary (Eds.), *Handbook of gender research in psychology* (Vol. 1, pp. 527–558). New York, NY: Springer.

Clemente, Carmine D. (1987). *Anatomy: A regional atlas of the human body* (3rd ed.). Baltimore, MD: Urban & Schwarzenberg.

Cochran, Susan D., Mays, Vickie M., Alegria, Magarita, Ortega, Alexander N., & Takeuchi, David. (2007). Mental health and substance use disorders among Latino and Asian American lesbian, gay, and bisexual adults. *Journal of Consulting and Clinical Psychology, 75,* 785–794.

Cochran, Susan D., Sullivan, J. Greer, & Mays, Vickie M. (2003). Prevalence of mental disorders, psychological distress, and mental health services use among lesbian, gay, and bisexual adults in the United States. *Journal of Consulting and Clinical Psychology, 71,* 53–61.

Cogan, Jeanine C., & Marcus-Newhall, Amy. (Eds.). (2002). Hate crimes: Research, policy, and action [Special issue]. *American Behavioral Scientist, 45*(12).

Cohen, Adam B. (2009). Many forms of culture. *American Psychologist, 64,* 194–204.

Cohen, David S. (2009). No boy left behind? Single-sex education and the essentialist myth of masculinity. *Indiana Law Journal, 84,* 135–187.

Cohen, Geoffrey L., Garcia, Julio, Apfel, Nancy, & Master, Allison. (2006). Reducing the racial achievement gap: A social-psychological intervention. *Science, 313,* 1307–1310.

Cohen, Jacob. (1969). *Statistical power analysis for the behavioral sciences.* New York, NY: Academic Press.

Coiro, Mary Jo. (2001). Depressive symptoms among women receiving welfare. *Women & Health, 32,* 1–23.

Coker, Ann L., Fisher, Bonnie S., Bush, Heather M., Swan, Suzanne C., Williams, Corrine M., Clear, Emily R., & DeGue, Sarah. (2015). Evaluation of the Green Dot bystander intervention to reduce interpersonal violence among college students across three campuses. *Violence Against Women, 21,* 1507–1527.

Coker, Ann L., Williams, Corrine M., Follingstad, Diane R., & Jordan, Carol E. (2011). Psychological, reproductive and maternal health, behavioral, and economic impact of intimate partner violence. In J. W. White, M. P. Koss, & A. E. Kazdin (Eds.), *Violence against women and children: Mapping the terrain* (Vol. 1, pp. 265–284). Washington, DC: American Psychological Association.

Colby, Ann, Kohlberg, Lawrence, Gibbs, John, Lieberman, Marcus, Fischer, Kurt, & Saltzstein, Herbert D. (1983). A longitudinal study of moral development. *Monographs of the Society for Research in Child Development, 48*(1/2), 1–124.

Colder, Craig R., Mott, Joshua A., & Berman, Arielle S. (2002). The interactive effects of infant activity level and fear on growth trajectories of early childhood behavior problems. *Development and Psychopathology, 14,* 1–23.

Cole, David A., Martin, Joan M., Peeke, Lachlan A., Seroczynski, A. D., & Fier, Jonathan. (1999). Children's over- and underestimation of academic competence: A longitudinal study of gender differences, depression, and anxiety. *Child Development, 70,* 459–473.

Cole, Elizabeth R. (2009). Intersectionality and research in psychology. *American Psychologist, 64,* 170–180.

Cole, Elizabeth R., & Stewart, Abigail J. (2001). Invidious comparisons: Imagining a psychology of race and gender beyond differences. *Political Psychology, 22,* 293–308.

Cole, Elizabeth R., & Zucker, Alyssa N. (2007). Black and White women's perspectives on femininity. *Cultural Diversity and Ethnic Minority Psychology, 13,* 1–9.

Cole, George F., Smith, Christopher E., & DeJong, Christina. (2015). *Criminal justice in America.* Boston, MA: Cengage Learning.

Coleman, Eli, Bockting, Walter, Botzer, Marsha, Cohen-Kettenis, Peggy T., De Cuypere, Griet, Fledman, Jamie L., . . . Zucker, Kenneth J. (2012). Standards of care for the health of transsexual, transgender, and gender-nonconforming people, version 7. *International Journal of Transgenderism, 13*(4), 165–232.

Collaborative Group on Hormonal Factors in Breast Cancer. (2002). Alcohol, tobacco and breast cancer: Collaborative reanalysis of individual data from 53 epidemiological studies, including 58,515 women with breast cancer and 95,067 women without the disease. *British Journal of Cancer, 87,* 1234–1245.

Collaer, Marcia L., & Hines, Melissa. (1995). Human behavioral sex differences: A role for gonadal hormones during early development? *Psychological Bulletin, 118,* 55–107.

College Board. (2010). *2010 college-bound seniors.* Retrieved from http://professionals.collegeboard.com

College Board. (2015). *2015 college-bound seniors: Total group profile report.* Retrieved from https://secure-media .collegeboard.org/digitalServices/pdf/sat/total-group-2015 .pdf

Collins, Lynn H. (2002). Alcohol and drug addiction in women: Phenomenology and prevention. In M. Ballou & L. Brown (Eds.), *Rethinking mental health and disorder: Feminist perspectives* (pp. 198–230). New York, NY: Guilford.

Collins, Patricia H. (1989). The social construction of Black feminist thought. *Signs: Journal of Women in Culture and Society, 14,* 745–773.

Coltrane, Scott, & Shih, Kristy Y. (2010). Gender and the division of labor. In J. Chrisler & D. McCreary (Eds.), *Handbook of gender research in psychology* (Vol. 2, pp. 401–422). New York, NY: Springer.

Comas-Diaz, Lillian. (1987). Feminist therapy with mainland Puerto Rican women. *Psychology of Women Quarterly, 11,* 461–474.

Comas-Diaz, Lillian. (1991). Feminism and diversity in psychology: The case of women of color. *Psychology of Women Quarterly, 15,* 597–610.

Comas-Diaz, Lillian. (2001). Hispanics, Latinos, or Americanos: The evolution of identity. *Cultural Diversity and Ethnic Minority Psychology, 7,* 115–120.

Comas-Diaz, Lillian. (2008). Spirita: Reclaiming womanist sacredness into feminism. *Psychology of Women Quarterly, 32,* 13–21.

Comas-Diaz, Lillian, & Greene, Beverly. (1994). *Women of color: Integrating ethnic and gender identities in psychotherapy.* New York, NY: Guilford.

Combahee River Collective. (1982). A Black feminist statement. In G. T. Hull, P. B. Scott, & B. Smith (Eds.), *All the women are White, all the Blacks are men, but some of us are brave* (pp. 13–22). Old Westbury, NY: Feminist Press.

Compas, Bruce E., & Luecken, Linda. (2002). Psychological adjustment to breast cancer. *Current Directions in Psychological Science, 11,* 111–114.

Condry, John, & Condry, Sandra. (1976). Sex differences: A study of the eye of the beholder. *Child Development, 47,* 812–819.

Confer, Jaime C., Easton, Judith A., Fleischman, Diana S., Goetz, Cari D., Lewis, David M. G., Perilloux, Carin, & Buss, David M. (2010). Evolutionary psychology: Controversies, questions, prospects, and limitations. *American Psychologist, 65,* 110–126.

Conkright, Lea, Flannagan, Dorothy, & Dykes, James. (2000). Effects of pronoun type and gender role consistency on children's recall and interpretation of stories. *Sex Roles, 43,* 481–498.

Conley, Terri D. (2010). Perceived proposed personality characteristics and gender differences in acceptance of casual sex offers. *Journal of Personality and Social Psychology, 100,* 309–329.

Constantinople, Anne. (1973). Masculinity-femininity: An exception to a famous dictum. *Psychological Bulletin, 80,* 389–407.

Conway, Francine, Hones, Samuel, & Speakes-Lewis, Amandia. (2011). Emotional strain in caregiving among African American grandmothers raising their grandchildren. *Journal of Women & Aging, 23,* 113–128.

Copen, Casey E., Chandra, Anjani, & Martinez, Gladys. (2012). *Prevalence and timing of oral sex with opposite sex partners among females and males aged 15 to 24 years* (National Health Statistics Report No. 56). Washington, DC: National Center on Health Statistics.

Corbett, Philip B. (2015, December 3). "Mx."? Did The Times adopt a new, gender-neutral courtesy title? *New York Times.*

Cordaro, Lucian, & Ison, James R. (1963). Psychology of the scientist: X. Observer bias in classical conditioning of the planarian. *Psychological Reports, 13,* 787–789.

Cordova, Matthew J., Cunningham, Lauren, Carlson, Charles, & Andrykowski, Michael. (2001). Posttraumatic growth following breast cancer: A controlled comparison study. *Health Psychology, 20,* 176–185.

Corral, Irma, & Landrine, Hope. (2010). Methodological and statistical issues in research with diverse samples: The problem of measurement equivalence. In H. Landrine & N. Russo (Eds.), *Handbook of diversity in feminist psychology* (pp. 83–134). New York, NY: Springer.

Correa-de-Araujo, Rosaly. (2016). Integrated health care for women of color with disabilities. In S. E. Miles-Cohen & C. Signore (Eds.), *Eliminating inequities for women with disabilities* (pp. 159–178). Washington, DC: American Psychological Association.

Corsi, Daniel J., Bassani, Diego G., Kumar, Rajesh, Awasthi, Shally, Jotkar, Raju, Kaur, Navkiran, & Jha, Prabhat. (2009). Gender inequity and age-appropriate immunization coverage in India from 1992 to 2006. *BMC International Health and Human Rights, 9*(Suppl. 1), S3.

Cortoni, Franca, Hanson, R. Karl, & Coache, Marie-Ève. (2010). The recidivism rates of female sexual offenders are low: A meta-analysis. *Sexual Abuse: Journal of Research and Treatment, 22,* 387–401.

Costello, Cynthia B., & Stone, Anne J. (Eds.). (2001). *The American woman 2001–2002: Getting to the top.* New York, NY: Norton.

Costello, Cynthia B., Wight, Vanessa R., & Stone, Anne J. (2003). *The American woman 2003–2004.* New York, NY: Palgrave/Macmillan.

Courtenay, Will H. (2000). Engendering health: A social constructionist examination of men's health beliefs and behaviors. *Psychology of Men and Masculinity, 1,* 4–15.

Cowell, Patricia E., Allen, Laura S., Zalatimo, Nadia S., & Denenberg, Victor H. (1992). A developmental study of sex and age interactions in the human corpus callosum. *Developmental Brain Research, 66,* 187–192.

Cox, William T. L., Devine, Patricia G., Bischmann, Alyssa A., & Hyde, Janet S. (2016). Inferences about sexual orientation: The roles of stereotypes, faces, and the gaydar myth. *Journal of Sex Research, 53,* 157–171.

Cralley, Elizabeth L., & Ruscher, Janet B. (2005). Lady, girl, female, or woman: Sexism and cognitive busyness predict use of gender-biased nouns. *Journal of Language and Social Psychology, 24,* 300–314.

Craske, Michelle G. (2003). *Origins of phobias and anxiety disorders: Why more women than men?* Oxford, UK: Elsevier.

Crawford, Mary. (2013). Meaning-making and feminist practice. *Psychology of Women Quarterly, 37,* 256–260.

Crawford, Mary. (2017). International sex trafficking. *Women & Therapy, 40,* 101–122.

Crawford, Mary, & English, Linda. (1984). Generic versus specific inclusion of women in language: Effects on recall. *Journal of Psycholinguistic Research, 13,* 373–381.

Crawford, Mary, & Kaufman, Michelle R. (2005). Sex differences versus social processes in the construction of gender. In K. Dindia & D. Canary (Eds.), *Sex differences and similarities in communication* (2nd ed., pp. 179–194). Mahwah, NJ: Lawrence Erlbaum.

Crawford, Mary, & Kimmel, Ellen. (1999). Promoting methodological diversity in feminist research. *Psychology of Women Quarterly, 23,* 1–6.

Crawford, Mary, & Popp, Danielle. (2003). Sexual double standards: A review and methodological critique of two decades of research. *Journal of Sex Research, 40,* 13–26.

Crenshaw, K. (1989). Demarginalizing the intersection of race and sex: A Black feminist critique of antidiscrimination doctrine, feminist theory and antiracist politics. *University of Chicago Legal Forum, 1989,* 139–167.

Crenshaw, K. (1991). Mapping the margins: Intersectionality, identity politics, and violence against women of color. *Stanford Law Review, 43,* 1241–1299.

Crick, Nicki R., & Grotpeter, Jennifer K. (1995). Relational aggression, gender, and social-psychological adjustment. *Child Development, 66,* 710–722.

Cromwell, Ronald E., & Ruiz, Rene A. (1979). The myth of macho dominance in decision making within Mexican and Chicano families. *Hispanic Journal of Behavioral Sciences, 1,* 355–373.

Crosby, Faye J., Iyer, Aarti, Clayton, Susan, & Downing, Roberta A. (2003). Affirmative action: Psychological data and the policy debates. *American Psychologist, 58,* 93–115.

Crosby, Faye J., Iyer, Aarti, & Sincharoen, Sirinda. (2006). Understanding affirmative action. *Annual Review of Psychology, 57,* 585–611.

Crose, Royda, Leventhal, Elaine A., Haug, Marie R., & Burns, Edith A. (1997). The challenges of aging. In S. Gallant, G. Keita, & R. Royak-Schaler (Eds.), *Health care for women: Psychological, social, and behavioral influences* (pp. 221–234). Washington, DC: American Psychological Association.

Cross, Catharine P., Copping, Lee T., & Campbell, Anne. (2011). Sex differences in impulsivity: A meta-analysis. *Psychological Bulletin, 137,* 97–130.

Crouter, Ann C., Manke, Beth A., & McHale, Susan M. (1995). The family context of gender intensification in early adolescence. *Child Development, 66,* 317–329.

Cui, Ming, Durtschi, Jared A., Donnellan, M. Brent, Lorenz, Frederick O., & Conger, Rand D. (2010). Intergenerational transmission of relationship aggression: A prospective longitudinal study. *Journal of Family Psychology, 24,* 688–697.

Cundiff, Jessica L. (2012). Is mainstream psychological research "womanless" and "raceless"? An updated analysis. *Sex Roles, 67,* 158–173.

Cutrona, Carolyn E., Russell, Daniel W., & Brown, P. Adama. (2005). Neighborhood context, personality, and stressful life events as predictors of depression among African American women. *Journal of Abnormal Psychology, 114,* 3–15.

Cvencek, Dario, Meltzoff, Andrew N., & Greenwald, Anthony G. (2011). Math-gender stereotypes in elementary school children. *Child Development, 82,* 766–779.

Daley, Ellen M., Perrin, Karen M., McDermott, Robert J., Vamos, Cheryl A., Rayko, Holly L., Packing-Ebuen, Jennifer L., . . . McFarlane, Mary. (2010). The psychosocial burden of HPV: A mixed-method study of knowledge, attitudes and behaviors among HPV+ women. *Journal of Health Psychology, 15,* 279–290.

Danaher, Kelly, & Crandall, Christian S. (2008). Stereotype threat in applied settings re-examined. *Journal of Applied Social Psychology, 38,* 1639–1655.

Danhauer, Suzanne C., Case, L. Douglas, Tedeschi, Richard, Russell, Greg, Vischnevsky, Tanya, Triplett, Kelli, . . . Avis, Nancy E. (2013). Predictors of posttraumatic growth in women with breast cancer. *Psychooncology, 22,* 2676–2683.

Daniels, Kimberly, Daugherty, Jill, & Jones, Jo. (2014). *Current contraceptive status among women aged 15–44: United States, 2011–2013* (NCHS Data Brief No. 173). Washington, DC: National Center for Health Statistics. Retrieved from http://www.cdc.gov/nchs/data/databriefs/db173.pdf

Dantzker, M. L., & Eisenman, Russell. (2003). Sexual attitudes among Hispanic college students: Differences between males and females. *International Journal of Adolescence & Youth, 11,* 79–89.

David, Henry P. (1992). Born unwanted: Long-term developmental effects of denied abortion. *Journal of Social Issues, 48*(3), 163–181.

David, Henry P., Dytrych, Zdenek, & Matejcek, Zdenek. (2003). Born unwanted: Observations from the Prague study. *American Psychologist, 58,* 224–229.

David, Henry P., Dytrych, Zdenek, Matejcek, Zdenek, & Schuller, Vratislav. (Eds.). (1988). *Born unwanted: Developmental effects of denied abortion.* New York, NY: Springer.

David, Henry P., & Matejcek, Zdenek. (1981). Children born to women denied abortion: An update. *Family Planning Perspectives, 13,* 32–34.

Davidson, Richard J., Jackson, Daren, & Kalin, Ned. (2000). Emotion, plasticity, context, and regulation: Perspectives from affective neuroscience. *Psychological Bulletin, 126,* 890–909.

Davidson, Richard J., & McEwen, Bruce S. (2012). Social influences on neuroplasticity: Stress and interventions to promote well-being. *Nature Neuroscience, 15,* 689–695.

Davis, Angela. (1981). *Women, race and class.* New York, NY: Random House.

Davis, Elizabeth Gould. (1971). *The first sex.* New York, NY: G. P. Putnam's Sons.

Davis, Mary C., Matthews, Karen A., & Twamley, Elizabeth W. (1999). Is life more difficult on Mars or Venus? A meta-analytic review of sex differences in major and minor life events. *Annals of Behavioral Medicine, 21,* 83–97.

Davis, Teresa L. (1995). Gender differences in masking negative emotions: Ability or motivation? *Developmental Psychology, 31,* 660–667.

Davison, Heather K., & Burke, Michael J. (2000). Sex discrimination in simulated employment contexts: A meta-analytic investigation. *Journal of Vocational Behavior, 56,* 225–248.

Davy, Zowie. (2015). The DSM-5 and the politics of diagnosis transpeople. *Archives of Sexual Behavior, 44,* 1165–1176.

Dawson, D. A., Grant, B. F., & Hartford, T. C. (1995). Variation in the association of alcohol consumption with five DSM-IV alcohol problem domains. *Alcoholism: Clinical and Experimental Research, 19,* 66–74.

de Beauvoir, Simone. (1952). *The second sex.* New York, NY: Knopf.

de Cadenet, A. (interviewer). (2016, January 12). Hillary Clinton exclusive interview. *The conversation with Amanda de Cadenet.* Los Angeles, CA: Lifetime Network Television.

De Cuypere, Griet, Sjoen, Guy T., Beerten, Ruth, Selvaggi, Gennaro, De Sutter, Petra, Hoebeke, Piet, . . . Rubens, Robert. (2005). Sexual and physical health after sex reassignment surgery. *Archives of Sexual Bheavior, 34,* 679–690.

de Jonge, A., Geerts, C. C., van der Goes, B. Y., Mol, B. W., Buitendijk, S. E., & Nijhuis, J. G. (2015). Perinatal mortality and morbidity up to 28 days after birth among 743,070 low-risk planned home and hospital births: A cohort study based on three merged national perinatal databases. *BJOG, 122,* 720–728.

de las Fuentes, Cynthia, Barón, Augustine, & Vasquez, Melba. (2003). Teaching Latino psychology. In P. Bronstein & K. Quina (Eds.), *Teaching gender and multicultural awareness* (pp. 201–220). Washington, DC: American Psychological Association.

de Lauretis, Teresa. (1991). Queer theory: Lesbian and gay sexualities, an introduction. *Differences, 3,* iii–xviii.

de Vries, Annelou L. C., McGuire, Jenifer K., Steensma, Thomas D., Wagenaar, Eva C. F., Doreleijers, Theo A. H., & Cohen-Kettenis, Peggy T. (2014). Young adult psychological outcome after puberty suppression and gender reassignment. *Pediatrics, 134,* 696–704.

Dean, Karol E., & Malamuth, Neil M. (1997). Characteristics of men who aggress sexually and of men who imagine aggressing: Risk and moderating variables. *Journal of Personality and Social Psychology, 72,* 449–455.

Deaux, Kay, & Emswiller, Tim. (1974). Explanations of successful performance on sex-linked tasks: What is skill for the male is luck for the female. *Journal of Personality and Social Psychology, 29,* 80–85.

Dedovic, Katarina, Wadiwalla, Mehereen, Engert, Veronika, & Pruessner, Jens C. (2009). The role of sex and gender socialization in stress reactivity. *Developmental Psychology, 45,* 45–55.

Delacoste-Utamsing, Christine, & Holloway, Ralph L. (1982). Sexual dimorphism in the human corpus callosum. *Science, 216,* 1431–1432.

DeLamater, John D., & Hyde, Janet S. (1998). Essentialism versus social constructionism in the study of human sexuality. *Journal of Sex Research, 35,* 10–18.

Delaney, Janice, Lupton, Mary Jane, & Toth, Emily. (1976). *The curse: A cultural history of menstruation.* New York, NY: Dutton.

Deligeoroglou, E. (2000). Dysmenorrhea. *Annals of the New York Academy of Sciences, 900,* 237–244.

DeLyser, Gail. (2012). At midlife, intentionally childfree women and their experiences of regret. *Clinical Social Work Journal, 40,* 66–74.

Denham, Susanne A., Bassett, Hideko H., & Wyatt, Todd M. (2010). Gender differences in the socialization of preschoolers' emotional competence. *New Directions for Child and Adolescent Development, 128,* 29–49.

Denmark, Florence L. (1993). Women, leadership, and empowerment. *Psychology of Women Quarterly, 17,* 343–356.

Denmark, Florence, Russo, Nancy F., Frieze, Irene H., & Sechzer, Jeri A. (1988). Guidelines for avoiding sexism in psychological research. *American Psychologist, 43,* 582–585.

Dennis, Jane A., Khan, Omer, Ferriter, Michael, Huband, Nick, Powney, Melanie J., & Duggan, Conor. (2012). Psychological interventions for adults who have sexually offended or are at risk of offending. *Cochrane Database of Systematic Reviews, 12,* CD007507.

Denzin, Norman K., & Lincoln, Yvonna S. (Eds.). (2005). *The SAGE handbook of qualitative research.* Thousand Oaks, CA: Sage.

Desmarais, Serge, & Curtis, James. (1997). Gender difference in pay histories and views on pay entitlement among university students. *Sex Roles, 37,* 623–642.

Deutsch, Francine M., LeBaron, Dorothy, & Fryer, Maury M. (1987). What is in a smile? *Psychology of Women Quarterly, 11,* 341–352.

Deutsch, Helene. (1944). *The psychology of women.* New York, NY: Grune & Stratton.

Deutsch, Maddie. (2014). Medical transition. In L. Erickson-Schroth (Ed.), *Trans bodies, trans selves* (pp. 241–264). New York, NY: Oxford University Press.

Deutsch, Madeline B. (2016). *Guidelines for the primary and gender-affirming care of transgender and gender nonbinary people* (2nd ed.). San Francisco, CA: Center of Excellence for Transgender Health.

Devries, Karen M., Mak, Joelle Y. T., García-Moreno, Claudia, Petzold, Max, Child, J. C., Falder, G., . . . Watts, Charlotte H. (2013). The global prevalence of intimate partner violence against women. *Science, 340,* 1527–1528.

Dey, Judy G., & Hill, Catherine. (2007). *Beyond the pay gap.* Washington, DC: AAUW Educational Foundation.

DeZolt, Denise, & Hull, Stephen. (2001). Classroom and school climate. In J. Worell (Ed.), *Encyclopedia of gender* (pp. 246–264). San Diego, CA: Academic Press.

Diamond, Lisa M. (2005). A new view of lesbian subtypes: Stable versus fluid identity trajectories over an 8-year period. *Psychology of Women Quarterly, 29,* 119–128.

Diamond, Lisa M. (2008a). Female bisexuality from adolescence to adulthood: Results from a 10-year longitudinal study. *Developmental Psychology, 44,* 5–14.

Diamond, Lisa M. (2008b). *Sexual fluidity.* Cambridge, MA: Harvard University Press.

dickey, lore m., Ducheny, Kelly M., & Ehrbar, Randall D. (2016). Family creation options for transgender and gender nonconforming people. *Psychology of Sexual Orientation and Gender Diversity, 3,* 173–179.

dickey, lore m., Hendricks, Michael L., & Bockting, Walter O. (2016). Innovations in research with transgender and gender nonconforming people and their communities. *Psychology of Sexual Orientation and Gender Diversity, 3,* 187–194.

Dickson, Lynda. (1993). The future of marriage and the family in Black America. *Journal of Black Studies, 23,* 472–491.

Diehm, Cynthia, & Ross, Margo. (1988). Battered women. In S. Rix (Ed.), *The American woman 1988–89.* New York, NY: Norton.

Diekman, Amanda B., & Murnen, Sarah K. (2004). Learning to be little women and little men: The inequitable gender equality of nonsexist children's literature. *Sex Roles, 50,* 373–386.

Diemer, Matthew A. (2002). Constructions of provider role identity among African American men: An exploratory study. *Cultural Diversity and Ethnic Minority Psychology, 8,* 30–40.

Dill, Karen E., Gentile, Douglas A., Richter, William A., & Dill, Jody C. (2005). Violence, sex, race, and age in popular video games: A content analysis. In E. Cole & J. H. Daniel (Eds.), *Featuring females: Feminist analyses of media* (pp. 115–130). Washington, DC: American Psychological Association.

Dillon, Sam. (2005, January 18). Harvard chief defends his talk on women. *New York Times.*

Dines, Gail. (2010). *Pornland: How porn has hijacked our sexuality.* Boston, MA: Beacon Press.

Dines, Gail. (2015, October 22). Why your father's Playboy can't compete in today's world of hard-core porn. *The Conversation.*

Dittmar, Helga, Halliwell, Emma, & Ive, Suzanne. (2006). Does Barbie make girls want to be thin? The effect of experimental exposure to images of dolls on the body image of 5- to 8-year-old girls. *Developmental Psychology, 42,* 283–292.

Division 44/Committee on Lesbian, Gay, and Bisexual Concerns. (2000). Guidelines for psychotherapy with lesbian, gay, and bisexual clients. *American Psychologist, 55,* 1440–1451.

Dohm, Faith-Anne, Brown, Melanie, Cachelin, Fary M., & Striegel-Moore, Ruth H. (2010). Ethnicity, disordered eating, and body image. In H. Landrine & N. Russo (Eds.), *Handbook of diversity in feminist psychology* (pp. 285–309). New York, NY: Springer.

Dolance, Susannah. (2005). "A whole stadium full": Lesbian community at Women's National Basketball Association games. *Journal of Sex Research, 42,* 74–83.

Dorgan, Joanne F., Baer, David J., Albert, Paul S., Judd, Joseph T., Brown, Ellen D., Corle, Donald D., . . . Taylor, Philip R. (2001). Serum hormones and the alcohol–breast cancer association in postmenopausal women. *Journal of the National Cancer Institute, 93,* 710–715.

Douglas, Karen M., & Sutton, Robbie M. (2014). "A giant leap for mankind" but what about women? The role of system-justifying ideologies in predicting attitudes toward sexist language. *Journal of Language and Social Psychology, 33,* 667–680.

Douglas, Susan J., & Michaels, Meredith W. (2004). *The mommy myth: The idealization of motherhood and how it has undermined all women.* New York, NY: Free Press.

Douvan, Elizabeth. (1970). New sources of conflicts in females at adolescence and early adulthood. In J. Bardwick, E. Douvan, M. Horner, & D. Gutman (Eds.), *Feminine personality and conflict* (pp. 31–43). Belmont, CA: Brooks/Cole.

Douvan, Elizabeth, & Adelson, Joseph. (1966). *The adolescent experience.* New York, NY: Wiley.

Dovidio, John F., Ellyson, Steve L., Keating, Caroline F., Heltman, Karen, & Brown, Clifford E. (1988). The relationship of social power to visual displays of dominance between men and women. *Journal of Personality and Social Psychology, 54,* 233–242.

Downey, Jennifer, Ehrhardt, Anke A., Schiffman, Mindy, Dyrenfuth, Inge, & Becker, J. (1987). Sex hormones in lesbian and heterosexual women. *Hormones and Behavior, 21,* 347–357.

Doyle, James A. (1989). *The male experience* (2nd ed.). Dubuque, IA: William C. Brown.

Doyle, Randi A., & Voyer, Daniel. (2016). Stereotype manipulation effects on math and spatial test performance: A meta-analysis. *Learning and Individual Differences, 47,* 103–116.

Drummond, Kelley D., Bradley, Susan J., Peterson-Badaali, Michele, & Zucker, Kenneth J. (2008). A follow-up study of girls with gender identity disorder. *Developmental Psychology, 44,* 34–45.

Dube, Shanta R., Anda, Robert F., Felitti, Vincent J., Edwards, Valerie J., & Croft, Janet B. (2002). Adverse childhood experiences and personal alcohol abuse as an adult. *Addictive Behaviors, 27,* 713–725.

Dube, Shanta R., Felitti, Vincent J., Dong, Maxia, Chapman, Daniel P., Giles, Wayne H., & Anda, Robert F. (2003). Childhood abuse, neglect, and household dysfunction and the risk of illicit drug use: The Adverse Childhood Experiences Study. *Pediatrics, 111,* 564–572.

DuBois, Cathy L. A., Knappe, Deborah E., Faley, Robert H., & Kustis, Gary A. (1998). An empirical examination of same- and other-gender sexual harassment in the workplace. *Sex Roles, 39,* 731–750.

Dugger, Karen. (1988). Social location and gender-role attitudes: A comparison of Black and White women. *Gender & Society, 2,* 425–448.

Dumond, Val. (2014). *S-H-E-I-T: A no-nonsense guide to writing and using nonsexist language.* Lakewood, WA: Val Dumond.

Dunn, Judith, Bretherton, Inge, & Munn, Penny. (1987). Conversations about feeling states between mothers and their children. *Developmental Psychology, 23,* 132–139.

Dunne, Eileen F., Unger, Elizabeth R., Sternberg, Maya, McQuillan, Geraldine, Swan, David C., Patel, Sonya S., & Markowitz, Lauri E. (2007). Prevalence of HPV infection among females in the United States. *Journal of the American Medical Association, 297,* 813–819.

Dunsmore, Julie C., Her, Pa, Halberstadt, Amy G., & Perez-Rivera, Marie B. (2009). Parents' beliefs about emotions and children's recognition of parents' emotions. *Journal of Nonverbal Behavior, 33,* 121–140.

Durik, Amanda M., Hyde, Janet S., Marks, Amanda C., Roy, Amanda L., Anaya, Debra, & Schultz, Gretchen. (2006). Ethnicity and gender stereotypes of emotion. *Sex Roles, 54,* 429–445.

Dutton, Mary Ann, & Goodman, Lisa A. (2005). Coercion in intimate partner violence: Toward a new conceptualization. *Sex Roles, 52,* 743–756.

Dweck, Carol, Goetz, Therese E., & Strauss, Nan L. (1980). Sex differences in learned helplessness: IV. An experimental and naturalistic study of failure generalization and its mediators. *Journal of Personality and Social Psychology, 38,* 441–452.

Dworkin, Andrea. (1987). *Intercourse.* New York, NY: Free Press.

Dye, Jane L. (2010). *Fertility of American women: 2008.* Washington, DC: U.S. Census Bureau.

Eagly, Alice H. (2009). The his and hers of prosocial behavior: An examination of the social psychology of gender. *American Psychologist, 64,* 644–658.

Eagly, Alice H., & Carli, Linda. (2007). *Through the labyrinth: The truth about how women become leaders.* Boston, MA: Harvard Business School Press.

Eagly, Alice H., & Crowley, Maureen. (1986). Gender and helping behavior: A meta-analytic review of the social psychological literature. *Psychological Bulletin, 100,* 283–308.

Eagly, Alice H., Eaton, Asia, Rose, Suzanna M., Riger, Stephanie, & McHugh, Maureen C. (2012). Feminism and psychology: Analysis of a half-century of research on women and gender. *American Psychologist, 67*, 211–230.

Eagly, Alice H., Johannesen-Schmidt, Mary C., & van Engen, Marloes L. (2003). Transformational, transactional, and laissez-faire leadership styles: A meta-analysis comparing women and men. *Psychological Bulletin, 129*, 569–591.

Eagly, Alice H., & Johnson, Blair T. (1990). Gender and leadership style. *Psychological Bulletin, 108*, 233–256.

Eagly, Alice H., & Karau, Steven J. (2002). Role congruity theory of prejudice toward female leaders. *Psychological Review, 109*, 573–598.

Eagly, Alice H., Karau, Steven, & Makhijani, Mona. (1995). Gender and the effectiveness of leaders: A meta-analysis. *Psychological Bulletin, 117*, 125–145.

Eagly, Alice H., Makhijani, Mona G., & Klonsky, Bruce G. (1992). Gender and the evaluation of leaders: A meta-analysis. *Psychological Bulletin, 111*, 3–22.

Eagly, Alice H., & Riger, Stephanie. (2014). Feminism and psychology: Critiques of methods and epistemology. *American Psychologist, 69*, 685–702.

Eagly, Alice H., & Wood, Wendy. (1999). The origins of sex differences in human behavior: Evolved dispositions versus social roles. *American Psychologist, 54*, 408–423.

Eagly, Alice H., & Wood, Wendy. (2011). Feminism and the evolution of sex differences and similarities. *Sex Roles, 64*, 759–767.

Eastwick, Paul W., Luchies, Laura B., Finkel, Eli J., & Hunt, Lucy L. (2014). The predictive validity of ideal partner preferences: A review and meta-analysis. *Psychological Bulletin, 140*, 623–665.

Eaton, Warren O., & Enns, Lesley R. (1986). Sex differences in human motor activity level. *Psychological Bulletin, 100*, 19–28.

Eccles, Jacquelynne S. (1994). Understanding women's educational and occupational choices: Applying the Eccles et al. model of achievement-related choices. *Psychology of Women Quarterly, 18*, 585–610.

Eccles, Jacquelynne S., Vida, Mina, & Barber, Bonnie. (2004). The relation of early adolescents' college plans and both academic ability and task-value beliefs to subsequent college enrollment. *Journal of Early Adolescence, 24*, 63–77.

Edwards, David A. (1969). Early androgen stimulation and aggressive behavior in male and female mice. *Physiology and Behavior, 4*, 333–338.

Edwards, Katie M., Turchik, Jessica A., Dardis, Christina M., Reynolds, Nicole, & Gidycz, Christine A. (2011). Rape myths: History, individual and institutional-level presence, and implications for change. *Sex Roles, 65*, 761–773.

Edwards-Leeper, Laura, Liebowitz, Scott, & Sangganjanavanich, Varunee F. (2016). Affirmative practice with transgender and gender nonconforming youth: Expanding the model. *Psychology of Sexual Orientation and Gender Diversity, 3*, 165–172.

Ehrensaft, Miriam K., Cohen, Patricia, Brown, Jocelyn, Smailes, Elizabeth, Chen, Henian, & Johnson, Jeffrey G. (2003). Intergenerational transmission of partner violence: A 20-year prospective study. *Journal of Consulting and Clinical Psychology, 73*, 741–753.

Eichenbaum, Luise, & Orbach, Susie. (1983). *Understanding women: A feminist psychoanalytic approach.* New York, NY: Basic Books.

Eisele, Heather, & Stake, Jayne. (2008). The differential relationship of feminist attitudes and feminist identity to self-efficacy. *Psychology of Women Quarterly, 32*, 233–244.

Eisenberg, Nancy, Cumberland, Amanda, & Spinrad, Tracy L. (1998). Parental socialization of emotion. *Psychological Inquiry, 9*, 241–273.

Eisenberg, Nancy, & Lennon, Randy. (1983). Sex differences in empathy and related capacities. *Psychological Bulletin, 94*, 100–131.

Eisenstein, Zilla R. (1982). The sexual politics of the New Right: Understanding the "crisis of liberalism" for the 1980s. In N. O. Keohane, M. Z. Rosaldo, & B. C. Gelpi (Eds.), *Feminist theory: A critique of ideology* (pp. 567–588). Chicago, IL: University of Chicago Press.

Ekman, Paul, & Oster, Harriet. (1979). Facial expressions of emotion. *Annual Review of Psychology, 30*, 527–554.

Elam-Evans, Laurie D., Yankey, David, Jeyarajah, Jenny, Singleton, James A., Curtis, C. Robinette, MacNeil, Jessica, & Hariri, Susan. (2014). National, regional, state, and selected local area vaccination coverage among adolescents aged 13–17 years—United States, 2013. *Morbidity & Mortality Weekly Report, 63*(29), 625–633.

El-Guebaly, Nady. (1995). Alcohol and polysubstance abuse among women. *Canadian Journal of Psychiatry, 40*, 73–79.

Eliot, Lise. (2009). *Pink brain, blue brain: How small differences grow into troublesome gaps—and what we can do about it.* Boston, MA: Houghton Mifflin.

Elliott, Diana M. (1997). Traumatic events: Prevalence and delayed recall in the general population. *Journal of Consulting and Clinical Psychology, 65*, 811–820.

Elliott, Diana B., & Simmons, T. (2011). *Marital events of Americans: 2009.* Washington, DC: U.S. Department of Commerce.

Else-Quest, Nicole M. (2012). Gender differences in temperament. In M. Zentner & R. Shiner (Eds.), *Handbook of temperament* (pp. 479–496). New York, NY: Guilford.

Else-Quest, Nicole M., & Hamilton, V. (2018). Measurement and analysis of nation-level gender equity in the psychology of women. In C. B. Travis & J. W. White (Eds.), *Handbook of the psychology of women*. Washington, DC: American Psychological Association.

Else-Quest, Nicole M., Higgins, Ashley, Allison, Carlie, & Morton, Lindsay C. (2012). Gender differences in self-conscious emotional experience: A meta-analysis. *Psychological Bulletin, 138*, 947–981.

Else-Quest, Nicole M., & Hyde, Janet S. (2016). Intersectionality in quantitative psychological research: I. Theoretical and epistemological issues. *Psychology of Women Quarterly, 40*, 155–170.

Else-Quest, Nicole M., Hyde, Janet S., Goldsmith, H. Hill, & Van Hulle, Carol A. (2006). Gender differences in temperament: A meta-analysis. *Psychological Bulletin, 132*, 33–72.

Else-Quest, Nicole M., Hyde, Janet S., & Linn, Marcia C. (2010). Cross-national patterns of gender differences in mathematics: A meta-analysis. *Psychological Bulletin, 136*, 103–127.

Else-Quest, Nicole, Mineo, Concetta C., & Higgins, Ashley. (2013). Math and science attitudes and achievement at the intersection of gender and ethnicity. *Psychology of Women Quarterly, 37*, 293–309.

Else-Quest, Nicole M., & Morse, Emily. (2015). Ethnic variations in parental ethnic socialization and adolescent ethnic identity: A longitudinal study. *Cultural Diversity and Ethnic Minority Psychology, 21*, 54–64.

Enns, Carolyn Z. (2004). *Feminist theories and feminist psychotherapies* (2nd ed.). New York, NY: Haworth.

Enns, Carolyn Z., & Byars-Winston, Angela M. (2010). Multicultural feminist therapy. In H. Landrine & N. Russo (Eds.), *Handbook of diversity in feminist psychology* (pp. 367–390). New York, NY: Springer.

Enns, Carolyn Z., & Sinacore, Ada. (2001). Feminist theories. In J. Worell (Ed.), *Encyclopedia of women and gender* (pp. 469–480). San Diego, CA: Academic Press.

Enserink, Martin. (2002). The vanishing promises of hormone replacement. *Science, 297*, 325–326.

Epperson, C. Neill, Steiner, Meir, Hartlage, S. Ann, Eriksson, Elias, Schmidt, Peter J., Jones, Ian, & Yonkers, Kimberly A. (2012). Premenstrual dysphoric disorder: Evidence for a new category for DSM-5. *American Journal of Psychiatry, 169*, 465–475.

Epstein, Marina, & Ward, L. Monique. (2011). Exploring parent-adolescent communication about gender: Results from adolescent and emerging adult samples. *Sex Roles, 65*, 108–118.

Erikson, Erik H. (1950). *Childhood and society*. New York, NY: Norton.

Espín, Oliva M. (1987a). Issues of identity in the psychology of Latina lesbians. In Boston Lesbian Psychologies Collective, *Lesbian psychologies* (pp. 35–55). Urbana: University of Illinois Press.

Espín, Oliva M. (1987b). Psychological impact of migration on Latinas: Implications for psychotherapeutic practice. *Psychology of Women Quarterly, 11*, 489–504.

Espín, Oliva M. (1993). Issues of identity in the psychology of Latina lesbians. In L. D. Garnets & D. C. Kimmel (Eds.), *Psychological perspectives on lesbian and gay male experiences* (pp. 348–363). New York, NY: Columbia University Press.

Etaugh, Claire. (1993). Women in the middle and later years. In F. L. Denmark & M. A. Paludi (Eds.), *Psychology of women: Handbook of issues and theories* (pp. 213–246). Westport, CT: Greenwood.

Etowa, Josephine, Beagan, Brenda L., Eghan, Felicia, & Bernard, Wanda T. (2017). "You feel you have to be made of steel": The strong Black woman, health and wellbeing in Nova Scotia. *Health Care for Women International, 38*, 379–393.

Everitt, Barry J., & Bancroft, John. (1991). Of rats and men: The comparative approach to male sexuality. *Annual Review of Sex Research, 2*, 77–118.

Evers, Andrea, & Sieverding, Monika. (2014). Why do highly qualified women (still) earn less? Gender differences in long-term predictors of career success. *Psychology of Women Quarterly, 38*, 93–106.

Fabes, Richard A., Martin, Carol L., & Hanish, Laura D. (2003). Young children's play qualities in same-, other-, and mixed-sex peer groups. *Child Development, 74*, 921–932.

Factor, Rhonda J., & Rothblum, Esther D. (2007). A study of transgender adults and their non-transgender siblings on demographic characteristics, social support and experiences of violence. *Journal of LGBT Health Research, 3*, 11–30.

Fagot, Beverly I., Rodgers, Carie S., & Leinbach, Mary D. (2000). Theories of gender socialization. T. Eckes & H. Trautner (Eds.), *The developmental social psychology of gender* (pp. 65–90). Mahwah, NJ: Lawrence Erlbaum.

Fairburn, Christopher G., Cooper, Zafra, Doll, Helen A., & Welch, Sarah L. (1999). Risk factors for anorexia nervosa. *Archives of General Psychiatry, 56*, 468–476.

Fairburn, Christopher G., Welch, Sarah L., Doll, Helen A., Davies, Beverly A., & O'Connor, Marianne E. (1997). Risk factors for bulimia nervosa: A community-based case-control study. *Archives of General Psychiatry, 54*, 509–517.

Fairchild, Halford H., Whitten, Lisa, & Richard, Harriette. (2003). Teaching African American psychology. In P. Bronstein & K. Quina (Eds.), *Teaching gender and multicultural awareness* (pp. 195–200). Washington, DC: American Psychological Association.

Falk, Patricia J. (1993). Lesbian mothers: Psychosocial assumptions in family law. In L. D. Garnets & D. C. Kimmel (Eds.), *Psychological perspectives on lesbian and gay male experience* (pp. 420–436). New York, NY: Columbia University Press.

Fallows, Deborah. (2005). *How women and men use the Internet.* Washington, DC: Pew Research Center. Retrieved from http://www.pewinternet.org

Faludi, Susan. (1991). *Backlash: The undeclared war against American women.* New York, NY: Anchor Books/Doubleday.

Faludi, Susan. (1999). *Stiffed: The betrayal of the American man.* New York, NY: HarperCollins.

Faludi, Susan. (2001, January 8). Don't get the wrong message. *Newsweek.*

Faludi, Susan. (2006). *Backlash: The undeclared war against American women* (15th anniv. ed.). New York, NY: Three Rivers Press.

Farmer, Melissa A., & Meston, Cindy M. (2007). Predictors of genital pain in young women. *Archives of Sexual Behaviors, 36,* 831–843.

Farr, Rachel H. (2017). Does parental sexual orientation matter? A longitudinal follow-up of adoptive families with school-age children. *Developmental Psychology, 53,* 252–264.

Farr, Rachel H., Forssell, Stephen L., & Patterson, Charlotte J. (2010). Parenting and child development in adoptive families: Does parental sexual orientation matter? *Applied Developmental Science, 14,* 164–178.

Farr, Rachel H., & Patterson, Charlotte J. (2013). Coparenting among lesbian, gay, and heterosexual couples: Associations with adopted children's outcomes. *Child Development, 84,* 1226–1240.

Farrow, Ronan. (2017, October 10). From aggressive overtures to sexual assault: Harvey Weinstein's accusers tell their stories. *New Yorker.* Retrieved from newyorker.com

Fassinger, Ruth E., & Israel, Tania. (2010). Sanctioning sexuality within cultural contexts: Same-sex relationships for women of color. In H. Landrine & N. Russo (Eds.), *Handbook of diversity in feminist psychology* (pp. 211–232). New York, NY: Springer.

Fasteau, M. F. (1974). *The male machine.* New York, NY: McGraw-Hill.

Fasula, Amy M., Carry, Monique, & Miller, Kim S. (2014). A multidimensional framework for the meanings of the sexual double standard and its application for the sexual health of young Black women in the U.S. *Journal of Sex Research, 51,* 170–183.

Fausto-Sterling, Anne. (1992). *Myths of gender* (2nd ed.). New York, NY: Basic Books.

Fausto-Sterling, Anne. (1993, October). Sex, race, brains, and calipers. *Discover, 14*(10), 32–37.

Fausto-Sterling, Anne. (2000). *Sexing the body: Gender politics and the construction of sexuality.* New York, NY: Basic Books.

Fausto-Sterling, Anne, Crews, David, Sung, Jihyun, García-Coll, Cynthia, & Seifer, Ronald. (2015). Multimodal sex-related differences in infant and in infant-directed maternal behaviors during months three through twelve of development. *Developmental Psychology, 51,* 1351–1366.

Federal Bureau of Investigation. (2001). Murder and non-negligent manslaughter. Retrieved from http://www.fbi.gov

Federal Bureau of Investigation. (2014). Crime in the United States by community type, 2014. Retrieved from https://ucr.fbi.gov/crime-in-the-u.s/2014/crime-in-the-u.s.-2014/tables/table-2

Feild, Hubert S. (1978). Attitudes toward rape: A comparative analysis of police, rapists, crisis counselors, and citizens. *Journal of Personality and Social Psychology, 36,* 156–179.

Feingold, Alan. (1995). Gender differences in personality: A meta-analysis. *Psychological Bulletin, 116,* 429–456.

Feingold, Alan, & Mazella, Ronald. (1998). Gender differences in body image are increasing. *Psychological Science, 9,* 190–195.

Feiring, Candice, Simon, Valerie A., & Cleland, Charles M. (2009). Childhood sexual abuse, stigmatization, internalizing symptoms, and the development of sexual difficulties and dating aggression. *Journal of Consulting and Clinical Psychology, 77,* 127–137.

Feng, Jing, Spence, Ian, & Pratt, Jay. (2007). Playing an action video game reduces gender differences in spatial cognition. *Psychological Science, 18,* 850–855.

Ferguson, Roderick A. (2004). *Aberrations in black: Toward a queer of color critique.* Minneapolis: University of Minnesota Press.

Fergusson, David M., Boden, Joseph M., & Horwood, L. John. (2008). Neonatal circumcision: Effects on breastfeeding and outcomes associated with breastfeeding. *Journal of Paediatrics and Child Health, 44,* 44–49.

Ferreira, Leandro, Santos-Galduróz, Ruth F., Ferri, Cleusa P., & Galduróz, Jose C. F. (2014). Rate of cognitive decline in relation to sex after 60 years-of-age: A systematic review. *Geriatrics & Gerontology International, 14,* 23–31.

Fidas, Deena, & Cooper, Liz. (2015). *The cost of the closet and the rewards of inclusion: Why the workplace environment for LGBT people matters to employers.* Washington, DC: Human Rights Campaign Foundation.

Field, Nigel P., Myong, Sophear, & Sochanvimean, Vannavuth. (2013). Parental styles in the intergenerational transmission of trauma stemming from the Khmer Rouge regime in Cambodia. *American Journal of Orthopsychiatry, 83,* 483–494.

Field, Nigel P., Om, Chariya, Kim, Thida, & Vorn, Sin. (2011). Second generation effects of genocide stemming from the Khmer Rouge regime in Cambodia: An attachment perspective. *Attachment and Human Development, 13,* 611–628.

Fields, Jason, & Casper, Lynne. (2001). *America's families and living arrangements.* Washington, DC: U.S. Census Bureau.

Fine, Cordelia. (2008). Will working mothers' brains explode? The popular new genre of neurosexism. *Neuroethics, 1,* 69–72.

Fine, Cordelia. (2017). *Testosterone rex: Myths of sex, science, and society.* New York, NY: Norton.

Fine, Michelle. (1988). Sexuality, schooling, and adolescent females: The missing discourse of desire. *Harvard Educational Review, 58,* 29–53.

Fine, Reuben. (1990). Anna Freud (1895–1982). In A. N. O'Connell & N. F. Russo (Eds.), *Women in psychology: A bio-bibliographical sourcebook* (pp. 96–103). Westport, CT: Greenwood Press.

Finer, Lawrence B., & Zolna, Mia R. (2016). Declines in unintended pregnancy in the United States, 2008–2011. *New England Journal of Medicine, 374,* 843–852.

Fingerhut, Adam W., Peplau, L. Anne, & Ghavami, Negin. (2005). A dual-identity framework for understanding lesbian experience. *Psychology of Women Quarterly, 29,* 129–139.

Finkelhor, David. (1984). *Child sexual abuse: New theory and research.* New York, NY: Free Press.

Firestone, Shulamith. (1970). *The dialectic of sex.* New York, NY: Bantam.

Fischer, Agneta H., & LaFrance, Marianne. (2015). What drives the smile and the tear: Why women are more emotionally expressive than men. *Emotion Review, 7,* 22–29.

Fischer, Agneta H., & Manstead, Anthony. (2000). The relation between gender and emotions in different cultures. In A. Fischer (Ed.), *Gender and emotion* (pp. 71–94). Cambridge, UK: Cambridge University Press.

Fischer, Agneta H., Rodriguez Mosquera, Patricia M., van Vianen, Annelies E. M., & Manstead, Antony S. R. (2004). Gender and culture differences in emotion. *Emotion, 4,* 87–94.

Fischer, Ann R., Tokar, David M., Good, Glenn E., & Snell, Andrea F. (1998). More on the structure of male role norms. *Psychology of Women Quarterly, 22,* 135–155.

Fisher, Bonnie S., Daigle, Leah E., & Cullen, Francis T. (2010). *Unsafe in the ivory tower: The sexual victimization of college women.* Thousand Oaks, CA: Sage.

Fisher, Maryanne L., Garcia, Justin R., & Sokol Chang, Rosmarie. (Eds.). (2013). *Evolution's empress: Darwinian perspectives on the nature of women.* New York, NY: Oxford University Press.

Fisher, Terri D. (2007). Sex of experimenter and social norm effects on reports of sexual behavior in young men and women. *Archives of Sexual Behavior, 36,* 89–100.

Fiske, Susan T. (1993). Controlling other people: The impact of power on stereotyping. *American Psychologist, 48,* 621–628.

Fiske, Susan T. (2010). Venus and Mars or down to earth: Stereotypes and realities of gender differences. *Perspectives on Psychological Science, 5,* 688–692.

Fisman, Raymond, Iyengar, Sheena S., Kamenica, Emir, & Simonson, Itamor. (2008). Racial preferences in dating. *Review of Economic Studies, 75,* 117–132.

Fitch, Roslyn H., & Bimonte, Heather A. (2002). Hormones, brain, and behavior: Putative biological contributions to cognitive sex differences. In A. McGillicuddy-De Lisi & R. De Lisi (Eds.), *Biology, society, and behavior: The development of sex differences in cognition* (pp. 55–92). Westport, CT: Ablex.

Fite, Jennifer E., Bates, John E., Holtzworth-Munroe, Amy, Dodge, Kenneth A., Nay, Sandra Y., & Pettit, Gregory S. (2008). Social information processing mediates the intergenerational transmission of aggressiveness in romantic relationships. *Journal of Family Psychology, 22,* 367–376.

Fitzgerald, Louise F., Weitzman, Lauren M., Gold, Yael, & Ormerod, Mimi. (1988). Academic harassment: Sex and denial in scholarly garb. *Psychology of Women Quarterly, 12,* 329–340.

Fivush, Robyn. (1989). Exploring sex differences in the emotional content of mother-child conversations about the past. *Sex Roles, 20,* 675–692.

Fivush, Robyn, Brotman, Melissa A., Buckner, Janine P., & Goodman, Sheryl H. (2000). Gender differences in parent–child emotion narratives. *Sex Roles, 42,* 233–253.

Fivush, Robyn, & Buckner, Janine P. (2000). Gender, sadness, and depression: The development of emotional focus through gendered discourse. In A. H. Fischer (Ed.), *Gender and emotion: Social psychological perspectives* (pp. 232–253). Cambridge, UK: Cambridge University Press.

Fivush, Robyn, & Zaman, Widaad. (2015). Gendered narrative voices: Sociocultural and feminist approaches to emerging identity in childhood and adolescence. In K. C. McLean & M. Syed (Eds.), *Oxford handbook of identity development* (pp. 33–52). New York, NY: Oxford.

Flannagan, Dorothy, & Perese, San. (1998). Emotional references in mother-daughter and mother-son dyads' conversations about school. *Sex Roles, 39*, 353–368.

Flouri, Eirini, & Buchanan, Ann. (2002). What predicts good relationships with parents in adolescence and partners in adult life: Findings from the 1958 British Birth Cohort. *Journal of Family Psychology, 16*, 186–198.

Foa, Edna B., Dancu, Constance V., Hembree, Elizabeth A., Jaycox, Lisa H., Meadows, Elizabeth A., & Street, Gordon P. (1999). A comparison of exposure therapy, stress inoculation training, and their combination for reducing posttraumatic stress disorder in female assault victims. *Journal of Consulting and Clinical Psychology, 67*, 194–200.

Foa, Edna B., Steketee, Gail, & Olasov, Barbara. (1989). Behavioral/cognitive conceptualizations of post-traumatic stress disorder. *Behavior Therapy, 20*, 155–176.

Foertsch, Julie, & Gernsbacher, Morton Ann. (1997). In search of gender neutrality: Is singular *they* a cognitively efficient substitute for generic *he*? *Psychological Science, 9*, 106–111.

Ford, Maureen R., & Widiger, Thomas A. (1989). Sex bias in the diagnosis of histrionic and antisocial personality disorders. *Journal of Consulting and Clinical Psychology, 57*, 301–305.

Forgays, Deborah K., Hyman, Ira, & Schreiber, Jesse. (2014). Texting everywhere for everything: Gender and age differences in cell phone etiquette and use. *Computers in Human Behavior, 31*, 314–321.

Foucault, Michel. (1978). *The history of sexuality: Vol. 1. An introduction* (R. Hurley, Trans.). New York, NY: Pantheon.

Fox, Jesse, & Potocki, B. (2016). Lifetime video game consumption, interpersonal aggression, hostile sexism, and rape myth acceptance: A cultivation perspective. *Journal of Interpersonal Violence, 31*, 1912–1931.

Frazier, E. (1939). *The Negro family in the United States.* Chicago, IL: University of Chicago Press.

Frazier, Patricia, Tashiro, Ty, Berman, Margit, Steger, Michael, & Long, Jeffrey. (2004). Correlates of levels and patterns of positive life changes following sexual assault. *Journal of Consulting and Clinical Psychology, 72*, 19–30.

Fredrickson, Barbara, & Roberts, Tomi-Ann. (1997). Objectification theory: Toward understanding women's lived experiences and mental health risks. *Psychology of Women Quarterly, 21*, 173–206.

Freese, Jeremy, & Meland, Sheri. (2002). Seven tenths incorrect: Heterogeneity and change in the waist-to-hip ratios of *Playboy* centerfold models and Miss America pageant winners. *Journal of Sex Research, 39*, 133–138.

Freud, Anna. (1928). *Introduction to the technique of child analysis* (Trans. L. P. Clark). New York, NY: Nervous and Mental Disease.

Freud, Anna. (1937). *The ego and the mechanisms of defense* (Trans. C. Bains). London, UK: Hogarth Press.

Freud, Anna. (1943). *War and children.* New York, NY: Medical War Books.

Freud, Sigmund. (1933). *New introductory lectures in psychoanalysis.* New York, NY: Norton.

Freud, Sigmund. (1948). Some psychical consequences of the anatomical distinction between the sexes. In I. Riviere (Trans.), *Collected papers* (Vol. V, pp. 186–197). London, UK: Hogarth Press.

Freyd, Jennifer J. (1996). *Betrayal trauma: The logic of forgetting childhood abuse.* Cambridge, MA: Harvard University Press.

Freyd, Jennifer J. (2003). Memory for abuse: What can we learn from a prosecution sample? *Journal of Child Sexual Abuse, 12*, 97–103.

Freyd, Jennifer J., Putnam, Frank W., Lyon, Thomas D., Becker-Blease, Kathryn A., Cheit, Ross E., Siegel, Nancy B., & Pezdek, Kathy. (2005). The science of child sexual abuse. *Science, 308*, 501.

Frieze, Irene H., & Chen, Karen Y. (2010). Intimate partner violence: Perspectives from racial/ethnic groups in the United States. In H. Landrine & N. Russo (Eds.), *Handbook of diversity in feminist psychology* (pp. 427–448). New York, NY: Springer.

Frieze, Irene H., Whitley, Barnard E., Jr., Hanusa, Barbara H., & Mchugh, Maureen C. (1982). Assessing the theoretical models for sex differences in causal attributions for success and failure. *Sex Roles, 8*, 333–334.

Frisch, Morton, Aigrain, Yves, Barauskas, Vidmantas, Bjarnason, Ragnar, Boddy, Su-Anna, Czauderna, Piotr, . . . Wijnen, Rene. (2013). Cultural bias in the AAP's 2012 technical report and policy statement on male circumcision. *Pediatrics, 131*, 796–800.

Fujita, Frank, Diener, Ed, & Sandvik, Ed. (1991). Gender differences in negative affect and well-being: The case for emotional intensity. *Journal of Personality and Social Psychology, 61*, 427–434.

Fulu, Emma, Miedema, Stephanie, Roselli, Tim, McCook, Sarah, Chan, Ko L., Haardörfer, Regine, & Jewkes, Rachel. (2017). Pathways between childhood trauma, intimate partner violence, and harsh parenting: Findings from the UN Multi-country Study on Men and Violence in Asia and the Pacific. *Lancet Global Health, 5,* e512–e522.

Furnham, Adrian, & Baguma, Peter. (1994). Cross-cultural differences in the evaluation of male and female body shapes. *International Journal of Eating Disorders, 15,* 81–89.

Gale, Joan E. (2006). The Family and Medical Leave Act: Lost in translation. In M. F. Kasten (Ed.), *Gender, race, and ethnicity in the workplace* (Vol. 2, pp. 119–142). Westport, CT: Praeger.

Gallant, Sheryle J., Popiel, Debra A., Hoffman, Denise M., Chakraborty, Prabir, K., & Hamilton, Jean. (1992). Using daily ratings to confirm premenstrual syndrome/late luteal dysphoric disorder: Part II. What makes a "real" difference? *Psychosomatic Medicine, 54,* 167–181.

Gallo, Linda C., Troxel, Wendy M., Matthews, Karen A., & Kuller, Lewis H. (2003). Marital status and quality in middle-aged women: Associations with levels and trajectories of cardiovascular risk factors. *Health Psychology, 22,* 453–463.

Gallup. (2002, September 3). Feminism: What's in a name? Retrieved from http://www.gallup.com/poll/6715/Feminism-Whats-Name.aspx

Galsworthy-Francis, Lisa, & Allan, Steven. (2014). Cognitive behavioural therapy for anorexia nervosa: A systematic review. *Clinical Psychology Review, 34,* 54–72.

Gannon, Linda, Luchetta, Tracy, Rhodes, Kyle, Pardie, L., & Segrist, Dan. (1992). Sex bias in psychological research: Progress or complacency? *American Psychologist, 4,* 389–396.

Garcia, Alma M. (1989). The development of Chicana feminist discourse, 1970–1980. *Gender & Society, 3,* 217–238.

Garcia-Moreno, Claudia, Jansen, Henrica A. F. M., Ellsberg, Mary, Heise, Lori, Watts, Charlotte, & Naved, Ruchira. (2006). Prevalence of intimate partner violence: Findings from the WHO multi-country study on women's health and domestic violence. *Lancet, 368,* 1260–1269.

Garrett, Michael T., & Barret, Bob. (2003). Two spirit: Counseling Native American gay, lesbian, and bisexual people. *Journal of Multicultural Counseling and Development, 31,* 131–142.

Garrett, Tanya, & Davis, John D. (1998). The prevalence of sexual contact between British clinical psychologists and their patients. *Clinical Psychology and Psychotherapy, 5,* 253–263.

Gartrell, Nanette, & Bos, Henry. (2010). US National Lesbian Family Study: Psychological adjustment of 17-year-old adolescents. *Pediatrics, 126,* 28–36.

Gastil, J. (1990). Generic pronouns and sexist language: The oxymoronic character of masculine generics. *Sex Roles, 23,* 629–643.

Gates, Gary J. (2013). *LGBT parenting in the United States.* Los Angeles, CA: Williams Institute.

Gatta, Gemma, Capocaccia, Riccardo, Coleman, Michel P., Glockler Ries, Lynn A., Hakulinen, Timo, Micheli, Andrea, ... Berrino, Franco. (2000). Toward a comparison of survival in American and European cancer patients. *Cancer, 89,* 893–900.

Gaucher, Danielle, Friesen, Justin, & Kay, Aaron C. (2011). Evidence that gendered wording in job advertisements exists and sustains gender inequality. *Journal of Personality and Social Psychology, 101,* 109–128.

Gavin, Lorrie, MacKay, Andrea P., Brown, Kathryn, Harrier, Sara, Ventura, Stephanie J., Kann, Laura, ... Ryan, George. (2009). Sexual and reproductive health of persons aged 10–24 years—United States, 2002–2007. *Morbidity and Mortality Weekly Reports, 58,* SS-6.

Ge, Xiaojia, & Natsuaki, Misaki. (2009). In search of explanation for early pubertal timing effects on developmental psychopathology. *Current Directions in Psychological Science, 18,* 327–331.

Geary, David C. (1998). *Male, female: The evolution of human sex differences.* Washington, DC: American Psychological Association.

Geary, David C. (2010). *Male, female: The evolution of human sex differences* (2nd ed.). Washington, DC: American Psychological Association.

Gee, Gilbert, Spencer, Michael, Chen, Juan, Yip, Tiffany, & Takeuchi, David. (2007). The association between self-reported discrimination and 12-month DSM-IV mental disorders among Asian Americans nationwide. *Social Science and Medicine, 64,* 1984–1996.

Gee, James P., Hull, Glynda, & Lankshear, Colin. (2000). *The new work order: Behind the language of the new capitalism.* Boulder, CO: Westview Press.

Gelman, Susan A., Taylor, Marianne G., & Nguyen, Simone P. (2004). Mother-child conversations about gender. *Monographs of the Society for Research in Child Development, 69,* 1–127.

General Social Survey, 1972–2012 [cumulative file]. (2012). Retrieved from http://www.icpsr.umich.edu/icpsrweb/ICPSR/studies/34802

Gentile, Brittany, Grabe, Shelly, Dolan-Pascoe, Brenda, Twenge, Jean M., Wells, Brooke E., & Maitino, Alissa. (2009). Gender differences in domain-specific self-esteem: A meta-analysis. *Review of General Psychology, 13,* 34–45.

Gentile, D. A., Lynch, Paul J., Linder, Jennifer R., & Walsh, David A. (2004). The effects of violent video game habits on adolescent attitudes and behaviors. *Journal of Adolescence, 27,* 5–22.

Gentry, Jacquelyn H. (1993, March). Women and AIDS. *Psychology and AIDS Exchange.*

Gerson, Helena, Sorby, Sheryl A., Wysocki, Anne, & Baartmans, Beverly J. (2001). The development and assessment of multimedia software for improving 3-D visualization skills. *Computer Applications in Engineering Education, 9,* 105–113.

Gervais, Sarah J., Vescio, Theresa K., & Allen, Jill. (2011). When what you see is what you get: The consequences of the objectifying gaze for women and men. *Psychology of Women Quarterly, 35,* 5–17.

Ghavami, Negin, & Peplau, L. Anne. (2013). An intersectional analysis of gender and ethnic stereotypes: Testing three hypotheses. *Psychology of Women Quarterly, 37,* 113–127.

Ghumman, Usman, McCord, Carly E., & Chang, Jessica E. (2016). Posttraumatic stress disorder in Syrian refugees: A review. *Canadian Psychology, 57,* 246–253.

Gidycz, Christine A., Orchowski, Lindsay M., & Edwards, Katie M. (2011). Primary prevention of sexual violence. In M. P. Koss, J. D. White, & A. E. Kazdin (Eds.), *Violence against women and children: Navigating solutions* (Vol. 2, pp. 159–180). Washington, DC: American Psychological Association.

Gifford, R. (1997). *Environmental psychology: Principles and practice.* Boston, MA: Allyn and Bacon.

Gil-Gómez, Ellen M. (2016). Lesbianas Unidas: Shaping nation through community activist rhetorics. *Journal of Lesbian Studies, 20,* 197–212.

Gilbert, Lucia A. (1993). *Two careers/one family.* Newbury Park, CA: Sage.

Gilbert, Lucia A., & Dancer, L. Suzanne. (1992). Dual-earner families in the United States and adolescent development. In S. Lewis, D. N. Izraeli, & H. Hootsmans (Eds.), *Dual-earner families: International perspectives* (pp. 151–171). Newbury Park, CA: Sage.

Gilbert, Lucia A., & Rader, Jill. (2001). Counseling and psychotherapy: Gender, race/ethnicity, and sexuality. In J. Worell (Ed.), *Encyclopedia of women and gender* (pp. 265–277). New York, NY: Academic Press.

Gilbert, Stefanie C., Keery, Helen, & Thompson, J. Kevin. (2005). The media's role in body image and eating disorders. In E. Cole & J. H. Daniel (Eds.), *Featuring females: Feminist analyses of media* (pp. 41–56). Washington, DC: American Psychological Association.

Gill, Diane L. (2001). Sport and athletics. In J. Worell (Ed.), *Encyclopedia of gender* (pp. 1091–1100). San Diego, CA: Academic Press.

Gilligan, Carol. (1982). *In a different voice: Psychological theory and women's development.* Cambridge, MA: Harvard University Press.

Gilman, Susan J. (2005). *Hypocrite in a pouffy white dress: Tales of growing up groovy and clueless.* New York, NY: Warner Books.

Gilpatrick, Naomi. (1972). The secret life of Beatrix Potter. *Natural History, 81*(8).

Ginorio, Angela B., Gutierrez, Lorraine, Cauce, Ana Mari, & Acosta, Mimi. (1995). Psychological issues for Latinas. In H. Landrine (Ed.), *Bringing cultural diversity to feminist psychology: Theory, research, and practice* (pp. 241–264). Washington, DC: American Psychological Association.

Ginorio, Angela B., & Martinez, Lorraine J. (1998). Where are the Latinas? Ethno-race and gender in psychology courses. *Psychology of Women Quarterly, 22,* 53–68.

Gladstone, Tracy R. G., Kaslow, Nadine J., Seeley, John R., & Lewinsohn, Peter M. (1997). Sex differences, attributional style, and depressive symptoms among adolescents. *Journal of Abnormal Child Psychology, 25,* 297–305.

Glass, Jon, & Owen, Jesse. (2010). Latino fathers: The relationship among machismo, acculturation, ethnic identity, and paternal involvement. *Psychology of Men & Masculinity, 11,* 251–261.

Glenn, Heidi. (2017, March 2). Fear of deportation spurs 4 women to drop domestic abuse cases in Denver. National Public Radio. Retrieved from http://www.npr.org

Glick, Peter, & Fiske, Susan T. (2001). An ambivalent alliance: Hostile and benevolent sexism as complementary justifications for gender inequality. *American Psychologist, 56,* 109–118.

Glick, Peter, Fiske, Susan T., Mladinic, Antonio, Saiz, Jose L., Abrams, Dominic, Masser, Barbara, . . . Lopez, Wilson L. (2000). Beyond prejudice as simple antipathy: Hostile and benevolent sexism across cultures. *Journal of Personality and Social Psychology, 79,* 763–775.

Glick, Peter, Lameiras, Maria, Fiske, Susan T., Eckes, Thomas, Masser, Barbara, Volpato, Chiara, . . . Wells, Robin. (2004). Bad but bold: Ambivalent attitudes toward men predict gender inequality in 16 nations. *Journal of personality and Social Psychology, 86,* 713–728.

Goeke-Morey, Marcie C., & Cummings, E. Mark. (2007). Impact of father involvement: A closer look at indirect effects models involving marriage and child adjustment. *Applied Developmental Science, 11,* 221–225.

Gohm, Carol L., & Clore, Gerald L. (2000). Individual differences in emotional experience: Mapping available scales to processes. *Personality and Social Psychology Bulletin, 26*, 679–697.

Gold, Ellen B., Colvin, Alicia, Avis, Nancy, Bromberger, Joyce, Greendale, Gail A., Powell, Lynda, . . . Matthews, Karen. (2006). Longitudinal analysis of the association between vasomotor symptoms and race/ethnicity across the menopausal transition: Study of Women's Health Across the Nation. *American Journal of Public Health, 96*, 1226–1235.

Gold, Rachel B., & Nash, Elizabeth. (2007). State abortion counseling policies and the fundamental principles of informed consent. *Guttmacher Policy Review, 10*(4), 6–13.

Gold, Steven N., Hughes, Dawn, & Hohnecker, Laura. (1994). Degrees of repression of sexual abuse memories. *American Psychologist, 49*, 441–442.

Goldberg, Abbie E. (2013). "Doing" and "undoing" gender: The meaning and division of housework in same-sex couples. *Journal of Family Theory & Review, 5*, 85–104.

Goldberg, Margaret E. (1995). Substance-abusing women: False stereotypes and real needs. *Social Work, 40*, 789–798.

Goldberg, Michelle. (2016, December 27). The empire strikes back. *Slate.* Retrieved from http://www.slate.com

Goldberg, Philip. (1968, April). Are some women prejudiced against women? *Transaction, 5*, 28–30.

Goldschmidt, Orly T., & Weller, Leonard. (2000). "Talking emotions": Gender differences in a variety of conversational contexts. *Symbolic Interaction, 23*, 117–134.

Goldstein, Joshua S. (2001). *War and gender.* New York, NY: Cambridge University Press.

Gollenberg, Audra L., Hediger, Mary L., Lee, Peter A., Himes, John H., & Buck Louis, Germaine M. (2010). Association between lead and cadmium and reproductive hormones in peripubertal U.S. girls. *Environmental Health Perspectives, 118*, 1782–1787.

Golombok, Susan, & Fivush, Robyn. (1994). *Gender development.* New York, NY: Cambridge University Press.

Golombok, Susan, Perry, Beth, Burston, Amanda, Murray, Clare, Mooney-Somers, Julie, Stevens, Madeleine, & Golding, Jean. (2003). Children with lesbian parents: A community study. *Developmental Psychology, 39*, 20–33.

Golombok, Susan, & Tasker, Fiona. (1996). Do parents influence the sexual orientation of their children? Findings from a longitudinal study of lesbian families. *Developmental Psychology, 32*, 3–11.

Golub, Sharon. (1992). *Periods: From menarche to menopause.* Newbury Park, CA: Sage.

Gone, Joseph P. (2009). A community-based treatment for Native American historical trauma: Prospects for evidence-based practice. *Journal of Consulting and Clinical Psychology, 77*, 751–762.

Gone, Joseph P. (2010). Psychotherapy and traditional healing for American Indians: Exploring the prospects for therapeutic integration. *Counseling Psychologist, 38*, 166–235.

Gonzales, Patricia M., Blanton, Hart, & Williams, Kevin J. (2002). The effects of stereotype threat and double-minority status on the test performance of Latino women. *Personality and Social Psychology Bulletin, 28*, 659–670.

Good, Glenn E., Robertson, John M., O'Neil, James M., Fitzgerald, Louise F., Stevens, Mark, Debord, Kurt, . . . Braverman, David G. (1995). Male gender role conflict: Psychometric issues and relations to psychological distress. *Journal of Counseling Psychology, 42*, 3–10.

Goodchilds, Jacqueline, & Zellman, Gail. (1984). Sexual signaling and sexual aggression in adolescent relationships. In N. Malamuth & E. Donnerstein (Eds.), *Pornography and sexual aggression* (pp. 233–243). New York, NY: Academic Press.

Goodman, Gail S., Ghetti, Simona, Quas, Jodi A., Edelstein, Robin S., Alexander, Kristen W., & Redlick, Allison D. (2003). A prospective study of memory for child sexual abuse. *Psychological Science, 14*, 113–118.

Goodman, Lisa A., & Epstein, Deborah. (2011). The justice system response to domestic violence. In M. P. Koss, J. D. White, & A. E. Kazdin (Eds.), *Violence against women and children: Navigating solutions* (Vol. 2, pp. 215–236). Washington, DC: American Psychological Association.

Goodwin, Paula, McGill, Brittany, & Chandra, Anjani. (2009). *Who marries and when? Age at first marriage in the United States: 2002* (NCHS data brief No. 19). Hyattsville, MD: National Center for Health Statistics.

Gooren, Louis J., Wierckx, Katrien, & Giltay, Erik J. (2014). Cardiovascular disease in transsexual persons treated with cross-sex hormones: Reversal of the traditional sex difference in cardiovascular disease pattern. *European Journal of Endocrinology, 170*, 809–819.

Gordon, Allegra R., Austin, S. Bryn, Krieger, Nancy, White Hughto, Jaclyn M., & Reisner, Sari L. (2016). "I have to constantly prove to myself, to people, that I fit the bill": Perspectives on weight and shape control behaviors among low-income, ethnically diverse young transgender women. *Social Science and Medicine, 165*, 141–149.

Gordon, Maya K. (2008). Media contributions to African American girls' focus on beauty and appearance: Exploring the consequences of sexual objectification. *Psychology of Women Quarterly, 32*, 245–256.

Gotta, Gabrielle, Green, Robert-Jay, Rothblum, Esther, Solomon, Sondra, Balsam, Kimberly, & Schwartz, Pepper. (2011). Heterosexual, lesbian, and gay male relationships: A comparison of couples in 1975 and 2000. *Family Process, 50*, 353–376.

Gough, Harrison G. (1957). *Manual for the California Psychological Inventory.* Palo Alto, CA: Consulting Psychologists Press.

Gould, Stephen J. (1987). *An urchin in the storm.* New York, NY: W. W. Norton.

Gowaty, Patricia A. (Ed.). (1997). *Feminism and evolutionary biology: Boundaries, intersections and frontiers.* New York, NY: Chapman & Hall.

Grabe, Shelly, & Else-Quest, N. M. (2012). The role of transnational feminism in psychology: Complementary visions. *Psychology of Women Quarterly, 36*, 158–161.

Grabe, Shelly, & Hyde, Janet S. (2006). Ethnicity and body dissatisfaction among women in the United States: A meta-analysis. *Psychological Bulletin, 132*, 622–640.

Grabe, Shelly, & Hyde, Janet S. (2009). Body objectification, MTV, and psychological outcomes among female adolescents. *Journal of Applied Social Psychology, 39*, 2840–2858.

Grabe, Shelly, Hyde, Janet S., & Lindberg, Sara M. (2007). Body objectification and depression in adolescents: The role of gender, shame, and rumination. *Psychology of Women Quarterly, 31*, 164–175.

Grabe, Shelly, Ward, L. Monique, & Hyde, Janet S. (2008). The role of the media in body image concerns among women: A meta-analysis of experimental and correlational studies. *Psychological Bulletin, 134*, 460–476.

Grady, Kathleen. (1979). Androgyny reconsidered. In J. H. Williams (Ed.), *Psychology of women: Selected readings* (pp. 172–177). New York, NY: Norton.

Graham, Cynthia A. (1991). Menstrual synchrony: An update and review. *Human Nature, 2*, 293–311.

Graham, Cynthia A. (2010). The DSM diagnostic criteria for female sexual arousal disorder. *Archives of Sexual Behavior, 39*, 240–255.

Graham, Cynthia A., Sanders, Stephanie A., & Milhausen, Robin R. (2006). The Sexual Excitation/Sexual Inhibition Inventory for Women: Psychometric properties. *Archives of Sexual Behavior, 35*, 397–409.

Grant, Jaime M., Mottet, Lisa A., & Tanis, Justin (with Harrison, Jack, Herman, Jodi L., & Keisling, Mara). (2011). *Injustice at every turn: A report of the National Transgender Discrimination Survey.* Washington, DC: National Center for Transgender Equality and National Gay and Lesbian Task Force.

Grant, Kathryn E., Compas, Bruce E., Thurm, Audrey E., McMahon, Susan D., & Gipson, Polly Y. (2004). Stressors and child and adolescent psychopathology: Measurement issues and prospective effects. *Journal of Clinical Child and Adolescent Psychology, 33*, 412–425.

Grantham, Tarek C. (2004). Multicultural mentoring to increase Black male representation in gifted programs. *Gifted Child Quarterly, 48*, 232–246.

Gray, Peter. (1992). *Men are from Mars, women are from Venus.* New York, NY: HarperCollins.

Green, Vanessa A., Bigler, Rebecca, & Catherwood, Di. (2004). The variability and flexibility of gender-typed toy play: A close look at children's behavioral responses to counterstereotypic models. *Sex Roles, 51*, 371–386.

Greenberger, Marcia D., & Blake, Deborah L. (1996, July 5). The VMI decision: Shattering sexual stereotypes. *Chronicle of Higher Education*, p. A52.

Greene, Beverly. (1994). African American women. In L. Comas-Diaz & B. Greene (Eds.), *Women of color: Integrating ethnic and gender identities in psychotherapy* (pp. 10–29). New York, NY: Guilford.

Greene, Beverly. (2000). African American lesbian and bisexual women. *Journal of Social Issues, 56*, 239–250.

Greenfield, Shelly F. (2002). Women and alcohol use disorders. *Harvard Review of Psychiatry, 10*, 76–85.

Greenhaus, Jeffrey H., & Parasuraman, Saroj. (1993). Job performance attributions and career advancement prospects: An examination of gender and race effects. *Organizational Behavior and Human Decision Processes, 55*, 273–297.

Greenwood, Dara N., & Lippman, Julia R. (2010). Gender and media: Content, uses, and impact. In J. Chrisler & D. McCreary (Eds.), *Handbook of gender research in psychology* (Vol. 2, pp. 643–670). New York, NY: Springer.

Gregersen, Edgar. (1996). *The world of human sexuality.* New York, NY: Irvington.

Greil, Arthur L., McQuillan, Julia, Shreffler, Karina M., Johnson, Katherine M., & Slauson-Blevins, Kathleen S. (2011). Race-ethnicity and medical services for infertility: Stratified reproduction in a population-based sample of U.S. women. *Journal of Health and Social Behavior, 52*, 493–507.

Grenyer, Brin F. S., & Lewis, Kate L. (2012). Prevalence, prediction, and prevention of psychologist misconduct. *Australian Psychologist, 47*, 68–76.

Grice, James W., & Seely, Elizabeth. (2000). The evolution of sex differences in jealousy: Failure to replicate previous results. *Journal of Research in Personality, 34*, 348–356.

Grier, William H., & Cobbs, Price M. (1968). *Black rage.* New York: Basic Books.

Grijalva, Emily, Newman, Daniel A., Tay, Louis, Donnellan, M. Brent, & Harms, Peter D. (2015). Gender differences in narcissism: A meta-analytic review. *Psychological Bulletin, 141,* 261–310.

Grinde, Donald A. (1977). *The Iroquois and the founding of the American nation.* San Francisco, CA: American Historian Press.

Grossman, Aryn L., & Tucker, Joan S. (1997). Gender differences and sexism in the knowledge and use of slang. *Sex Roles, 37,* 101–110.

Grossman, Michele, & Wood, Wendy. (1993). Sex differences in intensity of emotional experience: A social role interpretation. *Journal of Personality and Social Psychology, 65,* 1010–1022.

Guay, A. T., & Jacobson, Jerilynn. (2002). Decreased free testosterone and dehydroepiandrosterone-sulfate (DHEA-S) levels in women with decreased libido. *Journal of Sex and Marital Therapy, 28,* 129–142.

Guerrero, Laura K., & Jones, Susanne, M. (2006). Sex differences in emotional communication. In D. Canary & K. Dindia (Eds.), *Sex differences and similarities in communication* (2nd ed., pp. 241–262). Mahwah, NJ: Lawrence Erlbaum.

Guillamon, Antonio, Junque, Carme, & Gómez-Gil, Esther. (2016). A review of the status of brain structure research in transsexualism. *Archives of Sexual Behavior, 45,* 1615–1648.

Gullone, Eleonora, & King, Neville J. (1992). Psychometric evaluation of a Revised Fear Survey Schedule for children and adolescents. *Journal of Child Psychology and Psychiatry, 33,* 987–998.

Gura, Trisha. (1995). Estrogen: Key player in heart disease among women. *Science, 269,* 771–773.

Gurian, Michael. (2011). *Boys and girls learn differently! A guide for teachers and parents.* San Francisco: Jossey-Bass.

Gurian, Michael, & Ballew, Arlette C. (2003). *The boys and girls learn differently action guide for teachers.* San Francisco, CA: Jossey-Bass.

Gutek, Barbara A. (2001b). Working environments. In J. Worell (Ed.), *Encyclopedia of women and gender* (pp. 1191–1204). San Diego, CA: Academic Press.

Guthrie, R. V. (1976). *Even the rat was White: A historical view of psychology.* New York, NY: Harper.

Guttentag, Marcia, & Secord, Paul F. (1983). *Too many women? The sex ratio question.* Beverly Hills, CA: Sage.

Gutter, Belen T. (2002). *The construction and maintenance of bicultural competence: A phenomenological investigation and ecological perspective of African American women in the professions and executive management* (Unpublished doctoral dissertation). University of Wisconsin–Madison.

Guttmacher Institute. (2011). Testimony of Guttmacher Institute submitted to the Committee on Preventive Services for Women, Institute of Medicine. Retrieved from http://www.guttmacher.org/pubs/CPSW-testimony.pdf

Guyll, Max, Matthews, Karen, & Bromberger, Joyce. (2001). Discrimination and unfair treatment: Relationship to cardiovascular reactivity among African American and European American women. *Health Psychology, 20,* 315–325.

Gygax, Pascal, Gabriel, Ute, Sarrasin, Oriane, Oakhill, Jane, & Garnham, Alan. (2009). Some grammatical rules are more difficult than others: The case of the generic interpretation of the masculine. *European Journal of Psychology and Education, 24,* 235–246.

Ha, Nathan Q., Dworkin, Shari L., Martinez-Patiño, Maria J., Rogol, Alan D., Rosario, Vernon, Sánchez, Francisco J., . . . Vilain, Eric. (2014). Hurdling over sex? Sport, science, and equity. *Archives of Sexual Behavior, 43,* 1035–1042.

Hagen, D. Brienne, & Galupo, M. Paz. (2014). Trans* individuals' experiences of gendered language with health care providers: Recommendations for practitioners. *International Journal of Transgenderism, 15,* 16–34.

Hager, Lori D. (Ed.). (1997). *Women in human evolution.* London, UK: Routledge.

Haines, Elizabeth L., Deaux, Kay, & Lofaro, Nicole. (2016). The times they are a-changing . . . or are they not? A comparison of gender stereotypes, 1983–2014. *Psychology of Women Quarterly, 40,* 353–363.

Halberstam, Judith. (2012). Global female masculinities. *Sexualities, 15,* 336–354.

Hald, Gert M., & Malamuth, Neil N. (2015). Experimental effects of exposure to pornography: The moderating effect of personality and mediating effect of sexual arousal. *Archives of Sexual Behavior, 44,* 99–109.

Halim, May L., & Ruble, Diane. (2010). Gender identity and stereotyping in early and middle childhood. In J. Chrisler & D. McCreary (Eds.), *Handbook of gender research in psychology* (Vol. 1, pp. 495–526). New York, NY: Springer.

Halim, May Ling, Ruble, Diane N., Tamis-LeMonda, Catherine S., Zosuls, Kristina M., Lurye, Leah E., & Greulich, Faith K. (2014). Pink frilly dresses and the avoidance of all things "girly": Children's appearance rigidity and cognitive theories of gender development. *Developmental Psychology, 50,* 1091–1101.

Hall, Christine C. I. (2009). Asian American women: The nail that sticks out is hammered down. In N. Tewari & A. Alvarez (Eds.), *Asian American psychology: Current perspectives* (pp. 193–209). New York, NY: Routledge.

Hall, Elaine J., & Rodriguez, Marnie S. (2003). The myth of postfeminism. *Gender & Society, 17,* 878–902.

Hall, Gordon C. N. (1995). Sexual offender recidivism revisited: A meta-analysis of recent treatment studies. *Journal of Consulting and Clinical Psychology, 63,* 802–809.

Hall, Gordon C. N., & Barongan, Christy. (1997). Prevention of sexual aggression: Sociocultural risk and protective factors. *American Psychologist, 52,* 5–14.

Hall, Gordon C. N., Teten, Andra L., DeGarmo, David S., Sue, Stanley, & Stephens, Kari A. (2005). Ethnicity, culture, and sexual aggression: Risk and protective factors. *Journal of Clinical and Consulting Psychology, 73,* 830–840.

Hall, Judith A. (1984). *Nonverbal sex differences.* Baltimore, MD: Johns Hopkins University Press.

Hall, Judith A. (1998). How big are nonverbal sex differences? The case of smiling and sensitivity to nonverbal cues. In D. Canary & K. Dindia (Eds.), *Sex differences and similarities in communication* (pp. 155–178). Mahwah, NJ: Lawrence Erlbaum.

Hall, Judith A., & Friedman, Gregory. (1999). Status, gender, and nonverbal behavior: A study of structured interactions between employees of a company. *Personality and Social Psychology Bulletin, 25,* 1082–1091.

Hall, Judith A., LeBeau, Lavonia B., Gordon, Jeannette, & Thayer, Frank. (2001). Status, gender, and nonverbal behavior in candid and posed photographs: A study of conversations between university employees. *Sex Roles, 44,* 677–692.

Hall, Judith A., & Matsumoto, David. (2004). Gender differences in judgments of multiple emotions from facial expression. *Emotion, 4,* 201–206.

Halperin, David M. (2003). The normalization of queer theory. *Journal of Homosexuality, 45,* 339–343.

Halpern, Diane F. (1992). *Sex differences in cognitive abilities* (2nd ed.). Hillsdale, NJ: Erlbaum.

Halpern, Diane F. (2000). *Sex differences in cognitive abilities* (3rd ed.). Mahwah, NJ: Lawrence Erlbaum.

Hamilton, Brady E., Martin, Joyce A., Osterman, Michele J. K., Curtin, Sally C., & Mathews, T. J. (2015). Births: Final data for 2014. *National Vital Statistics Reports, 64*(12).

Hamilton, M. C. (1988). Using masculine generics: Does generic he increase male bias in the user's imagery? *Sex Roles, 19,* 785–799.

Hancock, Adrienne B., & Rubin, Benjamin A. (2015). Influence of communication partner's gender on language. *Journal of Language and Social Psychology, 34,* 46–64.

Hancock, Adrienne B., Stutts, Holly W., & Bass, Annie. (2015). Perceptions of gender and femininity based on language: Implications for transgender communication therapy. *Language and Speech, 58,* 315–333.

Hankin, Ben, & Abramson, Lyn. (2002). Measuring cognitive vulnerability to depression in adolescence: Reliability, validity, and gender differences. *Journal of Clinical Child and Adolescent Psychology, 31,* 491–504.

Hankin, Benjamin L., Abramson, Lyn Y., Moffitt, Terrie E., Silva, Phil A., McGee, Rob, & Angell, Kathryn E. (1998). Development of depression from preadolescence to young adulthood: Emerging gender differences in a 10-year longitudinal study. *Journal of Abnormal Psychology, 107,* 128–140.

Hankin, Benjamin L., Young, Jami F., Abela, John R. Z., Smolen, Andrew, Jenness, Jessica L., Gulley, Lauren D., . . . Oppenheimer, Caroline W. (2015). Depression from childhood into late adolescence: Influence of gender, development, genetic susceptibility, and peer stress. *Journal of Abnormal Psychology, 124,* 803–816.

Hanschmidt, Franz, Linde, Katja, Hilbert, Anja, Riedel-Heller, Steffi G., & Kersting, Anette. (2016). Abortion stigma: A systematic review. *Perspectives on Sexual and Reproductive Health, 48,* 169–177.

Hanson, R. Karl, Bourgon, Guy, Helmus, Leslie, & Hodgson, Shannon. (2009). The principles of effective correctional treatment also apply to sexual offenders: A meta-analysis. *Criminal Justice and Behavior, 36,* 865–891.

Harackiewicz, Judith M., Canning, Elizabeth A., Tibbetts, Yoi, Priniski, Stacy J., & Hyde, Janet S. (2016). Closing achievement gaps with a utility-value intervention: Disentangling race and social class. *Journal of Personality and Social Psychology, 111,* 745–765.

Hardie, Elizabeth A. (1997). Prevalence and predictors of cyclic and noncyclic affective change. *Psychology of Women Quarterly, 21,* 299–314.

Hare, Lauren, Bernard, Pascal, Sanchez, Francisco J., Baird, Paul N., Vilain, Eric, Kennedy, Trudy, & Harley, Vincent R. (2008). Androgen receptor repeat length polymorphism associated with male-to-female transsexualism. *Biological Psychiatry, 65,* 93–96.

Hare-Mustin, Rachel T., & Marecek, Jeanne. (1988). The meaning of difference: Gender theory, postmodernism and psychology. *American Psychologist, 43,* 455–464.

Harknett, Kristen, & McLanahan, Sara S. (2004). Racial and ethnic differences in marriage after the birth of a child. *American Sociological Review, 69*, 790–811.

Harper, Sam, Lynch, John, Meersman, Stephen C., Breen, Nancy, Davis, William W., & Reichman, Marsha C. (2009). Trends in area-socioeconomic and race-ethnic disparities in breast cancer incidence, stage at diagnosis, screening, mortality, and survival among women ages 50 years and over (1987–2005). *Cancer Epidemiology, Biomarkers & Prevention, 18*, 121–131.

Harrell, Shelly, Coleman, Ashley E., & Adams, Tyonna P. (2014). Toward a positive womanist psychospirituality: Strengths, gifts, and optimal well-being among women of African descent. In T. Bryant-Davis, A. Austria, D. Kawahara, & D. Willis (Eds.), *Religion and spirituality for diverse women: Foundations of strength and resilience* (pp. 49–70). Santa Barbara, CA: Praeger.

Harrington, Ellen F., Crowther, Janis H., & Shipherd, Jillian C. (2010). Trauma, binge eating, and the strong Black woman. *Journal of Consulting and Clinical Psychology, 78*, 469–479.

Harris, Christine R. (2002). Sexual and romantic jealousy in heterosexual and homosexual adults. *Psychological Science, 13*, 7–12.

Harris, David J., & Douglas, Pamela S. (2000). Enrollment of women in cardiovascular clinical trials funded by the National Heart, Lung, and Blood Institute. *New England Journal of Medicine, 343*, 475–480.

Harris, G. W., & Levine, S. (1965). Sexual differentiation of the brain and its experimental control. *Journal of Physiology, 181*, 379–400.

Harris, Gardiner. (2004, February 28). Pfizer gives up testing Viagra on women. *New York Times.*

Harris, Lisa H. (2012). Stigma and abortion complications in the United States. *Obstetrics & Gynecology, 120*, 1472–1474.

Hart, Linda L. (1990). Accuracy of home pregnancy tests. *Annals of Pharmacotherapy, 24*, 712–713.

Hartka, Elizabeth, Johnstone, Bryan, Leino, E. Victor, Motoyoshi, Michelle, Temple, Mark T., & Fillmore, Kaye M. (1991). A meta-analysis of depressive symptomatology and alcohol consumption over time. *British Journal of Addiction, 86*, 1283–1298.

Hartung, Cynthia M., & Widiger, Thomas A. (1998). Gender differences in the diagnosis of mental disorders: Conclusions and controversies of the DSM-IV. *Psychological Bulletin, 123*, 260–278.

Harvey, Elizabeth A., Friedman-Weieneth, Julie L., Miner, Amy L., Bartolomei, Rachel J., Youngwirth, Sara D.,

Hashim, Rebecca L., & Arnold, David H. (2009). The role of ethnicity in observers' ratings of mother-child behavior. *Developmental Psychology, 45*, 1497–1508.

Haslam, Nick, & Levy, Sheri R. (2006). Essentialist beliefs about homosexuality: Structure and implications for prejudice. *Personality and Social Psychology Bulletin, 32*, 471–485.

Hatcher, Robert A., Trussell, James, Guest, Felicia, Kowal, Deborah, Cates, Willard, Stewart, Felicia H., & Nelson, Anita L. (2004). *Contraceptive technology* (18th ed.). New York, NY: Ardent Media.

Hatzenbuehler, Mark L. (2009). How does sexual minority stigma "get under the skin"? A psychological mediation framework. *Psychological Bulletin, 135*, 707–730.

Hausmann, Markus, Slabbekoorn, Ditte, van Goozen, Stephanie H. M., Cohen-Kettenis, Peggy T., & Güntürkün, Onur. (2000). Sex hormones affect spatial abilities during the menstrual cycle. *Behavioral Neuroscience, 114*, 1245–1250.

Hayes, Eden-Reneé, & Swim, Janet K. (2013). African, Asian, Latina/o, and European Americans' responses to popular measures of sexist beliefs: Some cautionary notes. *Psychology of Women Quarterly, 37*, 155–166.

Hayes, Tyrone B., Collins, Atif, Lee, Melissa, Mendoza, Magdalena, Noriega, Nigel, Stuart, A. Ali, & Vonk, Aaron. (2002). Hermaphroditic, demasculinized frogs after exposure to the herbicide atrazine at low ecologically relevant doses. *Proceedings of the National Academy of Sciences of the USA, 99*, 5476–5480.

Hayman, Brenda, Wilkes, Lesley, Halcomb, Elizabeth, & Jackson, Debra. (2015). Lesbian women choosing motherhood: The journey to conception. *Journal of GLBT Family Studies, 11*, 395–409.

Hays, H. R. (1964). *The dangerous sex: The myth of feminine evil.* New York, NY: G. P. Putnam's Sons.

Haywood, A., Slade, P., & King, H. (2002). Assessing the assessment measures for menstrual cycle symptoms: A guide for researchers and clinicians. *Journal of Psychosomatic Research, 52*, 223–237.

Healy, Jack, & Eligon, John. (2016, June 17). Orlando survivors recall night of terror: "Then he shoots me again." *New York Times.*

Heflick, Nathan A., & Goldenberg, Jamie L. (2014). Seeing eye to body: The literal objectification of women. *Current Directions in Psychological Science, 23*, 225–229.

Hegarty, Peter, & Buechel, Carmen. (2006). Androcentric reporting of gender differences in APA journals: 1965–2004. *Review of General Psychology, 10*, 377–389.

Hegarty, Peter, & Pratto, Felicia. (2010). Interpreting and communicating the results of gender-related research. In J. Chrisler & D. McCreary (Eds.), *Handbook of gender research in psychology* (Vol. 1, pp. 191–214). New York, NY: Springer.

Heilman, Madeline E., & Okimoto, Tyler G. (2007). Why are women penalized for success at male tasks? The implied communality deficit. *Journal of Applied Psychology, 92,* 81–92.

Heiman, Julia R. (1975). The physiology of erotica: Women's sexual arousal. *Psychology Today, 8*(11), 90–94.

Heiman, Julia R. (2002). Sexual dysfunction: Overview of prevalence, etiological factors, and treatment. *Journal of Sex Research, 39,* 73–78.

Heiman, Julia, LoPiccolo, Leslie, & LoPiccolo, Joseph. (1976). *Becoming orgasmic: A sexual growth program for women.* Englewood Cliffs, NJ: Prentice Hall.

Helgeson, Vicki S. (2009). *Psychology of gender* (3rd ed.). Upper Saddle River, NJ: Pearson.

Helgeson, Vicki, Cohen, Sheldon, Schulz, Richard, & Yasko, Joyce. (2000). Group support interventions for women with breast cancer: Who benefits from what? *Health Psychology, 19,* 107–114.

Helgeson, Vicki, Cohen, Sheldon, Schulz, Richard, & Yasko, Joyce. (2001). Long-term effects of educational and peer discussion group interventions on adjustment to breast cancer. *Health Psychology, 20,* 387–392.

Helgeson, Vicki S., Snyder, Pamela, & Seltman, Howard. (2004). Psychological and physical adjustment to breast cancer over 4 years: Identifying distinct trajectories of change. *Health Psychology, 23,* 3–15.

Helms, Janet E., Jernigan, Maryam, & Mascher, Jackquelyn. (2005). The meaning of race in psychology and how to change it. *American Psychologist, 60,* 27–36.

Helmuth, Laura. (2000). Reports see progress, problems, in trials. *Science, 288,* 1562–1563.

Helwig, Andrew A. (1998). Gender-role stereotyping: Testing theory with a longitudinal sample. *Sex Roles, 38,* 403–424.

Hembree, Wylie C., Cohen-Kettenis, Peggy, Delamarre-van de Waal, Henriette, Gooren, Louis J., Meyer, Walter J., III, Spack, Norman P., . . . Montori, Victor M. (2009). Endocrine treatment of transsexual persons: An Endocrine Society clinical practice guideline. *Journal of Clinical Endocrinology Metabolism, 94,* 3132–3154.

Henderson-King, Donna, & Brooks, Kelly D. (2009). Materialism, sociocultural appearance messages, and paternal attitudes predict college women's attitudes about cosmetic surgery. *Psychology of Women Quarterly, 33,* 133–142.

Hendricks, Michael L., & Testa, R. J. (2012). A conceptual framework for clinical work with transgender and gender nonconforming clients: An adaptation of the minority stress model. *Professional Psychology: Research and Practice, 43,* 460–467.

Hendy, Helen M., Eggen, Doreen, Gustitus, Cheryl, Mcleod, Kelli C., & Ng, Phillip. (2003). Decision to leave scale: Perceived reasons to stay or leave violent relationships. *Psychology of Women Quarterly, 27,* 162–173.

Henggeler, Scott W., Letourneau, Elizabeth J., & Chapman, Jason E. (2009). Mediators of change for multisystemic therapy with juvenile sexual offenders. *Journal of Consulting and Clinical Psychology, 77,* 451–462.

Henley, Nancy M. (1977). *Body politics: Power, sex, and nonverbal communication.* Englewood Cliffs, NJ: Prentice-Hall.

Henley, Nancy M. (1995). Body politics revisited: What do we know today? In P. J. Kalbfleish & M. J. Cody (Eds.), *Gender, power, and communication in human relationships* (pp. 27–61). New York, NY: Psychology Press.

Henningsson, Susanne, Westberg, Lars, Nilsson, Staffan, Lundström, Bengt, Ekselius, Lisa, Bodlund, Owe, . . . Landén, Mikael. (2005). Sex steroid-related genes and male-to-female transsexualism. *Psyhoneuroendocrinology, 30,* 657–664.

Henrich, Joseph, Heine, Steven J., & Norenzayan, Ara. (2010). The weirdest people in the world? *Behavioral and Brain Sciences, 33,* 61–135.

Herbenick, Deborah, Reece, Michael, Schick, Vanessa, Sanders, Stephanie A., Dodge, Brian, & Fortenberry, J. Dennis. (2010). An event-level analysis of the sexual characteristics and composition among adults ages 18 to 59: Results from a national probability sample in the United States. *Journal of Sexual Medicine, 7*(SS05), 346–361.

Herdt, Gilbert H. (Ed.). (1984). *Ritualized homosexuality in Melanesia.* Berkeley: University of California Press.

Herdt, Gilbert H. (1998). *Same sex, different cultures.* Boulder, CO: Westview Press.

Herdt, Gilbert H. (2006). *The Sambia: Ritual, sexuality, and change in Papua New Guinea.* Belmont, CA: Wadsworth Cengage.

Herek, Gregory M. (1990). The context of anti-gay violence: Notes on cultural and psychological heterosexism. *Journal of Interpersonal Violence, 5,* 316–333.

Herek, Gregory M. (2000a). The psychology of sexual prejudice. *Current Directions in Psychological Science, 9*(1), 19–22.

Herek, Gregory M. (2000b). Sexual prejudice and gender: Do heterosexuals' attitudes toward lesbians and gay men differ? *Journal of Social Issues, 56,* 251–266.

Herek, Gregory M. (2010). Sexual orientation differences as deficits: Science and stigma in the history of American psychology. *Perspectives on Psychological Science, 5,* 693–699.

Herman, Judith L. (1981). *Father-daughter incest.* Cambridge, MA: Harvard University Press.

Hernández, Brenda, Ramirez Garcia, Jorge I., & Flynn, Megan. (2010). The role of familism in the relation between parent-child discord and psychological distress among emerging adults of Mexican descent. *Journal of Family Psychology, 24,* 105–114.

Hernandez, Ines. (1990, April). *American Indian women writers.* Colloquium presented at the University of Wisconsin–Madison.

Herndon, James G. (2010). The grandmother effect: Implications for studies on aging and cognition. *Gerontology, 56,* 73–79.

Herrett-Skjellum, Jennifer, & Allen, Mike. (1996). Television programming and sex stereotyping: A meta-analysis. In B. Burleson (Ed.), *Communication yearbook 1995* (pp. 157–185). Thousand Oaks, CA: Sage.

Hersey, Rexford B. (1931). Emotional cycles in man. *Journal of Mental Science, 77,* 151–169.

Hess, Ursula, Adams, Reginald B., & Kleck, Robert E. (2004). Facial appearance, gender, and emotion expression. *Emotion, 4,* 378–388.

Hess, Ursula, David, Shlomo, & Hareli, Shlomo. (2016). Emotional restraint is good for men only: The influence of emotional restraint on perceptions of competence. *Emotion, 16,* 208–213.

Hicks, Brian M., Blonigen, Daniel M., Kramer, Mark D., Krueger, Robert F., Patrick, Christopher J., Iacono, William, G., & McGue, Matt. (2007). Gender differences and developmental change in externalizing disorders from late adolescence to early adulthood: A longitudinal twin study. *Journal of Abnormal Psychology, 116,* 433–447.

Hill, Darryl B., & Willoughby, Brian L. B. (2005). The development and validation of the genderism and transphobia scale. *Sex Roles, 53,* 531–544.

Hilliard, Lacey J., & Liben, Lynn S. (2010). Differing levels of gender salience in preschool classrooms: Effects on children's gender attitudes and intergroup bias. *Child Development, 81,* 1787–1798.

Hines, Melissa. (2004). Androgen, estrogen, and gender: Contributions of the early hormone environment to gender-related behavior. In A. H. Eagly, A. E. Beall, & R. J. Sternberg (Eds.), *The psychology of gender* (2nd ed., pp. 9–37). New York, NY: Guilford.

Hines, Melissa. (2011). Gender development and the human brain. *Annual Review of Neuroscience, 34,* 69–88.

Hines, Melissa, Brook, Charles, & Conway, Gerard S. (2004). Androgen and psychosexual development: Core gender identity, sexual orientation, and recalled childhood gender role behavior in women and men with congenital adrenal hyperplasia (CAH). *Journal of Sex Research, 41,* 75–81.

Hines, Melissa, & Collaer, Marcia L. (1993). Gonadal hormones and sexual differentiation of human behavior. *Annual Review of Sex Research, 4,* 1–48.

Hitlan, Robert T., Pryor, John B., Hesson-McInnis, Matthew S., & Olson, Michael. (2009). Antecedents of gender harassment: An analysis of person and situation factors. *Sex Roles, 61,* 794–807.

Hochschild, Arlie. (1989). *The second shift: Working parents and the revolution at home.* New York, NY: Viking.

Hochschild, Arlie R. (1990). Ideology and emotion management. In T. Kemper (Ed.), *Research agendas in the sociology of emotions* (pp. 117–142). Albany: State University of New York Press.

Hochschild, Arlie. (2012). *The second shift: Working parents and the revolution at home* (Rev. ed.). New York, NY: Viking.

Hock, Alyson, Kangas, Ashley, Zieber, Nicole, & Bhatt, Ramesh S. (2015). The development of sex category representation in infancy: Matching of faces and bodies. *Developmental Psychology, 51,* 346–352.

Hodnett, Ellen, Gates, Simon, Hofmeyr, G. Justus, & Sakala, Carol. (2013). Continuous support for women during childbirth. *Cochrane Database of Systematic Reviews, 7,* CD003766.

Hofferth, Sandra L. (2003). Race/ethnic differences in father involvement in two-parent families. *Journal of Family Issues, 24,* 185–216.

Hoffman, Lois W. (1972). Early childhood experiences and women's achievement motives. *Journal of Social Issues, 28*(2), 129–155.

Hogue, Mary, DuBois, Cathy L. Z., & Fox-Cardamone, Lee. (2010). Gender differences in pay expectations: The roles of job intention and self-view. *Psychology of Women Quarterly, 34,* 215–227.

Hogue, Mary, & Yoder, Janice D. (2003). The role of status in producing depressed entitlement in women's and men's pay allocations. *Psychology of Women Quarterly, 27,* 330–337.

Hollander, Jocelyn A. (2016). The importance of self-defense training for sexual violence prevention. *Feminism & Psychology, 26,* 207–226.

Holmberg, Diane, & Blair, Karen. (2009). Sexual desire, communication, satisfaction, and preferences of men and women in same-sex versus mixed-sex relationships. *Journal of Sex Research, 46,* 57–66.

Holmes, Melisa M., Resnick, Heidi S., Kilpatrick, Dean G., & Best, Connie L. (1996). Rape-related pregnancy: Estimates and descriptive characteristics from a national sample of women. *American Journal of Obstetrics and Gynecology, 175,* 320–325.

Holroyd, Jean C., & Brodsky, Annette M. (1977). Psychologists' attitudes and practices regarding erotic and non-erotic physical contact with patients. *American Psychologist, 34,* 843–849.

Holtzworth-Munroe, Amy. (2000). A typology of men who are violent toward their female partners: Making sense of the heterogeneity in husband violence. *Current Directions in Psychological Science, 9,* 140–143.

Holtzworth-Munroe, Amy, Meehan, Jeffrey C., Herron, Katherine, Rehman, Uzma, & Stuart, Gregory L. (2003). Do subtypes of maritally violent men continue to differ over time? *Journal of Consulting and Clinical Psychology, 71,* 728–740.

Hook, Jennifer L. (2010). Gender inequality in the welfare state: Sex segregation in housework, 1965–2003. *American Journal of Sociology, 115,* 1480–1523.

hooks, bell. (2000). *Feminism is for everybody.* Cambridge, MA: South End Press.

Hopper, Elizabeth K. (2017). Trauma-informed psychological assessment of human trafficking survivors. *Women & Therapy, 40,* 12–30.

Horbach, Sophie E. R., Bouman, Mark-Bram, Smit, Jan M., Özer, Müjde, Buncamper, Marlon E., & Mullender, Margriet G. (2015). Outcome of vaginoplasty in male-to-female transgenders: A systematic review of surgical techniques. *Journal of Sexual Medicine, 12,* 1499–1512.

Horner, Matina S. (1969). Fail: Bright women. *Psychology Today, 3*(6), 36.

Hornstein, Theresa, & Schwerin, Jeri Lynn. (2013). *Biology of women* (5th ed.). Clifton Park, NY: Delmar Cengage.

Houseknecht, Sharon K. (1979). Timing of the decision to remain voluntarily childless: Evidence for continuous socialization. *Psychology of Women Quarterly, 4,* 81–96.

Howden, Lindsay M., & Meyer, Julie A. (2011). *Age and sex composition: 2010.* Washington, DC: U.S. Census Bureau.

Hoyt, William T., & Kerns, Michael-David. (1999). Magnitude and moderators of bias in observer ratings: A meta-analysis. *Psychological Methods, 4,* 403–424.

Hrdy, Sarah B. (1981). *The woman that never evolved.* Cambridge, MA: Harvard University Press.

Hrdy, Sarah B. (1999). *Mother nature: Maternal instincts and how they shape the human species.* New York, NY: Ballantine.

Hrdy, Sarah B. (2009). *Mothers and others: The evolutionary origins of mutual understanding.* Cambridge, MA: Harvard University Press.

Hrdy, Sarah B. (2013). Foreword: Overdue dialogues. In M. L. Fisher, J. R. Garcia, & R. Sokol Chang (Eds.), *Evolution's empress: Darwinian perspectives on the nature of women* (pp. xv–xix). New York, NY: Oxford University Press.

Hsu, L. K. George, Kaye, Walter, & Weltzin, Theodore. (1993). Are the eating disorders related to obsessive compulsive disorder? *International Journal of Eating Disorders, 14,* 305–318.

Huang, Cindy Y., & Stormshak, Elizabeth A. (2011). A longitudinal examination of early adolescence ethnic identity trajectories. *Cultural Diversity & Ethnic Minority Psychology, 17,* 261–270.

Hughes, Jean O., & Sandler, Bernice R. (1987). *"Friends" raping friends: Could it happen to you?* Washington, DC: Association of American Colleges.

Hulleman, Chris S., Godes, Olga, Hendricks, Bryan L., & Harackiewicz, Judith M. (2010). Enhancing interest and performance with a utility value intervention. *Journal of Educational Psychology, 102,* 880–895.

Humes, Karen R., Jones, Nicholas A., & Ramirez, Roberto R. (2011). *Overview of race and Hispanic origin: 2010.* Washington, DC: U.S. Census Bureau.

Hungerford, Thomas L. (2001). The economic consequences of widowhood on elderly women in the United States and Germany. *The Gerontologist, 41,* 103–110.

Hunter, John A., Figueredo, Aurelio J., Becker, Judith V., & Malamuth, Neil. (2007). Non-sexual delinquency in juvenile sexual offenders: The mediating and moderating influences of emotional empathy. *Journal of Family Violence, 22,* 43–54.

Hurtado, Aida. (2003). *Voicing Chicana feminisms: Young women speak out on sexuality and identity.* New York, NY: New York University Press.

Hurtado, Aida. (2010). Multiple lenses: Multicultural feminist theory. In H. Landrine & N. Russo (Eds.), *Handbook of diversity in feminist psychology* (pp. 29–54). New York, NY: Springer.

Hutchinson, Karen A. (1995). Androgens and sexuality. *American Journal of Medicine, 98*(Suppl. 1A), 1A111S–1A115S.

Hyde, Janet S. (1984a). Children's understanding of sexist language. *Developmental Psychology, 20,* 697–706.

Hyde, Janet S. (1984b). How large are gender differences in aggression? A developmental meta-analysis. *Developmental Psychology, 20,* 722–736.

Hyde, Janet S. (2002). Feminist identity development: The current state of theory, research, and practice. *Counseling Psychologist, 30,* 105–110.

Hyde, Janet S. (2003). The use of meta-analysis in determining the effects of child sexual abuse. In J. Bancroft (Ed.), *Sexual development* (pp. 82–91). Bloomington: Indiana University Press.

Hyde, Janet S. (2005a). The gender similarities hypothesis. *American Psychologist, 60,* 581–592.

Hyde, Janet S. (2005b). The genetics of sexual orientation. In J. S. Hyde (Ed.), *Biological substrates of human sexuality* (pp. 9–20). Washington, DC: American Psychological Association.

Hyde, Janet S., & DeLamater, John D. (2011). *Understanding human sexuality* (11th ed.). New York, NY: McGraw-Hill.

Hyde, Janet S., & DeLamater, John D. (2017). *Understanding human sexuality* (13th ed.). New York, NY: McGraw-Hill.

Hyde, Janet S., & Essex, Marilyn J. (Eds.). (1991). *Parental leave and child care: Setting a research and policy agenda.* Philadelphia, PA: Temple University Press.

Hyde, Janet S., Essex, Marilyn J., & Horton, Francine. (1993). Fathers and parental leave. *Journal of Family Issues, 14,* 616–641.

Hyde, Janet S., Fennema, Elizabeth, & Lamon, Susan J. (1990). Gender differences in mathematics performance: A meta-analysis. *Psychological Bulletin, 107,* 139–155.

Hyde, Janet S., & Jaffee, Sara R. (2000). Becoming a heterosexual adult: The experiences of young women. *Journal of Social Issues, 56,* 283–296.

Hyde, Janet S., Klein, Marjorie, Essex, Marilyn J., & Clark, Roseanne. (1995). Maternity leave and women's mental health. *Psychology of Women Quarterly.*

Hyde, Janet S., & Kling, Kristin C. (2001). Women, motivation, and achievement. *Psychology of Women Quarterly, 25,* 364–378.

Hyde, Janet S., Lindberg, Sara M., Linn, Marcia C., Ellis, A., & Williams, C. (2008). Gender similarities characterize math performance. *Science, 321,* 494–495.

Hyde, Janet S., & Linn, Marcia C. (Eds.). (1986). *The psychology of gender: Advances through meta-analysis.* Baltimore, MD: Johns Hopkins University Press.

Hyde, Janet S., & Linn, Marcia C. (1988). Gender differences in verbal ability: A meta-analysis. *Psychological Bulletin, 104,* 53–69.

Hyde, Janet S., & Mertz, Janet. (2009). Gender, culture, and math. *Proceedings of the National Academy of Sciences of the USA, 106,* 8801–8807.

Hyde, Janet S., Mezulis, Amy H., & Abramson, Lyn Y. (2008). The ABCs of depression: Integrating affective, biological and cognitive models to explain the emergence of the gender difference in depression. *Psychological Review, 115,* 291–313.

Hyde, Janet S., & Phillis, Diane E. (1979). Androgyny across the lifespan. *Developmental Psychology, 15,* 334–336.

Iachini, Tina, Coello, Yann, Frassinetti, Francesca, Senese, Vincenzo P., Galante, Francesco, & Ruggiero, Gennaro. (2016). Peripersonal and interpersonal space in virtual and real environments: Effects of gender and age. *Journal of Environmental Psychology, 45,* 154–164.

Ickovics, Jeannette R., Thayaparan, Beatrice, & Ethier, Kathleen. (2000). Women and AIDS: A contextual analysis. In A. Baum, T. A. Revenson, & J. Singer (Eds.), *Handbook of health psychology* (pp. 821–839). Hillsdale, NJ: Lawrence Erlbaum.

Ilies, Remus, Hauserman, Nancy, Schwochau, Susan, & Stibal, John. (2003). Reported incidence rates of work-related sexual harassment in the United States: Using meta-analysis to explain reported rates disparities. *Personnel Psychology, 56,* 607–631.

Impett, Emily A., Sorsoli, Lynn, Schooler, Deborah, Henson, James M., & Tolman, Deborah L. (2008). Girls' relationship authenticity and self-esteem across adolescence. *Developmental Psychology, 44,* 722–733.

Ingraham, Christopher. (2015, October 1). Shooting in Oregon: So far in 2015, we've had 274 days and 294 mass shootings. *The Washington Post.* Retrieved from www.washingtonpost.com

Institute for Women's Policy Research. (2007). *The economic security of older women and men in the United States.* Washington, DC: Author.

Institute for Women's Policy Research. (2010). *The gender wage gap: 2009.* Retrieved from http://www.iwpr.org

Insurance Institute for Highway Safety. (2016). General statistics. Retrieved from http://www.iihs.org/iihs/topics/t/general-statistics/fatalityfacts/gender

International Labor Organization. (2012). *Global estimate of forced labour 2012: Results and methodology.* Geneva, Switzerland: Author.

Inzlicht, Michael, & Kang, Sonia K. (2010). Stereotype threat spillover: How coping with threats to social identity affects aggression, eating decision making, and attention. *Journal of Personality and Social Psychology, 99,* 467–481.

Irvine, Jacqueline J. (1985). Teacher communication patterns as related to the race and sex of the student. *Journal of Educational Research, 78,* 338–345.

Irvine, Jacqueline J. (1986). Teacher-student interactions: Effects of student race, sex, and grade level. *Journal of Educational Psychology, 78,* 14–21.

Iverson, Katherine M., King, Matthew W., Cunningham, Katherine C., & Resick, Patricia A. (2015). Rape survivors' trauma-related beliefs before and after cognitive processing therapy: Associations with PTSD and depression symptoms. *Behaviour Research and Therapy, 66,* 49–55.

Jackson, Linda A., von Eye, Alexander, Witt, Edward A., Zhao, Yong, & Fitzgerald, Hiram A. (2011). A longitudinal study of the effects of Internet use and videogame playing on academic performance and the roles of gender, race and income in these relationships. *Computers in Human Behavior, 27,* 228–239.

Jacobi, Corinna, Hayward, Chris, de Zwaan, Martina, Kraemer, Helena C., & Agras, W. Stewart. (2004). Coming to terms with risk factors for eating disorders: Application of risk terminology and suggestions for a general taxonomy. *Psychological Bulletin, 130,* 19–65.

Jacobs, Jerry A., & Labov, Teresa G. (2002). Gender differentials in intermarriage among sixteen race and ethnic groups. *Sociological Forum, 17,* 621–646.

Jacobs, Sue-Ellen, Thomas, Wesley, & Lang, Sabine. (Eds.). (1997). *Two-spirit people.* Urbana: University of Illinois Press.

Jaffee, Sara, & Hyde, Janet S. (2000). Gender differences in moral orientation: A meta-analysis. *Psychological Bulletin, 126,* 703–726.

Jakubowski, Patricia A. (1977). Assertive behavior and clinical problems of women. In E. I. Rawlings & D. K. Carter (Eds.), *Psycho-therapy for women.* Springfield, IL: Charles C Thomas.

Jakubowski-Spector, Patricia. (1973). Facilitating the growth of women through assertiveness training. *Counseling Psychologist, 4,* 75.

James, Stanlie M., & Busia, Abena (Eds.). (1993). *Theorizing Black feminisms: The visionary pragmatism of Black women.* New York, NY: Routledge.

Jane, Emma J. (2016). "Dude . . . stop the spread": Antagonism, agonism, and #manspreading on social media. *International Journal of Cultural Studies.* Advance online publication. https://doi.org/10.1177/1367877916637151

Janowsky, Jeri S., Chavez, Bambi, Zamboni, Brian D., & Orwoll, Eric. (1998). The cognitive neuropsychology of sex hormones in men and women. *Developmental Neuropsychology, 14,* 421–440.

Janson-Smith, Deirdre. (1980). Sociobiology: So what? In Brighton Women & Science Group, *Alice through the microscope.* London, UK: Virago.

Jemal, Ahmedin, Siegel, Rebecca, Ward, Elizabeth, Murray, Taylor, Xu, Jiaquan, & Thun, Michael J. (2007). Cancer statistics, 2007. *CA: A Cancer Journal for Clinicians, 57,* 43–66.

Jena, Anupam B., Olenski, Andrew R., & Blumenthal, Daniel M. (2016). Sex differences in physician salary in U.S. public medical schools. *JAMA Internal Medicine, 176,* 1294–1304.

Jennison, Karen M., & Johnson, Kenneth A. (2001). Parental alcoholism as a risk factor for DSM-IV-defined alcohol abuse and dependence in American women: The protective benefits of dyadic cohesion and marital communication. *American Journal of Drug and Alcohol Abuse, 27,* 349–374.

Jerman, Jenna, Jones, Rachel K., & Onda, Tsuyoshi. (2016). *Characteristics of U.S. abortion patients in 2014 and changes since 2008.* New York, NY: Guttmacher Institute.

Joel, Daphna, Berman, Zohar, Tavor, Ido, Wexler, Nadav, Gaber, Olga, Stein, Yaniv, . . . Assaf, Yaniv. (2015). Sex beyond the genitalia: The human brain mosaic. *Proceedings of the National Academy of Sciences of the USA, 112,* 15468–15473.

Joffe, Carole. (2013). The politicization of abortion and the evolution of abortion counseling. *American Journal of Public Health, 103,* 57–65.

Johansson, Annika, Sundbom, Elisabet, Höjerback, Torvald, & Bodlund, Owe. (2010). A five-year follow-up study of Swedish adults with gender identity disorder. *Archives of Sexual Behavior, 39,* 1429–1437.

Johnson, Daniel P., & Whisman, Mark A. (2013). Gender differences in rumination: A meta-analysis. *Personality and Individual Differences, 55,* 367–374.

Johnson, Michael J., Nemeth, Lynne S., Mueller, Martina, Eliason, Michele J., & Stuart, Gail W. (2016). Qualitative study of cervical cancer screening among lesbian and bisexual women and transgender men. *Cancer Nursing, 39,* 455–463.

Johnston, Deirdre D., & Swanson, Debra H. (2004). Moms hating moms: The internalization of Mother War rhetoric. *Sex Roles, 51,* 497–510.

Joiner, Thomas E., Jr., Heatherton, Todd F., Rudd, M. David, & Schmidt, Norman B. (1997). Perfectionism, perceived weight status, and bulimic symptoms: Two studies testing a diathesis-stress model. *Journal of Abnormal Psychology, 106,* 145–153.

Joint Economic Committee Democratic Staff. (2016). *Gender pay inequality: Consequences for women, families and the economy.* Retrieved from http://www.jec.senate.gov

Jonason, Peter K., & Fisher, Terri D. (2009). The power of prestige: Why young men report having more sex partners than young women. *Sex Roles, 60,* 151–159.

Jones, C. A., Reiter, L., & Greenblatt, E. (2016). Fertility preservation in transgender patients. *International Journal of Transgenderism, 17,* 76–82.

Jones, James M. (2010). I'm White and you're not: The value of unraveling ethnocentric science. *Perspectives on Psychological Science, 5,* 700–707.

Jones, Jo, Mosher, William D., & Daniels, Kimberly. (2012). *Current contraceptive use in the United States, 2006–2010, and changes in patterns of use since 1995* (National Health Statistics Reports No. 60). Washington, DC: National Center on Health Statistics. Retrieved from http://www.cdc .gov/nchs/data/nhsr/nhsr060.pdf

Jones, Rachel K. (2011). *Beyond birth control: The overlooked benefits of oral contraceptive pills.* New York, NY: Guttmacher Institute.

Jones, Rachel K., & Jerman, Jenna. (2017). Abortion incidence and service availability in the United States, 2014. *Perspectives on Sexual and Reproductive Health, 46,* 3–14.

Jones, Rachel K., & Kavanaugh, Megan L. (2011). Changes in abortion rates between 2000 and 2008 and lifetime incidence of abortion. *Obstetrics & Gynecology, 117,* 1358–1366.

Jones, Rachel K., & Kooistra, Kathryn. (2011). Abortion incidence and access to services in the United States, 2008. *Perspectives on Sexual and Reproductive Health, 43,* 41–50.

Jones, Susan, & Myhill, Debra. (2004). "Troublesome boys" and "compliant girls": Gender identity and perceptions of achievement and underachievement. *British Journal of Sociology of Education, 25,* 547–561.

Jones, Susanne M., & Dindia, Kathryn. (2004). A meta-analytic perspective on sex equity in the classroom. *Review of Educational Research, 74,* 443–471.

Jordan-Young, Rebecca. (2010). *Brain storm: The flaws in the science of sex differences.* Cambridge, MA: Harvard University Press.

Joshi, Suchi P., Peter, Jochen, & Valkenburg, Patti M. (2011). Scripts of sexual desire and danger in US and Dutch teen girl magazines: A cross-national content analysis. *Sex Roles, 64,* 463–474.

Jourard, Sydney M. (1974). *Healthy personality: An approach from the viewpoint of humanistic psychology.* New York, NY: Macmillan.

Kaestle, Christine E., & Allen, Katherine R. (2011). The role of masturbation in healthy sexual development. *Archives of Sexual Behavior, 40,* 983–994.

Kahlenberg, Susan G., & Hein, Michelle M. (2010). Progression on Nickelodeon? Gender-role stereotypes in toy commercials. *Sex Roles, 62,* 830–847.

Kahn, Arnold S., Mathie, Virginia A., & Torgler, Cyndee. (1994). Rape scripts and rape acknowledgment. *Psychology of Women Quarterly, 18,* 53–66.

Kahn, Jessica A., Slap, Gail B., Bernstein, David I., Tissot, Abbigail M., Kollar, Linda M., Hillard, Paula A., & Rosenthal, Susan L. (2007). Personal meaning of human papillomavirus and Pap test results in adolescent and young adult women. *Health Psychology, 26,* 192–200.

Kahn, Joan R., García-Manglano, Javier, & Bianchi, Suzanne M. (2014). The motherhood penalty at midlife: Long-term effects of children on women's careers. *Journal of Marriage and Family, 76,* 56–72.

Kail, Ben L., Acosta, Katie L., & Wright, Eric R. (2015). State-level marriage equality and the health of same-sex couples. *American Journal of Public Health, 105,* 1101–1105.

Kalbfleisch, Pamela J., & Herold, Anita L. (2005). Sex, power, and communication. In K. Dindia & D. Canary (Eds.), *Sex differences and similarities in communication* (2nd ed.). Mahwah, NJ: Lawrence Erlbaum.

Kalish, Rachel, & Kimmel, M. (2010). Suicide by mass murder: Masculinity, aggrieved entitlement, and rampage school shootings. *Health Sociology Review, 19,* 451–464.

Kallstrom-Fuqua, Amanda C., Weston, Rebecca, & Marshall, Linda L. (2004). Childhood and adolescent sexual abuse of community women: Mediated effects on psychological distress and social relationships. *Journal of Consulting and Clinical Psychology, 72,* 980–992.

Kamerman, Sheila B. (2000). Parental leave policies. *Social Policy Report of the Society for Research in Child Development, 14,* 1–15.

Kandall, Stephen R. (1996). *Substance and shadow: Women and addiction in the United States.* Cambridge, MA: Harvard University Press.

Kantor, Jodi, & Twohey, Megan. (2017, October 5). Harvey Weinstein paid off sexual harassment accusers for decades. *New York Times.* Retrieved from nytimes.com

Kaplan, Helen S. (1979). *Disorders of sexual desire.* New York, NY: Simon & Schuster.

Kaplan, Helen S. (1995). *The sexual desire disorders: Dysfunctional regulation of sexual motivation.* New York, NY: Brunner/Mazel.

Kaplan, Helen S., & Owett, Trude. (1993). The female androgen deficiency syndrome. *Journal of Sex and Marital Therapy, 19,* 3–25.

Kaplan, Helen S., & Sager, Clifford J. (1971, June). Sexual patterns at different ages. *Medical Aspects of Human Sexuality,* pp. 10–23.

Karazsia, Bryan T., Murnen, Sarah K., & Tylka, Tracy L. (2017). Is body dissatisfaction changing across time? A cross-temporal meta-analysis. *Psychological Bulletin, 143,* 293–320.

Karg, Katja, Burmeister, Margit, Shedden, Kerby, & Sen, Srijan. (2011). The serotonin transporter promoter variant (5-HTTLPR), stress, and depression meta-analysis revisited: Evidence of genetic moderation. *Archives of General Psychiatry, 68,* 444–454.

Kaschak, Ellyn. (2001). Intimate betrayal: Domestic violence in lesbian relationships. *Women & Therapy, 23*(3), 1–5.

Kaschak, Ellyn, & Tiefer, Leonore. (2001). *A new view of women's sexual problems.* New York, NY: Haworth.

Katz-Wise, Sabra, & Hyde, Janet S. (2012). Victimization of lesbian, gay, and bisexual individuals: A meta-analysis. *Journal of Sex Research, 49,* 142–167.

Katz-Wise, Sabra L., & Hyde, Janet S. (2015). Sexual fluidity and related attitudes and beliefs among young adults with a same-gender orientation. *Archives of Sexual Behavior, 44,* 1459–1470.

Kawahara, Debra M., & Espín, Oliva M. (Eds.). (2007). *Feminist reflections on growth and transformation: Asian American women in therapy.* New York, NY: Haworth.

Kearin, Manette, Pollard, Karen, & Garbett, Ian. (2014). Accuracy of sonographic fetal gender determination: Predictions made by sonographers during routine obstetric ultrasound scans. *Australasian Journal of Ultrasound in Medicine, 15*(3), 125–130.

Keefe, David L. (2002). Sex hormones and neural mechanisms. *Archives of Sexual Behavior, 31,* 401–404.

Keel, Pamela K., & Heatherton, Todd F. (2010). Weight suppression predicts maintenance and onset of bulimic syndromes at 10-year follow-up. *Journal of Abnormal Psychology, 119,* 268–275.

Kegel, Arnold H. (1952). Sexual functions of the pubococcygeus muscle. *Western Journal of Surgery, 60,* 521–524.

Kelch-Oliver, Karia. (2011). The experiences of African American grandmothers in grandparent-headed families. *The Family Journal, 19,* 73–82.

Kelly, Janice R., & Hutson-Comeaux, Sarah L. (1999). Gender-emotion stereotypes are context specific. *Sex Roles, 40,* 107–120.

Kendler, Kenneth S., Bulik, Cynthia M., Silberg, Judy, Hettema, John M., Myers, John, & Prescott, Carol A. (2000). Childhood sexual abuse and adult psychiatric and substance use disorders in women: An epidemiological and cotwin control analysis. *Archives of General Psychiatry, 57,* 953–959.

Kerpelman, Jennifer L., & Schvaneveldt, Paul L. (1999). Young adults' anticipated identity importance of career, marital, and parental roles: Comparisons of men and women with different role balance orientations. *Sex Roles, 41,* 189–218.

Kessler, Ronald C., McGonagle, Katherine A., Swartz, Marvin, Blazer, Dan G., & Nelson, Christopher B. (1993). Sex and depression in the National Comorbidity Survey: I. Lifetime prevalence, chronicity, and recurrence. *Journal of Affective Disorders, 29,* 85–96.

Kessler, Ronald C., McGonagle, Katherine A., Zhao, Shanyang, Nelson, Christopher B., Hughes, Michael, Eshleman, Suzann, . . . Kendler, Kenneth S. (1994). Lifetime and 12-month prevalence of DSM-III-R psychiatric disorders in the United States: Results from the National Comorbidity Survey. *Archives of General Psychiatry, 51,* 8–19.

Kessler, Suzanne J., & McKenna, Wendy. (1985). *Gender: An ethnomethodological approach.* Chicago, IL: University of Chicago Press.

Kettrey, Heather H. (2016). What's gender got to do with it? Sexual double standards and power in heterosexual college hookups. *Journal of Sex Research, 53,* 754–765.

Key, Mary Ritchie. (1975). *Male/female language.* Metuchen, NJ: Scarecrow Press.

Khan, Omer, Ferriter, Michael, Huband, Nick, Powney, Melanie J., Dennis, Jane A., & Duggan, Conor. (2015). Pharmacological interventions for those who have sexually offended or are at risk of offending. *Cochrane Database of Systematic Reviews, 2,* CD007989.

Kibria, Nazli. (1990). Power, patriarchy, and gender conflict in the Vietnamese immigrant community. *Gender & Society, 4,* 9–24.

Kiecolt-Glaser, Janice K., & Newton, Tamara L. (2001). Marriage and health: His and hers. *Psychological Bulletin, 127,* 472–503.

Kiesner, Jeff. (2011). One woman's low is another woman's high: Paradoxical effects of the menstrual cycle. *Psychoneuroendocrinology, 36,* 68–76.

Kilbey, M. Marlyne, & Burgermeister, Diane. (2001). Substance abuse. In J. Worell (Ed.), *Encyclopedia of women and gender* (pp. 1113–1128). San Diego, CA: Academic Press.

Kilmartin, Christopher T. (2000). *The masculine self* (2nd ed.). New York, NY: McGraw-Hill.

Kilpatrick, Dean G., Resnick, Heidi S., Ruggiero, Kenneth J., Conoscenti, Lauren M., & McCauley, Jenna. (2007). *Drug facilitated, incapacitated, and forcible rape: A national study.* Washington, DC: U.S. Department of Justice.

Kim, Bryan S. K., Li, Lisa C., & Ng, Gladys F. (2005). The Asian American values scale. *Cultural Diversity & Ethnic Minority Psychology, 11,* 187–201.

Kim, Elaine H. (1990, Winter). "Such opposite creatures": Men and women in Asian American literature. *Michigan Quarterly Review, 29,* 68–93.

Kim, Janna L. (2009). Asian American women's retrospective reports of their sexual socialization. *Psychology of Women Quarterly, 33,* 334–350.

Kimball, Meredith M. (1989). A new perspective on women's math achievement. *Psychological Bulletin, 105,* 198–214.

Kimerling, Rachel, & Baumrind, Nikki. (2005). Access to specialty mental health services among women in California. *Psychiatric Services, 56,* 729–734.

Kimmel, Ellen B., & Crawford, Mary. (2001). Methods for studying gender. In J. Worell (Ed.), *Encyclopedia of women and gender* (pp. 749–758). San Diego, CA: Academic Press.

Kimmel, Michael S. (2000). "White men are this nation": Right-wing militias and the restoration of rural American masculinity. *Rural Sociology, 65,* 582–604.

Kimmel, Michael S. (2002, February 8). Gender, class and terrorism. *Chronicle of Higher Education, 48,* B11–B12.

Kimmel, Michael S. (2004). *The gendered society* (2nd ed.). New York, NY: Oxford University Press.

Kimmel, Michael S. (2006). *Manhood in America: A cultural history* (2nd ed.). New York, NY: Oxford University Press.

Kimmel, Michael S. (2008). *Guyland: The perilous world where boys become men.* New York, NY: HarperCollins.

Kimmel, Michael S., & Mahler, Matthew. (2003). Adolescent masculinity, homophobia, and violence. *American Behavioral Scientist, 46,* 1439–1458.

Kimmel, Michael S., & Messner, Michael A. (2001). *Men's lives* (5th ed.). Boston, MA: Allyn and Bacon.

Kimura, Doreen, & Hampson, Elizabeth. (1994). Cognitive pattern in men and women is influenced by fluctuations in sex hormones. *Current Directions, 3,* 57–60.

Kins, E., Hoebeke, P., Heylens, G., Rubens, R., & De Cuyprere, G. (2008). The female-to-male transsexual and his female partner versus the traditional couple: A comparison. *Journal of Sex and Marital Therapy, 34,* 429–438.

Kinsey, Alfred C., Pomeroy, Wardell B., Martin, Clyde E., & Gebhard, Paul H. (1953). *Sexual behavior in the human female.* Philadelphia, PA: Saunders.

Kitzmann, Katherine M., Gaylord, Noni K., Holt, Aimee R., & Kenny, Erin D. (2003). Child witnesses to domestic violence: A meta-analytic review. *Journal of Consulting and Clinical Psychology, 71,* 339–352.

Kjaersgaard, Kim S. (2005). Aging to perfection or perfectly aged? The image of women growing older on television. In E. Cole & J. H. Daniel (Eds.), *Featuring females: Feminist analyses of media* (pp. 199–210). Washington, DC: American Psychological Association.

Klatsky, Arthur L., Armstrong, Mary Anne, & Friedman, Gary D. (1992). Alcohol and mortality. *Annals of Internal Medicine, 117,* 646–654.

Klebanov, Pamela K., & Jemmott, John B. (1992). Effects of expectations and bodily sensations on self-reports of premenstrual symptoms. *Psychology of Women Quarterly, 16,* 289–310.

Klein, Kristi J. K., & Hodges, Sara D. (2001). Gender differences, motivation, and empathic accuracy: When it pays to understand. *Personality and Social Psychology Bulletin, 27,* 720–730.

Klein, Sabra L., Hodgson, Andrea, & Robinson, Dionne P. (2012). Mechanisms of sex disparities in influenza pathogenesis. *Journal of Leukocyte Biology, 92,* 67–73.

Klimes-Dougan, Bonnie, Pearson, Theresa E., Jappe, Leah, Mathieson, Lindsay, Simard, Melissa R., Hastings, Paul, & Zahn-Waxler, Carolyn. (2014). Adolescent emotion socialization: A longitudinal study of friends' responses to negative emotions. *Social Development, 23,* 395–412.

Kling, Kristen C., Hyde, Janet S., Showers, Carolin J., & Buswell, Brenda N. (1999). Gender differences in self-esteem: A meta-analysis. *Psychological Bulletin, 125,* 470–500.

Klump, Kelly L., VanHuysse, Jessica L., Burt, S. Alexandra, McGue, Matt, & Iacono, William. (2009). Genetic and environmental influences on disordered eating: An adoption study. *Journal of Abnormal Psychology, 118,* 797–805.

Knight, Raymond A., & Sims-Knight, Judith. (2011). Risk factors for sexual violence. In J. W. White, M. P. Koss, & A. E. Kazdin (Eds.), *Violence against women and children: Mapping the terrain* (Vol. 1, pp. 125–150). Washington, DC: American Psychological Association.

Knox, Sarah S., & Czajkowski, Susan. (1997). The influence of behavioral and psychosocial factors on cardiovascular health in women. In S. Gallant, G. Keita, & R. Royak-Schaler (Eds.), *Health care for women: Psychological, social, and behavioral influences* (pp. 257–272). Washington, DC: American Psychological Association.

Koch, Amanda J., D'Mello, Susan D., & Sackett, Paul R. (2015). A meta-analysis of gender stereotypes and bias in experimental simulations of employment decision making. *Journal of Applied Psychology, 100,* 128–161.

Kochanek, Kenneth D., Murphy, Sherry L., Xu, Jiaquan, & Tejada-Vera, Betzaida. (2016). *Deaths: Final data for 2014* (National vital statistics reports). Hyattsville, MD: National Center for Health Statistics.

Koenig, Anne M., Eagly, Alice H., Mitchell, Abigail A., & Ristikari, Tina. (2011). Are leader stereotypes masculine? A meta-analysis of three research paradigms. *Psychological Bulletin, 137,* 616–642.

Koepke, Sabrina, & Denissen, Jaap J. A. (2012). Dynamics of identity development and separation-individuation in parent-child relationships during adolescence and emerging adulthood: A conceptual integration. *Developmental Review, 32,* 67–88.

Koeser, Sara, Kuhn, Elizabeth A., & Sczesny, Sabine. (2015). Just reading? How gender-fair language triggers readers' use of gender-fair forms. *Journal of Language and Social Psychology, 34,* 343–357.

Kohlberg, Lawrence. (1966). A cognitive-developmental analysis of children's sex-role concepts and attitudes. In E. E. Maccoby (Ed.), *The development of sex differences.* Stanford, CA: Stanford University Press.

Kohlberg, Lawrence. (1969). Stage and sequence: The cognitive-developmental approach to socialization. In D. A. Goslin (Ed.), *Handbook of socialization theory and research* (pp. 347–480). Chicago, IL: Rand McNally.

Kosciw, Joseph G., Greytak, Emily A., Palmer, Neal A., & Boesen, Madelyn J. (2014). *The 2013 National School Climate Survey: The experiences of lesbian, gay, bisexual and transgender youth in our nation's schools.* New York: GLSEN.

Koss, Mary P. (2014). The RESTORE program of restorative justice for sex crimes: Vision, process, and outcomes. *Journal of Interpersonal Violence, 24,* 1623–1660.

Koss, Mary P., Abbey, Antonia, Campbell, Rebecca, Cook, Sarah, Norris, Jeanette, Testa, Maria, . . . White, Jacquelyn. (2007). Revising the SES: A collaborative process to improve assessment of sexual aggression and victimization. *Psychology of Women Quarterly, 32,* 357–370.

Koss, Mary, & Achilles, M. (2008). *Restorative justice responses to sexual assault.* Retrieved from http://vawnet.org/sites/default/files/materials/files/2016-09/AR_RestorativeJustice.pdf

Koss, Mary P., Bachar, Karen J., & Hopkins, C. Quince. (2003). Restorative justice of sexual violence: Repairing victims, building community, and holding offenders accountable. *Annals of the New York Academy of Sciences, 989,* 133–147.

Koss, Mary P., Bailey, Jennifer A., Yuan, Nicole P., Herrera, Veronica M., & Lichter, Erika L. (2003). Depression and

PTSD in survivors of male violence: Research and training initiatives to facilitate recovery. *Psychology of Women Quarterly, 27,* 130–142.

Koss, Mary P., Dinero, Thomas E., Seibel, Cynthia A., & Cox, Susan L. (1988). Stranger and acquaintance rape: Are there differences in the victim's experience? *Psychology of Women Quarterly, 12,* 1–24.

Koss, Mary P., & Figueredo, Aurelio. (2004). Change in cognitive mediators of rape's impact on psychosocial health across 2 years of recovery. *Journal of Consulting and Clinical Psychology, 72,* 1063–1072.

Koss, Mary P., Gidycz, Christine A., & Wisniewski, Nadine. (1987). The scope of rape: Incidence and prevalence in a national sample of higher education students. *Journal of Consulting and Clinical Psychology, 55,* 162–170.

Koss, Mary P., Goodman, Lisa A., Browne, Angela, Fitzgerald, Louise F., Russo, Nancy F., & Keita, Gwendolyn P. (1994). *No safe haven: Male violence against women at home, at work, and in the community.* Washington, DC: American Psychological Association.

Koss, Mary P., Wilgus, Jay K., & Williamsen, Kaaren M. (2014). Campus sexual misconduct: Restorative justice approaches to enhance compliance with Title IX guidance. *Trauma, Violence, & Abuse, 15,* 242–257.

Kost, K., Henshaw, S., & Carlin, L. (2010). *U.S. teenage pregnancies, births and abortions: National and state trends and trends by race and ethnicity.* New York, NY: Guttmacher Institute.

Koutsky, Laura A., Ault, Kevin A., Wheeler, Cosette M., Brown, Darron R., Barr, Eliav, Alvarez, Frances B., . . . Jansen, Kathrin U. (2002). A controlled trial of a human papillomavirus type 16 vaccine. *New England Journal of Medicine, 347*(21), 1645–1651.

Kozak, Megan N., Roberts, Tomi-Ann, & Patterson, Kelsey E. (2014). She stoops to conquer? How posture interacts with self-objectification and status to impact women's affect and performance. *Psychology of Women Quarterly, 38,* 414–424.

Krahé, Barbara, & Krause, Christina. (2010). Presenting thin media models affects women's choice of diet or normal snacks. *Psychology of Women Quarterly, 34,* 349–355.

Kravitz, Howard M., Ganz, Patricia A., Bromberger, Joyce, Powell, Lynda H., Sutton-Tyrrell, Kim, & Meyer, Peter M. (2003). Sleep difficulty in women at midlife: A community survey of sleep and the menopausal transition. *Menopause, 10,* 19–28.

Kreider, Rose M., & Ellis, Renee. (2011). *Number, timing, and duration of marriages and divorces: 2009* (Current Population Reports P70-125). Washington, DC: U.S. Census Bureau.

Krendl, Anne C., Richeson, Jennifer A., Kelley, William M., & Heatherton, Todd F. (2008). The negative consequences of threat. *Psychological Science, 19*, 168–175.

Kring, Ann M., & Gordon, Albert H. (1998). Sex differences in emotion: Expression, experience, and physiology. *Journal of Personality and Social Psychology, 74*, 686–703.

Kruger, Daniel J., Fisher, Maryanne L., & Wright, Paula. (2013). A framework for integrating evolutionary and feminist perspectives in psychological research. *Journal of Social, Evolutionary, and Cultural Psychology, 7*, 299–303.

Kubany, Edward S., Hill, Elizabeth E., & Owens, Julie A. (2004). Cognitive trauma therapy for battered women with PTSD (CTT-BW). *Journal of Consulting and Clinical Psychology, 72*, 3–18.

Kuhn, Deanna. (1976). Short-term longitudinal evidence for the sequentiality of Kohlberg's early stage of moral development. *Developmental Psychology, 12*, 162–166.

Kuhn, Thomas S. (1970). *The structure of scientific revolutions.* Chicago, IL: University of Chicago Press.

Kunda, Ziva, & Spencer, Steven J. (2003). When do stereotypes come to mind and when do they color judgment? A goal-based theoretical framework for stereotype activation and application. *Psychological Bulletin, 129*, 522–544.

Kurdek, Lawrence. (2005). What do we know about gay and lesbian couples? *Current Directions in Psychological Science, 14*, 251–254.

Kushner, Matt G., Sher, Kenneth J., & Beitman, Bernard D. (1990). The relation between alcohol problems and the anxiety disorders. *American Journal of Psychiatry, 147*, 685–695.

Kwong, Marilyn J., Bartholomew, Kim, Henderson, Antonia, & Trinke, Shanna J. (2003). The intergenerational transmission of relationship violence. *Journal of Family Psychology, 17*, 288–301.

LaCrosse, Jennifer, Sekaquaptewa, Denise, & Bennett, Jill. (2016). STEM stereotypic attribution bias among women in an unwelcoming science setting. *Psychology of Women Quarterly, 40*, 378–397.

Ladas, Alice K., Whipple, Beverly, & Perry, John D. (1982). *The G-spot.* New York, NY: Holt, Rinehart & Winston.

LaFrance, Marianne, Hecht, Marvin A., & Paluck, Elizabeth L. (2003). The contingent smile: A meta-analysis of sex differences in smiling. *Psychological Bulletin, 129*, 305–334.

LaFrance, Marianne, & Vial, A. C. (2016). Gender and nonverbal behavior. In D. Matsumoto, H. C. Hwang, & M. G. Frank (Eds), *APA handbook of nonverbal communication* (pp. 139–161). Washington, DC: American Psychological Association.

LaFromboise, Teresa D., Berman, Joan S., & Sohi, Balvindar K. (1994). American Indian women. In L. Comas-Diaz & B. Greene (Eds.), *Women of color: Integrating ethnic and gender identities in psychotherapy* (pp. 30–71). New York, NY: Guilford.

LaFromboise, Teresa, Choney, Sandra B., James, Amy, & Running Wolf, Paulette R. (1995). American Indian women and psychology. In H. Landrine (Ed.), *Bringing cultural diversity to feminist psychology: Theory, research, and practice* (pp. 197–240). Washington, DC: American Psychological Association.

LaFromboise, Teresa D., Heyle, Anneliese M., & Ozer, Emily J. (1990). Changing and diverse roles of women in American Indian culture. *Sex Roles, 22*, 455–476.

LaFromboise, Teresa D., Hoyt, Dan R., Oliver, Lisa, & Whitbeck, Les B. (2006). Family, community, and school influences on resilience among American Indian adolescents in the upper Midwest. *Journal of Community Psychology, 34*, 193–209.

Lahn, Bruce, & Page, David. (1997). Functional coherence of the human Y chromosome. *Science, 278*, 675–680.

Lakes, Kimberley D., & Hoyt, William T. (2009). Applications of generalizability theory to clinical child and adolescent psychology research. *Journal of Clinical Child and Adolescent Psychology, 38*, 144–165.

Lakoff, Robin. (1973). Language and woman's place. *Language and Society, 2*, 45–79.

Lakoff, Robin. (1975). *Language and woman's place.* New York, NY: Oxford University Press.

Lal, Shafali. (2002). Giving children security: Mamie Phipps Clark and the racialization of child psychology. *American Psychologist, 57*, 20–28.

Lamb, C. Sue, Jackson, Lee A., Cassiday, Patricia B., & Priest, Doris J. (1993). Body figure preferences of men and women: A comparison of two generations. *Sex Roles, 28*, 345–358.

Lamb, Douglas H., Catanzaro, Salvatore J., & Moorman, Annorah S. (2003). Psychologists reflect on their sexual relationships with clients, supervisees, and students: Occurrence, impact, rationales, and collegial intervention. *Professional Psychology: Research and Practice, 34*, 102–107.

Lamb, Lindsay M., Bigler, Rebecca S., Liben, Lynn S., & Green, Vanessa A. (2009). Teaching children to confront peers' sexist remarks: Implications for theories of gender development and educational practice. *Sex Roles, 61*, 361–382.

Lamberts, Steven W. J., van den Beld, Annewieke W., & van der Lely, Aart-Jan. (1997). The endocrinology of aging. *Science, 278,* 419–424.

Landor, Antoinette M., & Halpern, Carolyn T. (2016). Prevalence of high-risk sexual behaviors among monoracial and multiracial groups from a national sample: Are multiracial young adults at greater risk? *Archives of Sexual Behavior, 45,* 467–475.

Landrine, Hope. (1987). On the politics of madness: A preliminary analysis of the relationship between social roles and psychopathology. *Psychological Monographs, 113*(3), 341–406.

Landrine, Hope. (1988). Revising the framework of abnormal psychology. In P. Bronstein & K. Quina (Eds.), *Teaching a psychology of people.* Washington, DC: American Psychological Association.

Landrine, Hope, & Klonoff, Elizabeth A. (2001). Health and health care: How gender makes women sick. In J. Worell (Ed.), *Encyclopedia of women and gender* (pp. 577–592). San Diego, CA: Academic Press.

Landrine, Hope, Klonoff, Elizabeth A., & Brown-Collins, Alice. (1995). Cultural diversity and methodology in feminist psychology: Critique, proposal, empirical example. In H. Landrine (Ed.), *Bringing cultural diversity to feminist psychology* (pp. 55–76). Washington, DC: American Psychological Association.

Langer, S. J. (2011). Gender (dis)agreement: A dialogue on the clinical implications of gendered language. *Journal of Gay & Lesbian Mental Health, 15,* 300–307.

Langton, Lynn, Berzofsky, Marcus, Krebs, Christopher, & Smiley-McDonald, Hope. (2012). *Victimizations not reported to the police, 2006–2010* (NCJ 238536). Washington, DC: Bureau of Justice Statstics.

Larson, Reed W., Richards, Maryse H., & Perry-Jenkins, Maureen. (1994). Divergent worlds: The daily emotional experience of mothers and fathers in the domestic and public spheres. *Journal of Personality and Social Psychology, 67,* 1034–1046.

Larwood, Laurie, Szwajkowski, Eugene, & Rose, Suzanna. (1988). When discrimination makes "sense": The rational bias theory. In B. Gutek, A. H. Stromberg, & L. Larwood (Eds.), *Women and work: An annual review* (Vol. 3, pp. 265–288). Beverly Hills, CA: Sage.

Latu, Ioana M., Stewart, Tracy L., Myers, Ashley C., Lisco, Claire G., Estes, Sarah B., & Donahue, Dana K. (2011). What we "say" and what we "think" about female managers: Explicit versus implicit associations of women with success. *Psychology of Women Quarterly, 35,* 252–266.

Laumann, Edward O., Gagnon, John H., Michael, Robert T., & Michaels, Stuart. (1994). *The social organization of sexuality: Sexual practices in the United States.* Chicago, IL: University of Chicago Press.

Lavine, Howard, Sweeney, Donna, & Wagner, Stephen H. (1999). Depicting women as sex objects in television advertising: Effects on body dissatisfaction. *Personality and Social Psychology Bulletin, 25,* 1049–1058.

Lazarus, Arnold A. (1974). Women in behavior therapy. In V. Franks & V. Burtle (Eds.), *Women in therapy.* New York, NY: Brunner/Mazel.

Lazowski, Rory A., & Hulleman, Chris S. (2016). Motivation interventions in education: A meta-analytic review. *Review of Educational Research, 86,* 602–640.

Le Grange, Daniel, Lock, James, Agras, W. Stewart, Bryson, Susan W., & Jo, Booil. (2015). Randomized clinical trial of family-based treatment and cognitive-behavioral therapy for adolescent bulimia nervosa. *Journal of the American Acadmy of Child & Adolescent Psychiatry, 45,* 886–894.

Leaper, Campbell. (2015). Gender and social-cognitive development. In L. S. Liben & U. Muller (Eds.), *Handbook of child psychology and developmental science* (7th ed., Vol. 2, pp. 806–853). New York, NY: Wiley.

Leaper, Campbell, Anderson, Kristin J., & Sanders, Paul. (1998). Moderators of gender effects on parents' talk to their children: A meta-analysis. *Developmental Psychology, 34,* 3–27.

Leaper, Campbell, & Ayres, Melanie M. (2007). A meta-analytic review of gender variations in adults' language use: Talkativeness, affiliative speech, and assertive speech. *Personality and Social Psychology Review, 11,* 328–362.

Leaper, Campbell, & Brown, Christia S. (2008). Perceived experiences with sexism among adolescent girls. *Child Development, 79,* 685–704.

Leaper, Campbell, & Robnett, Rachael D. (2011). Women are more likely than men to use tentative language, aren't they? A meta-analysis testing for gender differences and moderators. *Psychology of Women Quarterly, 35,* 129–142.

Leaper, Campbell, & Smith, Tara E. (2004). A meta-analytic review of gender variations in children's language use: Talkativeness, affiliative speech, and assertive speech. *Developmental Psychology, 40,* 993–1027.

Lear, Martha W. (1973, January 28). Is there a male menopause? *New York Times Magazine.*

LeBreton, Marianne, Courtois, Frédérique, Journel, Nicolas M., Beaulieu-Prévost, Dominic, Bélanger, Marc, Ruffion, Alain, & Terrier, Jean-Étienne. (2017). Genital sensory detection thresholds and patient satisfaction with vaginoplasty in male-to-female transgender women. *Journal of Sexual Medicine, 14,* 274–281.

LeDoux, Joseph E. (1994). Emotion-specific physiological activity: Don't forget about CNS physiology. In P. Ekman & R. J. Davidson (Eds.), *The nature of emotion: Fundamental questions* (pp. 248–251). New York, NY: Oxford University Press.

Lee, Nikki C., Krabbendam, Lydia, White, Thomas P., Meeter, Marihn, Banaschewski, Tobias, Barker, Gareth, J., . . . Shergill, Sukhi S. (2013). Do you see what I see? Sex differences in the discrimination of facial emotions during adolescence. *Emotion, 13,* 1030–1040.

Lehmiller, Justin J., Vanderdrift, Laura E., & Kelly, Janice R. (2011). Sex differences in approaching friends with benefits relationships. *Journal of Sex Research, 48,* 275–284.

Leibbrandt, Andreas, & List, John A. (2015). Do women avoid salary negotiations? Evidence from a large-scale natural field experiment. *Management Science, 61,* 2016–2024.

Leiblum, Sandra R. (2000). Vaginismus: A most perplexing problem. In S. Leiblum & R. Rosen (Eds.), *Principles and practice of sex therapy* (3rd ed., pp. 181–202). New York, NY: Guilford.

Leinbach, Mary D. (1993). *Which one is the daddy? Children's use of conventionally and metaphorically gendered attributes to assign gender to animal figures.* Paper presented at the meeting of the Society for Research in Child Development, New Orleans, LA.

Leinbach, Mary, & Fagot, Beverly. (1993). Categorical habituation to male and female faces: Gender schematic processing in infancy. *Infant Behavior and Development, 16,* 317–332.

Lemieux, Suzanne R., & Byers, E. Sandra. (2008). The sexual well-being of women who have experienced child sexual abuse. *Psychology of Women Quarterly, 32,* 126–144.

Lenroot, Rhoshel K., Gogtay, Nitin, Greenstein, Deanna K., Wells, Elizabeth M., Wallace, Gregory L., Clasen, Liv S., . . . Giedd, Jay N. (2007). Sexual dimorphism of brain developmental trajectories during childhood and adolescence. *NeuroImage, 36,* 1065–1073.

Lenton, Alison P., Bruder, Martin, & Sedikides, Constantine. (2009). A meta-analysis on the malleability of automatic gender stereotypes. *Psychology of Women Quarterly, 33,* 183–196.

Leonard, David K., & Jiang, Jiming. (1999). Gender bias and the college prediction of the SATs: A cry of despair. *Research in Higher Education, 40,* 375–407.

Lepowsky, Maria A. (1993). *Fruit of the motherland: Gender in an egalitarian society.* New York, NY: Columbia University Press.

Lerman, Hannah. (1986). From Freud to feminist personality theory. *Psychology of Women Quarterly, 10,* 1–18.

Leslie, Sarah-Jane, Cimpian, Andrei, Meyer, Meredith, & Freeland, Edward. (2015). Expectations of brilliance underlie gender distributions across academic disciplines. *Science, 347,* 262–265.

Lev, Arlene I. (2013). Gender dysphoria: Two steps forward, one step back. *Clinical Social Work Journal, 41,* 288–296.

Levant, Ronald F. (2011). Research in the psychology of men and masculinity using the gender role strain paradigm as a framework. *American Psychologist, 66,* 765–776.

Levant, Ronald F., Hall, Rosalie J., Williams, Christine M., & Hasan, Nadia T. (2009). Gender differences in alexithymia. *Psychology of Men & Masculinity, 10,* 190–203.

Levant, Ronald F., & Richmond, Katherine. (2016). The gender role strain paradigm and masculinity ideologies. In Y. J. Wong & S. R. Wester (Eds.), *APA handbook of men and masculinities* (pp. 23–49). Washington, DC: American Psychological Association.

Levant, Ronald F., & Wong, Y. Joel. (2013). Race and gender as moderators of the relationship between the endorsement of traditional masculinity ideology and alexithymia: An intersectional perspective. *Psychology of Men & Masculinity, 14,* 329–333.

LeVay, Simon. (1991). A difference in hypothalamic structure between heterosexual and homosexual men. *Science, 253,* 1034–1037.

Levendosky, Alytia, Huth-Bocks, Alissa, & Semel, Michael A. (2002). Adolescent peer relationships and mental health functioning in families with domestic violence. *Journal of Clinical Child and Adolescent Psychology, 31,* 206–218.

Levendosky, Alytia A., Huth-Bocks, Alissa C., Semel, Michael A., & Shapiro, Deborah L. (2002). Trauma symptoms in preschool-age children exposed to domestic violence. *Journal of Interpersonal Violence, 17,* 150–164.

Levenson, Robert W., Carstensen, Laura L., & Gottman, John M. (1994). The influence of age and gender on affect, physiology, and their interrelations: A study of long-term marriages. *Journal of Personality and Social Psychology, 67,* 56–68.

Levine, Felice J., & Ancheta, Angelo N. (2013). The AERA et al. amicus brief in *Fisher v. University of Texas at Austin:* Scientific organizations serving society. *Educational Researcher, 42,* 166–171.

Levine, Michael P., Smolak, Linda, Moodey, Anne F., Shuman, Melissa D., & Hessen, Laura D. (1994). Normative developmental challenges and dieting and eating disturbances in middle school girls. *International Journal of Eating Disorders, 15,* 11–20.

Levine, Susan C., Vasilyeva, Marina, Lourenco, Stella F., Newcombe, Nora S., & Huttenlocher, Janellen. (2005). Socioeconomic status modifies the sex difference in spatial skill. *Psychological Science, 16,* 841–845.

Levinson, D. F. (2005). The genetics of depression: A review. *Biological Psychiatry, 60,* 84–92.

Levy, Gary D. (1994). High and low gender schematic children's release from proactive interference. *Sex Roles, 30,* 93–108.

Levy, Jere. (1976). Cerebral lateralization and spatial ability. *Behavior Genetics, 6,* 171–188.

Levy, Sheri R., & Macdonald, Jamie L. (2016). Progress on understanding ageism. *Journal of Social Issues, 72,* 5–25.

Levy-Agresti, Jere, & Sperry, Roger W. (1968). Differential perceptual capacities in major and minor hemispheres. *Proceedings of the National Academy of Sciences of the USA, 61,* 1151.

Lew-Williams, Casey, & Fernald, Anne. (2007). Young children learning Spanish make rapid use of grammatical gender in spoken word recognition. *Psychological Science, 18,* 193–198.

Lewis, Jioni A., & Neville, Helen A. (2015). Construction and initial validation of the Gendered Racial Microaggressions Scale for Black Women. *Journal of Counseling Psychology, 62,* 289–302.

Liben, Lynn S., Bigler, Rebecca S., & Krogh, Holleen R. (2002). Language at work: Children's gendered interpretations of occupational titles. *Child Development, 73,* 810–818.

Liddon, Nicole, Hood, Julia, Wynn, Bridget A., & Markowitz, Lauri E. (2010). Acceptability of human papillomavirus vaccine for males: A review of the literature. *Journal of Adolescent Health, 46,* 113–123.

Lightdale, Jenifer R., & Prentice, Deborah A. (1994). Rethinking sex differences in aggression: Aggressive behavior in the absence of social roles. *Personality and Social Psychology Bulletin, 20,* 34–44.

Lindberg, Sara M., Grabe, Shelly, & Hyde, Janet S. (2007). Gender, pubertal development, and peer sexual harassment predict objectified body consciousness in early adolescence. *Journal of Research on Adolescence, 17,* 723–742.

Lindberg, Sara M., Hyde, Janet S., Petersen, Jennifer L., & Linn, Marcia C. (2010). New trends in gender and mathematics performance: A meta-analysis. *Psychological Bulletin, 136,* 1123–1135.

Lindgren, Kristen P., Parkhill, Michele R., George, William H., & Hendershot, Christian S. (2008). Gender differences in perceptions of sexual intent: A qualitative review and integration. *Psychology of Women Quarterly, 32,* 423–439.

Lindsey, A. Elizabeth, & Zakahi, Walter R. (2005). Perceptions of men and women departing from conversational sex-role stereotypes. In K. Dindia & D. Canary (Eds.), *Sex differences and similarities in communication* (2nd ed.). Mahwah, NJ: Lawrence Erlbaum.

Lindsey, Eric W., & Mize, Jacquelyn. (2001). Contextual differences in parent-child play: Implications for children's gender role development. *Sex Roles, 44,* 155–176.

Lindsey, Eric W., Mize, Jacquelyn, & Pettit, Gregory S. (1997). Differential play patterns of mothers and fathers of sons and daughters: Implications for children's gender role development. *Sex Roles, 37,* 643–662.

Linn, Marcia C., & Hyde, Janet S. (1990). Gender, mathematics, and science. *Educational Researcher, 18*(8), 17–19, 22–27.

Linn, Marcia C., & Petersen, Anne C. (1985). Emergence and characterization of sex differences in spatial ability: A meta-analysis. *Child Development, 56,* 1479–1498.

Lippa, Richard A. (2006). Is high sex drive associated with increased sexual attraction to both sexes? *Psychological Science, 17,* 46–52.

Lippa, Richard A., Martin, Leslie R., & Friedman, Howard S. (2000). Gender-related individual differences and mortality in the Terman longitudinal study: Is masculinity hazardous to your health? *Personality and Social Psychology Bulletin, 26,* 1560–1570.

Lips, Hilary M. (1989). Gender-role socialization: Lessons in femininity. In Jo Freeman (Ed.), *Women: A feminist perspective* (4th ed.). Mountain View, CA: Mayfield.

Lipsey, Mark, & Wilson, David. (2001). *Practical meta-analysis.* Thousand Oaks, CA: Sage.

Lipton, Eric. (2005, September 9). Political issues snarled plans for troop aid. *New York Times.*

Liu, Tao, & Wong, Y. Joel. (2016). The intersection of race and gender: Asian American men's experience of discrimination. *Psychology of Men & Masculinity.* Advance online publication. http://dx.doi.org/10.1037/men0000084

Livingston, Jennifer A., Hequembourg, Amy, & Testa, Maria. (2007). Unique aspects of adolescent sexual victimization experiences. *Psychology of Women Quarterly, 31,* 331–343.

Livingston, Robert W., Rosette, Ashley S., & Washington, Ella F. (2012). Can an agentic Black woman get ahead? The impact of race and interpersonal dominance on perceptions of female leaders. *Psychological Science, 23,* 354–358.

Lock, James, & le Grange, Daniel. (2005). Family-based treatment of eating disorders. *International Journal of Eating Disorders, 37*(Suppl.), S64–S67.

Löckenhoff, Corinna E., Chan, Wayne, McCrae, Robert R., De Fruyt, Filip, Jussim, Lee, De Bolle, Marleen, . . . Terracciano, Antonio. (2014). Gender stereotypes of personality: Universal and accurate? *Journal of Cross-Cultural Psychology, 45,* 675–694.

Loftus, Elizabeth F. (1993). The reality of repressed memories. *American Psychologist, 48,* 518–537.

Lok, Ingrid H., & Neugebauer, Richard. (2007). Psychological morbidity following miscarriage. *Best Practice & Research, Clinical Obstetrics and Gynaecology, 21,* 229–247.

Loo, Robert, & Thorpe, Karran. (1998). Attitudes toward women's roles in society: A replication after 20 years. *Sex Roles, 39,* 903–912.

LoPiccolo, Joseph, & Stock, Wendy E. (1986). Treatment of sexual dysfunction. *Journal of Consulting and Clinical Psychology, 54,* 158–167.

Lorber, Judith, Coser, Rose L., Rossi, Alice S., & Chodorow, Nancy. (1981). On "The Reproduction of Mothering": A methodological debate. *Signs, 6*(3), 482–513.

Lott, Bernice. (1981). A feminist critique of androgyny: Toward the elimination of gender attributions for learned behavior. In C. Mayo & N. Henley (Eds.), *Gender and nonverbal behavior* (pp. 171–180). New York, NY: Springer-Verlag.

Lott, Bernice, & Maluso, Diane. (1993). The social learning of gender. In A. E. Beall & R. J. Sternberg (Eds.), *The psychology of gender* (pp. 99–126). New York, NY: Guilford.

Lovell, Vicky, Hartmann, Heidi, & Williams, Claudia. (2008). *Why Americans worry about retirement security, and why women worry more than men.* Washington, DC: Institute for Women's Policy Research.

Luce, Kristine H., Crowther, Janis H., & Pole, Michele. (2008). Eating Disorder Examination Questionnaire (EDE-Q): Norms for undergraduate women. *International Journal of Eating Disorders, 41,* 273–276.

Lueck, Kerstin, & Wilson, Machelle. (2011). Acculturative stress in Latino immigrants: The impact of social, socio-psychological and migration-related factors. *International Journal of Intercultural Relations, 35,* 186–195.

Lugones, M. C. (2010). Toward a decolonial feminism. *Hypatia, 25,* 742–758.

Lund, Emily M., & Thomas, Katie B. (2015). Necessary but not sufficient: Sexual assault information on college and university websites. *Psychology of Women Quarterly, 39,* 530–538.

Lytle, L. Jean, Bakken, Linda, & Romig, Charles. (1997). Adolescent female identity development. *Sex Roles, 37,* 175–186.

Lytton, Hugh, & Romney, David M. (1991). Parents' differential socialization of boys and girls: A meta-analysis. *Psychological Bulletin, 109,* 267–296.

MacArthur, Heather J., & Shields, Stephanie A. (2015). There's no crying in baseball, or is there? Male athletes, tears, and masculinity in North America. *Emotion Review, 7,* 39–46.

Maccoby, Eleanor E. (1998). *The two sexes: Growing up apart, coming together.* Cambridge, MA: Harvard University Press.

Maccoby, Eleanor E. (2002). Gender and group process: A developmental perspective. *Current Directions in Psychological Science, 11,* 54–58.

Maccoby, Eleanor E., & Jacklin, Carol N. (1974). *The psychology of sex differences.* Stanford, CA: Stanford University Press.

MacKinnon, Catharine A. (1982). Feminism, Marxism, method, and the state: An agenda for theory. *Signs: Journal of Women in Culture and Society, 7,* 515–544.

MacMillan, Harriet L., Fleming, Jan E., Streiner, David L., Lin, Elizabeth, Boyle, Michael H., Jamieson, Ellen, . . . Beardslee, William R. (2001). Childhood abuse and lifetime psychopathology in a community sample. *American Journal of Psychiatry, 158,* 1878–1883.

Macur, Juliet, & Schweber, Nate. (2012, December 16). Rape case unfolds on web and splits city. *New York Times.* Retrieved from http://www.nytimes.com

Maeda, Yukiko, & Yoon, So Y. (2013). A meta-analysis on gender differences in mental rotation ability measured by the Purdue Spatial Visualization Tests: Visualization of Rotations (PSVT-R). *Educational Psychology Review, 25,* 69–94.

Magaña, J. Raul, & Carrier, Joseph M. (1991). Mexican and Mexican American male sexual behavior and spread of AIDS in California. *Journal of Sex Research, 28,* 425–441.

Mahalik, James R., Locke, Benjamin D., Theodore, Harry, Cournoyer, Robert J., & Lloyd, Brendan F. (2001). A cross-national and cross-sectional comparison of men's gender role conflict and its relationship to social intimacy and self-esteem. *Sex Roles, 45,* 1–14.

Mahay, Jenna, Michaels, Stuart, & Laumann, Edward O. (2001). Race, gender, and class in sexual scripts. In E. O. Laumann & R. T. Michael (Eds.), *Sex, love, and health in America: Private choices and public policies* (pp. 197–238). Chicago, IL: University of Chicago Press.

Major, Brenda. (1989). Gender differences in comparisons and entitlement: Implications for comparable worth. *Journal of Social Issues, 45*(4), 99–115.

Major, Brenda. (1994). From social inequality to personal entitlement: The role of social comparisons, legitimacy appraisals, and group membership. In M. P. Zanna (Ed.), *Advances in experimental social psychology* (Vol. 26, pp. 293–355). New York, NY: Academic Press.

Major, Brenda, Appelbaum, Mark, Beckman, Linda, Dutton, Mary Ann, Russo, Nancy F., & West, Carolyn. (2009). Abortion and mental health: Evaluating the evidence. *American Psychologist, 64*, 863–890.

Major, Brenda, Barr, Leslie, Zubek, Josephine, & Babey, Susan H. (1999). Gender and self-esteem: A meta-analysis. In W. Swann, J. Langlois, & L. Gilbert (Eds.), *Sexism and stereotypes in modern society: The gender science of Janet Taylor Spence* (pp. 223–254). Washington, DC: American Psychological Association.

Majors, Richard, & Billson, Janet M. (1992). *Cool pose: The dilemmas of black manhood in America.* New York, NY: Simon & Schuster.

Malamuth, Neil M. (1998). The confluence model as an organizing framework for research on sexually aggressive men: Risk, moderators, imagined aggression, and pornography consumption. In R. Geen & E. Donnerstein (Eds.), *Aggression: Theoretical and empirical reviews* (pp. 229–245). New York, NY: Academic Press.

Malamuth, Neil M., Linz, Daniel, Heavey, Christopher L., Barnes, Gordon, & Acker, Michele. (1995). Using the confluence model of sexual aggression to predict men's conflict with women: A 10-year follow-up study. *Journal of Personality and Social Psychology, 69*, 353–369.

Malatesta, Carol Z., Culver, Clayton, Tesman, Johanna R., Shepard, Beth, Fogel, Alan, Reimers, Mark, & Zivin, Gail. (1989). The development of emotion expression during the first two years of life. *Monographs of the Society for Research in Child Development, 54*, 1–136.

Malm, Gunilla, Haugen, Trine B., Henrichsen, Trine, Bjørsvik, Cathrine, Grotmol, Tom, Saether, Thomas, . . . Giwercman, Aleksander. (2004). Reproductive function during summer and winter in Norwegian men living north and south of the Arctic Circle. *Journal of Clinical Endocrinology & Metabolism, 89*, 4397–4402.

Mandel, William. (1975). *Soviet women.* Garden City, NY: Anchor.

Manivannan, Anjali. (2015). Gender inequalities in access to information about Ebola as gender-based violence. *Harvard Human Rights Journal Online.* Retrieved from http://harvardhrj.com/

Mann, Karl, Hintz, Thomas, & Jung, Martin. (2004). Does psychiatric comorbidity in alcohol-dependent patients affect treatment outcome? *European Archives of Psychiatry & Clinical Neuroscience, 254*, 172–181.

Marchetti, Gina. (1993). *Romance and the "yellow peril": Race, sex, and discursive strategies in Hollywood fiction.* Berkeley: University of California Press.

Marcus, Dale E., & Overton, Willis F. (1978). The development of cognitive gender constancy and sex preferences. *Child Development, 49*, 434–444.

Marecek, Jeanne. (2012). The global is local: Adding culture, ideology, and context to international psychology. *Psychology of Women Quarterly, 36*, 149–153.

Marecek, Jeanne, Crawford, Mary, & Popp, Danielle. (2004). On the construction of gender, sex, and sexualities. In A. H. Eagly, A. E. Beall, & R. J. Sternberg (Eds.), *The psychology of gender* (2nd ed., pp. 192–216). New York, NY: Guilford.

Markus, Hazel R. (2008). Pride, prejudice, and ambivalence: Toward a unified theory of race and ethnicity. *American Psychologist, 63*, 651–670.

Marrazzo, Jeanne M. (2004). Barriers to infectious disease care among lesbians. *Emerging Infectious Disease Journal, 10*, 1974–1978.

Marrazzo, Jeanne M., Coffey, Patricia, & Bingham, Allison. (2005). Sexual practices, risk perception and knowledge of sexually transmitted disease risk among lesbian and bisexual women. *Perspectives on Sexual and Reproductive Health, 37*, 6–12.

Marsh, Herbert W., Martin, Andrew J., & Cheng, Jacqueline H. S. (2008). A multilevel perspective on gender in classroom motivation and climate: Potential benefits of male teachers for boys? *Journal of Educational Psychology, 100*, 78–95.

Marshall, Amy D., & Holtzworth-Munroe, Amy. (2010). Recognition of wives' emotional expressions: A mechanism in the relationship between psychopathology and intimate partner violence perpetration. *Journal of Family Psychology, 24*, 21–30.

Marshall, Grant N., et al. (2005). Mental health of Cambodian refugees 2 decades after resettlement in the United States. *Journal of the American Medical Association, 294*, 571–579.

Marsiglio, William, Amato, Paul, Day, Randal, & Lamb, Michael. (2000). Scholarship on fatherhood in the 1990s and beyond. *Journal of Marriage and the Family, 62*, 1173–1191.

Martin, Carol L., & Halverson, Charles F., Jr. (1983). The effects of sex-typing schemas on young children's memory. *Child Development, 54*, 563–574.

Martin, Carol L., Ruble, Diane N., & Szkrybalo, Joel. (2002). Cognitive theories of early gender development. *Psychological Bulletin, 128*, 903–933.

Martin, Del. (1976). *Battered wives.* San Francisco, CA: Glide.

Martin, M. Kay, & Voorhies, Barbara. (1975). *Female of the species.* New York, NY: Columbia University Press.

Martin, Nina. (2015, September 23). Take a valium, lose your kid, go to jail. ProPublica. Retrieved from https://www.pro-publica.org/

Martin, Sandra L., Macy, Rebecca J., & Young, Siobhan K. (2011). Health and economic consequences of sexual violence. In J. W. White, M. P. Koss, & A. E. Kazdin (Eds.), *Violence against women and children: Mapping the terrain* (Vol.1, pp. 173–196). Washington, DC: American Psychological Association.

Martinez, Gladys, Copen, Casey, & Abma, Joyce C. (2011). Teenagers in the United States: Sexual activity, contraceptive use, and childbearing, 2006–2010 National Survey of Family Growth. *Vital Health Statistics, 23*(31).

Marván, Maria L., & Cortés-Iniestra, Sandra. (2001). Women's beliefs about the prevalence of premenstrual syndrome and biases in recall of premenstrual changes. *Health Psychology, 20,* 276–280.

Marwha, Dhruv, Halari, Meha, & Eliot, Lise. (2017). Meta-analysis reveals a lack of sexual dimorphism in human amygdala volume. *NeuroImage, 147,* 282–294.

Marx, David M., & Roman, Jasmin S. (2002). Female role models: Protecting women's math test performance. *Personality and Social Psychology Bulletin, 28,* 1183–1193.

Mascaro, Jennifer S., Rentscher, Kelly E., Hackett, Patrick D., Mehl, Matthias R., & Rilling, James K. (2017). Child gender influences paternal behavior, language, and brain function. *Behavioral Neuroscience, 131,* 262–273.

Mast, Marianne S., & Sczesny, Sabine. (2010). Gender, power, and nonverbal behavior. In J. Chrisler & D. McCreary (Eds.), *Handbook of gender research in psychology* (Vol. 1, pp. 411–428). New York, NY: Springer.

Masters, William H., & Johnson, Virginia E. (1966). *Human sexual response.* Boston, MA: Little Brown.

Masters, William H., & Johnson, Virginia E. (1970). *Human sexual inadequacy.* Boston, MA: Little, Brown.

Matamonasa-Bennett, Arieahn. (2015). "A disease of the outside people": Native American men's perceptions of intimate partner violence. *Psychology of Women Quarterly, 39,* 20–36.

Mathews, T. J., & Hamilton, Brady E. (2005). Trend analysis of the sex ratio at birth in the United States. *National Vital Statistics Reports, 53*(20), 1–20.

May, V. M. (2015). *Pursuing intersectionality, unsettling dominant imaginaries.* New York, NY: Routledge.

Mazei, Jens, Hüffmeier, Joachim, Freund, Philipp A., Stuhlmacher, Alice F., Bilke, Lena, & Hertel, Guido. (2015). A meta-analysis on gender differences in negotiation outcomes and their moderators. *Psychological Bulletin, 141,* 85–104.

McArthur, Leslie Z., & Eisen, Susan V. (1976a). Achievement of male and female storybook characters as determinants of achievement behavior by boys and girls. *Journal of Personality and Social Psychology, 33,* 467–473.

McArthur, Leslie, & Eisen, S. (1976b). Television and sex-role stereotyping. *Journal of Applied Social Psychology, 6,* 329–351.

McCabe, J. (2009). Racial and gender microaggressions on a predominantly-White campus: Experiences of Black, Latina/o and White undergraduates. *Race, Gender & Class, 16,* 130–148.

McCarrey, Anna C., An, Yang, Kitner-Triolo, Melissa H., Ferrucci, Luigi, & Resnick, Susan M. (2016). Sex differences in cognitive trajectories in clinically normal older adults. *Psychology and Aging, 31,* 166–175.

McCarthy, Margaret M., & Arnold, Arthur P. (2011). Reframing sexual differentiation of the brain. *Nature Neuroscience, 14,* 677–683.

McClelland, David C., Atkinson, John W., Clark, Russell A., & Lowell, Edgar L. (1953). *The achievement motive.* New York, NY: Appleton-Century-Crofts.

McClintock, Martha K. (1971). Menstrual synchrony and suppression. *Nature, 229,* 244–245.

McClure, Erin B. (2000). A meta-analytic review of sex differences in facial expression processing and their development in infants, children, and adolescents. *Psychological Bulletin, 126,* 424–453.

McCormick, Cheryl M., & Teillon, Sarah M. (2001). Menstrual cycle variation in spatial ability: Relation to salivary cortisol levels. *Hormones and Behavior, 39,* 29–38.

McCormick, Naomi B. (1994). *Sexual salvation: Affirming women's sexual rights and pleasures.* New York, NY: Praeger.

McDonald, Justin D. (2000). A model for conducting research with American Indian participants. In *Guidelines for research in ethnic minority communities* (pp. 12–15). Washington, DC: American Psychological Association.

McEwen, Bruce S. (2001). Estrogen effects on the brain: Multiple sites and molecular mechanisms. *Journal of Applied Physiology, 91,* 2785–2801.

McEwen, Bruce A., & Milner, Teresa A. (2017). Understanding the broad influence of sex hormones and sex differences in the brain. *Journal of Neuroscience Research, 95,* 24–39.

McFarlane, Jessica, Martin, Carol L., & Williams, Tannis M. (1988). Mood fluctuations: Women versus men and menstrual versus other cycles. *Psychology of Women Quarterly, 12,* 201–224.

McFarlane, Jessica M., & Williams, Tannis M. (1994). Placing premenstrual syndrome in perspective. *Psychology of Women Quarterly, 18,* 339–374.

McGill, Brittany S. (2014). Navigating new norms of involved fatherhood: Employment, fathering attitudes, and father involvement. *Journal of Family Issues, 35,* 1089–1106.

McGlynn, Clare, Westmarland, Nicole, & Godden, Nikki. (2012). "I just wanted him to hear me": Sexual violence and the possibilities of restorative justice. *Journal of Law and Society, 39,* 213–240.

McHale, Susan M., Kim, Ji-Yeon, Dotterer, Aryn M., Crouter, Ann C., & Booth, Alan. (2009). The development of gendered interests and personality qualities from middle childhood through adolescence: A biosocial analysis. *Child Development, 80,* 482–495.

McHugh, Maureen C., & Hambaugh, Jennifer. (2010). She said, he said: Gender, language, and power. In J. Chrisler & D. McCreary (Eds.), *Handbook of gender research in psychology* (Vol. 1, pp. 379–410). New York, NY: Springer.

McHugh, Maureen C., Koeske, Randi D., & Frieze, Irene H. (1986). Issues to consider in conducting nonsexist psychological research: A guide for researchers. *American Psychologist, 41,* 879–890.

McKay, Ruth. (1978). One child families and atypical sex ratios in an elite black community. In R. Staples (Ed.), *The black family* (pp. 177–181). Belmont, CA: Wadsworth.

McKenry, Patrick C., & McKelvey, Mary W. (2003). The psychosocial well-being of Black and White mothers following marital dissolution: A brief report of a follow-up study. *Psychology of Women Quarterly, 27,* 31–36.

McKinlay, John B., McKinlay, Sonja M., & Brambilla, Donald J. (1987). Health status and utilization behavior associated with menopause. *American Journal of Epidemiology, 125,* 110–121.

McKinlay, Sonja M., Brambilla, Donald J., & Posner, Jennifer G. (1992). The normal menopause transition. *American Journal of Human Biology, 4,* 37–46.

McKinley, Nita M. (1998). Gender differences in undergraduates' body esteem: The mediating effect of objectified body consciousness and actual/ideal weight discrepancy. *Sex Roles, 39,* 113–124.

McKinley, Nita M., & Hyde, Janet S. (1996). The Objectified Body Consciousness Scale: Development and validation. *Psychology of Women Quarterly, 20,* 181–215.

McLanahan, Sara, & Adams, Julia. (1987). Parenthood and psychological well-being. *Annual Review of Sociology, 5,* 237–257.

McLean, Kate C., & Syed, Moin. (Eds.). (2015). *Oxford handbook of identity development.* New York, NY: Oxford University Press.

McLemore, Kevin A. (2014). Experiences with misgendering: Identity misclassification of transgender spectrum individuals. *Self and Identity, 14,* 51–74.

McLemore, Kevin A. (2016). A minority stress perspective on transgender individuals' experiences with misgendering. *Stigma & Health.* Advance online publication. http://dx.doi.org/10.1037/sah0000070

McMahan, Ian D. (1971, April). *Sex differences in causal attributions following success and failure.* Paper presented at the Eastern Psychological Association Meeting.

McMahan, Ian D. (1972, April). *Sex differences in expectancy of success as a function of task.* Paper presented at the Eastern Psychological Association Meeting, Boston, MA.

McMillan, Julie R., Clifton, A. Kay, McGrath, Diane, & Gale, Wanda S. (1977). Women's language: Uncertainty or interpersonal sensitivity and emotionality? *Sex Roles, 3,* 545–560.

McNally, Richard J., & Geraerts, Elke. (2009). A new solution to the recovered memory debate. *Perspectives on Psychological Science, 4,* 126–134.

McQuillan, Julia, Greil, Arthur L., Shreffler, Karina M., Wonch-Hill, Patricia A., Gentzler, Kari C., & Hathcoat, John D. (2012). Does the reason matter? Variations in childlessness concerns among U.S. women. *Journal of Marriage and Family, 74,* 1166–1181.

McWayne, Christine, Downer, Jason T., Campos, Rodrigo, & Harris, Robby D. (2013). Father involvement during early childhood and its association with children's early learning: A meta-analysis. *Early Education and Development, 24,* 898–922.

Mead, Margaret. (1935). *Sex and temperament in three primitive societies.* New York, NY: William Morrow.

Mead, Margaret. (1949). *Male and female.* New York, NY: William Morrow.

Mednick, Martha T. (1989). On the politics of psychological constructs: Stop the bandwagon, I want to get off. *American Psychologist, 44,* 1118–1123.

Mednick, Martha T., & Thomas, Veronica G. (1993). Women and the psychology of achievement: A view from the eighties. In F. L. Denmark & M. A. Paludi (Eds.), *Psychology of women: A handbook of issues and theories* (pp. 585–626). Westport, CT: Greenwood.

Meece, Judith L., Eccles-Parsons, Jacquelynne, Kaczala, Caroline M., & Goff, Susan B. (1982). Sex differences in math achievement: Toward a model of academic choice. *Psychological Bulletin, 91,* 324–448.

Meeus, Wim. (2011). The study of adolescent identity formation 2000–2010: A review of longitudinal research. *Journal of Research on Adolescence, 21,* 75–94.

Mello, Zena R. (2008). Gender variation in developmental trajectories of educational occupational expectations and attainment from adolescence to adulthood. *Developmental Psychology, 44,* 1069–1080.

Melloni, C., Berger, Jeffrey S., Wang, Tracy Y., Gunes, Funda, Stebbins, Amanda, Pieper, Karen S., . . . Newby, L. Kristin. (2010). Representation of women in randomized clinical trials of cardiovascular disease prevention. *Circulation: Cardiovascular Quality and Outcomes, 3,* 135–142.

Mendelson, Beverly K., Mendelson, Morton J., & White, Donna R. (2001). Body-esteem scale for adolescents and adults. *Journal of Personality Assessment, 76,* 90–106.

Mendle, Jane, & Ferrero, Joseph. (2012). Detrimental psychological outcomes associated with pubertal timing in adolescent boys. *Developmental Review, 32,* 49–66.

Meredith, Tami. (2013). A journal of one's own. *Journal of Social, Evolutionary, and Cultural Psychology, 7,* 354–360.

Merikangas, Kathleen R., He, Jian-ping, Burstein, Marcy, Swanson, Sonja, Avenevoli, Shelli, Cui, Lihong, . . . Swendsen, Joel. (2010). Lifetime prevalence of mental disorders in US adolescents: Results from the National Comorbidity Study–Adolescent Supplement (NCS-A). *Journal of the American Academy of Child and Adolescent Psychiatry, 49,* 980–989.

Merrill, Natalie, & Fivush, Robyn. (2016). Intergenerational narratives and identity across development. *Developmental Review, 40,* 72–92.

Meshkovska, Biljana, Siegel, Melissa, Stutterheim, Sarah E., & Bos, Arjan E. R. (2015). Female sex trafficking: Conceptual issues, current debates, and future directions. *Journal of Sex Research, 52,* 380–395.

Messner, Michael. (1990). Boyhood, organized sports, and the construction of masculinities. *Journal of Contemporary Ethnography, 18,* 416–444.

Meston, Cindy M., Levin, Roy J., Sipski, Marca L., Hull, Elaine M., & Heiman, Julia R. (2004). Women's orgasm. *Annual Review of Sex Research, 15,* 173–257.

Meyer, Ilan H. (2003). Prejudice, social stress, and mental health in lesbian, gay, and bisexual populations: Conceptual issues and research evidence. *Psychological Bulletin, 129,* 674–697.

Meyers, Diana T. (2001). The rush to motherhood—Pronatalist discourse and women's autonomy. *Signs: Journal of Women in Culture and Society, 26,* 735–773.

Michalik, Regina. (2001). Interview with Judith Butler interview. *Lola Press Magazine.* Retrieved from http://www.lolapress.org/

Mierop, Adrien. (2015). A nationally representative study of emotional competence and health. *Emotion, 15,* 653–667.

Mikolajczak, Moïra, Avalosse, Hervé, Vandorenland, Sigrid, Berniest, Rebekka, Callens, Michael, Van Broeck, Nady, . . . Milburn, Michael A., Mather, Ro, & Conrad, S. (2000). The effects of viewing R-rated movie scenes that objectify women on perceptions of date rape. *Sex Roles, 43,* 645–664.

Miles-Cohen, Shari E., & Signore, Caroline. (2016). *Eliminating inequities for women with disabilities.* Washington, DC: American Psychological Association.

Milgram, Stanley. (1965). Some conditions of obedience and disobedience to authority. *Human Relations, 18,* 57–76.

Milgram, Stanley. (1974). *Obedience to authority.* New York, NY: Harper & Row.

Mill, John Stuart. (1869). *The subjection of women.* (Reprinted in *Three essays by J. S. Mill.* London: Oxford University Press, 1966.)

Miller, B. A., Ries, L. A. G., Koasry, C. L., Harras, A., Devesa, S. S., & Edwards, B. K. (Eds.). (1993). *SEER cancer statistics review: 1973–1990* (NIH Publication No. 93-2789). Bethesda, MD: National Cancer Institute.

Miller, Casey, & Swift, Kate. (1995). *The handbook of non-sexist writing for writers, editors, and speakers.* London, UK: Women's Press.

Miller, Kathleen, Sabo, Donald, Farrell, Michael, Barnes, Grace, & Melnick, Merrill. (1998). Athletic participation and sexual behavior in adolescents: The different worlds of boys and girls. *Journal of Health and Social Behavior, 39,* 108–123.

Miller, Synthia L. (1983). Developmental changes in male/female voice classification by infants. *Infant Behavior and Development, 6,* 313–330.

Millett, Kate. (1969). *Sexual politics.* Garden City, NY: Doubleday.

Mills, Jacqueline, & Fuller-Tyszkiewicz, Matthew. (2017). Fat talk and body image disturbance: A systematic review and meta-analysis. *Psychology of Women Quarterly, 41,* 114–129.

Minuchin, Salvador, Rosman, Bernice L., & Baker, L. (1978). *Psychosomatic families: Anorexia nervosa in context.* Cambridge, MA: Harvard University Press.

Minze, Laura C., McDonald, Renee, Rosentraub, Erica L., & Jouriles, Ernest N. (2010). Making sense of family conflict: Intimate partner violence and preschoolers' externalizing problems. *Journal of Family Psychology, 24,* 5–11.

Mischel, Walter. (1966). A social-learning view of sex differences in behavior. In E. E. Maccoby (Ed.), *The development of sex differences.* Stanford, CA: Stanford University Press.

Mitchell, Karen S., & Mazzeo, Suzanne E. (2009). Evaluation of a structural model of objectification theory and eating disorder symptomatology among European American and African American undergraduate women. *Psychology of Women Quarterly, 33,* 384–395.

Mitchell, Kirstin R., Mercer, Catherine H., Ploubidis, George B., Jones, Kyle G., Datta, Jessica, . . . Wellings, Kaye. (2013). Sexual function in Britain: Findings from the third National Survey of Sexual Attitudes and Lifestyles (NATSAL 3). *Lancet, 382,* 1817–1829.

Mitchell, Valory, & Helson, Ravenna. (1990). Women's prime of life: Is it the 50s? *Psychology of Women Quarterly, 14,* 451–470.

Miville, Marie L., Mendez, Narolyn, & Louie, Mark. (2017). Latina/o gender roles: A content analysis of empirical research from 1982 to 2013. *Journal of Latina/o Psychology, 5,* 173–194.

Miyake, Akira, Kost-Smith, Lauren E., Finkelstein, Noah D., Pollock, Steven J., Cohen, Geoffrey L., & Ito, Tiffany A. (2010). Reducing the gender achievement gap in college science: A classroom study of values affirmation. *Science, 330,* 1234–1237.

Mizock, Lauren, & Hopwood, Ruben. (2016). Conflation and interdependence in the intersection of gender and sexuality among transgender individuals. *Psychology of Sexual Orientation and Gender Diversity, 3,* 93–103.

Mizock, Lauren, & Lundquist, Christine. (2016). Missteps in psychotherapy with transgender clients: Promoting gender sensitivity in counseling and psychological practice. *Psychology of Sexual Orientation and Gender Diversity, 3,* 148–155.

Mohamed, Besheer. (2016). A new estimate of the U.S. Muslim population. Retrieved from http://www.pewresearch.org/fact-tank/2016/01/06/a-new-estimate-of-the-u-s-muslim-population/

Mohanty, Chandra T. (2003). "Under Western Eyes" revisited: Feminist solidarity through anticapitalist struggles. *Signs, 28,* 499–535.

Mollen, Debra. (2006). Voluntarily childfree women: Experiences and counseling considerations. *Journal of Mental Health Counseling, 28,* 269–284.

Monahan, Lynn, Kuhn, Deanna, & Shaver, Philip. (1974). Intrapsychic versus cultural explanations of the "fear of success" motive. *Journal of Personality and Social Psychology, 29,* 60–64.

Mondschein, Emily R., Adolph, Karen E., & Tamis-LeMonda, Catherine S. (2000). Gender bias in mothers' expectations about infant crawling. *Journal of Experimental Child Psychology, 77,* 304–316.

Monroe, Scott M., & Reid, Mark W. (2009). Life stress and major depression. *Current Directions in Psychological Science, 18,* 68–72.

Monserud, Maria A., & Markides, Kyriakos S. (2017). Changes in depressive symptoms during widowhood among older Mexican Americans: The role of financial strain, social support, and church attendance. *Aging & Mental Health, 21,* 586–594.

Monte, Lindsay M., & Ellis, R. R. (2014). *Fertility of women in the United States: 2012.* Washington, DC: U.S. Department of Commerce, Economics and Statistics Administration.

Moore, Suzanne. (2016, October 12). The backlash against feminism has hit a new low with Donald Trump. *The Guardian.* Retrieved from https://www.theguardian.com

Morales, A., Heaton, Jeremy, & Carson, Culley. (2000). Andropause: A misnomer for a true clinical entity. *Journal of Urology, 163,* 705–712.

Morgan, Betsy L. (1998). A three-generational study of tomboy behavior. *Sex Roles, 39,* 787–800.

Morgan, Elizabeth M., & Thompson, Elisabeth M. (2011). Processes of sexual orientation questioning among heterosexual women. *Journal of Sex Research, 48,* 16–28.

Morris, Brian J., & Bailis, Stefan A., & Wiswell, Thomas E. (2014). Circumcision rates in the United States: Rising or falling? What effect might the new affirmative pediatric policy statement have? *Mayo Clinic Proceedings, 89,* 677–686.

Morris, Brian J., & Krieger, John N. (2013). Does male circumcision affect sexual function, sensitivity or satisfaction? A systematic review. *Journal of Sexual Medicine, 10,* 2644–2657.

Morris, Brian J., & Wiswell, Thomas E. (2013). Circumcision and lifetime risk of urinary tract infection: A systematic review and meta-analysis. *Journal of Urology, 189,* 2118–2124.

Morrison, Ann M., White, Randall P., Van Velsor, Ellen, & Center for Creative Leadership. (1992). *Breaking the glass ceiling: Can women reach the top of America's largest corporations?* (Updated ed.). Reading, MA: Addison-Wesley.

Mosher, William D., & Jones, Jo. (2010). Use of contraception in the United States: 1982–2008. *Vital and Health Statistics, Series 23*(29).

Moss-Racusin, Corinne A., Dovidio, John F., Brescoll, Victoria L., Graham, Mark J., & Handelsman, Jo. (2012). Science faculty's subtle gender biases favor male students. *Proceedings of the National Acadamy of Sciences of the USA, 109*, 16474–16479.

Moulds, Michelle L., & Bryant, Richard A. (2002). Directed forgetting in acute stress disorder. *Journal of Abnormal Psychology, 111*, 175–179.

Moulton, Janice R., Robinson, George M., & Elias, Cherin. (1978). Psychology in action: Sex bias in language use: "Neutral" pronouns that aren't. *American Psychologist, 33*, 1032–1036.

Moulton, Ruth. (1970). A survey and re-evaluation of the concept of penis envy. *Contemporary Psychoanalysis, 7*, 84–104.

Mouritsen, A., Aksglaede, L., Sørensen, K., Mogensen, S. S., Leffers, H., Main, K. M., . . . Juul, A. (2010). Hypothesis: Exposure to endocrine-disrupting chemicals may interfere with timing of puberty. *International Journal of Andrology, 33*, 346–359.

Moyer, A. (1997). Psychosocial outcomes of breast conserving surgery versus mastectomy: A meta-analytic review. *Health Psychology, 16*, 284–298.

Moynihan, Daniel P. (1965). *The Negro family: The case for national action*. Washington, DC: U.S. Government Printing Office.

Moynihan, Ray. (2014). Evening the score on sex drugs: Feminist movement or marketing masquerade? *BMJ, 349*, g6246.

Mozzafarian, Dariush, Benjamin, Emilia J., Go, Alan S., Arnett, Donna K., Blaha, Michael J., Cushman, Mary, . . . Turner, Melanie B. (2016). Heart disease and stroke statistics—2016 update: A report from the American Heart Association. *Circulation, 133*, e38–e360.

Muehlenhard, Charlene, Friedman, Debra E., & Thomas, Celeste M. (1985). Is date rape justifiable? The effects of dating activity, who paid, and men's attitudes toward women. *Psychology of Women Quarterly, 9*, 297–310.

Mulac, Anthony. (2006). The gender-linked language effect: Do language differences really make a difference? In K. Dindia & D. Canary (Eds.), *Sex differences and similarities in communication* (2nd ed., pp. 219–240). Mahwah, NJ: Lawrence Erlbaum.

Mulac, Anthony, Giles, Howard, Bradac, James J., & Palomares, Nicholas A. (2013). The gender-linked language effect: An empirical test of a general process model. *Language Sciences, 38*, 22–31.

Mumenthaler, Martin S., O'Hara, Ruth, Taylor, Joy L., Friedman, Leah, & Yesavage, Jerome A. (2001). Relationship between variations in estradiol and progesterone levels across the menstrual cycle and human performance. *Psychopharmacology, 155*, 198–203.

Munk-Olsen, Trine, Laursen, Thomas M., Pedersen, Carsten B., Lidegaard, Øjvind, & Mortensen, Preben B. (2011). Induced first-trimester abortion and risk of mental disorder. *New England Journal of Medicine, 364*, 332–339.

Muñoz-Laboy, Miguel. (2008). Familism and sexual regulation among bisexual Latino men. *Archives of Sexual Behavior, 27*, 773–782.

Murnen, Sarah K., & Smolak, Linda. (2000). The experience of sexual harassment among grade-school students: Early socialization of female subordination? *Sex Roles, 43*, 1–18.

Murnen, Sarah K., & Stockton, Mary. (1997). Gender and self-reported sexual arousal in response to sexual stimuli: A meta-analytic review. *Sex Roles, 37*, 135–154.

Murphy, Elaine M. (2003). Being born female is dangerous for your health. *American Psychologist, 58*, 205–210.

Murphy, Mary C., Steele, Claude M., & Gross, James J. (2007). Signaling threat: How situational cues affect women in math, science, and engineering settings. *Psychological Science, 18*, 879–885.

Murray, Kate E., & Marx, David M. (2013). Attitudes toward unauthorized immigrants, authorized immigrants, and refugees. *Cultural Diversity and Ethnic Minority Psychology, 19*, 332–341.

Murray, Laura K., Nguyen, Amanda, & Cohen, Judith A. (2014). Child sexual abuse. *Child and Adolescent Psychiatric Clinics of North America, 23*, 321–337.

Mustanski, Brian S., DuPree, Michael G., Nievergelt, Caroline M., Bockland, Sven, Schork, Nicholas J., & Hamer, Dean H. (2005). A genomewide scan of male sexual orientation. *Human Genetics, 116*, 272–278.

Myers, Linda J., Abdullah, Samella, & Leary, George. (2000). Conducting research with persons of African descent. In *Guidelines for research in ethnic minority communities* (pp. 5–8). Washington, DC: American Psychological Association.

Nadal, Kevin. (2013). *That's so gay! Microaggressions and the lesbian, gay, bisexual, transgender community*. Washington, DC: American Psychological Association.

Nadel, Lynn, & Jacobs, W. Jake. (1998). Traumatic memory is special. *Current Directions in Psychological Science, 7*, 154–157.

Nagata, Donna K., Cheng, Wendy, & Tsi-Chae, Amy. (2010). Chinese American grandmothering: A qualitative exploration. *Asian American Journal of Psychology, 1*, 451–461.

Nagoski, Emily. (2015). *Come as you are*. New York, NY: Simon & Schuster.

Najdowski, Cynthia J., & Ullman, Sarah E. (2009). PTSD symptoms and self-rated recovery among adult sexual assault survivors: The effects of traumatic life events and psychosocial variables. *Psychology of Women Quarterly, 33*, 43–53.

Naly, Claire, & Smith, A. (2015). *Twenty-first century feminism: Forming and performing femininity*. Baskingstoke, UK: Palgrave Macmillan.

Nanda, Serena. (2014). *Gender diversity*. Long Grove, IL: Waveland Press.

Napier, Jaime L., Thorisdottir, Hulda, & Jost, John T. (2010). The joy of sexism? A multinational investigation of hostile and benevolent justifications for gender inequality and their relations to subjective well-being. *Sex Roles, 62*, 405–419.

NASA. (2015). Biographical data: Ellen Ochoa, Ph.D. Retrieved from http://www.jsc.nasa.gov/Bios/htmlbios/ochoa.pdf

National Association for Single-Sex Public Education. (2011). Single-sex education. Retrieved July 9, 2011, from http://www.singlesexschools.org

National Cancer Institute. (2009). *Fact sheet: Human papillomavirus (HPV) vaccines*. Washington, DC: National Institutes of Health.

National Center for Education Statistics. (2010). *Digest of education statistics*. Retrieved from http://nces.ed.gov/programs/digest/d10_290.asp

National Center for Health Statistics. (2016). Key statistics from the National Survey of Family Growth. Washington, DC: Author.

National Congress of American Indians. (2013). *Policy insights brief: Statistics on violence against Native women*. Washington, DC: NCAI Policy Research Center.

National Lesbian & Gay Journalists Association. (2016). Stylebook. Retrieved from http://www.nlgja.org/stylebook/

National Science Board. (2008). *Science and engineering indicators 2008*. Retrieved from http://www.nsf.gov/statistics/seind08

National Science Foundation. (2011). *S&E degrees: 1966–2008*. Retrieved from http://www.nsf.gov/statistics/

National Science Foundation. (2017). Women, minorities, and persons with disabilities in science and engineering. Retrieved from http://www.nsf.gov/statistics/2015/nsf15311/tables.cfm

Native American Rights Fund. (2013). Let all that is Indian within you die! *NARF Legal Review, 38*(2), 1–11.

Natsuaki, Misaki N., Samuels, Danielle, & Leve, Leslie D. (2015). Puberty, identity, and context: A biopsychosocial perspective on internalizing psychopathology in early adolescent girls. In K. C. McLean & M. Syed (Eds.), *Oxford handbook of identity development* (pp. 389–405). New York, NY: Oxford University Press.

Navarette, Carlos D., McDonald, Melissa M., Molina, Ludwin E., & Sidanius, Jim. (2010). Prejudice at the nexus of race and gender: An outgroup male target hypothesis. *Journal of Personality and Social Psychology, 98*, 933–945.

Nelson, Jackie A., Leerkes, Esther M., O'Brien, Marion O., Calkins, Susan D., & Marcovitch, Stuart. (2012). Differences in African American and European American mothers' beliefs about negative emotions and emotion socialization practices. *Parenting: Science & Practice, 12*, 22–41.

Nelson, Nicole L., & Russell, James A. (2015). Children distinguish between positive pride and hubris. *Developmental Psychology, 51*, 1609–1614.

Nelson, S. Katherine, Kushlev, Kostadin, & Lyubomirsky, Sonja. (2014). The pains and pleasures of parenting: When, why, and how is parenthood associated with more or less well-being? *Psychological Bulletin, 140*, 846–895.

Neville, Helen A., Heppner, Mary J., Oh, Euna, Spanierman, Lisa B., & Clark, Mary. (2004). General and culturally specific factors influencing Black and White rape survivors' self-esteem. *Psychology of Women Quarterly, 28*, 83–94.

Newcombe, Nora S., Mathason, Lisa, & Terlecki, Melissa. (2002). Maximization of spatial competence: More important than finding the cause of sex differences. In A. McGillicuddy-De Lisi & R. De Lisi (Eds.), *Biology, society, and behavior: The development of sex differences in cognition* (pp. 183–206). Westport, CT: Ablex.

Newman, Denise L., Caspi, Avshalom, & Moffitt, Terrie E. (1997). Antecedents of adult interpersonal functioning: Effects of individual differences in age 3 temperament. *Developmental Psychology, 33*, 206–217.

Newton, Nicola, & Stewart, Abigail. (2010). The middle ages: Changes in women's personalities and social roles. *Psychology of Women Quarterly, 34*, 75–84.

Ng, Sik H. (2007). Language-based discrimination: Blatant and subtle forms. *Journal of Language and Social Psychology, 26*, 106–122.

Ngo, Thoai D., Park, Min H., Shakur, Haleema, & Free, Caroline. (2011). Comparative effectiveness, safety and acceptability of medical abortion at home and in a clinic: A systematic review. *Bulletin of the World Health Organization, 89*, 360–370.

Ngun, Tuck C., Ghahramani, Negar, Sánchez, Francisco J., Bocklandt, Sven, & Vilain, Eric. (2010). The genetics of sex differences in brain and behavior. *Frontiers in Neuroendocrinology, 32*, 227–246.

Niemann, Yolanda F., Jennings, Leilani, Rozelle, Richard M., Baxter, James C., & Sullivan, Elroy. (1994). Use of free responses and cluster analysis to determine stereotypes of eight groups. *Personality and Social Psychology Bulletin, 20*, 379–390.

Niewenweg, R., Smith, M. L., Walenkamp, M. J. E., & Wit, J. M. (2003). Adult height corrected for shrinking and secular trend. *Annals of Human Biology, 30*, 563–569.

Nikčević, Ana, & Nicolaides, Kypros H. (2014). Search for meaning, finding meaning and adjustment in women following miscarriage: A longitudinal study. *Psychology & Health, 29*, 50–63.

Nindl, Bradley C., Kraemer, William J., Gotshalk, Lincoln A., Marx, James O., Volek, Jeff S., Bush, Jill A., . . . Fleck, Steve J. (2001). Testosterone responses after resistance exercise in women: Influence of regional fat distribution. *International Journal of Sport Nutrition and Exercise Metabolism, 11*, 451–465.

No sexism please, we're Webster's. (1991, June 24). *Newsweek*, p. 59.

Nolen-Hoeksema, Susan. (1991). Responses to depression and their effects on the duration of depressive episodes. *Journal of Abnormal Psychology, 100*, 569–582.

Nolen-Hoeksema, Susan. (2001). Gender differences in depression. *Current Directions in Psychological Science, 10*, 173–176.

Nolen-Hoeksema, Susan, Wisco, Blaire E., & Lyubomirsky, Sonja. (2008). Rethinking rumination. *Perspectives on Psychological Science, 3*, 400–424.

Norris, Jeanette, Nurius, Paula S., & Dimeff, Linda A. (1996). Through her eyes: Factors affecting women's perception of and resistance to acquaintance sexual aggression threat. *Psychology of Women Quarterly, 20*, 123–146.

Norton, Arthur J., & Moorman, Jeanne E. (1987). Current trends in marriage and divorce among American women. *Journal of Marriage and the Family, 49*, 3–14.

Nosek, Brian A., Banaji, Mahzarin R., & Greenwald, Anthony G. (2002). Math = male, me = female, therefore math ≠ me. *Journal of Personality and Social Psychology, 83*, 44–59.

Nosek, Brian A., Greenwald, Anthony G., & Banaji, Mahzarin R. (2005). Understanding and using the Implicit Association Test: II. Method variables and construct validity. *Personality and Social Psychology Bulletin, 31*, 166–180.

Nosek, Brian A., Smyth, Frederick L., Sriram, N., Lindner, Nicole M., Devos, Thierry, Ayala, Alfonso, . . . Greenwald, Anthony. (2009). National differences in gender-science stereotypes predict national sex differences in science and math achievement. *Proceedings of the National Academy of Sciences of the USA, 106*, 10593–10597.

Nosek, Margaret A. (2016). Health disparities and equity: The intersection of disability, health, and sociodemographic characteristics among women. In S. E. Miles-Cohen & C. Signore (Eds.), *Eliminating inequities for women with disabilities* (pp. 13–38). Washington, DC: American Psychological Association.

Obedin-Maliver, Juno, Goldsmith, Elizabeth S., Stewart, Leslie, White, William, Tran, Eric, Brenman, Stephanie, . . . Lunn, Mitchell R. (2011). Lesbian, gay, bisexual, and transgender–related content in undergraduate medical education. *Journal of the American Medical Association, 306*, 971–977.

O'Brien, Laurie T., Blodorn, Alison, Adams, Glenn, Garcia, Donna M., & Hammer, Elliott. (2015). Ethnic variation in gender-STEM stereotypes and STEM participation: An intersectional approach. *Cultural Diversity and Ethnic Minority Psychology, 21*, 169–180.

O'Brien, Laurie T., & Major, Brenda. (2009). Group status and feelings of personal entitlement: The roles of social comparison and system-justifying beliefs. In J. T. Jost, A. C. Kay, & H. Thorisdottir (Eds.), *Social and psychological bases of ideology and systems* (pp. 427–441). New York, NY: Oxford University Press.

O'Brien, Laurie T., Major, Brenda N., & Gilbert, Patricia N. (2012). Gender differences in entitlement: The role of system-justifying beliefs. *Basic and Applied Social Psychology, 34*, 136–145.

O'Brien, Marion, Peyton, Vicki, Mistry, Rashmita, Hruda, Ludmila, Jacobs, Anne, Caldera, Yvonne, . . . Roy, Carolyn. (2000). Gender-role cognition in three-year-old boys and girls. *Sex Roles, 42*, 1007–1026.

O'Connell, Agnes N. (1990). Karen Horney (1885–1952). In A. N. O'Connell & N. F. Russo (Eds.), *Women in psychology: A bibliographical sourcebook* (pp. 184–196). Westport, CT: Greenwood Press.

Office of Civil Rights, Office of the Assistant Secretary. (2010, October 26). Dear colleague letter. Retrieved from https://www2.ed.gov/about/offices/list/ocr/letters/col league-201010.html

Ogletree, Shirley M., Fancher, Joshua, & Gill, Simran. (2014). Gender and texting: Masculinity, femininity, and gender role ideology. *Computers in Human Behavior, 31*, 49–55.

O'Hara, Michael W., & McCabe, Jennifer E. (2013). Postpartum depression: Current status and future directions. *Annual Review of Clinical Psychology, 9*, 379–407.

Oinonen, Kirsten A., & Mazmanian, Dwight. (2001). Effects of oral contraceptives on daily self-ratings of positive and negative affect. *Journal of Psychosomatic Research, 51,* 647–658.

Okamoto, Ikuhiro, Otte, Arie P., Allis, David, Reinberg, Danny, & Heard, Edith. (2004). Epigenetic dynamics of imprinted X inactivation during early mouse development. *Science, 303,* 644–649.

O'Keefe, Eileen S. C., & Hyde, Janet S. (1983). The development of occupational sex-role stereotypes: The effects of gender stability and age. *Sex Roles, 9,* 481–492.

Olson, Kristina R., Durwood, Lily, DeMeules, Madeleine, & McLaughlin, Katie A. (2016). Mental health of transgender children who are supported in their identities. *Pediatrics, 137*(3), e20153223.

Olson, Kristina R., Key, Aidan C., & Eaton, Nicholas R. (2015). Gender cognition in transgender children. *Psychological Science, 26,* 467–474.

Ong, Anthony D., Burrow, Anthony, Fuller-Rowell, Thomas E., Ja, Nicole M., & Sue, Derald Wing. (2013). Racial microaggressions and daily well-being among Asian Americans. *Journal of Counseling Psychology, 60,* 188–199.

Orchowski, Lindsay M., Gidycz, Christine A., & Raffle, Holly. (2008). Evaluation of a sexual assault risk reduction and self-defense program: A prospective analysis of a revised protocol. *Psychology of Women Quarterly, 32,* 204–218.

Orenstein, Peggy. (2011). *Cinderella ate my daughter: Dispatches from the front lines of the new girlie-girl culture.* New York, NY: HarperCollins.

Orenstein, Peggy. (2016). *Girls and sex: Navigating the complicated new landscape.* New York, NY: HarperCollins.

Ormerod, Alayne J., Collinsworth, Linda L., & Perry, Leigh, A. (2008). Critical climate: Relations among sexual harassment, climate, and outcomes for high school girls and boys. *Psychology of Women Quarterly, 32,* 113–125.

O'Sullivan, Lucia F., Graber, Julia, & Brooks-Gunn, Jeanne. (2001). Adolescent gender development. In J. Worell (Ed.), *Encyclopedia of gender* (pp. 55–67). San Diego, CA: Academic Press.

Oswald, Debra L., & Lindstedt, Kara. (2006). The content and function of gender self-stereotypes. *Sex Roles, 54,* 447–458.

Otterbein, Keith F. (1979). A cross-cultural study of rape. *Aggressive Behavior, 5,* 425–435.

Owen, Jesse, & Fincham, Frank D. (2011a). Effects of gender and psychosocial factors on friends with benefits relationships among young adults. *Archives of Sexual Behavior, 40,* 311–320.

Owen, Jesse, & Fincham, Frank D. (2011b). Young adults' emotional reactions after hooking up encounters. *Archives of Sexual Behavior, 40,* 321–330.

Owings, Maria, Uddin, Sayeedha, & Williams, Sonja. (2013). *Trends in circumcision for male newborns in U.S. hospitals: 1979–2010.* Atlanta, GA: Centers for Disease Control and Prevention.

Oyewumi, Oyeronke. (1997). *The invention of women: Making an African sense of Western gender discourses.* Minneapolis: University of Minnesota Press.

Oyewumi, Oyeronke. (2000). Family bonds/conceptual binds: African notes on feminist epistemologies. *Signs: Journal of Women in Culture and Society, 25,* 1093–1098.

Padawer, Ruth. (2016, June 28). The humiliating practice of sex-testing female athletes. *New York Times.*

Pahlke, Erin, Hyde, Janet S., & Allison, Carlie. (2014). The effects of single-sex compared with coeducational schooling on students' performance and attitudes: A meta-analysis. *Psychological Bulletin, 140,* 1042–1072.

Paige, Karen E. (1971). Effects of oral contraceptives on affective fluctuations associated with the menstrual cycle. *Psychosomatic Medicine, 33,* 515–537.

Paige, Karen E. (1973). Women learn to sing the menstrual blues. *Psychology Today, 7*(4), 41.

Palkovitz, R. (2002). Involved fathering and child development: Advancing our understanding of good fathering. In C. S. Tamis-LeMonda & N. Cabrera (Eds.), *Handbook of father involvement* (pp. 33–64). Mahwah, NJ: Lawrence Erlbaum.

Panjwani, Naaila, Chaplin, Tara M., Sinha, Rajita, & Mayes, Linda C. (2016). Gender differences in emotion expression in low-income adolescents under stress. *Journal of Nonverbal Behavior, 40,* 117–132.

Panksepp, Jaak, & Panksepp, Jules B. (2000). The seven sins of evolutionary psychology. *Evolution and Cognition, 6,* 108–131.

Parish, Susan, Mitra, Monika, & Iezzoni, Lisa. (2016). Health promotion and disease prevention for women with disabilities. In S. E. Miles-Cohen & C. Signore (Eds.), *Eliminating inequities for women with disabilities* (pp. 61–80). Washington, DC: American Psychological Association.

Parker, Kim, & Livingston, Gretchen. (2016). 6 facts about American fathers. Retrieved from http://www.pewresearch.org/fact-tank/2016/06/16/fathers-day-facts/

Parker, Kim, & Wang, Wendy. (2013). *Modern parenthood: Roles of moms and dads converge as they balance work and family.* Washington, DC: Pew Research Center.

Parks, Cheryl A., Hughes, Tonda L., & Matthews, Alicia K. (2004). Race/ethnicity and sexual orientation: Intersecting identities. *Cultural Diversity & Ethnic Minority Psychology, 10,* 241–254.

Parks, J. B., & Roberton, M. A. (2004). Attitudes toward women mediate the gender effect on attitudes toward sexist language. *Psychology of Women Quarterly, 28,* 233–239.

Parlee, Mary B. (1973). The premenstrual syndrome. *Psychological Bulletin, 80,* 454–465.

Parlee, Mary B. (1978). The rhythms in men's lives. *Psychology Today,* 82–91.

Parlee, Mary B. (1983). Menstrual rhythms in sensory processes: A review of fluctuations in vision, olfaction, audition, taste, and touch. *Psychological Bulletin, 93,* 539–548.

Parrot, Andrea, & Cummings, Nina. (2006). *Forsaken females: The global brutalization of women.* Lanham, MD: Rowman & Littlefield.

Pascoe, C. J. (2003). Multiples masculinities? Teenage boys talk about jocks and gender. *American Behavioral Scientist, 46,* 1423–1438.

Pascoe, C. J., & Bridges, Tristan. (2016). *Exploring masculinities: Identity, inequality, continuity and change.* New York, NY: Oxford University Press.

Pashler, Harold, McDaniel, Mark, Rohrer, Doug, & Bjork, Robert. (2009). Learning styles: Concepts and evidence. *Psychological Science in the Public Interest, 9,* 105–117.

Patterson, Charlotte J. (2000). Family relationships of lesbians and gay men. *Journal of Marriage and the Family, 62,* 1052–1069.

Patterson, Charlotte J. (2009). Children of lesbian and gay parents: Psychology, law, and policy. *American Psychologist, 64,* 727–736.

Patterson, Charlotte, J. (2017). Parents' sexual orientation and children's development. *Child Development Perspectives, 11,* 45–49.

Paulson, James F., & Bazemore, Sharnail D. (2010). Prenatal and postpartum depression in fathers and its association with maternal depression: A meta-analysis. *Journal of the American Medical Association, 303,* 1961–1969.

Peck, Joann, & Loken, Barbara. (2004). When will larger-sized female models in advertisements be viewed positively? The moderating effects of instructional frame, gender, and need for cognition. *Psychology and Marketing, 21,* 425–442.

Pedersen, Sara, & Seidman, Edward. (2004). Team sports achievement and self-esteem development among urban adolescent girls. *Psychology of Women Quarterly, 28,* 412–422.

Pedersen, William C., Miller, Lynn C., Putcha-Bhagavatula, Anila D., & Yang, Yijing. (2002). Evolved sex differences in the number of partners desired? The long and the short of it. *Psychological Science, 13,* 157–161.

Peplau, L. Anne. (1993). Lesbian and gay relationships. In L. D. Garnets & D. C. Kimmel (Eds.), *Psychological perspectives on lesbian and gay male experience* (pp. 395–419). New York, NY: Columbia University Press.

Peplau, L. Anne, & Conrad, Eva. (1989). Beyond nonsexist research: The perils of feminist methods in psychology. *Psychology of Women Quarterly, 13,* 381–402.

Peplau, L. Anne, & Garnets, Linda D. (2000). A new paradigm for understanding women's sexuality and sexual orientation. *Journal of Social Issues, 56,* 329–350.

Percec, Ivona, Plenge, Robert, Nadeau, Joseph, Bartolomei, Marisa, & Willard, Huntington. (2002). Autosomal dominant mutations affecting X inactivation choice in the mouse. *Science, 296,* 1136–1139.

Perez, Marisol, Ohrt, Tara K., & Hoek, Hans W. (2016). Prevalence and treatment of eating disorders among Hispanics/Latino Americans in the United States. *Current Opinion in Psychiatry, 29,* 378–382.

Pérez-Fuentes, Gabriela, Olfson, Mark, Villegas, Laura, Morcillo, Carmen, Wang, Shuai, & Blanco, Carlos. (2013). Prevalence and correlates of child sexual abuse: A national study. *Comprehensive Psychiatry, 54,* 16–27.

Perry, Armon R. (2013). African American men's attitudes toward marriage. *Journal of Black Studies, 44,* 182–202.

Perry, John D., & Whipple, Beverly. (1981). Pelvic muscle strength of female ejaculators: Evidence in support of a new theory of orgasm. *Journal of Sex Research, 17,* 22–39.

Perry-Jenkins, Maureen, Repetti, Rena L., & Crouter, Ann C. (2000). Work and family in the 1990s. *Journal of Marriage and the Family, 62,* 981–998.

Perry-Parrish, Carisa, & Zeman, Janice. (2011). Relations among sadness regulation, peer acceptance, and social functioning in early adolescence: The role of gender. *Social Development, 20,* 135–153.

Petersen, Jennifer L., & Hyde, Janet S. (2009). A longitudinal investigation of peer sexual harassment victimization in adolescence. *Journal of Adolescence, 32,* 1173–1188.

Petersen, Jennifer L., & Hyde, Janet S. (2010). A meta-analytic review of research on gender differences in sexuality: 1993 to 2007. *Psychological Bulletin, 136,* 21–38.

Peterson, Richard R. (1996). A re-evaluation of the economic consequences of divorce. *American Sociological Review, 61,* 528–536.

Petrosino, Jennifer M., DiSilvestro, David, & Ziouzenkova, Ouliana. (2014). Aldehyde dehydrogenase 1A1: Friend or foe to female metabolism? *Nutrients, 6,* 950–973.

Pettigrew, Thomas. (1964). *A profile of the Negro American.* Princeton, NJ: Van Nostrand.

Pheterson, Gail I., Kiesler, Sara B., & Goldberg, Philip A. (1971). Evaluation of the performance of women as a function of their sex, achievement, and personal history. *Journal of Personality and Social Psychology, 19,* 114–118.

Phillips, Louise H., & Henry, Julie D. (2008). Adult aging and executive functioning. In V. Anderson, P. Anderson, & R. Jacobs (Eds.), *Executive functions and the frontal lobes: A lifespan perspective* (pp. 57–79). Hove, UK: Psychology Press.

Phoenix, Charles H., Goy, Robert W., Gerall, Arnold A., & Young, William C. (1959). Organizing action of prenatally administered testosterone propionate on the tissues mediating mating behavior in the female guinea pig. *Endocrinology, 65,* 369–382.

Piccinelli, Marco, & Wilkinson, Greg. (2000). Gender differences in depression. *British Journal of Psychiatry, 177,* 486–492.

Piercy, Marge. (1974). *The token woman.* Amherst, MA: Feminist Arts Program of Everywoman's Center.

Pike, Jennifer J., & Jennings, Nancy A. (2005). The effects of commercials on children's perceptions of gender appropriate toy use. *Sex Roles, 52,* 83–92.

Pilkington, Neil W., & D'Augelli, Anthony R. (1995). Victimization of lesbian, gay, and bisexual youth in community settings. *Developmental Psychology, 23,* 33–56.

Pipher, Mary. (1994). *Reviving Ophelia: Saving the selves of adolescent girls.* New York, NY: Putnam.

Piran, Niva. (2001). Eating disorders and disordered eating. In J. Worell (Ed.), *Encyclopedia of women and gender* (pp. 369–376). San Diego, CA: Academic Press.

Pivo, Sarah, Montes, Jennifer, Schwartz, Shira, Chun, Jennifer, Kiely, Deirdre, Hazen, Alexes, & Schnabel, Freya. (2017). Breast cancer risk assessment and screening in transgender patients. *Clinical Breast Cancer, 17,* e225–e227.

Pizzey, Erin. (1974). *Scream quietly or the neighbors will hear.* London, UK: If Books.

Plant, E. Ashby, Hyde, Janet S., Keltner, Dacher, & Devine, Patricia G. (2000). The gender stereotyping of emotions. *Psychology of Women Quarterly, 24,* 81–92.

Plant, E. Ashby, Kling, Kristen C., & Smith, Ginny L. (2004). The influence of gender and social role on the interpretation of facial expressions. *Sex Roles, 51,* 187–196.

Pleck, Joseph H. (1975). Masculinity–femininity: Current and alternate paradigms. *Sex Roles, 1,* 161–178.

Pleck, Joseph H. (1981). *The myth of masculinity.* Cambridge, MA: MIT Press.

Pleck, Joseph H. (1992). Families and work: Small changes with big implications. *Qualitative Sociology, 15,* 427–432.

Pleck, Joseph H. (1995). The gender role strain paradigm: An update. In R. F. Levant & W. S. Pollack (Eds.) *A new psychology of men* (pp. 11–32). New York, NY: Basic Books.

Ploubidis, George B., Silverwood, Richard J., DeStavola, Bianca, & Grundy, Emily. (2015). Life-course partnership status and biomarkers in midlife: Evidence from the 1958 British birth cohort. *American Journal of Public Health, 105,* 1596–1603.

Polce-Lynch, Mary, Myers, Barbara J., Kliewer, Wendy, & Kilmartin, Christopher. (2001). Adolescent self-esteem and gender: Exploring relations to sexual harassment, body image, media influence, and emotional expression. *Journal of Youth and Adolescence, 30,* 225–244.

Polek, Carolee, & Hardie, Thomas. (2010). Lesbian women and knowledge about human papillomavirus. *Oncology Nursing Forum, 37,* E191–E197.

Pomerantz, Eva M., Altermatt, Ellen, & Saxon, Jill L. (2002). Making the grade but feeling distressed: Gender differences in academic performance and internal distress. *Journal of Educational Psychology, 94,* 396–404.

Pomerantz, Eva M., Ng, Florrie F.-Y., & Wang, Qian. (2004). Gender socialization; A parent × child model. In A. H. Eagly, A. E. Beall, & R. J. Sternberg (Eds.), *The psychology of gender* (2nd ed., pp. 120–142). New York, NY: Guilford.

Pope, Ken. (2001). Sex between therapists and clients. In J. Worell (Ed.), *Encyclopedia of women and gender* (pp. 955–962). New York, NY: Academic Press.

Porter, Natalie P., Geis, Florence L., & Walstedt, Joyce J. (1978, August). *Are women invisible as leaders?* Paper presented at the American Psychological Association Meeting, Toronto, Ontario, Canada.

Posavac, Heidi D., Posavac, Steven S., & Posavac, Emil J. (1998). Exposure to media images of female attractiveness and concern with body weight among young women. *Sex Roles, 38,* 187–202.

Poulin, François, & Pedersen, Sara. (2007). Developmental changes in gender composition of friendship networks in adolescent girls and boys. *Developmental Psychology, 43,* 1484–1496.

Pratto, Felicia, & Walker, Angela. (2004). The bases of gendered power. In A. H. Eagly, A. E. Beall, & R. J. Sternberg (Eds.), *The psychology of gender* (2nd ed., pp. 242–268). New York, NY: Guilford.

Prause, Nicole, & Graham, Cynthia A. (2007). Asexuality: Classification and characterization. *Archives of Sexual Behavior, 36,* 341–356.

Prentky, Robert A. (1997). Arousal reduction in sexual offenders: A review of antiandrogen interventions. *Sexual Abuse: A Journal of Research and Treatment, 9,* 335–347.

Prentky, Robert A., Gabriel, Adeena M., & Coward, Anna I. (2011). Treatment for perpetrators of sexual violence. In M. P. Koss, J. D. White, & A. E. Kazdin (Eds.), *Violence against women and children: Navigating solutions* (Vol. 2, pp. 115–136). Washington, DC: American Psychological Association.

Prewitt-Freilino, Jennifer L., Caswell, T. Andrew, & Laakso, Emmi K. (2012). The gendering of language: A comparison of gender equality in countries with gendered, natural gender, and genderless languages. *Sex Roles, 66,* 268–281.

Pridal, Cathryn G., & LoPiccolo, Joseph. (2000). Multielement treatment of desire disorders: Integration of cognitive, behavioral, and systemic therapy. In S. Leiblum & R. Rosen (Eds.), *Principles and practice of sex therapy* (3rd ed., pp. 57–84). New York, NY: Guilford.

Priess, Heather A., Lindberg, Sara M., & Hyde, Janet S. (2009). Adolescent gender-role identity and mental health: Gender intensification revisited. *Child Development, 80,* 1531–1544.

Propper, Catherine R. (2005). The study of endocrine-disrupting compounds: Past approaches and new directions. *Integrative and Comparative Biology, 45,* 194–200.

Pryor, John B., Giedd, Janet L., & Williams, Karen B. (1995). A social psychological model for predicting sexual harassment. *Journal of Social Issues, 51*(1), 69–84.

Pugliesi, Karen. (1992). *The social construction of premenstrual syndrome: Explaining problematic emotion.* Paper presented at the American Sociological Association Meeting, Pittsburgh, PA.

Quinn, Diane M., & Spencer, Steven J. (2001). The interference of stereotype threat with women's generation of mathematical problem-solving strategies. *Journal of Social Issues, 57,* 55–72.

Quinn, Paul C., Uttley, Lesley, Lee, Kang, Gibson, Alan, Smith, Michael, Slater, Alan M., & Pascalis, Olivier. (2008). Infant preference for female faces occurs for same- but not other-race faces. *Journal of Neuropsychology, 2,* 15–26.

Quinn, Paul C., Yahr, Joshua, Kuhn, Abbie, Slater, Alan M., & Pascalis, Olivier. (2002). Representation of the gender of human faces by infants: A preference for female. *Perception, 31,* 1109–1121.

Raag, Tarja, & Rackliff, Christine L. (1998). Preschoolers' awareness of social expectations of gender: Relationships to toy choices. *Sex Roles, 38,* 685–700.

Rabinowitz, Vita C., & Sechzer, Jeri A. (1993). Feminist perspectives on research methods. In F. L. Denmark & M. A. Paludi (Eds.), *Psychology of women: Handbook of issues and theories* (pp. 23–66). Westport, CT: Greenwood.

Radford, Eleanor J., & Hughes, Mark. (2015). Women's experiences of early miscarriage: Implications for nursing care. *Journal of Clinical Nursing, 24,* 1457–1465.

Raffaelli, Marcela, & Ontai, Lenna L. (2004). Gender socialization in Latino/a families: Results from two retrospectives studies. *Sex Roles, 50,* 287–300.

Raifman, Julia, Moscoe, Ellen, Austin, Bryn, & McConnell, Margaret. (2017). Difference-in-differences analysis of the association between state same-sex marriage policies and adolescent suicide attempts. *JAMA Pediatrics, 171,* 350–356.

Ramchandani, Paul G., Domoney, Jill, Sethna, Vaheshta, Psychogiou, Lamprini, Vlachos, Haido, & Murray, Lynne. (2013). Do early father–infant interactions predict the onset of externalising behaviours in young children? Findings from a longitudinal cohort study. *Journal of Child Psychology and Psychiatry, 54,* 56–64.

Ramey, Estelle. (1972, Spring). Men's cycles. *Ms.,* pp. 8–14.

Ramsey, Jennifer L., Langlois, Judith H., & Marti, Nathan C. (2005). Infant categorization of faces: Ladies first. *Developmental Review, 25,* 212–246.

Ransby, Barbara. (2000). Black feminism at twenty-one: Reflections on the evolution of a national community. *Signs: Journal of Women in Culture and Society, 25,* 1215–1222.

Rebelsky, Freda, & Hanks, Cheryl. (1971). Fathers' verbal interaction with infants in the first three months of life. *Child Development, 42,* 63–68.

Reed, Oakleigh M., Franks, Andrew S., & Scherr, Kyle C. (2015). Are perceptions of transgender individuals affected by mental illness stigma? A moderated mediation analysis of anti-transgender prejudice in hiring recommendations. *Psychology of Sexual Orientation and Gender Diversity, 2,* 463–469.

Reid, Pamela T., & Bing, Vanessa M. (2000). Sexual roles of girls and women: An ethnocultural lifespan perspective. In C. B. Travis & J. W. White (Eds.), *Sexuality, society, and feminism* (pp. 141–166). Washington, DC: American Psychological Association.

Reid, Pamela T., Haritos, Calliope, Kelly, Elizabeth, & Holland, Nicole E. (1995). Socialization of girls: Issues of ethnicity in gender development. In H. Landrine (Ed.), *Bringing cultural diversity to feminist psychology: Theory, research, and practice* (pp. 93–112). Washington, DC: American Psychological Association.

Reinharz, Shulamit. (1992). *Feminist methods in social research.* New York, NY: Oxford University Press.

Reskin, Barbara F. (1988). Occupational resegregation. In S. Rix (Ed.), *The American woman 1988–89.* New York, NY: Norton.

Rich, Adrienne. (1980). Compulsory heterosexuality and lesbian existence. *Signs, 5,* 631–660.

Ridgeway, Cecilia L., & Bourg, Chris. (2004). Gender as status: An expectation states theory approach. In A. H. Eagly, A. E. Beall, & R. J. Sternberg (Eds.), *The psychology of gender* (2nd ed., pp. 217–241). New York, NY: Guilford.

Riegle-Crumb, Catherine, & King, Barbara. (2010). Questioning a White male advantage in STEM: Examining disparities in college major by gender and race/ethnicity. *Educational Researchers, 39,* 656–664.

Riggle, Ellen D. B., Rostosky, Sharon S., & Horne, Sharon G. (2010). Psychological distress, well-being, and legal recognition in same-sex couple relationships. *Journal of Family Psychology, 24,* 82–86.

Riley, Joseph L., Robinson, Michael E., Wise, Emily A., Myers, Cynthia D., & Fillingham, Roger B. (1998). Sex differences in the perception of noxious experimental stimuli: A meta-analysis. *Pain, 74,* 181–187.

Riley, Joseph L., Robinson, Michael E., Wise, Emily A., & Price, Donald. (1999). A meta-analytic review of pain perception across the menstrual cycle. *Pain, 81,* 225–235.

Rind, Bruce, Tromovitch, Philip, & Bauserman, Robert. (1998). A meta-analytic examination of assumed properties of child sexual abuse using college samples. *Psychological Bulletin, 124,* 22–53.

Ro, Marguerite. (2002). Moving forward: Addressing the health of Asian American and Pacific Islander women. *American Journal of Public Health, 92,* 516–519.

Robertson, Nic. (2008, June 19). Rape is a way of life for Darfur's women. *CNN.* Retrieved from http://articles.cnn.com

Robinson, Dionne P., & Klein, Sabra L. (2012). Pregnancy and pregnancy-associated hormones alter immune responses and disease pathogenesis. *Hormones and Behavior, 62,* 263–271.

Robinson, Ira, Ziss, Ken, Ganza, Bill, Katz, Stuart, & Robinson, Edward. (1991). Twenty years of the Sexual Revolution, 1965–1985. *Journal of Marriage and the Family, 53,* 216–220.

Robinson, Margaret. (2017). Two-Spirit and bisexual people: Different umbrella, same rain. *Journal of Bisexuality, 17,* 7–29.

Robinson-Cimpian, Joseph P., Lubienski, Sarah T., Ganley, Colleen M., & Copur-Genturk, Yasemin. (2014). Are schools shortchanging boys or girls? The answer rests on methods and assumptions. *Developmental Psychology, 50,* 1840–1844.

Robnett, Rachael D. (2016). Gender bias in STEM fields: Variation in prevalence and links to STEM self-concept. *Psychology of Women Quarterly, 40,* 65–79.

Rocca, Corinne H., Kimport, Katrina, Gould, Heather, & Foster, Diana G. (2013). Women's emotions one week after receiving or being denied an abortion in the United States. *Perspectives on Sexual and Reproductive Health, 45,* 122–131.

Rodin, Judith, Silberstein, Lisa R., & Striegel-Moore, Ruth H. (1985). Women and weight: A normative discontent. In T. B. Sonderegger (Ed.), *Psychology and gender: Nebraska Symposium on Motivation* (pp. 267–307). Lincoln: University of Nebraska Press.

Rodin, Mari. (1992). The social construction of premenstrual syndrome. *Social Science and Medicine, 35,* 49–56.

Rodriguez, Ned, Ryan, Susan W., Vande Kemp, Hendrika, & Foy, David W. (1997). Posttraumatic stress disorder in adult female survivors of childhood sexual abuse: A comparison study. *Journal of Consulting and Clinical Psychology, 65,* 53–59.

Rogers, Baron K., Sperry, Heather A., & Levant, Ronald F. (2015). Masculinities among African American men: An intersectional perspective. *Psychology of Men & Masculinity, 16,* 416–425.

Rogers, Megan L., Halberstadt, Amy G., Castro, Vanessa L., MacCormack, Jennifer K., & Garrett-Peters, Patricia. (2016). Maternal emotion socialization differentially predicts third-grade children's emotion regulation and lability. *Emotion, 16,* 280–291.

Rogers, Stacy J., & White, Lynn K. (1998). Satisfaction with parenting: The role of marital happiness, family structure, and parents' gender. *Journal of Marriage and the Family, 60,* 293–308.

Rohner, Ronald P., & Veneziano, Robert A. (2001). The importance of father love: History and contemporary evidence. *Review of General Psychology, 5,* 382–405.

Roisman, Glenn I., Clausell, Eric, Holland, Ashley S., Fortuna, Keren, & Elieff, Chryle. (2008). Adult romantic relationships as contexts of human development:

A multimethod comparison of same-sex couples with opposite-sex dating, engaged, and married dyads. *Developmental Psychology, 44,* 91–101.

Romans, Sarah E., Clarkson, Rose F., Einstein, Gillian, Kreindler, David, Laredo, Sheila, Petrovic, Michele J., & Stanley, James. (2017). Crying, oral contraceptive use and the menstrual cycle. *Journal of Affective Disorders, 208,* 272–277.

Romans, Sarah E., Kreindler, David, Asllani, Eriola, Einstein, Gillian, Laredo, Sheila, Levitt, Anthony, . . . Stewart, Donna E. (2013). Mood and the menstrual cycle. *Psychotherapy & Psychosomatics, 82,* 53–60.

Rood, Lea, Roelofs, Jeffrrey, Bögels, Susan M., Nolen-Hoeksema, Susan, & Schouten, Erik. (2009). The influence of emotion-focused rumination and distraction on depressive symptoms in non-clinical youth: A meta-analytic review. *Clinical Psychology Review, 29,* 607–616.

Root, Maria P. P. (1995). The psychology of Asian American women. In H. Landrine (Ed.), *Bringing cultural diversity to feminist psychology: Theory, research, and practice* (pp. 265–302). Washington, DC: American Psychological Association.

Roper Center. (2011). http://webapps.ropercenter.uconn.edu

Rosaldo, Michelle Z. (1974). Woman, culture, and society: A theoretical overview. In M. Z. Rosaldo & L. Lamphere (Eds.), *Woman, culture, and society* (pp. 17–42). Stanford, CA: Stanford University Press.

Rosenkrantz, Paul, Vogel, Susan, Bee, Helen, Broverman, Inge, & Broverman, Donald M. (1968). Sex-role stereotypes and self-concepts in college students. *Journal of Consulting and Clinical Psychology, 32,* 287–295.

Rosenthal, Lisa, & Levy, Sheri R. (2010). Understanding women's risk for HIV infection using social dominance theory and the four bases of gendered power. *Psychology of Women Quarterly, 34,* 21–35.

Rosenthal, Marina N., Smidt, Alec M., & Freyd, Jennifer J. (2016). Still second class: Sexual harassment of graduate students. *Psychology of Women Quarterly, 40,* 364–377.

Rosenthal, Robert. (1966). *Experimenter effects in behavioral research.* New York, NY: Appleton-Century-Crofts.

Rosette, Ashleigh S., Koval, Christy Z., Ma, Anyi, & Livingston, Robert. (2016). Race matters for women leaders: Intersectional effects on agentic deficiencies and penalties. *Leadership Quarterly, 27,* 429–445.

Rositch, Anne F., Nowak, Rebecca G., & Gravitt, Patti E. (2014). Increased age and race-specific incidence of cervical cancer after correction for hysterectomy prevalence in the United States from 2000 to 2009. *Cancer, 120,* 2032–2038.

Rosnow, Ralph L. (1981). *Paradigms in transition: The methodology of social inquiry.* New York, NY: Oxford University Press.

Ross, C. E., & Mirowsky, J. (1988). Child care and emotional adjustment to wives' employment. *Journal of Health and Social Behavior, 29,* 127–138.

Ross, Catherine E., Mirowsky, John, & Goldsteen, Karen. (1990). The impact of the family on health: Decade in review. *Journal of Marriage and the Family, 52,* 1059–1078.

Roter, Debra L., & Hall, Judith A. (1997). Gender differences in patient-physician communication. In S. Gallant, G. Keita, & R. Royak-Schaler (Eds.), *Health care for women: Psychological, social, and behavioral influences* (pp. 57–72). Washington, DC: American Psychological Association.

Rothman, Emily F., Sullivan, Mairead, Keyes, Susan, & Boehmer, Ulrike. (2012). Parents' supportive reaction to sexual orientation disclosure associated with better health: Results from a population-based survey of LGB adults. *Journal of Homosexuality, 59,* 186–200.

Roubinov, Danielle S., Leucken, Linda J., Gonzales, Nancy A., & Crnic, Keith A. (2016). Father involvement in Mexican-origin families: Preliminary development of a culturally informed measure. *Cultural Diversity and Ethnic Minority Psychology, 22,* 277–287.

Rouse, Leah M. (2016). American Indians, Alaska Natives, and the psychology of men and masculinity. In Y. J. Wong & S. F. Wester (Eds.), *APA handbook of men and masculinities* (pp. 319–337). Washington, DC: American Psychological Association.

Rozée, Patricia D., & Koss, Mary P. (2001). Rape: A century of resistance. *Psychology of Women Quarterly, 25,* 295–311.

Rubin, Lillian. (1979). *Women of a certain age.* New York, NY: Harper & Row.

Ruble, Diane N. (1977). Premenstrual symptoms: A reinterpretation. *Science, 197,* 291–292.

Rucklidge, Julia J. (2010). Gender differences in attention-deficit/hyperactivity disorder. *Psychiatric Clinics of North America, 33,* 357–373.

Rudman, Laurie, & Fairchild, Kimberly. (2004). Reactions to counterstereotypic behavior: The role of backlash in cultural stereotype maintenance. *Journal of Personality and Social Psychology, 87,* 157–176.

Rudman, Laurie A., & Glick, Peter. (1999). Feminized management and backlash toward agentic women: The hidden costs to women of a kinder, gentler image of middle managers. *Journal of Personality and Social Psychology, 77,* 1004–1010.

Rudman, Laurie A., & Glick, Peter. (2008). *The social psychology of gender: How power and intimacy shape gender relations*. New York, NY: Guilford.

Rudolfsdottir, Annadis G. (2000). "I am not a patient, and I am not a child": The institutionalization and experience of pregnancy. *Feminism & Psychology, 10*, 337–350.

Rushton, J. Philippe. (1992). Cranial capacity related to sex, rank, and race in a stratified random sample of 6,325 U.S. military personnel. *Intelligence, 16*, 401–413.

Russell, Diana. (1982). *Rape in marriage*. New York, NY: Macmillan.

Russo, Nancy F. (1979). Overview: Sex roles, fertility, and the motherhood mandate. *Psychology of Women Quarterly, 4*, 7–15.

Russo, Nancy F. (2010). Diversity and women's mental health. In H. Landrine & N. Russo (Eds.), *Handbook of diversity in feminist psychology* (pp. 261–284). New York, NY: Springer

Russo, Nancy Felipe, & O'Connell, Agnes N. (1980). Models from our past: Psychology's foremothers. *Psychology of Women Quarterly, 5*, 11–54.

Ryan, Kathryn M. (2011). The relationship between rape myths and sexual scripts: The social construction of rape. *Sex Roles, 65*, 774–782.

Saarni, Carolyn. (1999). *The development of emotional competence*. New York, NY: Guilford.

Sachs-Ericsson, Natalie, Blazer, Dan G., Plant, Ashby, & Arnow, Bruce. (2005). Childhood sexual and physical abuse and the 1-year prevalence of medical problems in the National Comorbidity Survey. *Health Psychology, 24*, 32–40.

Sadker, Myra, & Sadker, David. (1985, March). Sexism in the schoolroom of the '80s. *Psychology Today, 19*, pp. 54–57.

Saez, Pedro A., Casado, Adonaid, & Wade, Jay C. (2009). Factors influencing masculinity ideology among Latino men. *Journal of Men's Studies, 17*, 116–128.

Salgado de Snyder, V. Nelly, Acevedo, Andrea, Diaz-Perez, Maria, & Saldivar-Garduno, Alicia. (2000). Understanding the sexuality of Mexican-born women and their risk for HIV/AIDS. *Psychology of Women Quarterly, 24*, 100–109.

Salisbury, Amy, Law, Karen, LaGasse, Lyn, & Lester, Barry. (2003). Maternal-fetal attachment. *Journal of the American Medical Association, 289*(13), 1701.

Salk, Rachel H., & Engeln-Maddox, Renee. (2011). "If you're fat, then I'm humongous!" Frequency, content, and impact of fat talk among college women. *Psychology of Women Quarterly, 35*, 18–28.

Salk, Rachel H., & Hyde, Janet S. (2012). Contemporary genetics for gender researchers: Not your grandma's genetics anymore. *Psychology of Women Quarterly, 36*, 395–410.

Salk, Rachel H., Hyde, Janet S., & Abramson, Lyn Y. (2017). Gender differences in depression in representative national samples: Meta-analyses of diagnoses and symptoms. *Psychological Bulletin, 143*, 783–822.

Salk, Rachel H., Petersen, Jennifer L., Abramson, Lyn Y., & Hyde, Janet S. (2016). The contemporary face of gender differences and similarities in depression throughout adolescence: Development and chronicity. *Journal of Affective Disorders, 205*, 28–35.

Salovey, Peter, Detweiler-Bedell, Brian T., Detweiler-Bedell, Jerusha B., & Mayer, John D. (2008). Emotional intelligence. In M. Lewis, J. M. Haviland-Jones, & L. F. Barrett (Eds.), *Handbook of emotions* (3rd ed., pp. 533–537). New York, NY: Guilford.

Sánchez, Francisco J., Martinez-Patiño, Maria J., & Vilain, Eric. (2013). The new policy on hyperandrogenism in elite female athletes is not about "sex testing." *Journal of Sex Research, 50*, 112–115.

Sanchez-Hucles, Janis, Hudgins, Patrick, & Gamble, Kimberly. (2005). Reflection and distortion: Women of color in magazine advertisements. In E. Cole & J. H. Daniel (Eds.), *Featuring females: Feminist analyses of media* (pp. 185–198). Washington, DC: American Psychological Association.

Sanday, Peggy R. (1981). The socio-cultural context of rape: A cross-cultural study. *Journal of Social Issues, 37*, 5–27.

Sanday, Peggy R. (1988). The reproduction of patriarchy in feminist anthropology. In M. M. Gergen (Ed.), *Feminist thought and the structure of knowledge* (pp. 49–68). New York, NY: New York University Press.

Sanday, Peggy R. (1990). *Fraternity gang rape*. New York, NY: New York University Press.

Sandberg, John F., & Hofferth, Sandra L. (2001). Changes in children's time with parents: United States, 1981–1997. *Demography, 38*, 423–436.

Sanghavi, Darshak M. (2006, October 17). Preschool puberty, and a search for the causes. *New York Times*.

Santos de Barona, Maryann, & Barona, A. (2000). A model for conducting research with Hispanics. In *Guidelines for research in ethnic minority communities* (pp. 9–11). Washington, DC: American Psychological Association.

Sasson, Isaac, & Umberson, Debra J. (2014). Widowhood and depression: New light on gender differences, selection, and psychological adjustment. *Journals of Gerontology, Series B: Psychological Sciences and Social Sciences, 69*, 135–145.

Sathyanarayana, Sheela, Grady, Richard, Barret, Emily S., Redmon, Bruce, Nguyen, Ruby H. N., Barthold, Julia S., . . . Swan, Shanna H. (2016). First trimester phthalate exposure and male newborn genital anomalies. *Environmental Research, 151*, 777–782.

Savin-Williams, Ritch C. (1998). The disclosure to families of same-sex attractions by lesbian, gay, and bisexual youths. *Journal of Research on Adolescence, 8*, 49–68.

Sax, Leonard. (2006). Six degrees of separation: What teachers need to know about the emerging science of sex differences. *Educational Horizons, 84*, 190–200.

Saxton, Marsha. (2016). Access to care: The heart of euity in health care. In S. E. Miles-Cohen & C. Signore (Eds.), *Eliminating inequities for women with disabilities* (pp. 39–60). Washington, DC: American Psychological Association.

Sayers, Dorothy. (1946). *Unpopular opinions.* London, UK: Victor Gollancz.

Sbarra, David A., Emery, Robert E., Beam, Christopher R., & Ocker, Bailey L. (2014). Marital dissolution and major depression in midlife: A propensity score analysis. *Clinical Psychological Science, 20*, 1–9.

Scherf, K. S., Elbich, D. B., & Motta-Mena, N. V. (2017, April 26). Investigating the influence of biological sex on the behavioral and neural basis of face recognition. *ENeuro.* doi:10.1523/eneuro.0104-17.2017

Schilt, Kristen, & Westbrook, Laurel. (2009). Doing gender, doing heteronormativity. *Gender & Society, 23*, 440–464.

Schmader, Toni. (2010). Stereotype threat deconstructed. *Current Directions in Psychological Science, 19*, 14–18.

Schmader, Toni, & Johns, Michael. (2003). Converging evidence that stereotype threat reduces working memory capacity. *Journal of Personality and Social Psychology, 85*, 440–452.

Schmidt, Ulrike, Magill, Nicholas, Renwick, Bethany, Keyes, Alexandra, Kenyon, Martha, DeJong, Hannah, . . . Landau, Sabine. (2015). The Maudsley Outpatient Study of Treatments for Anorexia Nervosa and Related Conditions (MOSAIC): Comparison of the Maudsley Model of Anorexia Nervosa Treatment for Adults (MANTRA) with Specialist Supportive Clinical Management (SSCM) in outpatients with broadly defined anorexia nervosa: A randomized controlled trial. *Journal of Consulting and Clinical Psychology, 83*, 796–807.

Schooler, Deborah, Ward, L. Monique, Merriwether, Ann, & Caruthers, Allison. (2004). Who's that girl: Television's role in the body image development of young White and Black women. *Psychology of Women Quarterly, 28*, 38–47.

Schuetz, E., Furuya, K., & Schuetz, J. (1995). Interindividual variation in expression of P-glycoprotein in normal human liver and secondary hepatic neoplasms. *Journal of Pharmacology and Experimental Therapeutics, 275*, 1011–1018.

Schulman, Kevin A., Berlin, Jesse A., Harless, William, Kerner, Jon F., Sistrunk, Shyrl, Gersh, Bernard J., . . . Escarce, José J. (1999). The effect of race and sex on physicians' recommendations for cardiac catheterization. *New England Journal of Medicine, 340*, 618–626.

Schulte, Erica M., Grilo, Carlos M., & Gearhardt, Ashley N. (2016). Shared and unique mechanisms underlying binge eating disorder and addictive disorders. *Clinical Psychology Review, 44*, 125–139.

Schultheiss, Oliver C., Wirth, Michelle M., Torges, Cynthia M., Pang, Joyce S., Villacorta, Mark A., & Welsh, Kathryn M. (2005). Effects of implicit power motivation on men's and women's implicit learning and testosterone changes after social victory or defeat. *Journal of Personality and Social Psychology, 88*, 174–188.

Schulz, Muriel R. (1975). The semantic derogation of woman. In B. Thorne & N. Henley (Eds.), *Language and sex: Difference and dominance* (pp. 64–75). Rowley, MA: Newbury-House.

Sczesny, Sabine, Formanowicz, Magda, & Moser, Franziska. (2016). Can gender-fair language reduce gender stereotyping and discrimination? *Frontiers in Psychology, 7*, 25.

Sczesny, Sabine, Moser, Franziska, & Wood, Wendy. (2015). Beyond sexist beliefs: How do people decide to use gender-inclusive language? *Personality and Social Psychology Bulletin, 41*, 943–954.

Seavy, Carol A., Katz, Phyllis A., & Zalk, Sue R. (1975). Baby X: The effects of gender labels on adult responses to infants. *Sex Roles, 1*, 103–110.

Sechzer, Jeri A. (2004). "Islam and woman: Where tradition meets modernity": History and interpretations of Islamic women's status. *Sex Roles, 51*, 263–272.

Sedgh, Gilda, Ashford, Lori S., & Hussain, Rubina. (2016). *Unmet need for contraception in developing countries: Examining women's reasons for not using a method.* New York, NY: Guttmacher Institute.

Sedgh, Gilda, Bearak, Jonathan, Singh, Susheela, Bankole, Akinrinola, Popinchalk, Anna, Ganatra, Bela, . . . Alkema, Leontine. (2016). Abortion incidence between 1990 and 2014: Global, regional, and subregional levels and trends. *Lancet, 388*(10041), 258–267.

Sedgwick, Eve K. (1990). *Epistemology of the closet.* Berkeley: University of California Press.

Segnan, N. (1997). Socioeconomic status and cancer screening. In M. Kogevinas, N. Pearce, M. Susser, & P. Boffetta (Eds.), *Social inequalities and cancer* (IARC

Scientific Publication No. 138, pp. 369–376). Lyon, France: International Agency for Research on Cancer.

Segura, Denise A., & Pierce, Jennifer L. (1993). Chicana/o family structure and gender personality: Chodorow, familism, and psychoanalytic sociology revisited. *Signs, 19*, 62–91.

Seidlitz, Larry, & Diener, Ed. (1998). Sex differences in the recall of affective experiences. *Journal of Personality and Social Psychology, 74*, 262–271.

Seidman, Ilene, & Pokorak, Jeffrey J. (2011). Justice responses to sexual violence. In M. P. Koss, J. D. White, & A. E. Kazdin (Eds.), *Violence against women and children: Navigating solutions* (Vol. 2, pp. 137–158). Washington, DC: American Psychological Association.

Séjourné, Natalène, Callahan, Stacey, & Chabrol, Henri. (2010). Support following miscarriage: What women want. *Journal of Reproductive and Infant Psychology, 28*, 403–411.

Selby, Jenn. (2014, January 15). Kate Moss in quotes: "Nothing tastes as good as skinny feels" and other career-defining statements from fashion's silent supermodel. *The Independent*. Retrieved from http://www.independent.co.uk

Selvin, Elizabeth, & Brett, Kate M. (2003). Breast and cervical cancer screening: Sociodemographic predictors among White, Black, and Hispanic women. *American Journal of Public Health, 93*, 618–623.

Servin, Anna, Nordenström, Anna, Larsson, Agne, & Bohlin, Gunilla. (2003). Prenatal androgens and gender-typed behavior: A study of girls with mild and severe forms of congenital adrenal hyperplasia. *Developmental Psychology, 39*, 440–450.

Sevelius, Jae M. (2013). Gender affirmation: A framework for conceptualizing risk behavior among transgender women of color. *Sex Roles, 68*, 675–689.

Shainess, Natalie. (1977). The equitable therapy of women in psychoanalysis. In E. I. Rawlings & D. K. Carter (Eds.), *Psychotherapy for women.* Springfield, IL: Charles C Thomas.

Shakespeare, Tom. (2005). Sex selection. *Nature Reviews Genetics, 6*, 666.

Shanor, Karen. (1978). *The sexual sensitivity of the American male.* New York, NY: Ballantine.

Shapiro, Alyson F., Gottman, John M., & Fink, Brandi C. (2015). Short-term change in couples' conflict following a transition to parenthood intervention. *Couple and Family Psychology: Research and Practice, 4*, 239–251.

Sharp, Gemma, Tiggemann, Marika, & Mattiske, Julie. (2015). Predictors of consideration of labiaplasty: An extension of the tripartite influence model of beauty ideals. *Psychology of Women Quarterly, 39*, 182–193.

Shaver, Phillip. (1976). Questions concerning fear of success and its conceptual relatives. *Sex Roles, 2*, 305–320.

Shaw, Lois B. (1984). Retirement plans of middle-aged married women. *Gerontologist, 24*, 154–159.

Shepard, David S. (2002). A negative state of mind: Patterns of depressive symptoms among men with high gender role conflict. *Psychology of Men and Masculinity, 3*, 3–8.

Sherman, Gary D., Rice, Leslie K., Jin, Ellie S., Jones, Amanda C., & Josephs, Robert A. (2017). Sex differences in cortisol's regulation of affiliative behavior. *Hormones and Behavior, 92*, 20–28.

Sherman, Julia A. (1971). *On the psychology of women: A survey of empirical studies.* Springfield, IL: Charles C Thomas.

Sherman, Julia A. (1978). *Sex-related cognitive differences.* Springfield, IL: Charles C Thomas.

Sherman, Linda A., Temple, Robert, & Merkatz, Ruth B. (1995). Women in clinical trials: An FDA perspective. *Science, 269*, 793–795.

Sherwin, Barbara B. (1991). The psychoendocrinology of aging and female sexuality. *Annual Review of Sex Research, 2*, 181–198.

Shields, Stephanie A. (1975). Functionalism, Darwinism, and the psychology of women: A study in social myth. *American Psychologist, 30*, 739–754.

Shields, Stephanie A. (2000). Thinking about gender, thinking about theory: Gender and emotional experience. In A. Fischer (Ed.), *Gender and emotion: Social psychological perspectives* (pp. 3–23). Cambridge, UK: Cambridge University Press.

Shields, Stephanie. (2002). *Speaking from the heart: Gender and the social meaning of emotion.* New York, NY: Cambridge University Press.

Shields, Stephanie A. (2005). The politics of emotion in everyday life: "Appropriate" emotion and claims on identity. *Review of General Psychology, 9*, 3–15.

Shields, Stephanie A. (2013). Gender and emotion: What we think we know, what we need to know, and why it matters. *Psychology of Women Quarterly, 37*, 423–435.

Shifren, Jan L., Braunstein, Glenn D., Simon, James A., Casson, Peter R., Buster, John E., Redmond, Geoffrey P., . . . Mazer, Norman A. (2000). Transdermal testosterone treatment in women with impaired sexual function after oophorectomy. *New England Journal of Medicine, 343*, 682–688.

Shifren, Jan L., & Schiff, Isaac. (2010). Role of hormone therapy in the management of menopause. *Obstetrics & Gynecology, 115*, 839–855.

Shih, Margaret, Pittinsky, Todd L., & Ambady, Nalini. (1999). Stereotype susceptibility: Identity salience and shifts in quantitative performance. *Psychological Science, 10*, 80–83.

Shih, Margaret, & Sanchez, Diana T. (2005). Perspectives and research on the positive and negative implications of having multiple racial identities. *Psychological Bulletin, 131*, 569–591.

Shiina, Akihiro, Nakazato, Michiko, Mitsumori, Makoto, Koizumi, Hiroki, Shimizu, Eiji, Fujisaki, Mihisa, & Iyo, Masaomi. (2005). An open trial of outpatient group therapy for bulimic disorders: Combination program of cognitive behavioral therapy with assertiveness training and self-esteem enhancement. *Psychiatry and Clinical Neurosciences, 59*, 690–696.

Shilts, Randy. (1993). *Conduct unbecoming: Lesbians and gays in the U.S. military, Vietnam to the Persian Gulf.* New York, NY: St. Martin's Press.

Shor, Eran, Roelfs, David J., Curreli, Misty, Clemow, Lynn, Burg, Matthew M., & Schwartz, Joseph E. (2012). Widowhood and mortality: A meta-analysis and meta-regression. *Demography, 49*, 575–606.

Shreffler, Karina M., Greil, Arthur L., & McQuillan, Julia. (2011). Pregnancy loss and distress among U.S. women. *Family Relations, 60*, 342–355.

Sidanius, Jim, & Pratto, Felicia. (1999). *Social dominance: An intergroup theory of social hierarchy and oppression.* New York, NY: Cambridge University Press.

Siegel, Jacob S. (1978). *Prospective trends in the size and structure of the elderly population, impact of mortality trends, and some implications* (Special Studies Series P-23, No. 59, 2nd printing, rev.). Washington, DC: U.S. Government Printing Office.

Signore, Caroline. (2016). Reproductive and sexual health for women with disabilities. In S. E. Miles-Cohen & C. Signore (Eds.), *Eliminating inequities for women with disabilities* (pp. 93–114). Washington, DC: American Psychological Association.

Silverstein, Louise B., & Auerbach, Carl F. (1999). Deconstructing the essential father. *American Psychologist, 54*, 397–407.

Simes, M. R., & Berg, D. H. (2001). Surreptitious learning: Menarche and menstrual product advertisements. *Health Care for Women International, 22*, 455–469.

Simon, J. G., & Feather, N. T. (1973). Causal attributions for success and failure at university examinations. *Journal of Educational Psychology, 64*, 45–56.

Simon, Robert J., Fleiss, Joseph L., Gurland, Barry J., Stiller, Pamela R., & Sharpe, Lawrence. (1973). Depression and schizophrenia in hospitalized patients. *Archives of General Psychiatry, 28*, 509–512.

Simoni-Wastila, Linda. (1998). Gender and psychotropic drug use. *Medical Care, 36*, 88–94.

Sinacore, Ada L., & Enns, Carolyn Z. (2005). Diversity feminisms: Postmodern, women-of-color, antiracist, lesbian, third-wave, and global perspectives. In C. Enns & A. Sinacore (Eds.), *Teaching social justice: Integrating multicultural and feminist theories in the classroom* (pp. 41–68). Washington, DC: American Psychological Association.

Singh, Anneliese A. (2013). Transgender youth of color and resilience: Negotiating oppression, finding support. *Sex Roles, 68*, 690–702.

Singh, Anneliese A., & dickey, lore m. (2016). Implementing the APA Guidelines on Psychological Practice With Transgender and Gender Nonconforming People: A call to action to the field of psychology. *Psychology of Sexual Orientation and Gender Diversity, 3*, 195–200.

Singh, Anneliese A., & McKleroy, Vel S. (2011). "Just getting out of bed is a revolutionary act": The resilience of transgender people of color who have survived traumatic life events. *Traumatology, 20*, 1–11.

Singh, Devendra. (1993). Adaptive significance of female physical attractiveness: Role of waist-to-hip ratio. *Journal of Personality and Social Psychology, 65*, 293–307.

Singley, Daniel B., Cole, Brian P., Hammer, Joseph H., Molloy, Sonia, Rowell, Alexander, & Isacco, Anthony. (2017, February 23). Development and psychometric evaluation of the Paternal Involvement With Infants Scale. *Psychology of Men & Masculinity.* Advance online publication. http://dx.doi.org/10.1037/men0000094

Singley, Daniel B., & Edwards, Lisa M. (2015). Men's perinatal mental health in the transition to fatherhood. *Professional Psychology: Research and Practice, 46*, 309–316.

Sirin, Selcuk R., McCreary, Donald R., & Mahalik, James R. (2004). Differential reactions to men and women's gender role transgressions: Perceptions of social status, sexual orientation, and value dissimilarity. *Journal of Men's Studies, 12*, 119–132.

Slevec, Julie, & Tiggemann, Marika. (2010). Attitudes toward cosmetic surgery in middle-aged women: Body image, aging anxiety, and the media. *Psychology of Women Quarterly, 34*, 65–74.

Smedley, Audrey, & Smedley, Brian D. (2005). Race as biology is fiction, racism as a social problem is real: Anthropological and historical perspectives on the social construction of race. *American Psychologist, 60*, 16–26.

Smiler, Andrew P. (2006). Living the image: A quantitative approach to delineating masculinities. *Sex Roles, 55*, 621–632.

Smith, Andrea. (2005). Native American feminism, sovereignty, and social change. *Feminist Studies, 31,* 116–132.

Smith, Christine A., Johnston-Robledo, Ingrid, McHugh, Maureen C., & Chrisler, Joan C. (2010). Words matter: The language of gender. In J. Chrisler & D. McCreary (Eds.), *Handbook of gender research in psychology* (Vol. 1, pp. 361–378). New York, NY: Springer.

Smith, David M., & Gates, Gary J. (2001). *Gay and lesbian families in the United States: Same-sex unmarried partner households.* Washington, DC: Human Rights Campaign.

Smith, Elke S., Junger, Jessica, Derntl, Birgit, & Habel, Ute. (2015). The transsexual brain: A review of findings on the neural basis of transsexualism. *Neuroscience and Biobehavioral Reviews, 59,* 251–266.

Smith, Howard L., & Grenier, Mary. (1982). Sources of organizational power for women: Overcoming structural obstacles. *Sex Roles, 8,* 733–746.

Smith, Jessi L., Cech, Erin, Metz, Anneke, Huntoon, Meghan, & Moyer, Christina. (2014). Giving back or giving up: Native American student experiences in science and engineering. *Cultural Diversity & Ethnic Minority Psychology, 20,* 413–429.

Smith, Tom W., Hout, Michael, & Marsden, Peter V. (2012). General Social Survey, 1972–2012. Retrieved from http://www.icpsr.umich.edu/icpsrweb/ICPSR/studies/34802?q=general+social+survey+2012+tom+smith

Smolak, Linda, & Striegel-Moore, Ruth. (2001). Body image concerns. In J. Worell (Ed.), *Encyclopedia of gender* (pp. 201–210). San Diego, CA: Academic Press.

Snowden, Jonathan M., Tilden, Ellen L., Snyder, Janice, Quigley, Brian, Caughey, Aaron B., & Cheng, Yvonne W. (2015). Planned out-of-hospital birth and birth outcomes. *New England Journal of Medicine, 373,* 2642–2653.

Snyder, R. Claire. (2008). What is third-wave feminism? A new directions essay. *Signs: Journal of Women in Culture and Society, 34,* 175–196.

Soares, Claudio N., Almeida, Osvaldo P., Joffe, Hadine, & Cohen, Lee S. (2001). Efficacy of estradiol for the treatment of depressive disorders in perimenopausal women: A double-blind, randomized, placebo-controlled trial. *Archives of General Psychiatry, 58,* 529–534.

Sohn, David. (1982). Sex differences in achievement self-attributions: An effect-size analysis. *Sex Roles, 8,* 345–357.

Sojo, Victor E., Wood, Robert E., & Genat, Anna E. (2016). Harmful workplace experiences and women's occupational well-being: A meta-analysis. *Psychology of Women Quarterly, 40,* 10–40.

Sokol-Chang, Rosemarie, Fisher, Maryanne L., et al. (2013). Letter of purpose of the Feminist Evolutionary Psychology Society. *Journal of Social, Evolutionary, and Cultural Psychology, 7,* 286–294.

Solomon, Sondra E., Rothblum, Esther D., & Balsam, Kimberly F. (2004). Pioneers in partnership: Lesbian and gay male couples in civil unions compared with those not in civil unions and married heterosexual siblings. *Journal of Family Psychology, 18,* 275–286.

Solomon, Sondra E., Rothblum, Esther D., & Balsam, Kimberly F. (2005). Money, housework, sex, and conflict: Same-sex couples in civil unions, those not in civil unions, and heterosexual married siblings. *Sex Roles, 52,* 561–575.

Sommer, Iris E., Aleman, André, Somers, Metten, Boks, Marco P., & Kahn, René S. (2008). Sex differences in handedness, asymmetry of the Planum Temporal and functional language lateralization. *Brain Research, 1206,* 76–88.

Sommers, Christina H. (2000). *The war against boys: How misguided feminism is harming our young men.* New York, NY: Simon & Schuster.

Sonfield, Adam, Hasstedt, Kinsey, Kavanaugh, Megan L., & Anderson, Ragnar. (2013). *The social and economic benefits of women's ability to determine whether and when to have children.* New York, NY: Guttmacher Institute.

Sonis, Jeffrey, Gibson, James L., de Jong, Joop T. V. M., Field, Nigel P., Hean, Sokhom, & Komproe, Ivan. (2009). PTSD and disability in Cambodia. *Journal of the American Medical Association, 302,* 527–536.

Spelman, Elizabeth V. (1988). *Inessential woman: Problems of exclusion in feminist thought.* Boston, MA: Beacon Press.

Spence, Janet T., & Buckner, Camille E. (2000). Instrumental and expressive traits, trait stereotypes, and sexist attitudes: What do they signify? *Psychology of Women Quarterly, 24,* 44–62.

Spence, Janet T., & Helmreich, Robert L. (1978). *Masculinity and femininity.* Austin: University of Texas Press.

Spence, Janet T., & Helmreich, Robert L. (1980). Masculine instrumentality and feminine expressiveness: Their relationships with sex-role attitudes and behaviors. *Psychology of Women Quarterly, 5,* 147–163.

Spencer, Michael S., Chen, Juan, Gee, Gilbert C., Fabian, Cathryn G., & Takeuchi, David T. (2010). Discrimination and mental health-related service use in a national study of Asian Americans. *American Journal of Public Health, 100,* 2410–2417.

Spencer, Steven J., Logel, Christine, & Davies, Paul G. (2016). Stereotype threat. *Annual Review of Psychology, 67,* 415–437.

Spencer, Steven J., Steele, Claude M., & Quinn, Diane M. (1999). Stereotype threat and women's math performance. *Journal of Experimental Social Psychology, 35,* 4–28.

Spies, M., Hahn, A., Kranz, G. S., Sladky, R., Kaufmann, U., Hummer, A., . . . Lanzenberger, R. (2016). Gender transition affects neural correlates of empathy: A resting state functional connectivity study with ultra high-field 7T MR imaging. *NeuroImage, 138,* 257–265.

Spitzer, Brenda L., Henderson, Katherine A., & Zivian, Marilyn T. (1999). Gender differences in population versus media body sizes: A comparison over four decades. *Sex Roles, 40,* 545–566.

Sprecher, Susan. (2014). Evidence of change in men's versus women's emotional reactions to first sexual intercourse: A 23-year study in a human sexuality course at a midwestern university. *Journal of Sex Research, 51,* 466–472.

Sprecher, Susan, Barbee, Anita, & Schwartz, Pepper. (1995). "Was it good for you, too?" Gender differences in first sexual intercourse experiences. *Journal of Sex Research, 32,* 3–15.

Sprecher, Susan, & Hatfield, Elaine. (1996). Premarital sexual standards among U.S. college students: Comparison with Russian and Japanese students. *Archives of Sexual Behavior, 25,* 261–288.

Srebnik, Debra S., & Saltzberg, Elayne A. (1994). Feminist cognitive-behavioral therapy for negative body image. *Women & Therapy, 15,* 117–133.

Stagl, Jamie M., Antoni, Michael H., Lechner, Suzanne C., Boucard, Laura, Blomberg, Bonnie B., Glück, Stefan, . . . Carver, Charles S. (2015). Randomized controlled trial of cognitive behavioral stress management in breast cancer: A brief report of effects on 5-year depressive symptoms. *Health Psychology, 34,* 176–180.

Stahlberg, Dagmar, Braun, Friederike, Irmen, Lisa, & Sczesny, Sabine. (2007). Representation of the sexes in language. In K. Fiedler (Ed.), *Social communication* (pp. 163–187). New York, NY: Psychology Press.

Stanton, Annette L., Lobel, Marci, Sears, Sharon, & DeLuca, Robyn S. (2002). Psychosocial aspects of selected issues in women's reproductive health: Current status and future directions. *Journal of Consulting and Clinical Psychology, 70,* 751–770.

Staples, Robert. (2006). *Exploring Black sexuality.* Lanham, MD: Rowman & Littlefield.

Stark-Wrobleski, Kim, Yanico, Barbara J., & Lupe, Steven. (2005). Acculturation, internalization of Western appearance norms, and eating pathology among Japanese and Chinese international student women. *Psychology of Women Quarterly, 29,* 38–46.

Starr, Christine R., & Zurbriggen, Eileen L. (2017). Sandra Bem's gender schema theory after 34 years: A review of its reach and impact. *Sex Roles, 76,* 566–578.

Steele, Claude M. (1997). A threat in the air: How stereotypes shape intellectual identity and performance. *American Psychologist, 52,* 613–629.

Steele, Claude M., & Aronson, Joshua. (1995). Stereotype threat and the intellectual test performance of African Americans. *Journal of Personality and Social Psychology, 69,* 797–811.

Steensma, Thomas D., McGuire, Jenifer K., Kreukels, Baudewijntje P., Beekman, Anneke J., & Cohen-Kettenis, Peggy T. (2013). Factors associated with desistence and persistence of childhood gender dysphoria: A quantitative follow-up study. *Journal of the American Academy of Child and Adolescent Psychiatry, 52,* 582–590.

Steil, Janice M. (2001a). Family forms and member well-being: A research agenda for the Decade of Behavior. *Psychology of Women Quarterly, 25,* 344–363.

Steil, Janice. (2001b). Marriage: Still "his" and "hers"? In J. Worell (Ed.), *Encyclopedia of gender* (pp. 677–686). San Diego, CA: Academic Press.

Steil, Janice M., & Hay, Jennifer L. (1997). Social comparison in the workplace: A study of 60 dual-career couples. *Personality and Social Psychology Bulletin, 23,* 427–438.

Steil, Janice, McGann, Vanessa L., & Kahn, Anne S. (2001). Entitlement. In J. Worell (Ed.), *Encyclopedia of women and gender* (pp. 403–410). San Diego, CA: Academic Press.

Steinhausen, Hans-Christoph. (2002). The outcome of anorexia nervosa in the 20th century. *American Journal of Psychiatry, 159,* 1284–1293.

Steinhausen, Hans-Christoph, & Weber, Sandy. (2009). The outcome of bulimia nervosa: Findings from one-quarter century of research. *American Journal of Psychology, 166,* 1331–1341.

Stephens, W. N. (1961). A cross-cultural study of menstrual taboos. *Genetic Psychology Monographs, 64,* 385–416.

Stepler, Renee. (2016). *Smaller share of women ages 65 and older are living alone: More are living with spouse or children.* Washington, DC: Pew Research Center.

Stermer, S. Paul, & Burkley, M. (2015). SeX-Box: Exposure to sexist video games predicts benevolent sexism. *Psychology of Popular Media Culture, 4,* 47–55.

Stern, Marilyn, & Karraker, Katherine H. (1989). Sex stereotyping of infants: A review of gender labeling studies. *Sex Roles, 20,* 501–522.

Stevenson, Michael R., & Black, Kathryn N. (1988). Paternal absence and sex-role development: A meta-analysis. *Child Development, 59,* 793–814.

Stewart, Abigail J., & Chester, N. L. (1982). The exploration of sex differences in human social motives: Achievement, affiliation, and power. In A. J. Stewart (Ed.), *Motivation and society* (pp. 172–218). San Francisco, CA: Jossey-Bass.

Stice, Eric. (2001). A prospective test of the dual-pathway model of bulimic pathology: Mediating effects of dieting and negative affect. *Journal of Abnormal Psychology, 110,* 124–135.

Stice, Eric, Gau, Jeff M., Rohde, Paul, & Shaw, Heather. (2017). Risk factors that predict future onset of each DSM-5 eating disorder: Predictive specificity in high-risk adolescent females. *Journal of Abnormal Psychology, 126,* 38–51.

Stice, Eric, Marti, C. Nathan, & Rohde, Paul. (2013). Prevalence, incidence, impairment, and course of the proposed DSM-5 eating disorder diagnoses in an 8-year prospective community study of young women. *Journal of Abnormal Psychology, 122,* 445–457.

Stice, Eric, Rohde, Paul, Gau, Jeff, & Shaw, Heather. (2009). An effectiveness trial of a dissonance-based eating disorder prevention program for high-risk adolescent girls. *Journal of Consulting and Clinical Psychology, 77,* 825–834.

Stice, Eric, & Shaw, Heather. (2004). Eating disorder prevention programs: A meta-analytic review. *Psychological Bulletin, 130,* 206–227.

Stinson, Frederick S., Dawson, Deborah A., Goldstein, Risë B., Chou, S. Patricia, Huang, Boji, Smith, Sharon M., . . . Grant, Bridget F. (2008). Prevalence, correlates, disability, and comorbidity of DSM-IV narcissistic personality disorder: Results from the wave 2 national epidemiologic survey on alcohol and related conditions. *Journal of Clinical Psychiatry, 69,* 1033–1045.

Stith, Sandra M., Rosen, Karen H., Middleton, Kimberly A., Busch, Amy L., Lundeberg, Kirsten, & Carlton, Russell P. (2000). The intergenerational transmission of spouse abuse: A meta-analysis. *Journal of Marriage and the Family, 62,* 640–654.

Stith, Sandra M., Smith, Douglas B., Penn, Carrie E., Ward, David B., & Tritt, Dari. (2004). Intimate partner physical abuse perpetration and victimization risk factors: A meta-analytic review. *Aggression and Violent Behavior, 10,* 65–98.

Stockard, Jean, Gray, Jo Anna, O'Brien, Robert, & Stone, Joe. (2009). Race differences in cohort effects on non-marital fertility in the United States. *Social Forces, 87,* 1449–1479.

Stöckl, Heidi, Devries, Karen, Rotstein, Alexandra, Abrahams, Naeemah, Campbell, Jacquelyn, Watts, Charlotte, & Garcia Moreno, Claudia. (2013). The global prevalence of intimate partner homicide: A systematic review. *Lancet, 382,* 859–865.

Stone, Lindsey B., Hankin, Benjamin L., Gibb, Brandon E., & Abela, John R. Z. (2011). Co-rumination predicts the onset of depressive disorders during adolescence. *Journal of Abnormal Psychology, 120,* 752–757.

Stoner, Susan A., Norris, Jeanette, George, William H., Morrison, Diane M., Zawacki, Tina, Davis, Kelly C., & Hessler, Danielle M. (2008). Women's condom use assertiveness and sexual risk-taking: Effects of alcohol intoxication and adult victimization. *Addictive Behaviors, 33,* 1167–1176.

Stoney, Catherine M. (2003). Gender and cardiovascular disease: A psychobiological and integrative approach. *Current Directions in Psychological Science, 12,* 129–133.

Story, Mary, French, Simone A., Resnick, Michael D., & Blum, Robert W. (1995). Ethnic/racial and socioeconomic differences in dieting behaviors and body image perceptions in adolescents. *International Journal of Eating Disorders, 18,* 173–179.

Stotzer, Rebecca L. (2009). Violence against transgender people: A review of United States data. *Aggression & Violent Behavior, 14,* 170–179.

Stout, Jane G., & Dasgupta, Nilanjana. (2011). When he doesn't mean you: Gender-exclusive language as ostracism. *Personality and Social Psychology Bulletin, 36,* 757–769.

Stover, Carla S., Easton, Caroline, & McMahon, Thomas J. (2013). Parenting of men with co-occurring intimate partner violence and substance abuse. *Journal of Interpersonal Violence, 28,* 2290–2314.

Straus, Murray A. (1980). Wife beating: How common and why? In M. A. Straus & G. T. Hotaling (Eds.), *The social causes of husband-wife violence* (pp. 23–36). Minneapolis: University of Minnesota Press.

Strickland, Bonnie R. (1988). Sex-related differences in health and illness. *Psychology of Women Quarterly, 12,* 381–399.

Striegel-Moore, Ruth H., & Bulik, Cynthia M. (2007). Risk factors for eating disorders. *American Psychologist, 62,* 181–198.

Striegel-Moore, Ruth H., Goldman, Susan L., Garvin, Vicki, & Rodin, Judith. (1996). A prospective study of somatic and emotional symptoms of pregnancy. *Psychology of Women Quarterly, 20,* 393–408.

Stroebe, Margaret. (2001). Gender differences in adjustment to bereavement: An empirical and theoretical review. *Review of General Psychology, 5,* 62–83.

Stroumsa, Daphna. (2014). The state of transgender health care: Policy, law, and medical frameworks. *American Journal of Public Health, 104*(3), e31–e38.

Su, Rong, Rounds, James, & Armstrong, Patrick I. (2009). Men and things, women and people: A meta-analysis of sex differences in interests. *Psychological Bulletin, 135,* 859–884.

Substance Abuse and Mental Health Services Administration. (2014). *Results from the 2013 National Survey on Drug Use and Health: Summary of national findings* (HHS Publication No. [SMA] 14-4863). Rockville, MD: Author.

Sue, David. (2000). Health risk factors in diverse cultural groups. In R. Eisler & M. Hersen (Eds.), *Handbook of gender, culture, and health* (pp. 85–104). Mahwah, NJ: Lawrence Erlbaum.

Sue, Derald Wing. (2010). *Microaggressions in everyday life: Race, gender, and sexual orientation.* Hoboken, NJ: Wiley.

Sue, Derald Wing, Capodilupo, Christina M., Torino, Gina C., Bucceri, Jennifer M., Holder, Aisha M. B., Nadal, Kevin L., & Esquilin, Marta. (2007). Racial microaggressions in everyday life: Implications for clinical practice. *American Psychologist, 62,* 271–286.

Sue, Stanley, & Sue, Derald W. (2000). Conducting psychological research with the Asian American/Pacific Islander population. In *Guidelines for research in ethnic minority communities* (pp. 2–4). Washington, DC: American Psychological Association.

Sullivan, Cris M. (2011). Victim services for domestic violence. In M. P. Koss, J. D. White, & A. E. Kazdin (Eds.), *Violence against women and children: Navigating solutions* (Vol. 2, pp. 183–198). Washington, DC: American Psychological Association.

Suls, Jerry, & Green, Peter. (2003). Pluralistic ignorance and college student perceptions of gender-specific alcohol norms. *Health Psychology, 22,* 479–486.

Sutherland, Hamish, & Stewart, Iain. (1965). A critical analysis of the premenstrual syndrome. *Lancet, 1,* 1180–1183.

Svarstad, Bonnie L., Cleary, Paul D., Mechanic, David, & Robers, Pamela A. (1987). Gender differences in the acquisition of prescribed drugs: An epidemiological study. *Medical Care, 25,* 1089–1098.

Svoboda, J. Steven. (2013). Circumcision of male infants as a human rights violation. *Journal of Medical Ethics, 39,* 469–474.

Swarns, Rachel L. (2004, August 29). "African-American" becomes a term for debate. *New York Times.*

Swim, Janet K. (1994). Perceived versus meta-analytic effect sizes: An assessment of the accuracy of gender stereotypes. *Journal of Personality and Social Psychology, 66,* 21–36.

Swim, Janet K., Aikin, Kathryn J., Hall, Wayne S., & Hunter, Barbara A. (1995). Sexism and racism: Old-fashioned and modern prejudices. *Journal of Personality and Social Psychology, 68,* 199–214.

Swim, Janet, Borgida, Eugene, Maruyama, Geoffrey, & Myers, David G. (1989). Joan McKay versus John McKay: Do gender stereotypes bias evaluations? *Psychological Bulletin, 105,* 409–429.

Swim, Janet K., Mallett, Robyn, & Stangor, Charles. (2004). Understanding subtle sexism: Detection and use of sexist language. *Sex Roles, 51,* 117–128.

Sykes, Bryan L., & Pettit, Becky. (2014). Mass incarceration, family complexity, and the reproduction of childhood disadvantage. *The Annals of the American Academy of Political and Social Science, 654,* 127–149.

Szymanski, Dawn M., Moffitt, Lauren B., & Carr, Erika R. (2011). Sexual objectification of women: Advances to theory and research. *The Counseling Psychologist, 39,* 6–38.

Tan, Anh, Ma, Wenli, Vira, Amit, Marwha, Dhruv, & Eliot, Lise. (2016). The human hippocampus is not sexually dimorphic: Meta-analysis of structural MRI volumes. *NeuroImage, 124,* 350–366.

Tan, Robert S., & Culbertson, John W. (2003). An integrative review on current evidence of testosterone replacement therapy for the andropause. *Maturitas, 45,* 15–27.

Tancredi, Annalisa, Reginster, Jean-Yves, Luyckx, Françoise H., & Legros, Jean-Jacques. (2005). No major month to month variation in free testosterone levels in aging males: Minor impact on the biological diagnosis of "andropause." *Psychoneuroendocrinology, 30,* 638–646.

Tannen, Deborah. (1991). *You just don't understand: Women and men in conversation.* New York, NY: Ballantine.

Tarasoff, Lesley A. (2016). "We exist": The health and well-being of sexual minority women and trans people with disabilties. In S. E. Miles-Cohen & C. Signore (Eds.), *Eliminating inequities for women with disabilities* (pp. 179–208). Washington, DC: American Psychological Association.

Task Force on the Glass Ceiling Initiative. (1993). *Report of the Governor's Task Force on the Glass Ceiling Initiative.* Madison: State of Wisconsin.

Tate, Charlotte C. (2013). Another meaning of Darwinian feminism: Toward inclusive evolutionary accounts of sexual orientations. *Journal of Social, Evolutionary, and Cultural Psychology, 7,* 344–353.

Tate, Charlotte C., & Ledbetter, Jay N. (2010). Oversimplifying evolutionary psychology leads to explanatory gaps. *American Psychologist, 65,* 929–930.

Tate, Charlotte C., & Pearson, Mercedes D. (2016). Toward an inclusive model of lesbian identity development: Outlining a common and nuanced model for cis and trans women. *Journal of Lesbian Studies, 20,* 97–115.

Taylor, Laramie D. (2005). All for him: Articles about sex in American lad magazines. *Sex Roles, 52,* 153–164.

Taylor, Pamela L., Tucker, M. Belinda, & Mitchell-Kernan, Claudia. (1999). Ethnic variations in perceptions of men's provider role. *Psychology of Women Quarterly, 23,* 741–762.

Taylor, Paul, Lopez, Mark H., Martínez, Jessica, & Velasco, Gabriel. (2012). *When labels don't fit: Hispanics and their views of identity.* Washington, DC: Pew Research Center. Retrieved from http://www.pewhispanic.org/2012/04/04/when-labels-dont-fit-hispanics-and-their-views-of-identity/

Taylor, R. (1976). Psychosocial development of black youth. *Journal of Black Studies, 6,* 353–372.

Taylor, Shelley E. (2006). Tend and befriend: Biobehavioral bases of affiliation under stress. *Current Directions in Psychological Science, 15,* 273–277.

Taylor, Shelley E., Klein, Laura C., Lewis, Brian P., Gruenewald, Tara L., Gurung, Regan A. R., & Updegraff, John A. (2000). Biobehavioral responses to stress in females: Tend-and-befriend, not fight-or-flight. *Psychological Review, 107,* 411–429.

Tebbe, Esther N., & Moradi, Bonnie. (2012). Anti-transgender prejudice: A structural equation model of associated constructs. *Journal of Counseling Psychology, 59,* 251–261.

Tedeschi, Richard G., Calhoun, Lawrence G., & Groleau, Jessica M. (2015). Clinical applications of posttraumatic growth. In S. Joseph (Ed.), *Positive psychology in practice: Promoting human flourishing in work, health, education, and everyday life* (2nd ed., pp. 503–518). Hoboken, NJ: Wiley.

Tedeschi, Richard G., Park, Crystal, & Calhoun, Lawrence. (Eds.). (1998). *Posttraumatic growth: Positive change in the aftermath of crisis.* Hillsdale, NJ: Lawrence Erlbaum.

Terman, Lewis, & Miles, Catharine. (1936). *Sex and personality.* New York, NY: McGraw-Hill.

Testa, Maria, VanZile-Tamsen, Carol, & Livingston, Jennifer A. (2005). Childhood sexual abuse, relationship satisfaction, and sexual risk taking in a community sample of women. *Journal of Consulting and Clinical Psychology, 73,* 1116–1124.

Theorell, Töres, & Härenstam, Annika. (2000). Influence of gender on cardiovascular disease. In R. Eisler & M. Hersen (Eds.), *Handbook of gender, culture, and health* (pp. 161–177). Mahwah, NJ: Lawrence Erlbaum.

Therrien, Melissa, & Ramirez, Roberto. (2000). *The Hispanic population in the United States: March 2000* (Current Population Reports, P20-535). Washington, DC: U.S. Census Bureau.

Thoman, Dustin, Arizaga, Jessica A., Smith, Jessi L., Story, Tyler S., & Soncuya, Gretchen. (2014). The grass is greener in non–science, technology, engineering, and math classes: Examining the role of competing belonging to undergraduate women's vulnerability to being pulled away from science. *Psychology of Women Quarterly, 38,* 246–258.

Thomas, Alexander, & Sillen, Samuel S. (1972). *Racism and psychiatry.* Secaucus, NJ: Citadel.

Thomas, Jerry K., & French, Karen E. (1985). Gender differences across age in motor performance: A meta-analysis. *Psychological Bulletin, 98,* 260–282.

Thomas, Rodney G. (2000). Daughters of the lance: Native American women warriors. *Journal of the Indian Wars, 1,* 147–154.

Thompson, Ashley E., & Voyer, Daniel. (2014). Sex differences in the ability to recognize non-verbal displays of emotion: A meta-analysis. *Cognition and Emotion, 28,* 1164–1195.

Thompson, Janice L. (1991). Exploring gender and culture with Khmer refugee women: Reflections on participatory feminist research. *Advances in Nursing Science, 13,* 30–48.

Thompson, Sharon H., Corwin, Sara J., & Sargent Roger G. (1997). Ideal body size beliefs and weight concerns of fourth-grade children. *International Journal of Eating Disorders, 21,* 279–284.

Thompson, Stacy D., & Walker, Andrea C. (2004). Satisfaction with parenting: A comparison between adolescent mothers and fathers. *Sex Roles, 50,* 677–688.

Thomson, Rob. (2006). The effect of topic of discussion on gendered language in computer-mediated communication discussion. *Journal of Language and Social Psychology, 25,* 167–178.

Thomson, Rob, Murachver, Tamar, & Green, James. (2001). Where is the gender in gendered language? *Psychological Science, 12,* 171–175.

Thornhill, Randy, & Palmer, Craig T. (2000). *A natural history of rape: Biological bases of sexual coercion.* Cambridge, MA: MIT Press.

Tiefer, Leonore. (1991). Historical, scientific, clinical, and feminist criticisms of "The Human Sexual Response Cycle" model. *Annual Review of Sex Research, 2,* 1–24.

Tiefer, Leonore. (1995). *Sex is not a natural act, and other essays.* Boulder, CO: Westview.

Tiefer, Leonore. (1996). Towards a feminist sex therapy. *Women and Therapy, 19,* 53–64.

Tiefer, Leonore. (2001). A new view of women's sexual problems: Why new? Why now? *Journal of Sex Research, 38,* 89–96.

Tien, Liang. (1994). Southeast Asian American refugee women. In L. Comas-Diaz & B. Greene (Eds.), *Women of color: Integrating ethnic and gender identities in psychotherapy* (pp. 479–504). New York, NY: Guilford.

Tjaden, Patricia, & Thoennes, Nancy. (1998, November). *Prevalence, incidence, and consequences of violence against women: Findings from the National Violence Against Women Survey.* Washington, DC: National Institute of Justice.

Tobin, Desiree D., Menon, Meenakshi, Menon, Madhavi, Spatta, Brooke C., Hodges, Ernest V. E., & Perry, David G. (2010). The intrapsychics of gender: A model of self-socialization. *Psychological Review, 117*, 601–622.

Tolman, Deborah. (2002). *Dilemmas of desire.* Cambridge, MA: Harvard University Press.

Tolman, Deborah L., Davis, B. R., & Bowman, C. P. (2016). "That's just how it is": A gendered analysis of masculinity and femininity ideologies in adolescent girls' and boys' heterosexual relationships. *Journal of Adolescent Research, 31*, 3–31.

Tolman, Deborah L., & Diamond, Lisa M. (2014). Sexuality theory: A review, a revision, and a recommendation. In D. Tolman & L. Diamond (Eds.), *APA handbook of sexuality and psychology* (pp. 3–28). Washington, DC: American Psychological Association.

Tolman, Deborah L., & McClelland, Sara I. (2011). Normative sexuality development in adolescence: A decade in review, 2000–2009. *Journal of Research on Adolescence, 21*, 242–255.

Tolman, Deborah L., & Szalacha, Laura A. (1999). Dimensions of desire: Bridging qualitative and quantitative methods in a study of female adolescent sexuality. *Psychology of Women Quarterly, 23*, 7–40.

Tompkins, Kyla W. (2015). Intersections of race, gender, and sexuality: Queer of color critique. In S. Herring (Ed.), *Cambridge companion to gay and lesbian literature* (pp. 173–189). New York, NY: Cambridge University Press.

Tompkins, Tanya L., Shields, Chloe N., Hillman, Kimberly M., & White, Kadi. (2015). Reducing stigma toward the transgender community: An evaluation of a humanizing and perspective-taking intervention. *Psychology of Sexual Orientation and Gender Diversity, 2*, 34–42.

Tong, Rosemarie P. (1998). *Feminist thought* (2nd ed.). Boulder, CO: Westview Press.

Tong, Rosemarie P. (2014). *Feminist thought: A more comprehensive introduction* (4th ed.). Boulder, CO: Westview Press.

Tooby, John, & Cosmides, Leda. (1992). The psychological foundations of culture. In J. Barkow, L. Cosmides, & J. Tooby (Eds.), *The adapted mind: Evolutionary psychology and the generation of culture* (pp. 19–136). New York, NY: Oxford University Press.

Tossell, Chad C., Kortum, Philip, Shepard, Clayton, Barg-Walkow, Laura H., Rahmati, Ahmad, & Zhong, Lin. (2012). A longitudinal study of emoticon use in text messaging from smartphones. *Computers in Human Behavior, 28*, 659–663.

Tram, Jane M., & Cole, David A. (2000). Self-perceived competence and the relation between life events and depressive symptoms in adolescence: Mediator or moderator? *Journal of Abnormal Psychology, 109*, 753–760.

Travis, Cheryl B. (1988a). *Women and health psychology: Biomedical issues.* Hillsdale, NJ: Lawrence Erlbaum.

Travis, Cheryl B. (1988b). *Women and health psychology: Mental health issues.* Hillsdale, NJ: Lawrence Erlbaum.

Travis, Cheryl B. (1993). Women and health. In F. L. Denmark & M. A. Paludi (Eds.), *Psychology of women: Handbook of issues and theories* (pp. 283–323). Westport, CT: Greenwood.

Travis, Cheryl B. (2005). Heart disease and gender inequity. *Psychology of Women Quarterly, 29*, 15–23.

Travis, Cheryl B., & Compton, Jill D. (2001). Feminism and health in the Decade of Behavior. *Psychology of Women Quarterly, 25*, 312–323.

Trentacosta, Christopher J., Davis-Kean, Pamela, Mitchell, Colter, Hyde, Luke, & Dolinoy, Dana. (2016). Environmental contaminants and child development. *Child Development Perspectives, 10*, 228–233.

Trentham, Susan, & Larwood Laurie. (1998). Gender discrimination and the workplace: An examination of rational bias theory. *Sex Roles, 38*, 1–28.

Tresemer, David. (1974). Fear of success: Popular, but unproven. *Psychology Today, 7*(10), 82.

Trimberger, E. Kay. (2005). *The new single woman.* Boston, MA: Beacon Press.

Trimble, Joseph E. (2003). Infusing American Indian and Alaska Native topics into the psychology curriculum. In P. Bronstein & K. Quina (Eds.), *Teaching gender and multicultural awareness* (pp. 221–236). Washington, DC: American Psychological Association.

Trinh, Sarah L. (2016). "Enjoy your sexuality, but do it in secret": Exploring undergraduate women's reports of friends' sexual communications. *Psychology of Women Quarterly, 40*, 96–107.

Trivers, R. L. (1972). *Parental investment and sexual selection* (Vol. 136). Cambridge, MA: Harvard University, Biological Laboratories.

True, Reiko Homma. (1990). Psychotherapeutic issues with Asian American women. *Sex Roles, 22,* 477–486.

Tsugawa, Yusuke, Jena, Anupam B., Figueroa, Jose F., Orav, E. John, Blumenthal, Daniel M., & Jha, Ashish K. (2017). Comparison of hospital mortality and readmission rates for Medicare patients treated by male vs. female physicians. *JAMA Internal Medicine, 177,* 206–213.

Tucker, Clyde, Kojetin, Brian, & Harrison, Roderick. (1995). A statistical analysis of the CPS supplement on race and ethnic origin. Retrieved from https://www.census.gov/prod/2/gen/96arc/ivatuck.pdf

Turchik, Jessica A., Hebenstreit, Claire L., & Judson, Stephanie S. (2016). An examination of the gender inclusiveness of current theories of sexual violence in adulthood: Recognizing male victims, female perpetrators, and same-sex violence. *Trauma, Violence, & Abuse, 17,* 133–148.

Twenge, Jean M. (1997). Attitudes toward women, 1970–1995: A meta-analysis. *Psychology of Women Quarterly, 21,* 35–52.

Twenge, Jean M. (1999). Mapping gender: The multifactorial approach and the organization of gender-related attributes. *Psychology of Women Quarterly, 23,* 485–502.

Twenge, Jean M., Campbell, W. Keith, & Foster, Craig A. (2003). Parenthood and marital satisfaction: A meta-analytic review. *Journal of Marriage and Family, 65,* 574–583.

Twenge, Jean M., Campbell, W. Keith, & Gentile, Brittany. (2012). Male and female pronoun use in U.S. books reflects women's status, 1900–2008. *Sex Roles, 67,* 488–493.

Tyler, Leona E. (1965). *The psychology of human differences.* New York, NY: Appleton-Century-Crofts.

Tylka, Tracy L., & Hill, Melanie S. (2004). Objectification theory as it relates to disordered eating among college women. *Sex Roles, 51,* 719–730.

Ullman, Sarah E., & Najdowski, Cynthia J. (2011). Vulnerability and protective factors for sexual assault. In J. W. White, M. P. Koss, & A. E. Kazdin (Eds.), *Violence against women and children: Mapping the terrain* (Vol. 1, pp. 151–172). Washington, DC: American Psychological Association.

Ullsperger, Josie M., & Nikolas, Molly A. (2017). A meta-analytic review of the association between pubertal timing and psychopathology in adolescence: Are there sex differences in risk? *Psychological Bulletin, 143,* 903–938.

Umaña-Taylor, Adriana J., Alfaro, Edna C., Bámaca, Mayra Y., & Guimond, Amy B. (2009). The central role of familial ethnic socialization in Latino adolescents' cultural orientation. *Journal of Marriage and Family, 71,* 46–60.

UNESCO. (2008). *Overcoming inequality: Why governance matters.* New York, NY: Oxford.

Unger, Rhoda. (1979). Toward a redefinition of sex and gender. *American Psychologist, 34,* 1085–1094.

UNHCR. (2017). U.S. resettlement facts. Retrieved from http://www.unhcr.org/en-us/588a14fc4

UNIFEM. (2009). *Who answers to women: Gender and accountability.* New York, NY: Author. Retrieved from http://www.unwomen.org/en/digital-library/publications/2008/1/progress-of-the-world-s-women-2008-2009-who-answers-to-women

United Nations. (2010). *Human development report 2010.* Retrieved from http://hdr.undp.org

United Nations. (2015). *The world's women 2015: Trends and statistics.* New York, NY: Author.

United Nations Development Programme. (2015). *Human development report 2015.* New York, NY: Oxford University Press.

University of North Carolina at Charlotte. (2017). Reduce the risk of becoming a rape victim. Retrieved from http://police.uncc.edu/crime-prevention-safety/sexual-assault-prevention/reduce-risk-becoming-rape-victim

UNODC. (2014). *Global report on trafficking in persons.* Vienna, Austria: United Nations.

U.S. Cancer Statistics Working Group. (2016). *United States cancer statistics: 1999–2013 incidence and mortality Web-based report.* Atlanta, GA: Centers for Disease Control and Prevention.

U.S. Census Bureau. (2007). The American community—Asians: 2004. Retrieved from http://www.census.gov

U.S. Census Bureau. (2010a). 2010 census data. Retrieved from https://www.census.gov/data.html

U.S. Census Bureau. (2010b, December). Current Population Survey, Annual Social and Economic Supplement, 2009. Retrieved from http://www.census.gov

U.S. Census Bureau. (2013). *Current population survey, 2013 annual social and economic supplement.* Washington, DC: Author.

U.S. Census Bureau. (2015). *Current Population Survey, June 1976–2014.* Washington, DC: Author.

U.S. Census Bureau. (2016a). *2011–2015 American Community Survey 5-year estimates.* Washington, DC: Author.

U.S. Census Bureau. (2016b). *2015 American Community Survey 1-year estimates.* Washington, DC: Author.

U.S. Census Bureau. (2016c). *Current Population Survey, 2015.* Washington, DC: Author.

U.S. Census Bureau. (2016d). *Decennial censuses, 1890 to 1940, and Current Population Survey, Annual Social and Economic Supplements, 1947 to 2016*. Washington, DC: Author.

U.S. Department of Defense. (2001). *Trends in enlistment propensity*. Arlington, VA: Author.

U.S. Department of Defense. (2011). Instruction: Number 6130.03. Retrieved from http://www.esd.whs.mil/Portals/54/Documents/DD/issuances/dodi/613003p.pdf

U.S. Department of Education. (2016). Civil rights data collection (CRDC) for the 2013–14 school year. Retrieved from https://www2.ed.gov/about/offices/list/ocr/docs/crdc-2013-14.html

U.S. Department of Education, National Center for Education Statistics. (2010). *Condition of education 2010* (NCES 2010-028). Washington, DC: Author.

U.S. Department of Justice. (2003). *Intimate partner violence, 1993–2001*. Retrieved from http://www.ojp.gov/bjs/

U.S. Department of Justice. (2005). *Homicide trends in the U.S.: Intimate homicide*. Retrieved from http://www.ojp.gov/bjs/

U.S. Department of Labor. (1992). *Pipelines of progress: A status report on the glass ceiling*. Washington, DC: U.S. Government Printing Office.

U.S. Department of Labor, Women's Bureau. (2000). 20 facts on women workers. Retrieved from http://www.dol.gov/dol/wb

U.S. Department of State. (2013). *Trafficking in persons report*. Washington, DC: Author.

U.S. Department of State. (2016). *Trafficking in persons report*. Washington, DC: Author.

U.S. Department of Transportation. (2005). *Traffic safety facts 2005*. Retrieved from http://www.nrd.nhtsa.dot.gov

Ussher, Jane M. (1996). Premenstrual syndrome: Reconciling disciplinary divides through the adoption of a material-discursive epistemological standpoint. *Annual Review of Sex Research, 7*, 218–251.

Uttal, David H., Meadow, Nathaniel G., Tipton, Elizabeth, Hand, Linda L., Alden, Alison R., & Warren, Christopher. (2013). The malleability of spatial skills: A meta-analysis of training studies. *Psychological Bulletin, 139*, 352–402.

Uttal, David H., Miller, David I., & Newcombe, Nora S. (2013). Exploring and enhancing spatial thinking: Links to achievement in science, technology, engineering, and mathematics? *Current Directions in Psychological Science, 22*, 367–373.

Uzzell, David, & Horne, Nathalie. (2006). The influence of biological sex, sexuality and gender role on interpersonal distance. *British Journal of Social Psychology, 45*, 579–597.

Vainapel, Sigal, Shamir, Opher Y., Tenenbaum, Yulie, & Gilam, Gadi. (2015). The dark side of gendered language: The masculine-generic form as a cause for self-report bias. *Psychological Assessment, 27*, 1513–1519.

Valanis, Barbara G., Bowen, D. J., Bassford, T., Whitlock, E., Charney, P., & Carter, R. A. (2000). Sexual orientation and health: Comparisons in the Women's Health Initiative sample. *Archives of Family Medicine, 9*, 843–853.

Valera, Eve M., & Berenbaum, Howard. (2003). Brain injury in battered women. *Journal of Consulting and Clinical Psychology, 73*, 797–804.

Van Anders, Sari M., Steiger, Jeffrey, & Goldey, Katherine L. (2015). Effects of gendered behavior on testosterone in women and men. *Proceedings of the National Academy of Sciences of the USA, 112*, 13805–13810.

Van Borsel, John, & Van de Putte, Anneleen. (2014). Lisping and male homosexuality. *Archives of Sexual Behavior, 43*, 1159–1163.

Van den Bos, Arne, & Stapel, Diederik A. (2009). Why people stereotype affects how they stereotype: The differential influence of comprehension goals and self-enhancement goals on stereotyping. *Personality and Social Psychology Bulletin, 35*, 101–113.

van der Pol, Lotte D., Groeneveld, Marleen G., van Berkel, Sheila R., Endendijk, Joyce J., Hallers-Haalboom, Elizabeth T., Bakermans-Kranenburg, Marian J., & Mesman, Judi. (2015). Fathers' and mothers' emotion talk with their girls and boys from toddlerhood to preschool age. *Emotion, 15*, 854–864.

Van Goozen, Stephanie H. M., Cohen-Kettenis, Peggy T., Gooren, Louis J. G., Frijda, Nico H., & Van de Poll, Nanne E. (1995). Gender differences in behaviour: Activating effects of cross-sex hormones. *Psychoneuroendocrinology, 20*, 343–363.

Van Lankveld, Jacques. (1998). Bibliotherapy in the treatment of sexual dysfunctions: A meta-analysis. *Journal of Consulting and Clinical Psychology, 66*, 702–708.

Vandello, Joseph A., & Bosson, Jennifer K. (2013). Hard won and easily lost: A review and synthesis of theory and research on precarious manhood. *Psychology of Men & Masculinity, 14*, 101–113.

Vandermassen, G. (2005). *Who's afraid of Charles Darwin? Debating feminism and evolutionary theory*. Lanham, MD: Rowman & Littlefield.

VanSickle, Caroline. (2015). Can the sex of hominin pelvic fossils be assessed using methods developed for recent humans? *American Journal of Physical Anthropology, 156*(S60), 312.

Vazquez-Nuttall, Ena, Romero-Garcia, Ivonne, & DeLeon, Brunilda. (1987). Sex roles and perceptions of femininity and masculinity of Hispanic women: A review of the literature. *Psychology of Women Quarterly, 11,* 409–426.

Vencill, Jennifer A., Tebbe, Elliot A., & Garos, Sheila. (2015). It's not the size of the boat or the motion of the ocean: The role of self-objectification, appearance anxiety, and depression in female sexual functioning. *Psychology of Women Quarterly, 39,* 471–483.

Veroff, Joseph, Douvan, Elizabeth, & Kukla, Richard. (1981). *The inner American: A self-portrait from 1957 to 1976.* New York, NY: Basic Books.

Vervecken, Dries, & Hannover, Bettina. (2015). Yes I can! Effects of gender fair job descriptions on children's perceptions of job status, job difficulty, and vocational self-efficacy. *Social Psychology, 46*(2), 76–92.

Vilain, Eric, & Sánchez, Francisco. (2012). Athletes' bodies, sexed bodies: Intersexuality in athletics. *Nature Reviews Endocrinology, 8,* 198–199.

Vishnevsky, Tanya, Cann, Arnie, Calhoun, Lawrence G., Tedeschi, Richard G., & Demakis, George J. (2010). Gender differences in self-reported posttraumatic growth: A meta-analysis. *Psychology of Women Quarterly, 34,* 110–120.

Vogeltanz, Nancy D., & Wilsnack, Sharon C. (1997). Alcohol problems in women: Risk factors, consequences, and treatment strategies. In S. Gallant, G. Keita, & R. Royak-Schaler (Eds.), *Health care for women: Psychological, social, and behavioral influences* (pp. 75–96). Washington, DC: American Psychological Association.

von Hippel, William, & Dunlop, Sally M. (2005). Aging, inhibition, and social inappropriateness. *Psychology and Aging, 20,* 519–523.

Vonk, Roos, & Ashmore, Richard D. (2003). Thinking about gender types: Cognitive organization of female and male types. *British Journal of Social Psychology, 42,* 257–280.

Voyer, Daniel. (1996). On the magnitude of laterality effects and sex differences in functional lateralities. *Laterality, 1,* 51–83.

Voyer, Daniel. (2011). Time limits and gender differences on paper-and-pencil tests of mental rotation: A meta-analysis. *Psychonomic Bulletin and Review, 18,* 267–277.

Voyer, Daniel, & Voyer, Susan D. (2014). Gender differences in scholastic achievement: A meta-analysis. *Psychological Bulletin, 140,* 1174–1204.

Voyer, Daniel, Voyer, Susan, & Bryden, M. Philip. (1995). Magnitude of sex differences in spatial abilities: A meta-analysis and consideration of critical variables. *Psychological Bulletin, 117,* 250–270.

Vrugt, Anneke, & Luyerink, Mara. (2000). The contribution of bodily posture to gender stereotypical impressions. *Social Behavior & Personality, 28,* 91–103.

Waite, Linda J., & Gallagher, Maggie. (2000). *The case for marriage: Why married people are happier, healthier, and better off financially.* New York, NY: Doubleday.

Waldfogel, Jane. (2001). International policies toward parental leave and child care. *The Future of Children, 11,* 99–111.

Walker, Alice. (1983). *In search of our mothers' gardens: Womanist prose.* San Diego, CA: Harcourt Brace Jovanovich.

Walker, Lawrence J. (1984). Sex differences in the development of moral reasoning: A critical review. *Child Development, 55,* 677–691.

Walker, Lenore E. (1980). Battered women. In A. Brodsky & R. Hare-Mustin (Eds.), *Women and psychotherapy.* New York, NY: Guilford.

Walker, Lenore E. (1991). Post-traumatic stress disorder in women: Diagnosis and treatment of battered women syndrome. *Psychotherapy, 28,* 1–9.

Walker, Lenore E. A. (2001). Battering in adult relations. In J. Worell (Ed.), *Encyclopedia of women and gender* (pp. 169–188). San Diego, CA: Academic Press.

Wallien, Madeleine S. C., & Cohen-Kettenis, Peggy T. (2008). Psychosexual outcome of gender-dysphoric children. *Journal of the American Academy of Child and Adolescent Psychiatry, 47,* 1413–1423.

Walsh, Margaret, Hickey, Crystal, & Duffy, Jim. (1999). Influence of item content and stereotype situation on gender differences in mathematical problem solving. *Sex Roles, 41,* 219–240.

Walsh, Mary R. (1977). *Doctors wanted: No women need apply.* New Haven, CT: Yale University Press.

Walters, Ellen E., & Kendler, Kenneth S. (1995). Anorexia nervosa and anorexic-like syndromes in a population-based female twin sample. *American Journal of Psychiatry, 152,* 64–71.

Walters, Karina L., & Simoni, Jane M. (2002). Reconceptualizing Native women's health: An "indigenist" stress-coping model. *American Journal of Public Health, 92,* 520–524.

Walters, Mikel L., Chen, Jieru, & Breiding, Matthew J. (2013). *The National Intimate Partner and Sexual Violence Survey (NISVS): 2010 findings on victimization by sexual orientation.* Atlanta, GA: Centers for Disease Control and Prevention, National Center for Injury Prevention and Control.

Walton, Greg M., & Cohen, Geoffrey L. (2003). Stereotype lift. *Journal of Experimental Social Psychology, 39,* 456–467.

Wang, Wendy. (2015). Interracial marriage: Who is "marrying out"? Retreived from http://www.pewresearch.org/fact-tank/2015/06/12/interracial-marriage-who-is-marrying-out/

Ward, Elizabeth, Jemal, Ahmedin, Cokkinides, Vilma, Singh, Gopal K., Carinez, Cheryll, Ghafoor, Asma, & Thun, Michael. (2004). Cancer disparities by race/ethnicity and socioeconomic status. *CA: A Cancer Journal for Clinicians, 54*, 78–93.

Ward, L. Monique, & Harrison, Kristen. (2005). The impact of media use on girls' beliefs about gender roles, their bodies, and sexual relationships: A research synthesis. In E. Cole & J. H. Daniel (Eds.), *Featuring females: Feminist analyses of media* (pp. 3–24). Washington, DC: American Psychological Association.

Ward, Russell A., & Spitze, Glenna. (1998). Sandwiched marriages: The implications of child and parent relations for marital quality in midlife. *Social Forces, 77*, 647–666.

Warne, Russell T., Yoon, Myeongsun, & Price, Chris J. (2014). Exploring the various interpretations of "test bias." *Cultural Diversity & Ethnic Minority Psychology, 20*, 570–582.

Warr, M. (1985). Fear of rape among urban women. *Social Problems, 32*, 239–250.

Warren, Karen J. (1987). Feminism and ecology: Making connections. *Environmental Ethics, 9*(1), 3–20.

Wasserman, Benjamin D., & Weseley, Allyson J. (2009). ¿Qué? Quoi? Do languages with grammatical gender promote sexist attitudes? *Sex Roles, 61*, 634–643.

Waters, Emily, Jindasurat, Chai, & Wolfe, Cecilia. (2016). *Lesbian, gay, bisexual, transgender, queer, and HIV-affected hate violence in 2015.* New York, NY: National Coalition of Anti-Violence Programs.

Watson, Laurel B., Robinson, Dawn, Dispenza, Franco, & Nazari, Negar. (2012). African American women's sexual objectification experiences: A qualitative study. *Psychology of Women Quarterly, 36*, 458–475.

Watzlawick, P. (Ed.). (1984). *The invented reality: Contributions to constructivism.* New York, NY: Norton.

Weaver-Hightower, Marcus. (2003). The "boy turn" in research on gender and education. *Review of Educational Research, 73*, 371–498.

Weissman, Myrna M., Bland, Roger, Joyce, Peter R., Newman, Stephen, Wells, J. Elisabeth, & Wittchen, Hans-Ulrich. (1993). Sex differences in rates of depression: Cross-national perspectives. *Journal of Affective Disorders, 29*, 77–84.

Weissman, Myrna M., & Klerman, G. L. (1979). Sex differences and the epidemiology of depression. In E. S. Gomberg & V. Franks (Eds.), *Gender and disordered behavior.* New York, NY: Brunner/Mazel.

Weisstein, Naomi. (1971). Psychology constructs the female, or the fantasy life of the male psychologist. *Journal of Social Education, 35*, 362–373.

Weisstein, Naomi. (1982, November). Tired of arguing about biological inferiority? *Ms.*, pp. 41–46.

Weitzman, Lenore J. (1986). *The divorce revolution.* New York, NY: Free Press.

Weller, Leonard, Weller, Aron, & Avinir, Ohela. (1995). Menstrual synchrony: Only in roommates who are close friends? *Physiology and Behavior, 58*, 883–889.

Welsh, Sandy. (1999). Gender and sexual harassment. *Annual Review of Sociology, 25*, 169–190.

Werner, Nicole E., & Crick, Nicki R. (2004). Maladaptive peer relationships and the development of relational and physical aggression during middle childhood. *Social Development, 13*, 495–514.

West, Candace, & Zimmerman, Don H. (1983). Small insults: A study of interruptions in cross-sex conversations between unacquainted persons. In B. Thorne, C. Kramarae, & N. Henley (Eds.), *Language, gender, and society* (pp. 102–117). Rowley, MA: Newbury House.

West, Jevin D., Jacquet, J., King, Molly M., Correll, S. J., & Bergstrom, Carl T. (2013). The role of gender in scholarly authorship. *PLoS ONE, 8*(7), e66212.

West, Suzanne L., Vinikoor, Lisa C., & Zolnoun, Denniz. (2004). A systematic review of the literature on female sexual dysfunction prevalence and predictors. *Annual Review of Sex Research, 15*, 40–172.

Wethington, Elaine. (2000). Expecting stress: Americans and the "midlife crisis." *Motivation and Emotion, 24*, 85–103.

Whatley, Mark A. (1993). For better or worse: The case of marital rape. *Violence and Victims, 8*, 29–39.

Whitbeck, Les B., McMorris, Barbara J., Hoyt, Dan R., Stubben, Jerry D., & LaFromboise, Teresa. (2002). Perceived discrimination, traditional practices, and depressive symptoms among American Indians in the Upper Midwest. *Journal of Health and Social Behavior, 43*, 400–418.

White, Tonya, & Ettner, Randi. (2007). Adaptation and adjustment in children of transsexual parents. *European Child and Adolescent Psychiatry, 16*, 215–221.

White House Council of Economic Advisers. (2016). *The gender pay gap on the anniversary of the Lilly Ledbetter Fair Pay Act.* Washington, DC: U.S. Department of Labor, Women's Bureau. Retrieved from https://archive.org/details/GenderPayGapIssueBrief

White House Council on Women and Girls. (2011). *Women in America: Indicators of social and economic well-being.* Retrieved from http://digitalcommons.ilr.cornell.edu/cgi/viewcontent.cgi?article=1804&context=key_workplace

White House, Office of the Press Secretary. (2017, August 25). Presidential memorandum for the secretary of defense and the secretary of homeland security. Retrieved from https://www.whitehouse.gov/the-press-office/2017/08/25/presidential-memorandum-secretary-defense-and-secretary-homeland

White Hughto, Jaclyn M., Pachankis, John E., Willie, Tiara C., & Reisner, Sari L. (2017). Victimization and depressive symptomology in transgender adults: The mediating role of avoidant coping. *Journal of Counseling Psychology, 64,* 41–51.

White Hughto, Jaclyn M., & Reisner, Sari L. (2016). A systematic review of the effects of hormone therapy on psychological functioning and quality of life in transgender individuals. *Transgender Health, 13,* 21–31.

Whitley, Bernard E., McHugh, Maureen C., & Frieze, Irene H. (1986). Assessing the theoretical models for sex differences in causal attributions of success and failure. In J. S. Hyde & M. C. Linn (Eds.), *The psychology of gender: Advances through meta-analysis* (pp. 102–135). Baltimore, MD: Johns Hopkins University Press.

Whorf, Benjamin L. (1956). *Language, thought, and reality.* Cambridge, MA: MIT Press.

Wichstrøm, Lars, & Hegna, Kristinn. (2003). Sexual orientation and suicide attempt: A longitudinal study of the general Norwegian adolescent population. *Journal of Abnormal Psychology, 112,* 144–151.

Widiger, Thomas A., & Settle, Shirley A. (1987). Broverman et al. revisited: An artifactual sex bias. *Journal of Personality and Social Psychology, 53,* 463–469.

Wierckz, Katrien, Van Caenegem, Eva, Pennings, Guido, Elaut, Els, Dedecker, David, Van de Peer, Fleur, . . . T'Sjoen, Guy. (2012). Reproductive wish in transsexual men. *Human Reproduction, 27,* 483–487.

Wilcox, Sara, Evenson, Kelly R., Aragaki, Aaron, Wassertheil-Smoller, Sylvia, Mouton, Charles P., & Loevinger, Barbara L. (2003). The effects of widowhood on physical and mental health, health behaviors, and health outcomes: The Women's Health Initiative. *Health Psychology, 22,* 513–522.

Willcutt, Erik G. (2012). The prevalence of DSM-IV attention-deficit/hyperactivity disorder: A meta-analytic review. *Neurotherapeutics, 9,* 490–499.

Williams, Colin J., Weinberg, Martin S., & Rosenberger, Joshua G. (2013). Trans men: Embodiments, identities, and sexualities. *Sociological Forum, 28,* 719–741.

Williams, Colin J., Weinberg, Martin, & Rosenberger, Joshua. (2016). Trans women doing sex in San Francisco. *Archives of Sexual Behavior, 45,* 1665–1678.

Williams, David R. (2002). Racial/ethnic variations in women's health: The social embeddedness of health. *American Journal of Public Health, 92,* 588–597.

Williams, Juanita H. (1983). *Psychology of women* (2nd ed.). New York, NY: Norton.

Williams, Linda M. (1992). Adult memories of childhood abuse: Preliminary findings from a longitudinal study. *APSAC Advisor, 5,* 19–20.

Williams, Linda M. (1994). Recall of childhood trauma: A prospective study of women's memories of child sexual abuse. *Journal of Consulting and Clinical Psychology, 62,* 1167–1176.

Williams, Melissa J., Paluck, Elizabeth L., & Spencer-Rodgers, Julie. (2010). The masculinity of money: Automatic stereotypes predict gender differences in estimated salaries. *Psychology of Women Quarterly, 34,* 7–20.

Williams, Melissa J., & Tiedens, Larissa Z. (2016). The subtle suspension of backlash: A meta-analysis of penalties for women's implicit and explicit dominance behavior. *Psychological Bulletin, 142,* 165–197.

Williams, Stacey L., & Frieze, Irene H. (2005). Patterns of violent relationships, psychological distress, and marital satisfaction in a national sample of men and women. *Sex Roles, 52,* 771–784.

Williams-Washington, Kristin N. (2010). Historical trauma. In R. L. Hampton, T. P. Gullotta, & R. L. Crowel (Eds.), *Handbook of African American health* (pp. 31–50). New York, NY: Guilford.

Willingham, Warren, & Cole, Nancy. (1997). *Gender and fair assessment.* Mahwah, NJ: Lawrence Erlbaum.

Willoughby, Teena. (2008). A short-term longitudinal study of Internet and computer game use by adolescent boys and girls: Prevalence, frequency of use, and psychosocial predictors. *Developmental Psychology, 44,* 195–204.

Wilsnack, Richard W., Wilsnack, Sharon C., Kristjanson, Arlinda F., Vogeltanz-Holm, Nancy D., & Gmel, Gerhard. (2009). Gender and alcohol consumption: Patterns from the multinational GENACIS project. *Addiction, 104,* 1487–1500.

Wilsnack, Sharon, Vogeltanz, N. D., Klassen, A. D., & Harris, T. R. (1997). Childhood sexual abuse and women's substance abuse: National survey findings. *Journal of Studies on Alcohol, 58,* 264–271.

Wilson, Edward O. (1975a, October 12). Human decency. *New York Times Magazine,* pp. 38–50.

Wilson, Edward O. (1975b). *Sociobiology: The new synthesis.* Cambridge, MA: Harvard University Press.

Wilson, Edward O. (1978). *On human nature.* Cambridge, MA: Harvard University Press.

Wilson, G. Terence, Grilo, Carlos M., & Vitousek, Kelly M. (2007). Psychological treatment of eating disorders. *American Psychologist, 62,* 199–216.

Wilson, William Julius. (1996). *When work disappears: The world of the new urban poor.* New York, NY: Knopf.

Wimpissinger, Florian, Tscherney, Robert, & Stackl, Walter. (2009). Magnetic resonance imaging of female prostate pathology. *Journal of Sexual Medicine, 6,* 1704–1711.

Winstead, Barbara, & Griffin, Jessica. (2001). Friendship styles. In J. Worell (Ed.), *Encyclopedia of gender* (pp. 481–492). San Diego, CA: Academic Press.

Winter, Sam, Webster, Beverly, & Cheung, Pui K. E. (2008). Measuring Hong Kong undergraduate students' attitudes towards transpeople. *Sex Roles, 59,* 670–683.

Wise, Phyllis, Dubal, Dena B., Wilson, Melinda E., Rau, Shane W., Böttner, Martina, & Rosewell, Katherine L. (2001). Estradiol is a protective factor in the adult and aging brain. *Brain Research Review, 37,* 313–319.

Wiswell, Thomas, Enzenauer, R. W., Holton, M. E., Cornish, J. D., & Hankins, C. T. (1987). Declining frequency of circumcision: Implications for changes in the absolute incidence and male to female sex ratio of urinary tract infections in early infancy. *Pediatrics, 79,* 338–342.

Wittig, Michele A. (1985). Metatheoretical dilemmas in the psychology of gender. *American Psychologist, 40,* 800–811.

Wittig, Michele A., & Skolnick, Paul. (1978). Status versus warmth as determinants of sex differences in personal space. *Sex Roles, 4,* 493–503.

Wizemann, Theresa M., & Pardue, Mary-Lou. (Eds.). (2001). *Exploring the biological contributions to human health: Does sex matter?* Washington, DC: National Academy Press.

Wolf, Naomi. (1991). *The beauty myth.* New York, NY: William Morrow.

Wolfe, Lahle. (2009). *2009—Women CEOs of Fortune 500 companies.* Retrieved from http://womeninbusiness.about.com

Wolfers, Justin, Leonhardt, David, & Quealy, Kevin. (2015, April 20). 1.5 million missing Black men. *New York Times.* Retrieved from https://www.nytimes.com

Wolpe, Joseph, & Lazarus, Arnold A. (1966). *Behavior therapy techniques: A guide to the treatment of neuroses.* New York, NY: Pergamon Press.

Wong, Y. Joel, Steinfeldt, Jesse A., Speight, Quentin L., & Hickman, Sarah. (2010). Content analysis of *Psychology of Men & Masculinity* (2000–2008). *Psychology of Men & Masculinity, 11,* 170–181.

Wood, Dana, Kaplan, Rachel, & McLoyd, Vonnie C. (2007). Gender differences in the educational expectations of urban, low-income African American youth: The role of parents and the school. *Journal of Youth and Adolescence, 36,* 417–427.

Wood, Julia T. (1994). *Gendered lives: Communication, gender, and culture.* Belmont, CA: Wadsworth.

Woods, Krystle C., Buchanan, Nicole T., & Settles, Isis H. (2009). Sexual harassment across the color line: Experiences and outcomes of cross- versus intraracial sexual harassment among Black women. *Cultural Diversity and Ethnic Minority Psychology, 15,* 67–76.

Woods, Nancy F., Mitchell, E., & Lentz, M. (1995). Social pathways to premenstrual symptoms. *Research in Nursing and Health, 18,* 225–237.

Woods, Nancy F., Mitchell, Ellen, & Lentz, Martha. (1999). Premenstrual symptoms: Delineating symptom clusters. *Journal of Women's Health and Gender-Based Medicine, 8,* 1053–1062.

Worell, Judith, & Johnson, Dawn M. (2001). Feminist approaches to psychotherapy. In J. Worell (Ed.), *Encyclopedia of women and gender* (pp. 425–437). New York, NY: Academic Press.

Worell, Judith, & Remer, Pam. (1992). *Feminist perspectives in therapy: An empowerment model for women.* New York, NY: Wiley.

Worell, Judith, & Remer, Pam. (2002). *Feminist perspectives in therapy: An empowerment model for women* (2nd ed.). New York, NY: Wiley.

World Health Organization. (2000). Gender disparities in mental health. Retrieved from http://www.who.int/mental_health/media/en/242.pdf

World Health Organization. (2006). *Fuel for life: Household energy and health.* Geneva, Switzerland: Author.

World Health Organization. (2009). Clinical features of severe cases of pandemic influenza. Retrieved from http://www.who.int/csr/disease/swineflu/notes/h1n1_clinical_features_20091016/en/

World Health Organization. (2011). *Taking sex and gender into account in emerging infectious disease programmes: An analytical framework.* Geneva, Switzerland: Author.

World Health Organization. (2017). Fact sheet: The top 10 causes of death. Retrieved from http://www.who.int/mediacentre/factsheets/fs310/en/

Wright, L. J., Kalantaridou, S. N., & Calis, K. A. (2002). Update on the benefits and risks of hormone replacement therapy. *Formulary, 27*(2), 78.

Wright, Logan, Schaefer, Arlene B., & Solomons, Gerald. (1979). *Encyclopedia of pediatric psychology.* Baltimore, MD: University Park Press.

Wright, Paul J., Tokunaga, Robert S., & Kraus, Ashley. (2016). A meta-analysis of pornography consumption and actual acts of sexual aggression in general population studies. *Journal of Communication, 66*, 183–205.

Wuethrich, Bernice. (2001). Does alcohol damage female brains more? *Science, 291*, 2077–2079.

Wyche, Karen F. (2004). African American Muslim women: An invisible group. *Sex Roles, 41*, 310–328.

Wyche, Karen F., & Rice, Joy K. (1997). Feminist therapy: From dialogue to tenets. In J. Worell & N. Johnson (Eds.), *Shaping the future of feminist psychology: Education, research, and practice* (pp. 57–71). Washington, DC: American Psychological Association.

Xhyheri, Borejda, & Bugiardini, Raffaelle. (2010). Diagnosis and treatment of heart disease: Are women different from men? *Progress in Cardiovascular Diseases, 53*, 227–236.

Xu, Jiaquan, Kochanek, Kenneth D., Murphy, Sherry L., & Tejada-Vera, Betzaida. (2010). Deaths: Final data for 2007. *National Vital Statistics Reports, 58*(19).

Yakushko, Oksana, & Espín, Oliva M. (2010). The experience of immigrant and refugee women: Psychological issues. In H. Landrine & N. Russo (Eds.), *Handbook of diversity in feminist psychology* (pp. 535–558). New York, NY: Springer.

Yavorsky, Jill E., Kamp Dush, Claire M., & Schoppe-Sullivan, Sarah J. (2015). The production of inequality: The gender division of labor across the transition to parenthood. *Journal of Marriage and Family, 77*, 662–679.

Yoder, Janice D., & Kahn, Arnold S. (1993). Working toward an inclusive psychology of women. *American Psychologist, 48*, 846–850.

Yoon, Eunju, Chang, Chih-Ting, Kim, Soyeon, Clawson, Angela, Cleary, Sarah E., Hansen, Meghan, . . . Gomes, Alexandrina M. (2013). A meta-analysis of acculturation/enculturation and mental health. *Journal of Counseling Psychology, 60*, 15–30.

Yoon, Eunkyung, Funk, Roni S., & Kropf, Nancy P. (2010). Sexual harassment experiences and their psychological correlates among a diverse sample of college women. *Affilia: Journal of Women and Social Work, 25*, 8–18.

York, J. L., & Welte, J. W. (1994). Gender comparisons of alcohol consumption in alcoholic and nonalcoholic populations. *Journal of Studies on Alcohol, 55*, 743–750.

Young, William C., Goy, Robert W., & Phoenix, Charles H. (1964). Hormones and sexual behavior. *Science, 143*, 212–218.

Yu, Douglas W., & Shepard, Glenn H., Jr. (1998). Is beauty in the eye of the beholder? *Nature, 396*, 321–323.

Zabin, Laurie S., Hirsch, Marilyn B., & Emerson, Mark R. (1989). When urban adolescents choose abortion: Effects on education, psychological status, and subsequent pregnancy. *Family Planning Perspectives, 21*, 248–255.

Zadnik, Elizabeth, Sabina, Chiara, & Cuevas, Carlos A. (2015). Violence against Latinas: The effects of undocumented status on rates of victimization and help-seeking. *Journal of Interpersonal Violence, 31*, 1141–1153.

Zahnd, Elaine, Grant, David, Aydin, May, Chia, Y. Jenny, & Padilla-Frausto, D. Imelda. (2010). *Nearly four million California adults are victims of intimate partner violence.* Los Angeles: University of California, Los Angeles, Center for Health Policy Research.

Zakriski, Audrey L., Wright, Jack C., & Underwood, Marion K. (2005). Gender similarities and differences in children's social behavior: Finding personality in contextualized patterns of adaptation. *Journal of Personality and Social Psychology, 88*, 844–855.

Zala, Sarah M., & Penn, Dustin J. (2004). Abnormal behaviors induced by chemical pollution: A review of the evidence and new challenges. *Animal Behaviour, 68*, 649–664.

Zaman, Widaad, & Fivush, Robyn. (2013). Gender differences in elaborative parent-child emotion and play narratives. *Sex Roles, 68*, 591–604.

Zaviačič, Milan, Zajíčková, Mária, Blažeková, Jana, Donárová, Lucia, Stvrtina, Svetoslav, . . . Breza, Ján. (2000). Weight, size, macroanatomy, and histology of the normal prostate in the adult human female: A minireview. *Journal of Histotechnology, 23*, 61–69.

Zea, Maria C., Asner-Self, Kimberly K., Birman, Dina, & Buki, Lydia P. (2003). The abbreviated Multidimensional Acculturation Scale. *Cultural Diversity and Ethnic Minority Psychology, 9*, 107–126.

Zeigler-Hill, Virgil, & Noser, Amy. (2015). Will I ever think I'm thin enough? A moderated mediation study of women's contingent self-esteem, body image discrepancies, and disordered eating. *Psychology of Women Quarterly, 39*, 109–118.

Zell, Ethan, Krizan, Zlatan, & Teeter, Sabrina R. (2015). Evaluating gender similarities and differences using meta-synthesis. *American Psychologist, 70*, 10–20.

Zeman, Janice, & Garber, Judy. (1996). Display rules for anger, sadness, and pain: It depends on who is watching. *Child Development, 67*, 957–973.

Zentner, Marcel, & Eagly, Alice H. (2015). A sociocultural framework for understanding partner preferences of women and men: Review of concepts and evidence. *European Review of Social Psychology, 26*, 328–373.

Zigler, Edward F., & Frank, Meryl. (Eds.). (1988). *The parental leave crisis*. New Haven, CT: Yale University Press.

Zilbergeld, Bernie. (1978). *Male sexuality*. Boston, MA: Little, Brown.

Zilbergeld, Bernie. (1999). *The new male sexuality* (Rev. ed.). New York, NY: Bantam Books.

Zilbergeld, Bernie, & Ellison, Carol R. (1980). Desire discrepancies and arousal problems in sex therapy. In S. R. Leiblum & L. A. Pervin (Eds.), *Principles and practice of sex therapy*. New York, NY: Guilford.

Zilbergeld, Bernie, & Evans, Michael. (1980). The inadequacy of Masters and Johnson. *Psychology Today, 14*(3), 28–43.

Zillman, Dolf, Weaver, James B., Mundorf, Norbert, & Aust, Charles F. (1986). Effects of an opposite-gender companion's affect to horror on distress, delight, and attraction. *Journal of Personality and Social Psychology, 51*, 586–594.

Zimmerman, Don H., & West, Candace. (1975). Sex roles, interruptions and silences in conversation. In B. Thorne & N. Henley (Eds.), *Language and sex: Difference and dominance* (pp. 105–129). Rowley, MA: Newbury House.

Zimmerman-Tansella, Christa, Bertagni, Paolo, Siani, Roberta, & Micciolo, Rocco. (1994). Marital relationships and somatic and psychological symptoms in pregnancy. *Social Science and Medicine, 38*, 559–564.

Zlotnick, Caron, Tzilos, Golfo, Miller, Ivan, Seifer, Ronald, & Stout, Robert. (2016). Randomized controlled trial to prevent postpartum depression in mothers on public assistance. *Journal of Affective Disorders, 189*, 263–268.

Zosuls, Kristina M., Ruble, Diane N., Tamis-LeMonda, Catherine S., Shrout, Patrick E., Bornstein, Marc H., & Greulich, Faith K. (2009). The acquisition of gender labels in infancy: Implications for gender-typed play. *Developmental Psychology, 45*, 688–701.

Zucker, Kenneth J., Lawrence, Anne A., & Kreukels, Baudewijntje P. C. (2016). Gender dysphoria in adults. *Annual Review of Clinical Psychology, 12*, 217–247.

Zuckerman, Miron, & Wheeler, Ladd. (1975). To dispel fantasies about the fantasy-based measure of fear of success. *Psychological Bulletin, 82*, 932–946.

Zuk, M. (2002). *Sexual selections: What we can and can't learn about sex from animals*. Berkeley: University of California Press.

Zurbriggen, Eileen L. (2010). Rape, war, and the socialization of masculinity: Why our refusal to give up war ensures that rape cannot be eradicated. *Psychology of Women Quarterly, 34*, 538–549.

Index